MW00769649

The ROBERT URICH Story

'An Extraordinary Life'

by Joe Martelle

The Robert Urich Story
By Joe Martelle

Published in the USA by:
BearManor Media
P O Box 71426
Albany, Georgia 31708
www.bearmanormedia.com

Paperback ISBN: 978-1-62933-456-1
Case ISBN: 978-1-62933-457-8
BearManor Media, Albany, Georgia
Printed in the United States of America
Book design by Robbie Adkins, www.adkinsconsult.com

Dedicated to…

Heather Menzies Urich,

Who loved Bob every moment of her life and who graciously devoted hours of her time to help me share his story. I am so grateful, Heather.

***And to my wife, Kimmie*,**

who who somehow manages to keep our home and life running smoothly while I write just one more line. Thank you, honey. You're the best.

Bob's life story, including his six year battle against cancer, is also dedicated to cancer survivors everywhere, who continue to wage war against their own health issues every minute of every day. There is never a break from fighting disease. As Bob Urich often said, "Don't ever quit or give up!" Continue to fight on with hope in your heart. God Bless.

The author also expresses his extreme gratitude to the following individuals: Annette Lloyd, Robbie Adkins, Sandra Grabman, Jill Wilson and, of course, Ben Ohmart. Without their assistance, a bio on Bob Urich would still remain just a dream.

Acknowledgements

Sat. April 21, 2018

First and foremost, a very special thank you to my beloved wife, Kimmie. It was at her suggestion that I write the story of our friend Bob's life and career in the first place. She graciously and unselfishly allowed me the necessary time and space to head off to my writing cave for hours on end to pen just one more additional word. It is with a great deal of personal sadness that I mention the passing of Bob's adoring wife, Heather. She left us all too suddenly on Christmas Eve 2017, after being diagnosed just one month earlier with inoperable brain cancer. This book never would have seen the light of day without her input and dedication to her husband, Bob. She kindly spent hours on the phone and through e-mail with me offering her personal memories of the man she loved so much. I deeply regret that after 3 ½ years of working so hard on Bob's bio, she passed before having an opportunity to read the final draft. However, I believe, somehow she is aware of its completion. I only hope she approves. I did my best to honor Bob's memory and now hers, as well.

Thanks to Bob and Heather's children, Ryan, Emily and Allison; Bob's sister Monica, brothers Tom and David, who always rose to the occasion when I needed to pluck an additional leaf from the Urich family tree. Thanks to Bob's cousin Jo-Jo Urich, Heather's sister, Sheila and brother Neil; also Bob and Heather's friends, especially Jack Fenwick, Tom DeLopez, Joni Darling, James Baquet, Dyrk Halstead, Joe Malone, Eric Caley, Roger Hobson, Johnny Lane, Judy Rice, Tony Hillery, Deidre 'Dee Dee' Miller Cohen, Peter Trevino, Katie Brunk Lupton, and Abby Wright who were privileged to know Bob and his family and graciously gave their time to offer their personal insight to help tell Bob's story. Thanks to Bob's long-time agent, Merritt Blake; producers, Duke Vincent and John Wilder; actor friends, Angela Cartwright, Tim Matheson, Chick Vennera, Joanna Kerns, Gary Lockwood, Sally Kirkland, Anson Williams, Emeril LaGasse, Dylan Daniels, and Kaj-Erik Eriksen; Steeler great, Rocky Bleier; physicians who kindly assisted the author with their insight regarding Bob's illness and treatment for synovial cell sarcoma, Dr. Larry Baker and Dr. Charles Forscher, and medical researcher, Cigall

Kadoch. My deep appreciation to the following members of Bob's graduating Class of 1964, at Toronto [Ohio] High for giving so generously of their time and comments: Lois Burchfiel Bradway, Tom Chip Coulter, Dohrman Crawford, Dave Harvilak, Terry Hunter, Bill Hutchison, Jim Lowery, Gregg 'Mr. Baseball' McKelvey, George Melhorn, Candace Parker Mindigo, Kay Gilchrist Murray, Lynn Vanich Popovich, Jim Ray, Teri Volsky Samstag, Tim Seese and Tom Smith with special thanks to Carolyn Motter Walker for always answering my incessant questions. Her insightful knowledge of the people and City of Toronto, Ohio helped make Bob Urich's life story complete. My heartfelt thanks to each of you. Please forgive my aging eyes if your name was inadvertently omitted.

Table of Contents

Dedications iii
Acknowledgements v
Preface: Author's friendship with Bob Urich ix
Dedication: Angela Cartwright xiv
Prologue: April day in Southern California xvii
PART I - '*He played by the rules*' 1
Chapter 1- Toronto Ohio • 'The Gem City' • Bob's hometown 1
2-History of the Urich Clan 11
3-Bob's Growing up years 14
4-Bobby, Rudy's Store and Hoppy 24
5-Meet the Urich Family 32
6-Bullies & Bob • Acting was in his stars • His first dramatic role . . . 56
7-Memories from Classmates • Growing up in Ohio in the 50's 65
8-Bob liked Candy • Youth Harbor • Doo-Wop • *Sound of Music* 85
9-Friday Night Lights • Rocky Bleier • Reverse Shuttle Hurdles 98
10-Football scholarship to Florida State University 114
PART II - '*He dared to dream big' [blue skying it]* 134
Chapter 11- Jack Fenwick • Michigan St. • Chicago-WGN
• Marriage • Acting 134
12-Burt Reynolds • La la land • *Bob & Carol, Ted & Alice* • Break-up . . . 146
13-Bob's film debut • Tim Matheson • *S.W.A.T* • Bob meets Heather . . 154
14-Wedding Bells • Heather's Family • Billy Crystal 170
15-Bob's take on acting • Joni Darling & Milton Katselas 183
16-TV Jargon • Johnny Galecki • Kaj Erik Erikson
• Dylan Daniels "*Blind Faith*" • Chick Vennera • Anson Williams . . 201
PART III - '*Bob played to win*' 226
Chapter 17- Bob's Hits Wheel of Fortune with *Vega$* • Duke Vincent 226
18-More on *Vega$* • Behind the scenes • Bob vs. the Champ • Sinatra . . 237
19-It's a Boy! • It's a Girl • Allison & Dee Dee • M-G-M Movie deal . . 263
20-*Spenser: For Hire* • John Wilder • Cast • Boston fire
• Spenser & Kid 291
21-The Redcoats • Boston's unique cast of characters
• This Old House 323

22-So long *Spenser*, bye bye, Boston • California here we come • J.W. . . . 341
PART IV - '*Courage was Bob's guide*'. 351
Chapter 23- *Lonesome Dove* • On the Trail • Tommy Lee Jones
• Robert Duvall 351
24-*American Dreamer* • *Lazarus Man* • A little Lump • The Bel-Air . . 370
25-Bob's safe sanctuary - West Lake CANADA 381
26-The Lump • Cancer Strikes • Dream sequence • *Lazarus* lawsuit . . 397
PART V - '*The Will to Win • Never Give Up*' 408
27-Bob through Heather's eyes 408
28-Living with cancer • Bob's extraordinary will to live
• His fear of snakes 438
29-Bob's final days • Service in L.A. & the lake Bob reaches out . . . 452
30-Family & friends remember Bob 471
Robert Urich's Memorial Service. 483
Epilogue: Finding a cure for Synovial cell sarcoma
• Cigall Kadoch, Dr. Charles Forscher. 490
After word: Tribute to Heather Menzies Urich. 493
**Filmography: Complete listing of Bob's films and television
series and appearances** 498
Index 538

Preface: Joe Martelle, the Author's friendship with Bob

It was Spring, 1985, I was on the radio in Boston with the late Andy Moes. We co-hosted a popular morning-drive Show, the *Joe and Andy Family* on 98.5-WROR.

I remember the time quite vividly. It was seven-thirty. We had just gone into our half-hour news break. Five glorious minutes to run to the bathroom, grab a cup of 'Joe,' or discuss what the heck we were planning to do with the next 25 minutes of our show! Even though we had a basic outline, we usually followed the 'flow-of-the-show' and where the listeners and callers took us, so our precious 5 minute break was usually spent laughing and joking around. This particular morning, Andy & I were leisurely sipping our coffee and kibitzing about a bit we successfully pulled off earlier. Just so you know, and humility aside, we enjoyed our own humor and quite often basked in it. We often told each other, we hoped our loyal listeners enjoyed our show as much as we did! It was fun! Our radio friend, Dick Syatt, who was on the air at ten each morning, down the hall, on our sister station, WRKO, would see us laughing and having a fun time and comment, "You guys are living in Disney World. You are so lucky!" By the way, we agreed!

The newscast was wrapping up and we were awaiting our cue to go back on the air. Our producer, Linda was in the adjacent studio. Through the control room window, we noticed she was wearing a huge smile, as she shouted over the intercom. "Robert Urich is on-the-line and wants to go on the radio with you!" Pushing the reply button, I laughed, and answered her with a smart-alecky reply, " ya, sure and right after him, put Jack Nicholson and Meryl Streep through to us." "Seriously," she shot back, "it really is Robert Urich! He wants to go on your show." At that time, Robert Urich was the big-name celebrity in town.

His new ABC-Television series, *Spenser: For Hire*–based on the Robert B. Parker detective novels–was filmed entirely on the streets in and around Boston. Bob was being driven to the filming location site in his motor home. His regular driver, Bobby McGuiness was a loyal listener and had us on that morning, which meant forced listening for Mr. Urich. Evidently, Bob, as our newest listener, liked what he heard. "Who are these guys?" He asked Bobby McGuiness. "They are outrageously funny." "Joe and Andy," McGuiness answered. "A couple of goof balls, but really nice guys. They host Boston's most popular morning Radio show. Ya, never know what's gonna come out of Andy's mouth. He's like a loose cannon. Joey, as the straight guy, does his best to keep Andy from goin' over the line. I listen to 'em every morning." Evidently, Bob wanted to join in on the fun and craziness that was uniquely part of our daily show. That particular morning, we were doing regular weekly feature, *Name that Disease* with our physician friend, Dr. Peter Masucci. Every Wednesday, Pete would call in with symptoms of a disease, then our listeners would call us trying to *Name that disease.* Pretty simple, aye? Well, we're talkin' about a couple of simple guys. Boston is one of the medical Mecca's of the ole U.S.A., and with many medical folks in our audience, we always came up with a winner. The contest was strictly for fun. It certainly wasn't for the cheap prizes we offered callers for their time and effort. Those itsy-bitty toys found in the bottom of a Cracker Jack box have a higher dollar value. Bob thought he could identify the disease of the week and asked Bobby to call our show. I don't recall if he correctly *named that disease*, but do know, we had a fun time with him on the air. Bob was a natural for radio. He was friendly, and funny.

Since it was the first time Bob and I spoke, we had yet to meet face to face. That would come later, and looking back on it, it's a wonder we developed any sort of friendship. It nearly ended before it got off the ground. Bob's initial call to our show was followed by many others, often made when he was on his way to another Boston location site. Much to the consternation of our competition, *the Joe & Andy Family* became the 'unofficial home on Boston radio' for Robert Urich and *Spenser: For Hire.*

A few mornings following Bob's initial call to our radio show, he was headed towards a downtown Boston location site for a day's shooting on *Spenser*. It was close by our WROR studio, which back then was located in the Harvard Medical Building at 3 Fenway Plaza. Bob decided to stop by to meet us in person.

Our receptionist met Bob at the elevator and escorted him down the hallway to our studio. You could tell by the way he walked into our room that the man had confidence and class. When he said "Hi," I must have had a look written all over my face of *I don't know what the hell TV shows you've worked on before Spenser, because I don't recognize you at all!* He must have sensed it. As I reached out to shake his huge hand, which totally engulfed mine, he smiled warmly and with a broad grin that would light up the darkest room, said, in a deep, low voice, "You don't have a clue as to who the heck I am, do you?" Oh, my word, I thought, the man is clairvoyant! He's reading my own thoughts! Standing before this giant of a man, now totally embarrassed, I honestly believed I had insulted him before opening my mouth. At any moment, I expected him to either pulverize me, or turn on his heel and vacate our studio faster than a dog on a big juicy ole bone.

Still gripping my outstretched hand, maybe just a wee bit tighter now, Bob calmly asked, "Joe, have you ever seen *Vega$*? Explaining in sort of a sarcastic way, "It's a little television series, that was sort of popular," and he added without sounding too braggadocios, "Well, I'm the guy in it."

Now, perspiring profusely, and wearing a crimson face, I did my best to weasel out of the difficult situation I found myself in. Stammering all over myself, I tried finding the right words. "Bob, you need to know, I'm an early to bed, early to rise radio guy. Getting up at 3 a.m. to do our show means I don't get to watch a lot of night-time TV. [Keep in mind, this was 1985, before the advent of DVR.] I'm in la la land before Vega$ airs!" Apologetically, I added, "Sorry, but I never watched it." To my surprise, Bob began laughing and proceeded to give me a huge bear hug! I thought, either, he's trying to squeeze the living bananas out of me or he's trying to ease any fears I may have that he was upset by what I said. "No problem," Bob smiled, and speaking in a low tone said, "My wife Heather and I never watched Vega$ either!" And with that we both burst out laughing! His ability to laugh at himself told me much about the man's character and from that moment, we became fast friends. Bob was someone I instantly liked. Over time, I learned much about him. We shared many of the same values, including love of family.We both grew up Catholic and had been altar boys and with small town values; we both loved sports, movies, radio and TV and music, good ole songs that our mom and dad used to sing. We also shared a deep appreciation for America and patriotism and what our country stands for. Bob Urich was both spirited and spiritual and a devout Catholic who loved the traditions and rituals of his faith.

Bob Urich had a code of honor that was striking. You'd be hard pressed to find a more caring guy than Bob when it came to his family and friends. He was devoted and loyal to his wife, Heather. He loved her and his family more than anything, and once said, "I like my work as an actor, but I love my family." Bob, could be very direct, but always tried to do so in a respectful way. There was never any hidden agenda with the man. He was a "What you see is what you get" kind of guy. He was every bit a real man with real emotions who wasn't afraid to show them. Like many of us, he wrestled with his own shortcomings, including his fiery quick release temper, which his brother David witnessed. "Bob could fly off the handle and into a rage in a heartbeat, depending on the circumstances. I saw him lose it a few times. He could blow off steam at the drop of a dime; particularly, when he saw someone treating another person in a disrespectful way. Bob also had an extremely low tolerance for anyone acting really dumb and stupid around him. Woe to the person who hurt his family or him. He could turn his back on you as if you never existed. Once, Heather asked him, "Doesn't it bother you at all that you never speak to that person anymore?" "Nope," Bob replied. "I can no longer trust him, so for me, he ceases to exist." He was honorable and had a great compassion for people. He was very unpretentious, and witty with a good sense of humor, and who loved to laugh. Bob was very engaging with his friends, allowing them to be themselves. That's why I believe, even to this day, back when we first met, he appreciated my total honesty about never seeing him on TV. He immediately sensed that I cared less about any celebrity status he had. I liked him from the beginning for being a genuinely nice guy, not some manufactured Hollywood bozo like so many actors who come complete with an out of control ego. Bob was a friendly, down to earth guy, who took great pride in saying, "I'm just a down- home kid from Ohio."

Bob Urich was endowed with the greatest gift an actor can have. . .talent. The viewing audience came to recognize it and made him one of the most popular stars ever on TV. Bob got all that he asked for and more. He certainly had material wealth, but he also had a lot more. He had the love of the people he touched and for my money that made Bob Urich one of the wealthiest people in the world.

I'm hoping after reading this story of Bob's life and career, you will see for yourself that my friend, Robert Urich had more than his share of life's ups and downs, but always did his best to remain thankful for the good times and to remain positive through the not so good. A man who loved his family and friends and in turn was loved by those of us who were fortunate to know him. The world is a better place because Bob was here. Most importantly, Bob was a good and decent man, who accomplished some wonderful things, and who was human like the rest of us. You will soon see that during his relatively short life span of 55 years, Robert Urich did lead an extraordinary life, and why years following his untimely passing, he is still revered and missed so much, by so many, including me. I am honored and privileged to share his story with you in the pages ahead.

The Robert Urich Story, An Extraordinary Life.
Joe Martelle, December 19, 2016[1]

L-R, Bob Urich, Joe Martelle [Author] Andy Moes [Joe's radio partner] set of Spenser: For Hire *in So. Boston 1985. Photo courtesy of Author.*

1 The date Bob would have been 70 years old.

Dedication: by Angela Cartwright

April 21, 2002 - By Angela Cartwright

This has been the longest week... a nonstop emotional ride through the portals of a person's life who was not ready to leave, and not ready to stop fighting, to the caverns of grief that a family must face and whose hearts have been torn by the disbelief... After the memorial for Robert Urich, everyone went to Heather's home and lingered in the rooms and on the balconies exchanging stories. There were some laughs, and some tears and a lot of staring at the green golf course, which spread like a tablecloth in front of them. How many times had Bob driven the course in his golf cart? Isn't it odd that Bob's favorite flower, lilacs, only bloom in April and he would pick this month to pass? How many calla lily bulbs had he planted here in front of his library door? My eyes rested on that empty chair on his library porch. How many days were as beautiful as this one. With the cerulean blue sky kissing the phthalo green grass... there would be no mixing colors if this day were to be painted, the colors would be right out of the tube.

Some of the bouquets were bigger than the front door, those only seem appropriate, for when Bob was in that house, he was bigger than life.

I hugged and spoke to people, some of them I only see occasionally. Familiar faces passed mine in the hallways, our eyes meeting in compassion and sadness. If I sat down right now I might never get up... if I cried right now I was afraid I would never stop... Heather stood in the entrance of her home for three hours greeting friends, and I knew she felt the same way. I wandered from room to room while the fragrance of lilacs lingered in the air...

The day was a dialogue of entrances and exits... food was there and then it was gone, wine glasses filled again and again, and the cerulean sky that turned midnight blue, gave birth to a million stars that had stayed dormant during the daytime but now glimmered overhead brighter than usual. I felt closer to the earth, further from the craziness, and the world moved at a gentler pace… You could really see the stars out here too…

...and I remember nine months ago in Canada. We sat around the fire pit after a gourmet meal that Bob had cooked from the the fresh vegetables Heather and I had gathered at the market stands earlier that day. Bob sat in his Adirondack chair, spread out his legs and leaned back to look at the stars. He was tall and strong and handsome, and we all followed his lead, stretching out our legs and looking up at the blanket of stars overhead. This was a different pocket of the world up here. Bob was so proud of this corner of the world that was his and he loved to share it.

The fire popped and crackled with the man-size fire he had built. Heather had brought out graham crackers, marshmallows and chocolate and we had all put in our two cents on how smores were to be cooked. How to melt the chocolate and maintain the integrity of the cookie, regretfully there was not a Girl Scout among us. Bob had delighted in the banter, told us where to place them on the stones to achieve the right blend of flavors, and I remember the firelight dancing on his smiling face. This was the simplest time, the happiest of times, with both our families around us. Bob had just been contracted to write his autobiography, and he struggled with how he would put it into words, this extraordinary life he had lived. He had also been reminded that his struggle with Sarcoma was not over and he would leave in a few days to begin a new treatment. There was hope...

It was decided that life should be kept as normal as possible the day after the memorial, so I drove out to Heather's again for her daughter's birthday party. That morning the birthday girl had asked her mother "if they could glue Daddy back together so he could come to her party." The little four year old was excited about the princess dress she had received, even putting on the crown and the diamond shoes, she didn't care much for the visit from Cinderella though. I'm sure she was wishing someone else would visit her. All the presents in the world would not replace the fact that someone was missing. Sadness sweeps over me like a wave on the shore. Bob has moved on now, to a peaceful place where he won't hurt anymore. Only those left behind will hurt now. But as someone close to me said, "I'd rather live 55 years to the fullest, then 80 empty years." In that there is comfort. Robert Urich, only 55 years old, really did live an extraordinary life. I sure will miss him.

Bold text indicates Robert Urich's own words, taken directly from his unfinished Journal,[1] which he had hoped one day to publish in book form. Sadly, he did not live long enough to complete his project. Having personally known Bob Urich, I can attest that he was a pretty terrific guy, a wonderful husband, father, brother and loyal friend who deserves having his story told. In fact, it is long over-due.

I feel privileged that Bob's wife, Heather, trusted me with her husband's memoirs. It was an awesome responsibility that I did not take lightly. In my own research, and writing, I have taken utmost care in transcribing Bob's words exactly as he wrote them in his personal journal. These are the actual happenings of his life and career, as he remembered, from his years growing up in his hometown of Toronto, Ohio through his life and career on stage and as a film actor and television star and personality. I hope you enjoy reading Bob's own words as much as I have had in transcribing them for you.

I also hope you will enjoy reading my personal thoughts coupled with comments obtained from hundreds of interviews with his family, friends, classmates and co-workers. With the late Heather Menzies Urich's invaluable input, I have endeavored to do my best to complete Bob's story. As you continue to read on, it is my wish that you will see for yourself that Robert Urich did lead an extraordinary life.

1 Heather informed the author that 'sometimes' Bob got a few things wrong when writing his story. They were only a few minor details, a misspelled name or two, or a place and not the all-important details of actual events. Since many of his journal entries were written during his final days, his illness [memory] may have contributed to him getting a few facts wrong, which she corrected along with assistance from the author's research.

PROLOGUE

An April morning in Southern California
Friday Morning, April 12th 2002

[**Bold typed words** and sentences are Robert Urich's, taken directly from his journal.]

It was a cool, beautiful Spring morning in Southern California. The kind of April day that's filled with the sweet scent of lilacs, honey-suckle and orange blossoms. The clean fresh ocean breeze off the Pacific ocean permeated the air. The salt stimulated one's nostrils and taste buds. It was a great day to be alive.

Playgrounds were filled with the voices of happy youngsters, golfers were teeing off, bike riders and joggers were doing their perfunctory morning work-out, while others busily headed off to work, class or shopping. It was the kind of gorgeous day the chamber of commerce wished they could bottle to include with brochures promoting itself 'why' sunny Southern California is the perfect place to live, work and play!

Suddenly, an ambulance siren breaks the peaceful serenity of the day.

Friday morning

April 12, 2002

Bob Urich called his older brother, Tom. "I'm in the mood for some home-style Halupki [stuffed cabbage], what'd ya say? I guess mine was the closest to tasting like our mom's," says Tom, and knowing Bob had been ill, happily replies, 'Sure. I'll fix up a batch and we'll bring it over tomorrow.' "Great! Can't wait! Thanks!" Little did Tom know those would be the last words he would ever hear from his younger brother, Bob. "I prepared the food that night, and we drove up the next day, Saturday," recalls Tom. "Bob and Heather lived exactly 25 miles–door to door–from my wife Judy and me. Driving, could take anywhere from 30 minutes to an hour, depending on time of day and traffic. On this particular Saturday, traffic was fairly light in the late morning. We were less than a mile from the gated entrance, when we saw an ambulance pass by. I said to Judy, 'oh God, I hope that's not Bob.'"

"As we approached the entrance to Sherwood Country Club, the guard at the gate confirmed my worst fears," exclaims Tom. "It was Bob in the ambulance!"

Noon - Saturday
April 12, 2002

Meanwhile, Bob, lying on the gurney inside the ambulance is fighting to stay alert as he slowly drifts in and out of consciousness. The drip, drip of the I.V. connected to his arm does little to sedate the pain in his chest, accented more from the slightest bump in the road the driver did his best to avoid, but doesn't. Glancing upwards through the window in the rear door of the ambulance, Bob notices the bright blue sky. It brings back memories of those special Spring days growing up in the small neighborly town of Toronto, Ohio.

"There is a softness to the air in the Ohio Valley in the springtime, and after a long, dark winter, I could not gulp enough of it down."

Suddenly, Bob is jolted from his memories by another bump from a pot hole. The ambulance driver, acutely aware of the seriousness of Bob's condition, apologizes. Bob, forcing a smile, shrugs it off as to good ole California infrastructure in need of repair. His thoughts race back, five years or so, to the first time this insidious disease, synovial cell sarcoma raised its vicious little head.

May 1996
Santa Fe, New Mexico

He was in Santa Fe, New Mexico filming a western series he loved. His dream of starring in a western series of his own had finally come true. Propelled across the land-scape by winds gusting up to fifty-five miles an hour, a tumbleweed appears out of nowhere. Robert Urich's driver, Billy Cardhart, slows down their 4-wheel drive vehicle to avoid hitting it.

Bob shifts a little in his seat and Billy, a quiet turn of a man from Seminole, Oklahoma, seems to sense something is on his mind.

When Bob arrived in Santa Fe to begin filming *The Lazarus Man*, Billy had signed on to drive him to and from the series location at the Hughes Ranch. As is the case with most people upon meeting congenial Bob for the first time, the two became fast friends. Billy mentioned to Bob he was one of his favorite actors, and he came out of retirement especially to drive him. His kind gesture moved Bob and made him feel special. After all, Billy had driven all the big stars that had come to Santa Fe to make westerns–Henry Fonda, Kirk Douglas and one of Urich's favorite pop singers, Dean Martin. Yes indeed, ole Billy Cardhart enjoyed his work as much as they enjoyed theirs.

Now, as they drive along buffeted by yet another of Northern New Mexico's legendary dust storms, Bob senses that Billy was keeping one eye on the road and the other on him. "It's gonna get worse," the old-timer says. It's something Bob already knows. Up at the crack of dawn, he always kept an eye on the forecast while swilling down half a pot of coffee and reviewing dialogue for the upcoming days work on the set. This particular morning, Urich grimaced as the meteorologist speculated that by afternoon the winds could be gusting to seventy miles per hour.

The weather in Santa Fe sure is a lot different than back home in Toronto, Ohio, Bob thinks to himself, desperately trying to ease the pain, by shifting his weight as he lies on the stretcher in the speeding ambulance. His thoughts drifting back to his hometown.

"Down over the hill, down by the river bank was dangerous, forbidden territory, for there was always the chance you would run into the Locke brothers, Arrie And Zannie. As tough as they were mean. They were always lurking and always looking to pick a fight. Down over the river bank was the low river bottom flood plane, dark and over-grown with reeds and tall grasses growing out of the rich verdant soil."

Jumbled thoughts of his days 'back home' race through Bob's mind, nearly as fast as the ambulance, which is speeding towards Los Robles Hospital.

"Some of the old Polish and Slavic men in the neighborhood had staked their claims, using this fertile land for large vegetable gardens... a good place to steal a warm tomato or two, or a cucumber. Usually, when I ventured there, I'd peal them with my Hopalong Cassidy pen knife, which I carried fastened to my belt with a recycled watch chain that kept me from losing it should it slip out of my pocket."

Bob, smiles slightly thinking how he took to carrying an old kitchen salt shaker in a faded army surplus knapsack for just those occasions.

"Those old gardeners knew more than tomatoes. On dark, cool, moonless nights in autumn, pumpkins and hard corn for throwing on porches on Halloween were ours for the taking."

Saturday, late morning
April 13, 2002

Robert Urich has collapsed in his home, after coughing up blood and is having difficulty breathing. "Do you want me to call 9-11?" anxiously asks his wife, Heather, as she tries her best to remain calm at the frightening sight. "Yes," is Bob's only reply.

He is now being rushed by ambulance to the nearby Los Robles Medical Center in Thousand Oaks, CA. The hospital is just a few miles away. Drifting in and out of consciousness, we can only imagine, Bob's thoughts are of times past…of his years growing up in his hometown of Toronto, Ohio on the banks of the mighty Ohio River. Stories of the river were exchanged and passed down from generation to generation.

"As children, we all heard the story of the night watchman at the power-plant loading dock, who slipped while taking a cigarette break, and being swept away. His body was found three days later, several miles downstream at Brown's Island. During the great flood of '36 the river rose to record levels. Those who heeded the warnings from the U.S. Army Corps of Engineers had their belongings loaded into rail cars." The rail-line occupied a favorable position about a hundred feet above the town itself. **"My grandfather, a wiry stick of a man with a shock of white hair with many fine qualities, cursing in his native Slavic tongue was not one of them." "His only precaution** [against the flood waters] **was to put the chickens in the kitchen. 'The river, he bellowed, would never come into the house.'**

"He and my grandmother, affectionately known as 'Baba,' and their thirteen children–seven sons and six daughters–watched the powerful river rise from a second-story bedroom window, and then from the rooftop as their neighbor's house was lifted from its foundation by the surging waters and floated down stream. All of my grandfather's chickens perish in the great flood of 1936."

***

It all happened such a very long time ago, as Bob desperately tries clearing the fogginess from his mind…and his time spent filming *The Lazarus Man* in Santa Fe.

May 1996
Santa Fe, New Mexico

Billy turns off Interstate 25 onto New Mexico Highway 285. It's the short cut to Clines Corners. If you kept going, you'd end up in Roswell, New Mexico, famous for the extra-terrestrials you probably read about or watched on television, who touched down there in the 1950s. It's a hilly road, winding through a valley of low-growing junipers and sage. In the distance is a broad plateau, scarred by a now defunct gold mine, the tailings still visible for miles by the naked eye.

Billy Cardhart was a great source of wisdom and entertainment for Bob Urich on those long drives out to the various ranch locations. One story is how he was born in the oil fields near Seminole, Oklahoma. "The country doctor rode out from town in a horse n' buggy to attend to my mother," Billy begins with a grin. "I was delivered on the dirt floor of a tent, which was part of a tent city similar to many that sprang up during the oil boom of the '20s and '30s. "'You done it right Mrs. Cardhart," the doctor proudly exclaimed. 'You have 'em small and let 'em grow.'"

Billy Cardhart's Uncle Irvin Medlock had owned the Kaiser-Frazier car dealership in Mallberg, Arkansas. He also spent his spare time preaching a Halleluiah gospel of fire-and-brimstone under a small tent on the outskirts of town. "Uncle Irvin fancied himself a man of God," says Billy, "and was persistent in his attempts at my redemption, regularly urging me to visit one of his weekly Friday night revivals. Tired of my uncle's constant pestering, I agreed to attend one of his prayer meetings.

Shortly after taking my seat on a hard wooden bench next to family, friends and grizzly oil workers in search of salvation," Billy recalls, "a couple of ladies from the congregation removed Uncle Irvin's shoes and began washing his feet. And now, Uncle Irvin, with his feet still wet, and filled with the Holy Spirit began jumping from bench to bench, while shouting in a wild frenzy, praises of a loving and forgiving God!"

"After the revival meeting," Billy continues, " I stayed to help clean up, stacking chairs and reflecting on the evening's events, while Uncle Irvin busily and happily, counted the take generously donated by those of a giving faith.

'Well, Billy, his uncle asked, 'were you filled with the Holy Spirit?'

"Yes sir," insisted Billy.

"Any man who could jump from bench to bench like that with wet feet without breaking his dang neck, has got to have God on his side!"

***

Stars or locals, the Spring weather is no respecter of persons in Santa Fe. Blustery skies can turn to snow storms as late as May, and newborn calves have frozen to death overnight on the open range as temperatures unexpectedly drop well below freezing. But, the most dangerous and least predictable seasonal change is the wind; wind that will blow incessantly from sunup to sundown and sometimes throughout the night, lashing at the mountains and the valley floor and hoisting blinding dust clouds that light from the most powerful halogen headlamps can't penetrate.

"This is shaping up to be such a day," says Billy in a slow drawl, and Bob detects a sense of verboten in the ole timers voice.

Peering out the window of the 4-wheel drive vehicle, Bob thinks to himself...

"Springtime comes reluctantly to these parts. Cold winds blow down from the majestic Sangre DeChristo and San Juan Mountains, which climb to thirteen thousand feet above Santa Fe, a long-time artist's haven and now a weekend refuge for Hollywood types. Writers, producers and directors come here for the solitude, the spectacular sunsets and the vast sky that seems to be held up by the mountain peaks. Oprah, Gene Hackman, Carol Burnett and Brian Dennehy–all have second homes here."

As beautiful as the mountains and Santa Fe can be, there's no place quite like home, as Bob's memory cells momentarily click away from Santa Fe and back to his Ohio roots.

Saturday April 13th 2002

Lying on a stretcher in the back of a speeding ambulance, bound for the local hospital in Thousand Oaks, California, Bob Urich is lapsing in and out of consciousness. A time his active mind is recalling various moments of his extraordinary life.

"The old men of Toronto Ohio had staked their garden claims, but to the youth of the neighborhood–down over the river bank' belonged to the Locke brothers. The Locke brothers controlled their domain with iron fists and bad attitudes. Their territory included the slag pile, an Edison power plant by product of gritty, glass-like ash left over from burning coal. While not officially 'down over the river bank,' the slag pile was close enough to be 'down over the river bank,' to suit the Locke brothers definition of their territorial boundary if they caught you there."

The slag pile extended out from River Avenue, across from St. Joseph's church where Bob was an altar boy. It's also where he attended grammar school. **"The pile was approximately a quarter of a mile long and half as wide. It dropped sharply on one side to an open grassy field and on the other side to the mouth of a ravine that filled during rainstorms in summer, and emptied into the river below, and at the edge of the slag pile was the Ohio river itself, swiftly moving and extremely powerful."**

Life itself is like the ebb and flow of a mighty river, complete with its twists and turns. On this beautiful Spring day, Bob Urich is fighting for his life, in the back of a speeding ambulance, yet, his mind travels back to his youth on another spring day on a bluff high above the Ohio River. From his vantage point, Bob spent many hours day-dreaming, and his unspoken relationship with the river continued through the years. He was inextricably drawn to the body of water by forces both basic and primordial.

"Even though, I could not quite see the river from my bedroom window, I could forever feel it's ubiquitous presence...dark, swirling currents that could carry you away. At thirteen years of age, I was inextricably drawn to this body of water. Often, I used the only excuse my parents considered legitimate for going anywhere near the river...fishing. I would tramp along the soft, sandy bank, cut branches from the river willows to cradle my fishing rod, cast homemade sinkers as far as I could out into the current, and wait for the familiar tap, tap, tapping on my line.

The tapping usually meant a catfish was calling, or the long, steady, real zinging pull signaled the more desirable white and black carp, and sometimes golden or a red carp like the ones you see nowadays in ponds in front of sushi restaurants. After supper, I would sit by the river until

dark, staring out into the flowing river and dream of where it might take me. The Ohio flowing majestically into the mighty Mississippi at Cairo, Illinois, down through Memphis and on to New Orleans and the Gulf of Mexico."

But the serenity of the riverbank just as often meant trouble, Bob writes in his journal.

"It was where you went to play with matches and smoke homemade cigars rolled from the broad leaves of a local tree we knew only as the 'stogie tree.' It wasn't unusual for a trip to the river to end with torn jeans and a bloody nose. Growing up in Toronto, we had some great fist-fights. It was the main recreation outside of high-school sports."

The Ohio River is where a youthful Robert Urich experienced a paradigm shift of life-changing magnitude. It was there, that he discovered with utmost certainty and clarity that he would be forever caught in another kind of current, a current of passions and dreams that would last a lifetime. **"Someday, I would be an actor!"**

Saturday
April 13th 2002

The speeding ambulance pulls to a stop directly in front of the emergency entrance to Los Robles Regional Medical Center. Doctors and nurses are at the ready. Bob is rushed inside to intensive care. Initial results are inconclusive, but it doesn't look good.

May 1996
Santa Fe, New Mexico, The Hughes Ranch

"Billy turns the SUV off the highway and through the gates of the Hughes Ranch, slowing to say "howdy" and "good morning" to the ranch foreman's wife, who watches over the main gate from the cozy confines of a double-wide trailer with a cup of coffee in her hand. Lying beneath the trailer is a black lab, her constant companion. He barely lifts his head as we pass on by. He's accustomed to all manner of strangers coming and going."

"Kevin Costner was launched into stardom on this ranch by his colorful performance in *Silverado*. And, the entire western town set was painted a monochromatic gray for Bruce Willis and the movie *Last Man Standing*." "As we approach the set, Billy finally asks the question

that has been on his mind since he picked me up: "'Why the pained expression, Robert?'"

When I don't reply, he gives it his best guess.

"They're going to pick up the show, ya know."

"The show he's referring to is *The Lazarus Man*. We just finished its first season, and renewal time is always tense for the cast and crew of any show."

"'They'd be damn fools not to renew," he continues. "Everybody I talk to says, 'you drive Robert Urich? We sure do like that Lazarus Man series of his; you tell him that for us."

"Oh, it's nothing," I say, but not very convincingly. Billy is using his best amateur psychology to try and lift me out of what he thinks is some sort of deep, dark pit of series-renewal dread.

"'They either will or they won't," I reply. Referring to whether or not the western series will be picked up for another season. "I've done all I can, Billy. Now it's up them." "'Well it sure is something that's on yer mind,'"he says, "'you making faces like that. I never seen you complain-in'…ever. Always ready to go, always leadin' the way! Hell's bells, that's why they call you a leadin' man, ain't it?'"**"Thanks for the kind words, Billy, but that's not why I'm making faces," trying to reassure him that everything was fine."**

"'Then what is it?,'" he asks again?

"Oh, I might as well tell him, I silently think to myself, or he's going to nag me through eternity. . ."Got this lump way down in my abdo-men…it's got me a little worried."

"'You want me to take you to the hospital?' Billy asks in an almost pleading way.

"No time today, Billy, but I'll check it out soon, I promise."

"'A lump's a lump,'" he says.

"His concern for the network, The Lazarus Man, and everything else suddenly pushed aside.

"I know."

"'You gotta take care of you, your family and then God,' urges Billy, "and the rest of them can just go straight to hell.'"

"I'm sure it's nothing to worry about," I say, smiling. [Bob doing his best to ease Billy's fears.]

"I was somehow cheered by the thought of 'the rest of them going straight to hell.'"

Bob & Billy drive the rest of the way in silence, except for the wind that howls outside, gathering clouds of dust and dirt, obliterating the sun and any chance for warmth.

"None of that lump stuff matters. Today, I'll put on my worn leather chaps and buffalo coat and ride my gray horse, Steel. Don't give two shakes about no damn lump today."

Suddenly, Bob Urich, seems reconciled to the matter. . .at least for the moment.

"Today, I get to be a cowboy!
I'm The Lazarus Man."

Bob standing in shadow on porch on his TV series The Lazarus Man, *Santa Fe, New Mexico, photo courtesy of James Baquet.*

Part I
Chapter 1

The Gem City and growing up on the Ohio River in Toronto...Ohio! Heavenly Bodies & Bob's horoscope

'Bob played by the rules'

"I think my longevity as an actor has a lot to do with where I come from–a blue-collar town in Ohio–and how I was raised: to work hard and respect other folks." Robert Urich

Toronto, Ohio, population around 8,000 when Bob Urich was growing up in the 50s and 60s. Not, Toronto, as in Canada, where Urich's wife, Heather was born, no, this Toronto is in Ohio; along with the neighboring states of Pennsylvania and West Virginia, they encompass an area known as the tri-states. Toronto, Ohio is nestled in the picturesque upper Ohio River Valley of Jefferson County with the majestic Ohio River flowing along its Eastern bank. Toronto is within a 2-hour drive to four metro cities; Pittsburgh is a 45 minute drive across the river to the East, Cleveland, a 2-hour drive NW, Columbus is 2 hours to the SW and Wheeling, WVA less than an hour to the South.

As legend goes, Mike Auver Myers, a scout during the Revolutionary War, was awarded the land[1] for outstanding service to his country. Later, his brother, George sold the land to John Depuy, who laid out the town and named it Newburg. The village consisted of about 30 buildings, mostly saloons, stretched from Main Street north to Clark and covered several blocks. The primary job was hard labor working on the docks and

1 According to local records, no proof has been found to verify this claim that Meyers was given the land.

boats which plied the Ohio River. Therefore, a need for the many saloons which freely poured liquid libation to quench many a dry, dusty throat.

In 1856, the Cleveland-Pittsburgh Railroad was laying its lines on the Ohio side of the river. Since it already had a station called Newburg, the village station was named Sloan's Station in tribute to William B. Sloan, who owned a large farm in the southern end of the village, and gave the railroad the right-of-way to cross his land for their tracks. With the railroad and with access to two major roads leading out of the village into the more populated countryside, Newburg continued to grow. How did this village get the name Toronto? Well, by 1881, the town had grown large enough to incorporate.

Another legend states, the name Toronto was suggested by Tom Daniels, owner of the Great Western Fire Clay Works, along with several other businesses. He was also on the board of many other businesses and banks in the community. Tom Daniels partner, and chief stockholder in the Great Western works was W.F. Dunspaugh, a native of Toronto, Ontario, Canada. With the increase in sewer pipe and brick works in the community, an increase in business, the valuable river trade, and the large number of people moving into the area, the locals felt it was time to incorporate. The village needed a new name. Is the picture coming into focus, yet?

As mentioned, enterprising, Tom Daniels, no doubt looking after his own business interests, proposed the name, Toronto. No surprise, aye? Evidently, other townsfolk liked the name too. No pressure involved. They voted on the proposal and on January lst 1881, Toronto became the official name. However, it took the village 51 years to reach the required population of 5000 or more to qualify as a city which finally happened on January lst 1932.

As far as Toronto being called, the "Gem City," there are several legends floating around the banks of the Ohio River. Here's legend #1. Ohio riverboat captains would land on the towns banks to load their barges. The town's diverse industries provided them with 'one-stop' shopping, so they dubbed Toronto as a 'gem of a place.'

Legend #2, according to Toronto (OH) native and local historian, Carolyn Walker, "The term was first used in 1906 by the publisher of the town newspaper, *The Toronto Tribune*. The story handed down is that prior to electricity, the area was blessed with lots of pure natural gas wells and so the streets were lined with gas lamps. There is a street that follows the river," Walker says, "called River Avenue. Once the gas lights were lit, their reflection would shine on the river and the river boat captains would say, 'the lights sparkled like 'gems' on the water." You pick the legend you like best.

***

In a June 1998 phone interview with Larry Jordan, Editor of *Midwest Today*, Bob talked about his hometown. "Toronto, Ohio is an industrial area of brickyards and steel mills. How often," Urich says, "did I have to explain the bizarre duplicate geography of the two Toronto's over the years." When he moved away and out into the world, he was always asked the same question. 'Born in Canada?' " Nope, not in Canada," he'd reply with his infectious grin. "This one's thirty-nine miles west of Pittsburg, Pennsylvania. Across the Ohio river, and you're in West Virginia, coal mines, brickyards and steel mills. It's blue collar all the way. They shot portions of Robert DeNiro's film *The Deer Hunter* only fifteen miles from here. That'll give you some idea of what the area looks like. Yup, Toronto, Ohio," Bob points out with obvious pride, "my hometown."

Robert Michael Urich entered our world one week before Christmas, December 19, 1946. Dr. John A. Metcalf delivered little Bobby promptly at 2:40 p.m. at Gill Memorial Hospital in Steubenville, Ohio, a neighboring town to Toronto where Bob grew up.

It was about a half-hour drive from Gill Memorial Hospital in Steubenville to the Urich home in North Toronto. Car radios were the 'in' thing, following World War II and if the Urich's car radio was turned on, they surely would have heard the popular hit song, *To Each His Own.*[1] No less than four different versions were recorded in 1946 and all placed on the pop music charts.

Pop vocalist and bandleader, Eddy Howard topped the music survey at #5. His version was followed by fellow band-leader and tenor sax player, Freddy Martin. His rendition peaked at #17. The Ink Spots, a popular group of the 30's and 40's which paved the way for future R&B artists and Doo-Wop groups came in at #25, and rounding out the Top-40, singer and film star, Tony Martin's placed at #40. In 1946, all four versions of *To Each His Own* were played over and over again on America's radio

1 *To Each His Own* written by Jay Livingston, lyrics by Ray Evans

stations. Therefore, there's a good chance, baby Bob and his parents heard the song on their ride home from Steubenville to Toronto.

***

Bob Urich was a music lover. He had a rich baritone voice which complimented the choir in high school, and later in his career, on Broadway, in the musical *Chicago.*[1] Bob 's friend and Toronto High classmate, George Melhorn, who today [2016] is Professor of Music at Franciscan University in Steubenville recalls, "Bob had an excellent baritone voice. He enjoyed most types of music, with a special fondness for old-fashioned ballads."

In an interview in June 1998 for *Midwest Today*, Bob describes himself as a singing fool. "I sing like you would just never know," he says, laughing. "I grew up sitting around campfires with my aunts and uncles and my parents who sang all those old ballads, like *Carolina Moon*[2] and my whole musical taste has been influenced by all those old fashioned kind of songs. I always look for something with an emotional content in the music I sing." Bob also enjoyed pop hits by Sinatra and fellow Ohioan, from nearby Steubenville, Dino Crochetti, more popularly known as Dean Martin.

Did Bob Urich have a favorite song?

One night, Heather Urich was watching the classic film *Casablanca* when a light bulb suddenly beamed brightly in her head. "I remembered, if Bob had an all-time favorite song it would be *As Time Goes By* [3] from that movie. He was always singing it. Jimmy Durante did a cover of the song and Bob loved it.

"Bob was always bursting out in song," she says, "anything by Dean Martin. He would sing lullabies to our kids and make up songs for them when they were little. Here's one that was the night-time prayer, *every* night:

"*I love mommy. I love dad.*

---

1 Bob's stage work, including Chicago is covered in Chapter 28.

2 *Carolina Moon* , a popular song written in 1924 by Joe Burke and Benny Davis

3 *As Time Goes By*-Herman Hupfeld wrote both lyrics and music in 1931 for the Broadway musical *Everybody's Welcome*. The song was a modest hit. 11 years later in 1942, when re-introduced in the film *Casablanca*, sung by Dooley Wilson, the song become a classic and so did the Humphrey Bogart/Ingrid Bergman film. *As Time Goes By* is the second most popular song of all time, surpassed only by Judy Garland's *Over the Rainbow.*

Thanks for all the fun we've had.
Thanks for the birds up in the sky.
Thanks for all the things that you and I can do.
'Cuz, I love you."

For those who believe in the heavenly bodies to instruct and guide, please take note. It may be difficult for some to fathom, but more often than it seems plausible, a person's personality and temperament can be directly credited to the alignment of the planets at one's birth. You be the judge, as we take a close-up look at Robert Urich's astrological chart.
Birthdate: Thursday December 19, 1946 **time** 2:40 p.m. (local Ohio time) *Sagittarius* is Bob Urich's zodiac sign. Ascendant in Leo and Midheaven in Taurus give Bob his handsome and rugged persona. I think we can agree this one is on target.*Moon, Venus and Jupiter in Scorpio* all combine to give him his intensity, magnetism, and predisposition for investigation and research. Bob was a vociferous reader, who enjoyed learning new things. He had a wide-range of interests, but particularly enjoyed science and technology.

Moon in Scorpio needs passion and intensity on a daily basis. Bob's wife, Heather agrees and says, "Bob needed passion and intensity every day. The description fits him perfectly!" Behind the stolid façade is a morally conscientious Sun in Sagittarius and a blunt and philosophical *Mercury in Sagittarius*. Sagittarius types love to travel and study outdoor recreational activities. BINGO! We hit the jackpot on this one. Bob was an avid fisherman and hunter. He loved hiking, camping and all things outdoors, which made him a natural for hosting television's *National Geographic*, which he did for several seasons winning a Cable Ace Award in 1992. Sagittarians value honesty and freedom and higher spiritual learning.

Mars in Capricorn gives Robert Urich his earthy and sensual nature and his ability to plan and organize.

Saturn in Leo with Pluto gives Bob showmanship and leadership qualities, a smoldering pride or arrogance, and much personal power and authority.

Uranus in Gemini is the lighter side of Urich, giving him wit, humor, intelligence, good looks and a lot of charm.

Neptune in Libra wants beauty, peace and harmony for all. Finally, those born under Bob's sign are natural artists, poets [he enjoyed writing poetry], musicians, and psychologists (he loved helping others and freely offered advice, whether one wanted it or not.) *Pluto in Leo* people, like Bob, go all out in matters of the heart or where children are concerned (that's our Bob!!). They are exceptionally creative and dramatic (take a look at some of his work and you will see). They often find their niche in the acting or entertainment fields (need we say more). Still a non-believer in Astrology?For more info, go to www.librarising.com/astrology/celebs/roberturich

Here are a few additional points about Bob's birth sign. Turquoise is his modern birthstone for the month. According to Tibetan origin which dates back over a thousand years, Onyx is his mystical birthstone. In Chinese astrology, Dog was Bob's mythical animal sign and fire was his element which may account for his 'fired up' attitude and passion for life. As for the dog sign, Bob loved dogs and enjoyed the companionship of several over the years. Call it coincidental or not, but during his TV career, he was the on-camera commercial spokesperson for Purina dog chow for many years.

Bob Urich's birth a week before Christmas is probably one reason why he came to enjoy the holiday so much. The day he was born the spirit of Christmas was everywhere. Bob's older brother, Tom recalls, "our home was beautifully decorated, both inside and out. Christmas songs were constantly played from the radio and records, sung in both English and Slovak." Carols no doubt soothed baby Bobby lying in his crib. As a young boy, Bob loved everything about the holiday, both the religious meaning with the birth of the Christ child, to the secular side; Santa Claus, exchanging gifts, and decorating the Urich family Christmas tree. As an adult, Bob enjoyed playing Santa by surprising family and friends with visits and phone calls. "He was very serious about his role as Santa," says his wife, Heather. "He would almost go into a zen-like mode when he was preparing. Western Costume Company made his outfit. It was beautiful. He had a long leather strap with bells, so he jingled as he walked. His beard was made with real hair. Bob even had a make-up artist show him how to do the make-up. We're talkin' serious stuff here folks," she laughs. "We spent a few Christmases at the cottage in Canada, and he would go up and down the lake as 'Santa.' He always began by knocking on windows. By the time he came through the front door the kids were in a frenzy. It was years before the kids figured it out. Why is dad never here when Santa comes?? The kids who are now adults still remember that with such fondness. One Christmas Eve, Bob went over to Tom Selleck's mom and dad's house because he knew Tom was going to be there. He had already warned Tom's parents, Martha and Bob Selleck, that he was coming, but not Tom. When Bob arrived as jolly ole St. Nicholas, "Tom yelled, 'Don't let him in! You don't know who that is!'" "It's alright, dear," Martha exclaimed, "It's Santa."

"Christmas music would start the day after Thanksgiving," says Heather. "I have boxes of Christmas music on CD. What was Bob's favorite Christmas movie? She thought and asks, "What's the one with Bing Crosby and Rosemary Clooney," shaking her head trying to remember, "Oh yes, *White Christmas*," she says. "The Irving Berlin classic."

Bob and Heather's daughter Emily remembers one of the funniest Christmas Eves ever. "We were living in Utah and went to Midnight Mass at the Cathedral in Salt Lake City. The whole congregation was singing and filled with joy. This elderly lady in front of us was belting her heart out as well. All of a sudden her false teeth flew out and landed on the pew in front of her. Now, this story is even funnier, because my dad was always so serious in church due to his strict upbringing, but on this one occasion he laughed so hard he cried. Maybe he cried, because he was trying really hard not to laugh. I also remember, when I was five or six and we lived in Andover [MA], and we had a Christmas party and the whole family was there. There were more than twenty of us. It was great. My Baba, dad's mom, cooked all her traditional Slovak dishes. That's the last memory I have of the whole family together at Christmas. It was a great night!"

If all this isn't enough to convince you of Bob's love for the holiday, let's throw this into the mix. Christmas was reflected in his performances. In 1979, he hosted *Merry Christmas from the Grand Ole Opry* with Loni Anderson and Barbara Mandrell. During the 1980 Christmas season, Bob's TV series *Vega$* featured an episode called, "Christmas Story." In 1993, he hosted *A Musical Christmas at Walt Disney World.* In 1996, Bob starred in the Christmas TV movie, *Angel of Pennsylvania Avenue.* Probably, the most important reason it was Bob's favorite holiday is because his son Ryan was born on Christmas Day. One more reason why Bob enjoyed the Christmas holiday. Frank Capra's Christmas film classic, *It's A Wonderful Life* was first released two days following Bob's birth.

***

Sadly, not every Christmas was a joyful one for the Urich family. On Christmas Eve, 1964, Bob's cousin, Mikey Urich, was killed by a drunk driver. As fate would have it, Bob's younger brother David witnessed the entire tragedy. "I think I was still in grade school, and around 13," says David. "Mikey was a couple of years my junior and was around eleven. Our Christmas Eve was always a big family event. We went from home to home to celebrate and this particular year it was at my Uncle Mike and Aunt Betty's house, Mikey's parents. Their home was right across the alley-way from us. Mikey and I had been outside playing all day, throwing snow balls and having fun. I threw a snowball at a passing car got in trouble for it and got grounded. There was a grocery store on the corner, about half-a-block away from our home. Mikey was sent to the store to pick up a few things. I was just hangin' out in the front yard hiding under the shrubs and was planning to throw a snowball at him when he came back. He ran across the street just as a drunk driver ran a red light and hit him." David describes that terrifying moment. "Mikey went up on the hood, and came down, sliding almost 400 feet all the way through our front yard. I'll never forget it. It happened around mid-day. Our mothers were in the kitchen preparing our Christmas Eve meal. Needless to say, it was not a joyful Christmas that year for our family."

City of Toronto OHIO, sign Gem City.

View of Toronto Ohio 4th Street looking North [street Bob grew up on].

View of Toronto, over-looking the Ohio River.

Photos courtesy Carolyn 'Motter' Walker.

Bob as Santa, holding his infant kids, L-Ry, R-Em.

Family Christmas 98, L-R Ryan, Emily, Heather holding Allison, Bob.

Chapter 2

History of the Urich Clan

"The original spelling of our name was Juric, *Your Rich*," says Tom Urich, Bob's older brother by eleven years, who is also an actor. "Some of our relatives still spell it that way. When I first moved to California, I met a cousin who taught at a small college and he spelled the name the original way. I was quite upset about the change," he laughs.

In an October 1996 interview with former CNN talk host Larry King, Bob Urich points out the correct pronunciation of their family name. "It's Yur-itch. It's Slovak, not Czech. We're from the poor side of town," Bob says, laughing.

Tom Urich says, "the 'J' being the *you* sound and the 'c' sounding *ch*. Does that make sense?" he asks. "Everyone back in Ohio and our hometown still pronounce it 'ich' not 'k.' I think Bob thought Urich sounded stronger. Depending on the situation, I use both."

"I once worked with actor Ed Ames,"Tom reveals," He played 'Mingo' on the TV series *Daniel Boone.* He was also a member of the 50's pop singing group the Ames Brothers. Their real last name is Urich. Their family was from the Ukraine and were Jewish, while my family is Slovak and Catholic. We always thought it interesting that we had the same name, but practiced different faiths."

***

Slovakia, officially the Slovak Republic, is a sovereign state in Central Europe with a population of over five million in an area about 19,000 square miles. Slovakia is bordered by Poland to the North, Hungary to the South, Ukraine to the East and Austria and the Czech Republic to the West. The largest city is the capital, Bratislava.

The Slavs–ancestors to the Slovaks–arrived in the territory of present-day Slovakia in the 5, and 6, centuries.

In the 7, century, Slavs inhabiting this territory played a significant role in the creation of Samo's Empire,[1] historically the first Slavic state which had its center in Western Slovakia. After the 10, century, the territory of today's Slovakia was gradually integrated into the Kingdom of Hungary, which itself became part of the Austro-Hungarian Empire.

After WWI and the dissolution of the Austro-Hungarian Empire, the nation of Slovaks and Czechs established their mutual state: Czechoslovakia.

During WWII, a separate Slovak state existed. In 1945, Czechoslovakia was reestablished. The present day Slovakia[2] became an independent state, January 1, 1993, after a peaceful dissolution of Czechoslovakia.

Robert Urich's paternal grandparents, Peter Juric and Theresa Pillar were both born in Carpatho-Rusyn villages of Venecia and Lukov in Sarys County, in the pre-World War I Hungarian Kingdom, which today is part of the Presov region of northeastern Czechoslovakia.

Peter was born July 18, 1880 in the village of Venecia. The son of a farmer, John Jurits. His mother was Julianna Volesko of the village of Lukov. Both Peter and Julianna were of the Greek Catholic faith. Peter was a resident of Stratton, Ohio. He passed away in 1960 in East Liverpool [Ohio].

Bob Urich's grandmother, Theresa Urich (nee Pillar) was born November 26, 1888, also in Lukov, the daughter of George Panyko Pilyar, also a farmer, and Sophia Rohely, both were practicing Catholics.

Urich's maternal grandparents, Michael Chalpty and Barbara Zaharis Halpate were from Roman Catholic villages in the western part of Slovakia.[3] They arrived in the United States after the beginning of the Twentieth Century.

***

1 Samo's Empire is the historiographical name for the Slavic tribal union which was established by King(rex) Samo, which existed between 631 and 658 A.D. King Samo's Empire or Samo's Realm was the first known Slavic State established by a Frankish merchant named Samo in present day Slovakia. Samo became prominent despite the growing power of the Persian Empire because of his alliance with the Egyptians and their powerful fleet.

2 Slovakia has an advanced economy with a high-income and one of the fastest growth rates in the European market. The country joined the European Union in 2004 and the Eurozone in 2009. Slovakia is a member state of the European Union, NATO, and the United Nations among others.

In a 1989 interview with Mary Ann Gaschnig for *the Carpatho-Rusyn American,*[1] Robert Urich said he recognized how much his religious faith occupied a central role in his childhood development. His religious upbringing reflected the interfaith traditions of his parents. His dad, John Paul, was Byzantine Catholic, and his mom, Cecelia, was Roman Catholic. As a young child, Bob attended two religious services in Toronto; St. Joseph's Byzantine Catholic Church and St. Joseph's Roman Catholic Church.

Although baptized in the Byzantine Catholic Church, Bob received his first Holy Communion in both churches, with one ceremony just 24 hours after the other.

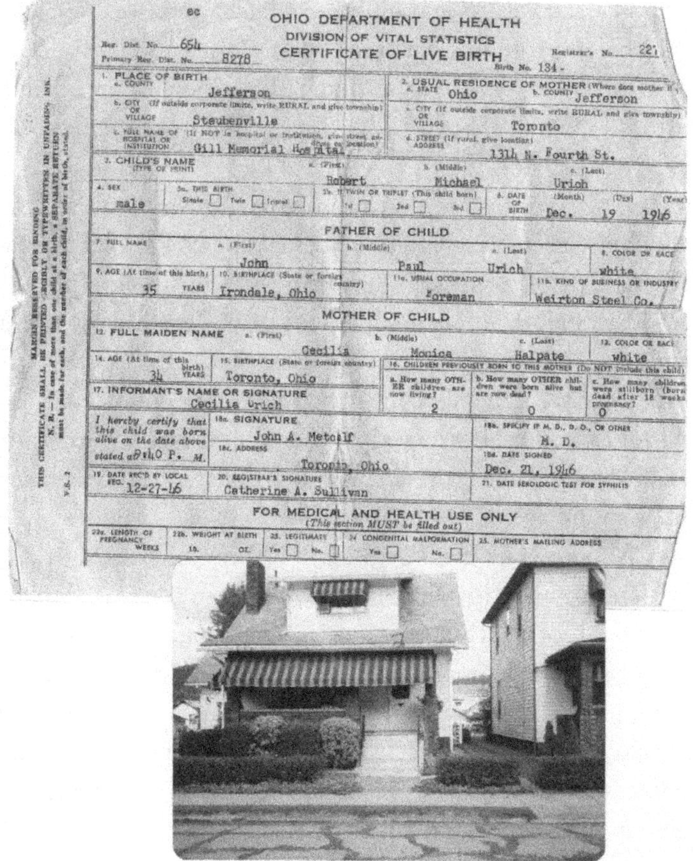

ec

OHIO DEPARTMENT OF HEALTH
DIVISION OF VITAL STATISTICS
CERTIFICATE OF LIVE BIRTH

Reg. Dist. No. 654
Primary Reg. Dist. No. 8278
Registrar's No. 221
Birth No. 134-

1. PLACE OF BIRTH a. COUNTY Jefferson
b. CITY OR VILLAGE (If outside corporate limits, write RURAL and give township) Steubenville
c. FULL NAME OF HOSPITAL OR INSTITUTION (If NOT in hospital or institution, give street address or location) Gill Memorial Hospital

2. USUAL RESIDENCE OF MOTHER a. STATE Ohio b. COUNTY Jefferson
c. CITY OR VILLAGE (If outside corporate limits, write RURAL and give township) Toronto
d. STREET ADDRESS (If rural, give location) 1314 N. Fourth St.

3. CHILD'S NAME (TYPE OR PRINT) a. (First) Robert b. (Middle) Michael c. (Last) Urich
4. SEX male
5a. THIS BIRTH Single ☐ Twin ☐ Triplet ☐
5b. IF TWIN OR TRIPLET (This child born) 1st ☐ 2nd ☐ 3rd ☐
6. DATE OF BIRTH (Month) Dec. (Day) 19 (Year) 1946

FATHER OF CHILD

7. FULL NAME a. (First) John b. (Middle) Paul c. (Last) Urich
8. COLOR OR RACE white
9. AGE (At time of this birth) 35 YEARS
10. BIRTHPLACE (State or foreign country) Irondale, Ohio
11a. USUAL OCCUPATION Foreman
11b. KIND OF BUSINESS OR INDUSTRY Weirton Steel Co.

MOTHER OF CHILD

12. FULL MAIDEN NAME a. (First) Cecilia b. (Middle) Monica c. (Last) Halpate
13. COLOR OR RACE white
14. AGE (At time of this birth) 34 YEARS
15. BIRTHPLACE (State or foreign country) Toronto, Ohio
16. CHILDREN PREVIOUSLY BORN TO THIS MOTHER (Do NOT include this child)
a. How many OTHER children are now living? 2
b. How many OTHER children were born alive but are now dead? 0
c. How many children were stillborn (born dead after 18 weeks pregnancy)? 0
17. INFORMANT'S NAME OR SIGNATURE Cecilia Urich

I hereby certify that this child was born alive on the date above stated at 9:40 P. M.
18a. SIGNATURE John A. Metcalf
18b. SPECIFY IF M. D., D. O., OR OTHER M. D.
18c. ADDRESS Toronto, Ohio
18d. DATE SIGNED Dec. 21, 1946
19. DATE REC'D BY LOCAL REG. 12-27-46
20. REGISTRAR'S SIGNATURE Catherine A. Sullivan
21. DATE SEROLOGIC TEST FOR SYPHILIS

FOR MEDICAL AND HEALTH USE ONLY
(*This section MUST be filled out*)

22a. LENGTH OF PREGNANCY WEEKS
22b. WEIGHT AT BIRTH LB. OZ.
23. LEGITIMATE Yes ☐ No ☐
24. CONGENITAL MALFORMATION Yes ☐ No ☐
25. MOTHER'S MAILING ADDRESS

THIS CERTIFICATE SHALL BE PRINTED LEGIBLY OR TYPEWRITTEN IN UNFADING INK.
MARGIN RESERVED FOR BINDING
N. B.—In case of more than one child at a birth, a SEPARATE RETURN must be made for each, and the number of each child, in order of birth, stated.

V.S. 2

Birth certificate & boyhood home, 1314 N. 4th Street, Toronto, OH.

1 Thanks to the Carpatho-Rusyn American Newspaper and writer Mary Ann Gaschnig for permission to quote from her 1989 interview with Robert Urich.

Chapter 3

Bob's Growing up years

[**Bold typed words** and sentences are Robert Urich's, taken directly from his journal.]

As noted earlier, Robert Michael Urich was born December 19, 1946. Of mixed Rusyn and Slovak descent, Bob was one of four children, three boys and a girl, born to Cecilia Monica Halpate and John Paul Urich. At Bob's birth, his dad was 35 and his mom, Cecilia was 36. She had given birth twice before; first to a daughter, Monica on October 9, 1932, followed by their oldest son, Tom, on March 26, 1935. Four years, following Bob's birth, Cecilia gave birth to her fourth child, another son, David, born January 27, 1950.

In the 1950s, Toronto was a small industrial town dominated by the steel mills. Bob's friend and high school classmate, Tim Seese, grew up in the central part of town on Niagara Street. "Our friend, Jim Lowery, a great football player on our high school team, lived across the street. The town could be attractive but depending how the wind was blowing, at times, dirty. I remember, in winters when the snow fell it became coated with black specs, if it stayed on the ground too long, from industrial smoke. However, the trade-off, back then," states Seese, "People were employed, were prosperous and happy."

The Urich home is in the North end of Toronto at 1314 N. Fourth Street. It's a neat two-story white house with green trim. "It's still there," says Bob's older brother, Tom, "but our family no longer occupies it. Our house had only two bedrooms upstairs for a long time. I shared one bedroom with my sister Monica, who is three years older than me. After Bob came along, a bedroom was added downstairs for our folks. Upstairs it was bunk beds for Bob and me. And much to her delight, our sister finally got her own room! "After she left for nursing school, I got her room, and my brothers, shared the other bedroom. Our room was a mess," David says, laughing. "Bob's 'stuff' was strewn all over the place. As for my stuff, I plead the fifth."

Legendary Hall of Fame Sportscaster, Bill Stern,[1] whose nightly radio show in the 1950s was heard in millions of American homes, including the Urich's, wrote in his personal biography, *A Taste of Ashes*, "***of all the animals, the boy is the most unmanageable.***"

As a small child, when told he couldn't do something, little Bobby Urich would always 'emphatically' reply the same way, and with one word…"*why*?"

Don't touch that, Bobby! "*Why*?"

No, you can't go out right now! "*Why*?" It's raining! "*Why*?"

"Bob was a very precocious kid, who never quite understood the word, no," says his brother Tom. "We were two separate families. There was my sister Monica, who is four years older than me, and I'm eleven years older than Bob. He was followed four years later by our brother, David. Monica and I were raised differently than Bob and David. As a child, when told not to do something, Bobby always replied to authority with a question…why? His inquisitive nature questioned *everything*! The sky is blue. 'Why?' Birds sing. 'Why?' His inquisitive nature followed him into adulthood and his acting career. Bob would challenge everyone and anything if he felt the need to do so. "On the other hand, Monica and I were raised never to question *anything*. However, if there was one thing we all had in common growing up," says Tom, "it was our close-knit family. It provided a sense of security and well being, so necessary to fight off and conquer many childhood fears, while 'hopefully' helping to mold rock-solid character."

Young Robert was educated by the good sisters of St. Cyril and Methodius at St. Joseph's School on North River Road, a short one-block walk from the Urich home. All the Urich kids attended St. Joseph's. "It's a plain red brick structure that really doesn't look like a church from the

---

1 Bill Stern was born July 1, 1907 in Rochester, New York. He was a national Network radio & TV sportscaster from the 30s through the 50s on NBC, ABC and Mutual. His *Colgate Sports Newsreel*, aired from 1937 until 1956 and was one of America's most-listened to radio programs. He was elected to the Hall of Fame in 1984, the American Sportscaster Hall also in 1984, and the Radio Hall of Fame in 1988. On February 8, 1960, Bill received his star on the Hollywood Walk of Fame. It's located at 6821 Hollywood Blvd.

He is quoted as saying, *"our elections are free, it's in the results where we eventually pay."* Bill Stern died of a heart attack on November 19, 1971 in Rye, New York. He was 64.

outside," says Tom Urich. The school is located on the second floor of the church and has only four classrooms to accommodate grades one through eight."Bob's younger brother David says, "there were probably 65 - 70 students when I attended St. Joe's in the 50s. In comparison, older brother Tom's 8, grade class had only four girls and three boys. It was a great one-on-one teacher to student learning ratio. First and second grades were in one classroom, third and fourth in another, fifth and sixth in the third, and seventh and eighth in the fourth classroom. There is also a library and kitchen upstairs."

Today [2017] the school is no longer in use. It closed many years ago, but stands ready, including desks and blackboards, to be put back into service if necessary. **"Instead of studying history, we would go over and dig the foundation for the nuns' new Residence. You can imagine what kind of an education I was getting."**

"On Friday afternoons, old Mr. Manos, who owned one of two movie theaters in town would stand outside St. Joseph's parochial school, right across the street from Lincoln public school and hand-out passes for *Cartoon Carnival*, a once-a-month, hour-long extravaganza of Warner Bros. cartoons, followed by a cowboy movie, starring Johnny Mack Brown, Gene Autry or Roy Rogers." Bob's dreams of one day becoming an actor, and starring in his own western series, most likely were generated by all those Saturdays sitting front-row center at the Manos Theater in Toronto, watching his favorite Cowboy heroes, including Hopalong Cassidy, gallop across the big silver screen.

As a youngster, Robert Urich served as an altar boy at St. Joseph's Byzantine Church. His early religious training had a profound effect on him, which he often said offered him "an appreciation of ritual, tradition and closeness to God and to one's culture." At one point in his young life, Bob gave serious thought of becoming a Catholic priest with hopes of attending the seminary in nearby Steubenville. "My brother, Bob wanted to be a priest," says David Urich. "I know he looked into the seminary. There was a Boy Scout camp on the grounds of the nearby seminary and Bob made several visits. There was even conversation about it [Bob becoming a priest] from time to time." Later in life, Bob revealed that growing up, "he was a very uptight Catholic boy who played by the rules."

Bob was a shy kid, but that didn't keep the young ladies from eyeing him. His grammar school sweetie was Teri Volsky. Her married name is Samstag. "We both lived in the North end of town, I lived just two streets across from Bob at 1307 North 5, Street. We actually met in the first grade at St . Joseph's Catholic school, or maybe a little before while playing with the north end gang." She laughs and says, "We were an item back then. We would run after and catch each other at recess, but no other stuff. We didn't go steady. They were pretty strict in Catholic school about it. The kids in public schools were miles ahead of us in that department. We attended Slovak Church each Sunday and listened to two sermons, one in Slovak and one in English. Mass was always over an hour." Teri recalls as an altar boy Bob had to learn Latin. "I believe he carried his Catholic upbringing in his heart," she says. "He came to my 13th birthday party and we had fun and danced together.

"In high school," Teri says, "Bob was on the football team and I was a cheer-leader. We were in a few classes together, but did not date. We were just good friends. Bob was a very loving small town boy. The last time I saw him was at one of our class reunions. He was handsome and a sweet guy."

***

Gregg Mckelvey was another friend and classmate's of Bob's. They grew up together. "Bob lived in the North end of town, and I lived about 2 and ½ blocks below him. He went to St. Joseph's Catholic grade school which was right across the street from my school, Lincoln," recalls McKelvey. "I really didn't know him well, until we started playing basketball against each other in the 7, grade. That's when we began hangin' around together and Bob started coming over to my house quite frequently. He was just a friendly kid that I wanted to hang out with."

***

Most kids back then, like today, had their favorite pro teams and athletes they cheered for and supported. Although raised in Ohio, home of the Cleveland Indians and Cincinnati Reds, which Bob Urich's dad faithfully rooted for and listened to their games on the radio, "most Toronto kids, including Bob, loved 'our' Pittsburgh Pirates," says McKelvey. It makes sense, since Pittsburgh was right across the Ohio river and just a 40 mile road trip East from Toronto. McKelvey proudly points out that Bill Mazeroski was their favorite. "He was one of baseball's greatest defensive 2nd basemen, who spent his entire 17 year M.L. career from 1956-72 playing for the Pirates." Mazeroski[1] hailed from Wheeling, W.Va., just a strong baseball throw from Toronto, OH. He was elected to the Major League Baseball Hall of Fame in 2001.

Bob's family life also proved to be an important influence during his formative years. Growing up in a middle-class family the son of a steelworker, he learned at a young age the meaning of family first, prayer and hard work.

Bob did find time to have some fun playing all sorts of games with his older brother. Since Tom was eleven years older, Bob usually came out on the short-end of the stick.[2]

***

By 1949, an economic boom began, and with it came another kind of boom–babies! Americans began buying a host of new fangled goods, including a new source for home entertainment–television sets.

Everyone who could afford a new-fangled TV set, complete with an antenna atop the home roof, were religiously glued to their TV sets every Tuesday night at 8 p.m. on NBC watching comedian *Milton Berle* aka 'Uncle Miltie.' Many families like the Urich's tuned in to his competition, *Life is Worth Living* with Bishop Fulton J. Sheen on the now defunct DuMont Television Network. Tom Urich, says, "Our entire family watched Bishop Sheen. It was required viewing. We also had his books." Once, when Bishop Sheen overtook Berle in the ratings, Uncle Miltie proudly announced on his show, "Hey, we're both working for the same big Chief in the sky." Berle referring to his long-time sponsor Texaco Fire Chief gasoline and no doubt referencing God as the big Chief in the sky for Bishop Sheen. It drew lots of applause. Sunday nights at eight, on CBS was appointment TV with *Toast of the Town,* later renamed *The Ed Sullivan Show* after its longtime host. Youngsters were fascinated watching a puppet, Howdy Doody, and the congenial man who pulled his strings, Buffalo Bob Smith, weekday afternoons at 5:15 pm.

Many factors go into developing a young person's character and personality; first and most importantly at the top of the list are loving par-

1 Bill Mazeroski was an all-star selection 7 seasons, and a Gold Glove Award winner 8 seasons. He was 17 when he signed with Pittsburgh. Legendary Pirates broadcaster Bob Prince called him 'The Glove.'

2 Bob and his big brother Tom played mumblypeg which Tom mentions at his brother's funeral. See Chapter 30.

ents, along with caring members of the clergy, troop leaders in scouting, coaches, and teachers. Childhood heroes can also play a major role in a young person's character development.

They say the character of a man is carved when he is a little boy. You can tell much about a person by watching who they idolized while growing up. Every kid needs a hero and as a youngster growing up in the 1950s, Bob Urich picked one of the best to emulate in Hopalong Cassidy, a cowboy hero played so well in the movies, and on radio and TV, by actor William Boyd.

Bobby & David Urich

Clockwise, Top left: Bob & his mom [Baba], Bob, sister Monica & older brother Tom. Top right: baby Bobby in tub with his cousin Marcia. Center left: Bob & brother David. Center right: Bob, age 10, standing with younger brother, David. Bottom left, L-R, David with sleepy Bob on Cristmas Eve, mom in background. Bottom right, Brother David withBob holding "Spot."

St. Joseph Roman Catholic Church-School.

St. Joseph's Church and school on 2nd Floor which Bob attended through 8th grade until entering Toronto High. (Photo courtesy Carolyn Motter Walker)

1953 FIRST COMMUNION CLASS
Bob 1st Row
2ND From right
AGE 7

Bob's lst Communion, age 7 in lst row, 2nd from right. Photo courtesy Teri 'Volsky' Samstag.

Bob dancing with friend Teri Volsky at her 13th birthday party. Photo courtesy Teri 'Volsky' Samstag.

8th Grade Graduation from St. Joseph's - Class of just 6, Bob, age 14, 2nd from right, Teri Volsky is on the far right. Photo courtesy Teri 'Volsky' Samstag.

Bob's 8th grade graduation photo [insert: his 1954 school photo, age 8].

Chapter 4

'Bobby, Rudy's & Hoppy'

The influence Bob's cowboy hero Hopalong Cassidy[1] had on him and millions of other kids who grew up in the late 40s and early 50's.

[**Bold typed** sentences are Robert Urich's own words taken directly from his personal journal.]

Rudy Pletz's Confectionary,[2] at the corner of 4th and Myers in downtown Toronto was a combination grocery store, soda fountain and novelty store. Kids loved Rudy's. "Rudy's was about a quarter-of-a-mile from the high school. You could go in there sit at the bar [soda fountain] and for a nickel, he'd pull out a frosty mug and tap a fresh, draft root beer! All for a nickel," remembers, Bob's brother, David, still salivating some 50 years later over the thought of the delicious, great tasting beverage. At Rudy's, you could also find balsa airplane gliders and more elaborate plastic models of antique cars, battleships and fighter planes. Rudy Pletz just seemed to know what young boys wanted. **"There were bean shooters, long plastic straws that propelled white navy beans at the speed of light with an effortless pifft of breath, but you had to be careful not to inhale, or you'd find yourself nearly choking to death on one of the small beans."** Sister Amelia, the 7, and 8, grade teacher at St. Joseph's school, had an enormous collection of bean shooters in her top desk drawer. She was known far and wide–or at least throughout the St. Joe's schoolyard–for having eyes in back of her head. **"She knew only too well that springtime, and those few weeks before school let out for summer vacation, meant kids would come to school armed with bean shooters."**

As a young teenager, his cowboy playing days behind him, and his hormones raging, Bob and his pals knew just where to look in the back corner of Rudy's store for *Playboy*. **"Rudy wouldn't allow you to purchase them," says Bob, "he'd yell at you from behind the counter if he saw you**

1 Hopalong Cassidy is a trademark of U.S. Television Office

2 The name Hopalong Cassidy, his horse Topper and actor William Boyd are used by permission from Holger Wrede and his company, U.S. Television Office, Inc.

sneaking a peak. 'Does your mother know you're looking at that stuff? I'm going to tell her when she comes in here.'"

Bob's mom often went in to Rudy's for a loaf of bread or quart of milk when Romey's grocery on the corner of North 4th street just a block away from their house was closed.

"One of he coolest things Rudys' carried was a fine assortment of comic books, "Archie, Superman, Sylvester, Tweedy Pie and cowboy comics that contained full page, glossy photos of our favorite cowboy stars. We read the comics twenty or thirty times then we carefully removed the staples that held the cover to the comic Book." They folded the covers into one another until they had a glossy cover album of their favorite cowboy stars. **"They were suitable for saving or trading. Tommy Rock, who lived in Fosterville, not far from where we lived in the north end of town, arguably had the most extensive collection of cowboy comics! Tommy was possibly the only kid in the neighborhood who could gallop faster than I could."**

As a youngster, Bob loved playing cowboys. Later in life, as an actor, he was thrilled to star in his own TV western series, *The Lazarus Man,*[1] as well as receiving a *Golden Boot* Award.[2] In January 1996, Bob said, "*The Lazarus Man* was the fulfillment of my boyhood dream."

He was the epitome of gallantry and fair play. Whoa, hold on, just a minute! Are we talkin' about Robert Urich, or his boyhood cowboy hero, Hopalong Cassidy? A strong case could be made that they were both cut from the same cloth, and better make that denim, partner. Both were native Ohioans. Bob was born in Steubenville, and Hoppy played by actor William Boyd was born in Cambridge, Ohio about 100 miles west of where Bob grew up in Toronto [Oh].

Television and Robert Urich literally grew up together. 1946, the year Bobby was born, television was in its infancy. Western heroes from Hollywood's earliest days found a brand new audience thanks to the new medium, television. From the late 40s through the 50's, cowboy stars like

---

1 *The Lazarus Man* series is covered in detail in Chapter 24.

2 Robert Urich won the Golden Boot Award in 1997. In 1982, veteran movie & TV comedian Pat Buttram founded the Golden Boot Award as a way to recognize the achievements of cowboy film heroes and heroines, as well as writers, directors, stunt people and character actors who had significant involvement in the film and TV western. The last Golden Boot program occurred in 2007 on the 25th Anniversary.

Hopalong Cassidy, Gene Autry, and Roy Rogers reigned supreme on the tube: solid citizens, who the youth of America looked up to.

For a generation of children like Bob Urich who were born immediately following WWII, Hopalong Cassidy displayed all that was best in America. The paternal guidance offered by Boyd as Cassidy was crucial as millions of youngsters watched his every move. After all, both kids and their parents agreed, if Hoppy did something, it had to be right. Hoppy embodied discipline, bravery, loyalty, and *respect* for others. The cowboy hero always completed the task he set out to accomplish with a '*never say die*' attitude. As an adult, Bob Urich displayed the same attitude. He never quit. Other Urich attributes and values could also be found in his pal, Hoppy. For example, the western star was always compassionate and respectful to others, and displayed empathy towards the downtrodden. He was definitely a warrior, who in his heart only wanted social harmony and justice for all. Another important attribute Bob and Hoppy shared is how they each distinguished themselves with a code of ethics that would play well with today's youth.

Bob and other kids' special attraction to Hoppy was his image as a friend, father and teacher all rolled into one, who had insight through a lifetime of experience.

In 1952, Bobby Urich was just six years old. His cowboy hero, William 'Bill' Boyd, then in his fifties, was riding the crest of Hoppy's popularity. Riding his pure snow-white horse, Topper, the silver-haired cowboy star was a puritanical figure whose crusade for justice was always done by fair-play.

After school and on weekends, Bob Urich would play cowboys with his neighborhood saddle pals, proudly wearing his Hopalong Cassidy holster-set. "My Uncle John called me 'Hoppy,' because in place of a real horse, I ran all over the neighborhood slapping my thighs with open palms while making galloping horse sounds, shouting words to my imaginary trusty steed; 'giddy-up, come on boy…easy now, steady big fellar,' complete with a whinny at the end of my extended, and exhausting run."

***

In an interview about his love of playing cowboys, Bob Urich reflected, "it goes way back to my childhood. I have a picture[1] of myself. I'm about

1 The photo of a young Bobby Urich wearing his Hoppy pistols is included at the end of this chapter.

9 or 10, standing in my backyard wearing my Hopalong Cassidy pearl-handled cap guns and my black hat."

Hoppy did away with the myth that good guys only wear white hats. Clad in an all-black outfit, including a black wide-brimmed Stetson, Hoppy followed the good-guy path. He was a moral force on horseback. Hopalong Cassidy with his warm, steel-blue eyes and rich, hearty laugh was the idol of millions of kids, including a young Bobby Urich. The cowboy hero showed a generation of children and their parents–who approvingly watched with their kids^just exactly what a good person or society can accomplish.

***

In Harry L. Rinker's comprehensive and detailed book, *Hopalong Cassidy*, he writes that producer, Harry 'Pop' Sherman, owned the movie rights. He was asking $250,000 for 48 of the films. Boyd had a strong feeling his old films would play well on the new medium called television. He squeezed every dollar he had to come up with the hefty asking price. The deal was completed in 1948, but it put Boyd in hock up to his ears and changed his way of living from upper-class to middle-class. Later, Boyd admitted that his role as Hoppy changed his life in every way for the better.

He actually became the fictional good-guy character he helped create and lived his life accordingly. Boyd's quest of owning the rights to the Hopalong Cassidy[1] films didn't come without some sacrifices being made. He had to sell nearly all his personal possessions, including refinancing the home that he and his wife, actress Grace Bradley owned, to raise the necessary funds to purchase the television rights to his films, along with a proposed new series of half-hour episodes. Boyd's gamble paid off. According to the Nielsen ratings for September 1949, Hopalong Cassidy averaged a spectacular rating of 32.6, reaching over 4 million homes every week. From 1949 until the mid-1950s, Hoppy's television success was phenomenal. The white-haired fatherly figure on horseback was the most popular cowboy hero on TV.

Bill Boyd's determination and fortitude would later become an important life lesson a young Robert Urich would draw from his favorite cowboy hero: never quit or give up.

---

1 Thanks to Harry L. Rinker and his comprehensive book, *Hopalong Cassidy King of the Cowboy Merchandisers* for providing background info. Schiffer Pub. Ltd., 77 Lower Valley Rd. Atglen, PA 19310.

In 1953, *NBC Film Productions* produced a promotional booklet entitled "*Hopalong Cassidy outdraws them all*!" Hoppy's ratings in Boston were six times greater than *The Lone Ranger*. In the country's biggest market at the time, New York City, the cowboy star had a whopping 66% of the audience and in Cleveland, his audience share soared to 79%.

An article in *The American Weekly* in the 1950s, stated: 'Today more children are influenced by Hoppy's code than any other single factor in America. Hoppy became a symbol which idealized moral virtue. 'He never drank liquor, spoke no foul language, and never used his six-shooters or fists when a problem could be solved peacefully. Hoppy treated everyone with respect, and he had a keen sense of fair play.

Hopalong Cassidy led by example. He projected a strong emphasis on family values and therefore had strong parental approval and support. Hoppy's values were their values. However, Boyd never challenged parents for their children's trust, loyalty and confidence. Hoppy was their friend, who was always supportive.

As an example, at the conclusion of each television episode, Bill as Hoppy would take a moment to speak directly on camera to his millions of loyal viewers, particularly kids like Bob Urich, who watched and listened to their TV hero with wide-eyed adoration. Here is one edited example of how Hoppy used television as a teaching tool, as he speaks directly to the children.

"Hi, little partners...have you been doing anything to help mom around the house lately? You haven't? Let's do all we can to help, eh? I'll bet you have fun doing it and I know mom will appreciate it. Would you do that for me?..."

In 1947, William Boyd explained the social direction of the way he would play Hoppy. "I had this idea, that perhaps westerns, which kids have always loved, could be used to teach them things like fair play and having respect for themselves and each other. I had a hunch, if I could make the right kind of westerns [his Hoppy films did succeed in accomplishing that], and not forgetting they had to be action pictures and good entertainment," Boyd adds, "I might even do my best to reduce crime among kids." As a moral force, Bill's hunch was never more obvious than in his membership in Hoppy's Troopers Creed. As a youngster, there is little doubt that Bob Urich took to heart every one of the ten points outlined to be a better citizen. Read on and you will see a lot of Hoppy's Creed reflected in the way Robert Urich conducted himself as an adult.

Here are Hoppy's Trooper's Creed and ten points to be a better citizen:

1. The highest badge of honor a person can wear is honesty. Be truthful at all times.
2. Your parents are the best friends you have. Listen to them and obey their instructions.
3. If you want to be respected, you must respect others. Show good manners in every way.
4. Only through hard work and study can you succeed. Don't be lazy.
5. Your good deeds always come to light. So don't boast or be a show-off.
6. If you waste time or money today, you will regret it tomorrow. Practice thrift in all ways.
7. Many animals are good and loyal companions. Be friendly and kind to them.
8. A strong, healthy body is a precious gift. Be neat and clean.
9. Our country's laws are made for your protection. Observe them carefully.
10. Children in many foreign lands are less fortunate than you. Be glad & proud you are an American.

Young Bobby Urich was one of Hoppy's kids in Ohio, who followed Hoppy's creed to the letter. At the same time, another six-year old kid named Billy was doing the same thing growing up in Arkansas. Bill Boyd as Hoppy would be proud to know that one of his cowboy kids grew up to be President of the United States. You see, little two-gun totin' Billy's full name is William Jefferson Clinton.

***

There was something special about Hoppy that captured the hearts and imagination of millions of kids, just like little Bobby Urich and Billy Clinton, who grew up in the 50's. William Boyd and his wife, Grace Bradley Boyd*never had children of their own. Instead, they adopted an entire generation of kids between the ages of five and fifteen. Boyd as Hoppy took it upon himself the huge responsibility of providing them with a set of values that served Bob and other kids in their adult lives.

***

In a 1995 interview, at the 100th birthday celebration of Bill Boyd's life, Boyd's widow, Grace Bradley Boyd[1] revealed that "Bill used to think of Hoppy as his good side. He was a Gemini," she says, "he truly believed that Hoppy was an integral part of himself. He put himself into Hoppy. You do not think of William Boyd as an actor who played Hoppy, Grace adds with a loving smile, "you think of them as one. Everyone called Bill, *Hoppy*."

Bill Boyd in his role as Hopalong Cassidy made wholesome, clean pictures. He never committed an act which he would be ashamed of later. Boyd used Hoppy's on-screen persona as a teacher of morality, of good over evil.[2] Most importantly, he taught youngsters through his role that a man can be courageous without being a bully and that he can have good habits without being a sissy. Boyd as Hoppy on radio, television and in his films, reflected all this, and in doing so, left an indelible positive mark on Bob Urich and the youth of America. There's little doubt, the positive qualities displayed by Bill Boyd as Hoppy greatly influenced young Mr. Urich. He grew up to be an outstanding person and one of the most popular television and film actors of his era. William Boyd would be proud to know, his young saddle-pal also followed in his boots, and became the star of his own television western series, *The Lazarus Man*.[3]

---

1 Joe Martelle, the author of this book, and his wife Kim met & interviewed Grace Bradley Boyd in 1995 at the 100th birthday celebration of William 'Hoppy' Boyd in Lone Pine, CA. The always pleasant and gracious Grace passed away in Dana Point, CA, in 2010. She was 97.

2 During the earliest days of the 20th-Century, three generations grew up with Hopalong Cassidy. They read about Hoppy's adventures in the novels and short stories written by his creator, Clarence E. Mulford who lived his remaining years in Fryeburg, Maine. Bill Boyd and his wife Grace took the train from L.A. to Maine to meet and visit with Clarence.

The original 'Hoppy' as depicted in stories was a drifter, who sometimes drank to excess, and was a two-fisted, tobacco chewing, gun-fighter. A vigilante who was always willing to take the law into his own hands. A far cry from what Bill Boyd projected in his role as Hopalong Cassidy. The name Hopalong Cassidy, his horse Topper and actor William Boyd are used by permission from Holger Wrede and his company, U.S. Television Office, Inc.

3 Read more about Bob's TV series, *The Lazarus Man* in Ch. 24.

Montage Photo designed by the author - Joe Martelle

Bobby, the cowboy kid and his cowboy hero Hopalong Cassidy and Bob as adult in his own western series, The Lazarus Man.

Chapter 5

Meet the Urich Family, Bob's Dad 'Papa John Paul and Mom, Cecelia 'Baba'

"Our mom and dad were God-fearing folks with extremely sound work ethics, good people and I'm proud to say that's the stock I come from."
- Robert Urich

[**Bold typed** words are Bob's own.]

Bob Urich's mom and dad were teenagers during the stock market crash of 1929. The ensuing great depression had made them and others a tough generation. They knew how to persevere, to keep going. They never allowed themselves to quit and give up.

"Our dad was a veteran," Bob's older brother, Tom, proudly proclaims. "He was born February 6, 1911 in Irondale, Ohio, one of fifteen children and raised in Stratton [Ohio]. Both towns are within ten miles of Toronto where he lived until his death in 1980. Our dad was drafted into the Navy, on March 9, 1944. He was 33 at the time." The war had been raging for three years and fighting on two fronts in Europe and the Pacific had taken its toll on the youth of America. The U.S. had no choice but to draft older, married men. "Dad was stationed in Virginia, and when the war ended, he was discharged, after serving a year and 9 months with a rank of Aviation metal smith, AM3C(t). His pay was $55.05 a month! He received an additional $24.70 as travel pay upon his discharge which enabled him to hop a bus and get back home to Toronto and his family."

The wartime economy of WWII–which ended in '45, the year before Bob was born–shifted to a peacetime one. Jobs and housing were difficult to find and consumer goods were scarce. Returning veterans who couldn't find jobs were known as members of the *52-20 Club*. Under the G.I. bill, they received unemployment pay of $20 for 52 weeks. "Dad loved music," says the Urich's oldest son, Tom. " He played the harmonica but was totally tone deaf, and couldn't carry a tune. I'm told, when he and mom were 'courting' they went dancing a lot. The Big Bands came through the Ohio area on one-night stands."

***

When Papa John Urich returned home to Toronto, he worked almost 50 years at Weirton Steel Mill in West Virginia.. The plant was about 12 miles from their home right across the Ohio River. Carolyn Walker, President of the Toronto [Ohio] Historical Society who kindly contributed invaluable information about the City for this book, says Bob's father crossed the bridge linking Toronto with Weirton to get to work at the mill.

Tom Urich recalls their Dad left their home in the north end and drove clear through the Toronto business district. "That's State Route 7[1], the same road, they later named a portion of in honor of my brother Bob," Tom proudly proclaims. "Dad would have taken the same route until the early 70's when the by-pass was completed." Carolyn Walker says, "When we were kids in the '50s the bridge was known as the Fort Steuben Bridge.It was imploded a couple of years ago. It had been replaced in the 80's by a large four-lane bridge, named, Veterans Bridge. The road always paralleled the Ohio River."

On his drive to work, 'Papa John,' as the boys called their dad, would have traveled through such small places as Costonia, and the Pottery Addition, named for Steubenville Pottery,[2] then he would pass by Ailakana and cross over the bridge, hoping there were no rock slides (which was often the case in rainy weather along that stretch of road). In the early years, it was a toll bridge. "The cost," Walker says smiling, "just ten cents! Their dadwould travel down Freedom Way to Weirton through the main business district to the mill which is located on both sides of the highway."

The town of Weirton, W. VA was built by the Weirton Steel Corporation. "Today (2017) it is a ghost of itself," says Walker, an authority on historical facts about the tri-state region. "Interestingly," she points out, "while called the Ohio River, the river really belongs to West Virginia. Some

1 State Route 7, the Robert Urich Interchange is in the North end of town where Bob grew up, off Alexander Street. In the late 1980s, the Toronto town council passed a resolution renaming Alexander St. in honor of Bob. There is a State sign at the south end of the city acknowledging Robert Urich's connection to the city.

2 Steubenville Pottery was known for the Russell Wright Line.

bridges are the responsibility of Ohio and some West VA.," but adds, " all bodies found floating in the river are investigated by West Va."

Bob's dad loved fishing at Uncle Rudy's camp in Canada, during their annual two-week Urich family summer vacation. "As much as he enjoyed fishing, dad never fished in the Ohio River," says Bob's younger brother David, "To my knowledge, he never did, which is strange, since we only lived a few steps away from the river. Perhaps, he simply didn't have time. Dad's pride and joy, and his only hobby, was his garden. Working three-different shifts at the mill, he really didn't have time to enjoy anything else, except our annual summer vacation at the lake." "He always had a big garden," adds older brother, Tom. "It was 50 by 40 yards, and filled with tomatoes, corn, beets, green beans, cabbage, all of which were canned for our winter meals." Watching their dad work his garden is probably how Bob acquired his love for tilling the soil. Throughout his life he always had to have a spot for his garden.

***

"While in high school, during summers, I worked at the same mill as dad," says Tom. "Dad worked three turns [shifts] at the mill; *three to eleven*, *eleven to seven* and *seven to three*. His shift changed every week. In fact, all three of us [his sons], our younger brother David, Bob and I worked the same shifts going through school." In a 1986 *Chicago Tribune* interview, Bob Urich admitted working at the steel mill was the worst job of his life. "Shoveling buckets of hot grease in a steel mill for eight hours a day was like being in hell. I wrote poetry during lunch break. My father worked in the mill all his life. So, I got to appreciate how tough his job was. He insisted that I work there during summer vacation from high school. He made sure I got the dirtiest, toughest, filthiest jobs so that I wouldn't wind up in the mills someday. And it worked," he says smiling. The stifling heat and back-breaking hard work at Weirton Steel Mill was more than enough incentive to keep young Robert fixated on his goal of doing more with his life.

Bob also came to realize anything in life worth having doesn't come easy. He knew to fulfill his dreams would require hard work.

"After his shift was over, dad would stop at the bar next door to the mill for about 60 seconds. That's about how long it took him and then we were out of there," says Tom Urich. "I barely had time for a sip of my beer. At home, dad would have a beer or two and a shot during the holidays, but that was about the extent of his drinking as I recall." Older sister Monica says, "dad never drank during the week while working, but did so on weekends and that's usually when his temper showed. The younger Urich kids, Bob and David remember their dad's drinking habits a little differently than their older siblings.[1]

Early Fall- 1960

At the end of each shift a parade of men at the main-gate of the 54-inch rolling mill at the Weirton Steel Company in Weirton, West Virginia. A picture appears on the front-page of the Steubenville Herald Star [1960], taken in front of this same gate.

"John F. Kennedy is reaching out to shake the hand of one of the exiting workers, asking for his vote in the upcoming Presidential election. The worker, lunch bucket under one arm, still wears his white hard hat. His face covered with dirt and grime of an eight-hour, all-night 11 to 7 shift seems to be looking down, as if in a hurry. Across the street from the main gate of the mill is the reason my father is in such a hurry. Darkened by years of billowing smoke stand a row of taverns, "beer joints."

Architecturally identical, these small rectangular buildings each featuring simulated-brick tar-paper fronts.

In small oval windows hang red glowing neon signs promoting the local beers. Iron City, Dusquane, Pabst Blue Ribbon and Strohs, the only fire-brewed beer. None of that prissy, designer beer, brewed in small batches.

"My father sits on a red vinyl bar-stool at ten after seven in the morning and downs a fishbowl–a large snifter shaped glass full of his favorite beer or draft." Probably a Carlings Black Label, since Bob remembers the Carlings commercial complete with their neat jingle: **"First a whistle, then, 'Hey Mable, Black Label, Carlings Black Label Beer.' Or, if it had been a particularly tough shift, dad would have a boiler maker; a shot of whiskey, Canadian Club or Four Roses, slugged back in one effortless well-rehearsed motion, chased by a small tumbler of beer."**

***

1 There was a huge age gap between siblings. Monica was 14 yrs older than Bob. Tom was eleven years older than Bob and 15 years older than younger brother, David. Some times people and things change over the years, as do people's memories of certain events in their lives.

"It's funny, our mom was a t-totaler," says Bob's brother, David. I bet I didn't see her have six drinks in all the years she was alive. Dad, on the other hand, no matter what time of day or night, morning or Midnight, after his shift was over and he was home, he would always have a couple of beers, eat his meal and go to bed."

***

Heather Urich believes that Papa John had a drinking problem. "I saw him go behind the bar when he thought nobody was looking. Bob told me that after working the night shift at the steel mill, he would stop at the bar and have a shot at seven in the morning."

His shift over at the mill, and after a customary 'pit stop' at the bar across the street, the Urich patriarch, John Paul, heads for home. He crosses the Fort Steuben Bridge, over the Ohio River from West Virginia into the State of Ohio and up Route Seven, a winding highway that follows the river for eight miles or so, and finally home to a man's man kinda breakfast. **"Fried eggs and pork chops, fried potatoes and onions."**

"The smell drifts up to my bedroom as I get ready for school. The next day my father proudly passes around the newspaper with Kennedy on the front page. He votes straight Democratic ticket that fall."

"Our dad's favorite meal were pork chops," says Tom Urich, recalling his father's set routine. "He would eat and leave the table while the rest of the family were just beginning. Papa John Urich did everything quickly, except give hugs. I can't remember one hug," sighs Tom. "He just didn't know how to express his emotions. But, Our dad did have a bit of a temper, all we sons inherited that, but thanks be to God, we all mellowed as we got older. Our father only had a fifth-grade education, but he was by no means dumb. In fact," says the elder Urich son, "I can visualize him to this day, sitting in his comfy chair in the family living room reading the dictionary. He was quite proud that he could name every state and their capitals."

***

"My father was a steel worker, he worked in the mill all his life–forty-five years–and his natural speaking voice was twenty-five decibels above ours because the machinery was so noisy." The Urich boys recall quite vividly their dad's hearing loss from the mill's loud noises. It was from the constant banging and clanking of the mills equipment," says Tom, eldest of the three Urich sons. "We found ourselves yelling at him just to be heard!" **"He shouted because he was hard of hearing, working**

in an environment where a man standing at your elbow would have to shout to be heard. To have a conversation with dad, you would have to shout at each other. Dad would speak at the top of his lungs, which was his normal speaking voice after shouting to be heard in the mill all day. My father calls to my mother to get him a beer." . 'CISLLY!' that's what he called my mother, 'GET ME A BEER!' He calls her Cislly with an accent over the C' giving it an explosive S' sound, an endearing Slavicversion of Cecelia. For years neighbors next door thought he was calling her silly."

1960 - Summer

Toronto Ohio

It's 1960, early summer 1960 in Toronto and the shaggy maples that line River Avenue are fully leafed, dark green, but they look more like black in color. Fourteen year old Bob Urich in his pony-league uniform[1] walks the 2 ½ blocks from his house to the baseball diamond near the high school. It's hot and sticky on this June afternoon, made even more humid by the river that flows just beyond the left field fence, yet the grinning youngster looks forward to put on the catcher's equipment; the orange and black shin guards, the chest protector and face mask with it's sweet, pungent smell of well-worn leather.

"I'm the only one on this team to wear this gear and it makes me feel like a special warrior. Just let somebody be foolish enough to try and steal home today! Cleats chew-up the ground, little puffs of chalk fly into the air, as the runner charges down the third base line heading for home and here comes the relay! Come on! Come on throw the damn ball, and the throw, a slow motion, crystalline moment. I block the plate with my knee and then CONTACT! Grunts, sweat flying and the joyful explosion...the indescribable rush of an athletic collision."

After a full-shift working at the mill, Papa John is there watching his young son play ball. Coming up to the plate, Bob spots his dad, as he takes his practice swings with two thirty-five inch Louisville sluggers.

---

1 In his pre-teen years, Bob played Little League baseball for the Titanium Metals Team.

They are solid Carolina ash, branded with Ralph Kiner's[1] signature. **"My father is lying in the grass on a small bank just down and outside the right field line. He's wearing a funny tweed hat to shade the sun from his eyes–like the one Rex Harrison wore in *My Fair Lady*. How much I love him and want to please him at this moment, this gruff tough shot and-a-beer guy. I know my dad can't see me smile, a smile that evaporates after two quick strikes. The coach yelling at me blurs a cacophony of sound coming from both dugouts. I step out of the batters' box."**

Bob's dad sits up taking his hat in one hand, he makes a downward motion with both his arms attempting to calm his son down. Is there any sound sweeter than the crack of a bat making contact with that white powdered sphere being launched into space!

"The ball flies over the center fielder's head and is still rolling as I round first base. I hit the bag at second in full stride and now I see the coach at third give the signal to slide, head long, stretched out...my hand reaching the bag a split second before the slap of the ball in the 3rd baseman's glove. Dazed and breathless I stand and dust myself off, glancing in my father's direction. He is already up and walking towards the car."

***

"My dad was a man of few words. He was also angry a lot because he was exhausted, and because he spent most of his life doing a job that brought no joy.

"Living a life that had no art to it, that lacked any creativity except for raising a family, my two brothers and sister with only an eight grade education. But those afternoons in the outfield still linger in my mind. Dad sprawled out like a day at the beach, his elbow on the ground propped in his hand, watching me play."

On pay-day, when he wasn't scheduled to work at the mill, Bob's dad would sometimes take him along when he went to pick up his pay-check.

---

1 Ralph Kiner was one of Major-League baseball's greatest right-handed hitters. During his ten-year career, 1946-55, he played for the Pirates, Cubs and Indians. He was the first National Leaguer to hit 50 home runs in a season, doing it twice. Back problems forced him off the field at age 32. He later became a coach with the Padres organization, and then a broadcaster with the New York Mets. Ralph Kiner was elected to the Hall of Fame in 1975. He passed away at age 91 on February 6, 2014 at his home in Rancho Mirage, CA.

"We would stop in one of those beer joints. He would sit at the bar and I would wait for him in a nearby booth sipping on a coke and munching tall stick pretzels. Dad cashes his monthly check and a vacation bonus, all tens and twenties. When we get home, he throws the money in the air and it flutters down like so many falling leaves.

We feel rich, even though it's probably only several hundred dollars. My motherand father laugh and carry on and bandy names like Rockefeller and Vanderbilt."

Bob's mom and dad are happy and grateful. The Urich house is a place for rejoicing, to give thanks for what they have. "Mom was big in the Catholic Church," says Bob's younger brother David. "Our home was literally a half-a-block away from the Roman Catholic Church. She would attend daily Mass to offer prayers and to praise God, and no doubt prayed that her sons avoided getting into any trouble," he laughs.

Bob's older brother, Tom had done summer theater–*Carousel* and *Carnival* which he played opposite Anna Maria Alberghetti in Rochester, New York. The Urich brothers remember going to watch their older brother in summer stock. "We'd take 4 or 5 days and head to St. Louis, Chicago or wherever he was appearing to catch his performance."

"The whole family went to Rochester to see my older brother in *The Boys from Syracuse*.

"It's the musical version of *Two Gentlemen of Verona*. Our seats were in the second row of the mezzanine. The curtain goes up and there's my brother on stage wearing a little toga with sandals laced up his legs, being fed grapes by a couple of girls. My father, in his customary loud voice, turns to my mother and say, "MY son is doing that for a living?"' The whole theater swung around to see who this was. To this day, I remember trying to crawl under the seat." Incredibly, Tom didn't hear it on stage. Later, when Bob told his brother about the incident, Tom was incredulous.

"'C'mon Bob, he didn't do that, did he? I would have heard him.'"

"I thought, how could you not hear him?

***

"Dad really never accepted my working in the theater," says Tom Urich. "'When are you gonna quit this nonsense and get a real job," he'd bellow. Tom smiles and adds, "After Bob's success, he kind of relented." **"The theater is not exactly something that you come home and announced**

to your boiler-maker-drinking father." "Hey, dad, I've decided to give up studying and anything practical and pursue an acting career." Even years after I actually committed to being an actor, I would come home and he'd just ask me when was I going to get a real job."

***

Two packs of cigarettes a day, the noise and stress of the mill with only two weeks off for vacation [some years, but not all] and it's no wonder Papa John Urich dies young. **"In the middle of telling a funny story to his own brother and sister, slapping his thigh and throwing his head back in laughter that turns into a gasp, my father has a heart attack and dies."**

"I soon realize that it is the most important day of my life. In my dad's death, I discover the meaning of fatherhood. Sadly and reluctantly, I accept the mantle, understanding in one cognitive moment all that he had done."

Bob Urich is thankful his dad got to see him have some success in his life. **"I bought him his first color TV set. I took him to Hawaii and he swam in a swimming pool in the winter time–that was amazing for him. I'd try to call home every Sunday, but one Sunday would slip into another and we'd be a month out and I hadn't spoken to him. Finally, I picked up the phone and called and then realized that he was not there. As with so many things in life, I didn't really miss him until he was not around."**

When his dad passed, Bob held his emotions in for a long time. He was the strong one at his dad's funeral.

"They gave him a military salute–the firing of the rifles and then taps, and the sending up the flag and all of that–because he was a veteran [Navy]."

"I was doing Vega$ at the time, and we got on the plane and flew back to town. It must have been six weeks before it all hit. And again, I think it corresponded with one of those time frames when he starts to...[in his journal Bob never completes his thought] **I began to sob. I cried for two days. This was my mourning."**

***

In his memory, and in his journal entry, Bob's father looms largest in the family history, but in reality, theirs was really a matriarchal society.

Cecelia Halpate Urich was born February lst 1912, in Toronto [Ohio]. "Mom was one of ten brothers and sisters," says her oldest son, Tom. "Three died very young and on my dad's side, five of the fifteen siblings died young. There were twins on each side of the family. Our mother was a life-long resident of the city. We called her Baba, which is Slovak for grandmother. Our mom was really the head of the family. I can't recall my father ever hugging me, all love came from her." Tom chuckles and says, "Mom was fun to be with, but she hated to lose at penny poker or any kind of card game."

"My mother was the one responsible for our schooling, our manners and the way we were raised and our work ethic. She made sure we went to church. She took care of the spiritual nature of our being. And she was not beyond carving a switch from the hedge and giving us a little swat on the bottom, either. Mom did it all. My father would resonate in the background with a sort of 'I told you so' kind of look."

"Mom was loved by all," says Tom Urich. "They even dedicated a cookbook to her *A Taste of Toronto*, published in 1994 by The Toronto [OH] Alumni Association." In the book,[1] Cecelia, or "Ceil" or "Baba" as she was called by family and friends writes, "When the children come home, I always try to have some of their favorite dishes, such as City Chicken, Scalloped Potatoes, Cabbage Rolls, Creamed Cucumbers, Buttermilk pie, Apple Dream squares and others."

"Mom was very religious," says her oldest son, Tom. "She was quite proud of the fact, her mother Barbara [Zahar] and father Michael [Halpate] helped build St. Joseph's Catholic Church, which we were all communicants of and became an important part of her life and that of our family. Mom never missed Mass, and helped keep the church clean and washed and ironed the altar cloths. Dad went to church, too, but not on a regular basis. However, he never missed a holiday." Tom's brother David makes this point, "Dad was Byzantine Catholic, but didn't start practicing until he started having heart and health problems. All of us were baptized Byzantine, but we were raised Roman Catholic. It wasn't a problem," he adds, "until it was time for our First Communion. I was supposed to

---

1 A Taste of Toronto, a cookbook published in 1994 to benefit the Toronto High School Alumni Association, is dedicated to Cecelia Urich. It is jammed with yummy recipes and info about the town and it's people. Copies are still available for eleven dollars, shipping included at PO Box 273, Toronto, OH 43964, or at www.TorontoHigh-SchoolAluminAssociation.

make it with my class at St. Joseph's, the Roman Catholic Church. But, the Byzantine priest said, 'no, no, he's ours! He has to make his first communion at our church first.'" Laughing, David says, "they were fighting over us."

"Our mother only went through eight grade," according to Tom, "but she was very bright and taught classes in the Catholic School." Before she married, Cecelia worked in a pottery plant painting the gold leaf decorations on dinner plates. Her sister Mary owned a dry cleaners and Cecelia worked there, too, pressing suits and shirts. During World War II, while her husband, John Paul was serving in the Navy, Cecelia and her sister Stella were air-raid wardens. "They wore hard hats and carried flashlights, the whole 9 yards," says her oldest son, Tom. "It was their job to patrol the streets of Toronto making sure the blackout rules were followed. She took her job very seriously," he says. Even tough, Tom was only seven or eight during the height of the war, he remembers seeing his mom decked out in her air-raid warden helmet.

In 1990, Cecelia Urich appeared in a video produced by The Toronto High Alumni in celebration of the 'All School-All Alumni Weekend.' She revealed, as a little boy, Bob was quite shy. "We called him Bobby Knight," referencing either the Toronto High Red Knights, or that *her* Bobby *was* her shining knight. During the interview, Cecelia also reminisced about her own childhood and growing up in the Gem City. "There was a clay and brick-lined, round, hut-like oven in the backyard where bread was often baked. "To test the wood-burning oven," she says, "paper was thrown in to see if it burned quickly. If so, then the oven was ready for bread." Ceil recalls making soap with her mother, the ice-wagon making deliveries; and the ice man chipping small pieces for the neighborhood kids on a hot summer day. "Now that was something special," she says, grinning.

Tom Urich smiles thinking about how their mom was a great cook. "She cooked all the time; stuffed cabbage rolls, roast pork, all Slovak dishes. Bob & I would often joke that she was the original June Cleaver," referencing the fictional mom on the 60s TV series, *Leave it to Beaver*.[1]

---

1 *Leave it to Beaver* was a popular family sit-com starring Jerry Mathers as the Beaver, and Tony Dow as his older brother, Wally. Their parents were played by Hugh Beaumont and Barbara Billingsley. It aired first on CBS from 1957-58, and on ABC from 1958-63.

Younger brother David agrees, " she was always baking cookies, just like Beaver's mom. Our home was a scene right out of *Ozzie & Harriet.*[1]"

The Urich brothers agree their mom was also a good singer an all-around great lady. Heather Menzies Urich, Bob's wife of 27 years says she got along well with Bob's mom, but that 'Baba' could run hot and cold.

"The thing is she came from an ultra Catholic Eastern block atmosphere. That's one thing, and also the issue of Bob being her shining star. We got along very well, and she treated me like her own. HOWEVER," Heather emphasizes with a smile, "I always had a strong sense if it ever came down to it, she would always side with Bob on anything, and everything. It never came down to it," she quickly adds, "but I sensed that in a big way. Baba's strength was the love she had for her family. She was an amazing cook. I believe her weakness, and don't we all have some, she had a tendency to be a bit pious. She was 'old school' and from a totally different era. I never saw Bob and his mom engage in any sort of petty arguments, Baba, would never go that far with him," Heather insists.

In 2002, shortly before his own death, Bob writes in his journal that he never really figured his mom out. **"Even after all this time, I still haven't figured my mom out. She's ninety years old. Just celebrated her ninetieth birthday. I wish I knew all the things that go through her head, but I only get bits and pieces, fragments. I'm not even sure where these pieces go. I don't honestly know how to go about asking her the questions on my mind. She is a remarkable woman and at ninety still has tremendous energy and spirit. She fell and broke her hip a few years ago while staying at our house and went through a period of dementia in the hospital from the trauma and the drugs. She didn't really know who I was. I would visit her and she would say, "'I have to get dinner ready and the ball gowns aren't set and the limo' s are coming in an hour.'" "It was quite frightening to witness. We didn't know what was going to happen. Fortunately, she snapped out of it and is back to her old self."**

Bob also writes in his journal that his mom was always on the 'doomy' [sp] side.

---

1 *Ozzie & Harriet* was one of network's longest running family comedies. It starred the 'real-life' Nelson family, Ozzie, Harriet and their two sons, David and Ricky. The popular series began on radio in 1944 and moved to television in 1952, for a total of 22 years on the air, all for the same network, ABC.

"I don't know if pessimism is the right word for her outlook on life–maybe wary realism. There is a sense of absolute pragmatism to her way of thinking that is born out of the depression, of having to do without. The fear that everything might vanish overnight never left her. Even when I was making lots of money and had become something of a celebrity–none of it phased her a bit. I'd be just starting in a new show and she'd say, "'Bob, save your money, you never can tell.'" And then, she'd ask me, "' By the way, what else are you doing?'" What am I doing? I'm working sixteen hours a day, Mom, and that's about all I'm doing."

Bob was good to his mom and dad.

Bob's brother David, remembers when Bob traveled extensively. "If Bob traveled to a city they [parents] had never seen, he took them along, or invited them. Wherever it was that they wanted to go, Bob made it happen, so mom and dad could see a little bit of the world. I thought that was pretty cool." Heather Urich says, "Papa John [Bob's dad] passed in 1980 when Bob was doing Vega$. Therefore, he did not get to travel as much with us as his mom, Baba. We took her many places, including Australia, where Bob filmed *Survive the Savage Seas.*"[1]

Through the years, and particularly following the passing of her husband, Baba spent time staying with Bob and Heather+ wherever they happen to be living, California, Park City (UT), Andover, (MA) or wherever, but she still maintained the original house where Bob and her other children grew up in Toronto, Ohio.

*Bob's older brother Tom says, their mom would also spend winters with them in California. He recalls, "mom would go to Bob and Heathers first, but after a few days, Bob would call, and say, "come get her, I can't deal with it."

Meet the Urich Family Bob's Mom - Baba

"When my mother gets ready to leave, she always gives the same speech: "'Well, I probably won't be back next year. I just won't be able to. I'll probably be dead and gone.'

"So, we've finally taken to calling her on it. We say, 'Yeah, Mom, we know, we're not even planning the next plane ticket.'"

***

1 Dylan Daniels played one of Bob's sons in *Survive the Savage Seas* and comments about the experience can be found in Chapter 16.

"It was a fall day, October 5, 2002, when Mom Urich passed away, six months following my brother Bob's death," says Tom. "She was devoted to him and simply could not accept the fact that he was no longer alive. She lost her will to live. Mom loved all her children, but I think Bob was her favorite." Bob's high school classmate and friend, Tim Seese, sees it differently. "Mrs. Urich was interviewed by local press after Bob became famous and was asked if she was proud of Bob. She replied that she was proud of <u>all</u> her children. Anyone who knew her would have predicted that would be her response."

Top left, young Bob [age 3] with his mom Cecelia an dad, John Paul. Top right- Bob's dad, John Paul in U.S. Navy uniform, WWII-courtesy Tom Urich. Lower left-Bob's dad with "Big Catch" after fishing at Uncle Rudy's camp. Lower right - Bobby, age 9 in Little League uniform played for Titanium Metals.

Chapter 5 (cont.)

"Bob's siblings"
Monica, Tom & David

[**Bold typed** words are Bob's own.]

Papa John and Cecelia Baba Urich raised four children, a daughter and three sons.

Bob and his siblings learned from their parents how to cope with life's ups and downs.

"I have an older sister, and two brothers, one older and one younger," says Bob.

Bob's Sister - Monica

[**Bold typed words** are Bob's own and taken directly from his personal journal.]

Bob's older sister, Monica[1] was the first born to their parents, Cecelia and John Paul. She was born October 9, 1932 and is fourteen years older than Bob.

Monica was eighteen when she left home for nursing school. "Bobby was just four. I like to say, he was my first child," she laughs. "I practically raised him. Everyone in the family always called me 'sissy.'" The name stuck until she married Conrad 'Connie' Rauch[2]. They were married for 63 years and have seven children. "My sons 'dubbed' me Chief and that is what they and my sons-in law call me.

"I have tons of photos of Bobby. One of my favorites show him wearing a fireman's hat while sitting in a little [toy] fire truck. I am almost sure," she adds, "I have a picture of Bob wearing his cowboy suit.[3] I can see him in it, standing in our back yard in Ohio."

---

1 The author spoke with Monica in telephone interviews and through e-mail in May 2015 & in April 2017.

2 Sadly, Monica's husband, Conrad 'Connie" Rauch passed away in March 2017 after struggling for a few years with health issues, including severe neuropathy.

3 The actual photo is included at the end of Chapter 4.

In his journal, Bob writes about his sister's seven children. **"One more brilliant than the next,"** Uncle Bob proudly proclaims. **"Four girls and three boys. "The summer after graduating [from college] I went to Dallas. My sister was livingthere at the time and invited me to stay with them. I got a commercial agent and even did a couple of Dr. Pepper commercials, including one with Dick Clark. I thought, well, this isn't a bad life. I lived with them for the summer!**

Monica's husband, Conrad or 'Connie' as he was called, graduated from Ohio State with a PhD in physics and engineering. Interestingly, Bob's older brother Tom roomed with Connie his first year at Ohio State. "My sister introduced us. I think so someone could keep an eye on her younger brother," he says, laughing.

Bob's Sister - Monica and older brother, Tom

"Later, in 1961-62, Tom recalls, "while playing summer stock in Dayton, I rented a room from Connie's mom." Proving once again, in the circle of life, we keep meeting the same folks, over and over.

"I watched Conrad prepare dinner night in and night out. Roast pork, roast beef, chicken dinners. Every kid would be sitting with food on their plate before he would even begin considering to put anything on his. Living with a big family like that, I learned more about generosity and being selfless than you would from a year of sermons."

Monica says, "Bob and I became friends later as adults, especially when he lived with us for a summer in Dallas. Bob could be moody," she says. "Sometimes, he would just get up and grab a book and wander off to another room to be by himself. When he became a star, folks back home treated him like a 'rock star.' Everyone loved him. With his new found celebrity status, Bob felt he had a lot to live up too. Sometimes, it was overwhelming and I believe it got to him once in awhile. He just had to retreat in to himself."

"My older brother, Tom has been influential in everything I do. He's always working. He's helped me with every Broadway show I've ever done. So, when I'm in a quandary about some part, I call Tom. He was very instrumental in my getting into the theater. He traveled around the country with the Air Force in their theatrical troop. Later on, he went to the Cincinnati College Conservatory of Music–that's where

he met his wife, Judy and got married. Tom got a degree in voice, and he and his wife went off to New York." [theater work]

Tom Urich has understudied every major lead on Broadway.

Bob's Older Brother, Tom

"My brother was never able to step out into the limelight. One review he got sums up his predicament. It reads, '*Tom Urich is better than the original.*' But, when they recast, they cast some soap star in the part. That's just the way it is on Broadway. They don't seem to want to take chances on people they know."

"Even though I was older, I looked up to Bob. It's supposed to be the other way around. I loved Bob," says Tom, "but I always had the feeling, he was never all that comfortable around me. He seemed to keep me at arms length. I'm not sure why. Our brother David feels the same way."

"We weren't close," says David Urich. "Don't get me wrong, Bob was always there when I needed a helping hand and I'm grateful, but close, no. When he was in his prime [as an actor] I bet we didn't see each other twice or three times a year.[1] He had his own circle of friends, mostly actor or producer types. I wasn't included in his circle. It's not that there was any animosity between us, it's just that we didn't have a lot in common. We were two different people."

"Once when Bob was a student at Florida State," says Tom, "I was appearing nearby in a stage production and thought I'd pay him a surprise visit. He was upset the way I was dressed. Evidently, he didn't approve of the color shirt I was wearing. Silly, aye? But, Bob was fastidious about certain things. He was complex.[2]"

When Bob received his Star on the Hollywood Walk of Fame in 1995,[3] among the invited guests in attendance was his brother, Tom.

At one point during the ceremony, Bob, kneeling before his star,* looked up, grinned and said, **"I owe everything to that man right over there,"** pointing to his 'big brother,' Tom.

---

1 This was not by design and no one is to blame. Bob's busy film location work kept him traveling a lot, while David was also working. Therefore, it was difficult for them to see each other as often as they liked.

2 The word complex is defined in the dictionary as "consisting of many parts." Bob's so-called 'complex' personality probably contributed to his versatility as a successful actor.

3 Bob's star is located at 7083 Hollywood Blvd.

Tom divulged *to the author* that he was surprised and grateful for Bob's comments, adding, "It was one of the few times he ever recognized me."

Today, at the tender age of 83 [2017] and semi-retired from show biz, Tom and his wife, Judy [an actress] spend most of their time babysitting and spoiling their grandkids. However, it's safe to say, he is not opposed to do an occasional audition, and with his magnificent set of pipes, [voice] still does voice-over and narration work.

Bob's younger brother, David

Bob's brother David, who is 3 ½ years younger was a freshman at Toronto High, when Bob was a senior. "I was always following in his footsteps. He was the athlete and I never was." Like most older brothers, Bob pushed David around a little. "Ya, he was a bully," he says, laughing. "He pushed me around a little. Actually," he admits, "I was Bob's pain-in-the-ass little brother. There was enough of an age difference[1] that we didn't have the same circle of friends. He didn't want me hangin' around his buddies. I was the music nerd and he was the athlete, so we didn't have the same friends." Tim Seese, a high school friend of Bob's, recalls David being a great kid and says, "Unfortunately, one day while climbing he fell out of a tree and broke his arm. From that day on he was known as Tarzan, and he took the nickname in good natured fashion."

"Bob was sort of a perfectionist," says David. "He always wanted to be the best. He had the athletic jock mentality.

"Bob was a good student and carried his classes well and that wasn't a problem," says his younger brother, "but he had this fixation of always being the best at everything."

In a December 18, 1981 interview with *The Mirror*, a Toronto High School news publication, Bob Urich readily admits he earned only B's and C's in high school. He goes on to say, "I had great drive and determination, and once I got into the real world, my 'A' grade was success."

***

David enjoyed sports, but couldn't participate. From the age of thirteen, he had trouble with his knees. "I had a disease called Osgood-Schlatter." It was named in 1903, after two physicians, Dr. Robert Osgood and Dr. Carl Schlatter. It is a disorder involving painful inflammation at the tibial

1 The younger Urich brothers, Bob and David were closer in age than they were with their older siblings.

tuberosity [the bony part] at the top of the shin to the lower portion of the kneecap. It is a very common cause of knee pain usually occurring in boys between the ages of 10 and 15. "Somehow, my tibia [more commonly called the shin bone] and fibula [thin bone between the ankle and the patella or knee cap] were growing faster than the rest of the bones in my leg. Little calcium deposits were forming between them. Instead of growing behind my knee, the bones would pop out over the top of my knee-cap. I wore these cylinder caps from my hips all the way down to my ankles. They tried to immobilize the knee. The first time, I had to wear them for six months. The second time, about three months. It didn't work, so I probably had 3 or 4 surgeries on each knee to remove the bone chips."

David was thirteen the first time he had surgery. "The last time was in 1971, when I was around 20 or 21, while serving in the Navy." If you're wondering how a guy with bad knees got accepted in the U.S. Navy, stick around, details coming right up.

"We grew up Catholic but didn't go to the Catholic High School in nearby Steubenville," says David, "because it was a 17 mile bus ride. Toronto High, the public high school was only about a 5 minute walk. So, our dad said, 'no way. You guys can walk to school!'"

Toronto High was a three-story structure and as fate would have it, most of David's Classes–you guessed it, were on the top floor. "Because of the issues with my legs, Bob or somebody else would have to carry me up to the third floor in the morning. When I didn't have a class or study hall, I'd just go into an empty classroom and wait for my next class to begin." Laughing, David says, "my nickname was 'rigor-mortis.' I had steel cleats on my shoes, so the guys would bend me over and push me around."

"One afternoon, Bob forgot to pick me up. I guess he got busy at football practiceand forgot about me waiting up on the third floor of our high school. Around 6 o'clock, the janitor came by and said, 'What're you doing here?' I said, I can't get down the steps. Well, he went to the dean and the dean went to the football field and really boxed Bob's ears, saying, 'don't ever leave your brother like that again.' After that incident, I don't believe he ever forgot me again.

"After high school, I went to college for a year and then enlisted in the service [Navy]. Our dad had served in the Navy in WWII, and before I left for boot camp he had some advice for me. 'Don't volunteer for anything and there are two things you've got to remember,' he warned. 'If they ever ask if you want to be an engineer, say, no. And, if they ask, do you have a driver's license, tell them no.' I asked, 'why?' 'Because, if you say, ya, I want to be an engineer, they'll hand you a shovel, and the guy who says, I have a driver's license, he'll get the wheel barrow.'"

Now, for the story of how David and his bad knees got to serve in Uncle Sam's Navy in the first place.

"When I enlisted in the Navy," he says, "it was smack dab in the middle of the Viet Nam conflict. They were hurting for bodies, and I think the standards were slackened. At the time, I had been without problems [with his knees] for a couple of years. They looked at my knees and decided things were o.k." Talk about scientific. Here's how the Navy decided David Urich's knees and the rest of his body were acceptable for duty, as he explains it. "They actually had me do some deep knee bends, then climb onto a table and jump off. I did this several times. I didn't fall when I landed, so the conclusion was that I was good to go. Unbelievable, right?," he laughs. But, that's not the end of David's story regarding his ailing knees and the U.S. Navy.

"The first of two ships I was on," he recalls, "was the USS LaSalle, LPD-3 home ported in Norfolk, VA. We were in heavy weather in the North Atlantic. I was on watch when we got hit by a big wave. I was knocked off my feet and fell down a flight of stairs. That's what messed up my knees again. I was operated on at the Portsmouth VA Naval Hospital. Upon my recovery, I was assigned to the USS Vreeland DE 1068 out of Charleston, SC." And as legendary newscaster, the late Paul Harvey would say, "and now...you know the rest of the story."

The U.S.S. Vreeland is the ship David Urich and his hurting knees were assigned to when he was discharged.

***

David Urich hates saying, "I'm a Viet Nam era veteran. I spent most of my time on an LPD-3 troop transport. We would go down from Norfolk [VA] to Moorhead City [N.C.] pick up a battalion of Marines out of Lejeune [No. Carolina] and take 'em over to Operations; pick em up later, bring em back for 2 weeks leave and they were off to Nam. The most combat I ever saw, I was on shore patrol [military police] once and got hit in the head with a beer bottle."

***

When David got discharged from the Navy around 1971, he went back to school on the G.I. Bill. Somewhere along the way, he got married and divorced. He was living in Columbus, Ohio and was in tough shape financially. "I didn't even have enough money for cab fare. Anytime, I needed financial need or help with a problem, Bob would always be the first to call. Bob would say to his brother, "alright, here's how we're gonna fix this. We got a spare bedroom. Why don't you come out here [Vegas] and stay with us. Throw everything you can fit in your car, forget the rest and come on out, which I did. At the time, I was driving a little Chevy Mazda," says Dave. "It was an economy car, around 2 years old and about all that I could afford. I was in Vegas living with Bob & Heather for about a month and he called me and said, 'park that car.' I said, 'what'd ya mean. What are you talking about?' I had a dream and a premonition. Park the car,' he repeated. I said, 'OK, and he got me another car. A week later, the Mazda that I got rid of was totaled in an accident. True story."

It wouldn't be the first or last time Bob would have vibes about certain people and events. His sister-in-law Sheila [Heather's sister] calls Bob psychic."Bob saved David's life in more ways than one."

"Bob was always there to bail him out," says Heather.

"He constantly had a net under his little brother. He bought him a car, a house, set him up in the catering business which serves food to the cast and crew of Television and film productions including Bob's series, Vega$. Bob was always there to do whatever he could to ensure David success, who always seemed to be running into a brick wall, emotionally."

David tells the story of when they were filming *Cannonball Run* starring Burt Reynolds at Burt's Appaloosa ranch in Florida. "I was the caterer on the film, and it's when I got to know Burt's dad. You see, the Burt in the family we got to know was his dad, 'Burt.' Burt, the actor, was called 'Buddy.' Ole Burt used to ride around in a golf cart in the shape of a Mercedes. He always had a Dalmatian in it with him. There was a tack store where they sold hay and clothing and that sort of thing. I was walking up this road to the store. I was looking for a pair of boots. Ole Burt pulls up and says, 'Hey, David, where ya goin?' "I'm going up to your store lookin' for a pair of boots," I replied.

'Well, get in, maybe I can get those for you at cost and you can save yourself a buck.'

"I said, that'll be great and jumped on board."

"'You know,' ole Burt says, with a squint in his eye, 'we have something in common. We'll have to get together.'

"I'm thinking. O.K., now what could we possibly have in common, so, I ask.

"Ole Burt smiles and says, 'Well, we **don't** have a last name!'

"'You're always Bob's brother and I'm Burt's dad.'"

***

Later during David Urich's film career, "I finally gave up the catering business. It's a thankless job in the film industry," he laments.

"You have to get up really early, and be on the set before the film crew and cast show up. I lost interest. But, because of my catering business, I had to drive the vehicle on to the lot where the production was being filmed to set up, so I had been a member of the Teamsters union. That's when I moved into the transportation end of film production." **"He's been the top guy on Jim Carrey movies and also ran the show on the hit series, *Six Feet Under*."** "Yes, I did five seasons on *Six Feet Under* on HBO," says David. Then I moved to picture car coordinator, and as the PCC,[1] did the 2nd and 3rd *Transformer* films and also *The Avengers*. I was an active Teamster for nearly 28 years before retiring." All the long hours and traveling can do a number on one's marriage. "I worked a lot of hours," says David. "I was married when I started, but it was over when we were done. Ya, there was a divorce in their somewhere," he laughs. Today [2017] David Urich is happily married to his third wife, Janet. They live in Massachusetts.

1 PCC or Picture Car Coordinator is responsible for any action vehicles you see in a movie, cop, stunt cars, etc. "You meet with the producers and director to get an idea of what they need [vehicles] says Dave Urich "and you fulfill those needs."

Bob's sister Monica with late husband Conrad "Connie" Rauch, relaxing at Bob & Heather's home on West Lake CANADA, July 15, 1998. Also photo of Bob's brother Tom and his family, Christmas 2017, Tom on left wearing glasses, his wife Judy on far right in photo. Photo courtesy Tom Urich.

3 Urich brothers, L-R, David, Tom and Bob [insert Bob, Dave & Tom (in glasses.)

Chapter 6

Bullies and Bob's First Dramatic Performance

"On the ridge above the Ohio River there is always a breeze as if created by the movement of the water itself. It's a perfect spot for flying a kite, like the new one I purchased at Rudy Pletz's corner grocery, soda fountain and novelty store. These days you can't get me out of sporting good stores." Robert Urich

Bullies & Bob

[**Bold typed words** are Bob's own from his personal journal and used with permission.]

Young Bob Urich's gaze was fixated on the bright red kite emblazoned with a snarling back cat, with its homemade tail of rags, climbing steadily out over the Ohio River. Total purchase price of this paper high flyer: twenty-five cents. Three rolls of string at ten cents each, thirty cents. Total investment, fifty-five cents. With the price of mowing a lawn at around two-dollars, no small investment.

"Slowly, I fed it line and watched it dip and wobble and then rise.

Suddenly, my thoughts were disrupted by the crunch of clod-hoppers, black ankle-length boots on slag* and even before I turned, I knew who was standing behind me and why they were there.

"'What are you doin' out here?'" asked Pete, one of the infamous Locke Brothers.

"Flying my kite." I offered in my most reasonable voice.

"'You heard what he said. What the hell you doin' out here,'" repeated his brother, Arnie, ignoring what I thought had been a complete and satisfactory answer.

"Nothing," I said, "just flying my kite...just flying my new kite, that's all."

They were not a pleasant crew. Zannie was the younger of the brothers and clearly under the control of his older brother, Arnie. They wore their hair chopped short, home haircuts that appeared to have been administered by a very dull knife. Their heads were covered with scabbed-over sores. Zannie had a fresh cut under his left eye and Arnie, a little taller than his brother, sported a large crescent slice across the bridge of his runny nose. They gave the singular impression of never having bathed. Their unwashed jeans were almost black from wear and both had on dirty T-shirts. A pack of Camels protruded from Arnie's rolled-up sleeve.

"Standing next to the Locke Brothers was Pete Matches, older, maybe seventeen, a full foot taller than the rest of us with a crude, hand-pounded silver ring on the middle-finger of his right hand serving more as a weapon than a fashion statement, and guaranteed to cut through flesh in a fistfight. There were rumors that Pete Matches carried brass knuckles."

"'What in hell's name do you think you're doing," Arnie said. It wasn't a question.

"I told you, flying my kite."

"'Let it go," demanded Pete.

"What?"

"Let it go," he said, "or Zannie's going to beat you up."

"Why?"

"You don't think I can? Piped up, Zannie.

"Yes...uh...no, it's a new kite. I just bought it down at Rudy's."

Bobby Urich appeal to reason didn't appear to be working and was met with cold, blank stares.

"I was probably going to get my ass kicked for having the audacity to be flying a new kite out over this wondrous river, out on "their slag pile." I'd been in scraps before but was not known in the neighborhood for my pugilistic efforts. I had been taught not to fight, to just walk away, and to stay away from those who did."

Once in the alley that separated Bob's house from his Uncle John Sweda's, he got in a fight with Larry Coppa, a pudgy Italian kid who lived two houses down.

"My cousin Angie tried to break it up as we rolled around on the ground, landing one ineffective punch after another. Blinded by the rage, I bit Angie on the hand leaving teeth marks. At least that was her version. To this day, I do not remember biting her. But this was different, this was not Larry Coppa, I actually liked Larry Coppa. His dad, Peanuts Coppa, made the best tomato sauce and pizza ever. This was serious, with no chance for retreat, with no hope of being rescued by Cousin Angie."

Bobby knew, walking away would not be an option this time. We would definitely be talking bloody nose or broken teeth. If brass knuckles entered the picture, maybe even broken bones. Pete, getting a little impatient, repeated his demand.

"'Let go of the kite.

"Now, it wasn't one of the most intelligent decisions I've ever made, but I shouted may response, 'No! I won't, dammit, and you can't make me.' Actually, it only *felt* like I was shouting--it was more of a mumble, really. 'No.' I choked out, 'you can beat me up if you want, but I'm not letting go of the kite.'"

While the dialogue progressed, Bob was slowly rolling in the string, hand over hand, hoping against hope that the inevitable would somehow miraculously change and the confrontation would take a new direction or that Bob could land the kite before the brawl.

"Zannie, it occurred to me was a little more reluctant than he appeared. Bullies often are reluctant fighters. Arnie gave him a push forward, closing the six-foot gap between us to a couple of feet--striking range. Zannie pushed me backwards, but without conviction, and taunted me to push back."

Even among these neighborhood toughs there was a certain 'code of honor,' a protocol to follow. They needed Bobby to resist, to shove back, so as not to make this an unprovoked attack, so that when details of the fight were discussed later, the justification for whom pushed and shoved whom first, could be debated.

"I let him shove me back even closer to the edge of the slag pile and the long drop to the river below. And all the while, I'm winding in the string of the kite."

"'No,' I said again, my voice breaking a little less this time."

Something wasn't working for these bullies. Something elemental had shifted and Pete Matches sensed it. Slight resistance is supposed to be followed by a plea for mercy. To regain control, Pete methodically, and purposefully fished the brass knuckles from his back pocket, slipped them on his right fist and said, "let it go."

"'Let it go,' he repeated, taking a small step forward.

"'It's a new kite and I'm not letting it go.'"

Then came a pause that lingered like twilight. Zannie looked back at Arnie and they both looked over to Pete. Bob never shifted his gaze from Pete; he's the leader, the one to watch.

"'Okay,' Pete said, 'then start crying.'

"'What?'

"'Start crying! If you don't start crying, Zannie's going to beat you up.'"

Now, this new command sounded strangely similar to Bob's parents' logic. *If you don't stop crying, I'm going to give you something to cry about.*

"That was logic often used by my parents and never made sense to me. Couldn't they see that I already had something to cry about?"

The shift, it became clear, was profound. Bob's kite was no longer at risk. Pete wasn't going to do the dirty work. They were bargaining for a lesser concession. If Bob would just cry, show weakness, vulnerability, acknowledge that this was indeed their domain, he could beat the rap and they would have a good laugh at his expense and be able to tell the story all over the neighborhood.

"Pete's face was turning crimson. He was pissed and he wanted to be done with this kid stuff. No glory here. 'I said, start crying,' he yelled.

"I really didn't feel like crying, but without considering another course of action, in that instant, I embraced that moment and everything that had led to it and on command, summoned from some unknown place, tears formed and ran down my face, my voice wavered with fury, and an outraged monologue was born in my throat.

"'This is my kite, I earned the money to buy it and you have no right to do this,' I said. Then I cried, wailed with the anguish of the righteous and oppressed. Even as I sank to my knees, my voice grew stronger and clearer. Lost in the moment, my head bowed, I released the kite... because it was my moment, my place, my river, my kite and I could release if I chose and there was nothing they could do to alter that cosmic truth."

When Bob looked up, the Locke brothers were slowly backing away, looking a little confused. They turned and ran towards the River Avenue and home. Pete Matches did not move. A tight smile formed on his face, but in his eyes there was no amusement, no sense of conquest or ridicule, but a hint of what seemed to be ... respect.

"Ignoring him, I turned my back and watched the black cat kite flutter down towards a watery death in the muddy Ohio River. It slipped below the tree line and vanished.

The crying stopped as easily as it had begun and when I turned back around, Pete and his brass knuckles were no where to be seen. With the taste of warm, salty tears in the corners of my mouth, I began to laugh and hop and holler and do a little jig."

At a young age, Bob Urich had turned in his very first dramatic performance. Perhaps, not exactly Oscar winning quality, but certainly convincing enough to drive the bullies away.

Chapter 6 (cont.)

Acting was in Bob's stars

Acting was in Bob's Stars

Bob Urich was destined from an early age to become an actor.

In a 1998 interview with *Midwest Today*, Editor Larry Jordan asked Bob Urich if he knew when growing up that someday he would pursue an acting career.

"Yes. From the very beginning," he replied.

"It was strange. I knew most people cock an eyebrow when I say this, but I can remember being an infant in a crib, not having the benefit of speech and seeing light coming through a Venetian blind in the window. It struck the wall and the floor of my parent's bedroom and I was aware of the way the light made me feel. At that moment, I knew that someday those feelings, and how I felt about that sort of thing would be important in the work that I chose to do."

Bob's grammar school classmate, Teri 'Volsky' Samstag, remembers Bob enjoyed being on stage.

***

"Even back in high school I was thinking about acting," recalls Urich in a 1990 interview with his hometown newspaper, the *Toronto Tribune*.[1]Bob's first high school play was a three-act comedy, *Don't Take My Penny*. Another of Bob's classmates, Dohrman Crawford, was also in the play. "Bob had the lead. I was the only one who could do a French accent," he laughs, "so I became the French dress designer, Henri. One of our scenes required Bob to tangle me up and toss me on the floor. I remember it mostly because I broke my watch."

The Senior Class play was performed Saturday night, April 18, 1964. Tickets cost just seventy-five-cents for adults and fifty cents for children. Today, a candy bar costs more.

---

1 The Toronto Tribune served the 'Gem City' from 1879 until it's final issue in 1990.

"I remember Bob's performance at our senior talent show," says his classmate and friend, Tim Seese. "Bob sang *Maria*[1] from *West Side Story*. I don't believe I had ever heard him sing before. He was great and all... and I do mean ALL... the girls were swooning." Another of Bob's classmates, Terry Hunter says, "One of my favorite memories of him during high school was the time he sang '*Marie*' from *West Side Story* for a talent assembly. Let's put it this way," Hunter says," the guy could act, but he couldn't sing." Interesting, since most people in attendance thought Bob sang pretty well. Proving once again, 'different strokes for different folks.' Today, Terry Hunter lives in Hawaii with his wife, artist Nancy Vilhauer. He is mostly retired after a career as a TV news reporter/photographer/editor. He still does a weekly movie review on local television.

***

"I never met Bob's older brother, Tom, who was an actor," recalls Tim Seese. "I think he had a strong influence in Bob's eventual career choice. In one way, Tom, opened a whole new world to us. I was told Tom Urich was a friend of singer, satirist Tom Lehrer. Bob had some of Lehrer's albums and we listened laughing hysterically to the *Element* song, *Makes a Fellow Proud to be a Soldier* and many others." It wasn't any one particular film or play that got Bob Urich interested in acting–he was just drawn to it. His brother, Tom, proceeded Bob into show business and was a great influence on his decision to become an actor. "Tom was doing theater in New York, while we were in school," says Bob's friend, Bill Hutchison. "He sort of pulled Bob in that direction."

[**Bold typed words** are Bob's own and taken directly from his personal journal.]

"My brother Tom was the one to give me my first acting lessons in the kitchen of our tiny wood frame house, when he came home from college.

"I asked him, 'how do you act?'

---

1 Maria is from the popular Broadway musical, West Side Story. Music was written by Leonard Bernstein and lyrics by Stephen Sondheim. The American classic is based on the book by Arthur Laurents and is set in N.Y.'s upper West side in the mid 1950s. Two rival gangs, the all-white Jets and the Puerto-Rican Sharks duke it out with a pulsating music score and incredible dance numbers. The play had it's Broadway premiere in 1957, directed by Jerome Robbins, who also choreographed it. It's about two star-crossed lovers, ex-gang member, Tony, who falls for Maria , the younger sister of Bernado, the leader of the Sharks.

"'Well, give me that dish towel,' he said. [Bob was doing dishes and had a towel in his hand.]

"'OK,'" he said, 'don't get intimidated when I ask you for it.' Then he said, 'Give me the towel. I SAID GIMME THE TOWEL!'"

"No, I'm not going to give you the towel."

"'That was good. Now you ask me for the towel.'"

"Pretty soon we were rolling around on the floor fighting over the towel. He gets up, puts the dish towel down and says, 'There, you just had your first acting lesson.'

"It was a good one. It was about intention. The meaning of the words you say. How many different ways something can be said."

For Bob, it was all very refreshing and new, but he couldn't imagine for the life of him there was a way that somebody could make a living at it.

***

Bob's high-school steady, Candy Patrick Mindigo says Bob was a talented actor and singer. "He was always singing. Bob's brother Tom was an actor and he could sing as well. We went to New York to see Tom in *The Fantasticks.*[1] We really enjoyed that and spending time with Tom and his lovely wife [Judy]."

Candy also remembers something prophetic Bob said to her one evening. "We were out on a date, and he said, 'I think something great is going to happen to me in the future.'

I just looked at him because he was dead serious. I told him, I believed it too."

1 *The Fantasticks* is a 1960 musical with music by Harvey Schmidt and lyrics by Tom Jones.

Bob as early thespian in St. Joseph's School play, Bob as the King. Photo courtesy of Teri Volsky.

Toronto High Sr. Class Play, Don't Take My Penny, *Bob's high school sweetie, Candy Patrick standing lst on left side of photo. Bob is standing on stairs, 3rd boy up on left. Photo courtesy Holtzmann Studio.*

Chapter 7

"Toronto High"
and
Memories from Bob's classmates and friends

Author's note: In August 2016, I reached out to Bob Urich's classmates at Toronto High School - the graduating Class of 1964 - hoping a couple would respond to my request for their personal memories of Bob. Within a week, I was pleased to hear from seventeen class members! My sincerest thanks to them for taking time to reply. Robert Urich's story would be incomplete without their personal reflections and insightful comments. I am most grateful and happy to include them in this chapter.

Toronto High School Red Knights

Toronto High School was first built in 1889 and the first graduating class boasted four students. The second building was built in 1900 and served until 1926. The stadium[1] and football field were added in 1930 and the gym in 1939. According to Toronto historian, Carolyn Walker, "each time the number of children increased it necessitated the need for bigger buildings. Toronto schools have maintained its independence for 128 years–no small feat," she says, "in a day of consolidations. Bob Urich's and my class of 1964 was the 75th class to graduate. Bob and every Toronto High Freshman had to learn the words to the school alma mater.

"Hail the Colors, Red and White
Keep them waving day and night,
Shout thy name as years pass by,
Til our banners reach the sky."

1 In 1985, the stadium was officially named Clarke Hinkle field in honor of the 1927 T.H.S. grad, who played football for Bucknell Univ. and in the NFL for Green Bay. He is a member of the NFL Hall of fame.

Kathyrn Hammon, Toronto High's Dean of Girls, always seemed to have girls kneeling before her. No, it was not some sort of pledge to her royal highness, nothing like that, she was checking to make sure the hem line of every girl's skirt touched the floor.Miss Hammond always seemed to know what was going on in each girl's life, the good and the not the not-so-good. When confronted, one woman recalls, "it was always better to tell her the whole story, because she probably already knew the truth anyway!"

It was her smile, and her sense of sincerity that made each girl feel as though she were the most important person in the world, particularly when you needed her shoulder to cry on. When she saw you coming, she would greet you with, "how're you doing, old buddy?" There is little doubt every girl who attended Toronto High during the 1960s took a little piece of Kathryn Hammond with her into adulthood.

Across the hall and a short walk from Ms. Hammond's office was her counterpart, Bob Hughes, the Dean of Boys. If you happen to pass by his office, you would most likely see him checking missing belt loops and shirt tails. But, you would also see him in deep discussion with a student who had gone to him with a problem. You could always tip-toe away feeling confident that another issue was being resolved. Mr. Hughes always wore a welcoming smile for everyone.

It's hard to believe in today's permissive society that, at one time, our public high schools actually had a Dean of Boys, along with a Dean of Girls. It's even harder to believe in today's world of 'wear what you want,' that Miss Hammond was busy checking hem lines on skirts, while Mr. Hughes was busy looking for shirt tails sticking out! Bob Urich knew that Bob Hughes' duty was to keep every young man at Toronto High on the 'straight and narrow,' so he made sure he was squared away at all times. As a student Bob worked in Mr. Hughes' office and looked up to him with a great deal of admiration.

In 1990, at Toronto High's all-school reunion, Bob Urich was the guest M.C. He was introduced on-stage by his one-time Dean of students, Bob Hughes. Everyone present could instantly see there was tremendous respect between them as they warmly greeted each other.

***

"Bob was super good at everything in high school," says his classmate, Lois 'Burchfield' Bradway, who today lives in Richmond, Indiana. "We had some classes together and he and I worked in the Dean of Boys office. Bob and our Dean, Mr. Hughes were always discussing his [Bob's] sports successes and the roles he played in our school plays. They both entertained me, those many fifty plus years ago.

Growing Up in the 50's in Toronto Ohio

"He was an excellent student, athlete, actor and a real gentleman, unlike some of his immature cohorts," Lois Bradway says, laughing. "I didn't know Bob well, but even though he was a 'jock' he spoke to everyone, and didn't act like he was better than anyone else. We never hung out or had any social life together, because I was too shy to talk much to anyone. However, I felt comfortable being around Bob."

***

Some times, Toronto teens in the 50s and 60s would shoot pool at Leo's pool room, or Frogs, says Bob's classmate and fellow football tri-captain Bill Hutchison.[1] "Frogs was like going in to an old bar," he says. "It had wooden floors and you could get pop and chips, but there was no drinking since kids would go in. I didn't spend a whole lot of time there," he insists. "Noonan's drug store, owned by Jack and Florence Battles, is where I worked for about 3 ½ years. I did general errands, cleanup, and carried ice-cream containers. Our close friend and classmate, Joel Lamantia's aunt, Mary worked out front. She made the most delicious peanut butter fudge for Noonan's popular ice cream sundae's. If Bob Urich or anyone was down-town," says 'Hutch,' [the name his friends call him], "They'd come in to Noonan's for ice cream or a Coke. It was a local stop in spot. Toronto teens, like Bob Urich, hung out at Noonans, everyone did. As you walked in there were booths along the outside wall. Working at the pharmacy, helped me make the decision to become a pharmacist. Mike Popovich, a pharmacist, bought Noonan's. He was my mentor. I worked for him when home from college and in the summer."

Bob Urich and just about every other Toronto teen consumed gallons of cherry cokes and cheese crackers at Noonan's every Saturday

1 Bill 'Hutch' Hutchison played football at Ohio Northern Univ. for 4 years,. Invited to try out with the CFL, Toronto Argonauts, instead, he elected to attend pharmacy school. He met his wife, Christine, who was from Rocky River [OH] while in college. They have two sons, 2 grandsons and a granddaughter. He worked for Gray Drug as district manager , and later for Walgreens and Medco Mail order company until retiring in January 2013. 'Hutch is a prostate cancer survivor.

afternoon, after a movie at the Rex Theater in the Nolan Building right at the corner of 4th and Main. The other theater in town, the Manos, was a regular Saturday date night for couples going steady.

"We would also stop by Rudy's for a frosty root beer," says Tom Urich. "It was only about 5 or 6 blocks from our house. You could get a Coke and a burger there." It was a scene right out of the popular 1950s based TV show, *Happy Days.*[1] Thinking back to those happy days, Gregg McKelvey says, "I went there [Rudy's] probably 5 days a week. They sold penny candy. You could go in there with ten or fifteen cents and buy all sorts of stuff; sugar babies, root beer barrels, red and black licorice, tiny wax bottles filled with sweet liquid, candy cigarettes, all sorts of goodies. I liked Jaw breakers the best," says Gregg, who also recalls, Rudy's had a lemon-based drink that he really went for most of the time. McKelvey points out that since the 'hang out' was located close to the high school, kids would go there for lunch. "There was a lunch counter with stools, and also a few booths, but I lived three houses from the high school, so I just went home for lunch."

"Rudy's was also the place we stopped at on the way home from summer morning football practices," says Urich's fellow tri-captain, Tim Seese. "Rudy's special lemon lime drink helped us rehydrate. Then we'd go back for the afternoon practice session." "Rudy's last name was Pletz," says McKelvey. "He and his sister, who lived above the store, ran it for years. Then one day it just closed down. I guess as early as the 1970s. It just sat there vacant, almost as a landmark to all us kids who hung out there. They finally tore it down and today, he says wistfully, "like so much of Toronto, it's just a vacant lot."

Toronto native, Carolyn Walker graduated from Toronto High, Class of 1964 with Bob Urich. She remembers their first days as Freshmen. "Everyone entering high school is a little nervous and Bob was no exception,. He attended St. Joseph's grammar school through eight grade so he was probably meeting some kids for the first time. One thing that impressed me about Bob," she says, "he was always very polite and respectful of others. He was never flashy, very athletic and smart. I shared some

---

1 Happy Days was a popular sitcom depicting life in the 1950s. It aired on ABC-TV [1974-84 and starred Ron Howard, Henry Winkler, Don Most, Erin Moran, Tom Bosley, Marion Ross & Anson Williams. Anson directed Bob in the TV series, *Love Boat-The Next Wave*. Read more in chapter 15 and acting.

classes with Bob and we were in choir together." Carolyn witnessed close-up Bob's 'juggling act' in order to honor his activities. "Another quality which impressed me about Bob," she adds, "if he committed himself to a project, you could be sure he would not stop until itwas finished, and if he showed up late because of conflicting schedules, he would always be apologetic. In the summer, Bob was a lifeguard at the [town] pool," Walker says, with a smile. His warm 'hello' and always welcoming smile, almost made the mile walk from her house to the town pool worth the effort in the hot Ohio summer sun.

Kay 'Gilchrist' Murray says she was Bob's girlfriend their Sophomore year. "It was from October to December 1962. I don't remember us actually going on a date. His 16th birthday was in December, so he didn't even drive yet. He walked me home from football and basketball games and the local teenage hangout, Youth Harbor. There wasn't much of a connection between us and we realized, we should just be friends."

Lynn 'Vannich' Popovich also went to high school with Bob. "He was such a wonderful person," she fondly remembers, "Kind, funny, athletic and of course very handsome. Bob always had that sweet smile on his face. Everyone loved him. I followed his career, and of course, we were all devastated to lose him way too soon."

"I always thought of him as an easy-going guy with a good sense of fun," says Bob's classmate, Dohrman Crawford.[1] "He was enjoyable to be around. We referred to him as 'Luigi' for some reason now forgotten. Bob, Roy Glass and I used to play a fair amount of golf together [golf was one of Bob's passions], at a club built in the 1920s. I believe today it is named Cedar Hills.[2] Bob used to get a little hot under the collar playing

---

1 Dohrman Crawford graduated from Miami Univ. in 1968 and became an Air Force pilot, serving in Viet Nam as a Forward Air Controller, flying the 0-1 Birddog. He says, he got to fly some incredible planes, including the F-100 Super Sabre, the F4C Phantom II and the F15 Eagle. Dohrman was the first F15 Squadron Commander in the Air Guard, where he served 15 years, before joining Delta Airlines, where he flew for 31 years. He still works for Delta as an instructor. He resides in Atlanta with his wife of 48 years, Susan, which he proudly says, "anyone meeting her would instantly agree that I am a very lucky man."

2 Gregg McKelvey, Bob & Dohrman's classmate, says, back in the 60s there were three golf courses in the Toronto area; Dyer was private, but there was also Belle View in Steubenville, Highland in Wellsville and Rayland, today called Mazeroski's but back then called Vinecliff. He makes no mention of a Cedar Hills.

golf and was an excellent club thrower, for which we rode him unmercifully," says Crawford.

"To all of us in our hometown of Toronto, he'll always be 'Bob,' says his pal, Tom 'Chip' Coulter. "We never called him Robert. Our families came from a little town called Stratton [OH]. They knew each other long before Bob and I came along. Toronto is a small town, around 8,000, when we were growing up in the 50s and 60s. Every one knew every one else. "Chip remembers Bob being a really good athlete. "As kids, he went to Catholic grammar school, St. Joseph's. I went to Roosevelt, but we competed against each other in basketball. When we weren't competing against another team, we played pick-up ball against each other. Later, we played basketball together in high school. I was a power forward and Bob was a point guard." At 6' 2" Chip points out, "Bob was tall for basketball back then. He wasn't a ball-hog, but a real team player. He was a studious type. I think that's how he picked up the name, Igor. He was a laid back kinda guy. A real gentleman and well-mannered but also a man's man," says Coulter.

Bob's pal and classmate, Chip Coulter says, "To the best of my knowledge, Bob never got in any kind of trouble. He was a straight-shooter. You know, back then, you were told to be home for supper at six, you'd better be there and on time. That's just the way it was, and with school, sports and other activities, you didn't have time to get into any serious trouble. And, as mentioned, our town was so small," he laughs," you couldn't get away with anything, even if you tried. One thing people may be surprised to learn about Bob," says Chip, "was his 'quick' wit. He always had a comeback if cornered." Bill Hutchison, another of Bob's friends and classmates, says, "In high school you were either quick-witted or you got run over. Bob wasn't one who tried to be funny. He was just naturally witty. People probably wouldn't think it, but Bob was a funny guy. He had a little bit of comedian in him." Later, in his professional life, Bob often did stand up comedy at L.A. venues. "He loved doing it," says his wife, Heather, "and was quite good."

After high school, Chip Coulter played Major League ball for 7 years with the St. Louis Cardinals organization. Later, he was traded to the Mets. "I was sitting on the bench," says Chip, when he admitted to the manager, 'I think I wanna go home.' He looked at me and said, "'Chip, hang in here. I'll use you once in a while as a pinch hitter. You can always go back to the steel mills.'" So, I stayed. After the season ended, they sent Coulter a contract. "I just threw it up on the mantle. I was a carpenter by trade during the 'off-season' and was a happy guy. I forgot all about the contract, until one day, the director of player personnel, Joe McDonald called and said,"'Chip, we need that contract. Are you gonna sign it?'"

"I told him I'd think about it…and I did. I got to thinking' about all the long bus rides, time spent away from family and so on. My wife[1] said, 'Chip, what are ya gonna do?' I said, 'I'm quittin.' I decided to retire from baseball. My decision came right out of the blue. I had always wanted to end my major league career on my terms. I never wanted to be released. I called Joe McDonald[2] and said, 'Hey Joe, I'm not comin' to spring training. I'm done!' 'Well,' he says, 'We have coaching. We can put you in a rookie league as a 'player-coach,' whatever way you want to work it, Chip.' I rode those buses all those years. I said, 'No thanks, I'm gonna stay here and work.' It was the best move I ever made. I never regretted it. I'm a happy person. I married my 2nd wife, Georgia Swearingen, who I had known my whole life. I have my health. I golf, ride bicycles, and canoe." With an air of contentment, Chip Coulter adds, "I've got the perfect life. I'm a fortunate person."

***

Chip Coulter recalls one phone call he received from Bob Urich which stands out in his mind. "After we graduated from high school [1964] I had no contact with Bob until 1969, when I got called up with the Cardinals. I was in Chicago. I believe Bob was working at a radio station there. [WGN][3] "I'm not sure what he was doing. He called me up and said, "'Chip, it looks like you're doing pretty good.' I said, ya, for the moment. Baseball is a day to day thing. "How you doin,' Bob?"

"'Not well,' he said. 'I'm thinking about tossing it in and going back to the steel mills in Toronto.' I distinctly remember how disgusted he sounded with everything."

---

1 Chip Coulter's first wife, Jill Scott died at a young age, 41. They had one daughter.

2 Joe McDonald was a member of the New York Mets organization between 1965 and 1980 in various positions, including director of scouting, dir. of minor league operations, and eventually Gen. Mgr. 75-79.

3 Bob was not happy in sales at WGN, He longed to be an actor. He got caught moonlighting as one, which was against company policy and was promptly fired. Sometimes, good things come wrapped-up in strange circumstances. Read more about Bob's Chicago days in Chapter 11.

"Now Bob wasn't the type to quit anything," says Chip.

That was the last time I spoke with him. A short while later, I heard Burt Reynolds lent him a hand and Bob had gone out to Hollywood, and lived with him for a while until he got settled. I guess that when his career took off."

***

"Bob possessed leadership qualities," says classmate, Dave Harvilak. He was out-going and had no problem talking to anyone about any subject matter. He was tri-captain of the football team[1] and that takes leadership for others to turn to you for advice or answers. He was always in school plays, too. When you get chosen for numerous positions throughout your school years, others, like teachers, as well as students look up to you. I distinctly recall, Bob had the honor of being our high school flag bearer at school assemblies. Bob and John Daily, the other Flag bearer, would start at the back of the auditorium, while 'Pomp and Circumstance' played. The entire student body would stand while Bob & John walked down both aisles, climbed the stairs to the stage, and placed the American flag in one standard and our school flag in the other. We would all recite the school pledge. My dad," says Dave, "Nicholas Harvilak, a 1934 Toronto High graduate wrote the words to our alma mater."

"In high school, Bob was a natural born leader because of his wide-range of talent, in athletics, music and drama," says Bob's classmate, Jim Lowery. "He was confident, and he knew what he wanted to accomplish. Bob trusted in his training. Even though, he did not enjoy or necessarily crave the public eye. I believe Bob's talent always cast him in leadership roles that automatically placed him at the front of the line."

Bob was in the limelight many times because of his personality and leadership abilities. "It's funny," recalls Bob's classmates, Jim Ray.* Bob never sought to be a leader, but somehow, he always seemed to find himself cast in the role. Bob and I ran across each other while playing Junior high basketball. In the 50s, there were 3 or 4 junior high schools in Toronto and they each had their own basketball team. But, high school is where I really met Bob. He was never Robert, always Bob. He had a pleasant personality. I remember, he got along with everyone, whether it was in choir, sports or dramatics."We were in ensemble together for 2 or

1 Bob was tri-captain his senior year at T.H.S., along with Bill Hutchison and Tim Seese. For more info see Chapter 9,'Friday Night Under the Toronto Lights.'

3 years," says Jim Ray.[1] "Bob was a consummate pro in drama and also in athletics. In a small town like Toronto, you do everything. Bob was also a perfectionist. He always expected you to do it the right way and to do your best. To be selected captain of the football team+ was a big deal in Toronto. Classes were pretty competitive and Bob was a good student. I don't remember him [Bob] getting into any kind of trouble. He was quite busy with classes, athletics, and stuff. He didn't have time for anything else. Several of Bob's friends mentioned that Toronto is so small, it was impossible to get away with anything, so no one even tried." One way to keep kids out of trouble: keep em' busy!

Another of Bob's high school classmates, Tom Smith, who today lives with his wife in Oro Valley, Arizona described Bob in one word, Genuine. "He was never a phony. You knew where you stood with him, and most importantly, "he never did forget his humble start in Toronto. The 'Gem City' as the sign at each end of the town states. My uncle always told me," Tom Smith adds with a chuckle, "they left out the letter 'R.'"

"I remember Bob early on as this scrappy kid from the north side of town," says Tim Seese. "We competed against each other in a baseball game prior to high school, but we definitely became friends in high school. Toronto is a small town, but it wasn't until high school that everyone of the same age attended one school."

"One of my first memories of Bob was running into him at a Toronto High School varsity basketball game. We must have been freshmen and in the stands watching the game. More accurately, I was watching and Bob was announcing the game. He was giving a play by play description of the action down on the court. I expected him to stop after a while, but he didn't. He was immersed in his announcing and actually good at it. Maybe, this was an early predictor of life in the entertainment world for him."[2]

---

1 Jim Ray spent a total of 44 years in the Toronto & Addison School districts including Assistant Superintendent . Now retired, he and his wife Marilyn have three grown children. He enjoys singing with a Gospel group.

2 After graduating from Toronto [OH] high school, Bob received a bachelor's degree in Radio and Television Communications from Florida State Univ. in 1968, and in 1971, received a Master's degree in Broadcast Research and Management from Michigan State. His first job after college was in fact, in radio, as a sales rep at WGN-AM-Chicago. A job he loathed. He much preferred to be on-the-air than selling it.

"Bob and I double dated" says Tim Seese. "Bob drove his dad's Ford. I remember it being dark red or maroon. It was a late model and quite nice. My dad purchased a '57 Chevy convertible which was my car of choice. I believe, Bob's steady had moved out of the area our senior year and I had broken up with mine. It became our practice to drop in on Betty Ansell and Jackie Haynes, usually every Sunday night. Bob was interested in Betty and I in Jackie. I don't remember the circumstances but Betty was living with Jackie's family at the time. We would drop in unannounced although it was probably hardly unexpected after the first few occurrences," he says with a grin. "Bob's former steady girlfriend, Candy became a nursing student at one of the local hospitals. She and Bob fixed me up with one of her nursing school friends. I remember that I had to walk past the morgue in the basement to reach the nursing dorm, so that is hard to forget."

Bob's Toronto High Classmates Remember

Tim Seese says he would be remiss if he didn't mention that Bob was a handsome guy. "I remember one Christmas when he was at our house. Our family bought him a shirt or sweater as a gift. He had to try it on to assure that it fit. To this day, I remember that my older sister and even my mother were telling him how nice he looked. Bob was one of the standout people in our class. He was well liked and truly a nice guy."

***

Bob's senior year at Toronto High, the Class of 1964, the world was in turmoil. Lives were being turned upside down: the war in Viet Nam was heating up as the U.S. became increasingly more involved in Southeast Asia. Then a bit of reality about the 'real world' touched every student. Each one remembers exactly where they were as news came in that President John F. Kennedy had been assassinated in Dallas. It seems everywhere you looked people were sad and in a funk.

Bob and his classmates also lived through personal tragedies with the loss of very special people in their young lives. Linda Tarr, who would have graduated with them in 1964, met her death in a tragic car accident; Eugene Leasure, who served as a custodian at the high school, died suddenly. Mr. D.W. Hoover, music director in the Toronto schools for years, died during Bob's senior year, and Ralph Cope, a minister in the Church of Christ, also passed in 1964. He was well-known to students as an avid basketball fan, always present in the front row of the bleachers supporting Bob and his teammates, win or lose.

In 1964, the stability of high school students around the country was shaky. The world had become a much smaller place. Countries they had only read about in history class suddenly became front-page news stories and household names. Through it all, Bob and his classmates were encouraged by Toronto High's administration.

Growing up in the 1950s in Toronto Ohio

They felt 'safe and secure,' surrounded by people, not just in the classrooms, but by the community who cared about the young people of Toronto. Bob often said, "We were all lucky to have strong teachers and administrators who cared about us. They motivated us to do better!" In doing so, they helped mold Robert Urich into a successful man, and to his credit, he never forgot them or his small-town Ohio roots.

After graduation, Bob and his classmates had a few options, including college. Thanks to his prowess as a punter, Bob won a scholarship to Florida State University. For others, it was college, marriage or the service. Jobs were prevalent in 1964, at least in Toronto. There was the new Titanium plant, the power plants were expanding, and a few miles across the Ohio River in West Virginia, Weirton Steel, where the Urich family labored for years, was still a viable option.

However, by 1967, the choices became fewer and fewer for young men. Enlist or be drafted. College deferments and being married made little difference when it came to serving Uncle Sam. It was almost a given, if you were young and physically fit, the day you received your high school diploma, you could count on the next day, receiving greetings from the President of the United States.

Bob's classmate, Jim Lowery was one of many who served in the military. "The Viet Nam War was going strong, and I went in the Air Force for four years. After being discharged, I settled in Southern California, got a job, married my wife, Carol and we started a family. As time went on, my mother, who was friends with Bob's mom, would fill me in on what was going on with Bob and his acting career. I saw him many times on TV and in some movies. We caught up with each other at school reunions."

[**Bold typed words are Bob's** and taken directly from his journal.]

"We golfed and reminisced about old times. He was very busy all the time, but he would call me at times to catch up on things. He never changed. He was always good old Bob."

Bob's classmates remember

Bob Urich's success never changed the size of his hat. He never lost touch with his roots in the Ohio Valley and never lost sight of where he came from. Bob's wife, Heather, says, "at the height of his popularity and success as an actor, he delighted telling others, 'I'm still this kid from a small town in Ohio.' Bob was one small town boy who took his hometown pride all the way to Hollywood. He took great pride saying, 'Toronto is unique. It's worth preserving. I'm proud to be from Toronto…Ohio!'"

Terry Hunter, who says he is 'mostly retired' after working almost 30 years in TV news in Hawaii, also graduated from Toronto High with Bob. "Bob was very popular in high school and well-liked by everyone. Many years after we graduated, he came back to be the major speaker at our all-school reunion, he was the perfect celebrity, gracious and friendly to all. Not a trace of phoniness."

Returning 'back home' after being away for a while can be an emotional experience. The old times, old places and familiar faces back in his hometown of Toronto, helped to keep Bob Urich 'grounded' as he liked to say.

"I remember coming home to Toronto, Ohio, after I was in my first TV series–all the guys in the neighborhood were plumbers, carpenters and day laborers–and what they all wanted to know was when was I going to get a real job?

'What do you mean,' I said, 'I have a job. I do a show.'

'Yeah, sure,' they said, 'but that's only an hour a week. What do you do with yourself the rest of the time?'"

Distinguished Alumni

"I remember one time, after he became a huge star, Bob came back home to Toronto to visit," says his pal, Chip Coulter. "We have two one-way streets in our small town. North 4 runs South and goes right through the main part of town. Ron Anderson, Tommy Johnson and me, and someone else were walking down the street and we saw this car parked right in front of the 5 & 10 store, headed the wrong way. As we walked past the driver, Ron taps me on the shoulder and says, 'Do you know who that is?' I said no because it was difficult to see the person. He had a hat on and was wearing sun glasses and was kinda slouched down behind the wheel. I never would have recognized him. We walked up to the car, tapped on the window and said, 'Hey, we don't care if you are a big celebrity, you're not supposed to be parked there!' Bob rolled down the window and was laughing. He got a big kick out of it. We rode him about it all through

the years. He always took our ribbing good naturedly. Bob never changed. The last time I saw him was at his dad's funeral. I remember talking to his Mom. I heard Bob had been ill and learned of his passing from Carolyn Walker, of our Alumni Association. We've lost a lot of our classmates and now, we're at the age, where every day is a good day when we wake up," says Chip Coulter.

July 7, 1990

In July 1990, Bob Urich was one of six distinguished alumni recognized at the High School All-School Reunion. A press conference was held at the J.T. Karaffa Middle School honoring Bob and the others. Bob graduated with the THS Class of 1964-other honorees were Edna Tarr Beck, Class of 1925, Donald L. Humphrey-1947, Joseph T. Karaffa-1942, Francis Jane Shaffer-1937 and Robert D. Wise-Class of 1932.

Coming Back Home to Visit

Urich fondly recalled his involvement with various high school activities for an article in the Steubenville, Ohio *Sunday Herald-Star.* "I was very active in sports," and shaking his head with disappointment, Bob says, "I still can't believe we lost to Winterville [local school] in '62 on the last play of the game. I was a tackle and punter on the football team and tri-captain my senior year," and jokingly adds, "my jersey was # 75 in the program but #1 in their hearts. Football was such a cultural event and seeing all the scores on TV was a big thing." Bob was an active participant in many high school activities, including football, basketball and track. Bob and his teammates still hold a school record for the 'reverse shuttle relay event.'[1] Tim Seese was one of the football tri-captains, along with Bill Hutchison and Bob. "I don't remember him getting a big head over his

1 The reverse Shuttle Hurdle event is explained in Chapter 9.

successes," he says. "Bob always seemed to be modest and quick to give praise to others. Later in my business career, when I was evaluating talent for our team," says Seese,[1] "I would look for someone that possessed what we called the whole package. Bob had the whole package."

The Same old Bob

"Over the years, Bob Urich never changed," says his long-time friend and Toronto High classmate, Gregg McKelvey. "It was in the mid-1970's, and I hadn't seen Bob since our 1964 high school graduation," he recalls. "The Ohio Valley was holding it's annual Dapper Dan[2] Charity event at St. John's Arena in Steubenville. Bob was invited to speak at the event, along with many other distinguished people from the Ohio Valley area. Most were involved with sports, but since Bob was so well-known, he was one of the celebrities invited that year. An area had been set aside before the event started, where you could meet n' greet the guest speakers. I was standing in that area," says Gregg, "when Bob saw me. He immediately came over to me. 'Hi Gregg, how are you?' he said, reaching out to shake my hand. It was just like we saw each other all the time. We talked about old times for a few minutes. You never would have guessed that he was a well-known celebrity. He seemed exactly like the Bob I remembered. Nothing like he was any better than anyone else there. He was a very humble guy. Bob even invited me to visit him while he was filming his show in Vegas. 'Here's the address where I'm staying. Please come out and visit us,'" he urged his long-time friend. By the time, Gregg got around to visiting Vegas, filming had ended on his television series [Vega$] and Bob was gone. Gregg McKelvey only saw Bob once after that evening. "It was at one of our class reunions. He brought his wife Heather with him. She was just like Bob,

---

1 Tim Seese hung up his cleats after high school and took the academic route to the Univ. of Cincinnati, graduating with a BS in Metallurgical Engineering, followed by a MBA from Harvard Grad School of Business. His career began with G.E. then moved to the medical device business., holding several senior management positions in the industry, including CEO and board member. He says, the highlight of his career was as Pres. of Exactech Inc., a manufacturing company of orthopedic implants. Tim Seese is retired. He and his wife, Sharon have two children, Brian and Kristin. They've lived in Gainsville, Fl. since 1991. Currently his passion is off-shore fishing and flying radio-controlled airplanes.

2 Dapper Dan was a sports related charity event which honored local athletes from the Ohio Valley, from both Ohio and West Virginia who had outstanding years in high school and college sports.

friendly and kind to everyone." Bob's classmate, Jim Ray, echoes what others have said about the man. "For all of Bob's ability and all the things he did in his life, he was always a small town guy. Very low key.

"After he became famous, he would come back to Toronto to visit. He wanted no parades or any fanfare. He just wanted to come back home and visit his parents and some friends. I specifically recall," says Ray, "Bob wanted to quietly come in to town and quietly leave. Enter through the backdoor and exit the same way. The town wouldn't always let him do that, but he sure tried. He did not like the 'notoriety' his fame brought him. In fact, not only didn't he like it, but he didn't enjoy it. Bob never wanted to be famous. However, he did want to be great at everything he tried. "Bob would rather spend time with his family. Our kids were pretty much the same age as Bob and Heather's. When he did come home to Toronto, he would call me up and say, 'Jim, let's do something.' One time, we went to a carnival of all places. It was never anything big with Bob, just fun things to do."

Bob's cousin Jo-Jo Urich, a life-long resident of Irondale, Ohio, a town North of Toronto, agrees on how Bob craved privacy. "Yes, indeed, Bob always wanted to keep a low profile whenever he came back home. I'd get a phone call from him and he'd say, 'get a canoe and let's go down Yellow Creek. Just don't tell anyone.'" Jim Ray, a retired Toronto school administrator, is quite familiar with the old Toronto High. "We were all sad about the old high school being torn down, but, in Ohio, you have to deal with the facilities commission. If you're gonna build with the State, you gotta do what the State says. You have to build a new building on their terms." Listening to him describe the old high school, you immediately get the feeling that Jim Ray misses the old place as much as anyone.

"The old T.H.S. had a full auditorium with a nice stage that would seat about 750-800 people," Ray says. "We also had a separate gym. Now, it's called a cafetorium with a little stage, but it's nothing like the old high school. They also tore down the old stadium. It's not nearly as nice or big as it was, but they don't have the crowds like they use to have either. When we were in high school, in the '60s, there were probably 1600 kids in the school district in Toronto. Today, there's probably around 900 at most." Today [2017], according to Tom Urich, "the new high school is about two miles from where the old one majestically stood for so many years. It is now a parking lot for the football and baseball stadium." Heather Urich says, "Bob would be devastated to know his glorious old high school was torn down to make way for a new one."

Jim Ray remembers, "At our first all-school [classes] reunion in 1990, I picked Bob up at the airport in a limousine, provided by Clark's Funeral Home. Bob thought that was hysterical and couldn't stop laughing. So, we're riding home and it was coming up to the 4th of July weekend. That's when we use to have the all-school reunions," Ray points out. "Now, they're held over Labor Day weekend. 'Does the city still have fireworks?' Bob asked. 'No,' I said, 'We couldn't afford them.' 'We've got to have fireworks,' he Said, and asked me to call the fireworks people, so I did. 'You won't believe this,' I said on the phone, 'but I have Robert Urich sitting here in my living room and he insists we've got to have fireworks.' 'Oh my,' he says, 'I'm a great fan!' Now this is Thursday, and we only have a few days to get it all together for Saturday. The guy says, 'OK. I'll get you the fireworks. No problem. We'll have 'em there for you!'"

Bob and Toronto's Fireworks

"Now, here's the really interesting part," as Jim Ray continues. "All the guy wanted was an autographed picture of Bob in exchange for the fireworks. Now, mind you, Bob paid for the fireworks, but he didn't want people to know it. I only know all this, because I was standing right there beside him in my living room when he talked to the guy on the phone. The cost was probably somewhere around five thousand dollars. I don't know the exact amount, but Bob had to pay the city because they [fireworks people] billed the city of Toronto for the fireworks. Bob didn't want anyone to know he paid for them. He didn't want to come off as a show-boat! I said, 'OK; don't worry. I won't say anything,' so we simply announced that we added fireworks to the weekend events. It was a great fireworks display," exclaims Jim Ray. "And the city still does it every year, all because Bob Urich, back in 1990, brought back the tradition of fireworks on the 4th of July to his hometown."

***

Providing fireworks for Toronto wasn't the only generous thing Bob did for his hometown. The Robert Urich Scholarship began in 1978-79. It awarded $1000.00 every year to a graduating senior who had music or drama in his/her future plans. It was presented for 31 straight years. The Urich family ended the award after Bob died.

Toronto [Ohio] High School Building, built in 1926, the last graduating class was in 2013, before students entered the new Jr./Sr. High complex.

Dean's Assistants
First Row – Donna Utzler, Norma Talimine, Kathy Kruise, Miss Hammond, Mr. Hughes, Terry Hunter, Bob Urich, Greg Murray. *Second Row* – Evelyn Pinkerton, Linda Joy, Sandy Ranton. *Third Row* – Rita McGrath, Jackie Haynes, Beverly Jones, Barbara Harper, Connie Karaffa, Kathy Rosser, Lois Burchfield.

Dean's assistant's, Bob is front row, 2nd from right.

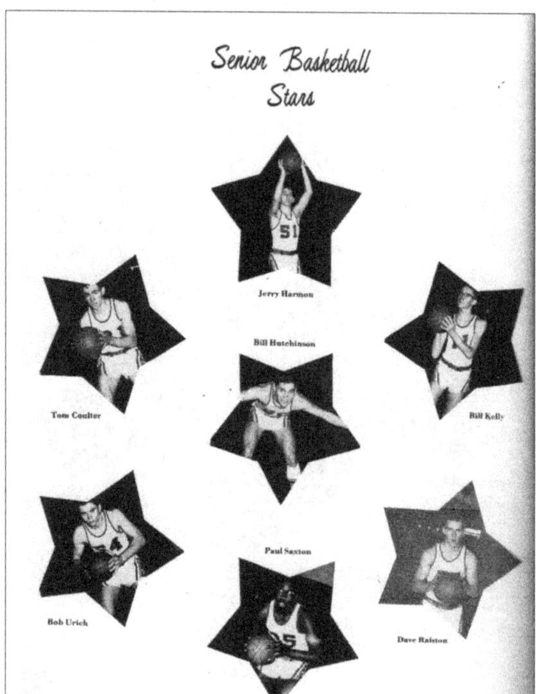

Toronto High Senior Basketball Stars, Bob Urich left lower star.

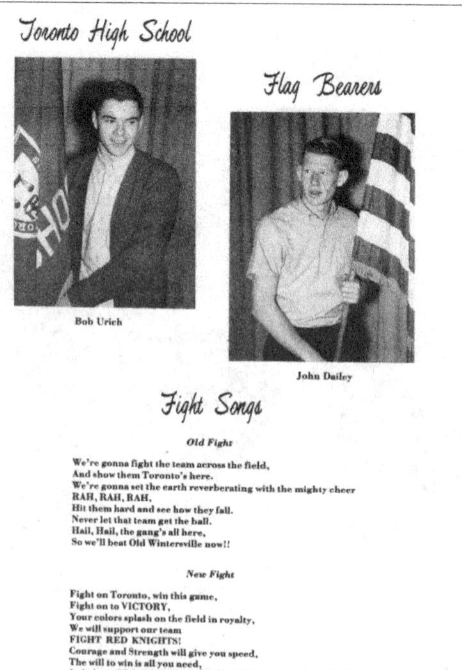

Toronto High School

Flag Bearers

Bob Urich

John Dailey

Fight Songs

Old Fight

We're gonna fight the team across the field,
And show them Toronto's here.
We're gonna set the earth reverberating with the mighty cheer
RAH, RAH, RAH,
Hit them hard and see how they fall.
Never let that team get the ball.
Hail, Hail, the gang's all here,
So we'll beat Old Wintersville now!!

New Fight

Fight on Toronto, win this game,
Fight on to VICTORY,
Your colors splash on the field in royalty,
We will support our team
FIGHT RED KNIGHTS!
Courage and Strength will give you speed,
The will to win is all you need,
So let's go RED KNIGHTS, let's FIGHT, FIGHT, ON TONIGHT,
We know you can win this game!

Toronto [Ohio] High School

Toronto High. Flag bearers, Bob Urich & John Dailey.

Sunday Herald -Star

SUNDAY, JULY 8, 1990, STEUBENVILLE, OHIO

Vol. 185 No. 32 SINGLE COPY 75¢

Robert Urich comes home for THS reunion

GIMME A T. Actor and Toronto High School alumnus Robert Urich leads a cheer of T-O-R-O-N-T-O during activities at the Toronto High School All-School Reunion Saturday, while Toronto Mayor Robert Wilson looks on.

Herald -Star Staff Photo

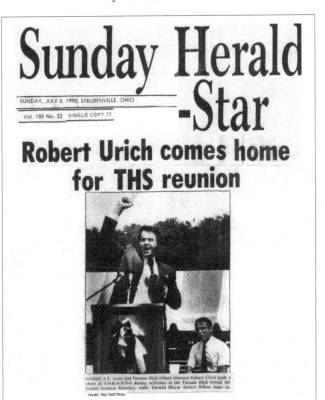

Sunday Herald-Star, *"Bob Returns Home," July 1990. Photo courtesy of Carolyn 'Motter' Walker.*

Clark's Limo, they picked Bob up at airport in this hearse. He loved it. Photo courtesy of Carolyn 'Motter' Walker.

Bob & his graduation Class of '64 at their reunion held in July 1990–Bob is standing in 2nd row, 2nd from right. Photo courtesy of Carolyn 'Motter' Walker.

Chapter 8

Bob liked *Candy*...Patrick, *that is, his High school steady . . . Youth Harbor Doo-Wop Time*

Bob Urich's high school sweetheart, Candy Patrick, was born in Pittsburgh, and lived in the little town of McKeesport until she was sixteen. In 2016, thanks to the Toronto High Alumni Association, Candy was located living in Los Altos California, happily married for the past 48 years to Richard Mindigo, a retired environmental engineer. In a phone interview with the author, Candy says, "I met my husband in Columbus [Ohio], when he was a student at Ohio State and I was there for my nursing classes. Richard had been in ROTC and after graduating was a Lieutenant in the Air Force. We got married in 1969. They transferred him to Beale Air Force base in Cal., where he was stationed for 4 years with the rank of Captain. We lived in Yuba City and raised two sons, Ryan, 39 and Mark, 36. We have two grandsons, Zachary, and Tyler."

"My dad got a job at a titanium plant in Toronto," says Candy, "so we moved there in 1962, my sophomore year. I got to know Bob in Mr. Wilson's history class my junior year. I don't know about being his [Bob's] first girlfriend," she laughs, "but we did date our junior and senior years. Our first official date was a movie in Steubenville, the town next to Toronto. After, the movie, we went to an Italian restaurant for spaghetti and if my memory serves me correctly, probably a meatball sandwich. As far as our dating, Bob and I would go to a movie from time to time at the Manos theater in town, or bowling at Toronto Lanes. Sometimes, just like on our first official date, we'd go to nearby Steubenville to catch a movie. Bob was a shopper. He loved to shop, so we'd also go shopping in Pittsburgh [45 minute drive East] and come home. It wasn't anything real exciting," she says, "but we had fun."

"We did go to Pittsburgh to see the Rolling Stones and that was exciting! I have no idea the cost of our tickets but I bet they were cheap compared with today's prices! Nobody had their own car back then and Bob took his dad's. It was a Ford something or other, but I can't recall the model," says Candy. "Bob and I were life-guards at the town pool, which was easy for us, since we both loved being in the water. I remember Bob was always singing. We enjoyed music and liked listening to Barbra Streisand and Johnny Mathis, two of our favorites. Bob and I had a lot in common. We even laughed at the same things," and adds with a smile in her voice, "Every now and then, we'd have a great laugh over some silly little thing. He had Czechoslovakian heritage like me, and we called our grandmothers Baba. His mother [Cecelia] was wonderful. I loved her. Years after Bob and I had gone our separate ways, I still visited Cecelia whenever I went back to Toronto see my parents, who are both now deceased."

Candy Patrick Mindigo is reflecting on her high school boyfriend, Bob Urich. Her thoughts drifting back over fifty years. "Bob was one of the finest people I knew. He was a true gentleman, kind, thoughtful, and very positive. Back then, I was Catholic.[1] We both had a strong faith and went to church together a lot. One thing people may be somewhat surprised to learn about Bob. He was very spiritual and a devout Catholic.[2] Spiritual in the sense," she explains, "that Bob was older than the rest of us [not in age, but his thinking]. He was an old soul. He thought very deeply about life and things. He was a much more 'spiritual' being than others may have thought."

"Bob was very outgoing," she says. "He could walk into a room, and not knowing who he was or what he did or anything, and he could instantly connect with people."

Looking back at her high school dating years with Bob Urich, Candy Patrick recalls something Bob said to her. "'You make me appreciate the little things in life.' At first, I thought it didn't mean much, but as I pondered it," she says, "it meant a lot to me, because we both loved the small things in life; nature, music, good Czech food…the sweetness of life and

---

1 Today Candy is of the Presbyterian faith and is extremely active in her church. June 3, 2016, in celebration of her 70th birthday, Candy officially retired after 48 years in the nursing profession with Stanford Hospital [today Stanford Healthcare].

2 In his youth, Robert Urich gave serious thought about attending the seminary and becoming a priest.

slices of grace in our lives. Something else I really liked about Bob, he was soft-spoken but also had a great sense of humor. I liked that," says Candy. "When I had a tendency to get a little too serious, Bob always had a way of looking at it in a more positive way. He could lighten the moment, so you'd feel comfortable with him. After a football or basketball game, win or lose, I remember Bob being more even-keeled. Not too down, or too up. More like, we'll get 'em next time. He was like that about life and other things, too.

"Bob was definitely a romantic, very thoughtful," Candy says smiling at the thought. "I love plums and once he brought me one with a bow around it. I thought that was so sweet. He was very sentimental and could shed a tear if he was touched by something. Bob and I memorized the following poem which had an anonymous author. I still remember it, even after all these years. It was a poem we both liked, so here goes."

"Oh the comfort, the inexpressible comfort of feeling safe with a person. Neither having to weigh thoughts nor measure words, but pouring them all out, the chaff and the grain together, keeping what is worth keeping and with a breath of kindness, blow the rest away."

"At Christmas, we exchanged gifts. One time, Bob gave me a small painting, an oil on canvas that I loved. Not sure what happened to it. Over the years it got lost in the shuffle.

"I remember once taking Bob to meet my grandparents in Pennsylvania. They were Czech and enjoyed meeting him and he enjoyed them very much. He was very respectful of family. There were many times we had dinner at his home. His mother 'Baba' was a good cook, especially when it came to homemade chicken soup, my fave," Candy smiles, thinking about the tantalizing tasty memory of his mom's cooking.

At Toronto High, Candy and Bob had some fun times together. "We were in a school play together. It was called *Don't Take My Penny.* The premise, "I wanted to be an actress, and I was going out to Hollywood and he [Bob's role] didn't want me to do that. It's funny because he's the one who ended up being an actor, and I became a nurse."

Bob and Candy's high school relationship was more than puppy love. There was even talk of marriage one day.

"After High school, Bob and I dated for a couple of years. He was at Florida State on a football scholarship. I went to Kent State for a year and then to nursing school [Ohio Valley School of Nursing] at a hospital in

Steubenville. When I went away to Kent State we were still dating at the time and sending letters back and forth. Bob would also send me poetry. I kept the letters for years, but can't find them. I think my mom may have done some major house-cleaning. I remember having an 8x10 picture of Bob in a frame that I took with me. One of the gals walked in my room where I had the picture. Now, make no mistake, Bob was a strikingly good-looking guy. She looked at the photo, took it and placed it out in the hall with a note that read, 'Man of the year!' Bob's photo remained on display in the hallway for about a month," she says, smiling. "I made a trip to visit him at F.S.U.. There were lots of pretty girls there."

Sometimes, distance has a way of breaking even the strongest bonds. "Long-distance relationships are hard, so I think ours ended after a few years," she says. "I'm not sure who broke up with whom. It just went away."

One thing that never went away was Bob and Candy's enduring friendship. "We had gone our separate ways and somehow, after we both were married, we connected on several occasions in California. The first time was when Bob and first wife, Barbara, lived in Marina Del Rey. My husband and I visited and had dinner with them. She had a beautiful smile and was gorgeous. I remember thinking, Bob married a woman who looked like that! I figured they were happy. I was moving forward with my life with my husband and two wonderful sons and living a good life in Los Altos [CA]." Later, the two couples went skiing at Squaw Valley.

Candy recalls another time they got together after Bob became a huge celebrity. "My husband Richard thought very highly of Bob. We were driving an RV down to Southern Cal. for a football game. Ohio State was playing. It may have been the Rose Bowl. I called Bob and said, 'how 'bout if we stop by to say hello?' 'Sure,' he said. He was married to Heather and we had a really nice visit. I liked her from the get go. She has a wonderful personality. Talk about a genuinely nice person. She and Bob also visited us in our tiny condo in Sunnyvale [CA]. We went out to the pool area to chat. You could see how much they were in love. I remember thinking, 'Bob has the right person.' I was so happy for them. I'd love to tell Heather how many times I've seen *Sound of Music,* how we loved it, and how I sing *Do-Re-Mi* to my grandsons." Not to worry, Candy, somehow, I feel Heather will get your message.

Heather Menzies & *The Sound of Music*

Bob Urich's devoted wife, actress Heather Menzies Urich played the oldest daughter Louisa in the 1965 screen version of *The Sound of Music.* She was 15 at the time. It's a musical from the book by Howard Lindsay and Russel Crouse and based on the real-life story of the von Trapp family, one of the world's best-known concert groups during the period immediately preceding WWII. Music is by Richard Rodgers with lyrics by Oscar Hammerstein II. It opened on Broadway in 1959, starring Mary Martin and Theodore Bikel. It won five Tony Awards. The songs have become standards, including *My Favorite Things, Edelweiss, Climb Every Mountain, Do-Re-Mi* and the title song, *The Sound of Music.* It was the final musical written by Rodgers & Hammerstein. Oscar died of stomach cancer nine months after the play opened. The film version, starring JulieAndrews as Maria, and Christopher Plummer as Capt. Von Trapp, was released on April 1, 1965 by 20th Century Fox. Heather says, "no one ever expected the film to become a classic."

Candy Mindigo remembers another time they visited Bob and was so surprised to learn something about him that she thought was so unusual. "He had a friend with him from Tennessee[1] or some place, who kept talking about them shooting quail. Bob looked at me, and I looked back, shaking my head in a disbelieving way. 'I know, I know! You never thought I could shoot anything,'[2] he said. 'You're absolutely right,' I replied.

"The last time I saw Bob [before his passing]," remembers Candy, was when he came to San Jose [CA] as the spokesman for the American Cancer Society.

Youth Harbor

The Toronto High commemorative booklet, *100 Years of Excellence,* published in 1989 thanks to the generous donation of Larry W. Anderson, Class of 1960, describes Youth Harbor as a converted bank building [Union Bank] at the north west corner of Clarke and Fourth Streets in Toronto. Youth Harbor first opened to the youth of the city in 1943.

---

1 Visiting Bob at the time was his fishing and hunting companion, Dr. Dyrk Halstead, a Nashville [TN] operating room physician, who comments on Bob and his friendship in Ch. 30.

2 Heather says, later in life, Bob gave up shooting any type of game. "He really preferred fishing, particularly fly-fishing, and she proudly boasts, "he ate everything he caught."

"When I was in high school, in the early '50s," says Bob Urich's older brother, Tom, "It was a safe place to go and hang out, especially on Friday nights after the football games." Toronto native and Bob's classmate, Gregg McKelvey agrees. "That was the place in town. If it wasn't for Youth Harbor, it would have been bad."

When the 1960's happened, Youth Harbor was still *the place* to hang out in a safe environment. Bob Urich and his high school steady, Candy Patrick, along with other teens, gathered there to shoot the breeze, play ping pong, dance and have fun.

The basement at Youth Harbor had ping-pong and pool tables. The ground floor had a dance floor and meeting place. There were no tables and chairs. Instead, benches were placed along the walls. Gregg McKelvey recalls, "the boys and girls had to dress appropriately. I don't think shorts were allowed. It was dress pants for the guys. Saturday was dress-up night. Everyone looked much nicer than most of the kids do today."

The person in charge, who for many years served as chaperone, was a diminutive lady named S. A. Grill. "Everyone loved Mrs. Grill," says Bob Urich's grade school girlfriend Teri Volsky. Over the years, it has been a mystery of sorts as to what her initials S. A. stood for. Thanks to the detective work of 'Sherlock' Walker, better known as Carolyn, we can now reveal some important background info about Mrs. Grill. With a little help from the 1940 census, Carolyn believes her real name was Mary Bella.

Youth Harbor

As far as the mystery surrounding her initials S.A.: they are her husband's. He was a teacher and administrator in Toronto. An article in the *Toronto* [OH] *Tribune,* dated Thursday, May 24, 1962, reads, "Mrs. Grill was honored by the Toronto Civic Club." The article also states *that she has been in charge of Youth Harbor since May 8, 1944 and through the years has contributed her time, energy, understanding and love to the youth of the community.* Many Toronto High alumni completely agree, and proudly state, "Mrs. Grill was not only our advisor but a friend who took an interest in each and every one of us." One thing for sure, Mrs. Grill certainly had part in starting many lasting romances by climbing up on the juke box enclosure and turning on the bright light signaling a 'girl's choice,' or "o.k, this is a guy's choice." She also made sure no one got rowdy or was drinking. If so, you were promptly and politely asked to leave.

A slow song by Johnny Mathis, crooning *Chances Are,*[1] signaled 'snuggle-up' time, while a fast song by the Beatles made the old bank walls reverberate from the heavy rock n' roll beat! "I definitely attended the dances at Youth Harbor," says Tim Seese. "I became seriously interested in the opposite sex starting in the seventh grade. I believe we were allocated a certain time slot at Y.H. for 7th and 8th grade separate from high school participants." However, Tim stayed away from Youth Harbor his freshman year. "There was a custom of 'de-pantsing freshmen. It was just like it sounds. Upper classmen would take the pants off freshman boys going to or mostly after leaving the dance, put the pants on a nearby front porch and then the 'victim' had to recover them. This was all the more embarrassing," he says, "If you were walking a girl home."

"During our sophomore year after the coast was clear," continues a smiling Tim Seese. "Most of us, including Bob and I, returned to Youth Harbor." We were now preying on the first year girls as the new class of freshman boys cowered away."

Candy Patrick, Bob Urich's girlfriend in high school has fond memories of Youth Harbor. "I loved dancing at the place [Y.H.]. It was a safe place to gather. I would never miss a chance to go dancing. Usually, Friday or Saturday night, all of us headed for the place. Folks just showed up, and dancing and chatting took off from there." When asked whether Bob [Urich]was a good dancer, she replies, "I don't remember, but he was good at everything, so I am sure he was a good dancer!" Candy likes fast dancing. "I love the Supremes, Beatles and Beach Boys. At Youth Harbor, we'd dance and then go out for pizza. I still love to dance," she says, "I love going to weddings so I can dance," she says laughing.

Attending a dance at Youth Harbor turned out to be a lucky night for Bob and Tim's friend and classmate, Gregg McKelvey. "I met Chris, my future wife,' there, I was a sophomore and she was a freshman. We actually had met several weeks before for about 5 minutes, but I saw her at Youth Harbor one night in September 1962. She had on a skirt and blouse and looked really nice. I finally got the nerve to ask her to dance.

---

1 *Chances Are* with music by Robert Allen with lyrics by Al Stillman was huge hit for pop singer Johnny Mathis, reaching #1 on the Billboard pop music charts September16, 1957, and #1 on Cash Box, October 12, 1957.

"I believe the first song we danced to was *Stranger on the Shore*[1] by Acker Bilk. I wouldn't call it 'our' song," he says with a grin, "but we both love that song." After a couple of dances, Gregg asked Chris if he could walk her home. She said, yes and 48 years later, they are still together and still dancing.'[2]

Youth Harbor was open, Thursday, Friday and Saturday nights. According to Bob's classmate, Jimmy Ray, 'I don't believe there was an admission charge, but you needed a pass to get in.' Junior high kids were there from 7-9 and high school students, 9 to 11.' "It's all gone now. Just an empty parking lot," says Bob's classmate, Chip Coulter. "It was pretty nice." 'I think more people were upset to see Youth Harbor torn down than the high school," adds Gregg McElvey. "It was torn down within the last few years," says Ray. "When we were kids growing up, there were no empty lots in Toronto. Now, there are corner lots everywhere where they've torn buildings down. I'm afraid, our ole home-town doesn't look the way it did back in the 1950's and 60's." "It's so sad to see so many places you loved, all gone," says McKelvey.

***

You could say Bob Urich was one heck of an active student-athlete at Toronto High. During his four years, he played basketball, football and ran track. He also did quite a few school plays and participated in the school talent shows. With his great baritone singing voice, Bob was the student choir master of an eighty-voice student choir, a member of the SPBSQSA[3] and also sang with a doo-wop group.

George Melhorn, another of Bob Urich's high school classmates, says, "Bob's acting skills and athletic endeavors are well-known," but doubts his music talents are. "Bob had an excellent baritone voice. In Ohio, we have solo/ensemble contests. He sang and I accompanied him on the

---

1 *Stranger on the Shore* is an instrumental piece for clarinet written by Acker Bilk, born Bernard Stanley Bilk [1-28-29] in Pentsford Somerset England. Acker Bilk wrote the song for his young daughter, 'Jenny' and originally named it after her. Used as the theme for a BBC serial *Stranger on the Shore*, thereafter it became the title. First released in the UK; later in the U.S. It became a #1 hit on Billboard, March 7, 1962.

2 Gregg and Chris McKelvey have been married for 48 years and have two boys, Keith & Eric. He worked as a claims Rep & Ops Analyst for 32 years for the Social Security Admin. in Steubenville [OH]. He retired in September 2001and they are both enjoying life in Mesquite, Nevada – but maybe not the triple-digit summer temps.

3 Society for the Preservation of Barber Shop Quartet Singing in America.

piano. One song he sang was a hit back in the 60's for Andy Williams, *Can't Get Used to Losing You.*[1] Bob sang it beautifully as I played the piano."

Bob's Singing Voice & Doo Wop

Melhorn adds, "If my memory serves me correctly, Bob earned a superior rating each year. He and I also sang together in a men's ensemble. D.W. 'Don' Hoover was our music instructor."

Dave Harvilak was also Bob's classmate. They also sang together in high school in the double quartet group. "We went to Canton Central Catholic for the regional competition in the double quartet category. We received a '1,' which earned us a trip, about 5 weeks later, to the state finals at Kent State University. We only received a '2' at states but enjoyed the experience. I remember, while waiting for our score about five of us were sitting in the stands in the KSU gym and getting restless. All of a sudden," Harvilak says, "someone began snapping their fingers in rhythm [it may have been Bob] and we began singing Dion's *A Teenager in Love*[2]with Dave Ralston singing lead. Ralston was always razzed by the girls about looking like Rick Nelson. He even had Ricky's eyes and eyebrows some details, huh," Harvilak says, laughing. Ego aside for the moment, Harvilak proudly boasts, "We had great harmony with no accompaniment. We decided right then and there to form a doo-wop group.

Doo Wop is a genre of music which achieved mainstream popularity in the 50's and and early 60s, an era when Bob Urich and his classmates were growing up. Built upon 4-part harmony with falsetto leads, baritone and bass singers, doo-wop was one of the most popular music styles of the time and was instrumental in launching the Rock n' Roll period in American pop music.

Doo Wop Time

Doo Wop featured both fast and slow beats, as exhibited in many hit songs of the day, from Dion and the Belmonts finger-poppin, *I Wonder*

---

1 *Can't Get Used to Losing You* written by Jerome 'Doc' Pomus and Mort Shuman was recorded by Andy Williams in December 1962 and spent 4 weeks on Billboard hitting #2 in March 1963. Cashbox ranked it #1.

2 *A Teenager in Love* was a hit by Dion [DiMucci] and the Belmonts. Written by Jerome 'Doc' Pomus & Mort Shuman. It got as high as #5 on Billboard, April 27, 1959.

Why[1] to the 5 Satins' smooth melodic ballad, *In the Still of the Night,*[2] perfect for couples to cuddle-up to while slow dancing. Some other examples of great doo-wop music from the early fifties include *Gee,*[3] a 1953 summer-time hit for the Crows and *Sh-boom* by the Chords in 1954. The group the Moonglows displayed beautiful harmony with their soft n' easy hit *Sincerely*, released in 1955. The Del-Vikings, *Come Go With Me* and *Lil' Darlin'* by the Diamonds, both released in 1957, and *Get A Job* by the Silhouettes[4] in 1958 are further examples of great doo-wop harmony. These are only a few examples of the thousands of doo wop hits. A complete listing would take volumes to fill.

Bob and the other members of their newly formed doo wop group got together a few nights a week to practice at Ricky's home, oops, that's Dave Ralston's house. "Other members in our group were Brent Wilson, who also played the bongos, Bob and me," says Harvilak, who sang bass on all their songs. "Bob sang Richie Valens hit *Donna,*[5] and *Can't Get Used to Losing You.* Thinking back to those fun days, he says, "I can still see Bob sitting on a stool, while we stood beside him, and George [Melhorn] played piano."

The 'nameless' Doo Wop Group

"You know, funny thing," Dave recalls, "No one seems to remember the name of our group. Sorry about not remembering it, but I do know at the

1 *I Wonder Why* was the lst hit for Dion & the Belmonts, in May 1958. It reached #22 on Billboard.

2 *In the Still of the Night* was a hit in September 1956 for the 5 Satins, and reached #6 on Billboard's pop chart.

3 *Gee* by the Crows was released in June 1953. It was #2 on the R&B charts and #14 on pop charts. It was the groups' only hit song but is credited as being one of the first cross-over hits of the rock n' roll era, going from R&B to Pop music charts. Thereby coining the phrase, 'a crossover hit.' *Sh-boom* peaked at #2 on the R& B charts and # 9 on Billboards pop chart. It was their only hit song.

4 *Come Go With Me* by the Dell-Vikings got as high as the #4 spot on Billboard in March 1957. *Lil Darlin'* by the Diamonds almost made it to #1 on Billboard, but settled in at #2 in September of 1956. *Get A job* was #1 in January 1958 for the Philadelphia group, the Silhouettes. Sadly, it was their only hit.

5 *Donna* was written & sung by Ritchie Valens. The song scored as high as #2 on Billboard, December 1958. Valens was tragically killed in a plane crash 2 months following the release of the song on February 3, 1959, The crash also took the lives of Rock stars, Buddy Holly and J.P. Richardson (the Big Bopper). Buddy Holly served as the inspiration for Don McLean's hit song, *Bye-Bye Miss American Pie,* released in December 1971, it was #1 on Billboard for four consecutive weeks.

time," he insists, "it was a good one, but it is lost in my memory bank over the past 53 years. I even asked Dave Ralston, but he couldn't remember the name either."

The nameless doo-wop group which included Bob Urich never made the 'big time,' but the boys had fun performing locally at their Senior Day talent show, and at a few other venues in and around their hometown of Toronto.

"Summer came," Dave Harvilak[1] says, "and we were all busy with part-time jobs and some of the guys were on their way to college, so our singing doo-wop group was about a 4-month short-lived stint. We sure had fun doing that, though," says a smiling Mister Bass Man.

Oh, one other note, before we close the musical chapter on the story of Toronto High's *nameless* doo-wop group featuring Bob Urich. We can't have them go nameless, so what'd ya say, we give them one. Let's see...

Well, since Toronto High is the home of the Red Knights, and Bob and the rest of the doo-wop group sang what today are known as 'classic hits,' what do you say we call the group the *Classic Knights.* Let the author know if you think it's a hit or a miss.[2]

---

1 After high school, Dave Harvilak joined the FBI in a clerical position before being drafted. He spent 2 years in the US Army, with a year in Viet Nam [October1966-October 67] and says, "I was proud to have served." After service, he rejoined the FBI using his G.I. bill to earn a college degree, while working full-time with the bureau. Dave retired as an agent in July '04. He and his wife, Aly have lived in Mesquite, NV since 2008. Like Bob Urich and the rest of their classmates and doo wop members, Dave remains ever loyal to his Ohio roots. So much so, that he started an Ohio State Buckeyes Club. He and about 20 others in their Sun City community, including his long-time friend and Toronto high classmate, Gregg McKelvey, get together at various sport pubs to watch every Ohio State football game and root for their Bucks.

2 You can contact the author [Joe Martelle] at his publisher's website at www.bearmanormedia.com.

Bob (on right) and his hi-school steady Candy Patrick visit his older brother Tom, on left in NYC. Tom also an actor was appearing on Broadway.

Youth Harbor, where Toronto Ohio teens gathered to dance & socialize

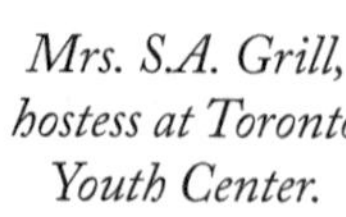

Mrs. S.A. Grill, hostess at Toronto Youth Center.

Honored By Civic Club

MEMORIES - Mrs. S. A. Grill, center, is shown being presented a bouquet of roses by Mrs. Paul Jones, president of the Toronto Civic Club. Seated on the right is Bertha Jacobs, Wellsburg, close friend of Mrs. Grill. Photo by Holtzmann.

Bob & gang as freshmen[1961] in Gregg McKelvey's basement, L-R, standing, William Roy Glass, Bob U., Gregg McKelvey & Don Lucas, sitting, Terry Hunter. Photo courtesy Gregg McKelvey.

Music Contest State Winners

Top, *Left to Right:* Dan Smith, Tom Campbell, Barry Stewart, Bob Urich, Lee Graubner, Pat Lloyd. ***Bottom, Left to Right:*** Jim Rey, Christine Cattrell, George Melhorn, Bryant Evans.

Music Contest State winners, Bob standing in back row, 3rd from right. Photo courtesy Toronto Ohio Yearbook.

Bob & classmates at their T.H.S. class reunion in July 1990, L-R, Dave Harvilak, Heather & Bob, Chris & Gregg McKelvey. Photo courtesy Gregg McKelvey

Chapter 9

Friday Night Lights in Toronto

In the Ohio Valley, High School Football is like a religion

Friday Night Lights in Toronto

[**Bold type** indicates words and sentences written by Bob Urich and taken directly from his journal.]

A full moon rises over the Allegheny Mountains and the Ohio River. A dozen barges at a time filled with ore and coal flashing their spot-lights along the bank to navigate this turn in the river, sounding their horns… a long low blast that echoes up and down the valley [Ohio] floor. **"On a half-mile plateau above it lies our high school stadium, a Roosevelt WPA[1] project.** The stadium known as Hinkle Field is named after 1927 Toronto High grad Clarke Hinkle, who went on to play football at Bucknell and in the NFL for Green Bay. **"On one side a large concrete set of bleachers, with turret-like structures on either end that house the home and visitors' locker rooms. A half-dozen arched openings with barred gates gives it the look of a mini Ohio State University stadium in Columbus. This is where the home crowd sits, the visitors relegated to what appears to be temporary bleachers on the riverside of the field."**

The TV series, *Friday Night Lights*[2] had to be based on football night in Toronto Ohio! Friday night football in the Ohio Valley is more than just another sporting event. **"It is a tradition that in it's fervor defies any rational explanation. The freshly caulked field with the yard markers lined-out on the field itself, yards of red and white crepe paper flying in the breeze from the goal posts, and from the large double gate at the south end of the field enters the hundred and ten strong Toronto**

1 WPA -(Works Project Admin.) part of Pres. F.D.R's New Deal plan in 1936 which employed millions of unemployed workers in various programs; new roads, bridges, building America's infra-structure.

2 *Friday night Lights* a TV series about a high school football team in the fictional town of Dillon, Texas, based on the book by Buzz Bissinger and the 2004 movie of the same name. It aired on NBC-TV, 10-3-06, until its final episode, February 9, 2011.

Red Knight marching band." It seems half the town is in attendance and some Friday nights 3,000 fans are on their feet as the football team comes charging onto the field bursting through the paper banner held by the cheerleaders.

"I am one of the tri-captains, my senior year, and lead the way. Forget about the Oscars and the Emmys. This is bigger. It's football night in Toronto, Ohio!!"

***

In a 1990 interview with the *Steubenville Herald*, Bob Urich talks about his ability as a kicker while playing football at Toronto High. "I was very active in sports," and he says with obvious disappointment, while shaking his head, "I still can't believe we lost to Winterville in '63 on the last play of the game." The game Bob is referring to was against Toronto's arch rival, Wintersville High, Friday night October 12, 1963 at Toronto High Stadium. Bob was a junior and played tackle, but was known for his punting prowess. Bob's teammate, Jim Lowery, played safety and returned punts and kickoffs. He vividly remembers Urich's kicking ability. "Bob could punt a football about as high and far as anyone I have ever seen in high school. He was great at kickoffs too." It was Bob's strong kicking leg that landed him a full football scholarship to Florida State University.

The *Steubenville Herald*, a newspaper based in the neighboring town to Toronto, tells the story:

It was a battle of sturdy defenses. Both Wintersville Warriors and the Toronto Red Knights were fired-up for the big battle of rivals and several goal lines stands punctuated the action! Toronto's coach Bob Khoenle's Red Knights took the early lead on the first play of the game when junior Bob Urich, Toronto's kicking ace, kicked to the Wintersville goal line. Tyrone Harris, a 175 pound halfback retrieved the punt but was trapped in his own end zone for a safety. Late in the 3rd quarter, Harris would more than make up for his error. It was rock em, sock em time and a battle of both defenses through the remainder of the first half. Toronto led Wintersville by a slim two point lead, 2 to 0 at the half.

In the 3rd quarter, Tyrone Harris, the same running back who got trapped in his own end zone on the very first play of the game to give Toronto a 2 point lead, carried the ball on 14 of 16 plays, finally diving in from the 1 yard line to make the final score, *WintersvilleWarriors* 6, *Toronto Red Knights* 2.

The *Steubenville Herald* reported that the spectacular punting of Bob Urich and the terrific defensive play of both teams were highlights of the closely fought game. The accolades tossed Bob Urich's way apparently did not make up for the sting of the loss, which he still felt some 25 years later! Bob Urich was a tough competitor who in every way was a winner, and who didn't like to lose.

Bob's teammate, Jim Lowery says, "Bob was an outstanding athlete, tough and strong, and quite the competitor. During the summer before our senior year, a bunch of us got together and worked out to get in shape for the football season. We decided to do a 'pick-up' game of touch. On one play, Bob rushed a punt and was accidentally kicked in his lower groin area.[1] It caused him severe pain and he could hardly walk. We all felt bad, and the next day a few of us went over to see him. He was still in pain but in good spirits and as usual, he found humor in it. It took Bob quite awhile to recover and in condition to play, but he did come back. I can't remember how long he was out. At least a couple of weeks. We were worried that he wouldn't be ready for two-a-day practices in mid-August, but Bob made it. He was a fighter in every way. "Bob had a great senior year as our left tackle and punter," says Lowery, "along with being one of our three football captains."

Bob, A Natural Born Leader

"Bob and I became teammates and good friends in high school," says Tim Seese. "He played right tackle and I played right end, lining up next to him on the football team. Back in those days [50s & 60s] it was common to play both offense and defense and we did that for the most part. Our senior year, Bob, Bill Hutchison and I were named Tri-Captains. It was quite an honor and put pressure on us to play our best and provide leadership to the team. Bob was a standout player and clearly a leader. As I remember, hehad a very strong work ethic.[2] He worked hard at sports,

1 As a youngster, with his body developing, Bob received numerous injuries to that particular part of his body. It makes one wonder, as an adult, how much of a factor his childhood injuries played in his contracting his rare cancer, synovial-cell sarcoma which attacked the soft tissue in his groin area.

2 Bob's strong work ethics carried over to his acting career, as pointed out by producer Duke Vincent in the Vega$ chapter 17.

music, extracurricular activities, and his summer jobs. Bob set a very good example to follow, as he led by example. He was persistent in developing himself in many areas. He also had a very good personality and was always pleasant to be around. Bob displayed a broad range of interests and was friendly with a wide-group of people, but most importantly," Tim says, "Bob had a good moral compass and set a great example in that area for us to follow."

Toronto High's third football tri-captain, Bill Hutchison, agrees with Tim on Bob's leadership ability. "Bob Urich was a natural born leader. He respected others, was a hardworker and was fun to be around. He had that magnetic personality a leader needs. I also remember he was a good player. Ohio Valley football was aggressive and Bob was reasonably aggressive. He was a little bit taller than the rest of us and ended up playing on the line, but Bob could have played any position. He was that good," says Hutchison.

***

"I especially remember one night game," says Tim Seese, "when I received the hardest hit of my high school career by none other than Bob Urich!"

The Hardest Hit

Bob's high school football teammate, Tim Seese recalls the hardest hit he ever received. "We were playing defense and on one play I had stopped the ball carrier. He was still standing [the player] but making no further progress. Out of the corner of my eye, I saw Bob running across the field at full speed preparing to finish off the runner. The opposing player also saw Bob racing at him. At the last minute, he turned away and as I held on, he positioned me just in front of Bob. I absorbed the full impact some place in my back as all three of us hit the ground! As I slowly got up, I facetiously said to Bob, "nice tackle." He grinned and jokingly replied, "next time, get out of the way."

In an interview with his home-town newspaper, *The Toronto Tribune,*[1] Bob Urich describes himself as being a 'fairly decent athlete.' "I always loved playing sports. There were vacant lots across where I lived and we played football for hours on end all day Saturday. My favorite team, like

---

1 *The Toronto* [OH] *Tribune* was a newspaper published from 1879 until 1990

most of the other kids in my neighborhood were the Steelers." Later, during his successful career as an actor, one can only imagine the elation Bob felt when cast to play Pittsburgh Steeler great Rocky Bleier in the story of his life. Rocky was one of the most popular Steeler players ever to don their uniform.

Rocky Bleier

Rocky Bleier was born and raised in Appleton, Wisconsin. He picked up his nickname as a baby. "As first born of the family, my dad was proud, as all parents are," Bleier says. "Guys would ask my dad, 'how's that new kid of yours?' And he would say, 'Aw, you should see him. He looks like a little rock sitting in that crib. He's all muscles.' So, from then on, they'd say, "Hey Bob, 'how's that little rock of yours?' The name stuck and that's how I got it," says Robert 'Rocky' Bleier.

Rocky graduated from Xavier High School in 1964, where he was team captain in both football and basketball. In football, he was a three-time all-state selection at running back and won all-conference honors at both linebacker and defensive back. Bleier played college football at the University of Notre Dame. In 1966, his junior year the 'fighting Irish' won the national championship. He was team captain his senior year. In 1968, Rockywas selected in the 16th round of the NFL/AFL draft by the Pittsburgh Steelers. In December of that year [1968], after his rookie season, he was drafted again, this time by Uncle Sam's Army. Rocky volunteered for duty in Viet Nam.

As a Specialist 4th class, he was shipped out in May 1969 assigned to Company C, 4th Battalion, 31st Infantry 196th Light Infantry Brigade as a squad grenadier, operating a grenade launcher.

On August 20, 1969, while on patrol in Hiep Duc, Rocky Bleier's platoon was ambushed in a rice paddy. He was shot and wounded in the left thigh. While he was down, an enemy grenade landed nearby, bounced off a member of his platoon, sending shrapnel into Rockys' lower right leg. As a result of the blast, he lost part of his right foot. Later, he was awarded the Bronze Star and Purple Heart. While recovering in a hospital in Tokyo, doctors told Bleier he would never play football again. Around the same time, Rocky received a post card from Steelers owner, Art Rooney which read, 'Rock, the team's not doing well. We need you. Art Rooney.' It was just the motivation Rocky needed. Later, he said, "when you have somebody take the time and interest to send you a postcard, something they didn't have to do, you have a special place for those kind of people.'

After several surgeries, Rocky Bleier was discharged from the military in 1970 and began his informal workouts with his Steeler teammates. He couldn't walk without pain, let alone run with the ball, but he kept at it. Because of his lengthy hospitalization, his playing weight of 212 pounds dropped to 180. Rocky was placed on injured reserve for the season, but returned in 1971 playing on special teams. He spent two additional seasons working hard to get his leg and body back in condition to get increased playing time. He was waived by the team on two occasions, but he never quit. Bleier said, he worked hard so that some time in the future, he didn't have to ask himself, 'what if?'

In 1974, his 'never quit' attitude paid off. Rocky earned a spot in the Steelers starting line-up. In addition to being a great lead blocker, Rocky was the second of the Steelers' rushing weapons directly behind their primary running back, Franco Harris. In 1976, he and teammate Harris rushed for over 1,000 yards. Bleier played in the first four Steeler Super Bowl victories and caught the touchdown pass from quarterback Terry Bradshaw that gave Pittsburgh a lead the team would never surrender in Super Bowl XIII.

Rocky Bleier* retired after the 1980 season as the Steelers' fourth all-time leading rusher. *Fighting Back: The Rocky Bleier Story* is a gritty story of positive determination. It is one of the most inspiring in the history of sports and Bob Urich gave his all to the role. Richard Herd played Steelers coach, Chuck Noll and Bonnie Bedelia played Rocky's girlfriend.

In a phone interview [July 15, 2016] with the author, Rocky Bleier reminisced about the good times he had 'hangin' out' with Bob Urich. "I flew to Vegas on a Monday to meet with Bob. I had to be back in Pittsburgh for practice on Tuesday."

"We stayed at the Desert Inn [the location site for Urich's TV series, *Vega$*]. Bob and I had never met before. Into the casino, bigger than life, walks Bob Urich, complete with that mischievous grin. There was no question that he was Dan Tanna," says Rocky with a smile. As he strolled past the roulette wheel, Bob threw down some money. Maybe twenty bucks. I can't remember the exact amount. It could have been a hundred. He wins! Nonchalantly picks up his winnings and continues to walk out without missing a beat. He was calm, cool and collected," recalls Bleier. "I knew I had met the real Dan Tanna."

"Later," the Rock says, "Bob and Heather flew into Pittsburgh and stayed with us for a few days. It was sort of a get to know each other time. That's when Bob and I realized we had so much in common. Catholic upbringing, we both played football and in our careers, we both had our own struggles."

"On the set, Bob was playing a scene with actress, Bonnie Bedelia. She played my girlfriend and later my wife in the film," says Bleier. "I didn't think Bob was playing me very well, so I walked over and in a low voice, I told him so. I said, I would never say that or act that way. Bob grinned and softly said, 'OK Rock.' He was being nice to me and under his breath I'm sure he was thinking, f_ _k him. Who does he think he is. I'll play it my way, which of course, he did," says Rocky, laughing.

"My one regret is that I didn't cultivate the friendship," says Bleier. "It was my own insecurity. I didn't feel that I was in the same league as Bob. I assumed he hung out with producers and other celebrities. I felt, he traveled in a different circle than me, and I didn't fit in. Today, I realize that wasn't true and wish I had stayed in touch. How sad to think that way. People are people, regardless of their position in life," Rocky admits. "Thinking back, I'm sure Bob dealt with his own insecurities only on a different level."

The circle of life often brings people together in ways we can never imagine. One can't help but wonder if Rocky Bleier's[1] never-quit attitude somehow served as an inspiration later in Bob's life during his own hard-fought battle against cancer.

***

For the longest time, whenever you walked into the Urich home in Andover, MA, and into their library, your eye would immediately catch the Steeler helmet Bob wore while filming Rocky Bleier's story. It was proudly displayed on the corner of his antique desk. A desk which weighed almost as much as a Volkswagen. How he managed to get that big heavy

---

1 Today Rocky Bleier is author of the book *Don't fumble your retirement* and is a speaker on retirement and financial management. He runs Bleier Zagula Financial with his business partner Matt Zagula, 'Rocky' is the father of four children and as of this writing lives with his second wife, Jan Gyurina in Mt. Lebanon, Pennsylvania. Rocky and the author spoke by telephone.

desk all the way from Texas–where they filmed *Lonesome Dove*–to their home in Andover, MA still remains material for an episode of 'Unsolved Mysteries."One day, while visiting the Urich home, he teasingly asked the author to lift one corner of the desk. "Go ahead, try and lift it," he challenged me while proudly stating, "now that's real heavy antique western wood, Joe! I brought it all the way home from Texas!" One thing is true about Bob Urich. He had to have the very best of everything, even sometimes it proved to be the heaviest! I couldn't budge it.

***

Bob had a great sense of humor and loved having a good time. "I remember one especially fun time," recalls Bob's high school football teammate, Jim Lowery.

Cabbage Rolls and the football team

"Bob's mom, Cecelia was a great cook," he says An opinion which seems to be shared by many Toronto Ohio townsfolk even to this day. "One time she made her famous homemade cabbage rolls for all the senior football players. They were so good," as he smacked his lips thinking back to those good ole days.

"During our senior year, Bob's dad had a recreation room built in their basement. My dad and I built it," Lowery says. "I would help him out whenever I had a few hours to spare. As I recall, the walls were dark paneling and one wall was greenish, almost a jade color permastone. On graduation night [1964] my family and others celebrated in the Urich's new rec room! As mentioned, Bob loved having a good time. After we ate," Jim says, "We all went down to the playroom to 'hang out.' That's when Bob brought out a tape recorder. We all sat around, full of gas and he taped us as we flatulated as only virile young men can do. When Bob played the explosive gastric sounds back, we laughed until our sides hurt. We had tears in our eyes from laughing so hard. Teenage boy humor? You bet, but we had great fun and always enjoyed each other's company."

"Years later, my wife and I attended Bob's funeral. After the service I spoke with his mom, Cecelia. She remembered me right off and we talked of things she remembered we did during our high school days. Through misty eyes, she managed a slight smile, as she recalled the night she made the homemade cabbage roll."

Bob's senior year in football, the Toronto Red Knights won 6 and lost 4, but defensively, they shut out 4 teams with an opening season win over Springfield Local 12-0…a 30-0 shut-out of Carrolton…a 26-0 win over Mingo and a lopsided 67-0 win over Jefferson Union! What a powerhouse of a football team!

Bob, the track star

[**Bold typed words are Bob's** and taken directly from his journal.]

In the springtime, Bob Urich ran track, the 120-yard high hurdle. Rehearsals for the school play were happening at the same time, so if he wanted to take part in track, he had to run from where he was rehearsing to the starting line.

"I would be in my sweats, in the school auditorium across the street rehearsing the school play under the direction of longtime English teacher Anthony Carissimi. They'd send a freshman to let me know it was last call for the high hurdles. He would come running down the aisle yelling, 'They're ready. They're ready, you better get going.' I'd jog up and down the auditorium aisles, my way of limberingup–cross the street, down the full length of the stadium to the starting line, peel off my sweats and make it there just as Bob Hughes, our dean of boys and the starter, raised his black pistol for the start of the race. I'd run the race. More times than not, I won. It's kind of embarrassing to say that, but that's the way it was." When Bob crossed the finish line, he'd just keep on going…running right down the line through the big double gates and just keep running, up into the high school and go right back to rehearsal.

"In those heady days, I had no idea what life had in store for me. What kid does?"

Bob and his Toronto High track teammates, Bill Hutchison, Joel Lamantia and Tim Seese still hold a school record for the shuttle hurdle relay event. However, no mention to 'confirm' their accomplishment is available, nor does anyone seem to know exactly what the 'reverse shuttle relay' event is all about. We turned to Tim Stried at the Ohio High School State Athletic Association for help. He had not heard of the event either, and handed us off to his track administrator, Dale Gabor, who cleared things up for us.

Reverse Shuttle Hurdles

"The 'reverse shuttle hurdles," Dale explains, "is a reference to the manner in which they are run. For example, the lead off hurler in lane #1 would run North-to-South, runner 2 would run South-to-North in lane 2. The 3rd runner would run North to South in lane 1, and the number four runner would run South-to-North in lane 2. In this manner," he continues, "the finish line is in the same place as the starting line."

"I feel certain that part of the problem in finding any information is due to the fact that the 'shuttle hurdles' is not sanctioned or recognized event by the NFHS,"[1] says Gabor. "It is certainly allowable, but not recognized. You generally find the shuttle hurdles run at large invitational where you have a lot of athletes, but as you know, some schools can barely find one good hurdler, let alone four! As is often the case, I would surmise the 'stadium record' [at Toronto] is just that, a stadium record only since it is not a recognized event." Dale Gabor, OHSAA, Director of Cross Country and track and field says, "This is a little like events such as the 'shot put relay' or 'discus relay.' In these cases, you have 3 throwers and add the best throws to determine who wins. Is this an allowable event? Yes. Is it approved or sanctioned by the NFHS? No. I think this is exactly what you have with the shuttle hurdles," explains Dale Gabor.

The Toronto High School track record for the reverse shuttle hurdles, which Bob Urich and his three teammates set their senior year [1964] was run in a time of 58.8. Head coach Ralph Anastasia took over the duties from Harry Tarr in 1963. It was during this time until 1984 that Toronto High practically dominated this sport in the upper Ohio Valley.

Bob and his teammates

"It just seemed like one sporting season slipped into the next."

Bob was a tri-captain on the football team his senior year, a starter on the basketball team and also ran track.

"Who had time to get in trouble? The notion of drugs was non-existent as far as I can remember. As a senior, the big temptation was this thing called three-point-two beer. Watered down. Towards the end of your senior year, when you were about to graduate, the big deal was to

---

1 NFHS is the National Federation of High Schools

buy a quart of Pabst-Blue-Ribbon or Mamms beer and go down over the river bank by the little marina."

Bill Hutchison remembers one particular night 'down at the marina' when they were seniors. "Our classmate, Joel Lamantia's cousin, Pat, was a junior at Catholic Central in neighboring Steubenville, he was with us and had a few too many *Iron City* beers. The rest of us were o.k., so we took Pat to Bob's house and threw him in the shower, clothes and all, to sober him up. Bob's mom was there and was very tolerant of what was happening," Hutchison says, laughing. That was about the extent of their rowdiness, if you even want to call it that. It was more like young men out to have a good time.

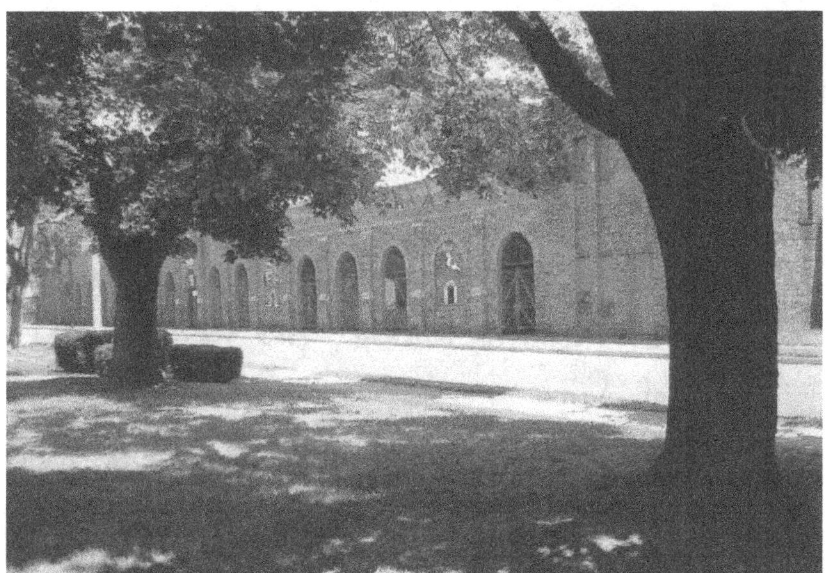

Toronto High School football stadium, Hinkle Field. Photo courtesy Toronto Ohio Alumni Association.

T.H.S. Tri captains in football, Bob's Senior year 1964, L-R, Bob, Bill Hutchison and Tim Seese. Photo courtesy Tim Seese.

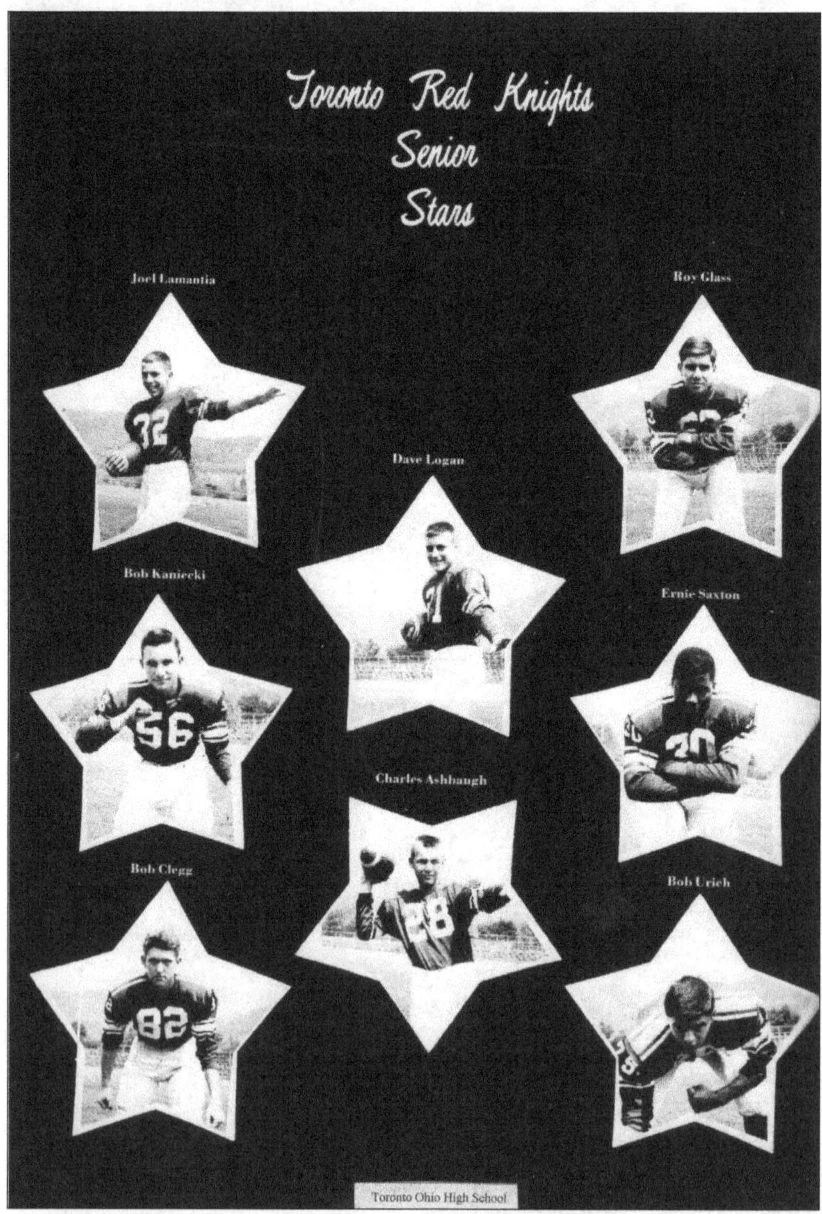

T.H.S. Red Knights Senior Football Stars, Bob lower right.

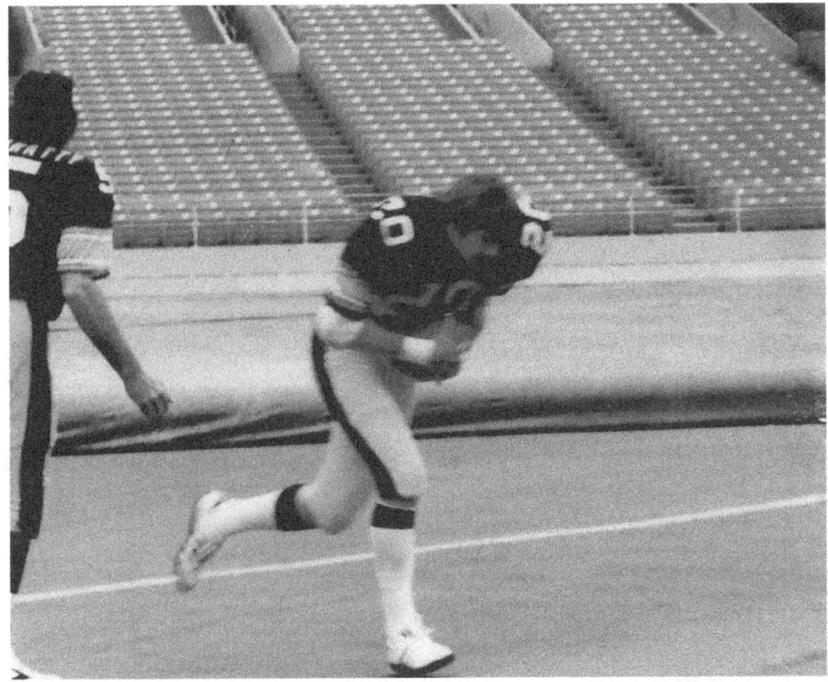

Scene from The Rocky Bleier story "Fighting Back" *starring Bob as Rocky, shown running with the ball.*

Bob in Steeler uniform standing with his mom, Baba.

Bob with arm around Rocky Bleier.

Bob running hurdles in track, Bob is on right.

Bob's T.H.S. graduation photo 1964.

Prom night for Bob & friends, L-R, Tim Seese, Jackie Haynes Taylor, Betty Ansell Bouhan & Bob. Photo courtesy Carolyn 'Motter' Walker.

Carolyn 'Motter' Walker in front of Toronto Main Street Museum.

Chapter 10

Football Scholarship to F.S.U.

Bob's teammates Jack Fenwick and Tom DeLopez & Michigan State

In Bob Urich's high school senior year, the coaches sent films of their student athletes around to different colleges.

Bob's Senior year and Scholarships

[**Bold type** indicates words and sentences written by Bob Urich and taken directly from his journal.]

"I got letters of invitation or scholarship offers inviting me to come and visit every university in Ohio. Ohio University, Ohio State, Bowling Green and some bigger out-of-state schools, too: Perdue, Miami, Florida State and the University of Florida. I wondered what it would be like to go to school in Florida. I'd soon find out."

In February 1964, Bob decided to check out the University of Miami in sunny Florida.

"Do you remember Joe Mira and George Mira,[1] the All Americans? They took me around and got me drunk for the first time in my life. That's what they all did.

They drank." Someone broke into the dormitory where Bob was staying and stole all his toiletries. He had been given twelve dollars for travel money and he lost that playing poker to these guys he met on the plane.

"They were two guys from Pennsylvania, who were also being recruited. I didn't realize what was happening. They took all my money. They stole all my stuff and the next day I had a hangover and I had to meet the head coach. I went, "Oh, my God! What am I going to do?"

1 Both Mira brothers played football at the Univ. of Miami (Fl) George Mira played Q.B. and later played in the NFL with the 49ers.

The next day they were having mini drills. They were throwing passes and making guys sprint. They looked at Bob, who wasn't very big and said, "And what do you do?"

"I said, Well, I punt, sir." They said, "Okay, let's see you punt." I took my shoes off and in my bare feet I hit four or five fifty-yarders in a row. They took me back into the office and offered me a no-contact contract. They said, "All we want you to do is kick. That is all you've got to do," I said, "Thank you."

"The next week when I went home, my mom asked me, "How did it go?" I said, "Mom they broke into my room and they took my Old Spice." That's all I could think about." Bob Urich had seen the University of Miami and didn't really like it. **"It didn't feel like a campus to me. It didn't feel like a college town. I wanted the perfect Ivy League looking school, ivy-covered, Georgian brick, gothic architecture."**

In late February of Bob's senior year he left Pittsburgh International Airport in a snow storm. Destination…Tallahassee, Florida, home of the Florida State Seminoles! **"When we landed in Tallahassee it was a sunny seventy-eight degrees. Pine forests everywhere and this little tiny country airport. That was it. I was hooked on Florida. On the drive into campus the recruiting coach drove by the Seminole Reservation,park-like acreage with a lake in the center. Sailboats, water skiing and beautiful girls picnicking on the lawn. My only question was, where do I sign?"**

On the campus of Florida State they took Bob to the Westcott Building. **"It's a gothic castle. It's everything I dreamed it would be. This beautiful Georgian brick building with big old oak trees, and Spanish moss hanging, and ivy growingon the walls. I thought, "Wow, this is it." I decided right there on the spot."**

At Florida State the school colors are garnet and gold. The various football teams were designated according to jersey color. **First team offense was white, first team defense was garnet. The second string offense was gold, second string defense wore blue. The freshmen were in green, and then there was orange–about as far away as you could get from garnet and gold. That was the team I was on."**

Bob was surrounded by these high school All Americans and All Staters on the team. Dawn patrol meant showing up in the stadium at five-thirty in the morning.

"They always announced the names for dawn patrol the night before football practice. Burkhart, Smith, Urich."

"I'd say, "Wait a minute, I was in bed at ten o'clock last night."

"Oh, it doesn't matter, you'll miss tomorrow–be there."

Bob didn't know if they were trying to run him off, but would say to him,

"Where were you last night?"

"I'd reply, Well, the School of Music was doing *The Merry Widow*, and I'd never seen an operetta."

And, they would go, "What? What are you talking about?"

Dawn Patrol was physically and mentally draining.

"You started out at the center of the field and ran across the field and up a hundred and thirty-eight rows, back down to the center and back up again. That designated one complete trip. Tallahassee in the winter actually has ice up there at the top of the stadium. You ran five to ten complete loops with some assistant coach who didn't want to be up at the crack of dawn, anyway, yelling at you.

***

Bob's sophomore year at Florida State he was a red shirt in football.

"I did not want to be a red shirt. That seemed like failure to me. Red shirt is an accepted procedure at the college level where you serve a year of eligibility–you practice but you don't play the games. All colleges conduct red-shirt programs.

It's a five-year program. For me, it felt like five years in college."

"It wasn't what I wanted to do. You're supposed to go to college and graduate and go out and do something else."

During Spring practice sessions, Bob was still wearing an orange jersey.

"The first and second string offense would go against this puny orange defense and just beat us to a pulp, and then they'd get a break, and I realized, well, they are at least getting a play break but we'd go every play."

One day at football drills, Bob went up against a guy who was second string center. An All-American from Georgia.

"I thought, you know what? This guy isn't that tough. He's a little bit bigger than me, but I think he's a damn cry baby. He's always getting hurt. The quarterback would snap the ball and hand it off to a running back," Bob explains–**"it was a block-and-tackle job. The idea is to shake off the block and tackle the ball carrier. I would maneuver around in**

line so I could get up against this guy. Every time he came up, I would make sure I was in front of him. I would just go all out and knock him down. Knock him on his back, cause him to fumble and basically try to humiliate him. He was bigger and probably more talented than I was, but I just didn't want to wear an orange shirt any more!

So after I'd done that a few times, the coach grabbed me by the collar like I had done something wrong! "You want that white, gold jersey, son?"

"Yes, sir." "You do that one more time and you've got it."

"He [the coach] doesn't care about me. He's trying to motivate the other guy, so he makes us go again and again and again."

Bob knocked the ball out one more time, made a tackle another time. He just went at him. They had to pull him off the guy.

"I was screaming and crying and foaming at the mouth. I may have bitten him. I don't really know. Might have been his jersey, I bit, actually."

"That's it," the coach says. He pulls the gold jersey off this guy. Gave him the orange one and puts the gold one on me.

I was in heaven."

The whistle blows and suddenly the drill is over and Bob runs up to the main practice field, which looks like a game field. It looks like a golf course. Beautifully laid out. All limed and the grass is green. It was wet and rainy that day in spring. The first string center, Jonathan Stephenson, started the scrimmage and twisted his ankle.

"They took the white jersey off him [Stephenson] and gave it to me. So in a matter of about twenty minutes, I went from orange to white. First string offensive center. I wasn't in shape and didn't know the plays, but I was wearing a white jersey. I came into the huddle and the quarterback didn't even know who I was. It was wet and slippery and on the first snap the quarterback and I had a bad exchange and the ball was fumbled. After a second straight fumble, Bill Peterson, the head coach got very wound up."

Coach Peterson was the father of modern-day football at Florida State. He served as head football coach for ten seasons, from 1960-69. He brought the 'wide open' San Diego passing offense to FSU and in doing so developed some of the decades greatest teams and players.

"Coach Peterson is wearing a gold jacket with a garnet and gold hat. He was always mixing up his words. He'd say things like, "I'm gonna

invite ya to…" and instead of saying, "Coach Peterson's party," he would say, "Coach Partisan's peter." He was full of blows to the head."

"It was wet and muddy, and the coaches all had towels on their hips. After the third fumble, Coach Peterson came running up to me and said, "Wipe, your hands off son!" I had mud all over them. He thrust his hip out to me so I could use the towel hanging there, but I was so nervous I wiped my hands right down the front of his gold jacket.

Bob heard Coach Peterson mumble to himself, as he walked away,

"My God, That's the best Florida State has to offer!"

***

The following Saturday was a Sping game. Bob kept the gold jersey. The other guy's name was Jonathan Stephenson. They got him well in a hurry. He was the first-string center and Bob was second-string center, alternating with the first string.

"I played against Alabama, Georgia and Georgia Tech. Johnny Stephenson was this wonderful kind of guy who I spent a lot of time with. Our lockers were next to each other, and because we were both centers, Johnny and I roomed together on road trips. That's what the coaches would do: have quarterbacks bunk with quarterbacks, defense guys with defense guys, so they could learn the plays from each other."

Years later, while performing in the play *The Hasty Heart* at the Kennedy Center in Washington, Bob Urich came across his ole friend and college football teammate, Johnny Stephenson. Sadly, his journey ended with a visit to the Viet Nam Memorial.[1]

Bob Urich's interest in acting found him hanging around the theater department, sneaking in to rehearsals and watching from the back of the theater. **"I can remember going past the music building at Florida State. It was near the English Department and sitting in the stairwell, listening to the arias and the scales and people playing instruments. It's really all I thought about at the time. I thought, "Now, that's what I *really* want to do. I want to go to Broadway. I want to learn to sing and act."**But, in reality, Bob knew, it was the football scholarship that brought him there.

"I felt obligated to spend as much time as I could on the field."

---

1 Read the full account of Bob's visit to the Viet Nam Memorial Wall in Chapter 15 *Bob's Take on Acting*.

"I didn't think it would go down very well with my father if I got a theater degree, so I majored in television and radio broadcasting."

On school breaks, Bob would head home to Ohio.

"Mrs. Kokal, this old Polish lady who lived next door, would always ask me a bunch of questions. I came back home from the first quarter of being at Florida State and she said, "Bobby, what are you studying in school?"

I said, "Well, Mrs. Kokal, I go to the Florida State University and ..."

"Ah! Florida."

I said, "Well, no. Florida *State*. Florida and Florida State, Mrs. Kokal is like Army and Navy...like Notre Dame and USC. You understand?

"Ah yes, Florida. So, Bobby, what for you study there in Florida?"

"It's Florida State, Mrs. Kokal, and I'm studying television and radio."

"You know something, Bobby, I got a little snow on channel seven. Will you take a look at my set? "Um, well, that's not exactly what I'm doing there, Mrs. Kokal." She could never understand that I went to school at *Florida State* University and wasn't fixing radios and television sets. She was a big college football fan; she loved Notre Dame. When they played USC or Miami, she was glued to her radio. She was the first person in the neighborhood to get a television set."

According to the entry in Bob's journal, Mrs. Kokal's son Davey had three gorgeous sisters. **"I would just go over to stare at them and dream about them at night. Sherry, Ruthie and Elaine Kokal were just gorgeous girls. Blonde and picturesque with parted lips. Beautiful girls. I was just this kid going over there to watch TV. Mrs. Kokal on Saturdays, always sat there with rapt attention listening to Notre Dame football on the radio and wondering if I could fix her TV set."**

It was at Florida State, on the gridiron field where Bob met Jack Fenwick. They roomed together their first two years at the football players' dorm, Sally Hall, and went on to become life-long friends. They were recruited by legendary coach, Bobby Bowden, who at the time was an assistant under F.S.U. head coach, Bill Peterson, who like Bob was from Ohio and also a graduate of Toronto High, Class of '39. Peterson was head coach at FSU for ten seasons. The rise of FSU football to national prominence is due in large part to the Peterson era. His teams compiled a record of 62-41-11 and made four bowl appearances.

Bob's freshman year, 1964, as a member of the team, FSU defeated Oklahoma 36-19 in the Gator Bowl. For you trivia buffs, the game marked Bob's first ever appearance on national television. Two years later, FSU lost to Wyoming in the Sun Bowl. In the 1967 Gator Bowl, FSU, thanks to a tremendous second half rally, tied Penn State 17-17. The final Peterson-FSU bowl appearance in 1968 saw the Seminoles lose a narrow 31-27 decision to LSU in the inaugural Peach Bowl. Bill Peterson was elected to the FSU Hall of Fame in 1979. He passed away August 5, 1993.

"Bobby Bowden," says Fenwick, "was the one who came up to Ohio and recruited both Bob and me along with about 3 or 4 other guys to come down to FSU. Then he left and came back later as head coach. Our defensive coach was Bob Harbison, who was there for many years. Fenwick recalls Bob hurting his right ankle. "He lost a year of eligibility. Our coaches took note of how hard he played." **"I played some football at Florida State. I always joke that I played almost as much football as Burt Reynolds *says* he did. He gave the university a million dollars. It's amazing how your stats go up when you contribute that kind of money. They go through the roof. I used to go to dinner at Burt's house in Bel Air which was a shrine to Florida State. More power to him. He did go to school there for a while, but I really got tired of hearing what a big football star Burt Reynolds was."**

One night, Bob was planning to have dinner at Burt's, so he called Vaughn Mansha, thenthe athletic director at Florida State.

"I said, I'm going to Buddy's house for dinner." That's what everybody calls him.

"You gonna go see Buddy?"

"Yes sir, I am. Would you do me a favor?" "Sure. I love you on that new show."

"Can you tell me how many times he carried the ball and for how many yards?" "I don't remember exactly, it was eleven times for twenty-two yards or something."

That's all I need to know. Thank you, sir!"

Bob heads over to Burt's house, armed with the information.

"Burt starts with the football stories. I talked him on. But Burt is so charming and so much fun to be at a dinner party with that there is no way one-upsmanship would ever come into it–you just let it go. Jokes

involving Buddy's football feats would now require us to go all the way out of the stadium and into the parking lot."

***

Fellow teammate, Tom DeLopez, who also roomed with Bob and Jack, remembers Bob being a good athlete. "At FSU, on a football scholarship they played you at many different positions. Bob got moved to center and took many blows directly to the head.

Back then, they were part of the game and actually encouraged," says DeLopez. In Bob's freshman year and in his sophomore year, he was a first team center," recalls Jack Fenwick. "We ran plays against the varsity. He took a lot of forearm hits from Jack Schinholster who played nose guard. He was known for his punishment to centers with 'forearm shivers,' a technique used by football linemen to deliver a devastating blow to their opponent by using their forearm, almost as a weapon.

In 1965, Bob was moved up to the varsity as a back-up center, but also played on the kickoff team which is what he was doing when he took a knee to the side of his head and helmet on a kickoff return against Alabama. "We all took hard hits back then," says Fenwick. "It was nothing to 'get your bell rung' in almost every full scrimmage or game."

Concussions can be cumulative.[1] Surely Bob's were and getting 'knocked out' in the Alabama game, along with headaches and other issues drew more attention to the problem. It resulted in Bob being sent for tests after that [Alabama] game," he says.

"Bob got a concussion and did not get normal EEG's [for years]," says Tom DeLopez, "so he had to quit playing." "I remember," adds Fenwick, " Bob being upset when told his football playing days were over. Many years later, before all the concussion issues that have come up in football, Bob and I were talking, and doctors told him that he probably could

---

1 In 2017 a study of the brain of deceased NFL players [donated by family members for research] show that out of 111 NFL players, 110 showed signs of C-T-E [Chronic Traumatic Encephalopathy] disease, which symptoms include, memory loss, depression and sometimes suicidal behavior. The finding also shows the disease can be caused by a cumulative affect of blows to the head over time, which contributes to serious health issues later in life, after their playing days are over. More info on 'concussions' related to blows to the head in football and other sports can be found in the book, *Head Games* by Dr. Chris Nowinski, co-founder and Exec. Dir. of Concussion Legacy Foundation.

have continued to play with what little they knew at that time. However, if you go by today's standards, I say, no way!" And, Jack emphasizes, "I bet if Bob were still with us today at age 70, or 71, who knows what complications there might be."

"I could no longer play football but did not want to lose my scholarship. I was still on the team handling stats and helping out wherever I could."

"Yep, that was required back then," says Jack Fenwick. "If you had an injury and could not play, to remain on scholarship, you were expected to be at practice to assist with equipment, laundry, work with the teams trainer, etc. A lot of guys would not do it and walked away from the scholarship.[1] Not Bob. He remained on scholarship a F.S. U. for his four years." Tom DeLopez, who was a year ahead of both Bob and jack remembers,"Bob's scholarship had an injury clause so it was good for four years. I injured my Shoulder," he says, "and that was the end of my football career, too."

Bob Perrone at the F.S.U. Noles Fans website, kindly checked info on Bob Urich's Football playing days at Florida State in the FSU handbook guides.

"During his [Urich's] time at FSU, Freshmen couldn't play on the varsity, so although he was there in '64 he would have been on the freshman team. He played in 1965 as a sophomore. His number was 55. Bob was a lineman [center] and not a starter, so exactly how many games he played is unknown because stats on participation were not kept." Perrone further explains, "unless you were a starter or generated some stats back then; ex: passes, catches, runs, punts, punt returns, tackles and so on, you could have gone in the game and never received credit. In 1965," he says, "players played both ways so he was a center on offense and either a middle guard or linebacker on defense. In 1966 [Bob's Jr. year] he was in the media guide but wasn't given a number, so he probably didn't play[2] that year.

As mentioned, the football players' dorm was Sally Hall. Jack Fenwick remembers it opened their freshman year, in the fall of 1964. "It was the first dorm ever to have air conditioning. "The room was nothing special. It certainly wasn't well decorated, at least not that I recall." Jack describes

---

1 A few years later there were law suits that changed injury and eligibility.

2 Bob Perrone is correct. Bob's concussion prevented him from playing football his Junior and senior years.

Bob Urich as being independent and traveling to the beat of a different drummer. "I certainly would not describe Bob as being a 'wild child.'" Fellow teammate Tom DeLopez agrees. Laughing, he says, "I have no wild stories to tell about Bob. He talked about Candy, his girlfriend back in high school. We never dated much the first two years. We were too busy with classes and football practice.

Besides, both of us were pretty broke. We only got $15 per month for laundry."

Today, with the high cost of living, fifteen dollars would probably only cover cleaning a couple of shirts and a pair of pants for a single day! "As players, we got movie passes to the three movie places at that time in Tallahassee. When a new movie came out, we walked to the theater." Jack points out, "movie passes were the only freebies we received."

"We didn't have a car and I remember we only triple dated once. We had a fraternity brother who had a car. We found some dates and we all ended up going to a drive-in movie. It was nothing special." Thinking back to their F.S.U. Days, Fenwick says, "I remember, Bob dating some girl in college, or tried to, but she went off with some other guy. Ahh, dumped again. The story of our lives," he laughs. " I think it might have been our freshmen year, we had a long weekend off. Bob and I went with another player from Jacksonville to visit him at his house. He had a girlfriend and she set us up with dates." Smiling, he continues, "we ended up going downtown to see the movie *The Sound of Music.* Little did we know at the time, we got to see Bob's future wife, Heather, performing at 15 years old. Years later, after they married, we kidded her about being so young. Bob said he felt he had robbed the cradle."

"Once Bob stopped going to practice and got into the radio and TV program at FSU," says Jack, "He started acting in some plays." Tom DeLopez, remembers listening to Bob's first radio play. It was broadcast over FSU's campus radio station. "Bob invited Fenwick, myself and one other fellow to listen to the show. He wouldn't tell us what it was about until we got to where he had set up a radio, which was not in the dorm. We lived in the football dorm and he didn't want to be razzed for months. It was a wise move on his part. Bob played a blind soldier on a train during WWII. As I remember, the program lasted about 20 minutes, but that was 50 years ago," says Tom. Memory lapses can & do occur.

Bob and life at F.S.U.

"Bob had a good sense of humor," says Jack. "But, was more reserved. He took life a little more seriously than we other guys, not just around the frat house but around other players." Their friend and teammate, Tom DeLopez says, "Bob was always a gentleman and a scholar." "However, he was not shy or reticent about giving you his honest opinion on any and every subject, whether you wanted to hear it or not," says Fenwick.

When asked to describe Bob's temperament and if he ever lost his temper and had a short fuse, Jack paused for a moment. "No, I wouldn't say he had a short fuse, but he could be impatient with people, particularly those who were disrespectful.[1]

A couple of things which stand out in my memory about Bob are religion and politics. He was Catholic and attended church services regularly, and politics is something we never discussed or thought about during our college days."

"After our first two years as roommates, I think Bob moved to an apartment with some fraternity brothers, not the fraternity house," recalls Fenwick. Bob, Tom DeLopez and I were members of Lambda Chi, but I distinctly remember Bob did not want to live in the frat house. He was serious about his studies and thought the house would be a distraction. He was probably right. I never lived there either. I had to live in the dorm with the other football players." "For us," says Tom DeLopez, "the fraternity was a chance to be around calmer, more rational people than at the dorm. The frat did party, but Lambda Chi always won the scholarship trophy and was also first or second in the intramural athletic competition."

FSU Years & Lambda Chi Alpha

This may come as a total surprise to many members of the Lambda fraternity, known for its many macho football members, but in the early 1970s, New York City's gay activists selected the Greek letter *lambda* as its

---

1 **Authors note**: in my numerous interviews with Bob's family and friends for his bio, every person mentioned if you wanted to set the normally cool guy off just show signs of being rude and disrespectful. It was one of Robert Urich's few hot buttons.

emblem.[1] In *More Than You'll Ever Be* by Joseph P. Goodwin[2] it reads, "the lower case Greek letter lambda carries several meanings. First, it represents scales and thus balance. The Greeks considered balance to be the constant adjustment necessary to keep opposing forces from overcoming each other. The hook at the bottom of the right leg of the lambda represents the action required to reach and maintain balance. To the Spartans, lambda meant unity. They believed that society should never infringe on anyone's individuality and freedom. The Romans adopted the letter to represent 'the light of knowledge shed into the darkness of ignorance.' Finally, in physics the symbol designates energy change. Therefore, lambda with all its meanings is an especially apt symbol for the gay liberation movement, which energetically seeks a balance in society and which strives through enlightenment to secure equal rights for homosexual people."

1966 - Bob's Junior year at F.S.U. - Talent Contest

In Bob's junior year at Florida State there was a talent contest for theater majors. It was conducted by Eddie Foye III, from the famous theatrical family. He had been traveling around the country, touring the various colleges and universities.

1966 - Bob's Junior year at F.S.U.
Talent Contest

"There was this one little girl, Janey Nelson who had chickened out of the contest earlier, and dropped out of her scene. Then at the last minute, she decided she wanted to do it, but there were no students left to play opposite her, so she asked me to do the scene with her."

Bob wasn't even in the theater department at that time, but figured, what the heck.

"She and I did this little scene from *The Rainmaker*.[3] The competition lasted all weekend, and by Sunday afternoon, it was time for the awards and the announcements." Everyone in the theater department

---

1 In no way does the author or publisher wish to imply that Lambda Chi Fraternity is associated with gay activists. A more definitive explanation on lambda as a symbol of gay/lesbian rights can be found in *The Encyclopedia of Homosexuality* pub: 1989, Indiana Univ. Press: Bloomington [pg. 26].

2 *More Than You'll Ever Be* by Joseph P. Goodwin, pub. 1989 Indiana Univ. Press

3 *The Rainmaker* would also play a pivotal role later in Bob's acting career. Read more in chapter 11.

was excited because there was the possibility that Eddie Foye was going to award a screen test to the winner.

Foye had just come from the University of Alabama and somebody there had gone to Hollywood as a result of the competition. The same was true from another contestant from the University of Texas.

"Towards the end of the event the auditorium was packed. We did this scene. Janey was very talented and sang beautifully."

At the end of the presentation, Eddie Foye said, "I've seen a lot of talent here this weekend. You've got an extraordinary theater program. But of all the people I've seen in my two days here–and don't get me wrong," encourages Foye, "you all should keep working and stay with it. But there are two young people here who should definitely consider the theater as a career. I suggest they go directly to New York or Hollywood to study, because they are going to make it!"

Bob writes in his journal, **"Then he pulled the two of us out. We'd won the talent scout contest–we were given certificates and a little medal. Everyone there knew I wasn't even in the theater program, so I was getting scowls and dirty looks from the other participants."**

The next day Bob received an irate call from the head of the theater department.

"He was actually upset with me.

"Urich," he said. "What is your major?"

"Television and radio, sir," I said. "So how did you get into that competition? Don't you know that was just for theater majors?"

"Well, I knew that but this girl asked me and she was stuck with a part and there was nobody left to perform with her and ..." He calmed down and said, "Ok. You're taking Acting 101 next year." "Yes sir," I said.

Jack's memories of Bob

"Bob, couldn't sit still for very long." recalls his life-long friend, Jack Fenwick. "He always had to be doing something and on the go. On one occasion, my wife and I were visiting Bob and Heather at their beautiful lake front cottage in Canada. He got me up early and said, 'come on, Jack, up and at 'em. Breakfast is on and after that, we're goin' fishing.' I looked outside and the water was really rough. It didn't matter to Bob. He had made up his mind and that was that. We were going fishing, come hell or high water. No matter how rough the lake was!"

"Another time, we were all sitting around a campfire. It was sort of an outdoor fire-pit, in front of their cottage. A nice family gathering spot to shoot the breeze after eating."

"Suddenly, Bob jumps up and says, 'I need to fly back to California. I'll be back in a couple of days.' And with that, he left. He drove about 200 miles to the airport in Toronto [Canada]."

"I also remember another time, we were sitting around enjoying each others' company. Looking around, I realized Bob was no longer with us, so I got up to go look for him. He had quietly slipped away to the other side of the cottage, and was stretched out on a blanket reading a copy of his script." Jack insists Bob wasn't being rude. It was just his independent nature kicking in. He had something on his ever-active mind he needed to do and was going to do it. Period.

Fenwick, the TV consultant

After college, Jack Fenwick and Bob Urich remained in touch. Not such was the case with Tom DeLopez. "I only spoke with Bob once after college," he admits. "Of course, I was pleased for his success as an actor, but we weren't close."

Jack became involved in police work in Tallahassee. "It was around the early 70s. I was Deputy Director of the Division of Criminal Investigations with the Florida Department of Law Enforcement.

"Bob was doing the television series *S.W.A.T.* He'd call me up to get pointers about police work," says Jack. "Things like, the type of equipment we used; body armor, different weapons and so forth. I became sort of his consultant. I thought it was funny. Here he was playing the role of this guy on TV, which was my profession in 'real' life."

Bob continued to lean on his long-time friend--for help in crafting story ideas for his TV series, *Vega$*. Jack mentions how it came to be while fishing. "We started fishing together when Bob and Heather got their place up in Canada [West Lake]," he says.

Bob gets a little help from his friend, Jack

"Conversations began about my police work. Like most of us in law enforcement and/or the military, we all have things that happen to us.

The 'good, the bad and the ugly,' so to speak, along with the funny. Bob said, 'These incidents could be used in a show or a movie. It's exactly what writers are looking for. They could use them,' he insisted. At the time Bob was doing *Vega$* and I was Deputy Director of the Criminal Investigations Div. in Tallahassee. 'Why don't you come out to California and sit down with the writers and tell them incidents or some of the stories that you told me,' suggested Bob. He offered to buy my plane tickets and said, we could stay with them. So, I accepted." Jack and his wife stayed with Bob and Heather for about two weeks at their place in Oxnard, about 30 miles north of L.A. He had a sailboat and we had a great time." Fenwick met with the writers at Bob's office at the studio. A tape recorder rolled as Jack related actual police incidents that he had been involved in. As a result of Fenwick's help, quite often, Bob could be heard humming the song, "I'll get by with a little help from my friends."[1]

Jack Fenwick recalls another time, around 1983 or 1984, when Bob was looking at another project for TV. "He was going to play the part of a State Agent in Florida, working on drug cases, homicides, organized crime. . .BUT, just before they could start filming, they [TV] came out with Don Johnson, so Bob's project never came out. I think it was around the time, he and Heather moved to Boston and Bob started doing *Spenser: For Hire.*[2] It was real close. I'm pretty sure they had the script written, and they were ready to film the pilot when *Miami Vice* debuted."

Jack Fenwick[3] says, "I saw some things I talked to Bob's writers about show up on the *Spenser: For Hire* series." Ironically, in 1985, ABC in its infinite wisdom debuted Bob's show, *Spenser*, Friday nights at 10:00pm, directly opposite. . .you guessed it. . .*Miami Vice*. which had premiered the

1 *With A Little Help from my Friends by the Beatles* was written by John Lennon & Paul McCartney. It was a hit in May 1967 from their album, Sgt. Pepper's Lonely Hearts Club Band.

2 Bob's series, *Spenser: For Hire* is covered in detail in Chapter 20.

3 **Author's note**: As of 2017, Jack Fenwick and his wife Clair were living on their farm in Tennessee. He was working for the Evans Rep Group, along with running a group of eight retired law enforcement firearms trainers/SWAT guys who do equipment demos for the products they represent. Companies like SureFire, Springfield Armory, Trijicon, Mossberg and Blue Force Gear. "I thought about retiring," he told the author in a telephone interview, "But, it does not hold a lot of interest for me." Always the outdoorsman, Jack enjoys going up to Alaska for Spring steelhead fishing with one of his sons and back again, in the fall for a brown bear hunt., along with more fishing which sounds better than retiring. "Besides," he says," If I retired here on our farm, I would find too much work to do!"

year before and had a huge loyal following and was top rated. Jack remembers Bob saying, "the reviews for *Spenser* were pretty good, but they [ABC] dropped it before it ran one more year and residuals would kick in."

***

Bob in Florida State Univ. football uniform #55.

Bob's head football coach F.S.U. Bill 'Pete' Peterson.

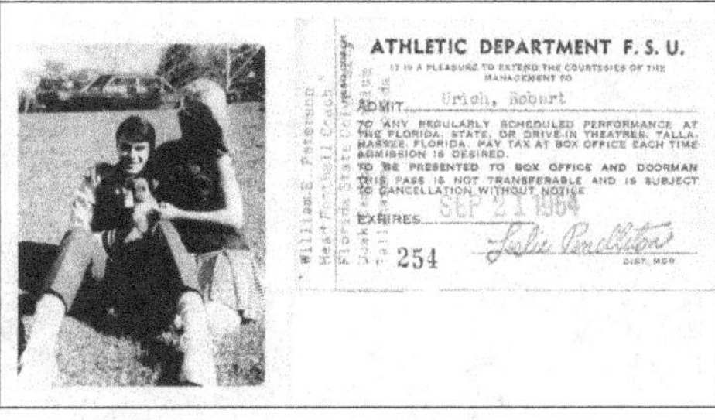

ATHLETIC DEPARTMENT F. S. U.

IT IS A PLEASURE TO EXTEND THE COURTESIES OF THE MANAGEMENT TO

ADMIT Urich, Robert

TO ANY REGULARLY SCHEDULED PERFORMANCE AT THE FLORIDA, STATE, OR DRIVE-IN THEATRES, TALLAHASSEE, FLORIDA. PAY TAX AT BOX OFFICE EACH TIME ADMISSION IS DESIRED.

TO BE PRESENTED TO BOX OFFICE AND DOORMAN

THIS PASS IS NOT TRANSFERABLE AND IS SUBJECT TO CANCELLATION WITHOUT NOTICE

EXPIRES SEP 21 1964

254 Leslie Pendleton

DIST. MGR

Bob sitting w/F.S.U. coed and his Athletic pass

Bob hoisting on high a Florida State U. cheerleader.

Bob sitting with two young ladies on set of WFSU-TV show he hosted. L-R, Janie Milton, Bob and Jennifer Pierson.

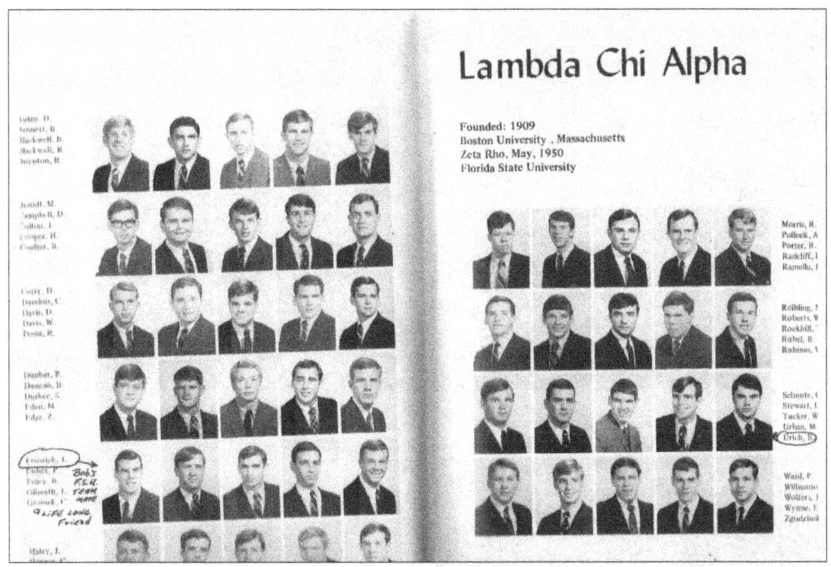

Bob's fraternity Lambda Chi Alpha, Bob's photo along with his roommate and life-long friend Jack Fenwick, courtesy F.S.U. Yearbook.

Bob standing by WFSU-TV Mobile Unit.

Bob w/parents on graduation day at Florida State.

Bob in cap & gown F.S.U. degree Arts/Sciences.

Bob & Jack Fenwick fishing buddies.

PART II
Chapter 11

Michigan State
Chicago - WGN Radio
Moonlighting as an actor
First marriage

Bob in Dallas & Michigan State

[**Bold typed words are Bob's taken directly from his personal journal.**]

Following Bob's graduation from Florida State in the Spring of 1968, he headed for Dallas.

"My sister lived there with her family and invited me to stay. I got a commercial agent and did a couple of Dr. Pepper commercials, one with Dick Clark. I thought, well, this isn't a bad life. My older brother, Tom had done some summer stock there–Oklahoma and all that kind of stuff–at the Casa Maria Theater in FortWorth. I suppose in an alternate universe I could have stayed in Dallas and got started there, tipped around the world and done commercials and industrial films and that might have led to something. Then again, this is part of that chaos theory. If I'd made that choice, where would my life be today. Would I have met Heather? Would I have children? Would I live in Sherwood?[1]

Would I be a lonely bachelor living in a penthouse somewhere reading his press clippings."

Bob had already been accepted at Michigan State graduate school, but now he had other plans. He didn't want to wait any longer to launch his acting career. Four years of college had been quite enough, thank you.

---

1 This entry from Bob's journal was written shortly before he passed in April 2002 while living in Sherwood.

"I thought I'd stay where I was and follow my acting career. I told my mom, "I'm not going back to school. I'm going to act."

"My mom said, "No, you're not. You've been accepted at Michigan State, and you are going to Michigan State, and that is that."

Bob and Michigan State

Bob's mom, Cecelia, was the one who was interested in her 'Bobby Knight' getting an education. **"She was the one who encouraged me. I came back from Florida State and then went on to Michigan State. Going for an M.A. was unusual for someone with my background. Neither of my parents had even been to college."**

Bob was twenty-one and already had a degree in communications, but felt he had absolutely nothing to offer an employer in a legitimate job.

"I could have got some lower entry job, but I just wasn't ready. I went home and told my parents that I wanted to go to graduate school. My mom is the one who encouraged me to go for it. She always had an idea what she wanted her children to be."

In the fall of 1968, Bob packed his bags and headed off to East Lansing, Michigan, home of the 'Spartans' at Michigan State University. Some famous Michigan State Alumni include one-time NBA Super-star Magic Johnson, former Major League baseball players Steve Garvey and Kirk Gibson, and actors James Caan and of course, Robert Urich. But, back then, long before his celebrity status, Bob didn't have any money. No fame or fortune. He lived in the basement of a woman's house, shoveling snow and mowing lawns for rent money, while majoring in broadcast research.

"One of the things I did to get my Master's degree was demographic research for WRVR-FM, the Riverside Church radio station in New York. They were having their license challenged by a special interest group. The station was owned by the Rockefeller Foundation, but do you think they were going to part with any of their billions of dollars to hire a research firm to look into their listener base? No."

Michigan State & Broadcast research

Instead, the Rockefeller Foundation called Michigan State and asked the research department for help. **"Do you have a couple of students over there who could do the research? One of the things you have to do**

as a broadcaster is prove that you are operating in the public interest and have a community of listeners."

At the age of 22, Bob and another student headed for Manhattan.

"I went out with my twelve-dollar briefcase and my three-piece suit. We walked the streets of Manhattan interviewing community leaders for the project. We interviewed George Mulcahey, the President of the New York Stock Exchange, film critic Judith Crist[1]and Cardinal Cushing. Two twenty-year olds conducting a survey of the community on the relevance of WRVR for the FCC. But, we did it and as a result, WRVR kept their license."

***

The summer of 1969, Bob won the Pierre Andre Memorial Award at one of the nation's most prestigious radio stations, WGN Chicago. **"They hired me as an intern and offered me a job as an account executive in one of the largest radio stations in the world, WGN. Meanwhile, I was still thinking about acting. Whenever you wanted to find me, I'd be hanging around with Ray Raynor and *Bozo the Clown*."**

Chicago Days

[Bold-typed words are Bob's –taken directly from his personal journal.]

"They did *Bozo the Clown* 'live' from the WGN[TV] studios. I'd be down in the studios or hanging out with Roy Leonard or Wally Phillips,[2] the stations top radio personalities. They were big celebrities at the time."

It's no big secret that Bob really hated his job in radio sales. Instead of calling on time buyers and advertising agencies, he would go to Wrigley Field and catch the Cubs playing a double header. **"I'd go to the broadcast booths and Jack Brickhouse and Lou Boudreau would be doing the play-by-play coverage and color [on the games]."**

Bob thought he was really getting away with something. However, there was one slight problem, as he explains in his journal.

"On each desk at the station, they would leave the radio on for commercial checks. There was a radio sitting on the general manager's desk

1 Judith Crist was an American film critic. She appeared regularly on NBC's *Today* show from 1964-78.

2 Both radio personalities are profiled in the author's book, *Radio Pro*; pub: 2013 bearmanormedia.com

as Lou goes, 'well, we're happy to have all our people from WGN here today. We have a couple of radio execs down here. Robert Urich is here with Jim Smith and they are enjoying the ball game.' Needless to say that required a little explaining."

WGN, then, part of the Tribune Company[1] had a very strict rule against moonlighting. No, outside jobs of any type. Period. It was also a very conservative company. White shirts, ties. No colored shirts. You couldn't wear loafers. **"Well, I wasn't going to wear that stodgy stuff. I'm wearing yellow shirts and red ties, and the station manager says to me, 'Urich, about your shirt there.'**

"Oh, I'm sorry, sir but I can't afford to buy new shirts. Not on my salary. This is the only one I own." So they left me alone. I actually had two shirts."

Pursues his dream of becoming an actor

"Meanwhile, I was doing okay learning this business, which was boring as hell, selling radio time."

On weekends Bob, striving to keep his dream alive of one day becoming an actor, studied acting, on Saturday mornings at the Actor's Studio in downtown Chicago. He also studied voice at the University of Chicago. Biding his time, figuring how to make a break.

"My voice coach was in the Fine Arts Building. I'd walk up the stairs, and there would be Miss Chichelo teaching romance languages. On the next floor there would be the Chicago Ballet. The next floor was a French teacher and then two people playing piano and violin in the hallways. One day my voice teaches said, "Robert, I don't know if you know this or not but I'm the chairman of the United Jewish Fund drive here and I'm wondering if you would like to make an extra hundred bucks?"

At the time, Bob was making a hundred and twenty-five dollars *a week* at WGN.

In two weeks at the Opera House, a black tie affair is held for the fund drive. It's five hundred dollars a seat. Irv Kupcinet, a syndicated columnist for the *Chicago Sun Times* is hosting the affair. Before the program

---

1 Tribune Company not only owned WGN Radio & Television but the Chicago Tribune Newspaper syndicate. In fact, WGN's call letters originally stood for World's Greatest Newspaper.

begins, the U.S. flag and the Israeli flag will drop from the flys at the opera house. They are enormous flags, flags as big as your house. Next, they play both national anthems. Then this young Israeli soldier, played by Bob Urich, dressed in fatigues stands center stage. He gives an emotional speech before this five-hundred-dollar-a-seat black tie audience to benefit the United Jewish Fund.

"I put on the uniform. I'm in my army fatigues in my straight off the battlefield make-up, looking up heroically, tears running down my face."

Bob plays a heroic Israeli soldier

"I walk center stage and looking up heroically, tears running down my face, deliver the speech about the noble cause of the Israeli youth: 'while the youth of America are burning their draft cards, carousing and smoking pot, the youth of Israel are fighting for their Nation on the twenty-fifth anniversary of their country.'"

Bob speech is interrupted five times with applause. Then a stranding ovation.

"I'm hooked. I'm an actor. I'm walking off stage and Irv Kupcinet[1] grabs me and says, 'You're a brave lad and that was beautiful, an inspiring speech. Son, tell me, what's it really like over there?'

I said, 'Beats the hell out of me.'

He said, 'What? You're not a soldier?'

'No sir, I'm an actor.'

He was nonplussed. 'An *actor*? You're an actor? You're not a soldier? You're an Actor?'

I said, 'Yes, an actor.'

So he starts to make his entrance and stops right at the apron of the stage and says, 'Hey kid, at least tell me you're Jewish.'

'Roman Catholic.' I replied.

He said, 'Well, you're good. Stick with it.'"

You're Fired !

The next day at the radio station [WGN] Bob almost makes it past reception on his way to his little cubicle when the receptionist says, "Marv [Marv Astrin-the Sales Manager] wants to see you at once.

---

1 Irv Kupcinet was a Chicago writer and newspaper columnist for the *Chicago Sun Times*. He was also a TV talk show host and radio personality.

"Marv calls me in and says, 'Have a nice weekend?'

'Oh, it was alright,' I reply.

'Anything special happen?'

'No.'

'Do you happen to have a seating plan of the opera on you?'

'Excuse me?'

He goes, 'Well, I do. That's where I was sitting. Dead row center. Caught your whole performance.'

Now where did I think Marv Astrin,[1]esteemed Jewish community leader, would've been on Saturday night?

He said, 'Tell me, Urich, what do you want to be when you grow up?'

I said, 'I think I want to be an actor.'

'Are you nuts? There are guys in my office every day once a day looking for your job. You could be running the station in twenty years.'

I thought, 'Oh, God forbid.'

He then said, 'So you want to be an actor, huh?'

I said, 'Yeah. I really think that's what I want to do.'

He said, 'Okay. I'm going to give you a little boost. You're fired.'"

Fortunately or unfortunately for Bob, the person who ran the research department had an appendicitis that same week. He developed some complications and couldn't return to work as soon as he thought he could. They asked Bob to stay on a while longer. **"I ran the research department for almost that whole summer [70 or 71], and by the end of the summer, I knew for certain what I *didn't* want to do. That was the beginning of my acting career. I was going to be a great actor like David Garrick[2] or Laurence Olivier. I'd play Richard III and Hamlet. I'd suffer and bare my soul nightly. I'd drive my Mazerati through Malibu Canyon, read scripts in my pool, be adored by thousands of women around the world, and wear shades to protect my eyes from the flashbulbs every time I walked through an airport."**

Bob had already taken the first step in his dreams of becoming an actor...he got fired.**"I hated my job at WGN–good riddance, but now**

1 Marv Astrin, later was V.P at WGN Radio. He passed away at age 84.

2 David Garrick [1717-1779] was an English actor, theater manager, playwright and producer, who influenced nearly all aspects of theatrical practice throughout the 18, century.

I was broke with no immediate prospects. I hadn't actually been cast in anything yet–no roles. I was just this young kid trying to find my way who knew nothing about the town or how the business worked, and to tell the truth, I knew very little about acting. But I was studying at the Actor's Studio in Chicago and I was *looking* for roles."

It was during this time that Bob met and married his first wife, Barbara Rucker."We met in Ted Liss'[1] acting class," she says." "I was born and raised in the Chicago area, Arlington Heights, about a block from Prospect High which I attended."

Bob's Ist wife

Barbara says she began modeling and got commercial work when she was thirteen. "My agent said, 'You need to get some acting lessons.'" Her mom did community theater, so Barbara loved the idea of acting. She signed with Shirley Hamilton, and ultimately was introduced to acting coach, Ted Liss. "I was there a couple of weeks, when one day in walks Robert Urich! 'Holy Cow,'" she says excitedly. "I was the first one to greet him. Ted said, 'I need to put you two together in a scene.' I said, 'I just met the guy.' 'That's o.k.,'" he replied. "I want you to exchange numbers and get together. So, we did," she says, laughing. "The scene Bob & I were in was one of those Neil Simon things and the chemistry was instant. I was in my twenties and that had never happened to me before. Bob was also in his early twenties. He was a gentle soul and very modest, but when he got on stage, he just exploded."

"Six months after we met," Barbara says, "we were engaged. We got married pretty quickly, probably within a year. My dad was not happy, 'You're marrying an actor,' he yelled! We had a wonderful wedding. Bob was Catholic. I'm not. In fact," she reveals, "I was about the only person in my family who was even slightly religious. At age six I went to church by myself looking for God. We had a big wedding, like 125 people. It was January and we went to Acapulco on our honeymoon. Bob got sick, so

---

1 Ted Liss an actor-training coach and performance Arts icon. He decided to share his acting skills with others and turned hundreds of everyday folks into top-notch stars of stage, screen and TV. He operated the Ted Liss Studio for performing Arts at his North Side Chicago home from 1946, until his sudden passing from a heart attack at age 72, on March 5, 1992. As of 2017, the school he started, the Chicago Actors studio still continues, under the direction of Ted's former student, Edward Dennis Fogell.

here I am sitting by the pool writing postcards: 'Oh, we're having a wonderful time,'" she laughs.

Actor Mark Hampton worked Chicago theater in the early 70's. He knew and worked on stage with Barbara. They had appeared together in *Plaza Suite*, which starred the talented actor/comedian, Sid Caesar. The play was presented at the Drury Lane Theater on Chicago's south side.

"The theater operated year round to near capacity [98%]," Hampton recalls. "Interestingly, the marquee routinely made no mention of the 'play,' just the star. In our case, it was something like... ***October 21, - December 1, SID CAESAR!"***

"I had done the national tour of the play, and was excited to return to Chicago and the Lane theater. It's where I worked during my college years at Northwestern and I grabbed at the chance to work with the great Sid Caesar. Unfortunately, it was during Sid's zombie period. Off alcohol, bone thin, he sipped club soda with a slice of lime and stared straight ahead. His manager, H.F. Green–called 'H'–did all the talking. Sid did the acting. If someone engaged Sid in conversation, a look of panic came into his eyes. He succinctly and politely responded as best he could, with 'H' jumping in to provide the color commentary [details]. One weekend 'H' had to go away on business and left Sid alone. The stage manager was supposed to 'take care' of Sid. But, something went wrong and Sid pulled a refrigerator over on himself. So that was the environment. I did have one glimpse of the great Sid,"[1] recalls Hampton. "An improvised moment, not in rehearsal, but in a performance which made it better. As the waiter, in *Plaza Suite*, I delivered champagne and handed him [Sid] the check. One night, instead of simply signing it and handing it back to me, as we had done up until then, he turned me around, bent me forward, used my back as a desk and got a laugh. It was a momentary glimmer of the 'great' Sid Caesar I remembered." Actor Mark Hampton had three small roles in *Plaza Suite*. "I was a bellhop in Act 1,a Puerto Rican waiter in Act II and bridegroom in Act III."

---

1 Great is the word to describe talented Sid Caesar. He was a vaudeville star who worked the borscht circuit from the Catskills to Florida before moving to television then in it's infancy. Sid was one of TV's first popular comedic talents, co-starring with Imogene Coca in *Your Show of Shows*. A 90 minute variety show on NBC [1950-54]. Supporting players included equally talented Carl Reiner and Howard Morris.

Bob & Barbara

"Bob Urich's first wife, Barbra Rucker played the secretary in act II. I believe she had come from modeling into acting," Hampton says. "She was a real dazzler, and one of the sweetest people ever. She was utterly without ego about her looks. She was also very, very dedicated to acting. I remember her jumping rope in her dressing room to warm-up."

"I lived in downtown Chicago," he says. "Barbara picked me up every day and drove us out to the theater on the south side. It was during those daily drives that I heard about her life with Bob. This beautiful woman with this handsome husband and a seemingly perfect life. They were in their first year of marriage, but it seemed like they were on an extended honeymoon. She would recount simple things they did together, like what they had made for dinner last night, but with such enthusiasm and appreciation for this life they were sharing that the facts of the actual event were immaterial. Nothing remarkable," he continues, "but what made it remarkable [and special] was they had done it together."

Mark Hampton[1] and Bob met at the theater. "He would meet her after work. He was her male counterpart. Tall, and handsome, a very sweet guy. He seemed to love that she was acting. I don't know why I think that–just a feeling I got from him rather than fromactual conversation. I do know they were both into acting."

***

There's lots of regional theater in the Chicago area. Bob started banging on doors. Eventually, he joined the repertory company at the Arlington Park Theater. **"The Arlington was a beautiful theater in the round, but it burned to the ground. Some kind of mobster payment that didn't get made."**

Chicago Theater & Bob

"Ann Southern attempts to seduce Bob, on stage"

One of the first plays Bob was in at the Arlington was *Father of the Bride.*

"Believe it or not, David Hasselhoff and I played brothers. I remember David chiding me because, in his opinion, I'd been doing repertory

1 Mark Hampton and the author chatted about Bob & Barbara via e-mail [from June 15, thru June 30, '15].

theater for too long. I'd been at the Arlington Theater a year before he'd arrived and he thought I'd over-stayed my time and missed the boat. I was now too old to make it, he told me. He actually seemed to feel a little sorry for me."

Bob writes in his journal that in regional theater, you do a lot of stuff–they call it the straw-hat circuit. You do different plays every three weeks. **"We did *Follow the Blind* with Don Ameche; *Lovers and Other Strangers*** [Renee Taylor & Joseph Bologna's romantic comedy] **with Janis Paige."** In another production, Bob was the ingénue in a play called *Personal Appearance* with Ann Sothern. **"She was really getting up there in years by that time, so all the lights in the theater had these pink jells on them to make her look younger. She would glow pink. Unfortunately, it made the rest of us look like a bunch of Hollywood Indians."**

There is a scene in the play where she [Sothern] seduces Bob–or attempts to.

"I'm this young man on the sofa and she starts coming on to me, unbuttoning my shirt. Every day in the performance, she'd get further and further and further down the front of my shirt, unbuttoning the buttons. Finally I sewed the buttons shut. I left the top three–but the rest of them were sewed. "We were in the scene that night and she got to button number four and she tugged on it and tugged on it, and of course it was sewn shut. "When she saw what was going on she glared at me. I could see the fire in her eyes and then she just went *ummpphh* and ripped the shirt open."

"Buttons flew all over the stage. When we got off stage, she said, 'Don't you *ever* do that again.' She also never tried to go below the third button again either."

***

After a year and a half of repertory work, at Chicago's Ivanhoe, Arlington Park and Pheasant Run Theaters, Bob came to a crossroads.

"I was no longer an ingénue and it didn't look as if I was going to become a star any time soon, either.

Producer David Lonn took Bob aside and explained the facts of theater life and how the system worked. **"The Arlington would import a star from Hollywood as a headliner to bring in the audiences, and then they'd fill the cast out with local actors. The moment had come where I either had to become a star myself, or be relegated to small parts or**

character roles...or get out of the business altogether–because big male stars were not going to want me on stage with them."

It was at that juncture Burt Reynolds showed up in town to star in *The Rainmaker.* **"Rhoda Snedleton, a wonderful actress was also in the cast. Jim Burroughs of future sit-com fame–*Cheers, Will & Grace*–was the director. Like me, Burt had gone to Florida State, but he's eleven years older than I am. Still, somehow he knew I'd gone there."**

Barbara took Bob over to her agency, because at the time Shirley Hamilton[1] was doing theater with Burt Reynolds and she figured it would be a good way for them to meet. It proved to be a wise decision. Shirley became Bob's agent during the remainder of his time in Chicago.

Burt Reynolds & Bob

When it came time for the actual auditions for the stage production of Richard Nash's *The Rainmaker,* Bob wasn't feeling that confident about his odds in the role as Burt Reynold's younger brother. **"Maybe I didn't have a chance, because of what the producer had said–that they were going to cast somebody younger. I went down and did my audition and it went well. As I walked back up the aisle, I saw Burt Reynolds sitting way in the back. His only remark was, 'Good looking young man. Get him out of here.' Followed by the patented Burt Reynolds laugh. I thought, 'Well, that's that.' I was getting a little despondent when he added, 'Hey kid. You're good. Some day you'll fill this theatre. You're going to be great in this part.'"** That's all Bob needed to hear. He and his acting career were off to the races!

***

Burt Reynolds and Bob Urich had a lot of things in common, but to Bob, Burt was a Movie Star. **"I was just a kid starting out, so it wasn't like we were on the same planet. He was a very big deal by then, flying off to do *The Tonight Show with Johnny Carson.*** Around that time, Burt did that infamous nude layout for Cosmopolitan–so naturally the play got a lot of attention. It was sold-out from opening night on. **"Woman went crazy over Burt. Screaming and shrieking when they saw him,**

1 Shirley Hamilton was a Chicago talent agent who represented hundreds of models, singers, theater and film & TV actors, including Jim Belushi, Daryl Hannah, and Bob Urich during his pre TVacting days in Chicago theater. Shirley Hamilton was 90 when she passed of natural causes, September 15, 2011.

bringing copies of the magazine to be signed by him. Burt could walk on stage and twitch his mustache and the place would start screaming. It was unbelievable. I thought, 'Wow! Now that's power.'"

Bob's first wife, actress & model Barbara Rucker. Photo courtesy, Barbara Rucker.

Bob with his mentor Burt Reynolds, backstage in D.C. at play Hasty Heart which Burt produced and starred Bob & his wife, Heather, circa 1984.

Chapter 12

La La Land, Burt Reynolds and Bob and Carol, Ted and Alice, and Bob and Barbara

Burt & Bob

[**Bold-typed words are Bob's –taken directly from his personal journal.**]

"Burt Reynolds was very instrumental in our lives," says Barbara Rucker. "His agent and manager came from California to see the final performance [of *The Rainmaker*]. After, they took us to dinner. They were most complimentary but said, 'you're not going to go anywhere if you stay in Chicago, you've got to come to L.A. Come out, we'll find you a place to live.'"

"Burt was very generous to me. After the show closed he said, 'Look, Bob, you need to move from here. I'm going to New York to do a couple of movies, but you need to get West.' He introduced me to Dick Clayton[1] who was his agent at the time. I called Clayton and he said, 'Yeah, I'd like to work for you.' Work for *me*? Finally, I felt I was on my way up. I had a big time agent–Clayton had been James Dean's agent. There are a lot of guys who went out to L.A. who never even got an agent."

In February Bob and Barbara sold everything at a farewell party, and along with their dog, Mimsy, jumped in their 1971 Chevy Malibu and headed West.

Years later, in an interview with writer Frank Sanello, Bob had high praise for the city. "I lived in Chicago from 1970 to 1972. It may be the greatest city in North America. It's a compilation of a lot of little neighborhoods with all the good stuff a big city has like sports and a

1 Dick Clayton also represented many Hollywood luminaries, including Burt Reynolds, Jane Fonda, and Farrah Fawcett. He died from heart failure, September 29, 2008. He was 93.

great orchestra. And wonderful neighborhood bars. It's just a super town. "Someday I see myself living there again," says Urich. However, fate would intervene.

"We moved to L.A. and right into Burt's home," says Barbara. "He was involved with Dinah Shore at that time, and she couldn't have been more delightful. When we pulled up in his [Burt's] drive way, he had this 3-story garage and his assistant lived upstairs.

Bob in La La Land

Burt came downstairs to greet them. "Welcome guys," he said. "I'm going out of town [to New York] why don't you just move in here for a few months, 'cause I have to go shoot a movie." Barbara remembers she and Bob thinking, "Is this a dream?" "Dinah came running into the house and said, 'oh, excuse me, I just need to hang a few more curtains.' We were both awestruck, Burt couldn't have been more wonderful. He was great." **"Burt was my patron and my friend. He offered to let us stay there [in his home]. This was not an isolated act on his part. He was always helping people, always putting people in the business and always putting his friends to work and for that he is above the rest. I don't know of anybody who has done that quite the way he has."** Bob and Barbara lived at Burt's house for a while before he got his first role.

"In my early days in Hollywood, I felt a little like George O'Leary, the coach at Georgia Tech who embellished his resume, got hired as the football coach at Notre Dame, and when they found out, they fired him."

Bob made up his resume too. What else could he do? It was a classic *Catch 22* situation: You can't get a job if you haven't worked. If you haven't worked, you don't have a resume. It all began for Bob, falsifying or if you prefer 'embellishing' his resume when he began banging around Chicago looking for acting jobs, as he explains in his journal.

"I made up this resume of all the parts I knew I *could* have done. I'd done one little production in a workshop or I'd done a scene from *The Crucible*. I'd make up little parts I'd played at the *Paper Mill Playhouse* in Des Moines–that kind of stuff. Nobody would check, nobody even knew these theaters existed except little small-town producers who knew all those venues."

Bob's first TV roles

"When I would get a legitimate credit–say, when I did *Father of the Bride* with Don Ameche and David Hasselhoff. I'd put that at the top and I'd scratch the imaginary *Music Man* off the bottom. It was like a chain letter."

Agent Dick Clayton took Bob around to the studios, introducing him to people. Bob got to meet a lot of TV producers through him, but not much in the way of movies.

"I started getting small parts–very small parts. Bad-kid roles. My first TV role was in 1972, on *The FBI* [episode: The Runner] **I had five lines. I played a guy** [David Stroud] **who gets knocked out with one punch by David Soul. A year later we were both testing for the same lead in a series. That is how fast things can happen. It may have been *Vega$* actually.**[1] Bob was quite active in 1973, appearing first in *Marcus Welby M.D.* appearing as Mike Lowry in the episode *Death is only a Side Effect*, and in *Owen Marshall: Counsel of Law* as Gavin Cord in the episode *A Girl Named Tham.*

"In *Kung Fu*, I played a leader of a gang [Greg Dundee] **responsible for the murder of Chinese rail workers. The theme of the episode was racism. The town elite think we're going to get away with it. I stand trial and they think I'm going to get off–instead I break down on the stand and confess and cry and get sentenced."**

***

Rounding out 1973 came *Bob and Carol and Ted and Alice.* Bob was excited to be cast in a new television series which was based on what had been a very successful movie. **"Ann Archer was Carol, Anita Gillette played Alice, David Speilberg was Ted and I played Bob. They made it into a series and took all the teeth out of it."**

Bob and Carol, Ted and Alice

"When I was twenty-five, I described it as a turkey. Now, I'd probably say, the Producers' failure to commit to it fully condemned it to mediocrity." The opening episode of *Bob & Carol, Ted and Alice* had them swimming naked.

---

1 *Vega$* Producer Duke Vincent says, to the best of his knowledge David Soul never auditioned for *Vega$*. However, Bob's long-time friend, Tom Selleck did. Read more about it in Chapter 17, *Vega$*, Bob's Wheel of Fortune.

"We were actually going to get nude in a pool on a sound stage at Warner Bros. on the Columbia set. It was supposed to be a big secret, but as I pulled into the studio that morning, even the guard at the gate knew about it. 'So, you're gonna get naked today, huh Bob?' They all knew. I went onto the set and there were bleachers set up so that the network [ABC] **and everybody else could watch."**

Leo Penn[1] was directing the pilot. They had a heated tank on the old Paul Lynde set and a real kidney shaped swimming pool. In the episode, after dinner the foursome is supposed to slip out of their bathrobes and go swimming naked. **"The time comes and there's a lot of nervous clicking of dishes and laughing conversation, and then Ted is the one who really wants to go skinny-dipping, says, 'Ok, it's time.' I start to peel off my bathrobe and I hear this noise. I say, 'What is that humming sound?' From the top of the rafters, one of the gaffers, who didn't realize we were rolling yet, shouts down, 'It's the pump. We're trying to keep the water warm for you guys.' Leo Penn said, 'Cut. Cut.' He came over to me and shook my hand. 'Bob,' he said, 'that gaffer just paid you the highest compliment that any actor can be paid.' It was actually a line from the script, my first line, in fact. We all wound up in the swimming pool, but you didn't actually have nudity on TV of course [back then]"**

Bob and Barbara move on

"You saw a little tush, but this was just the beginning. ABC cropped out anythingand everything that was even remotely controversial. They shied away from all the issues–which was what the series was going to be all about; free love and sexuality.

It didn't happen." "The first night we were up against ferocious competition...*Sonny & Cher* [a top-ten rated show on CBS] **and *Adam 12*–which was a big hit on NBC."** A new show thrown into the middle of two established shows is almost a kiss of death, and is difficult to survive. It's tough even today to be a hit when you are up against established shows that have been on the air for a while and have developed an audience. **"It's**

---

1 Leo Penn was an actor, but decades on Hollywood's black-list in the 40s and 50s had stalled his career and eventually led him to direct, primarily in television. He directed over 400 hours in prime time TV, including *Ben Casey, Police Story, Kojak, Matlock* and *St. Elsewhere*. Leo is the father of actors Sean and Chris Penn. He passed away in September 1998.

tough to launch into a new time slot. We did 12 episodes and then they cancelled the show."

In the meantime, Burt came back from doing the movies and Bob and Barbara moved out. "We couldn't stay in Burt's house all the time," says Barbara. "We moved into a one bedroom apartment in the marina. We were just unloading all our stuff trying to get settled in when my agent calls and says, "You got the job with Sheraton. You've got to be in Tokyo on Monday, so start packing honey." Earlier, Barbara had auditioned for the role with the advertising agency [BBDO] They had screened everyone to be the voiceand image for the Sheraton Hotel Corporation's new Ad campaign, "Follow Me," implying wherever you go, you'll find a Sheraton. "It was a fabulous deal," she says. "Afive-year contract to do all their commercials, radio, print, everything. They picked mebecause I was a new face. I couldn't pass it up, you know what I mean, but it was so unfair to him [Bob]." At the time, the couple had been married for about a year and a half.

Newlyweds were separated...a lot

"Bob was very supportive," she says, "and never said, 'don't do this,' but it [my job] wasn't good for his ego." After Japan, Barbara flew to Germany and just about every other place in the world. "He [Bob] went back to acting classes and I was jumping around, all over the place." The newlyweds found themselves separated a lot. Long-distance relationships are never easy, and Bob and Barbara's was no exception.

"It just wasn't fair to him. I just didn't know it was going to be so extensive, travel-wise,but it was a fabulous experience. It was wonderful for employment, and making money. Don't get me wrong. It isn't as glamorous as everyone thinks it is, and it was a lot of hard work, but I was also having the time of my life. Bob was working but not doing as well as he wanted to, but things started happening for him. It was crazy with all my traveling. Bob was very supportive," but she adds, "you can't nurture a relationship if you're not there. I wasn't gone the whole time, but it [traveling] took a toll on our relationship."

Barbara also says, when they were together he didn't talk to her a lot. She describes herself as 'a lifter-upper.' "I need somebody I can spring off and tell anything to and feel sheltered. My biggest fear," she readily admits, "is that I would become *Queen of the Hop*. I didn't want that, but it was hard not to believe your own 'stuff,' [publicity] because people were so wonderful."

"I remember, we had rented this house in the Hollywood Hills. It was all glass, really pretty. We were walking around the outside, trying to decide where we were going to put the flowers and the bushes. I said, 'what do you think about right here?' And, he said, 'my thoughts are my own.' I'm thinking, 'Oh, really. O.k., I'm just asking you about the flowers.'" Barbara says, "It really scared me."

"When I would ask Bob, 'what's wrong?' he'd say, 'Nothing's wrong! Nothing's wrong. Why do you keep bringing that up?'" Barbara thinks it was because he got reprimanded all the time [when he was growing up]. "It was always a negative with a positive," she says. "It wasn't a positive with a positive. I'm not blaming him. It was just a different atmosphere than I was used to."

Heather Urich feels differently about being able to communicate with Bob. She says Bob always talked to her. "He loved to walk and talk. He wasn't the kind of guy to put headphones on and go for a run. He wanted to talk the whole time. We never had a problem communicating about anything."

Marital experts say 'communication' along with compatibility are important keys to a solid marriage. Evidently, what Bob didn't have with Barbara, including two-way communication, he found with Heather.[1]

***

"Barbara and I were living in Nichols Canyon at the time. She had been on one of her commercial tours to Rome, Spain, Hawaii–that makes for a very heady romantic atmosphere. By the time she got home from that tour, it was pretty much over. She told me she was leaving me. That same afternoon, they told me they were canceling *Bob & Carol, Ted & Alice.* It was rock bottom time."

Note: Sometimes, the passing of time can play tricks with our memory. In an e-mail from Barbara to the author, dated: January 20, 2015, regarding the length of her marriage to Bob, she wrote; "She and Robert married in 1968 and divorced in 1974."However, in 1968, Bob was studying

---

1 Anyone who observed the couple for more than a few minutes could see how crazy in love they were with each other. Bob and Heather Urich were happily married for 27 years until his passing in 2002.

for his Masters at Michigan State. He didn't move to Chicago until 1970, where he met Barbara in acting class and they later married.

The break-up of Bob's first marriage

Bob was devastated over the break-up of his marriage with Barbara. He thought it was his fault. He went to see a psychologist that some friends had recommended.

"It was the fastest cure on record. I walk in to the psychologist's office.

'So tell me what happened,' he asks me.

"I tell him Barbara left me.

" 'Well, would you say she left you because you were abusive?'

"No, I tell him, I wasn't. I was loving and devoted.

" 'Then she left you because you were crass and thoughtless.'

"Actually, I don't think you could say that either. I was never thoughtless...and rarely crass."

" 'Then she left you because you're a bad human being and not worthy of love.'

"No, of course that's not true."

" 'No? So none of it's true, so who knows why? She's got her agenda and you've got yours. Whenever you start feeling bad about stuff like this, just hold a trial and you can make up whatever you want to make up about what happened. Hold the trial. Find yourself guilty. Deal out the punishment and get on with your life.'"

"I went, WOW!! That was great.

"He said, 'I'll see you next week at two o'clock.'

"What for? First of all, I can't afford eighty bucks a pop to come here and number two, you've cured me."

Bob Urich & Ann Archer in their 1973 TV Series, Bob & Carol, Ted & Alice, *which was based on the popular movie of that time. Bob played Bob and Ann was Carol.*

Chapter 13

Tim Matheson
Bob's film debut - Magnum Force
Bob meets the love of his life
and, in turn
Heather Menzies meets her shining knight

Bob meets Tim Matheson

[**Bold-typed words are Bob's –taken directly from his personal journal.**]

Tim Matheson [phone interview with author: Sat. 11a.m. MT 10-29-16].

Tim Matheson says the first time he met Bob Urich was in 1973. "It was on the set of Clint Eastwood's blockbuster film, *Magnum Force.*[1] Bob was the one guy on the film who was nice to me of the four of us who played rogue motor-cycle cops in the film." Urich neglected to tell the producers he had no previous experience riding a motorcycle. "I lied," says Bob. "When I went down the ramp, I was supposed to peel off but I ran over the others, just knocked em all down. Clint stood there and laughed." Neither Bob nor the bikes were seriously injured.

During filming in San Francisco, Matheson says, "Bob and I hung out a little. It was a pretty quick shoot. Clint couldn't have been nicer to us and was so cordial. But, as I recall, we didn't have a lot of scenes together. On day one, we had the shooting range scene together, it was an interior shot with Clint. I think that was one of the few times we were all together in a scene. There were doubles and David [Soul] had his scenes with Clint,

1 In the 1973 Warner Bros. block-buster movie, *Magnum Force*, Bob and Tim were cast as sharp-shooting, raw, young renegade cops. Tim played Phil Sweet, Bob was Mike Grimes, the role marked Urich's feature-film debut. Let's be honest, If you had to hand-pick a film and a movie-star to make your film debut, you couldn't ask for more than to be cast in a Clint Eastwood flick. Rounding out the four vigilante cops were David Soul as John Davis and Kip Niven as Alan 'Red' Astrachen. By the way, astrachen is a popular variety of apple grown in Central California.

but we really didn't have much to do in that regard. The funny thing about the hotel which, I believe, was at the corner of Lombard and Van Ness, is they used it as a staging area for some of the vehicles in the movie. This one car was a pimp mobile, which we 'allegedly' as vigilante cops shot this pimp to death in it. It was a white Cadillac with a furry interior, and after the scene, it was covered in blood, all over the car, on the outside and inside. And, the funny part is, they parked it in the hotel parking lot, (laughing)! I often wondered what guests of the hotel thought when they walked outside and saw this friggin car with blood stains all over it."

"After working on the film, I came back home," recalls Matheson. "That's when I received a call from Bob. During that time, I had purchased a one-acre piece of property in the Hollywood Hills. It was a main house with a guest house. The main house was divided into two apartments, an upstairs and downstairs, but for privacy they were not connected. I couldn't afford to live in the main house," Matheson adds, laughing, "so I lived in the guest house which looked like an English-style cottage. Besides, it was cheaper, and the main house had tenants which I inherited when I bought the place in 1972."

"In 1974, Bob was going through a divorce [from first wife Barbara Rucker]," Matheson says, "and was looking for a place to rent. He had been living in a little apartment up in Nichols Canyon, was getting ready to move out, and needed a place."Do you know of a place?" Bob asked. "Coincidentally," Tim replied, "the people who were staying [in the downstairs of my main house] have given notice. Now, I don't know if it's a place you'd like, or be good for you, but if you need a place right now, you can move in on an interim basis. Bob came over looked at it and liked it. It was a really cutelittle place."

For a period of time Bob lived there alone. It was a really cute little place. **"I guess it's as close as I ever came to that Thomas Kincade cottage I've always coveted. For a period of time, almost a year, I lived there alone. I spent that year trying to get a job and reading every self-help book imaginable, everything from Erich Fromm's *The Art of Loving* to *I'm OK, You're* OK to the reports from Esalen. I read all of Joseph Campbell."[1]**

---

1 Joseph Campbell [3-26 1904-10-30-198] author of *The Power of the Myth* was an American writer, Mythologist and lecturer.

Bob Meets Heather

What came out of all this for Bob is something he describes as his three principles. **"My three principles are…first, you have to get your personal life in order. Then you have to get your creative life focused and only then, take care of business. I think those three dynamics still work concurrently with each other. If any of them are out of phase, the other two suffer."**

***

Bob writes in his journal that Tim Matheson always seemed to have his nose to the pavement. "He knew what was going on in town." Bob, on the other hand, admits that he never knew what was happening.

"One day Tim came over and tells me about an upcoming commercial audition and showed me the latest *Playboy*. In the magazine was a pictorial: "Whatever Happened to those Girls in *Sound of Music*?" There is a three-page spread on Heather–nude pictures, but a very seventies version. There was always something covered up."

Actually, the first time Bob and Heather saw each other was much earlier at Joni Darling's acting class. An actor friend of theirs introduced them in a hallway. She was on her way to the restroom and it was one of those passing greeting kind of things, like, "Hi, how are you?"

"At that point, I was single. I couldn't get pretty girls to even say 'hello' to me. I went to the audition and the room is abuzz. All the guys are buzzing, because it's *her*. There was Heather at the cattle call." The Playboy article had just come out and they're all talking about her and she's obviously feeling the heat. Bob saw how they were pairing up couples for the audition and quickly sprung into action.

Bob's Take on Meeting Heather

"I said to the guy in front of me, 'Do you mind if I go ahead of you?' 'No,' he said, 'That's fine with me.' It didn't even occur to him what I had in mind. They began pairing up the couples and when it came to my turn I got paired up with Heather to go to the reading. Now the guy with whom I'd switched places twigged. 'Wait a second,' he said. 'She was meant to go with me.' 'No, I don't think so,' I said, 'I think they've already paired us up. Sorry.'"

Bob was delighted, but Heather–always skeptical of other actors of the male species–looked at him like he had three heads. Later, she admitted, "at that point, the last thing I needed in my life was another chiseled-jaw actor."

"I pretended that I had no idea who she was or about any *Playboy* pictorial. We went into the audition together and got called back. We got the parts. They were of a young couple getting married. It was a commercial for Libby's *on the table, table, table*–corned beef hash. The couple gets married and there is this huge wedding down on Wilshire Boulevard in a big Presbyterian church."

In the commercial, the first day they're married, the bride makes the groom corned-beef hash. The viewer sees it frying up on the stove. The marriage begins to disintegrate when he notices she's making him 'hash' for dinner. Then she shows him it's *Libby's* corned beef and how it browns up *soooo* nicely in the pan and that makes everything okay! Apparently, Bob as the groom is a brand-name kinda guy.

"They shoot the wedding sequence and they're throwing rice and there's '*Just Married*' on the back of the limo as we drive away. Heather is in a wedding gown and I'm in a tuxedo. I said, While we're dressed like this, why waste it? "Why don't we get married and have a great party? And, her exact words were, 'Drop dead!' She must have thought, what a line!"

Heather later admitted, she had been going through a period where she didn't want anything to do with actors.

"She had this wall up. Don't talk to me. Don't look at me. Heather had been to a lot of auditions and was used to being hit on by actors with a smooth line of talk. She probably thought, here comes another jerk with a chiseled jaw who's full of himself. She thought I was one of those slick, conceited Hollywood actors when she met me. A guy on the make, and she was partially right. But about my being slick, mostly wrong. I've always been anything but. I play slick guys sometimes. I'm not even exactly sure what that means."

Actually, Bob always played guys who were sure of themselves. If women came on to Dan Tanna, he would just smile and put them off. The same thing with Spenser.

Heather's memory of meeting Bob

Los Angeles
April 10, 1974

Heather Menzies almost made it. Her hand was on the door handle of her little blue VW convertible. Fifteen more seconds and her life would have taken a completely different turn.

"We had been filming a commercial all day," she recalls. "A one-day shoot for Libby's corned beef hash." Later, she and Bob would joke, if the relationship didn't work out, we could say, "Libby's made hash out of our lives! We were playing a newly married couple. We got married in one scene, complete with rice being thrown and wedding bells bonging. We were standing, facing each other in front of a church on

Wilshire Blvd and Gayley Ave, waiting for the word, "action."

"Bob looked down at me and said, "As long as we're dressed like this why don't we go ahead and do it." I think I muttered the words, drop dead, or over my dead body or something to that affect," says Heather, while thinking, "another egotistical chiseled jaw in Hollywood...just what I *don't* need!"

Bob believes Heather misjudged him. "I was a virgin until I was 21," he says. "The first woman I ever slept with was my first wife."[1] At that time in her life, her guard was up when it came to men, particularly good looking Hollywood-actors. She had recently been divorced[2] from one of those acting types and did not want to go down that road.

Heather had actually met Bob once before. "Occasionally," she says, "I would drop in on an acting class that Joan Darling taught over on Melrose Ave in L.A. I was on my way outside during a break. My friend, David Hayward was in the hallway talking to someone. As I passed, he said, 'Heather, meet Bob Urich. Bob this is Heather Menzies,'

I said, 'nice to meet you,' and continued on my way. Funny, David never remembered the exchange. Years later, Bob and Heather not only remember it, but what each other was wearing, where they were standing, what the light was like...*everything*!

---

1 Source: an October 23, 1978 *People* article with Sue Reilly.

2 Heather's first marriage was to Tom Cluett, an acting student at the time, whom she met through a friend, actor, Michael Douglas. She was twenty at the time and says, "Tom was a brilliant guitarist but his family was well-off and he had little ambition and wasn't motivated in life." Heather was the total opposite. They married, December 21, 1969 and divorced four years later in 1973, but remained good friends.

April 1974 - Heather remembers Libby's commercial audition

Heather recalls that she and Bob read together at the first commercial audition for Libby's, but at the call back, she was scheduled to read with another actor. "They often did that," she says. "It is common practice at auditions to see who looks best with whom."

"All of a sudden, I noticed things switched and I was back reading with this Robert Urich guy!" Years later, Bob admitted to Heather that he asked the guy to switch. He made up a story that he had to attend another audition and time was tight. After the first audition, when Bob returned home, he was greeted by his friend, neighbor and landlord, Tim Matheson. Tim owned two houses, next door to one another, at the top of Ellington Drive in the Hollywood Hills. He lived in one and rented the other to Bob.

"So, who did you read with at the audition?" Tim asked.

"Heather Menzies," Bob replied.

"Oh, I know Heather. I've worked with her," Tim says, smiling. "Come over here. I want to show you something." He pulled out a copy of *Playboy* that featured an 'expose' on Heather which had been published a few months earlier. "Oh, so that's Heather," Bob exclaimed, beaming brightly. He went back to the second audition on a mission!

"At the end of the one-day shoot, I was tired and looking forward to heading home," Heather says. "I also wasn't sure about this chiseled jaw guy with the dry wit," she admits. "All the ladies on the set were swooning over him all day long. He was in true form. I made it out to the parking lot, my hand on the door handle, when behind me, I hear, 'Wait a minute, slow down. I just want to talk to you.' I stopped and turned around.

"There, standing in front of me appeared to be a completely different person than the one I had been working with all day. The smart aleck had disappeared. He even looked a little bit vulnerable. He was wearing exactly what he had been wearing in the hallway that day at acting class. A blue shirt, sleeves rolled up, glasses on his nose and impossibly handsome."

Bob writes in his journal that he felt Heather was "running away from something."

"Perhaps I was," she says, recalling that momentous time in her life.

"But, Bob reached out and stopped me. Life, as I knew it, changed in an instant."

***

Now that Heather's planned escape in her blue VW had been foiled by young Mr.Urich, he asked her to go out with him. "I couldn't see Bob that night. I had a date, so we made plans to meet the next day."

"A friend of mine [Spencer Milligan] was going sailing and I invited her along. She said, Okay." Heather thought, "Well, that's during the day and if it doesn't go well, I can excuse myself that evening. Bob picked me up on the Saturday morning and off we went to Marina Del Rey. **"I picked her up at her house and I knew this guy had stayed the night. We spent the day and evening together and ended up going to the movies."** Our memories can play tricks on us. Here's Heather take on their first date.

"We sailed all day, picnicked at sea with Spencer[1] and his then girlfriend. At the end of the day we went off to Benihana's for dinner. Bob and I were strangely quiet with each other all day. But there was an undercurrent of comfort."

Bob remembers the day a little differently.

"She didn't speak two words to me the whole day. Totally silent through the whole day and into the evening."

So much for depending on the accuracy of our memory cells.

One thing Bob and Heather both agreed on...after their initial date they were seldom apart. **"After that** [their initial date] **I may have spent a night or two in my own place by myself. She did the same. But, after that, we were together all the time."**

Bob and Heather get together

"After that first day, we were very seldom apart," she says. **"We've been together ever since.[2] One of the things that apparently impressed her [Heather] about me was that I didn't have to constantly talk.[3] I wasn't continually selling some kind of line of goods to her. She was thinking,**

---

1 Later, Spencer played Heather's big brother in the TV movie, *The Keegans* which was released May 3, 1976.

2 Bob's wrote these words in his journal before his passing in 2002.

3 During Bob's lst marriage to Barbara Rucker, she mentions, he [quote] "did not talk to her."

he's so powerful and sure of himself that he doesn't always have to be talking. Meanwhile, I'm thinking, boy am I boring!"

Heather had put some money away and had planned to take a trip to Europe. She was going through a period in her life where she wanted to take off, and back-pack throughEurope, staying in hostels. "I planned to fly to Scotland to see my family and then hitchhike around Europe, sleeping in Hostels. I would stay as long as my money lasted," she says. "My airline ticket was purchased and I was leaving in less than a month."

Bob writes, **"The last thing she wanted to do was get involved with an actor. She wanted to get as far away from Hollywood as she could. She was twenty-three years old, and that's what you do when you're twenty-three. You want freedom, possibility, open-endedness. I was a little daunted."**

"One day, Bob turned to me, and asked if I was really going to go. I said, 'Yes. Do you want to go with me?'"

"Um," I said, "I have no reason why I can't go, too. Why not?"

"We paid the utility bill and took off."

"Now this is a guy who always had a plan," Heather says, smiling. "Even when he said he didn't have a plan... he had a plan. So, his response was very much out of character.

So, off we went to *fall in love* in Europe."

Bob and Heather Fall in love

Their friends thought they were crazy. The young lovers had only known each other for a few weeks and here they were jetting off to Europe together. "Of course, hitchhiking and hostels were out now," she says, laughing. "After all, Bob had an American Express card! So we rented a car and stayed in B&B's. **"We lived on my American Express card until we ran out of money. About three weeks."**

"We made our way from the Isle of Sky all the way down to Paris," remembers Heather. "We stayed at the Le Bon Hotel on the Left Bank. We were on the top floor of this small very quaint dwelling. It had one of those creaky cage elevators operated by a young girl with red lipstick and a cigarette constantly dangling out of her mouth. She looked like an extra from a 1940's Bogie and Bacall movie who was sent directly over from central casting! "The wall paper of the room was dark maroon and flocked. The louvered windows opened to a spectacular view of the Eiffel

Tower. Bob read poetry to me while I bathed in the antique bathtub complete with its ornate legs."

Fondly looking back, Heather says, "I think that room is where two souls became one and we knew at that moment we would be living our lives as one."

One day, following their return from their European junket, Heather came over to visit Bob. **"I asked her, should we go feed your cat, Smudge or stay here and feed my dog Mimsy?"**[1] **"Maybe we should *go get* my cat," she said.**

So they went and got the cat and she and her cat moved in with Bob and his lil doggie.

Bob and Heather's little cottage

"It was a tiny place, up in the Hollywood Hills, but we loved being there. It looked like the Snow White and the Seven Dwarfs cottage."

"It was rather quaint and it stood right behind the Hollywood Bowl. At night, Heather and I could hear the music from the bowl wafting over the hill. We'd sit on our back porch and listen."

"We loved that little cottage," Heather recalls wistfully. "Some of our happiest times were spent there. Bob, Tim and I were struggling actors back then. Some days we had work, other times, nothing. That's just the way it was. We didn't care, we were young and having fun! Whenever anything broke down, Tim would always gather up his toolbox and come over to fix it. Handyman? No way. Appliance guy? Forget it!," she laughs, "but he gave it his best shot. We prayed for an audition or two that might lead to work." Bob would pass the time trying to convince himself that one day he would be a working actor.

"I would say, well, one thing I know for sure, I'm going to work in August." Then he'd say... **"I'll surely get a reading for a part in August. In September,** [he'd tell himself] **"when the season gets going, they'll have to be casting. I know I'll get it. And, of course, nothing. It went on month after month. So, I would entertain myself with the thought**

---

1 Mimsy was part Chihuahua and beagle and was named after a line in Alice in Wonderland & Jabberwocky. Smudge was an all-white cat with a black spot on his forehead.

of being a writer or writing a screen play,[1] which I did." To counter his daydreaming, or 'blue-skying it' as he would say, Bob grew a huge vegetable garden. Heather remembers that special spot really well. "There was a little flat spot up the hill out back of the cottage and that's where Bob had his garden. He had asked Tim Matheson, who was our landlord, if he could renovate the spot."

"I had nothing else to do, so I would go up there in the morning as if it were a full-time job and I would chop and rake and dig, before I started planting."

Bob's Garden

Bob chopped brush and cleared away the over-growth of weeds and vines that had been there for well over fifty years. One morning, while clearing and digging around he discovered that underneath all that brush and vines was a foundation for an old wall. **"It was like an archaeological dig, I learned it was a garden an ole German guy had created. There were fruit and berry trees and rows of perennials coming up and it had all been covered over. In the end I had this spectacular little garden. We lived off the vegetables from that garden. Every day, we would go up and see what was ready. Beans, zucchini and tomatoes. We even planted corn."** Their other unemployed acting friends would come over for dinner. **"Stuffed Zucchini again?" they'd sigh. "Well now listen, I'd say, I could probably stuff it with something new. How about bringing a pound of hamburger?"** "That garden sustained us during many an actor's slow time. Bob loved getting his hands dirty," smiling, as Heather remembers how he enjoyed growing green beans, squash, and tomatoes. "Is there anything tastier thana fresh tomato right out of the garden," she asks, smacking her lips. "He'd spend the entire day up there with a hoe." Quickly adding, "That's hoe, as in a farming tool!" To pass the time, Bob and Heather played the soliloquy game. **"We'd stand on this old broken down picnic table in the shade of a tree–one of us would stand on the table and recite one of Shakespeare's soliloquies. While reciting one would squirt the other with the garden hose. The objective of the game was to get through the soliloquy without laughing or crying. Sometimes both**

---

1 The screenplay was entitled "*Screen Door Summer.*" It was all about Bob's adventures growing up in the 1950's & 60s, some of which took place at his beloved safe sanctuary, West Lake in Canada, which is covered in detail in Chapter 25.

took place. Because in those days, it was hard struggling and trying to make it in town and the ritual with the hose was a metaphor for that. It made the struggle a little easier. A little more bearable."

Their little cottage in the Hollywood Hills

"My property in the Hollywood Hills went through all sort of permutations,"Tim Matheson explains. "I bought 3 ½ acres next door to it, sub-divided, sold pieces off, but I always kept the little cottage that I lived in. I rented it out at times, and I also used it as a small place for me to stay when I was working in L.A. My marriage ended to Megan Murphy [divorced in 2012] about five years ago, and what do I do? I bounce back to L.A. and land in the cottage that I lived in back in 1973! I'm actually in the planning stages of building a larger house in the area where Bob had his garden. The new main house will be right next door to the guest house. I'll always keep that place. The little house is in a very special area. The woman I married, Jennifer Leak, who was in *Yours, Mine and Ours+* with me, had lived in the place and that's how I found it." "One day back then, says Matheson, "I was talking to the owner of the place and he said, "well, I'm going to sell it. And, I said, well, I'll buy it. I took it off his hands, and that was 45 years ago back in 1971-72.'"

"Bob liked the place, too," says Tim. "I remember the day he moved in. I was helping him. There were moving trucks. I filled my car up, and his car up. He and Heather were not together then, as his marriage to Barbara was breaking up. I never met her and don't even remember who Barbara was…I never made her acquaintance. But, as I recall, it seemed [the break-up] to happen fast. Boom it was over, and he jumped over here and into this place," recalls Matheson. "In 1975, Bob met Heather and she moved in with him."

During their time living in the little Hobbit type cottage Bob and Heather had very little money, but they didn't care. Acting jobs were rare and very few came their way, but they were still doing what they loved to do, pursuing an acting career, and they were having fun while moving in that direction.

Acting classes and relaxing

They spent their days going to auditions and attending Milton Katselas'[1] acting class two nights a week at the Beverly Hills Playhouse. Acting class was a family atmosphere."We were always rehearsing scenes with one another," Heather reminisces. "We would perform them on-stage for Milton's critique. Every once in a while, one of us would land a job and there would be cause for celebration. We socialized with our classmates, and would cheer each other on when one of us landed an acting assignment. A lot of great talent and success came out of that class," she proudly boasts. "Cheryl and David Ladd, Tom Selleck, Bruce Boxleitner, Catherine Bach, Patrick Swayze. Ann Archer met her future husband Terry Jastrow in that class."

***

On Friday nights, Bob and Heather would relax by occasionally sharing a joint. The love birds were no different than millions of Americans in the 1970s who gave pot a try, at least once. Plain and simply stated, most people who smoke 'weed' claim they do so, because, "it makes them feel good." Regular users of cannabis have repeatedly stated, it puts them in a state of euphoria, feeling happy and to let all one's troubles go.[2]

Researchers say, cannabis modifies how the brain perceives, retrieves, organizes and stores sensory information, whether the information is a song melody, an association stored in one's memory bank, or a pain signal from a pinched nerve. The function ability of this modification is how our brain works and is often considered of value to the cannabis user.

Cannabis

Cannabis, or 'Pot' as it is more commonly referred to also reportedly contains substances that mimic those naturally produced in the human body which are responsible for the regulation of pain threshold, appetite, memory and metabolism. It wasn't until recent years that cannabis was

1 Milton Katselas was born in Pittsburgh on December 22, 1933. He was a director, producer and famous Hollywood acting coach and instructor. He openly challenged his acting students to face their own weaknesses and problems so that they could better face those of the people they played. He said, "it was important for the butcher to be able to watch a performance of a butcher on stage and say, "that's how I do it!" Milton Katselas was 75 when he died of a heart attack on October 24, 2008.

2 These finding do not in any way suggest the endorsement or the use of cannabis by the author or publisher.

prescribed to patients suffering from chronic pain. Physicians have discovered that cannabis is a remarkable plant and is worthy of further study for medicine and more.

Dr. Sebastian Marincolo authored a book *High: Insights on Marijuana* which examines the use of cannabis through the lenses of evolutionary psychology. Some medical benefits of cannabis include stimulating appetite and reliving nausea in cancer patients. During Bob Urich's[1] radiation and chemo treatments, he would 'occasionally' smoke cannabis to relieve nauseousness.

Marijuana is also known to relieve the symptoms of Multiple Sclerosis, glaucoma, and PTS [Post Traumatic Stress] Syndrome.

Sundays with Strother Martin

On Sundays, Bob and Heather would sometimes head out to Strother Martin's[2] house on Lake Malibu. You may recall, Strother was famous for the line in *Cool Hand Luke*, "What we have here is a failure to communicate."

"Strother played my father," says Heather, "in the film *Ssssshhh* and kind of took on the role in real life. Strother and his wife, Helen had open house on Sundays and you never knew who was going to show up."

"Strother adored Bob, so sometimes it was just us. Once Jason Robards showed up... just imagine, an afternoon shooting the breeze with Jason Robards! Strother Martin knew everyone!"

***

Tim Matheson recalls 1975 as the year Bob's career took off. He had done his first series, *Bob & Carol, Ted & Alice* in 1973, followed by an episode of TV's *Marcus Welby*; a film, *Killdozer*, a pilot for Jack Webb, *The Specialists*,[3] along with guest starring on *Gunsmoke* as Manolo, the son

---

1 When Bob was undergoing treatment for cancer, the subject of smoking pot to relieve his pain came up. "Not without me," his wife Heather insisted, laughing.

2 Strother Martin was a popular character actor, best known for his role in *Cool Hand Luke* starring Paul Newman. He also co-starred in 6 of John Wayne's films. 3 days before his death on August 1, 1980 from a heart attack, he said, "no man can achieve immortality. We don't live for what comes after we are dead, but for what we can achieve in this life. It's the only chance we have."

3 In the pilot, *The Specialist* was the only time in his 30 year acting career that Robert Urich was credited using another name other than his own. Producer, Jack Webb felt Urich was too ethnic sounding and convinced Bob, who was playing Dr. William Nugent, to use the name Robert York.

of a Sheepherder. Heather remembers Bob's role quite vividly. "EVERY SINGLE night before each day of filming that Gunsmoke episode, I put Bob's hair up in pin curls, so it would nice and curly in the morning for the character he portrayed."

1975 was the big break-out year for Robert Urich. Bob's career was in high gear thanks to Aaron Spelling and his TV series, *S.W.A.T.* Bob landed the role of Officer Jim Sweet. "Yes, fortune struck and Bob got a series!!" gushes Heather. "We could actually buy vegetables in the super market for a while."

It was Urich's pal and mentor, Burt Reynolds, who convinced Aaron Spelling, the series executive producer, to allow Bob to audition for the part in *S.W.A.T.* Spelling was impressed with Urich's reading and cast the strapping, good-looking 29-year-old. Bob exploded on the screen as one of the Viet Nam War veterans in a *Special Weapons and Tactics* squad led by Lt. Dan "Hondo" Harrelson, played by Steve Forrest, as they tackled dangerous criminals and violent situations. Other cast members included Rod Perry, Mark Shera and James Coleman.

S.W.A.T.

S.W.A.T. was a mid-season replacement which gathered high enough ratings to warrant a second season. However, complaints from anti-violence campaigners caused the series to be cancelled after 37 episodes.[1] Colin Farrell reprised the role in the movie version years later.

***

"Bob was one of those guys–not me, I wasn't one," says Matheson, "but Bob was going from one series to another. I looked at Bob as a role model. Funny, every time I looked out my window there'd be a big G.D. limo picking him up. I remember thinking, "someday, all those freakin' limos picking him up will be picking me up," he says, Laughing. "Bob was a big star and I was just knockin' around trying to make ends meet."Tim is actually being quite modest while singing the praises of his friend, Bob. It is true that Bob received top billing in *S.W.A.T.*, and not to down-play his success in any way, but nevertheless, it was only his 2nd 'starring' series. At the same time, [1975]Tim Matheson, already had seven series* under his

1 S.W.A.T was canceled in 1976 due to it's violent content. In re-runs today, 2017, the series seems milquetoast in comparison to other present day produced series of the same genre.

belt, including two very successful westerns, *Bonanza* during the 1972-73 season, in which Tim starred as Griff King in 15 episodes, and earlier from 1968-70, he co-starred in 24 episodes of *The Virginian* as Jim Horn. "Ya, but they weren't anything like the one's Bob was in," Tim chimes in, once again down-playing his own accomplishments. "Bob knew who he was. He wasn't competitive with me," says Tim, "And was always gracious and encouraging. He was just a regular Joe, who didn't have any of those mental illnesses that are so common among us actors."

Bob loved working in his garden!

Bob in TV pilot, The Specialist. *It was the only time in his 39 year acting career that he used a different name. At the Producer, Jack Webb's urging – who said Urich sounded "too ethnic"--- he used the name Robert York as Dr. William Nugent.*

Cast of TV Series S.W.A.T. *Bob U. standing on left with Steve Forrest in center, also pictured, Rod Perry, Mark Shera and James Coleman. Insert photo of series Producer Aaron Spelling.*

Chapter 14

Heather's Family *"Wedding Bells"*

Wedding Bells

[**Bold typed words are Bob's, taken directly from his journal.**]

Bob & Heather were living together in Tim Matheson's rental house, when Bob's mom and dad came to visit. **"That weekend was tense,"** Bob notes in his journal. **"I didn't know how to tell them what my situation was with Heather. Finally, I told them the night before when I met them at the plane. My father walked down the steps from the airplane. This was when they still had the steps down from the plane. The first thing he said was not, 'Great to see you son,' or 'great to be in California for the first time.'" What he said in his sophisticated way was, 'If she's good enough to live with, she's good enough to marry.'[1] Okay, I said, and that was that."**

Bob says he gave Heather a microscopic engagement ring. **"You'd have to use the Hubbell telescope to find the diamond. Where is that ring now? It's in the vault, probably, though I have a sneaking suspicion Heather hocked it."[2]**

***

Since, he was now making decent money, starring in *S.W.A.T.*, the couple asked themselves, "why should we continue renting? Let's buy a house!" They packed up and left their cozy English-style cottage for new 'digs' at 4911 Carpenter Avenue in North Hollywood. Today in 2017 that section of Los Angeles is known as Valley Village. "I recently drove past it," says Heather, "and other than a few changes, it still looks the same. If my position were different, I'd buy it back. I loved that place." "While we were in escrow [waiting to close]," Heather remembers, "we would drive

1 Bob gave the same advice to the author who had been living with a lady for 5 years. Not sure it was Bob's words or not, but they broke up. A few years later, Mar 1995, the author married Kim, the girl of his dreams.

2 Actually, Heather had the ring made into a necklace, which remained amongst her most precious mementoes.

over and park the car under a tree across the street and just stare at it, and ask ourselves, "What have we done? We've gone from paying $250 a month rent to Tim and now we have to come up with $500 a month in mortgage. How in the world are we going to pull this off?"

It was during the filming of his series *S.W.A.T.* that Bob asked Heather to marry him. "I was a guest in one of the episodes. One day, after the filming at 20th Century Fox, and on our way home, we stopped at a restaurant, *The Captain's Table* on La Cienega Blvd in Hollywood. He actually got down on his knee in the restaurant and asked me," she says.

Their friends thought they were crazy, that it would never work. "I was what was referred to in those days as a 'flower child,'" says Heather, laughing, "And he owned Brooks Brothers shirts. We came from diametrically different backgrounds. Bob's father, John Paul Urich was a tough 'shot and a beer' foreman at a steel mill in Toronto, Ohio. My father, George Scottie Menzies was a commercial artist, a wanderlust from Scotland, who painted landscapes and portraits. He finally took a job with an outdoor advertising agency so we would have food on the table. As a youngster, we lived in South Florida and we finally landed in Los Angeles where I pursued my dream of the theater. They said my dad had a problem with alcohol, but I never saw it," she says. "Mary, my mom, would tell me he was an alcoholic but I never personally witnessed it, so it never affected me. I'm not saying he was or wasn't an alcoholic, but my mother always told me he was. My mom was so anti-dad that I wasn't allowed to speak to him for a number of years. They both went through a lot during WWII. He fought with Scotland's 51st Highland Division." Heather's brother Neil adds, "Our dad's unit was used as a blocking diversion to stop the advancing Germans to allow other troops time to escape at Dunkirk. Most of the men in his company were either killed or captured. He was captured by the Nazi's at St. Valerie, France, marched into Germany and held a P.O.W. for five long years. He escaped a few times but was always recaptured. The longest he was free was 3 days. The difficult terrain made it impossible to get away."

Heather's parents

"My mother was in the ATS [Women's Army in London] during the blitz," says Heather. "She was a plotter. Her job was to track incoming German planes so Allied artillery could shoot them down before they dropped their bombs on the city. Mom claims she never missed one and I believe her. One bomb nearly killed her. She was at a theater, but the bomb destroyed the entrance, not where she was seated. My mother used to say, my dad sat with his feet up during the war, while she was out shooting down planes. In my eyes, they were both heroes. Following the war, her mom visited the POW camp in Germany where her husband had been held. It had been converted to a senior living center. She sent her husband a post-card of the place with the inscription, "Would you like me to make you a reservation?" Heather believes both her parents suffered from PTSD, "But nobody knew what it was called back then, or how to treat it. They didn't give everyone a play-book on how to get through it [the war]."

Heather's Mum

Heather admits, she and her mother had a strained relationship. "She was narcisstic and bi-polar back in the day before it was even diagnosed. To help prove my point," she says, "let me share a story about how I actually learned I got the role as Louisa in *The Sound of Music*, which involves my mother. They told me on a Friday, they would let me know the following Monday if I got the part. It's now Monday, school's out and I hadn't heard anything. I'm thinking, o.k., I didn't get it. I would have heard by now. My mom would have sent a note to the principal, and they would have notified me to call home. I walk home, consciously or not, careful not to step on any cracks on the sidewalk. I get home and I hear my mother splashing in the bathtub. I'm in the hallway with my forehead pressed against the bath-room door, and ask, 'mom, did I get it?'

"Through the closed door comes her reply. 'Heather, your sister has an interview in twenty minutes, for a commercial. Please go outside and get her and get her dressed.' I ask again, 'Mom, did I get it?' Her reply, 'We're running late, can you just go get her and get her dressed.' Again, I ask. 'Mom, did I get It?' 'Could you just go get her and get her dressed!' 'Mom, did I get it?' 'YES, honey, NOW will you go get your sister!' In that brief exchange, in that very moment, my life changed," says Heather. "I'm screaming and cheering because at that point I had a lot invested in the part. I kept getting called back, time and again, the uncertainty, the waiting. Even though I was only fourteen, I still wanted it. My mother had that information all afternoon! If it were me, I would have gone to the principal and said, you've got to pull her out of class to tell her the good news. I guess my mother didn't tell me because she was a bit of a narcissus. Guess she thought, o.k., she got it and that's that. Maybe, she didn't realize how much it meant to me, or maybe she didn't really care. It changed me. We went for a period of time, about four years, where we didn't speak. So, when people ask me, how did you find out you got the role in *The Sound of Music*, that's my story. I can tell it in such a way as to make it sound really cute, but looking back, it's not the tell-tale sign of a good thing. It caused some serious issues."

"It was Bob who actually helped me repair the relationship with my mom. One day he said to me, "You know Heather, you don't get to choose who your mother is. What you need to do and *what we're gonna do* is find a common ground. He set out to do that and he did. He helped repair the relationship to the extent that it could be repaired. We went over to her place on Sunday afternoons and had dinner and hung out. He ingratiated himself to her and like me, she loved and adored him."

"Bob helped me create that common ground, so at least I could be civil with my mom. Now that I'm older, I can look at it objectively and say, o.k. I'm gonna give her a get out of jail 'free' pass. She had a lot of reasons to be the way she was. It was difficult growing up with that. I had my work [acting] and if I didn't have that I don't know how I would have survived."

"My brother [Neil] and sister [Sheila] didn't survive. My brother is kind of emotionally scarred. He never left home. Father died of a heart attack in 1982, then mom died in 1987 of cancer. She was a smoker. My brother never left home, because he couldn't. My sister has always suffered from anxiety, extreme anxiety and I know where it came from. As a kid [teen years] I'm out there working with Robert Wise, Shirley Knight[1] and all these people giving me a purpose of self-worth and for me that was my salvation. I ran away from home when I was eighteen," she says. "I snuck out in the middle of the night.I had everything packed and hidden under my bed. I had a friend back his Chevy, you know the one with

---

1 Robert Wise was a legend in Hollywood for decades as a director and producer. He won numerous awards, including Academy Awards for best director for *West Side Story* and *The Sound of Music*.

Accomplished actress, Shirley Knight was a contract player at WB, appearing in TV series, like *Maverick, Sugarfoot* and *Cheyenne*. She also made more than 50 films, and won an Academy Award as best supporting actress in *Dark at the Top of the Stairs*. She is also a life-member of the Actor's Studio.

the open bed in the back, [El Camino?] into my driveway. I loaded it up and we were gone. That's the time when my mom didn't speak to me for probably about four years. She would do that. She would shun you. Half the time I didn't even know why I was being shunned. It first happened when I was six years old."

Bob was raised in one small town surrounded by family and friends. It was middle-class existence at its best. "As for me," Heather says," I never went to the same school more than two years in a row."

Wedding Day

"All my relatives stayed behind in Scotland, while my mother and father constantly sought greener pastures. While Bob was sweating it out on the football field at Florida State University, I was running all over the hills of Austria singing *Do Re Mi* with Julie Andrews and the Von Trapps."

"The living room of our house on Carpenter Avenue is where Bob and I got married November 21, 1975. What an unforgettable day," Heather sighs, "I was late for my own wedding." Smiling and shaking her head in amusement, she remembers, "we didn't have any furniture, so we rented chairs for people to sit on from Abby Rents,"as she thinks back to that special day. "We picked up bagels and cold cuts from Arts Deli, around the corner. My wedding dress was something I picked up during my lunch hour."

"The cast from *S.W.A.T.* was there, along with Strother and my family and of course, Milton [Katselas, acting coach]. Actor Chick Vennera was Bob's best man, and his first wife, Joanne DeVito, was my maid of honor.

"We had decided to get married on a Friday. We hadn't planned on me working that day. Hey, it's an actor's life," she says, "peaks and valleys, feast or famine."

Heather was in the middle of filming *The James Dean Story.* She played Dean's ollege girlfriend. The final scene of the day is where Steven McAttie[1] who played Dean, explodes in an angry tirade and beats her up. The wedding is set for 7:00 pm. It is now 5:00 pm.," Heather laments. "I'm in Santa Monica with no end in sight."

As Time Goes By

---

1 Actor Stephen McHattie of Scottish/Irish descent is from Antigonish, Nova Scotia Canada, home to St. Francis Xavier, a university the author attended. Proving once again, it is a small world after all.

Meanwhile, in the living room at 4911 Carpenter Avenue in North Hollywood, everything is set for their wedding. Just one slight problem. No Heather.

"A half hour goes by, no Heather. An hour and still no Heather. An hour and a halflate for her own wedding. The director of the show she was in had promised her she would be done by four-thirty." "I need to be out of here by four," she told him. "I'm getting married this afternoon." "Don't worry," he said. "No problem, we'll work around it."

Four-thirty came and went and there were still several scenes to go. Heather was eventually released around eight o'clock. "I drove like a maniac and flew in the back door, covered in fake bruises, which I had to wash off before joining Bob. Of course,the jokes had already started about me standing Bob up," she says, laughing. **"The whole room had been waiting for a couple of hours. Finally, when Heather came flying through the door, holding her script, her sweater tied around her shoulders, her hair flying, she looked like she had just gone ten rounds with Mike Tyson."** In the last scene they'd shot that day, she'd been beaten up. She was still wearing her make-up–busted lips, blood and bruises, puffy eyes. Her face was covered with

black and blue bruises. **"Oh, hello darling," I said, as she entered and introduced her. "This is the girl I'm going to marry. She is a bouncer down at the Kit Cat Club."** "It was the best party I've even been to," says Heather.

Marriage By-laws

Prior to exchanging their nuptials, Bob & Heather drew up a marriage contract of sorts. Actually, it was more like a code of conduct. "We wrote down these by-laws before we got married," she says. "We didn't call them rules." They each promised to follow them faithfully to keep their marriage intact.

"One by-law states, neither party could never bring up anything from the past and put that in the present situation. "That was a huge no, no," says Heather. They also agreed never to get up and walk away and leave the room and no slamming doors! "You had to sit there and discuss it, whatever the issue was at hand. Stay in the room until we came to a conclusion and worked it out. It was always very calm," she insists but adds,

"Of course, it got emotional, "but you can be emotional without yelling and screaming." Sound advice for every married couple.

"We miraculously managed to come up with the mortgage payments for our new home by booking commercials and a guest spot here and there," she recalls. "A friend from our acting class, Jonathan Axelrod, decided he didn't want any material possessions anymore and sold off everything he had. We bought all his hand-me-downs and furnished the house. We even had dishes to eat off!"

Trouble brewing in Paradise

Every marriage has its own intrinsic peaks and valleys. Heather says she and Bob only experienced one hiccup, as she calls it, in their marriage. "Bob was always so supportive of my pursuit as an actor. My career was going through a bit of a nose dive and my confidence was waning. Bob said, 'I'll help you with this.' He got me into Milton Kaselas'[1] class and that's when things started taking off for me. All of a sudden, I was making it and he wasn't. It was about a year and a half into our marriage when we faced a marital discord. I was doing *Logan's Run*, and taking home $2,000 an episode. Not exactly chicken feed for 1977. At the same time, Bob was out of work. He was experiencing one of those down periods, that all we actors go through. Now, keep in mind, prior to my work on *Logan's Run,* we had both been on the same wave-length, a couple of struggling actors trying to make it in Hollywood. We came into the partnership as equals, financially, career wise and every other wise. All of a sudden. I was 'making it' and he wasn't. That's a tough pill for anyone to swallow, especially, the male ego. The only time a problem occurred between us in our marriage was when I was making the money!"

"Bob had done stuff, like *Bob & Carol, Ted & Alice* and *SWAT* and then things shifted. He was up for the TV series, *Man From Atlantis* that Patrick Duffy ended up doing. Then he was up for a movie about Howard Hughes that Tommy Lee Jones wound-up doing. Bob was very frustrated! He seemed to be coming in second with everything and that doesn't pay the rent. You don't get a silver medal when you come in second in the game of life," she adds. "Nothing seemed to be breaking for him and he didn't like it one bit. It seemed like one thing after another. It was always

---

1 Milton Katselas was one of Hollywood's premier acting instructors and coaches. You can read more about the man in Chapter 15.

another case of *almost* for Bob. Here I was starring in *Logan's Run,"* says Heather, "and he was at home."

It was very difficult for Bob not to be the breadwinner. Call him old-fashioned, but nevertheless, that's the way it was and it did NOT set well with him. It didn't help matters that Gregory Harrison,[1] her co-star on *Logan's Run*,[2] was a handsome dude. Heather recalls one evening when Greg came over to their house to meet Bob and to go over some lines. After Greg left, Bob was standing in the kitchen and said, "I don't like it. He's far too good looking and he's far too smart."

Heather says, Bob looked at the situation emotionally, while she viewed it philosophically. "I know what acting [love scenes] is all about. It's called choreography." When you're working, and this is really important as an actor, she emphasizes, "you have to be in a situation where you can trust. I've been in situations where I didn't trust and that's really hard. It limits you in terms of what you will allow yourself *to do* and *to be*, and the places where you could go [in one's role]. You also have to trust your 'real life' partner and vice-a-versa. If you don't, there's a problem."

Now, having said that, Heather admits, "Bob wouldn't be human if he weren't a little jealous. Especially in a situation like the one I was involved in. Greg and I were in every scene, in every episode, working together fourteen hours a day." It's easy to see why in Bob's mind, Heather working side by side and so closely with Gregory Harrison on *Logan's Run* was a bad situation. "Now, I wouldn't be human," she says, "if I didn't get jealous, too. Let's face it. Bob was working with beautiful women, but I knew his heart and besides, acting is a job. But, she does acknowledge that "Bob really had a hard time with me going to work with Greg every day. Deep down inside, Greg knew that Bob didn't like him. And, complicating the situation, Bob wanted and needed to be the bread-winner. Here I was starring in a television series and bringing home the money. He was home trying to land acting jobs. Bob struggled with all that and I must admit," she says, "I resented that struggle and told him so. I'm the one getting up at 5 in the morning, so don't give me a hard time about it."

---

1 After *Logan's Run* ended, she and Harrison remained friends.

2 *Logan's Run*, the Sci-fi series based on the movie aired on CBS, September 1977 until January 1978. Gregory Harrison played Logan 5, a young man who chose to escape from the Domed City. Heather played Jessica 6, who escaped with him. She enjoyed her role and co-star Harrison became one of her long-time friends.

"In the middle of all that, like halfway through the run of *Logan's Run*," Bob got *SOAP* and *Tabitha*. He was doing two shows simultaneously."

Bob's a working actor again

"Bob was working again and it put the issue [the breadwinner dilemma] to rest. That'sthe only real hiccup or serious issue in our marriage that I can honestly recall," says Heather.

It wasn't long after that brief but dark period in their marital lives that lady luck shined down on them. Bob and Heather had three television series between them ALL at the same time. Heather was filming *Logan's Run* at MGM and Bob was running back and forth between two studios doing *Tabitha* with Lisa Hartman and *Soap* with Billy Crystal.

"Eventually, I got another part in a series, the role of talk show host [Paul Thurston] **in *Tabitha*, a kind of glib 'Ted Knight' type. I then wanted to try out for the lecherous tennis pro,** [Peter] **on *Soap*, but ABC wouldn't let me. They didn't want me in two of their shows at the same time. In the end, they didn't like the guy they'd cast in *Soap* and called me back and asked if I could squeeze them both in."**

So, on Mondays and Wednesdays, Bob would head to one studio for one show andTuesdays and Thursdays, he would go to another studio for the other.

"I would sneak away to do Soap–it was done in front of a 'live' studio audience.

At the same time, Heather was doing a show called *Logan's Run*."

"It was a crazy, busy time. Bob and I made an agreement between us never to book any public appearances or interviews on a weekend. Nothing to do with show business, at least as the song goes, *Never on Sundays*! Heather found herself missing the days when they were broke and living off their vegetable garden. "Before we got married," she says, thinking back in time, "we had no money. Zero money. We were growing vegetables out of the back yard of the place we were renting. We would go up there every night to see what veggies we could pull out to eat."

Bob and Heather's Early Marriage Days

"We were living in this little tiny Peter Rabbit of a house for $250 a month, trying to get work as actors, while going to Milton Katselas' class and being with that whole group of people we met in his class. It was an innocent time. When I look back on those days, when we were flat out broke, eating out of our garden, going to Milton's class and trying to shape out a living as actors in Hollywood with absolutely no 'back-up' plan, those times were really magical. I think the foundation of our relationship and marriage was based on those magical times."

Tabitha[1] was similar to *Bewitched* except it was about a little girl who possessed magic powers while growing up. It starred Lisa Hartman as Tabitha Stevens, the now-grown-up daughter of *Bewitched's* Darren and Samantha Stevens.

"*Tabitha* didn't last long. *Soap* did!"[2] I was relegated to the first thirteen episodes [*Soap*] and then I got killed off. Robert Mandan and Billy Crystal were in it. Billy was great to work with and later had his own talk and variety show.[3]

"When Billy had his own variety show,* he called me and said, 'Remember that funny thing we used to do, playing horns without horns. We'd make horn sounds with our mouths. Trumpets and coronets and saxophones? Well, I want you to come on the show and do the horns. What do you think we should do?'

I said, 'We get a whole orchestra of guys playing horns and we'll do an old-fashioned '30's love tryst between the singer and the band leader and the head horn player.' So, that's what we did. It was very silly.

None of the musicians had instruments, but we all had slobber bibs on."

Billy Crystal & Bob

Fifteen years following Bob's passing, Heather attended Billy Crystal's one man show, *700 Sundays on Broadway*, a highly entertaining autobiography. "They were in *SOAP* together," she says. "Bob did Billy's Variety Show, and in turn, Billy did Bob a favor by appearing as a guest on the pilot for Bob's proposed TV talk show.[4] "I went backstage to say hi, because Bob adored Billy. I gave him a hug, and kinda had to remind him

1 *Tabitha* aired on ABC-TV, September 10, 1977 - August 25, 1978.

2 *Soap* ran on ABC, September 13, 1977-April 20, 1981.

3 *The Billy Crystal Comedy Hour* had a brief run on NBC, January 30 through February 27, 1982, Saturday nights at ten.

4 Bob did a couple of episodes for a proposed daily television talk show. Guests, including, Billy Crystal were featured, Bob's brother Tom Urich was the announcer, there was an Orchestra and Bob even crooned a couple of songs. It would have been a perfect venue for warm, friendly, Bob. The pilot was never picked up by the networks, which is a shame, because viewers would have loved it. Read more in Ch. 27.

who I was, she says, laughing. It had been awhile. 'Oh my God!,' he said, 'Heather!' He hugged me and whispered in my ear, 'Bob had the goods.' Meaning, that he had everything it took to be a success, which he was. Heather proudly points out that Bob really could do it all. "He could act, sing, dance, do drama, comedy, action stuff. You name it. The man could do it and with relative ease. Not many people know that about Bob," she says with a smile. "Well, not until now and this book."

Bob & Heather's wedding day, Nov. 21, 1975. L-R, Heather's mom, Mary, Heather & Bob, Heather's sister Sheila, her brother Neil and their dad, George Menzies.

Heather Menzies swearing 'Menzies Tartan" at age 13, shortly before she auditioned and won the role of Louisa in the classic film Sound of Music.

CBS-TV photo: Courtesy Heather Menzies Urich

Heather in her TV Series, Logan's Run, *she played Jessica 6, pictured with her co-stars, Gregory Harrison and Randy Powell.*

TV Series, SOAP, *Bob starred in first season 1977, Bob Urich & Billy Crystal in background on right. Bob played Peter Campbell, Crystal was Jodie Dallas. In foreground is Richard Mulligan who played Burt Campbell.*

Bob as host of Christmas Special from The Grand Ole Opry, *Jan. 1981 on ABC-TV.*

Chapter 15

Bob', the Actor
His coaches, Joni Darling & Milton Katselas

"Acting is a melding of intellect and spirit, but basically, it ain't that tough. It's a no-brainer folks." Robert Urich, *TV Guide,* November 9, 1996

When he shall die, take him and cut him out in little stars, and he shall make the face of heaven so fine that all the world will be in love with night and pay no worship to the garish sun.

- Shakespeare's Romeo & Juliet

Bob's Acting Career

"Even when his acting career soared to great heights, Robert Urich kept his feet on the ground!"

To recap, Bob first got the acting bug while in high school and college, appearing in several plays. After graduating from Florida State University with a B.A. in Communications and speech and from Michigan State with an M.A. in broadcast research, Urich further developed his acting skills in community theater in Chicago. He was helped along the way by being fired from his sales position at WGN Radio. Moonlighting, in Bob's case, as an actor, was strictly against company policy. While in the Windy City, Bob studied acting under Ted Liss. His agent was Shirley Hamilton. Bob made his Chicago stage debut in Renee Taylor and Joseph Bologna's romantic comedy [his favorite acting genre] *Lovers and Other Strangers*. He appeared in other productions at the Ivanhoe, Arlington Park and Pheasant Run Theaters.

"His professionalism was 'exemplary'" said his life-long friend, Burt Reynolds. It was Reynolds who helped launch Bob's acting career in Chicago. In 1972, Urich co-starred as Burt's younger brother in a stage production of *The Rainmaker* and it was Reynolds who encouraged Bob to head to L.A., even letting him to stay at his home until he got settled. Burt also introduced Bob to his long-time agent, Dick Clayton who got

Bob his first TV first role on the *F.B.I.* Bob also picked up the role of a vigilante motorcycle cop in Clint Eastwood's feature film *Magnum Force.* Urich only had 5 lines, but was grateful for the opportunity to stand shoulder to shoulder with one of Hollywood's biggest stars. If you had to pick one star and action film to kick-off your big screen debut, you'd be hard pressed to find one bigger and better than Clint Eastwood's *Magnum Force.* In Hollywood, Bob and Heather studied acting under Joni Darling and Milton Katselas.

Dramatic Arts Instructor, Joni Darling

Boston born Joan 'Joni Darling' Kugell entered show business as an actress on the New York Theater scene in the 1960s. She became a fixture on television in the 70's with a starring role on *Owen Marshall: Counselor at Law.* Joni made the leap from acting to directing and quickly made history as one of the first and most successful directors in television. She was the first woman nominated for an Emmy for directing, four times, winning one. She was nominated two times for a Directors Guild of America Award, winning one. Highlights of her directing career include directing the memorable *Mary Tyler Moore Show* episode, "Chuckles Bites the Dust" and a classic *M*A*S*H* episode, "The Nurses," which *TV Guide* calls the greatest episode ever for the way the show portrayed women in a positive fashion.

"The Art of Expression"

Referring to herself as a Dramatic Arts instructor, Joni Darling was a natural when it came to mentoring talent. She believes one of the keys to great acting is 'honesty,' as she describes in an April 2014 interview with writer, John D'Amico. "I teach acting a lot," she says, "and one of the things I think is so fascinating about it is that you do need to find in the landscape of your own life experiences metaphorical experiences for the ones that the character goes through in the play. Then you have to kind of arrange them in order. They're all in you," she points out, "but they're not necessarily arranged in the same manner that they are inside the character. After you've done that, it really is all of you and your life experiences, but then you have to deliver it in the kind of style of the character. In other words, if it's somebody who's very quiet or if the character is very flamboyant, the same things are going on in the flamboyant person as the quiet person, but it's just the style of expression that changes." Bob Urich had honesty in his acting.

The son of a blue-collar steel-mill worker, in an interview in *Total TV*, Urich said his father instilled in him "the principle that nothing comes without hard work." That attitude came in handy for his role in the made for television film, *Captains Courageous* which was based on the Rudyard Kipling classic. In this 1996 version, Urich plays a staunch disciplinarian who transforms a spoiled brat of a youth into a mature young man. Bob says he based his role as Capt. Matt Troop on his own dad. "My father was a man of few words," he recalled. "During summer vacation from school, he made sure I got the dirtiest, toughest, filthiest jobs so that I wouldn't wind up in the mills someday. And it worked."

Urich strongly believed that the more you experience life, it only adds to what you can draw on as an actor, instead of just your acting ability or imagination.

Joni Darling first met Bob Urich through a friend, Bob Hamilton, who was a writer at Universal. "At the time," she recalls, "he was with his first wife [Barbara Rucker], also an actress, and they both came to my class. Bob and I hit it off immediately. He was definitely my type...an athlete and an actor. At that time, he was really talented, and worked very hard."

"My husband and I spent social time with him. He was subsequently divorced but I don't remember much about that. Bob and I would go sailing together and on one trip he told me that he thought he was getting pretty serious about a girl named Heather. I don't remember if she was in my class yet. I was introduced to her at one of Universal's [Studio's] many official functions, since I was on a Universal TV series at the time. We referred to those meetings as 'the ubiquitous universal shrimp.' I was thrilled that she [Heather] was the one Bob was interested in. She was and is such a nice person. Eventually, Heather came to my acting class So, I say, if you didn't get a job, you might get a mate," says Joni Darling with a laugh.

Heather Urich says, "Joni Darling was a huge influence in both Bob's life and mine."

Talent coach - Milton Katselas

Milton Katselas, like Joni Darling, was a great motivator of talent.

Bob and Heather Urich also took acting classes from Milton Katselas. Born in Pittsburgh, February 22, 1933, he died of heart failure on October 24, 2008. He was 24 when he began teaching acting in New York after observing a class that failed to impress him. "When I teach," he said in a 1998 interview in *Buzz* Magazine, "my job is to bring out whatever is possible. It's *not* my job to push the ejector seat on somebody's dreams."Milton Katselas was a talented acting teacher, writer and director. He was nominated for a Tony Award for directing the Broadway debut of *Butterflies Are Free*, and headed west for Hollywood to direct the 1972 film adaptation, and decided to stay. Milton showcased his talent as a teacher through the Beverly Hills Playhouse for over 20 years. His students included, Anne Archer, Alec Baldwin, Jim Carrey, David Cassidy, George Clooney, Tyne Daly, Ted Danson, Bruce Davidson, James Farentino, Michelle Pfeiffer, Kate Hudson, Cheryl Ladd, Mimi Rogers, Tom Selleck, Patrick Swayze, Chick Venerra, Barry Williams and hundreds of others, including Bob and Heather Urich.

"Bob was always so supportive of me and my desire to act," says Heather. "He actually got me into MiltonKatselas' class, telling me, 'If you get into Milton's class it will drop-kick your career into the end zone' and it did! Just getting involved with those people helped my career. My confidence was waning and I was going through a little bit of a nose dive."

Katselas is quoted saying, "When you're having motivation problems, don't say, 'come on I can do it.' It's better to say, 'don't flinch.'" He was a master when it came to inspiring actors to reach deep within themselves to find success. He had a common sense approach to acting and had a huge heart for actors, teaching them to respect oneself and not to get burned out by the industry. "He taught the importance of ethics," Heather says, "like showing up on time. I was surprised something like that needed to be taught. He also taught how to handle the business. How to be your own director, and to 'trust' yourself, because he believed most directors in television are traffic cops."

Heather says Bob was a good listener in Katselas' classes. "He was always very engaged and very vocal, especially early on. He would actually disagree with Milton but in a respectful way. Bob always added different perspectives on acting. On the other hand, Milton always had to draw me out, I was so shy."

"The thing I came away with most from Milton's class," says Heather, "was that I am captain of my own ship. And, to call auditions 'meetings.' As an actor, I have the right to decide if I want to work with these people, to make it an even playing field. Don't go to auditions with my hat in my hand." Many actors will tell you flat-out, auditions scare the living bananas out of them. Heather was always nervous before an audition, but thanksto Katselas' acting classes, she learned how to cope with the process and adds, "It was a well-learned lesson from his classes."

Michelle Pfeiffer was another Katselas student. Appearing on *Inside the Actors Studio*, she noted, "Milton taught actors to second-guess your first superficial choice in how a role should be played, which prepares actors so that you are a little director-proof."

Auditions can be scary

"Milton's classes also taught us how to handle auditions and not be nervous." Heather recalls. Bob, on the other hand, seemed to thrive on the audition process. His attitude was always, "give me the ball. I can do this." Once, Bob Clark [director of *A Christmas Story*] was interviewing for a role in *Turk 182*. Bob wanted it badly, but couldn't get through to the right people. "I'm going to New York," he told me. "I'll find out what hotel he's staying at, call him from the lobby and tell him I want to see him about the part!' Who does that?" Heather asks, laughing. Bob did and got the part of fire-fighter Terry Lynch.

The primary reason talent is so apprehensive about auditioning is fear of rejection. Let's look at it from the actor's perspective. They want the gig, and in turn, want the producers, or whomever is conducting the audition, to pick them. You want the job, or you wouldn't be auditioning in the first place. So, you put your heart and soul into your performance, doing your best to secure the part, while quite often, auditioning in the presence of total strangers, which even seasoned pros find extremely unnerving. When you're finished, no one wants to hear, "We'll be in touch. Thanks for your time…next!"

***

"It got to the point when Bob could teach Milton's class, and about the time he did *Vega$* he stopped going. The fact that we were living in Vegas was also a consideration. I kept going for the first year of his series. Flying back n' forth each week until our son, Ryan was born. I went back to Milton's class in the early 80s then stopped when we moved to Boston for the *Spenser* series. I actually started Milton's Masters class in 2004 and went a few times, but didn't think I wanted to continue in that direction. Bob attended his classes for about four years. I went off and on for ten. The fee was $125 per month. I'm sure the Master's class was more expensive but Milton didn't charge me."

Bob - The Actor

In a three-decade long acting career, tall, handsome Urich moved effortlessly from action-adventure roles to romantic comedy, to westerns. He could do it all, from pathos to comedy, starring in 16 television series, a record which still stands to this day. Bob's presence in weekly television, starring in action series like *S.W.A.T.*, *Vega$* and *Spenser: for Hire* increased his popularity and made him a household name.

The Hollywood Reporter described Bob Urich as television's version of Harrison Ford, both known for playing "everymen in danger." Bob even took a page from the *Star Wars* genre starring in the 1984 feature-film *The Ice Pirates*. The science fiction space spoof developed a huge cult following, but rarely did Urich venture into feature film work, preferring to stick with his successful television career. However, Heather says, Bob regretted not doing more film. "He was sort of stuck in TV Land," she says, "and never was able to make that jump to motion pictures."

Duke Vincent, who produced Bob's series *Vega$* says "it remains one of the great Hollywood mysteries why Bob didn't make it big on the big screen. He certainly had all the necessary qualifications. He was talented and handsome, but back then, in the 70s and 80's, with a few exceptions, like Jim Garner, Burt Reynolds, Sally Field and Steve McQueen, few successfully made the transition. You were either a TV actor or a film actor." Urich's long-time manager Merritt Blake agrees. "I think, Duke's reasoning as to the difficult transition from TV star to film star recognition is perhaps the main reason, but of course Clint Eastwood and a few others were exceptions. Instead of a badge of honor, it was almost some sort of stigma that Bob was known as Mr. Television. 'Over here' we make 'movies,' is how many Hollywood producers looked at things."

Why Didn't Bob transition to Movies?

Bob's friend and fellow actor, Chick Vennera, says, "Back then was a time when you either did film or you did television." "It was a point of frustration for Bob," says Urich's wife, Heather. "He felt as though he was pegged as a TV star. He had a couple of goes at the cinema, *Endangered Species* and *Turk 182*. . . but neither of those films made the numbers [box office-wise]. Bob was always a bit frustrated by that," she says. "He never felt that he was better than his acting friends, but he believed he was *as good* as them." It wasn't that he didn't appreciate the success television offered him, and his loyal fan support, but he longed to make films with 'meatier' roles. "Sometimes, he would do a film for TV that he didn't particularly like," says Heather. "Susan Lucci is a doll but whenever Bob needed to do something for financial reasons, he'd say, "Well, it looks like I'm going to have to do a Susan Lucci movie."

Fast forward to November 1996. Bob was undergoing chemo for synovial cell sarcoma[1] when he was interviewed for *TV Guide* by Daniel Howard Cerone. In his office, Bob gestures to the boxes and boxes of get-well cards and letters of support he's received from his many fans. "They tell me there's another five boxes," he says, smiling. "We've already responded to 2000 letters. My family is helping me sort through all the mail. They're from all over the planet." You get a feeling Bob is touched and most grateful for the care, affection and support he is receiving, as he reaches down and randomly rips open an envelope. "Here's a packet of organic ginger tea somebody wants me to take. It's just endless, books, videos, cures." Bob knew many people who got cancer and felt they were robbed. He didn't feel that way. He believed it was just another challenge to overcome.

Bob would often say, "You have to believe in the prognosis." On the other hand, his wife, Heather believed, "Living with the diagnosis was the most difficult part. You hope that once you're cured, and once it's behind you, it really is behind you. But, there's always that lingering seed of doubt, that it could happen again. It's kind of like the wolf at the door, or poltergeist under the bed. Will he ever really go away? There's that fear," she says, "You don't think about it all day long, but it creeps up on you in the middle of the night." Many nights, sleep did not come easy for

1 A rare cancer which attacks the soft tissue of the body first diagnosed earlier in August, 1996.

Bob. After he felt Heather was asleep, or thought she was, he would get up, and walk around in the quiet of the darkness and ponder their future.

Following his treatment, and after he gets healthy, Bob hoped to be able to turn down luke-warm roles and hold out for stronger film work, which was his life-long dream. "Not that I'm going to abandon television," he stressed, "If I were just doing movies, there wouldn't be 10,000 letters in my office right now," smiling that infectious Urich grin. Producer Aaron Spelling, who cast Urich in the TV action series, *S.W.A.T.* and later as Dan Tanna in *Vega$* said there was a reason Bob kept turning up in series after series. "No matter what you put him in, the audience loved him. They may not have liked every series he was in, but they always loved Bob. He was a brilliant actor who always gave life to the character he played in a way that made the person seem so real. *Vega$* producer, Duke Vincent says, "Bob was outstanding in his many roles both in TV and film. His greatest asset as an actor was that he didn't *act* a character, he *became* the character. He *was* Dan Tanna for me in *Vega$* and later he *was* Spenser in the great Robert B. Parker's *Spenser: For Hire.*"

Bob, the Actor

[Bold typed words are Bob's, taken directly from his journal.]

Actor Chick Vennera, who worked with Bob on *Vega$,* agrees with Vincent. "Bob became the person he was playing. He was a very skilled actor and knew how to tap into those skills as needed." Over the years, Bob developed a certain amount of technique of his own.

Bob finished a film a few years before his passing called, *Aftermath.* His co-stars included Meredith Baxter and Diane Ladd.

"I still don't know what they did with it at CBS. *Aftermath* takes place a year after a father has sexually molested his daughter and how he has been rehabilitated and tries to come back into the family. A lot of the scenes were done on a black limbo[1] set where I'm being questioned and queried by a psychiatrist. I talk and I reveal that I've been molested by my own father and that I allowed him to do what he wanted. It quieted him down and made him less angry and I sobbed through the whole thing. Now, I have never been molested." Urich says, at that point, you just have to trust the material and the director and start clean with a clean slate.

1 A black limbo set is an inexpensive way to create a simple but elegant background for all cameras.

"Try to be totally relaxed. Stuff bubbles to the surface if you're playing the truth of the moment. But, this is clearly an area I think the producers are still a little nervous about. Movies [about sexual abuse] **that were made after this one** [*Aftermath*][1] **have come and gone–and they still have not aired that one. We had a really good director** [Lorrain Senna] **and I've seen some of the footage. It's well-crafted, a powerful film. I've seen moments that are very, very powerful. It's just the subject matter. Somebody feels like it's not time to let it out yet, but it will air at some point.**

How to cry on cue

People would occasionally ask Bob, "how do you cry on cue? How can you do something as intimate as that on a set with dozens of people eating donuts, drinking coffee, reading newspapers and books while you're trying to cry?

"Well, there are several schools of thoughts on the matter. "I can cry on camera, if and when, they want me to do so. If I think it's appropriate I'll do it. My feeling is that it isn't always absolutely necessary–no matter what the script says–to cry in a scene, to have tears running down your cheeks. It's not a physical accomplishment the way being able to dance or sing is, for instance. One theory is that if you cry, you relieve the audience of the obligation to cry. You take that away from people who are watching. In the crying game, I tend towards this school of thought, physically, and technically, crying is easy. Making other people cry is the real challenge."

When he goes to the theater, as a member of the audience, Bob Urich says, he turns in his acting card. **"But, still, you can't help getting bothered by awful, phony, pitiful attempts to cry on screen. There's a scene in *Last Tango in Paris* where Marlon Brando is pretending to cry over his mother's grave or casket. What I recall of it is not the pathos, but what was he doing? As an actor, all I could think of was 'Why? Why this three-card-monte emotion, Marlon.' I don't care if it is Marlon Brando. He shouldn't have attempted it if he couldn't do it with feeling. If it's not there, don't do it. That's my rule. Maybe, it was his attempt at self-pity, but whatever it was it was not very effective. An emotion like**

---

1 *Aftermath* was finally released in Germany on January 10, 2003, almost a year after Bob's passing.

crying has to be born of something true, honest and real. It can't be a gimmick. This is the way people react to pain, for God's sake, not some technique."

"Usually the tears come when you least expect them."

As an actor, Bob knew the more you experience life, it only adds to your acting ability. **"There was a scene I had to do in *Turk 182*[1] on a bench over-looking a river against the New York skyline with Tim Hutton–who at the time was being less than thoughtful as an actor. It was a rebellious time for him. He'd leave the set in his wardrobe and stay out all night and come in with the same wardrobe, and be late and not want to change for the appropriate scene. 'Well, hell, I'll just wear this,' he'd say. He had very little respect for me. In his eyes, I was just a television actor."**

It was a scene, Bob recalls, "that if ever my character was ever going to break down, this would be the spot. **"It's towards the end of the day, about three o'clock in the afternoon in the summertime in Manhattan, and a storm is coming in. It's getting dark and it started to rumble. . . And the wind is flapping and they've got guys holding down the tarps. The lights are set, the scaffolding is up, and it's like, 'Come on. God damn it. *Cry*!! We're running out of time here.'"**

It's a long scene where Bob's character explains his life. He had been a firefighter. A New York Fire Department guy, who's been put on disability leave. He'd been injured saving a kid, but was off-duty when it happened, so they won't pay him any disability severance pay. He has headaches. He has problems with his back and arms and he's cracking up a bit. **"The scene is highly emotional and I'm trying every trick there is to start crying, and then it occurs to me that I'm not really paying attention to the truth of the moment and what the scene is all about. It was about loss. It was about something that he personally would never recover from, something he loved. He was born to be–a fire-fighter– and that he would never be able to do it again."**

The Fact of the Moment

Out of desperation, Bob comes up with the idea that he would tell the story as a joke. **"I start to tell this joke and I'm laughing. I say, 'You know**

1 Turk was the nickname of the character he played [Terry Lynch] His fire dept. I.d. number was 182.

the way Danny is. When we have a five-alarm and we jump on the truck and the ladder company is behind us and they are all throwing us the bird because we're racing over to see who can get there first and playing games and, you know...we pull up and we're at the scene–the house is burning.' And, so Danny, he runs up to the house and we're running behind him and we've got the Halligan[sp] tools[1] and we're bringing those and I'm saying, 'Danny! Come on, grab the hose.' And, he's just standing there. He's just standing in front of the door."

Bob's laughing as he tells the story as a joke but right in the middle of it, he realizes Danny can't move.

"I can barely continue on film. I forced myself to keep going, as you often do in life, and that's when I begin to cry. I realized at that point it was about Danny's loss. And about losing that thing that was most dear to him. . .but I told the story as a joke, laughing and crying at the same time. It was *not* trying to cry that made the moment work. It was a realization of *what the moment meant*. It was being in the flow of telling a story/joke. Laughing and in the embracement of the laughter, the guy begins to cry. He's laughing and the tears are running down his face. That was the fact of the moment."

"Those are the kinds of moments you pray to have happen to you as an actor, but it doesn't always work out that way. Still, you have to have the courage to try it. You have to have the ability to say, 'Well, what's the worst I could do? I look foolish.' I learned a long time ago that when you are acting, there is no inappropriate behavior. You can't look foolish. It may not always be watchable, but I never feel embarrassed about anything I do."

Another technique on how to cry on cue

"So, how do I cry in movies? Is it something sad in my life that I summon up at those moments? Well, not exactly. If you take a very close look, you will notice that I have very few nostril hairs left. If you take a pair of tweezers and just pluck a nostril hair, I guarantee you will come to tears."

At one point in his successful acting career, Bob and Heather were performing in the play *The Hasty Heart* at the Kennedy Center in Wash-

---

1 Holloran tool is a crow-bar [one piece rod] made of aircraft steel and nickel plated. It is used by the FDNY to allow easy penetration with maximum leverage. Experts say it is the best forcible entry tool available.

ington, D. C. At the end of its run, President Ronald Reagan and his wife, Nancy [see photo] came to see the play because he had played the part of an American soldier in the movie version.

"I played a Scotsman and at the very end of the play I decide I don't want to die alone. It's a very emotional scene, but there were times when, having cried night after night, I just got cried out. I felt like I couldn't cry anymore. I had done the play for three months and the night before I hadn't really been able to cry and I thought, well, I'm starting to fake it. I don't have anything to cry *about* any more. I just can't cry anymore." The next Morning, Heather and Bob went for a walk in D.C. and stopped off to see the Viet Nam Memorial.

"It's below ground level, almost as if we were hiding the monument, as if we were ashamed of it. You have to walk down into this low area–in other words, it's subterranean. Open, but subterranean. We were jogging and jogged past the black granite memorial. I wasn't being disrespectful. I just wasn't thinking about what I was doing."

A park ranger came up to Bob and said, "I would think you'd want to show a little more consideration for the guys who paid with their lives over there. Do me a favor, don't run or jog through this area." **"All I could think of was that if those guys had the chance, they would want to be running, too.**

"At either end of the monument there is a big plastic encased book. It looks like the Manhattan phone book about ten times over."

Bob had heard that Johnny Stephenson– the guy he had roomed with and who taught him the football plays at Florida State the spring he made the team–had been killed in Viet Nam. **"He was always smiling, always mild mannered. I went through the book, looking for his name. I knew he was from Tallahassee. I ran my finger down the list of names. I got to the bottom of this page where it read, "Johnny Stephenson, Tallahassee, Florida, killed in action, July 7, 1970. I started to sob uncontrollably. Heather had to hold me and I just cried and cried and cried…and I thought what am I thinking of? How can I possibly say I don't have anything to cry about?**

Needless to say, that night, I wept for Johnny and for all the soldiers, Marines and service members who died and I wept for all these people who didn't come home from that war."

Bob was Driven

John Wilder[1] was producer for the first season on *Spenser: For Hire*. Wilder says, "Besides his obvious good looks and physicality, I think Bob's greatest assets as an actor were his intelligence and work ethics. He was a very smart man, who knew his own strengths and weaknesses. Bob knew what he felt worked for him on film. I remember," says Wilder, "the first scene I directed him in, and his request that I shoot it from an angle he felt best presented his features. Having been an athlete, Bob understood the kind of discipline it takes to succeed at any endeavor and he worked hard at his craft."

Bob was driven. He didn't necessarily want to be famous, but he did want to be great. Quite often, much to one's chagrin, greatness and fame go hand in hand. Because of his God-given talent and acting ability, coupled with his handsome good looks and never say die positive attitude, Bob never quit. Perhaps, due to his ability as an athlete, Bob was always more inclined to say, "Give me the ball. I can run with it. I can do this, just watch me." To his credit, he enjoyed a new challenge. Earlier in his career, a network executive told him that he and Tom Selleck (who had starred together in *Bunco*, a pilot for a projected TV series which didn't sell) didn't have enough talent between them to ever be a success. Neither gave up on their dreams. Bob went on to star in *Vega$* and Tom in *Magnum, P.I.* In 1996, at age 50, in the prime of his life, Bob faced the biggest challenge of his life. He was hit squarely between the eyes with the scariest words a human hopes never to hear: You have cancer. And not just any cancer, but one of the rarest forms of the disease in the world, synovial-cell sarcoma, which has a low survival rate.[2]

"The yellow note pad"

Robert Urich never shied away from auditioning for a role.

Even though he had hit shows like *Vega$, Spenser: For Hire* and *Lonesome Dove* under his belt, he knew he couldn't rest on his laurels and dwell on his past successes.

Bob was a man of great faith. His driving force was his belief that his talent was a gift from God and believed He could take it away just as

1 John Wilder comments farther in the *Spenser: For Hire* Chapter 20.

2 Bob's disease and his Will to Win is covered in detail in chapters 26 and 30.

quickly. Bob never wanted to tempt God by not being prepared to perform to the best of his ability every time he stepped before a camera or on stage. He never allowed himself to take his 'gift from God' for granted. His faith made him work all the harder.

"Bob was constantly reinventing himself," says Heather Urich.

In 2000, at age 54, Bob wanted the role as Jerry McKenney on *Emeril* starring famous chef Emeril LaGasse. The producers wanted to cast a younger man. Bob convinced them he was the right man for the role, auditioned and got the part. His attitude, whether battling his illness or auditioning for a part was always the same…never give up.

Bob had strong work ethics. He also had many different ways in which he prepared himself for various roles. One summer day in 2017, Heather accidentally discovered one such way; a discovery which initially left her somewhat bewildered and in a state of total shock. "Recently," she begins, "I was rummaging around and cleaning up at our summer cottage at the lake in Canada. I came across a yellow note pad which was shoved in a drawer in a small table in the front room. It was Bob's handwriting.

"At first glance, I didn't quite understand what I was reading."

It read "*My wife said I should get in touch with my feelings…learn to cry and I did…and I got really good at it. I cried when Kevin Costner played catch with his dad. I cried when Robert Redford played catch with his son…*I *cried when Kirk Gibson hit that home run for the Dodgers, good baseball makes me cry…Now that I've started crying I can't stop. Now it's a good soufflé that makes me cry…I'm the only man in America who cries over Indian pudding, but you see it's all the same. It's about perfection, that's what makes me cry. My wife divorced me. She just left me one day and I never shed a tear…not one.*"

After reading it for the first time, the words, "*My wife left me*, and *divorce*," jumped off the page! Heather completely confused thought, Good Lord what's this all about? At first glance, she didn't understand what she was reading. After all, the two pages in Bob's own handwriting, obviously had been placed in that drawer by him many years ago. He had been gone now for fifteen years, so it's not like she could confront him with it. The yellow legal-size memo pad had been untouched for all these years. She read the pages over a few more times before suddenly realizing it was a monologue or 'character description' Bob had written about a character he was playing on *Emeril.* "Whew," as she breathed a sigh of relief.

Bob would often describe –in his own words and in his own way–a character he was playing. It was just another way he prepared himself as an actor for the role. Here is the complete text–in his own handwriting–for you to see.

Bob as Capt. Matt Troop in the film Captain's Courageous.

Bob with his son, Ryan, 'sword-fighting' on set of film Ice Pirates.

L-R, Pres. Ronald Reagan, Bob, Nancy Reagan, Burt Reynolds, Heather; back stage Kennedy Center Washington, D.C. Bob & Heather co-starred in play Hasty Heart. *Burt was Producer. During Reagan's acting years, he was cast in the film version.*

Bob & Tom Selleck starring in TV pilot BUNCO, *it never aired as regular series.*

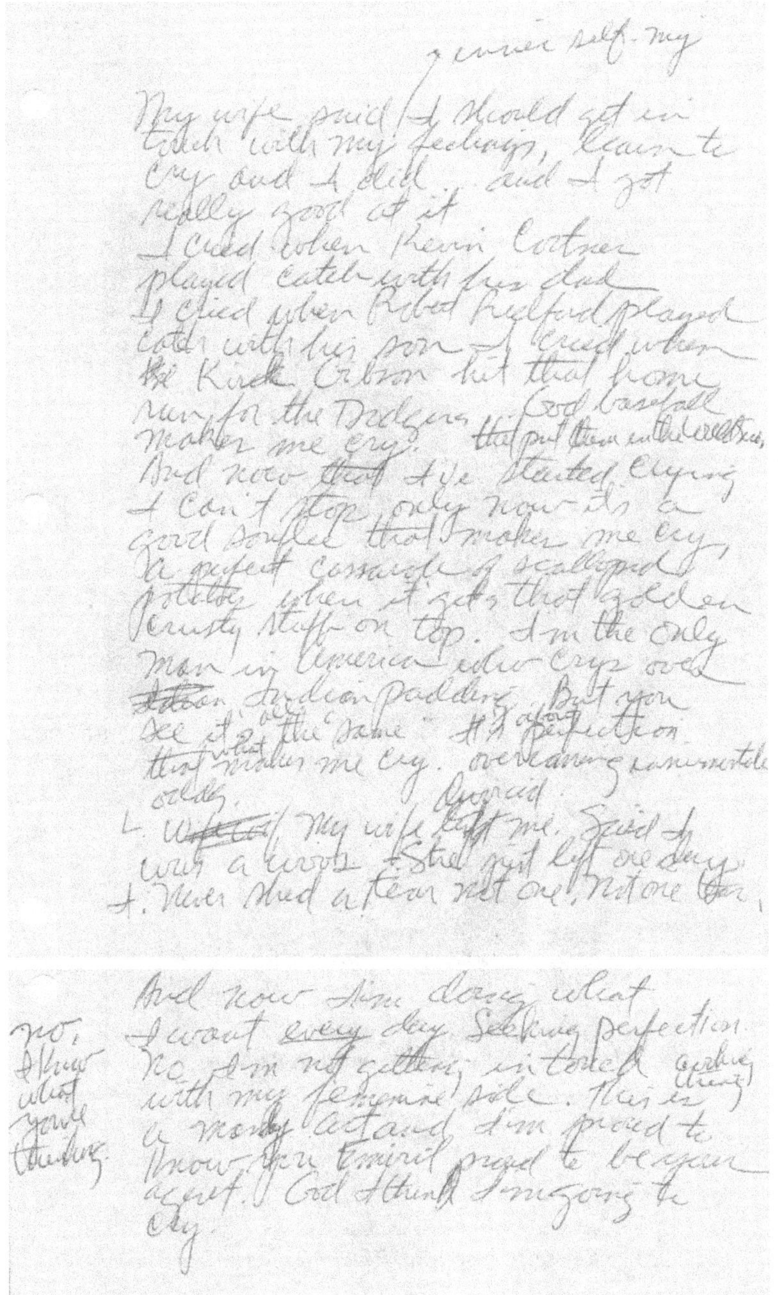

inner self - my

My wife said I should get in touch with my feelings, learn to cry out and I did. and I got really good at it.

I cried when Kevin Costner played catch with his dad

I cried when Robert Redford played catch with his son I cried when Kirk Gibson hit that home run for the Dodgers God baseball makes me cry. that put them in the World Series.

And now that I've started crying I can't stop only now it's a good souflee that makes me cry, a perfect cassarole of scalloped potatoes when it gets that golden crusty stuff on top. I'm the only man in America who crys over Indian pudding. But you see it's all the same. It's perfection that makes me cry. overcoming insurmountable odds.

4. My wife left me. Said I was a wuss. She just left one day.

I. Never shed a tear not one, not one tear.

And now I'm doing what I want every day. Seeking perfection. No, I'm not getting in touch with my feminine side. This is a manly act and I'm proud to know you Emeril proud to be your agent. God I think I'm going to cry.

No, I know what you're thinking.

Part 1- Bob's own hand-writing as he describes the character, Jerry McKenney, he played on NBC-TV's Emeri*(his final series.) Heather accidentally discovered the note-pad while cleaning out a desk drawer at their cottage in Canada in 2016, 14 years following Bob's passing.*

Bob golfing with his friend, Emeril LaGasse circa 2001.

Chapter 16

TV Jargon and Shop Talk
Bob's Take on Acting

[Bold typed words are Bob's own, taken exactly as written from his personal journal.]

Every business has its own shop talk. But with TV, it's not just the jargon that's different–*everything* is different. It bears little resemblance to reality, unreal in every sense of the word.

"The amazing thing, given it's Byzantine methods of operation is how anything ever gets made at all. The process of casting and re-writing a half-hour sit-com is as bizarre as the quest for the next Dalai Lama."

"A TV stage set is different from the ordinary life it supposedly represents in every way imaginable. Beginning with the fact that in real life you can't count on a laugh every 30 seconds. The way you eat, talk, walk and sit down are different. It's a looking glass world. Even the physics are different. I'll show you how you sit down on a couch in a TV show."

"When you see someone sit down on a couch in a TV show or a film, they don't just plunk themselves down the way you do in your own living room. If an actor just plunked himself down all hell would break loose. The camera guy would have a fit. He wouldn't be able to follow you. The director would say, 'Bob, what's the matter with you, you know you can't do that. Let's try it again.' You've got to *g-l-i-d-e*...slide yourself into your seat the way Groucho Marx used to sit down when he's chatting up the dowager Margaret Dumont. Gliding into place allows the cameraman to make a nice smooth shot. That's what's called doing a Groucho."

TV jargon - Midget on a Half Apple

In Hollywood film vernacular, a midget is a little light. A little midget light.

"Usually, a light that highlights your eyes. Sometimes the way you're positioned, especially in a close-up, obscures your eytes and the director will say, 'I can't see his eyes,' so they use these midget spots to light up areas that are in shadow.

An apple in television parlance is a box. **"It comes from the movies when they used apple crates to raise up a short actor like Alan Ladd** [he was 5' 6"] **in a scene. There are guys who put their kids through college renting boxes to the film industry. They used little wooden boxes. Today, you'll see gaffers [workers] during their lunch hour cutting [small] pieces of plywood, screwing them together, laminating and varnishing them and putting hand holds on them so you can grab them."**

They come in various sizes and heights. There's a quarter apple, a half apple and a full apple. **"For example, if you're in a scene which requires you to sit on a table, and the cameraman is trying to frame you, but he can't get you in his shot, he'll say, 'We need a couple of quarter apples to raise the table.' So, they bring in two-quarter-size boxes and put one box under either end and the table comes up and suddenly the frame looks good. That kind of stuff gets done all the time. Adjusting reality is the whole game. So, a midget on a half-apple would be a little light they put on a half an apple box and they bring it down here and they shine it in your eyes and they put a single or a double on it and they go, 'Okay, looks good.' So now you have light bouncing in your eyes so when they do the close-up your eyes sparkle. Ah, Hollywood!"**

It's Funny! It's Hysterical! It's a Disaster!

A half-hour comedy–you go in on a Monday to do a table read. It is exactly like it sounds. Talent and an astounding number of people get a copy of the script and you read it out loud. In the early stages of the show, there could be a hundred people on board.

Robert Urich explains the machinations behind a television sitcom.

"They all want to give their opinion. Bear in mind, that, first of all, this has nothing to do with the show and absolutely nothing to do with acting. They're there just because they want to hear the actors they've paid all this money for read the material written by top writers. Essentially, they want to sit there and laugh and congratulate themselves on what a wonderful job they've done assembling this mighty force of

talent. Network heads will be there–Jeffrey Zucker[1] of NBC and Ted Harbert and all their minions. All their young executives who are up and coming are there; show-runners and–those in charge of comedy development, VP's in charge of production and on and on. They all sit in chairs like at a theater club dinner while the actors sit at tables with their names on them–as if they don't know who we are. It's a little like a courtroom setting. Sometimes, it's in a conference room, other times it is done right on the stage where the show is done."

When Bob did a table read for *Late Boomers*, a show Burt Reynolds was going to do, there were easily a hundred and fifty people present–and it was a Sunday. **"Burt's opening remark was, 'Usually when I perform in front of this many people, I wear make-up.'"**

Burt ended up blowing his stack that Sunday morning on the first day of rehearsal."

A Dog and Pony Show

"They pulled the plug on the show and that was that. It never materialized. We were all sent home. They must have thought this was the tip of the iceberg. If it was going to begin like this on the first day, after weeks of readings and meetings, there was no point in continuing with it. As to what specifically he was mad about that day, there is no answer. With Burt you never know."

"You sit in font of all these people. The pressure is on. It's really a dog and pony show. You don't have any time to actually work on your role or fashion a performance, or create a character of any kind, so it doesn't really in any way relate to the final product. You've not really found a voice for your character. But, you try to make it sound funny without having any of the answers an actor needs before the character comes to life."

Bob believes you fall into the worst possible habits you can get into on a half-hour comedy show. **"It's almost sketch comedy, complete with indicated moves and gestures and sometimes, even set vocalizations. If you say something funny once, they implore you to say it the same way the next time, even though the reason for having said it, no longer exists. They might even eliminate the line in front of it, but still want**

---

1 Jeffrey Zucker was formerly, CEO of NBC, and as of 2017 is President of CNN. Ted Harbert in 2017 was Chairman of NBC broadcast/cable and prior to was Chairman at ABC Enter.

the line repeated in exactly the same way. It's American surrealism in action. It's like acting by the numbers. When you get to that spot over there, they want you to turn and deliver the punch line, or give a reaction look to a punch line." It's not uncommon for a director to say, 'Okay...I'll be cutting to you.' Oh, you want me to do what? React? Make a face, look disgruntled, surprised?"

"It's a little difficult to think about your life's work when you're being asked to just flip through your *Guide To Standard Sit-Com Expressions.* Believe me, the only criteria that is used all the time is the laugh. It's a case of, well, we are going to do a bit here and a bit here and it's like a little shtick here, and a little shtick there and it's like the worst possible discipline you can imagine. Bite-size acting."

Lucille Ball and Desi Arnaz invented the form, but there was something pure about them, back then, says Bob.

"By now, after 50 years of formula sit-coms...it's definitely a half-breed, half-brain, mechanical laugh machine. Plus you have all the technical restrictions of filming with none of the freedom of film. The material is not tried or true, or tested–like theater. In theater, you begin working on a play...it goes into workshop, then it goes into previews and then it goes out-of-town. And only then do they bring it in.

It all takes place over a long period of time."

Bob says, "with a half-hour comedy, the day you sit down in front of that crowd of people to read the play for the first time, you say to yourself, **"Oh, this material is just *great*! It's going to be a wonderful show–brilliant. This is so funny. Either that, or they just sit there stone-faced like you are from another planet and how dare you think that you could be funny. No matter what happens, it is a very strange dynamic. Either way, in the middle of the regearsal period, inevitably, it all falls apart! Panic sets in. Everone has convinced themselves now that it is *not* funny.It's not going to work, and no audience on earth is going to think this is funny.**

A Dog and Pony Show

"Because the network guys come in at the end of the first day, you literally have one day to get it up on it's feet to where you can block it. You go from set to set and you do the scenes. You move around in a very restricted area–it's pretty much set where you're going to be and where

you are going to deliver a line. Then, the network people come in again and sit in a little row of chairs and watch it. It's like soaking the pickles on the first day you can them."

"If it isn't perfect the first time," Bob continues, "If it is not funny, they start changing it." **"It's a disaster! It's like, everybody go back home. Go back to your houses. There is nothing to see. The minute you do the table read, Gary Goldberg[1] will say, 'Okay, we're *all* going to go to work. You guys are *not* funny. We're going to punch it up to *make it* funny.' And all the writers stay up all night working on it. They sleep in their offices. It's a hard job, making these shows funny."**

On a typical sit-com, the script changes from Monday to Tuesday to Wednesday. Different colored scripts; lavender, green, buff pages and cherry colored pages. Even on the final Thursday, Bob says, you have to ask, **"Is it set now? Can I work on it? Because, guess what? Tomorrow at five o'clock the audience is coming in. It's not like you had a year of Neil Simon fixing the script–the lines are funny whether or not you *thought* they were funny. When Neil Simon runs his funny lines, there's a pretty good chance that it's going to be funny to an audience, too. Why? Because, it's honest. It comes from truth. And, we laugh as we see ourselves faced with the same predicament. We recognize truth in the situation."**

Bob says, in the half-hour world of sit-com television, honesty and truth are irrelevant. **"Once you take away the very things comedy is based on, nobody can tell anymore what's funny and what's not, so everybody is consulted–the secretary, the assistant to the assistant producer, the hairdresser, the hairdresser's niece. "**

Everyone is consulted, except the actors.

One time, Jeffrey Tambor and Bob were once struggling with a scene during their lunch break when in walked director, Sam Wiseman.

"'What are you guys doing?' Wiseman asked. 'You're just wasting your time. Forget about it, go make some phone calls.'

A bunch of phone calls? We're working. We're trying our best to make something out of this and he tells us we are wasting our time!!"

Bob cleared the room.

---

1 Gary Goldberg wrote and produced the Robert Urich TV series, *American Dreamer* which was one of Bob's personal favorite roles. His real life wife, Heather got to play his deceased wife on an episode.

"I thought the audacity. I said, here we are doing whatever we can and there's no respect for the actor."

The writers go away and they come back with a whole new script, says Bob.

"The color of the paper the script is written on starts off white and the next day it's pink. Sometimes, it's substantially changed and sometimes, it's just little minor things. But the network, who has had the scripts and story idea for weeks and weeks–maybe even months–they are now just getting around to thinking about it.

And, then it starts; "Now, in the main scene…maybe it shouldn't be about a birthday.

Maybe it should be about a dog and pony in outer space."

"Sometimes, you're reading the new version and you don't even recognize it. Oh, so now it's about puppies in a cookie factory. Then the next day, the pink script becomes a blue script, because it's changed again. And, every day you run it again.

Blocking[1] day is generally Thursday and that's when they bring in all the technicians. **"Now, you've got all the cameras there. The cameras are rehearsing the moves in concert with the actors. You can't do a half-hour comedy with three cameras. It just doesn't work. There are usually four and sometimes even more than that. It's a ballet of machinery and sets. Walls are flying, the floor is covered with tape marks with each camera and each factor in the move."**

So, when you watch a half-hour TV comedy and you see two people walk from the left side of the stage –[on your screen]–to the right side, what you don't see is that everything is moving together.

"Four cameras, four operators, four focus pullers, four cable guys–all in concert, plus at least four sound guys with big booms over a stage and all of it going on simultaneously. And, you're trying to act with all that going on," says Bob.The cameras are like dinosaurs and are moving and changing positions. Then, there's the lighting which has to follow all the movements–it's set in certain positions, and once that's determined that's where the actors have to wind-up on shooting day.

---

1 Blocking generally means a rehearsal of the actors movements and setting up where the actors are to be positioned for each scene, to set up the camera shots, lights etc.

It Had to be You

In September 1993, Bob Urich starred in his 12th TV series, playing Mitch Quinn on the CBS sit-com, *It Had to be You*. The series aired Friday nights at eight. It was about the awkward romance of an unlikely couple. Laura Scofield, a high-powered, socially prominent Boston book publisher played by Academy Award winning actress, Faye Dunaway.[1] Bob played a carpenter she hired to build her a bookshelf. Despite the obvious social gap between the lady publisher and the surprisingly literate blue-collar carpenter, the chemistry between them was explosive and powerful stuff. Evidently, critics viewed it differently and panned it. The series only survived for a month and was canceled[2] after filming just 7 episodes.

"She [Dunaway] **was horrified at the lighting, because she had spent her entire career as a movie star. Her profile would take hours to light by some of the world's renowned DP's [directors of photography] Not because she needed it. She's a beautiful woman. That's just how long it took. Hours to light just one little thing.**

When she saw how they lit her on TV, she said, 'Oh, my God. Are you kidding me?' She was shocked. Because when you sit on a sofa on a TV set–and you always see people sitting on sofas–the lights are hung in such fashion that it casts these awful shadows across your face. The lighting is not good."

Now the audience comes in and it's warm-up time. Sometimes, there is a band. Everybody is laughing. The announcer walks out and they all applaud. **"The show goes on you start the process where the writers come up between takes and say, 'That worked. That was good and it was in sync with the audience, too. Let's keep that.'"**

Behind the Scenes of the Show

Sometimes an audience will get a joke, they'll laugh and sometimes they won't. **"If a line's not working a writer will come over to you and**

1 Faye Dunaway won an Academy Award for her role in *Network*. She also won 3 Golden Globe Awards.

2 Rumors say the show was canceled for various reasons including difficulties behind the scenes. Bob's brother Tom, a distinguished actor himself was visiting the *It Had To Be You* set one day and observed the following: "Faye walked on the set, looked at the color scheme and said something to the affect, 'this will never do' and walked off. They had to repaint the set which didn't sit well with the rest of the cast, production people and a studio audience who had to sit around waiting."

say, 'Okay, they didn't laugh at that one, so this time, try this line right here.' They change the joke right on the spot. They start punching it out. It's an amazing process."

Having said this, Bob adds, "there isn't an actor who works in the field who doesn't cherish working in TV. Because, when all is said and done, it's the most civilized process in the entertainment industry."

"After what I've just told you it might sound like insanity, but as an actor, it's quite humane. You show up ten o'clock on Monday morning, you have a read-through, sometimes, you rehearse a little bit and then they send you home. Sometimes, they just send you home. Then they re-write. Then on Tuesdays, you block it and rehearse a lot more and have a nice lunch and there's always an entertaining star coming to the set or somebody, or some kind of a press thing and then you go home at five o'clock. Then, on show day, you go in at noon or eleven o'clock and you're out of there by nine-fifteen, and you go home, We all go to some restaurant together for dinner and talk about what a great time it was."

Then the show goes on the air. The numbers come in, and if those numbers quickly dwindle, and it doesn't get the ratings they're looking for, the honeymoon is over and they pull the plug.

"Other times, you go on-the-air and have a hit and the network shows off–there's a hundred people at the network who feel it's all their doing."

Bob's take on the acting profession

According to Bob, **"Unlike television, movies do not provide a civilized schedule. On Monday morning, when I start a new movie, I'll probably have a five-thirty a.m. call somewhere in Malibu Canyon. That means getting up at four in the morning. And before the first day of shooting on a movie, the night before, no matter how well prepared you feel, you don't sleep, because you're afraid, you're going to be late. I'll drive down some dirty, muddy road and there will be a little trailer that is going to be freezing cold. I'll go into a makeup room and meet people that I have never met before."**

On a movie there are such long breaks between your parts that as an actor, you have to continuously remind yourself that it's a play and every piece belongs somewhere. **"It's like working on a puzzle from the inside**

out, because they don't very often have the time or the money to shoot in sequence."

The first day of the movie, Bob sleeps with Ann Archer. He also shoots the scene where he comes to the rescue on horseback. In the story-line, a lot happens before that and a lot happens after that.

"But you sort of have to lead up to it your mind," says Bob.

"I have little cues that I create for myself on a written page. I will say, this happened. That happened. Here is where we arrive. You have to go through that whole process, otherwise, you don't know where to begin.

When working on a movie, Bob reads the script over and over and over.

"Can you do scene seventeen?'

"Oh yes, sure. I can do any scene you want."

"Do you want to do seventeen or scene twenty seven-B, or if you want me to do 37C with a number one apple...or scene forty-two A, I am prepared to do it."

"If they shot the whole movie backwards, starting from the last page, I could handle it," he says.

In 1981, Bob and Heather starred in the Kenley Players summer theater production in Dayton Ohio of Neil Simon's *Barefoot in the Park.* John Kenley's name was synonymous with summer theater in Ohio from 1957 until 1995. Kenley remembered Bob as a perfectionist. Quite often, he would go over a scene a dozen times to get the comedic timing just perfect. Bob considers it his job to have the entire movie or play in his head, which is what he always did.

"It takes a long time and a lot of work, but it's the way I work."

Bob was a stickler when it came to dialogue and overall writing for his scripts. He learned well from his acting instructor, Milton Katselas, one of Hollywood's best. It was Milton who ingrained in Bob that "actors should seek out writing that is interested in humanity rather than cleverness or glib emotion." Bob's work ethic was extremely high. He demanded only the best performance from himself and expected it from those he worked with. "Bob really connected with kids, particularly young actors, and took them under his wing," says his wife, Heather. "Johnny Galecki* who played Bob's young son in his TV series, *American Dreamer,* was always over our house. He was only 15 at the time."

Jonny Galecki

Johnny's folks had returned to the Chicago area to live and Johnny was on his own. Galecki[1] was living in a studio apartment in Burbank and rode his motorcycle to the studio every day. "Bob didn't like the fact he was all alone in L.A. and offered him a room we had over our garage. It didn't work out," says Heather, "because Johnny was a smoker and Bob wanted no part of that." Bob would be pleased to know that today, Galecki is a 'former' smoker. He quit in 2007, shortly before the 8th season of his work on the *Big Bang Theory* began.

Whenever Bob needed a young man to play a role in one of his pictures, he would always ask if Johnny was available. That's how much he respected Galecki's talent and work.

Bob Urich was a people magnet. People just seemed to navigate towards Bob. He was a friend to everyone, like Kaj Erik Erikson.

Kaj Erik [pronounced KaiErik] was 17 when he played opposite Bob in the television film version of Rudyard Kipling's classic, *Captains Courageous.* A story of a hard and dangerous life at sea, and a young boy who grows up really fast through hardship and tragedy. "Bob was drawn to the story for a couple of reasons," says his wife. " He was a book collector, who enjoyed collecting Asprey leather-bound first editions. Classics, like *Captains Courageous* and others, including his all-time favorite, *Wind in the Willows.* "I still have that one. No way could I part with it," Heather noted, "but the rest I sold. I just didn't have room for them."

Captains' Courageous - Bob enjoyed mentoring kids

Another reason the film appealed to Bob was his love of the sea and boats of all types. The original film version of *Captains Courageous* starred Spencer Tracy and Freddie Bartholomew. The re-make with Bob was filmed off the coast of Vancouver, British Columbia and aired April 21, 1996, a few months before he was first diagnosed with cancer. It is the type of movie that you never want it to end, thanks to Michael Anderson's skillful directing, John McGreevey's excellent script and Bob's fine

1 Source: L.A. Times article 2012. Johnny Galecki was born in Belgium where his dad was stationed in the U.S. Air Force. He and his family moved to Chicago when he was three. In 1989, at age 13, he played Chevy Chase's son Rusty in *National Lampoon's Christmas Vacation.* In 1992, he was cast as David Healy on *Roseanne.* In 2017, co-starring with Jim Parsons on the *Big Bang Theory* his salary is reportedly more than one-million per episode.

acting, which tore at your heart. The film was faithful to the heart and spirit of the original Kipling classic of a hard and dangerous life at sea, and a boy who grows up fast through hardship and tragedy.

Kaj Erik Erikson played Bob's young son and shipmate in the film. He gives Bob high marks as both a friend and mentor. "I met him at a very pivotal point in my life and career," he recalled, during an April 2016 interview with the author. "I was just starting to really understand working [as an actor] and dissecting scenes. Bob's notes and willingness to run lines with me was an invaluable lesson. We shot the film for a month on a boat. Setting sail every morning and returning to port late at night. Our space was limited, so when we weren't shooting and on lunch break, we'd go fishing off the side of the boat. That's when Bob and I talked about 'life' and about acting. It's my favorite memory of Bob. He was an amazing actor, and a kind and amazing man."

Survive the Savage Sea

In 1992, Bob Urich and Ali MacGraw starred in an ABC-TV Movie of the Week, *Survive the Savage Sea*. The movie is about courage and survival at its best. Shot around the Great Barrier Reef in Queensland, Australia, this is the true-life story of Jack and Claire Carpenter, who realize his life-long dream to go to sea, by selling the family farm and uprooting their four kids to buy the yacht Providence.

They wind up spending 37 days at sea waiting to be rescued after their boat is capsized by whales. This movie is Robert Urich at his best, probably because he is right at home on the water. It also may be due to the fact he is surrounded by his real-life family; wife Heather, their thirteen year old daughter Emily and fifteen year old son, Ryan who plays one of Bob's sons. Critics say It is one of the best disaster films to come out in the early 1990's.

Dylan Daniels

Actor Dylan Daniels was nine when cast as Bob's other son, Timmy. "It was my first acting job," says Dylan. "My brother David and I were cast for the same role. I had all the lines and close-ups, while he was used in distance shots and stunts. The day came to do the table read and meet the cast [1990] It was the first time I met Robert," he says. "I had been abused a few years earlier and was painfully shy. I was very closed off and quiet and this situation made me very nervous." Dylan was watching Robert and Ali MacGraw talking. "They looked over at me and my brother, and Robert said, 'Let's meet our other sons.' I don't know if it was something in Robert's tone when he spoke," says Daniels, "but I realized I had to step up and meet people, so I pushed the shy side of me aside. I remember meeting Ali first, and then Robert held out his hand and I shook it. It was like an instant warm feeling. All shyness towards the man I had before just vanished. I felt very comfortable around him."

"Robert introduced us to his real son Ryan, who played my older brother in the film and we instantly got along. We did the table read, and in those few hours a bunch of strangers became a family and friends. During the filming, I grew very close to Robert and Ali." Dylan was the youngest of the cast, but fell right into the acting side very easily. "I wasguided by Robert. He was impressed how I was willing to listen and learn."

Bob made you feel safe

"I'd spend free time playing with Ryan or sitting on Robert's lap going over scenes. I spent a lot of time talking to Robert about acting and he explained the basics to me. We also talked about life and what an adventure we all were on. There was something so welcoming and warm about who this man was that words can't really describe. He was like a shining light in a big dark world that people rarely find, let alone to be taken under his wing and treated like part of his family. He radiated an all around comfortable energy, a good one-of-a-kind soul people hope to meet. Over the course of the shoot," says Dylan,"he became the only man I'd ever call a second father. I felt very safe around both he and Ali, but Robert was like a big teddy bear, always giving hugs and smiles."

Dylan Daniels, now in his early thirties, shares his emotional ordeal of being abused. "As far as what happened to me before meeting Robert I think it should be told," he says. "Bob helped me by finally talking about it, and getting it out there maybe I can finally let that pain go, so I don't mind you using it [my story]. I was eight and only lived in Australia for a few months, when the dad of one of my friends assaulted me in a sleep over. I don't have many memories from back then. Therapists call it a mind black out. It was only when I started working on the film did I start to have memories. Don't get me wrong," he says, "I have little clips of memory that are there after the event but very few. Robert helped me by finally talking about it and getting it out there. I felt comfort and peace,"

Daniels explains, "something I had lost and Robert brought it back to me. The movie and Robert brought me back out of the dark."

Dylan Daniels recalls working with Bob Urich in the early 90s on the film *Survive the Savage Sea.* "Any actor will tell you that water films are the worst films to work on."

"Sitting in six inches of water for 11 weeks will take its toll on people's moods. But Robert always kept everyone in cheerful spirits, even on hard days. In eleven weeks, I think I only ever saw him get frustrated twice. The first time was just one of those script lines that the word 'letters' always came out as 'lettuce.' So, after a few takes, he asked to take a break. After that, on random days, we'd leave a bowl of lettuce in his dressing room. He always got a good laugh out of it."

"The second time was during a night shoot in a water park wave pool for the big storm scene in the picture. If I remember correctly, we started shooting around 1:00 a.m. It was in the low 40's, and the water was ice cold. The rain water was even colder, so we'd do some takes getting hit with cold rain and cold water from the dump tanks. We all had partial wetsuits on under our costumes, but it didn't help much. When we had breaks, we'd get out, dry off and warm up. I didn't have a trailer with a heater so Robert and Ali let me warm up in theirs. We were about 6 hours into filming when the cold was just too much for all of us. Robert spoke up and said, 'Enough is enough. It's too damn cold for the kids. This is the last time we are getting back into that boat tonight. It's cold and we are all running the risk of getting sick. This is the last time! One more take and we are done.' We shot one more take and called it a night."

"One day we were shooting up North in Queensland when the weather got so bad," says Dylan, "they had to build a makeshift sound-stage in a storage unit. The scene in the film is after the flying fish jumps into the life raft. No one could figure out what would look real to eat as raw fish. I told them we could use fresh Ahi Tuna. Back then sushi wasn't a big thing. They took the idea and bought some tuna."

Dylan Daniels & Survive the Savage Sea

"Robert, Ali, Ryan and just about everyone else hated the taste. I loved it and had eaten it many times. So, they had a spit bucket [for obvious reasons] and when everyone would fake eating the fish, I was really chewing on it! Robert had them put chocolate on it to try to hide the flavor."

Bob always had a way to make even the long days end with a smile.

"Even on that long night, in the cold water at the wave park, we all had a good time warming up before heading home for the next days call," says Daniels, smiling. "While shooting on location in Port Douglas one time, Robert didn't believe that the replica dingy we were using to film would really sail. So, at the end of the day he told the crew to unhook us and he'd sail us back to the main yacht. Laughing and cheering with us, the whole way he was amazed it really worked."

"After the film wrapped Robert invited me to spend the summer with he and his family. He jokingly asked if he could keep me, but due to school I had to decline which was a let down for me. I don't like to talk about the loss," [Bob's passing in 2002] "but I will say, this man was a second father figure to me. He was so down-to-earth and really was a one-of-a-kind soul that everyone loved to be around, and I truly was blessed to have him help direct my life at such a young age."

***

Bob believed strongly that young actors should learn as much as they can about the history of their craft. "They should study the actors, writers and directors who have shaped what we do today," he said. "The colorful history of the cinema and the theater is filled with challenging writing that is interested in humankind and real communication.

"Every person who aspires to be a successful actor should be interested in the history of our business. Seek out information. It's out there and available." Urich urged them to read it. "Educate yourself and learn about the profession you love."

Bob plays himself and His Anti-self

Sometimes, Bob will act out his part at home, particularly if the voice is important–like the western he was doing, *The Lazarus Man.* **"The language is not my language, so I say it out loud, just so I get used to the language. Just so I find a way of embodying what the writer is trying to create. As an actor, what you can't do is ever deny who you are and what you're about. You can't play less intelligent than who you are. I don't think you can, anyway. There has to be a part of yourself in any character you play in order for it to work. There are only two things I was taught to do. You need to discover how you are like the character and how you are NOT like the character. In the way you are like the character, you don't have to work on it. You've already got that one taken care**

of. If the character is stingy, self-centered and sometimes moody, and has verbal explosions from time to time, I don't need to work on that," says Bob. **"I have seen myself do all those things. I go, oh yeah, okay. I got that moment. That doesn't mean I behave that way today or every day. But, I remember a time when I stormed out of a room, or threw a plate of linguine at the wall and watched it slide down the wall to the horror of my wife, Heather and our family. So sure, I can do that again. I know exactly what it felt like. I can remember what the silence in the room felt like. I can remember how embarrassed I felt. The way my face flushed after I did it."**

Bob's wife, Heather remembers that moment, too.

"The kids and I just looked at the wall as the macaroni slowly slid down. I looked at Bob and as calmly as I could be under the circumstances, said, 'I'm not picking it up. The bucket and mop are right over there, go to it,' and continued enjoying my meal."

Bob says he doesn't need more than a pinch of Stanislavski's[1] magical technique. **"I can just hypnotize myself into the scene,"** he says, asking himself, **"What if I *were* in this situation? I have a reservoir of moments stored up, emotions, times in my life that may not be identical, but are close enough to work. Then there are those moments where there is no way to connect to *anything* you've ever done."**

A good example is Bob's film role in *Blind Faith*.

Blind Faith is based on the real-life book by Joe McGinniss. Bob Urich plays Rob Marshall, a wealthy businessman who is accused of murdering his wife to collect insurance money to pay off his gambling debts. In preparing for the role, Bob, said, "I can't find anything in the man that I can identify with. Why anyone would want to kill their lovely, devoted wife, the mother of their children to collect insurance money is beyond me." Being a pro, Bob pulled off the role and gives an excellent portrayal of the weak and self-absorbed husband and father.

---

1 The Stanislavski method of acting was developed in the early 20thCentury at the Moscow Theater by Konstantin Stanislavski. It is a set of techniques meant to create realistic portrayals of character. The goal is to have a perfect understanding of the motivations, obstacles and objectives of a character in each moment. Actors use the technique for realistic plays, when trying to present an accurate portrayal of normal life. The Stanislavski method is not the same as method acting which goes even further into becoming a character.

If *Blind Faith* isn't Urich's best work it has to rank near the top of his lengthy body of work which spanned nearly three decades.

Blind Faith

Blind Faith hits an emotional home-run in telling the victim's side of the story. The loving relationship between Maria Marshall and her three sons is the cornerstone of the film. It makes the viewer realize the depth of suffering from such a senseless crime. The mother's love is contrasted with her husband's self-absorbed obsession with his own needs.

Actress Joanna Kerns, who plays Maria Marshall in *Blind Faith*, recalls it was the first time she worked with Bob. "He was wonderful, but, he was troubled by the role and the man he was asked to play. Robert Marshall[1] murdered his wife, the mother of their children, on her birthday." Bob had a tough time getting his mind around that. "Who acts that way," he said. Usually he could find some piece of himself to inject into the character he was playing. Not this time. This guy was evil, through and through.

In Bob's own words, taken directly from his journal, he describes another way to playa role when you've never been there before, and have nothing to draw from?

"How do you play, 'Oh my God. The plane is going down.' And, you're at the controls. Having never been there and hoping you never will. My way of thinking, a certain calm would come over you. There is a certain kind of instinctual sense that works. 'What if" has always worked for me.

Bob recalls a very famous story about director Alfred Hitchcock and actor Bruce Dern.**"Hitchcock told Bruce to go to the second story window, draw back the drapes, take a drag on a cigarette, look out the window down at what would be the street, exhale, let the curtain drop and walk away. And Bruce Dern as any responsible actor would do, said, 'What am I looking at?' Hitchcock again told him, 'Just go to the window. Take a drag off the cigarette. Look out the window, exhale and let it drop.' So Bruce did as he was told.**

"Later on, Dern is sitting in the screening room. He sees himself walk to the bedroom window, draw back the drapes and take a puff off the cigarette. Then, the camera cuts to the street where his wife is

---

1 The imprisoned Robert Marshall began writing Urich pleading his innocence and asking for Bob's help. It's not known if Bob ever responded.

coming out to do some shopping. Two men grab her. Throw her in the back of a car and it speeds away. Bruce Dern exhales, lets the curtain fall back into place and walks away. It's the most chilling moment in the movie. If Hitchcock had told him what he was seeing or what he was doing, he would have reacted. He would have ended up acting out something which would have been too much. No reaction was the perfect reaction."

In an interview with TCM's Robert Osborne, distinguished actor Peter O'Toole said, "Eighty percent of acting is using one's voice." All Bob Urich had to do was open his mouth and speak. His resonant voice immediately commanded your attention.

"Bob was a consummate pro who totally understood TV," says his friend and fellow actor Tim Matheson. "By that I mean, he showed up, knew his lines and did his job. He was also one of those people that wasn't full of himself, which in itself, is so rare."

Bob had a photographic memory when it came to learning his lines. One, look at a script and he was "finished," meaning he had done his homework, knew the script and had explored the character he was about to play. "I don't recall Bob ever bringing home a script to memorize his lines," says his wife Heather. "On the other hand, I always worked with a friend to learn my lines. We would bounce lines back and forth really fast." She continues, "If you know your lines inside and out and say them really fast, then you'll have no problem adding emotion and feeling to them later." It was a trick Heather learned from legendary screen actor, Garson Kanin.

Author's note:

When I played myself, a morning-drive radio personality on an episode of ABC-TV's long-running soap, *Ryan's Hope*, I was under the impression that my appearance would be nothing more than a quickie cameo and void of any lines. When they handed me the script, I nearly freaked out! There was line after line of dialogue which I needed to memorize. Quickly, I turned to my acting pal, Bob Urich for his sage advice. Without hesitating, he said, "Get a tape recorder [you remember those things, don't you]. Read the entire script–and I mean read everyone's lines–into the recorder, then when you come to your lines, STOP the recorder and say them!" I did as Bob kindly suggested and it worked beautifully. Learning my lines the Robert Urich way was a piece of cake.

Here's another valuable point about acting from Bob. He did not believe in the theory of good and bad acting. **"I believe either it's working as it should be or it isn't. Just like when you write. I don't think there is any such thing as bad writing. It's just that you aren't really doing it."**

Bob's Take on Acting

"Method acting. I think there are as many methods as there are actors. I think if you do a certain preparation–if you do A, B, C, a version of D will always take place. It's when you get lazy and go, 'Oh, I don't want to do any of these scenes, I know what this is going to be, this is going to be a D.' Just a quick little moment and then they go, 'Yeah. That's fine. Print it and let's move on.' Then you see it and you yell, 'Oh God, what was I thinking? Why didn't I do something there?'"

Bob recalls once when he was working with Dennis Dugan.

"He was a fine director and after I had finished a scene, he came up to me and said, 'That was amazing. You know, nobody is going to watch that and it's never going to be in the movie, but that was really something.' So. It wasn't usable, but then not everything is. Can you imagine if a writer were judged by every word he/she wrote? You see a manuscript by Hemingway or Proust and there is version after version—-pages crossed out, dozens of additions scribbled in the margin...notes pasted on. You realize it's a process. It's the same as acting.

"Sometimes, you get out of your own way and just *do the moment* and rely on the filmmaker, the director and the editor to put it together."

Bob says he is always shocked that stuff goes where it goes.

"Oh, that's where it went? Here I thought I was doing this wonderful moment and it doesn't go there at all. It does seem to fit there now.

"Often times, I watch my own work and I go, it's that place between. 'Just don't stand there. Do something!' And other times, I'll say, 'Don't do so much, it's too busy. Just stand there.' It's always a funny thing to watch your own work."

"Maybe the answer is in this idea of 'Flow.' When you're engaged fully, so engaged in fact that you forget what time it is and that you are hungry and have forgotten to eat–that's when the acting is the best. That's also a function of the material and the people you are around. I am so tired of being the best thing in a lousy movie. '*Once again Robert Urich aspires to and reaches well beyond the material.*' I am getting a little

weary of that review." Good reviews and bad movies. An actor's life is not a function of picking bad movies. **"All you can do is pick the people and the material."**

Sometimes, Bob honestly believed he did so much television he felt like shouting, "God, you give me eight months on a feature film and I'll win awards, too."

"You do an episode on television and you do twelve pages of dialogue a day and it's done in six days. In a movie, they do two or three or four pages a day and maybe only keep one. You rehearse for several weeks before they even begin filming and then they don't commit it to film until somebody [upstairs] feels like there is something real going on. You don't have that luxury on television [at least not when Bob was acting on television fifteen years ago]."

In many ways, it's good training for an actor because you have to stay focused. Bob says he doesn't necessarily get better because of the number of takes.

"I've done miniseries where it took this actress, seventeen, eighteen, twenty takes and she just got worse and worse and worse with each take. I thought her first take was brilliant and the director kept on having her do it over and over again. It got to a point where she was just wooden and unemotional. Maybe that was what the director was going for."

Then they turned the camera on Bob.

"I did my version twice. He printed the second take. I thought, it just must take me a lot less time to get lousy. I don't know."

There were days when Bob felt he wasn't doing it [acting] properly, or he didn't feel good, or circumstances were going against him, but that's true of any art form. **"Peter Finch came to our acting class once, and began talking about a scene he did in *Network*. He said that at four o'clock in the morning your director is drunk, the actor you're doing a scene with has forgotten his lines and you just do the best you can. Sometimes, those moments wind up on film."**

Bob says, **"When he finally stopped making it personal at that level his work changed. The funny think about it is that realization came at a very late time in my career. I still think there's a performance or two left in me worth watching. I think now that my best work might be ahead of me, except I haven't created a career where people are offering**

me the kind of roles that a fifty-five year old man[1] could be doing in the movies. Gene Hackman is already doing them.

In acting, it's a matter of being able to put aside the things that belong to your youth. Some actors I know would be more compelling to watch if they would stop looking at films they did when they were in their 20s and 30s and begin again."

Bob and Chick Vennera

Actor Chick Vennera performed on Broadway as Sonny in *Grease* in 1973. In 1975, he was off to L.A. to study under acclaimed director and teacher Milton Katselas. It was in Milton's class that Chick first met Bob and Heather.

Later, he was best man at their wedding. For the next two years Chick acted in various roles on television and film. He returned to New York to do the play *Jockeys* [directed by Katselas]. "I rehearsed a year on *Jockeys*," he says. "I won the Theater World Award for the role as Angel. Two weeks later, the show closed. I said, 'What am I gonna do now?' Bob, who made a habit of always lending a hand if needed, called and said, 'Why don't you come out here. I've got an extra bedroom.' That's what I did until I got back on my feet again." In 1978, Chick Vennera was cast as Mitch Costigan in the pilot episode of *Vega$*, no doubt getting the role due to his acting ability, but it didn't hurt that his pal, Bob, was star of the series.

***

Bob believed strongly that as an actor it was important to reinvent yourself at a certain stage and age in your career. **"If you've been performing over a long period of time, you're liable to get bogged down in a body of work. Anything outside of that is unknown to producers and directors. They have no idea what I've done. They think of me as just some guy who starred in a TV series once. It takes a tremendous amount of energy and effort to offset that kind of perception. Sometimes, I don't know if it's worth it."**

When Bob was doing *Vega$*, he appeared in a film with Cheryl Ladd. *When She Was Bad* was about child abuse, which was a serious and timely topic–the theme being that child abuse isn't only perpetrated by sick and disturbed people, unfortunately, it's all too common. Punishment

1 Bob wrote in his journal, about his feelings as an actor at age 55, shortly before his passing.

becomes child abuse when it's for the sake of the parent. The subtext of the movie was the pressure of trying to maintain a happy family lifestyle, making everything perfect, just the way it appears in TV sitcoms.

Bob's take on Acting

"I played Bob Morgan, a not too sympathetic husband. A guy who is constantly humiliating his already stressed-out wife."

Bob had known Cheryl going back to when they took acting classes together with Milton Katselas. It was an interesting career move for them as Bob points out in his journal.

"I thought this particular role would take me away from the slicker image I had projected in *Vega$*, and Cheryl, after all, was in *Charlie's Angels*. ABC was not thrilled with the project but because it was produced by David and Cheryl Ladd they went ahead with it. The film was painful to do but it turned out extremely well. It was one of the first TV movies dealing with the subject, and it sparked a lot of controversy. People went wild when it aired. There were protests at the network."

When Bob signed on to do the project, his agent said, "Don't worry, Bob. No one will be able to accuse you of being a slick, pretty boy in this show." And, that's exactly why he took the role, as Bob explains. **"At a certain point in your career you realize there's only so much time left to do what you want to do. After two years on *Vega$*, I desperately needed to find roles as far away from the macho characters I always get cast as. It gave me something to do other than drive and shoot! Somehow in the end, it all evaporated. This is painful for me to admit, but it seems to me almost everything I've done–from magic golfers to serial killers–has been ignored. I do movie after TV movie, after miniseries and somehow after the film, the subject could be outrageous as cannibalism in the suburbs of necrophilia, it doesn't matter, I become invisible again. That's partly what was so painful about getting cancer. I wasn't satisfied. I wasn't *finished*. I was still trying to make my mark on the world.**

Bob reveals in his memoirs, the film he and Cheryl did together evidently didn't do much for her career either. **"She's still perceived as a *Charlie's Angels* babe. *Vega$* came out of Aaron Spelling's *Charlie's Angels* bag of tricks, so what did I expect? We were all caught up in the Spelling mill of bikini-clad show girls, careening sports cars and poolside antics. When**

you hear your producer, Aaron Spelling, saying publicly that your show is 'candy for the mind,' your heart sinks."

Bob truly believed that no matter how you may try to break out, if you were going back to that series [*Vega$*] whatever you did in the meantime wasn't going to illicit the kind of weight it might have otherwise.

"If I'd quit the first year of *Vega$* and done a couple of films, my whole career might have been different. It's the chaos theory. But, when you're twenty-five or twenty-six[1] and someone says you're going to star in a TV series it was like pie in the sky. I thought, they couldn't be talking about me, could they?"

One Sunday, Bob was leafing through the newspaper and the entertainment section, reading out loud, **"Well, I'm sure glad I'm not in *that* film. Gee, I really don't want to see that one–what a disaster. How did that one ever get made? Who are these people? Very occasionally, I'll say, 'Well, now there's one I'd like to have done.' But that's one out of how many? I'll go, 'Wow! I'll remember that and I want to see that guy in something else.' My wife [Heather] will say, 'Who?'**

"I say, 'But you know, of course, that he's a card-carrying member of the FLC.'

"'The what?' 'Well, the f_ _king*[2] lucky club.'"

Spring 2001

"I don't even know how you get in to see people for substantial roles in these movies anymore. You talk to an agent today and it's like, 'What are you nuts? We've got movie stars out of work. *They're* taking other jobs.' So, I've been looking at other things…and it's not just a cop out—I don't think. There's a lot of actors who would do anything for a part. I don't know that I care about it that much."

Sometime in early 2000, Bob was offered the chance to direct a low budget feature. **"I started working on a project a year and a half ago, but it required a certain amount of money to actually be able to get it done. You always hear stories about, 'Well, we did it very economically. It took us nineteen years, but it only cost us a hundred grand.' The budget for this particular movie was very low, A million bucks."**

---

1 Whether knowingly or not, Bob knocked a few years off his age. Born in 1946, he would have been 32 when Vega$ first aired in 1978, but his point is well taken.

2 Bob hardly ever swore. He believed those who did were unable to express themselves properly. He rarely if ever used the "F" bomb.

The budget for the movie Bob was supposed to direct was very low, considering the costs of making motion pictures today.

"A million bucks–which sounds like a lot of money for an independent film, but not if they hand you a script where they want stuff to blow up. You just can't do it. It's not that I'm not interested in quiet little stories, I am, but that's not what I've been offered so far. Some simple story that's worth telling–-that you could do for a million bucks. No problem. You get a terrific actor who wants to play the part.

I'm still looking around for that kind of thing."

Towards the end of his life, Robert Urich's final television series was '*Love Boat–The Next Wave*. Anson Williams, who played Potsie on *Happy Days,* directed Bob on two episodes. "He was such a pro," Anson recalls, "showed up on time, knew his lines and always brought an air professionalism to the set. Everyone enjoyed being around him."

"Oh ya, one final thing about acting, at least from my perspective," says Bob, smiling. **"You know the three stages of an actor's career:**

Who is Robert Urich?

Get me Robert Urich.

Get me a Robert Urich type.

Then there's Red Skelton's version: ***youth, middle age and gee, you look good.***

I currently find myself straddling middle age, and gee you look good and whatever happened to Robert Urich?"

Never one to be a braggadocio, ever humble, Bob Urich never gave himself enough credit for his extensive and impressive body of television, film and theater work. You will find a complete listing of his work under Filmography at the conclusion of this book.

Bob & Heather appearing on-stage in Dayton Ohio in Henley Players Production Barefoot in the Park, *1981.*

Dylan Daniels & Bob appearing in the film Survive the Savage Sea, *1992.*

Actress & friend, Joanna Kerns; Bob's co-star in film Blind Faith.

Bob & actress Cheryl Ladd in film When She Was Bad.

PART III
Chapter 17

Bob Hits Pay Dirt with his own Wheel of Fortune

"VEGA$"
Part 1

[**Words typed in bold ink** are Bob's and are taken directly from his journal.]

It's late Friday afternoon. The sun is beginning to dip in the desert and against the horizon is a brilliant red sunset. The lights of the city slowly start to flicker on. It's not quite dark yet. Robert Urich walks into the casino…which is still half empty except for a sea of green felt tables. The promise of winning hangs in the air like some opiate.It's the beginning of a Vegas weekend. Friday night blurs into Saturday, and by Sunday morning around eight, there are people stubbing out their twelfth pack of cigarettes and throwing their last chip onto the pile.

"I'm waiting for my wife to come down to dinner, so I've got some time on my hands. I get into a game of Black Jack/Twenty One. I'm alone at the table when a guy in a tailored business suit sits down. The dealer obviously knows him. 'Good evening doctor,' says the dealer, and my first thought is that he is a doctor of cards, or perhaps, dice. Turns out, he's just a doctor from Dallas. A plastic surgeon. The cocktail waitress is there with his drink as soon as he sits down. She already knows what he's drinking. I'm impressed. The doctor pulls out a wad of fresh one-hundred-dollar bills and puts two hundred dollars on two different locations.

He loses. Both hands.

He then pulls off four-hundred more dollars and loses again.

Peels off four-hundred more and loses that.

Peels off another four-hundred and loses that, too.

Okay, now I'm seriously impressed. I figured must have nerves of steels–or a helluva lot of money."

Vegas Casino's

"None of his losses phase the doctor one iota. After exhausting the dollar bills in one pants pocket, he reaches over and takes out another wad and when he's lost all that he goes in his breast pocket and loses all that money, too. By the time he's had two drinks, he's lost almost fifteen thousand dollars. Twenty minutes ago he was this polished, gleaming, suave guy. His eyes sparkled. He was smiling and confident. Suddenly, he's become a stuttering, blubbering fool. 'I seem to have just had a bad run here,' he said, in a dazed voice. 'I seem to have lost all of my money,' he says, like a sleepwalker having a bad dream. 'I don't even have anything for the girl.' Yeah, well, that's the least of your worries, I think, as he stumbles off. I tip the girl."

People go to Vegas and lose huge amounts of money. It's almost as if they go to lose money. One Monday morning, Bob was shooting an episode of *Vega$* at the Desert Inn. The place is virtually empty at six-thirty in the morning; that's why they are there. The original deal with the casino stated producers could only shoot at the casino, during 'off-hours' when it was less crowded.

"Over in the Baccarat pit–the Baccarat crew are always in tuxedos– there is a handsome young guy in a lavender silk shirt and black gabardine slacks. He has an enormous mound of chips in front of him, a mountain of chips, that I'm told have been slowly dwindling all night long.

"Who's that? I ask.

"The heir to the Anaconda fortune. I've been getting calls all night about this.

"From whom? I want to know, his wife and family?

"Nah. From the people over at Caesars, from the people at the Sands and the people at the Frontier."

"What gives?"

"Well, this guy comes in about once a month, bringing ten million dollars with him, and he stays until he loses it. Sometimes, it's the weekend and sometimes, it's a week. I've been getting these calls all night long from casino managers complaining that I need to send him back over there."

"So, he can lose money over there, too?" I ask.

"Well sorts, but it's more they think they're owed, which I don't personally see."

"How's that?"

"Well see, this guy went to Caesars and won five million, and then he went over to the Frontier and won another two. Now, he's here at the Desert Inn and he's losing it all. They figure it's their money he's losing over here at the Desert Inn; they want us to send him back over there so he can lose the money back into their own casino."

Something to do with honor among thieves, I guess."

The one time Bob Urich hit $200 on the slot machines, a passerby recognized him from the show [*Vega$*] and figured the thing was rigged.

Bob Urich hit the Wheel of Fortune when cast in Producer Aaron Spelling's 1978 ABC television series, *Vega$*.

Bob was doing a show called *Soap* for ABC when he got the part in *Vega$*.

"I've been feeling like time is running out for me–it always is for actors. Sure, I'm making a fairly good living playing slick talk show hosts [on *Tabitha*] and lubricious tennis pros [*Soap*], but I have to make a move soon or I'll be stuck in the limbo of 'I-know-that-actor-from-somewhere.'"

One day Bob heard from his agent, Merritt Blake, that ABC was looking for a young detective for a new series set in Las Vegas. They had made an exhaustive search to find the right actor to cast for the part, but were not satisfied with anyone they auditioned. **"Aaron Spelling,[1] the producer of this new show, had seen me a year or two earlier and talked about using me in a new *Mod Squad* series he was thinking about doing. In the end, they decided not to do it, but Spelling remembered me from that screen test and wanted to see me. So, I head over to 20th-Century Fox and meet with Aaron Spelling."**

Spelling hands Bob two scenes to read. One scene takes place in a room and the other one is out in the alleyway. At the audition is another young actor, Bart Braverman, whom they were considering for the role of Binzer, and ex-hood and Dan Tanna's sidekick.

"I've always hated that word 'sidekick,' but in this case, it was a pretty accurate description of the character. Bart Braverman Binzer."

---

1 Aaron Spelling's name attached to any TV series in the 70s & 80s usually signaled a hit, from *Beverly Hills 90210, Fantasy Island, Vega$* to *Love Boat.*

Vega$ and Channeling Dan Tanna

"It occurred to me that if I'm going to play this Dan Tanna character every week, he'd better be a character *with* character, with some dimension to him beyond the standard P.I. clones that were proliferating TV at the time."

It was at that exact moment that Bob's personal and professional creativity came into play. **"I asked if I can write my own screen test. They're a little taken aback at the arrogance of an actor wanting to write his own lines. So am I."**

First, they shoot the scene in the alleyway. No sooner did they begin acting out the scene than Bob discovered something very alarming happening to his sidekick.

"He's having a fit. He [Bart] had epilepsy and would have seizures right in the middle of a scene–he'd blank out, be unable to even remember his name.

Sometimes, he'd completely lose the power of speech. He'd just stand there and stare with tears running down his face. People would come running over and I would tell them to stay back. 'It's okay, we're just talking here.' Bart would be speaking absolute gibberish. Then he would slowly come out of it and start smiling at me.

"'Who are you?' he'd ask me.

"I'm Bob. You're Bart. We're doing a screen test."

"'Oh, okay, I get it.'"

Then, they head inside and they do the other scene. They're about to wrap it up when Bob says, **"Uh, just a second, if you don't mind. I kinda want to do this monologue[1] I've written."**

Words typed in bold ink are Bob's and are taken directly from his journal.

In the monologue, Bob describes the character he's playing, how he lives and why he lives in Vegas. The whole time Bob is walking around, tossing a football, going into the refrigerator, taking out a beer, popping it open. He sits down on the sofa and looking directly into the lens while continuing to toss the football up and down explains who the guy is.

The next day, Bob gets a call from one of Aaron's top guys, Bret Garwood. He says, **"Hey Bob, guess what? Maybe I'm not supposed to tell**

---

1 Quite often Bob would write a description about the character he was playing. Read more in chapters 15 and 16.

you this, but Fred Silverman[1] looked at the screen test and saw your monologue and said, 'That's the guy, that's the character. Hire him.'"

***

For the next three years, from 1978-1981, Urich played Dan Tanna, a Viet Nam vet, who works as a private investigator in Las Vegas, Nevada, the gambling Mecca of America. Ironically, Bob's long-time friend, Tom Selleck, also auditioned for the lead role. "Yes, I interviewed him for Dan Tanna," says *Vega$* producer, Duke Vincent, "but I thought his voice was pitched too high for his Marlboro Man looks. He got it down and became a star [on *Magnum P.I.*]"

Bob Urich as Dan Tanna, equipped with his magnetic charm, helped solve crimes surrounded by roulette wheels, blackjack games, and poker tables in and around Las Vegas casinos. Tanna makes it quite clear he is not a bodyguard, nor does he do divorces. He mostly rescues lovely ladies in distress.

Note: Fox didn't begin television network programming until 1986 with the *Late Show Starring Joan Rivers*. The animated *Simpsons* was the first major hit for the Network, first airing December 17, 1989. As of this date, [2019] 30 years later, it is still as popular as ever and still being televised.

Vega$

Dan Tanna lives on the Las Vegas Strip next to Circus, Circus Hotel in the theatrical props warehouse owned by the Desert Inn Hotel and Country Club which he converted into his living place. A cool feature of Dan's pad allows him to park his shiny 1957 red T-Bird in his living room. His office at the Desert Inn[2] is owned by multi-millionaire Philip Roth, played by legendary film star, Tony Curtis. The office is complete with an array of hi-tech gear for its time, including an answering machine that physically picks up the phone off the hook and into the mic of a

---

1 Fred Silverman served as programming head at three major television networks, ABC, CBS and NBC, and was head of ABC from 1975 until 1978. The *Vega$* pilot aired on ABC-TV in 1977 on Silverman's watch.

2 The Desert Inn opened April 24, 1950 and remained in operation until August 28, 2000. It was the fifth resort to open on the Strip. The Desert Inn was imploded on November 16, 2004 to make way for the Wynn & Encore Resorts. The Desert Inn's most famous guest was Howard Hughes, who arrived on Thanksgiving Day 1966, renting the hotel's entire top two floors. He later bought the hotel when asked to vacate.

tape recorder. Roth has the detective on retainer, but "Dan the Man" also works for all the casinos and seems to know everyone, including a host of celebrities who wander through each episode, often playing themselves.

The *Vega$* guest list is impressive, and features big name stars of the day, including Dean Martin, June Allyson, Sid Caesar, Cesar Romero, Shelley Winters, Melanie Griffith and even the ace of pool sharks, Minnesota Fats and heavyweight boxing champ, Muhammad Ali. With such a powerful celebrity guest line-up, *Vega$* was perhaps the most star-studded private eye show in the history of television. With the exception of a few episodes filmed in Hawaii and San Francisco, *Vega$* was filmed entirely in Las Vegas. In fact, *Vega$* is believed to be the first television series produced entirely in Las Vegas.

Dan Tanna's name was inspired by producer Aaron Spelling's favorite L.A. restaurant, Dan Tana's [the character got an extra N in the surname], at 9071 Santa Monica Blvd in West Hollywood, which opened back in 1964 and remains a popular dining spot [2017].

In a *Los Angeles Times* article [July 6, 2003], *Vega$* producer Duke Vincent tells staff writer Robert W. Welkos how he persuaded the real Dan Tana to lend his name to the television series. "Dan Tanna was the man whose name we had in the script of the original *Vega$* pilot," says Vincent. "I became aware that there was a man in L.A. whose name was Dan Tana who is in the restaurant business. I asked our people, 'Anybody call Dan Tana and say, by the way, we're using your name in this pilot, do you mind?' They said, 'No, are we supposed to do that?' And, I said, 'What! Are you nuts! Of course, you're supposed to do that! Get him on the phone!' I managed to locate the real Dan Tana on a golf course in Britain and crossed my fingers. He said, 'Send me a copy of the pilot.' I said, 'I can't. I've got to deliver it to ABC tomorrow. He said, 'What would you do if you were me?' I said, 'Dan, I'd say, yes, because although you are now famous, I will make you even more famous.' He said, 'I'll take a chance,' and over the phone from London, he gave me his permission, and the rest is history."

Dan Tanna was a ruggedly handsome, fun-loving private eye who, when not keeping a watchful eye inside casinos on the Vegas Strip, could be seen outside cruising behind the wheel of his 1957 cherry-red Thunderbird convertible, which came complete with all the latest electronics of the day. Seated beside him, his constant companion, a long barreled .357 Magnum.

"On Sundays," Duke Vincent says, "Bob loved driving the T-Bird down the strip. When people saw him, they'd yell, 'Hey, Dan Tanna!' Bob would smile and wave his trusty Magnum in the air. Crowds would cheer and go ballistic. They loved him and he loved it! There's no question his ability to become the character he played was a big plus, which led to his success and popularity. Later, he did the same thing with *Spenser.*

Bob once described Dan Tanna as "a guy who wears wool jackets and a leather vest in 120 degree heat." Heather Urich says, "I remember the set always had an ice bucket and everyone would dip towels in the ice water and drape the towels around their necks to try and cool down." Something different and cool about the show was Dan driving his red T-Bird straight into his living room. Many fans of *Vega$* fondly remember that gorgeous car. During a TV talk-show interview, Urich commented, "that car got more fan mail than I did!" The car was not the only beneficiary of the popularity of the show.

"When we went to Vegas in 1977 to film the pilot it was in the doldrums," insists Duke Vincent. "When we went on-the-air with the show, the city was not doing well at all. Suddenly, everybody wanted to see the Vegas we were portraying with Dan Tanna and the T-Bird." Vincent said he could not make a deal to film the show with a hotel that was owned by the mob. With the exception of the Howard Hughes hotel, the Desert Inn, all the hotels were owned by the mob. "So, I made a deal with the Desert Inn and Burt Cohen, who was Pres. and CEO of the place to do the show there. After the pilot episode aired, we asked Burt what he thought of the show. 'It's the worse piece of junk I've ever seen,' he said." Never one to give up, Vincent, a former Navy pilot who in the 1960s flew with the popular Blue Angels flight demonstration team, convinced Cohen to allow them to shoot future episodes at the hotel. "He wasn't exactly thrilled with the idea. 'I can't shut down the hotel,' he said, 'so you can shoot. You'll have to shoot after hours from 3 o'clock in the morning until 7 A.M.' I said, okay, fine, whatever it takes, so that's what we did. Now the show goes on the air, and it's a smash hit," says Duke.

"People begin to come to the hotel to see where the show is shot, hoping to meet Dan [Bob]. So, Burt comes up to me and says, 'Maybe, you can shoot whenever ya want.' I said, really? He says, 'Ya, I'll make it work.' So, now, we start working normal hours, no longer restricted to filming at three in the morning!"

"Another four or five weeks go by and Burt comes up to me and says, 'Hey Duke, how many of those red-T-Birds do you have?' 'What are you talkin' about,' I said. 'I got two. One is a stunt car and the other one is a show car. Why?' 'Well, you only shoot here [at the Inn] a couple of days a week, right?' I said, correct. 'Well,' he says, 'when you're not shooting could you please leave one of the cars parked at the front door entrance.'" Laughing, Vincent says, "In a little over a month, we went from you can only shoot after hours to could you please park one of your cars out front so people driving by the Desert Inn will think Dan Tanna is home and come into the casino." Ah, the power of television!

In an April 2002 interview with the *Las Vegas Sun*, Burton Cohen, whose resort was the primary filming location for *Vega$* had words of praise for Bob Urich. "There was not one ounce of temperament in him as an actor," says the former President of the Desert Inn. "He brought a sense of seriousness to his role as Dan Tanna but always appeared as though he had fun doing it."

By the way, the next time, you dig out your DVD copy of *Vega$*[1] and turn it on, watch when Dan Tanna strolls in the Desert Inn. In the background, you'll hear, "paging Burt Cohen. . .Mister Burt Cohen." Duke Vincent, the producer and show runner [head writer] on *Vega$* knew it didn't hurt to stroke the ego a little of the man in charge, Burt Cohen.

Vega$

[**Bold typed words** are Bob's, taken directly from his personal journal.]

Duke Vincent says they shot the pilot, which was written by Michael Mann, in 1977.[2] **"He also wanted to direct it, but they wouldn't let him. The way he wrote the pilot was darker and had a little more edge to it than what the series eventually became. The pilot, the way it was originally written was very film noir."**

"We had a fifty-two national share pilot. I didn't even know what the number meant. It means that over half of all the TV sets that were on,

1 According to producer, Duke Vincent each episode of *Vega$* cost $750,000. to produce.

2 Michael Mann is a film director, screenwriter and producer. His major films, include *The Aviator* based on Howard Hughes life, *Last of the Mohicans* starring Daniel Day Lewis, *Heat* with Al Pacino & Robert De Niro and *Ali* with Will Smith. His films mix artistry with music and are noted for emotional intensity.

were watching *Vega$*. We were selling plenty of toothpaste for ABC. The pilot got such high ratings when it aired, the ABC programming brass thought we could do no wrong. It was a little like being the captain of the Titanic. Everyone was going around saying we couldn't sink. It was encouraging–but also a bit alarming."

"I've seen stories about how the Dan Tanna character was based on this or that private eye, but it's nonsense. Some guy looking to make a buck."

"There was no real-life model for Dan Tanna. Michael Mann created *Vega$* out of whole cloth. If he got him from anyone, it would be the popular radio detective, Phillip Marlowe. All other *Vega$* accoutrements in terms of the car, the clothes and all of that, came from Aaron Spelling, the wardrobe department or myself."

"Dan Tanna was an updated version of Raymond Chandler's private investigatorPhillip Marlowe complete with that attitude, '*Down these mean streets a man must go…*' But being in the seventies, and this being an Aaron Spelling production, he's a slicker, shallower quantity. He [Dan Tanna] **walks around in Bermuda shorts and air-brushed Hawaiian shirts and always has a bet going."**

Who Is Dan Tanna?

Bold typed words are Bob's own and taken directly from his personal journal.

"If Dan Tanna was in a casino waiting for somebody, he would be playing kino, or if he were driving to an appointment, he'd be listening to a Laker game because he had a point spread. That kind of guy. The script was way ahead of its time."

Vega$ showcased the old corrupt Los Angeles of Raymond Chandler,[1] only transferred to Las Vegas. The series encapsulated all the corruption of the big city underworld, complete with gangsters and petty hoods. Bob says it was hard work staying smooth for the part.**"I shave using a straight razor when I get up in the morning. By the time I get to the set**

---

1 Raymond Chandler's *Phillip Marlowe* was a wise-cracking hard-drinking tough private eye who was quietly contemplative and philosophical who enjoyed chess, who is morally upright and does not dish out violence just to settle scores. Chandler was 51 when his first full-length novel *Big Sleep* was published in 1939. Seven more novels were published during the last two decades of his life. His last, *Playback*, was released when he was 70. Phillip Marlowe was featured in the movies and on radio and television.

I have to shave again with an electric razor. Then, around 4 o'clock, it's time to shave off the whiskers once again. And even with all that shaving the make-up artist has to put powder on my face after every scene.

"In truth, Dan Tanna wasn't that original a creation. He was probably the 720th P.I. on TV with a wardrobe of unbuttoned flashy shirts, who was fast with the quips, fond of women and had a supernatural knack for solving cases. "I'm nothing like that," says Bob. **"If anything, I hope my own helplessness gave the character a bit more dimension. I don't know what kind of inner life you imagine Dan Tanna would have–although in my audition monologue I did have to give him one–mine, or at least my own compounded with the kind of movie tough guys we've all grown up on. But, I know I'm nothing like him in any other way. Dan Tanna was always sticking a gun in somebody's nose. I haven't been in a fight since I was ten."**

"Dan Tanna was a bad dude when he had to be. Get them with my fists was his moniker. If I had to handle the situation like that, I would have been killed a long time ago.

"The television series *Vega$* basically followed the theme of the pilot, but the pilot was done in a series of vignettes with a down and dirty Dan Tanna prowling through the bars and casinos, which gave it a certain dark feeling and momentum. Somehow the inventiveness and bite of the pilot was missing from the actual series."

Urich says, "Aaron Spelling in his wisdom [Bob actually credited with handing him his career] – knew what the audience wanted back then. They wanted a certain slickness and polish–they wanted a Vegas with glitter, shoot-outs and lots of pretty girls. He was right."

To this day, many believe that *Vega$* was a spin-off of *Charlie's Angels*. Any confusion may lie in the fact that both shows were produced by Aaron Spelling. However, Dan Tanna and *Vega$* was not introduced on *Charlie's Angels*, but in a pilot which aired as an ABC-TV Movie of the week on Tuesday, April 25, 1978. Five months before the 3rd season premiere of *Charlie's Angels* on Wednesday, September 13, 1978, the episode *did* feature a cameo appearance by Bob as Dan Tanna. The crossover was simply used to promote *Vega$* as an upcoming, regular series which debuted one week later on Wednesday, September 20, 1978.

Bob hits the Wheel of Fortune with his hit Television series, VEGA$, *1978-81.*

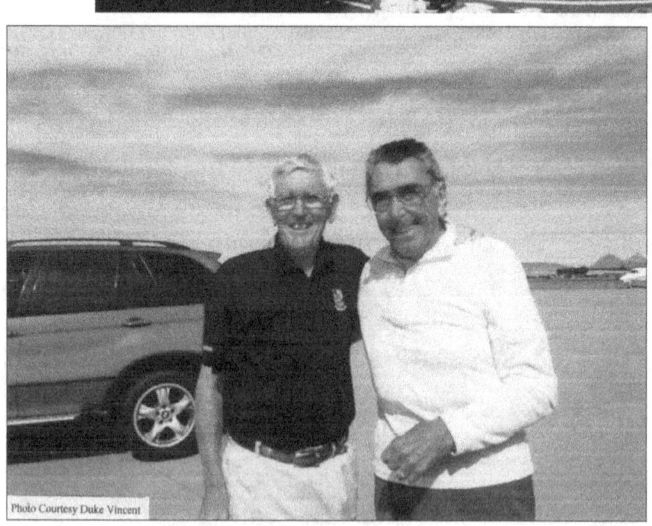

2017, 'Duke' Vincent, on right, Producer of Vega$ *with Admiral Denny Wisley, former leader with Blue Angels at Pensacola Naval Air Station. 'Duke' once flew as aviator with Blues.*

Chapter 18
"*VEGA$* "
Part II
Behind the Scenes
'off camera'

Bob, *Vega$* & the Ladies

Bob was handsome and the women loved him. One day during shooting of *Vega$* it got so bad with woman flaunting all over him that Bob called his wife Heather. "Can you please come over to the set and bring Ryan [their infant son] with you? Maybe if these women see you," he pleaded, "they will finally realize I'm married and in love with you and only you and they'll leave me alone!" It worked. . .but only for a little while. Bob's charm and good looks couldn't keep the throngs of female admirers away.

Tennis pro Johnny Lane[1] met Bob Urich when Bob, Tom Selleck and their wives were vacationing in Hawaii. "Hawaii had always been a favorite vacation spot for Bob.When I met Robert, I was in Hawaii and I was the touring pro of a little village resort on the big island. Since I was the touring pro I wasn't there all the time but I just happened to be there that day. So, these two big guys, Robert and Tom…I mean, I'm five-eleven and they towered over me. They wanted to hit some tennis balls. There were three courts right there in the lava area over-looking the ocean, a beautiful, beautiful site. Robert and Tom were literally belting balls out of the park, or at least out of the tennis court. Bob drove one ball about a mile nearly into the ocean," says Johnny, "And, Selleck wasn't much better hitting behind him. 'Hey guys, this is tennis, not baseball,' I laughingly said, as we shook hands. They were having fun, so I said, 'okay, let's take these old balls, not the new ones and line up this way [facing the ocean] and see who can hit it the furthest down into the ocean.' We became friends pretty quick. I'm a pretty easy goin' guy from down South, originally from

1 Today [2017] Johnny Lane is director of the tennis program at the Las Vegas Country Club

Mississippi. Ya know, if I can do it tomorrow, I'm gonna do it tomorrow," he laughs. I'm a very laid-back type of personality."

Bob & the Tennis Pro

"I ended up staying there longer because of these two guys, and actually didn't show up for one of the tournaments I was supposed to go to, because I was having so much fun with them. They left and I finished up my duties with the hotel. I got hurt and called Bob to see how he was doing that's when he said, 'Why don't you come to Las Vegas?' By the way, at that time, I had no idea Bob was an actor. I had never been to Vegas. My home-town is about 450 people and I never had been to the big city. Even though I traveled a bit, playing [tennis] around the world, I'm still a small-town kid.

"I get off the plane in Vegas and I've got all my racquets and gear with me and there's a limousine driver at the airport who has a sign which reads, 'Mister Lane.' I went up to him and in a joking way said, 'Look my last name is Lane. I'll go with you if you can't find one.' He said, 'Hey dude is your name, Johnny?' I said, 'Ya.' 'Get in.' I had never been in a limo and I get in and people are looking at me like I'm somebody. The limo takes me over to a warehouse to see Robert and ya know, there are cameras, the director's chair and fake little sets and stuff and I see Robert standing over next to the catering table. He's actually making coffee in one of those big over-sized 50 gallon urns. I went over and gave him a big hug and said, 'Hey man, how ya doin! Holy mackerel, do you work on this movie set?' And, he goes, 'No, Johnny, I'm the star of the show.' About that time, the director said, 'Mr. Urich we have you ready.' That's when I found out Bob was an actor. I had a back injury and tennis was on the back burner for awhile, and Bob asked me to stick around. I guess my job was his 'dialogue' coach. If you listen to my Southern accent, you'll know right away, I'm not one to be giving any dialogue lessons. I was also Vice President of Urich Productions, which I had no idea what that meant."

"Here I am, a 21 year-old kid," says Johnny Lane, "living at the Desert Inn, in the suite next to Bugsy Siegel and I'm thinking, I'm never going back to tennis, this is great. For the next three years I worked with Robert. He had a home at the Las Vegas Country Club Estates at 1096 Vegas Valley Drive [Johnny rented after Bob moved out]. Working withhim was way out of my comfort zone but was so much fun. He was such a good guy.

"There was one time, Heather was at *the Golden Door*, which I guess is a work-out place in Southern Calif. Robert and I were back in Vegas. That week's episode of the show featured a very beautiful actress. I can't recall her name. It may have been Lisa Hartman? We were downstairs at the Desert Inn, and Bob says, 'here's a hundred bucks go play the slot machines.' I said, 'Where you goin?' He said, 'I'm goin' over to so and so's room and we're gonna rehearse some lines.' 'What? Maybe, I should be doin' that,' I said. So, he heads out the dressing room door, heading over to wherever this actress' room was. Now, I'm thinking, 'gosh-damn it, I can't believe he's doin' that. I hope he really is going to rehearse lines,' because I looked up to Robert, almost like an older brother. Thirty seconds later, he comes walking back through the door, grabs the hundred dollars out of my hand and says, 'Gimme that, let's go gamble ourselves.' Now, I'm not sure why he changed his mind. Maybe it was the look I gave him or something in my voice, whatever, I was relieved. His intentions could have been the simplest thing on the planet, but you hear all this stuff about Hollywood, the casting couch and it makes your mind wander. He was a very good lookin' guy and women were constantly approaching him. But, as far as I personally know," says Johnny Lane, "Robert never wavered in his love for his wife Heather and remained faithful to her in spite of constant temptation."

Johnny Lane says he never really saw Bob get overly upset. "My nature is not to get upset too. I can usually talk my way out of most things," says Lane.

"Bob was the same way. I gravitate 'like to like.' In other words, I don't want to gravitate to someone I don't want to be around. Both he and Heather have this mannerism that is very comfortable to be with which I like. Growing up with my mom, dad and two sisters in a small town in Mississippi, there's not a whole lot to get upset about."

"I don't think I ever saw Robert get mad. I do remember one time, he got upset with himself. He had bought a home up in Oxnard [CA]. A beautiful place and we had gone to the store to buy television sets. He had to get a pretty big deal, because he wasn't buying one, it was more like ten. He wanted one for about every room where they would fit. I remember he was driving up the 101 and I could sense he was a little pissed that he had purchased so many television sets. He was kinda mumbling and stuff and I thought, how can I lighten the air a little. While he was driving I took one of the brown bags that had some of the cable stuff, punched a couple of holes in it, and stuck the bag over my head. I was seated way over in the passenger seat of the truck he had rented to transport all the TVs, and I wasn't saying a word. I'm looking straight ahead through the eye holes in the bag. All of a sudden, I hear him stop talking and feel the truck swerve a little. We almost went off the road because he was laughing so hard. I think he enjoyed having me around for a little comic relief."

"There were only a couple of times I saw him get really upset," Johnny reminisces. One time was on the set of *Vega$* when he wasn't too thrilled with me. He had to do this intimate scene and it was his birthday. I hired a guy to come over wearing a guerrilla suit. What a mistake! That didn't go over well. He was pissed about that."

Johnny Lane & the gorilla guy

Bob's sister-in-law, Sheila Menzies was on the set that day. She saw the guy in the gorilla suit get off the elevator. "I thought, 'Oh, Oh, Bob's not going to like this.' I think Bob took his acting seriously, and birthday or not, the gorilla suit was bad timing. When I saw what was happening," she says, "I took off in the opposite direction."

"Another time I saw Bob upset," says Lane, "is when he was duck hunting up in Ontario. He was shooting left and right and could never hit anything. He was really upset [with himself] but a lot of people do that. There was another time when we were also up in Canada at the lake. He had these really old fishing lures that were across the top of the mantel [in his cottage]. I was up there with a buddy of mine, staying for a week and doing some fishing. Well, my buddy had grabbed one of those lures, put it on his line and threw it out there, saying, 'God, look at the action on this thing. It floats so well.' I said, 'where'd you get that thing? It wasn't in the tackle box.' He said, 'I got it above the mantel.' I yelled, 'reel that in, quickly!' While he was reeling it in a pike grabbed that lure. He brings it up in the boat. I'm beating the crap out of the pike, so I can get the lure out of his mouth. All of a sudden the line breaks. I jump into the water, grab that pike and pull the lure out of it's mouth. 'Come on!' I said. 'We gotta go to an Arts and Crafts place right away!' We cleaned it up and put it [the lure] back on the mantel, but it didn't quite look the same. Bob was a little angry about that. But, I never saw him angry on the set or show any emotion towards anyone that may make one think, 'Okay, I'm not gonna work with this guy.'"

In spite of the gorilla suit incident, Johnny says, "He and Bob had a close friendship and a great working relationship for about three years." When it ended, Lane swears it had nothing to do with any guy in a gorilla suit…

"After *Vega$* got cancelled, we all went up to his cottage in Canada. During that time, I was also getting antsy to go back into tennis. You know when you're with somebody pretty much almost 24/7, you tend to get into each others' way. There were some times when we stepped on each others' toes. One time, he was having construction work done on his house and dealing with a banker. When the banker suggested something, rather than let Bob give his input, I put my input in. You see, I got to know him [Bob] so well, that I would say, 'he's gonna want to do it this way or that way.' This one time at the bank, I started to sign for him, because I had signed his name so many times. He looked at me really strange, almost as if to say, 'well Johnny I can do that.' I went, 'Oh sh_ t!' So, I think we both kinda got in each other's way a little bit. We did not part on bad company by any shape, fashion or form," he insists. "It just seemed time for both of us to move on.

"I was offered a position at the Las Vegas Country Club. I told Robert I'm going back to the Country Club because there's a position. When something comes up, let me know. I started working with kids and had a big following with them, which I enjoy. He went on to do [two TV series] *Gavilan* and *Spenser: For Hire*. And, I ended up staying at the club. Bob and I stayed in touch over the years. Every time I saw Bob after that, it was always a great big hug and 'how ya doin,' man.' In fact," Lane says, "We had a trip set-up to go fly-fishing down at the four corners in the San Juan's, when he went into the hospital for the final time."

Bob was an everyday guy

"Bob liked being more with the common man. He wasn't wrapped up in the world of the movie business," says Lane. "As far as I'm concerned, Bob looked at it [acting] as a means to an end so he could support he and his family. Don't get me wrong, I think he loved every minute of what he did. It's not an easy job being an actor. You know I deal with a lot of celebrities here at the Club, and I see the good and the bad. Bob was a really good guy. I was with him in so many situations, and he was always the same whether it was sailing a boat, going to the grocery store, or standing in front of a camera, or waiting in line to get an airline ticket, whatever it might be and in all those different cenarios, I gotta say the wow factor with him was just that. He wasn't anything different than that. What you saw with Bob was the real person. A real *good* guy."

Bob was a mensch

"Bob was a mensch," says *Vega$* Producer, Duke Vincent. Mensch is a Yiddish expression meaning *of integrity and honor*. "He was a terrific guy and a pleasure to work with. Everybody loved Bob. The thing that impressed me more than anything else about him was his high work ethics. He never, ever complained. We shot *Vega$* six days a week on location in triple digit desert heat! When we began shooting the show at the Desert Inn in June 1977, Bob was the sole star. Of course, there was a supporting cast, but unlike other shows which have leading stars, Bob was it! A normal day for us was twelve hours, but it was never that. It was always 14, 15 or 16 hours. When you figure he had to get up an hour or two early to get to the set on time and when he got home, he had to learn his lines for the next day, you're talking at least an 18-hour work day. That didn't leave much time for Bob to spend with Heather and his family. On top of that," Duke says, "We weren't shooting under normal studio conditions."

Duke and Bob

"We were shooting on location which was basically a desert. I mean, that's what Las Vegas is…a desert, where it's 102 degrees. Bob's running around in a 1957 Thunderbird with no air conditioning with the windows up. He never complained. Basically, the joke going around," says Vincent. "he did *Vega$* for us and we fried him, and he did *Spenser* in Boston and they froze him. This poor bastard couldn't get a break," he says, laughing. Whether he was frozen or fried, Bob was easy to work with and a good guy.

"That's why I say he was a mensch. He never complained. Bob never said, 'I can't do that.' He did about 85% of his own stunts. He loved doing that, but it made me crazy. If he got hurt, where the hell would I be, but he insisted he wanted to do it, and I reluctantly said, okay, fine. . .and closed my eyes when he'd do a stunt."

"The only thing Bob ever asked me to do was at the end of the first season...and I wrote a ton of shows on my typewriter. Notice I said, typewriter and not computer. Bob asked me, 'Duke, do you think you could write a show where maybe I get a Saturday and Sunday off?' I said, 'Robert, you got it! I will do that.' Bob looked at me and said, 'if you can do that I'd appreciate it.' That's the kind of man he was. Bob came to work every single day, never late. He knew his lines. He never f%#* up a scene, nothing."

"On the other hand, our other 'star,' Tony Curtis, was the complete opposite of Bob. Talk about oil and water," Vincent says, "I loved Tony but he was a handful. He was a huge star and I loved him. We had a great relationship, but I said to him, 'you know, Tony, getting you to the set on time, knowing your lines and keeping you sober is like herding a room full of cats.'"

Tony Curtis and Will Sampson

Tony Curtis told an interviewer, "Being on *Vega$* is great. So many people respond to me, it is fabulous. It's like having a kind of Alzheimer's where everyone knows you and you don't know anyone."

Will Sampson - Harmon Two-Leaf

One of the regulars on *Vega$* was Will Sampson, a full-blood Muscogee/Creek native American. The 6-foot-7, 240-pound man played Dan Tanna's Viet Nam buddy, Harmon Two Leaf. "Will liked to drink a bit," says producer Duke Vincent. "One day, he didn't show up on the set. I sent the assistant director to the motel where he was staying. He calls and says, 'I think he may be here, but I'm banging on the door and nobody will come out and I can't get the room key from the owner.' Bob said, 'What's wrong?' I told him and he says, 'Will loves me. Not to worry, come on. I'll go with you.' So, we hop in my car and drive to the motel. Duke says to the manager, 'Give me the key to the room. Whatever the hell it was I can't remember. I know it was on the first floor.' He says, 'I can't do that.' I said, 'Let me put it to you this way. Either you give me the key right now, or I will put you in the hospital, what would you rather do?' He looks at Bob, and Bob says, 'You better believe him.' The guy recognized Bob, and says, 'If you say so Mr. Tanna. I'll give him the key.' So, we get the key, go down to the room and knock on the door. No answer. I put the key in and open the door. There's Will on the bed, totally gone. On the floor of the room are half a dozen empty vodka bottles. So, I go over and I think he died. 'Will, Will,' I say, 'wake up!' He does and takes a swing at me. I duck and the momentum of his swing throws him right into Bob's arms. Will says, 'Is that you?' Bob says, 'Ya, do you want to waltz or do the lindy?' [1940s jitterbug]. I broke up," Duke says, laughing. "Where Bob came up with that who knows. He was a very funny guy."

On the set of *Vega$*

Bob had a great sense of humor. He and Bart Braverman, his partner Benji Binzer on *Vega$,* loved playing practical jokes on Phyllis Davis, who played Bea, and Judy Landers, who was Angie on the show. "Both girls were very well-endowed," says Duke, smiling. "Before the days of political correctness, Bob and Bart pulled off some pranks. Nothing scandalous," assures Vincent. "Just fun stuff, like hiding their bras"

A stage-hand on *Vega$* says it was fun working with Urich. "Unlike a lot of actors, he was very cognizant of the crew. He enjoyed cutting up with the guys on the set.

Veteran actor Gary Lockwood, who is probably best remembered for his starring role as the young Marine Corps officer on the 1960s television series, *The Lieutenant,* was a guest star on *Vega$*. "Bob was a nice guy," says Lockwood. "He played college football and so did I and we got along. Funny thing I remember about *Vega$*," he says, "was the actor's strike happened around that time and I never got paid. Later, I went back to do some additional scenes and I finally got paid. I never forgot that."

In 1978, Bob's friend, Francis 'Chick' Vennera was cast as Mitch Costigan in the pilot episode of *Vega$,* but he longed to do more movies. "After we filmed the *Vega$* pilot, I left for London to play Danny Ruffelo opposite Richard Gere in the film *Yanks.* In the meantime, my agent and Duke [Vincent] were in negotiations to get me in there [on *Vega$*]. After doing *Yanks,* I went back to Vegas. When I walked into the make-up room, there was a copy of *American Film* magazine lying right there. It had Richard Gere and my picture on the front cover. Needless to say, it did not make for a congenial atmosphere. It was kinda strange. It was one of those things that you get caught in the middle of something uncomfortable," says Chick.

"I was really proud of doing *Yanks* and I had already done *Thank God It's Friday.* I was on my way while Bob remained in television."

Chick Vennera believes if Bob had lived he would have eventually broken through to do major film roles, because the whole thing has changed. "What film was is not anymore," he says. "Television is better right now than a lot of the movies being made. HBO [Showtime] and all that good stuff that's going on. I think it was Julianna Margulies who said, back then that 'Movies were for adults and television was for kids.' Today, it's all changed," says Vennera. Chick did two additional episodes of *Vega$*. "Around the time Bob hurt his shoulder, he and I began having creative differences. We squabbled a lot. The tough personalities we played on the show kinda carried over to our clash in real life. So, we weren't speaking for a while. When you're the lead in a TV series, there's a lot of pressure that goes along with that 'fat check.' It goes with the territory. We all have our dark side. Look," Vennera candidly says, "I played sports with him. Believe me, he could get down and dirty, like all of us. That doesn't mean he's a bad guy. Bob was human. At that time, Bob and I were at odds. It was uncomfortable on the set so I walked. Looking back, we needed time to cool down and be friends again."

Later, after a much-needed cooling off period, Bob and Chick both came to the sensible conclusion that their friendship was more important than petty arguments, so they jumped in Bob's car and drove all the way from Las Vegas to Ontario, Canada and Bob's cottage on the lake, hashing things out along the way. Their friendship survived and remained intact until Bob's passing.

Vega$ played an important role in tourism for the city. People came to Vegas to visit the set to watch them film the series. The Dan Tanna character made such an impression that people who came to town would ask where he lived.

One Vegas resident had a near brush with Bob. He was crossing the busy street near the old Desert Inn. "My girlfriend and I were admiring the sites of Vegas–it was a lot different back then–when this convertible swerved to miss me and not by much, I might add. I felt the breeze against my leg as it passed by at a rapid speed. I looked at the car and noticed the license plate, 'TANNA.' I looked at the driver and realized it was Robert Urich. Since then, I've always admired his acting, but admired his driving skills more!"

Those who knew and worked with Bob, or those who simply bumped into him in the streets of the Casino capital while he was filming *Vega$*, all said the same thing. He was a nice guy. An article in the *Las Vegas Review Journal* [December 6, 2014] mentioned Bob and the crew spent several days filming at Rancho Circle, off Rancho Drive. Stephanie Stallworth was just five when she and her family moved there and has fond memories of growing up in the circle. She remembers Bob Urich filming his series there. "It must have been in the middle of winter because it was snowing and Robert Urich actually had a snowball fight with us." No matter who you talked with in Vegas–hotel workers, cabbies, everyday folks–inevitably the subject of the phoniness of Hollywood types came up. However, everyone had nice things to say about Bob, and his honest sincere manner in the way he dealt with the public. He was highly regarded and truly liked–and this in a town that sees mega stars come and go every single day.

Bob and the Champ on *Vega$*

[**Words typed in bold ink** are those of Bob's and are taken directly from his journal.]

Speaking of mega-TV stars, Bob certainly didn't come off as one, nor did he receive star treatment from the producers during the show's first season. His dressing room was little more than a utility trailer pulled behind one of the equipment trucks. However, during the second season, his standing had risen considerably and changed dramatically when Aaron Spelling visited the set.

"Aaron ordained that henceforth, I should have a motor home at my disposal. Ahh,luxury and comfort at last–until it got commandeered by a guest star."

Bob writes in his journal there was no shortage of talent in Las Vegas and the producers drew generously from the pool of guest stars including Wayne Newton and others who were in Vegas to do casino shows. But, according to Bob, no one created more excitement than Muhammad Ali. **"The Champ was coming to town for a title fight–strictly as a spectator–and our staff immediately went to work to recruit him for a cameo role. It would be a quick shot at sunset; Ali doing roadwork on a desert byway. Dan Tanna pulls alongside and they have a brief conversation as Ali jogs, three or four lines from the champ and Tanna peels away. It was a great idea!"**

Ali was supposed to arrive at four o'clock. A new motor home, identical to Bob's was brought to the set and parked adjacent to his.

'We waited. Four-fifteen, no Ali. Four-twenty, no Ali. We were getting anxious. The scene had to be shot before sunset."

Finally, a little after four-thirty, a caravan of black limos arrived and parked along the highway. Bob watched through the window of his motor-home as the door flew open and observed as bodyguards stepped out, one by one, followed by the champ.

"I realized they were not going to the coach provided for Ali, but were headed in my direction. The bodyguards entered first, each giving the place the once-over. Then Ali entered.

"Hello," I said, extending my hand. "I'm Robert Urich."

Ali nodded without smiling. I had seen that look in the ring a few times. "It's nice to meet you," I said. "It's so wonderful for you to do the show.

"Uh, excuse me champ," I began and realized five sets of eyes were boring into me.

"Ah, sir. . .champ. . .this is my dressing room. Yours is the one next door." He looked around slowly and said, "Well, this one will be just fine. I'll take this one. Thank you very much."

Bob quickly realized that when you are dealing with a guy who one-punched Sonny Liston into a stupor in the boxing ring, you lose all sense of motor-home proprietorship. **"I grabbed my coat and my script and left him with my beloved dressing room. One of my treasured mementos of *Vega$* is a photograph of Ali with his arm gripping my neck and delivering theatrical rabbit punches to my jaw."**

Vega$ producer Duke Vincent recalls another incident involving Bob. "There was an empty warehouse next to the Stardust hotel. In the show, Dan Tanna lives in a warehouse and drives his car into the place that is his bedroom and office."

Behind the scenes on Vega$-Bob's Accident

"From the Vegas Strip, Bob had his remote and would open the door and drive into the [empty] warehouse. Then, we'd cut and open on the actual set that we had built. So, one day, Bob says to me, 'Duke, I'm going to drive on to the set and when I'm coming in, I'll scream, 'The brakes, the brakes! And, I'll crash into the wall.' I said, 'You'll wreck the set.' He said, 'No, no. I won't hit it that hard. I just want to make 'Don' crazy," referring to director, Don Chaffey, who directed 17 episodes of *Vega$*. "He was one of our best," says Vincent. Born in East Sussex, England on August 5, 1917, prior to his work on *Vega$*, Chaffey had directed popular television series *the Avengers, Robin Hood* and others. Following *Vega$,* Don worked on two other Urich television series, *Gavilan* and *Spenser: For Hire*. His other 'big name' directing credentials include *Charlie's Angels, Fantasy Island, T.J. Hooker, MacGyver* and *Mission Impossible.*

"So, Bob drives on to the set," says Vincent, "and yells, 'The brakes!' And, of course, the whole crew doesn't know what's going on and are yelling, 'Oh, my God. He's going to hit the wall! Is he gonna get hurt?!' Well, when Bob slammed on the brakes, in fact, they didn't fail, but they skipped a little and he hit the wall pretty hard! No seat belt back in the day, and Bob launches into the steering wheel, hitting his head."

"Everybody panics, including me," says Duke.

"We run over to the car, drag him out and he's out cold, like a light.

"We lay him on the floor. I said, 'Get a medic over here. Get an ambulance,' and Bob starts laughing, and says, 'Duke, how'd I do? Was that a good shot?' He wasn't hurt at all. He faked the whole God damned thing. It had to be one of his best performances!"

Vega$

[**Bold typed words** are Bob's own taken from his own journal.]

One misnomer about the show is most everyone assumed Bob and the cast and crew were all carousing in the casinos until dawn and having a wild old time–but truth be known, they all went home after working. They were so exhausted from the 16-hour days filming in 108 degree Las Vegas heat. Under such conditions and long hours, is it any wonder a little levity was in order to keep one's sanity.

There was another time on *Vega$* when Bob did pass out, and it was not a faux pass. They were filming at the Frontier Hotel. In the script, Bob is in the audience guarding a notable. On-stage is a guy doing a song and dance routine with a cane.

"The cane turns out to be a gun or some ridiculous thing. I'm in the first row of The cocktail tables. They call, 'action,' and this guy dives off the stage."

He was a first-time stunt guy who got a little overly exuberant and forgot the cardinal rule of stunting, as Bob explains in his journal.

"When you fall like that, both performers have to have their hands free. That's how you control the situation. Instead, he wraps both arms around my arms and we *both* land on my right shoulder, which causes a complete separation of the AC joint. It doesn't break the skin, but you can see the bone protruding through the skin."

The pain is so intense Bob passes out. He awakened to a circle of faces staring down at him. **"Where am I? What's going on? I'm starting to hear voices, things are coming back into focus and I hear the head stunt guy say, 'He's okay. This happens all the time. He'll be fine. I'll pop his shoulder back. It just popped out of place.' Now, I'd probably say that, too, if I was him, but this guy wants to put his foot in my armpit and maneuver my shoulder back into place. At that point, I become very alert."**

Drill a hole in his collarbone

"You know what?" I say. "That's not something I want you to attempt."

"'Trust me,' he says. 'It's going to be okay.'"

"No, it isn't going to be okay. Go . . . Away."

That's when they decide to take Bob, or Captain Courageous, as he is now called, over to Sunrise Hospital. For a while, he is left lying on a gurney, because sometimes a dislocated shoulder will roll back into place once the pain subsides.

"The doctor says to me, 'Bob, you have to fill out this whole questionnaire. I didn't have my glasses with me , so I sad, 'can you just read them to me?'

He said, o.k.

Do you have a pacemaker? Because the metal in the pacemaker can be a potential problem.

No, I said.

Do you have any kind of metal implant?

I said, no.

Any bridges in your mouth?

No.

Do you have a penile implant?

Excuse me, I said.

Well, it's a ...

I know what it is! I said. NO, can we have the next question, please.

What about tattoo eyeliner?

I said, what?

Well some people have tattoo eyeliner which can make your eyes kind of water and get red and irritate the eye. I said, maybe you should ask the guy with the penile implant.

They wanted to give Bob a bunch of pain killers but. . .he refused.

"I want to know when you're hurting me," I tell them. "I want to know *why* it's hurting. The doctor gets up on the table and places his foot in my armpit. He starts maneuvering my arm, which only did more damage. Then a truly bizarre thought occurs to him. 'I can see now,' he says, 'We have quite another situation going on here. What we'll do is we'll drill a hole in the bloke like the size of a ballpoint pen tip and then wire it closed and in six weeks time, you'll be fine.'"

"You're not drilling a hole in my collarbone or anywhere else, I tell him."

Meanwhile, the producers are rushing around trying to get Bob a flight back to Los Angeles. At the time, Western Airlines flew back and forth to Vegas, but they are booked solid. Next, they called Aaron Spelling and within fifteen minutes the entire first class section of the next Western flight became available.

"They took me onto the airplane and laid me down on two seats and flew me to L.A. A private car took me to Cedars Sinai Hospital. In the meantime, Spelling's people had called Robert Rosenfelt, a lovely man who was the Oakland Raiders team doctor, their head orthopedic guy."

Bob's separated shoulder

Dr. Rosenfelt and the staff took Bob into a private room and gave him a shot of Demerol to ease the pain. Only one problem: at the time, he didn't know he was allergic to it. He had a horrible reaction.

"The room begins to spin. I hear people saying, 'We're losing him. Better get the antidote. Get the syringe.' The nurses are crashing into metal tables full of instruments, running to get the antidote. I can hear everything that's going on. They give me a shot and the whole thing starts to come back into focus."

Dr. Rosenfelt wraps Bob's shoulder and packs it in ice. "We'll just keep it tightly wrapped," he says, "And, I think it will grow back together and be just fine."

Later that night, the ice begins to melt. Bob has the shakes and shivers as the icy water pours down his back,

"I ring the bell and this nurse from Manila walks in. I tell her what's happened and she says, 'Just get up. You getting up now, okay?'"

"'No,' I tell her, 'You don't understand. I *can't*. I can't move.' She's yanking on me, trying to get me to sit up and the pain was excruciating. 'Leave me alone!' I shout. 'You don't know what you're talking about.'"

Bob writes in his journal. She had just come on duty and didn't have a clue what was going on with him and his condition. It took Bob an hour to sit upright, before he could get up and go to the bathroom.

"After I got out of the hospital, I recuperated at a beach house we had at the time in Oxnard [CA] in Ventura County. We had a little sailboat. It was bliss. That's where I stayed for six weeks and rested and healed."

The show must go on

One day, while recuperating, Bob got a call from Duke Vincent. "Robert, you know," he says, "We have five shows cut together, all ready to go, except for those sequences where you talk on the phone in the little red T-Bird." The first season of *Vega$* was shot on the street. But the show became so popular that people would gather around when we were filming and wave and yell at the camera. The end result they could not get a good shot. So, they went to old rear screen projection that they used in old MGM movies years ago.

"They found this old guy who knew how to do it. They brought a huge rear screen projector onto the sound stage–it took up the whole back of the sound stage. They had huge fans blowing my hair so it looked as if I were driving."

"Bob," Duke said, "if you could come in and somehow do all those little scenes with the phone in the car and all that would be great." **"There were all these bits and pieces that they needed to shoot. That way they could finish the episodes and we'd stay on schedule and make all our air dates, etc. I said, OK, I think I can do that.**

They sent a private Learjet to Oxnard to pick Bob up and fly him to Vegas and take him right to the sound stage. **"They have the whole thing setup. The T-Bird and the fans, the rear screen is all ready to go. My arm is still in a sling–I still can't lift my arm. The script girl would show**

me the three or four lines of dialogue and she would read the off-camera stuff. I'd get in the car–there was a phone in the car.

Bob was the first guy on television to have a phone in his car–probably the first guy in America. The phone sat in the center console. They roll the cameras. Bob reaches over and can't lift the phone out of the cradle. In fact, he can't even lift the phone, period!

"They went, 'Oh no. What are we going to do?'

""Let me ask you this, guys,'I said, 'Can you stop the cameras and then frame up like another five or six inches?'

"'Sure, we can do that.'

"'Does it look ok?' I asked.

"'Looks fine.'"

Here's how they wound up pulling things off with the car phone scenes: They cut the shot through the steering wheel so you couldn't see Bob's hand under the steering wheel. They had somebody else moving the steering wheel, so you would see it turning. Bob took his left hand and cradled the phone under his right elbow grasping it. When they called "Action," he would throw the phone up and into position."

"More times than not, it looked like I was whacking myself in the head with the phone. I had a bruise the size of a San Fernando Valley tomato on the side of my face at the end of the day."

Urich & Sinatra

Bob Urich had always wanted to see Sinatra perform in Vegas.

"I had seen a lot of big headliners, but never Sinatra. He was coming to Caesars soI had my folks at the show [*Vega$*] make a few calls and you bet there were complimentary tickets waiting for me for the first show on Saturday night."

The cast and crew of *Vega$* always worked on Saturdays and that Saturday night, they worked late–right up until the last minute.

"I didn't think I was going to be able to make the show, but just in the nick of time they sprung me. Heather met me, and we jumped in a limo, dashed across town, pulled up in front of Caesars and ran in as if they were waiting for us–my ego working overtime here!"

Bob goes on to describe in his journal that "it was ten minutes past show time. The house lights were still up and people were buzzing and having cocktails.

"I introduced myself and the maitre d' said, 'Oh yes, right this way, Mr. Urich.' He took us down to a big beautiful booth. The equivalent of fifth row center. No sooner had I sat down than Tilly, this guy who was Sinatra's famous Sergeant-at-arms comes over and says, 'Mr. Urich, I'm Tilly. I'm Frank's guy and I just wanted to know if it would be o.k. if tonight during the performance if Frank introduced you?'

I'm thinking, is he kidding? Frank Sinatra's going to introduce this kid from Ohio? That he even knows who I am–I thought was astounding.

"I would be honored, I say."

Bob was wearing a sport coat, and had on a necktie. He was all dressed up. The lights go down, and Bob recalls that it was all very smooth and rehearsed. Out walks Sinatra and he begins singing. No chat, no intro. He sings one song and then another and then a third song. . .

"And, then he did a thing where he squints into the spotlight and the house lights come up about half way. 'There are a few people in the audience I want you to meet,' he says. 'Some people who have taken this country by storm. Ladies and Gentlemen, the most beautiful of the Charlie's Angels is here with us tonight, Jaclyn Smith.' Jaclyn Smith stands up. Then he points to the right, 'Over here, we've got a man who walked on the moon and how many people can say that? Ladies and Gentlemen, Buzz Aldrin.' Buzz Aldrin stands up. Then he says, 'Now the young man I want you to meet who has taken America by storm and they all love him, he's a hero for all the ages."

Now, Bob is all excited and is straightening his tie and getting up out of his seat when Sintara says, 'Ladies and Gentlemen, **Hank Aaron**.' Hank Aaron stands up and bows.

"The lights went down and he finished the show and he never mentioned my name. I thought, Frank Sinatra, o,k. for you. I never did like that guy afterwards. Besides, I always liked Dean Martin's singing better, anyway. He was born in Steubenville, the town next to where I grew up in Toronto, Ohio."

Bob writes in his journal, "Vegas is an artificial City with real gangsters." **"These gangsters would come around and extend courtesies, lay all these gifts on you. When our son Ryan turned one year old, a custom leather bomber jacket with his name embroidered on it was delivered to our house, a gift from one of their casinos."**

"I'm asking myself, what is a one-year old going to do with a bomber jacket? But, you had to be careful, because some day they might call in their markers and when they did you were expected to reciprocate. It was a wild place. Everything was available. Then again, I was this straight-laced family guy."

Behind the Scenes in Vegas

Bob writes in his personal journal that the Vegas valet parkers ruled the town. **"They were the people who knew what was going on, but nobody seemed to care. A guy named Elliott was the only guy who ever tried to befriend me. He was at the Aladdin Casino. He'd been indicted on seven counts of horse race fixing. Occasionally, he'd call me up and ask me to put his son to work as a stand in. He'd offer me comp tickets to see this and that and it was always a question of knowing who not to say yes to. When friends came to town, I'd say, 'you want to see so and so? I think I know where I can get tickets.' Later on, his son Bobby came looking for me in Boston when we were doing *Spenser.* He wanted a similar job to the one he had on *Vega$*. He ended up working for a week and then said, he had 'other stuff to do' and disappeared."**

Bob always tried to get the writers to put more humor into the *Vega$* scripts. **"I thought it was one of my strong suits. The wise-cracking P.I. was something that the script writers would write occasionally, but they weren't all that good at."**

"When funny little things would happen, instead of letting them play, they would cut them out or cut around them. I love moments in a scene where something unexpected happens. However, in *Vega$*, those mistakes or accidental bits of business inevitably got taken out in an effort to make everything perfect."

As an example, Bob describes a scene where he is making popcorn.

"During the action, I drop the top of the popcorn jar into the pan and fish it out. But when the scene played they cut it out. There's such a thing as being too smooth."

Bob says, "There was a certain style to television in the 1970s. And in *Vega$*, style took precedent over content, and sometimes, even over common sense."

Urich recalled getting scripts that had absurd scenes in them.

"After doing the series for a year or two, I would try and fix these absurdities. There would be a little desert town and the bad guy has me with my hands tied behind my back–on my knees–and a .357 magnum is held to the back of my head, and the script reads, 'And, Dan gets the drop on him.'" I'd say, 'Now, how in God's name, do you get the drop on somebody when there's a gun to the back of your head and you're on your knees and your hands are tied?' The director would say, 'Well, you make a quick move and you kick over the thing.'

"'What are you talking about, he'd've shot me eight times by then, reloaded and shot me another six,' I say.

"In the end," Bob notes in his journal, **"You just figure something out with the director. You create a diversion, some bit of business and it works–most of the time.**

"These scripts were not only written fast, they'd been recycled. The same story-line would show up in one of their other series. At the time there were a bunch of similar P.I. shows like *Starsky and Hutch* and *The Streets of San Francisco.*[1]

There were a ton of cop shows+ being done and the same guys who wrote *Vega$*[2] wrote for all of them. They would recycle the same script over and over, just changing the names."

***

They filmed *Vega$* all over the city. Sometimes, unexpected things happened. Like the night they were shooting a scene in a parking lot outside a casino. Inside, perennial Vegas entertainer Wayne Newton was set to perform. According to actor Alan Campbell, who was in the audience, when Newton opened his mic to sing, out came another voice from the speakers, shouting, "*Dan Tanna! Don't move or I'll shoot.*" Evidently, the film crews' mic was picked up by the sound equipment on stage. Being a pro, Newton quickly ad-libbed something like, ahh, Dan Tanna. You never know where he's going to turn up!

---

1 *Starsky & Hutch* aired on ABC-TV from September 1975 to August 1979, starring Paul Michael Glaser as Det. Dave Starsky and David Soul as Det. Ken 'Hutch' Hutchinson. Antonio Fargas played 'Huggy Bear' their flamboyant informant. *The Streets of San Francisco,* also aired on ABC-TV from September 1972 until June 1977, starring Karl Malden as Det. Lt. Mike Stone and Michael Douglas as Inspector Steve Keller [Richard Hatch played Insp. Dan Robbins during the final season]

2 During the years *Vega$* aired,1978-81, there were at least eleven other police dramas on network television.

The End of *Vega$*

"*Vega$* was a smash hit when we went on the air," says producer Vincent. "We debuted with a 42 share of the audience, and we remained a smash hit through all three seasons it aired on ABC. But what finally hurt the show was the M-G-M hotel fire where people got hurt. Suddenly Vegas was not a wonderful place to go anymore. It lost its luster," he says. According to Duke, "I think when we went off the air we had a 29 or 30 share. It dropped precipitously from where it had been and ABC dropped us. They figured Vegas was not glamorous. Of course, that wasn't true and two years later, it was business as usual.

Writing in his journal, Bob has his own theory on why the show was dropped. **"By the third [and final] season of *Vega$*, we were pretty much an established show. They, meaning our producers, wrote a very violent script. It was against the grain. At the time, the pressure was on Hollywood to curtail violence on television. All these studies were coming out about how television violence adversely affected children, even though the violence then wasn't very graphic. You hear a gun shot and then you see someone fall. You couldn't even show the gun shot and the victim falling in the same shot. It was a part of the code."**

"The code determined that the violence actually was very unrealistic. If you saw a little trickle of blood that was a big deal. A lot of times they would cut around it and not even use it. But the moral majority was screaming about violence on TV. It all came down to a head when a script came down that was so gratuitously violent the network balked. It was based on a true incident that took place in San Diego called the Bob's Big Boy Massacre. "

Vega$ Gets Canceled

"A guy walks into a diner intending to kill one of the people standing in line, someone second from the end. But, if he walks in and shoots the second guy from the end, there'll be witnesses, so he shoots everybody. It's a massacre. We did a show based on it and Tony Thomopoulous, the head of ABC at the time, said, 'You can't air that. I'm going to have parent groups and church groups crawling over me for promoting violence.' Duke Vincent, who was Spelling's right-hand man said, 'Who cares what they think? We're a hit. We're going to continue to make shows and you're going to continue to air them.'"

Bob's friend, Johnny Lane, recalls one meeting he was privy to, when things got a little heated between the ABC brass and Aaron Spelling. "I remember, we were over at Aaron Spelling's house. Robert and I were throwing bread at each other because he wasn't really interested in what was going on. He was interested, but wasn't, if you know what I mean. Aaron Spelling wanted a little bit more from ABC and they said, no and Spelling said, 'Well, I'm gonna pull *Vega$*.' And to the best of my recollection" says Lane, "the meeting ended kind of abruptly. It wasn't long after that they cancelled *Vega$*."

***

"Later in the year at the announcement of the show's cancellation in May [1981], **Tony Thomopoulous pulled me aside and said, 'I wasn't going to lose that pissing contest. I'm not going to be told what I can or cannot do. If I don't want something on the air, it's not going on the air. We're going to be good citizens and good neighbors and we're going to cancel his show.'"**

Bob wondered why cancel the show instead of just cutting down on the violence?

"Go figure." Bob believes the real reason *Vega$* got canceled was political. **"The woman in charge of programming at ABC who'd okayed *Vega$* had left and Tony Thomopoulous**[1] **became head of the Network. When you have a changing of the guard, the new king of the hill has the knife out for his predecessor's shows. We did a thirty-nine national share** [of the total TV audience] **–that's serious numbers and we got canceled. Meanwhile, the clones of *Vega$* proliferated. *Magnum P.I.* in large measure was a takeoff of *Vega$*. Same character."**

Bob admits that at one time he used to go around saying things like, **"My macho image is killing me."** But, he says, **"I needn't have worried about getting type-cast as that kind of character. It never turned out to be the case. I would have thought the natural progression for a guy starring in a show like *Vega$* would be to go into action movies. Have an agent segue [me] right into the kind of roles that Arnold Swartzenegger or Wesley Snipes or Bruce Willis ended up doing. Hey, I mean, Bruce Willis came out of a half-hour sit-com** [*Moonlighting*, which was actually an hour-long show]**."**

---

1 Tony Thomopoulous joined ABC in 1973, eventually was elevated to Pres. of the ABC Broadcast Group. He left the Network in 1985.

It makes sense that Bob Urich would have been a most likely candidate for action hero roles in the movies.

"But no one ever saw that in me," Bob says and quickly adds, **"Not that I would've wanted to spend a career doing it…but then again, I could've made a huge killing.**

Oh, well."

***

Bob always wanted to get a revisit with his ole pal, Dan Tanna. Perhaps, a TV movie going back and redoing the characters thirty years later.

Bob wanted to re-visit Dan Tanna

"*Family Affair* and *The Brady Bunch* have done reunion movies. Shows that weren't nearly as popular. *Vega$* achieved an almost iconic status for a lot of television viewers, but in spite of that, no one's been able to get a TV movie made. I came close one season several years ago. I pitched a story to one of Aaron's right hand men and I knew I was getting through to them when everybody at lunch began telling back to me the story I'd just pitched. 'Great. Brilliant!' the exec said.

"'That's a great idea,' another one said. 'Why don't we do that?'

"'Ok. We'll get right on it.'

"'The next day Aaron's right-hand man calls and says, 'What if we do a detective show in Freeport in the Bahamas?'

"'What are you talking about?' I said.

"'Well, we just wanted to do something a little different with you.'"

***

Bob Urich never did get to wear the wool jacket and leather vest again as Dan Tanna, but he did get to make one final appearance in Vegas. It was on April 24, 2000 at his old stomping grounds, the Desert Inn.[1] for a weeklong celebration and celebrity golf tournament in celebration of the 50th Anniversary of the hotel. The following day, April 25, a time capsule was buried on the grounds in a granite burial chamber.

Date to be re-opened: April 25, 2050.

---

1 Bob Urich died April 16, 2002, and two years following his passing, the grand dame of Vegas Casinos met her own fate. On November 16, 2004, the Desert Inn was imploded to make way for the new kid on the strip, the Wynn and Encore Resorts. It is rather certain that the time capsule survived the blast. Check in, come 2050, for an update!

Let's hope someone had the foresight to include a DVD copy of Bob's hit TV series *Vega$* tucked neatly inside the pocket of his well-worn tweed blazer or leather vest.

Bob & his long-time pal, Tom Selleck playing Backgammon on vacay in Hawaii.

L-R, Actor Chick Vennera, Bob & Johnny Lane at Urich's home/West Lake.

Bob's birthday on set of Vega$, *L-R, his mom, Heather & their son Ry & Bob.*

Bob & Bart Braverman, who played Dan Tanna's s inept assistant Binzer on Vega$.

Bob with Vega$ *cast members, L-R, Tony Curtis, Judy Landers & Phyllis Davis.*

Bob on phone while driving red T-Bird on Vega$.

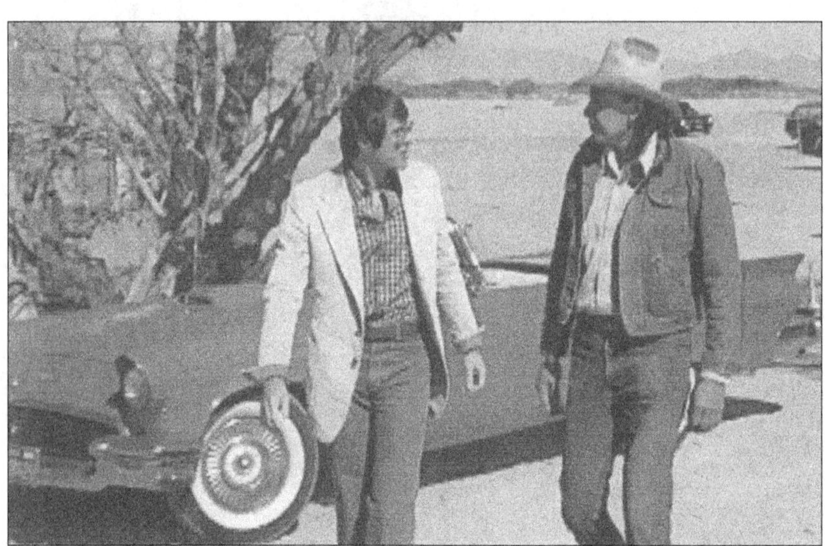

Bob with fellow Vega$ *cast member Will Sampson.*

Bob with Vega$ *crew in Hawaii. Bob with finger gesturing #1 sign is wearing shades and white hat standing in center behind camera.*

Chapter 19

"It's A Boy !"
Bob & Heather's Kids
Ryan, Emily & Allison

"It's A Boy !"

[**Words typed in bold ink** are Bob's and are taken directly from his journal.]

Heather recalls that after her television series *Logan's Run* got cancelled she became pregnant. "We were never not trying and we were over the moon," she confides. "The first miscarriage broke my heart, but after the second and third my spirit was starting to fade. We wanted a family from the very beginning. We knew this, and must admit," she says, "we had a lot of fun trying to make those babies, but still no luck."

The first year of *Vega$,* Heather was still working and still attending Milton Katselas' classes. "I would spend Friday through Monday in Vegas and then get on a plane for L.A., and go back n' forth. It was o.k., because it was only a 45-minute flight. I got into a routine of doing it. Bob's schedule of shooting *Vega$* was so busy throughout the week that I didn't feel badly about leaving him, and he could focus on the series. I would attend Milton's class on Tuesday night, go to auditions and even did a pilot. So, during that time, I was still very active in my career and contributing to our 'kitty.'"

It was summer 1978, during the second season of filming *Vega$*. After a multitude of fertility treatments that bore no discernable reason for the infertility, the couple finally had hope on the horizon. Bob writes in his journal. **"Heather and I were becoming very frustrated and ultimately, we decided to adopt. We were introduced to Tom Miller, then head of Catholic Charities in Las Vegas. We were put on an adoption list and waited and waited for a very long time."** Heather remembers, "We had no idea how long it would take. We had heard it could take up to seven years."

"We were living in Vegas part of the year where we had a condo. But, we'd come home to L.A. for Christmas, because that's what we always did."

"It's A Boy !"

North Hollywood
Christmas Day 1978 - 12:25 p.m.

Heather remembers the date and time very well. "The only reason I remember is because we were late. I had glanced at the clock. We were supposed to be at my parent's house for Christmas dinner by 12:30 p.m. and it was now 12:25. Bob was lying on the floor of our bedroom–as was his custom–lying on his back on the floor with his hands clasped behind his head–contemplating–staring at the ceiling. He wasn't dressed, just in his underwear and we needed to get going. His glazed over look was not in the getting going mode."

"'He's here,' he said.

"'Who's here?' I said.

"'Our baby is here,' he said.

"He just had a feeling it was imminent. I thought he was hallucinating," she says.

The next day the couple were getting ready for a little party they were having. **"Heather was doing the cooking. She was crazed. I was out shopping with my father. We'd been trying to get tickets to go to Hawaii. We wanted to take my parents to Hawaii for Christmas and were disappointed because there were no plane seats available. When I called the travel agent and told him I wanted four tickets to Maui, he said, 'Getting into Maui right now? Are you crazy? This is Christmas. I can't get you into Hawaii on a canoe. You can't get a seat for love or money.'"**

"Bob was out running a few errands and the phone rang. It was the adoption agency in Vegas," says Heather. "Someone on the other end of the line was telling me, 'it's a boy!'

"I was pretty confused and answered, 'What's a boy?' 'You have a beautiful baby boy who was born on Christmas Day at ***12:25 P.M.***' [This wouldn't be the first or last time Bob would be psychic about something] 'You need to come get him,' the voice at the other end of line happily insisted. Evidently, they had sent the letter notifying us of the impending birth to our condo in Vegas, but we were in North Hollywood for Christmas."

"I pull in the driveway. Heather comes dashing out the front door."

"I'm screaming, crying, joyous. At first," she says, "Bob thought this was all about getting those last-minute airline tickets to Hawaii that had been unattainable."

"See, I said to my dad, 'I knew if anybody could, that travel agent would get us into the hotel.' We step out of the car and Heather runs up to us and says, 'It's a boy!

Can you believe it? It's a boy!'"

I didn't know what she was talking about. That was a most astounding moment in my life."

"My sister Sheila," says Heather, "grabbed a camera and caught the life changing moment on celluloid. Bob and me in the driveway, holding each other up."

Not only were flights to Hawaii unavailable, so were all flights to Las Vegas. The joyous couple resorted to hiring a private plane. Heather, Bob and his mom, fly to Vegas with a fully-loaded diaper bag to pick up their son, Ryan Michael Urich…just 3 days old.

"We're in our condo [in Vegas] **pacing back and forth looking out the window. A car pulls up and out steps two people. One is carrying a baby.**

"They knock on the front door and say, 'The way we do this here, we present the baby to the father and the father gives the baby to the mother.' That was the beginning."

There was one important stipulation with the adoption agency that one parent had to not work outside the home for six months. "It's a very Catholic organization and maybe they felt one parent needed to be at home with the baby. They may have changed the rules now," says Heather, "times have changed, but that was the stipulation at the time. So, what am I supposed to do?" Call Aaron Spelling and tell him that Bob can't continue doing *Vega$*? "That wasn't going to happen, I want to tell you, Joe [addressing the author], I welcomed it. I went wow. I'm a mom. I'm no good at multi-tasking anyway. How am I supposed to fly back n' forth from Vegas to L.A. I didn't want to miss any steps. I had wanted this [the baby] for so long," she says, "and I didn't feel like I'd be giving anything up by stopping [her career] for that period of time."

"We had a little advance notice for our second child [Emily] and had a couple of diapers on hand," Heather says laughing. "But, I just didn't want to do it [acting] anymore. I wanted to focus on my family and be there for Bob and the kids. I didn't want to be an absentee parent. So, when Ry and later Em came along, I said, 'o.k., I'm done.'"

Bob did not in any way tell or advise Heather to curtail her acting career. "It did not come from him," she empathizes. "It came from me."

Bob and Heather & the kids/Love Boat

"We were always trying–or not trying–to try having a baby," says Heather. "I made it to four months once and was hospitalized with bed rest. At the time, we were in Canada for the summer and Bob was in NYC filming the movie *Turk 182* with Timothy Hutton. I remember flying my sister, Sheila, up to take care of Ry and Em, who were 2 and 4 years old at the time, while I lay on my back in little Picton Ontario hospital. When premature labor started, Bob chartered a plane and came to be my side. We were devastated by our loss, but we had two kids at home, and all I wanted to do was get home to them."

"Later, when Ryan and Emily were in high school, Bob and I found ourselves talking about having a third child. It wasn't until a few years later, after he completed cancer treatment that we decided to adopt our third child, Allison. At the time, Bob was in the middle of filming the TV series, *Love Boat: The Next Wave*. Yes, he was captain of *The Love Boat*. Aaron Spelling offered him the lead as Captain. It was the remake of the original 70's series which starred Gavin MacLeod as Captain. Bob and I had done a couple of episodes of the original, but he didn't want to do it. He told me, 'Heather, I can't be captain of *The Love Boat*. It will ruin my career. But, I can't say no to Aaron, I owe him my career.' So, I said, 'Here's what you do. You ask Uncle Aaron for an obscene amount of money and tell him you will only work three days a week. He'll *never* go for that.' The following day, when I asked Bob how it went. He looked at me, grinned and said, 'Looks like I'm the next Captain of the Love Boat!' Well, as it turned out, he loved doing it and what an amazing time we had. The kids and I were able to go on one of the cruises because it fell during spring break. They each had their own cabin and we never saw them," she laughs. "All I asked of them was that they not fall off the boat."

Allison Grady Urich

"When we decided to join Bob for one of the cruises," she says, "We were a little nervous about leaving the birth parents of our unborn baby behind. We were afraid they might change their minds while we were gone and take off. We need not to have worried as everything turned out just fine. Allison Grady Urich was born April 18, 1998 and immediately stole her daddy's heart." More on Allie coming up later in this chapter.

James Baquet was a teacher at Campbell Hall School in North Hollywood when Ryan was a sixth-grader. Before James shares with us how he and Ryan first met, we'll let him tell you about his first two encounters with Ryan's dad, Bob Urich.

"He was walking across the school quad. I said, 'Hi, Mr. Urich. How are you?' And, he ignored me. Irrepressible jerk that I was, and probably still am, over two decades later, I ran around in front of him and stuck my face in his and asked, 'ARE YOU ALL RIGHT?' Startled, he took a step back and said, 'Oh, sorry, I was just thinking about something.'

Our second encounter was at the school picnic. When we were introduced, he said, 'Ryan says you wanted to be a priest and then commenced to give me his Catholic *bona fides*–"I have a friend who's a Monsignor," yada, yada, yada.' I guess Ryan forgot to tell him I wanted to be an Episcopal priest."

James Baquet really got to know Bob in early 1995, when Heather called and asked if he would come up to Park City [Utah], where they were living at the time, and tutor Ryan. "'For how long?' I asked. 'The rest of the school year.' So, I put my apartment in storage, shipped my books to the Philippines and moved to Park City. I was nervous in anticipation of our meeting–and completely relaxed when we met."

Bob & James Baquet

"Robert and I were from similar backgrounds–blue-collar, he grew up about 45 miles down the Eastern border of Ohio from my mom's hometown of Youngstown. We had similar life experiences and so on. But, all of that is external," says Baquet. "What really clicked was that we were both seekers, readers, thinkers. I imagine that sensitivity must come through in some of the writings he left behind. If I recommended a book–Rilke's *Letters to a Young Poet* and Jon Kabat-Zinn's *Wherever You Go, There You Are*, which were hot at the time–he would not only read it but buy copies for others. Despite his great success, Robert was still a blue-collar boy, as am I," says James. "He was immune to the trappings of fame and stardom, and despite the difference in our worldly status, when we were together, we were just Bob and Jim. He was no snob. We'd talk about everything from movies to family to philosophy to history to reminiscences of childhood. He was a voracious reader, and not a quick, but a deep thinker."

"One of my favorite things about Bob was when I'd toss an idea out there–as teachers often do–and he'd say, "aw, that's horsesh*t!' And then we'd talk and talk and talk. Sometimes he'd end up agreeing with me, sometimes I with him. Sometimes, there was no resolution, but it was always the camaraderie, and being together that was important, not the conclusion. Once at the dinner table, Bob said, 'Hey Heather, maybe we should keep Baquet around after the kids go off to school, and he can teach us all the stuff we should have learned in high school.' He even told a reporter that I was the family's resident academic adviser. I loved him for his attitude towards personal growth.

"We talked a LOT about his illness when he was back in L.A. and undergoing treatment. Most of it was fairly philosophical. I never remember him talking about 'what would happen *if*,' as his attitude was pretty much '*it isn't going* to happen.' But, we did talk about the sweetness of life and the importance of sucking up as much goodness as possible–just what you'd expect from the man."

James Baquet says, "I am proud to have had the love, support and trust Robert and Heather gave me, but none of this is about *me*. It speaks to the kind of man he was, that he would pal around with a humble school teacher, take the guy into his home and even pay him to be around on set [*The Lazarus Man*] just for the chance to improve himself. Bob could have sat down and talked with almost anyone in the world, but he chose to spend a lot of time with me, and for that I'm grateful."

Now that you know how James Baquet met Bob, here's how he met Bob's son, Ryan. "We were on a school-sponsored camping trip near Malibu. On one of the hikes, I was 'sweep,' responsible for keeping the stragglers moving. Ryan was the chief straggler, but not because he was shirking. Rather, his innate curiosity was so strong that he just couldn't walk past the most boring twig or pebble without checking it out! So, he and I interacted quite a bit as I answered his questions the best I could."

The following year Ryan, now in seventh grade, found himself in Mister Baquet's English class where his inquisitiveness continued. "Students often try to get a teacher 'off-track' telling old 'war stories' and what-not," says Baquet. "Teacher learns to say, "If you're really interested, come back and ask me at lunch or after school. This usually kills the campaign. Ryan asked plenty of seemingly distracting questions. But unlike any other kid I ever taught, he would come back later, on his own time, to get answers!"

Ryan and his teacher

"It was his [Ryan's] attitude toward the world that made me say an immediate 'Yes!' when Heather asked me to come to Park City and tutor him. Well that, and the fact that I was unemployed at the time. As his former teacher," says Baquet, "I'd say his positive adjectives are respectful, loyal to the teachers who had nurtured him, inquisitive, smart, and quick-thinking. The negatives; hyper, scattered, seemingly lazy because his energies were not always directed to the task at hand, and potentially sarcastic because of his misused wit."[1]

***

Heather believes her son's time spent at Campbell Hall was most beneficial. "I'm sure his time at Campbell Hall provided fundamentals that helped guide him in his academic life," she says. "He was there in kindergarten and first grade. Then, we moved to the Boston area when Bob was filming *Spenser: For Hire*, and Ryan and Emily attended St. Augustine in Andover [MA] in the town where we lived. When we moved back to California, Ry was in fourth grade and again attended Campbell Hall until we moved to Park City. Along the way and during our travels, he went to Brooks in North Andover where, in his second year, he managed to get himself thrown out.[2] He went back to Campbell Hall for his senior year. He got his BS in Biology at Cal Poly San Luis Obispo." Heather says, "It took him a bit more than four years, because the school shut down in the summer [budget cuts] and he had two more courses to take before receiving his diploma." Ryan next attended and graduated from Ross University School of Medicine in Miramar, Florida, and in

1 In all fairness, James Baquet's observations of Ryan's behavior were made over 20 years ago, when Ryan was a teen.

2 Apparently, Ryan got caught smoking a joint. The school had a zero tolerance policy for substance abuse.

Dominica, West Indies. Today, Dr. Ryan Urich is an infectious disease hospitalist at Lovelace Medical Ctr. in Albuquerque, New Mexico.

Ryan Urich was a challenge for his dad

"I have one other story about Ryan Urich," says James Baquet.[1] "On the last day of seventh grade, we were on a class trip to Disneyland. Ryan was typically rambunctious on the bus until I said, 'Ryan Urich! If you don't settle down, you're going to spend the day with me!!' Thoughtfully, and not at all in a wise-ass way, he looked at me and asked. 'What rides would we go on?' He was merely considering his options. At lunch time that day he found us [the teachers] knowing perhaps, I'd head for the only Mexican place in Disneyland, and ate his final lunch with the teachers instead of his friends. Since my time with him in Park City, I have seen little of Ryan. The last time was the weekend of his dad's funeral [April 2002]."

Ryan Urich, like most healthy young teenage men, proved to be quite the 'challenge' for his dad. He always seemed to 'push the envelope' and along with it, his dad's buttons. It's not unusual for the young bull in a family to occasionally challenge the authority of the senior bull. Ryan is the first to admit that he was quite the handful for his dad. "I was a pain in the butt," he says. But according to "Ry-guy," as the family calls him, he and his dad only had one major brawl. "We only had one that I can recall. It occurred at my high school graduation party. Dad came up to my bedroom and asked, 'Where's your sister?' I flipped him some wise-ass answer, which apparently ticked him off. He dove at me and tackled me. We rolled around on the floor, almost like a scene in the movies; a lot of action without anyone getting seriously hurt. I knew some wrestling moves and managed to move out from under him. My dad, evidently realizing his actions, got up and walked away. No damage was done to either of us," Ryan says, laughing. "The next day, everything was back to normal. He came into my room, stretched himself out on floor with his hands clasped behind his head. His usual position when he wanted to talk. 'So, what's up?' he said. He was fine. That's the only time I can honestly say, we had any sort of altercation," says Ryan, "If you even want to call it that."

When Ryan's mom was asked about the incident, she simply said, "My memory is foggy about that night," laughs and cops the fifth. Then adds, "this most likely happened in California, when we had a graduation party

---

1 You can read more of James Baquet's friendship with the Urich's at his blog site.

for Ryan. I wasn't in the room at the time, because I don't remember it. Ryan was on the wrestling team in high school, so I'm sure it was his graduation party. Emily was busy out front taking car keys away from kids she felt were not fit to drive home." Em was 17, Ry was 19. She was always a good Samaritan who looked after her big brother and his wayward friends.

"On good days," Heather says, "father and son enjoyed fly fishing and went pheasant and quail hunting together. "When we lived in Park City, sometimes Ry and his dad would ski together, but Ry got too good for any of us to ski with him. Bob was always looking for new ways he and the kids could spend more time together."

April 2015

Heather Urich, reflecting on their son's actions, which sometimes his dad vehemently opposed, particularly his use of pot, says, "I think his father's diagnosis spun his head around quite a bit," she says. "Ryan kind of went off on me recently, telling me how horrible he felt about how he gave his dad a hard time when he was a kid [teenager], and how he wasted that time with him by being such a pain. I told him, you have to appreciate what you had with him. I reminded him of all the things his dad did for him and with him, like Cub Scouts. And how his dad went to every single one of his Little League games that he could attend. All the things he and his dad did together; the trip they took by themselves to Costa Rica on National Geo; a trip to Cairo and the pyramids. I reminded Ry of how he got to act and 'hang out 'with his dad on some of his movies and also an episode of *Spenser: For Hire*." When asked if he enjoyed acting, Ryan replied, "Not really, but it gave me a chance to spend time with my dad." Heather mentions one fun trip they took by themselves. "It was a fishing trip to Alaska. Bob taught Ry how to fly-fish. They brought back on dry ice the most amazing salmon I have ever tasted in my life!"

"Bob did have a way of intimidating Ryan's friends," she says. "He had a thing about teenagers wearing ball caps in the house. He'd actually rip them off their heads as they walked in. His confront level was pretty high if someone acted like a jerk or was disrespectful in any way, he would have no qualms about letting them know how he felt."

As a freshman biology major at Cal Poly at San Luis Obispo, Ryan would mess with his classmates by telling them his dad was a milkman or something like that." Bob believed at that point in Ryan's life, he felt the pressure of being the son of a famous actor. "He was very sensitive to just being Ryan." As an outlet, Ry turned to drugs, most often pot. His usage most likely caused by bullying when he was a youngster. When Ry was extremely young, he had to endure the taunts of classmates about his adoption. A classmate told him that being adopted meant he didn't have any real parents. "When a crisis like that arises," emphasizes Heather, "It's a time you have to have discussions with your kids. Bob and I never made a secret of our childrens' adoption. Instead, we stressed from their earliest days how special they are. We told them, 'We picked you because you are so special.'"

Ryan and his Dad

"Ry was just three days old when Bob held him on his shoulder," says Heather, patting his little bottom and while he was burping formula all over his daddy. Bob told him, 'I want you to know you are special. You're adopted and thank God you're here.'" The couple helped all their kids work through any identity crisis they may have had with love and hugs. They believe it's important to tell your kids sooner rather than later that they are adopted. Heather remembers when a major celebrity came up to Bob at the airport. He never met the person before, but somehow he knew we had adopted kids. He asked Bob when we told our kids they were adopted. Bob told him his story and he replied, 'My son's nine and we haven't told him yet!' Bob was floored."

When their kids were teens, Bob would still kiss them goodnight. His schedule was long. "Sometimes the kids are in bed when I leave in the morning, and when I come home late at night. So, I'd wake them up just to give them a hug." They never seemed to mind being awakened at one in the morning with a kiss. "Even if they did, we wouldn't stop doing it," says Heather. Ryan says his dad was a great guy. "He was always willing to try something new. I was a regular beach bum and fancied myself a pretty good surfer. I guess dad thought it was a good way for us to spend more time together, so he bought a surf board, because he knew I was into it in a big way. I can still see him trying to get up on that board! It didn't work. He wiped out! I told him, 'Dad, you're gonna kill yourself.' So that was that." Ryan remembers he and his dad went hiking and camping a lot. There's little doubt, he inherited his great love of the outdoors from his dad, but didn't reciprocate that love for surfing back to his dad. "No way," laughs Ryan.

It's a Girl, **Emily** *And another girl,* **Allison**

"It's a Girl, Emily arrives !"

Bob and Heather's second adoption, daughter Emily, was also through Catholic Charities. "I was in Los Angeles," says Heather, "when Bob got the call about Emily's arrival. We knew it was imminent but didn't quite know exactly when. I had to get back to Vegas immediately. There was a fog rolling in at the airport and a chance the plane wouldn't be able to take off. We ended up taking off early with a fraction of the folks on board. I arrived in time and Emily was brought to us that day. Emmy was a very sickly baby and toddler. We couldn't understand why she kept getting sick. She had ongoing urinary track infections and bladder problems. We finally found out what was wrong when we lived in Boston and she ended up at Boston Children's Hospital. She had a combination of two problems at birth which were not diagnosed until she was four. Emmy had ongoing urinary track infections and bladder reflexes that were defective and not closing all the way. The contaminated urine was backing up into her kidneys and destroying them little by little. In fact, one of her kidneys had already atrophied quite a bit. "We were so worried and concerned, our little girl underwent a 6-hour bladder implant surgery to correct the problem."

The tests and surgery they performed were very invasive, and Em remained hospitalized for two agonizing weeks. It was quite an ordeal for an adult to undergo, let alone a four-year-old child. "I got someone to take care of Ryan," she says, "while I stayed in the hospital with Em. Bob came over everyday after working on *Spenser*. "What a time that was," she sighs. "Thankfully, the end result was a healthy little girl, and two very grateful and relieved parents."

Meet Emily

"When my brother and I were growing up," Em says, "both our parents were strict disciplinarians. If we were going to be late for curfew, dad wanted to know *who we were with*, *where we were* and *how he could reach us*! At the time, I thought, geez, he's pretty strict but now, with children

Urich children at their Baptismals. Top L-R, Terry & Teril Foutz holding baby Ryan, his God parents, Heather & Bob w/priest. Bottom left, Heather holding their baby daughter Emily, Bob holding their son, Ryan. Bottom, right: L-R, Emily & her brother Ryan holding their baby sister, Allison

of my own, I realize more than ever that he acted the way he did because he loved us and cared for us so much. As we grew older, it was more difficult receiving the silent treatment from our parents. Their look of total disappointment in us hurt more than being yelled at." Their father didn't tell them how to live their lives, she says. He lived his life and let them watch him do it. As a father, Bob led by example.

"After I was at boarding school for awhile [Holderness in New Hampshire] and came home to visit, dad could see that both my brother Ryan and I were growing up. He treated us differently. I mean, as young adults, my brother and I discovered for the first time that our dad had a sense of humor. As a youngster," Em explains, "you never look at your parents as being funny. As we grew older, and went out to dinner with them and their friends, we could see how quick he was with one-liners and hear him tell funny jokes, some even dirty." Em's mention of her dad sharing a dirty joke somehow just doesn't fit Robert Urich's squeaky clean image. However, it does make him real.

Emily says, "Dad was fun to be around. I don't believe he ever said, 'Oh today, I'll spend time with Ry or Em.' He'd just ask me, 'Hey, you want to go golfing or fishing today?' The best gift dad ever gave me was making his family a priority. One thing that stands out in my memory is how he always made sure that with every opportunity he was offered through his work, that he thought we would enjoy or benefit from, he would do his best to include us. Thanks to dad, we traveled all over the world."

Emily & her dad

"For example," remembers Emily, "we traveled to Disney World at Christmas, and got to go behind the scenes from Niagara Falls to Hawaii, Australia and so many other places. The experiences they provided while being with our dad were the best gifts possible.

"Dad also loved the holidays. He made us think *all of them* were his favorite, but I think Thanksgiving was his favorite. My favorite holiday memory was a recurring one; cooking with my dad on Thanksgiving. We did it every year. I also have great memories of showing up at my Aunt Judy and Uncle Tom's home the last Christmas my dad was alive in December 2001. I was supposed to work that Christmas,[1] so my parents

1 Read more about Bob and what Christmas meant to him in Chapter 1.

didn't think I'd be able to be with them. At the last minute, I was able to get a few nights off. I called my Aunt and Uncle and made arrangements to surprise my parents. I flew back home and arrived at their house and remember both my parents cried. Of course, at the time, none of us knew how truly special that Christmas* would be until after dad passed a few months later in April [2002]. That entire holiday was a special occurrence in my life. At the time of my dad's passing, we had developed a really close friendship. I considered him my best friend." Em admits, "after dad died, mom and I were estranged for awhile. Part of the reason is she couldn't stand my first husband. I went to Canada and sort of dropped out. She and my brother thought I just took off on them and in a way I guess I did, but I had to find myself." Em's mom adds, "that's true," but insists they still spoke on the phone. Heather believes it was because they needed their own space back then. We were all grieving in our own way. At one point, I yelled at Ryan and asked him to leave my home. It was an extremely emotional time for all of us. Today we are all close again. I love my kids."

"I went back to school in my early thirties and got my nursing degree." Today, it's quite apparent Emily has found herself. She and her second husband Steve Notaro have children from their previous marriages. Em is an RN at Belleville General Hospital in Belleville, Ontario Canada and says, "she and her mom are much closer now."

Emily & Abby

Abigail Wright is one of Emily's best friends. For the past 16 years, Abby, as her friends call her, has worked as a professional stage manager, including eleven years with Cirque du Soleil in Vegas. In 2017, Abby was Manager of Entertainment Operations for the *Wizarding World of Harry Potter* at Universal Studios - Hollywood.

Abby and Emmy first met in 1999 at Occidental College. Em was a freshman and Abby was a sophomore. "We lived in the same dorm and were best buds though college. Em was the most practical one in the group. I could depend on her. She was always so supportive and loving. What impressed me most about Emily was her ability to give. When we were younger she met a lot of people who didn't always have the bes-tintentions, yet she never lost her optimism. She was always giving and loving. Her work ethic also impressed me so much. She is an incredibly hard worker. Not at all the spoiled child of a film star. When we were in college she was a Cutco knife seller and was so passionate about doing a good job. She was the best seller in her group.

"Even though Em grew up knowing movie stars and was well off financially, she was always grounded," recalls Abby. "I met and saw her dad a handful of times. He had cancer when we met but he was always joyful and loving. He treated me as one of the family even though I didn't know him that well. He was always accessible to Emily and never acted like a 'movie star.'"

Em's friends

"Emily's mom is a lovely woman, but I know Emily got along with her father better as a college student."

"I distinctly remember one time when I was spending the night at Em's home," says Abby. "It was my birthday. When we went to bed, her dad's name came up. He had passed the year before. Em played a tape where her dad voiced a children's book idea he had about a mouse doing something a human would do. It may have been a farmer. Sorry, I don't remember exactly. Em started crying saying her dad was always coming up with great ideas. She kept apologizing because it was my birthday and here she was crying. I remember comforting her and thinking grief never ends, it just changes. I was honored to be able to comfort her that night and that she felt she could be vulnerable with me."

Abby and Emily are still in touch, usually through Facebook and e-mails. "We aren't as close as we used to be," says Abby. Primarily because she is in Canada and I am on the West Coast [Calif] but I love her very much and know if she needed me I would be there in a moment and vice versa. Although we don't get to see each other I still consider her a close friend, whom I care for deeply. Emily is a remarkable woman."

Katie Brunk Lupton is also a friend of Emily's. Katie grew up in Aurora, Colorado. She grew up performing and at age 14, an agent visited Denver and picked her and a few other kids to come out to Los Angeles for a pilot. Katie's parents were very supportive, and off they went to Los Angeles. "I had two very successful pilot seasons," she says, "And, finally when I was 16 and about to start my junior year in high school, we moved to L.A. My dad was looking for a new job and the best one happened to be in Los Angeles at the time, and it's where I wanted to be to start a career. All the cards lined up, so we moved."

Emmy & Katie

"Like I said," Katie smiles, "I have very supportive parents. They put me in a private high school, Campbell Hall that was just down the street from our new home, mainly because it was the only school that had a spot for me and was close by that would allow me to audition and work. That is where I met Emily."

"Em had been at the school previously, had left for a bit and was now returning. Se we were both sort of new and neither of us jived really well with the other students in our class. Therefore, we were drawn to each other. I had no idea who her dad was. His name was not familiar to me as I didn't watch a lot of TV growing up. I just liked Em for Em. And, she didn't care, like a lot of the other students there, that I came from a small town, or that my parents weren't famous, or that I didn't have a car. She and I became really close. One thing that always impressed me about Em was her work ethic. She worked her tail off, sometimes, 2 or 3 jobs at a time. She made her own money rather than depending on her parents. She always worked hard in school even though it came easier to her than it did for me. She's a very determined, bright woman." Katie admits, "I struggled a lot finding my place in that school [Campbell Hall]. Thank goodness I had her, I spent a lot of time at her house and her family welcomed me just like part of their own. They were very accepting of me. I spent the night a lot. We worked on projects together there and her parents even helped us host a party."

After graduating from high school, Emily and Katie went to Europe together with Em's boyfriend at the time and a mutual friend of theirs. Katie says, "I stood by Em through a tough relationship with that boyfriend and she was there when I met my boyfriend [today, her husband]."

"Em was there when I started college at USC and we would talk and hang out all the time. The summer following my freshman year of college, Em and I decided to live together for those few months. We both wanted some independence. We were just sort of always there for each other. We supported each other. Em's sadness was my sadness, my happiness was her happiness. We went through it all together. After my husband proposed to me, she was the first person we called. Em even had us over to celebrate and decided to open one of her dad's bottles of champagne, but she didn't quite pay attention to the label. Turns out it was a 20-year-old bottle of Dom Perignon! *Sorry, Mr. Urich.* We still laugh about that. Her brother Ryan was there and pointed it out saying something like, 'Do you know what year this bottle is? Oh, he's gonna kill you.' Of course my fiancé and I panicked, feeling really horrible, but he (Mr. Urich) never said a word, at least not to us. If he said something to Em, I wasn't aware of it. But, she thought it was hilarious, which led me to believe that he wasn't all that upset."

Katie and Emily stayed in touch, even after Em moved to Canada. They talked all the time and e-mailed each other through each others' marriages and babies. They especially made a point of calling on each other's birthdays. "Neither of us ever really loved our birthdays," Katie laughs, "and we figured that way, we could at least brighten the other one's day with a call."

"We have always forgiven each other for our short comings and loved each other in spite of them when others wouldn't and I'm not sure that is something that can be erased even with distance. To this day, Em is the only one that calls me 'Kat.' I am so happy that she is happy and thriving. She deserves it. I will always love Em. We have a very deep, very special friendship."

Katherine 'Katie' Brunk Upton is still acting and lives in Los Angeles with her husband of 13 years, Jake, and their daughter and son.

Allison

Bob and Heather's third child, their second daughter, Allison [Allie] Grady Urich, was adopted through a private attorney. "Our precious gift was born on April 18, 1998. We were all in the delivery room and I got to cut the umbilical cord," says Heather, who looking back on that special day says how happy and excited they all were. "We had to leave her there for a day, which was so difficult for us, but we were able to take her home the following day. We were concerned about the paparazzi [with Bob's illness and all] so he didn't come with Emily and me to get her.

"When Allie came along, we were living in a house we rented in Toluca Lake because the kids wanted to finish high school at Campbell Hall. At the time, we were in the process of building our home in Thousand Oaks at the Sherwood Country Club. It's a beautiful spot at the base of the Santa Monica Mountains. We started building in 1999 and moved in 2000 after Bob did the *Chicago* [musical] tour.

It was before the *Chicago* tour that Heather knew she needed help caring for infant Allie. "I began interviewing people and when I met Dee Dee [Deidre Miller Cohen]. We immediately bonded. I wanted someone I could 'hang' with, and she was the one."

"We were together a lot [Allie and me]," says Dee Dee, "especially when Bob didn't feel good or when Heather understandably couldn't do it. It was on me. We were and are bonded. Big time. She was my best friend, we had each other's number from the day we met, and I knew this kid was going to change me, and she has. As a baby, she was joyful, quick, and fun to be with. When she would cry in the back seat, I would match and mimic her exact cry in volume, screech and squeal. It would stop her dead in her tracks. She would bolt upright in her car seat and stare at me quietly. It immediately stopped her! It was so strange, but so great! And, it worked every time! Allie was also deep. She would look straight into your eyes and put her little hand on your cheek and you'd feel like bawling. She wasn't a baby about trying foods, even though she was a baby. She would just gobble it. If she made a face, I'd say, 'Oh, come on!' And, she'd open her little trap and swallow it."

"That kid is a warrior, she rolls with anything and everything," says Dee Dee. "She rode roller coasters since she was 2 and 3 years old. She'd go stand in line by herself on the tot rides. I'd wave at her if I was too big to ride. She would just sit by whomever and just go for it. Allie got pretty upset when she didn't get her way which is pretty normal for a child. Being sad would make her mad. I think what upset her the most in her 'time outs' with me was me ignoring her. Which was not easy, who wants to be in time out? Ever? When she was little," Dee Dee recalls, "Allie had some issues with kids bullying and we talked about how to handle it. She faced them and usually won them over. And, when she didn't, she moved on better than any adult ever would."

"Allison loved being silly, being free, giggling is her specialty," says her former sitter, Dee Dee Miller. "She loves to have fun. She's a PARTY! Her smile was and is magic.

"Allie's a fast learner. I was very repetitive with her. We stuck to a tight routine. She knew with me, I meant what I said. One time, we had bought her a Magna-Doodle and she had a marker in the back seat. If you draw on a Magna-Doodle with a marker, it's all over. I was driving and saw her checking to see if I was looking. She had been ignoring my requests for the marker. I told her, 'Don't do it. If you draw on that, I'm going to pull over and throw the whole thing out.' I saw her thinking about it, then look up at me in the rear mirror, then look at the marker...and she went for it. Effed it up real good. I drove into a RiteAid parking lot, pulled into a spot in front of a trash can. I asked for the Magna-Doodle and she handed it right over. No problem. I was perplexed. I was looking for tears. I was looking to teach her a lesson. I took it, and marched right up to the trash can and dramatically held it up and dropped that sucker in the can. I was the only one who wanted to cry. She looked at me as a bitchy 30-year-old, then looked out her window, as if to say, get in, let's go buy me another Magna-Doodle. I did not. But, later she said, 'I'm sorry about the car ride.' Now, keep in mind, she was four at the time. It was crazy, she would have these very adult moments and understanding of way more than people gave her credit for. To this day, I have a very hard time not bossing her around when she comes to visit. But part of me knows she likes it. I think it makes her feel loved and feel the structure we had back then. Allie is very brave and wants to belong. You just want to hug her and she needs hugs." Dee Dee says, "I was her nanny, God-mom, auntie, sister, warden, boss for roughly 8 years, but we still remained close even when she moved away."

Heather, Allie and Dee Dee

"Heather was kind enough to continue to send her to stay with me. Allie still has a room in our home. She is my family and I love her very much. Her mom knows that and respects our bond, which means the world to me. I honestly consider her 'our daughter' because once Bob passed, it was really us, Heather and I who shared Allison. We spent a lot of time at the beach, at school, shopping and in restaurants talking. And, when Heather was there, it was three broads. Allison Urich is the bravest person I know. She was brave as a baby, a tot, a kid, a teen, and she is brave as an adult. She could have a nail in her foot and you wouldn't know it. She is that good at putting on a happy face. By the way, so is Heather. She's tough, too. One time, Heather had a bloody blister when we were walking about in New York City. She didn't tell me till the end of the day, showed it to me. It was like hamburger. Tough chicks, Allie and her mom!

Allie has very thick armor, built in. She's strong, and sadly, too good at goodbyes."

Bob used to say that she [Allie] seemed to come from a planet where there was no baggage. Meaning she was a very happy little camper. Emily is especially close to Allie and always has been. She always wanted a little sister and today, she is like another mom.

Dee Dee Miller Cohen believes Allie's strength comes from both her mom and dad. "Bob was a strong person. And God help anyone who displayed a lack of respect for others in his presence.[1] I saw him explode a few times. Once at a stranger in a crosswalk. I think the guy pushed a lady. Bob turned around and shocked the guy. He screamed and got in his face, towering over him and put him in his place. It flipped a switch in him… It was actually incredible," she says.

Dee Dee and Bob

"If it were someone besides Bob, not a celebrity, and not a giant of a man, it would have been a pretty crazy thing for an everyday person to confront a stranger in that way. I think a lot of people that are huge [in size] kind of use their bodies as an intimidating tool. I know a big girl who I've experienced this with. They feel more powerful, size-wise. I think it gives people a false sense that 'they're the boss,' the leader, or in Bob's case, *the protector*. It was great to see justice happen and I'm glad the guy scampered off and didn't have a weapon, you know what I mean? I liked that when Bob did explode. It was over pretty quick. When Bob was really pissed," Dee Dee recalls, "You could feel it coming, quiet, powerful, thunderous, like, oh f_ _ k is Bob mad? He'd come in stewing or be deep in thought and you just knew to stay away from him. Bob didn't like stupidity. He could be a little cutting with his comments, like if Heather and he were in a tiff, or if he was upset with his son Ryan, my eyes would go huge. I'd think, No! Don't say that in front of me. Bob was normal and he didn't like moron moments," she adds, laughing.

The Urich's Sherwood Home in California

"A lot of homes in Sherwood are Georgian in design but ours was more Cape Cod in style," Heather points out. "We built it based on the designs of Robert AM Stern who was Bob's favorite architect. He was so

1 You can read about Bob's reaction to Bob Duvall's lack of respect on the set of *Lonesome Dove* in Chapter 23.

enamored with his work. Stern designed quite a few notable homes in the Hamptons and Westchester County, New York. "We didn't have him design our home because he was $3000. a minute. Well, that's a bit of an exaggeration," she laughs, "but you get the gist. As it turned out, we found a local architect who had studied under Stern. He built us a beautiful home. The lot was $800,000, and I think, it cost 1.8 to build."

"Back then, the initiation fee for membership at Sherwood began at $200,000. When Bob died, the club made me sell the membership. I thought it was a family membership, and even if it was in his name I would inherit it like everything else. Not so. They put it up for sale the day he died. I could re-join, but it was at a price that was a lot more." To her credit, Heather never harbored any ill feelings towards those responsible for such an insensitive move. "No, we loved living there," she says, "We used all the facilities. Even though we had a pool, Sunday afternoons we would head over to the club house pool as did most everyone else who had kids. It was like a spontaneous pool party. Hockey great Wayne Gretzky and others brought their kids. The club made the best curly fries. Bob loved the Jack Nicklaus-designed golf course which is considered one of the best. We could walk out our door and tee off. One thing Bob truly enjoyed doing was after the course closed for the day, he could go out with little Allie after dusk and putt around. She had her own little mini set of clubs. It was Bob's favorite of all the places we lived. He said he wanted to live there for the rest of his life. . .and he accomplished that goal."

"Over the years, we lived in different places," Heather remembers, "We lived in North Hollywood and Sherman Oaks before renting in Vegas, and before Boston. We fell in love with New England and rented a place outside Boston in Weston. Our 'Money Pit house' was in Andover, MA. After *Spenser*, we moved back to CA, and Encino. Next, we moved to Utah and lived in two houses in Park City, and built one in Deer Valley, which I referred to as The Inn. It was too big. It had 5 levels and 3 stories. Our bedroom was on the 3rd floor, and had an elevator to the kitchen. Em's bedroom was on the first floor, next to the theater and wine room. The house was so big, Ryan had his own wing."

The Many Houses of Bob & Heather's

Sheila Menzies recalls how much her sister hated living in that house.

"The house or 'Inn,' as Heather called it, was above Park City in what I called, Bald Eagle, which was really Deer Valley," says Sheila. "She called me one day, crying, because it was overcast and snowing. I lived down the mountain from them in Park City and the sun was out. She was not a happy girl in that house." Some visitors often said, you could hardly open your car door because the force of the wind was so strong. "They didn't live there very long," says Sheila. "Bob got an offer he couldn't refuse."

After Bob died, Heather kept the Sherwood house for two years and sold it for around $3.3 million. "I really didn't want to live there without the membership. There was a profit and I bought a cute English cottage in Toluca Lake close to the school I wanted Allie to attend. She was on the list to go to a school closer to the Sherwood house but my life at that time seemed to be moving closer to town [L.A]. We lived there for four years but decided that I really didn't want to raise a teenager alone in Los Angeles. So, I sold the house in Toluca Lake, moved back to Utah and bought one in Park City.

"In 2013, after graduating, Allie and I moved to our cottage at the lake in Canada. And, the beat goes on."During this time, Heather also maintained a New York City residence, and Allie lived with her sister Emily in Canada, while attending high school.

In 2017, Allie moved to her own apartment, her first. It affected her mom emotionally, in a way she never expected. Heather's little Allison was all grown up. "Allie's leaving was so difficult and more traumatic than I ever expected," say Heather. "It was so hard to see her go."

August 2017 - Ontario Canada
Heather Urich's own writings

There's no right of passage for teenage boys in our society. They have a tendency to want to go away and do their own thing and having to fight to find their own identity.

"Ryan, the beautiful baby boy is now 38 years old and has a little boy and two girls of his own which Bob would have adored. Ry's dad doesn't know he found his passion and direction in life. He didn't see his son graduate from Ross University School of Medicine. Ry couldn't save his dad, so perhaps, he can save someone else was his reason for following this path, and today [2017] is an infectious disease hospitalist at Lovelace Medical Center in Albuquerque, New Mexico. Emily also found her calling in medicine and caring for others as an RN at Belleville General Hospital in Belleville, Ontario Canada. She is married for the second time and is a mother. Our third child, Allison [Allie] was only four when she lost her daddy. Today," writes Heather, "she is 19 and in college in Canada. Bob isn't here to see the fine young adults his children have grown up to be. As a lasting tribute to his dad, Ryan designed the cemetery marker, a cross, where some of his dad's ashes are interred in the tiny church cemetery, just a short walk from our family cottage on West Lake."

"Bob doesn't know any of this," writes Heather, concluding her journal entry about her children – all of whom she loves so much.

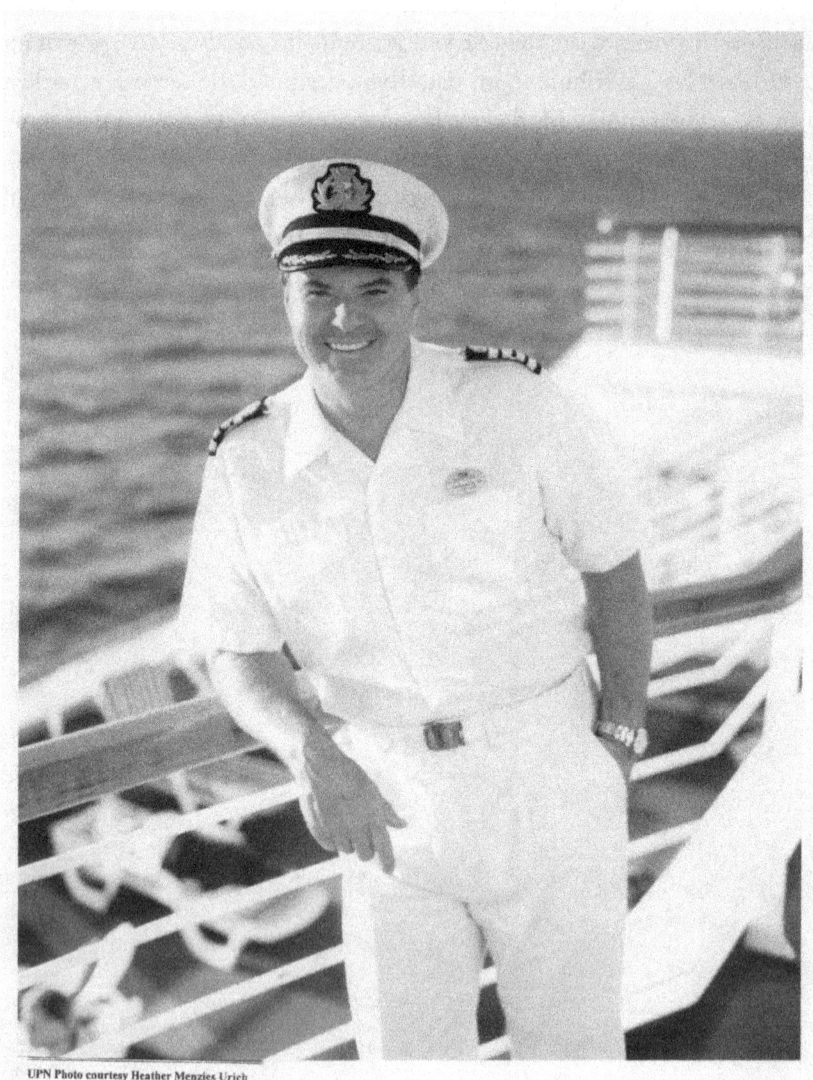

UPN Photo courtesy Heather Menzies Urich

Bob as Capt. Kennedy, skipper of the UPN's Love Boat: The Next Wave.

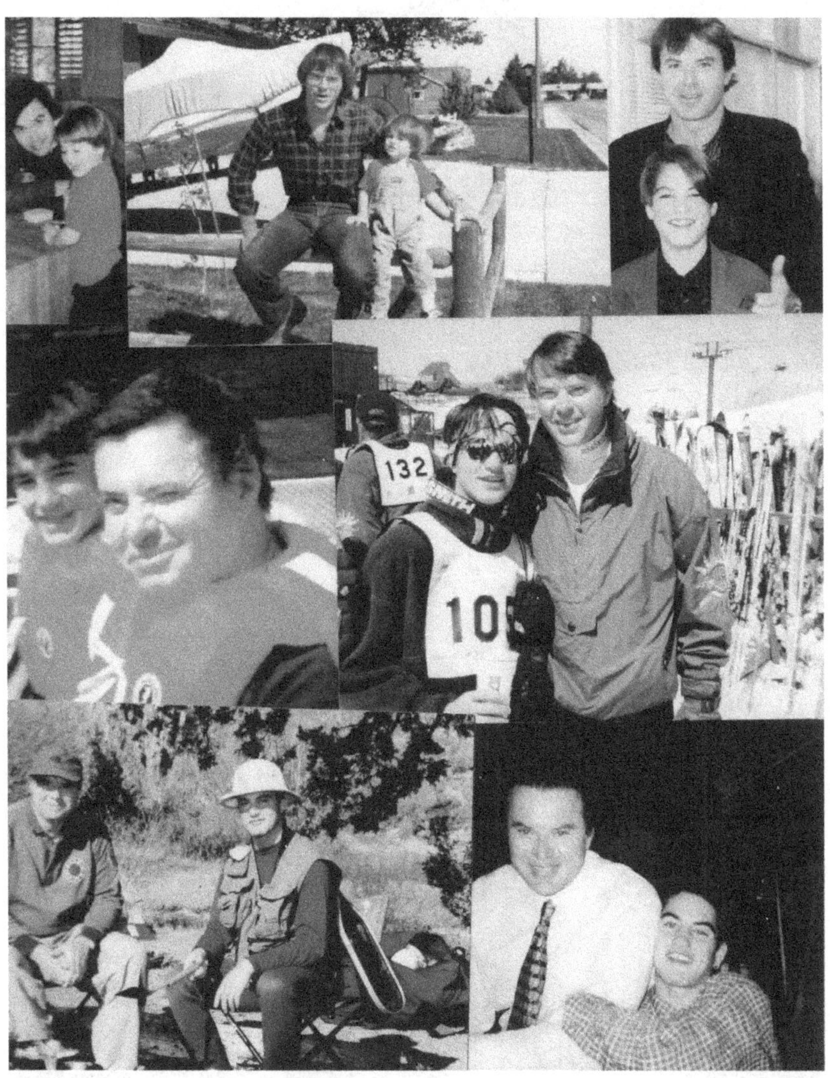

Bob & son Ryan through the years.

Emily with her dad preparing Thanksgiving at their Sherwood CA home, 2001.

Bob, his mom 'Baba' and Emily at their home, Park City Utah circa 1990's.

Top left, Bob teaching Ryan how to swim, top right, Bob teaching Emily how to swim. Bottom photo, L-R, Ryan, Allison and Emily - the last photo Bob took of his kids.

Family group on rocks. L-R, Bob, Em, Heather & Ry, photo taken before Allison was born.

Bob teaching Allison all about the game of golf.

Bob face painting with Allie his last summer at his beloved West Lake – Canada, 2001.

Chapter 20

The Big Screen Beckons as M-G-M Calls ***BOSTON*** *And* ***Spenser: For Hire !***

Sometimes in television everything comes together at just the right time and place. The script, the cast, the crew and production values are all top-shelf. These important factors create as one can only describe it as pure 'Magic.' Such was the case with the pilot film "*Promised Land*" based on Robert B. Parker's novel featuring popular private eye, *Spenser: For Hire*. The film, shot entirely on location in the streets of Boston, is brilliantly played by popular actor, Robert Urich. The 2-hour film was so well-received that *Spenser* was developed into a regular weekly series which had a three-year run on the ABC-Television Network. Following its successful airing, several feature films based on the detective, also starring Robert Urich, were produced and aired on the Lifetime Network.

Boston & Spenser

After Bob's hard-hitting television series *Vega$* was cancelled, he set his sights on becoming a film star. Even though he enjoyed playing the role of Dan Tanna and was grateful for the success the show brought him, he was tired and worn out from the exhausting six-day work schedule. In a February 1982 UPI interview with Hollywood columnist Vernon Scott, Urich talked about his grueling schedule. "It was a vigorous six day week with fifteen hour work days," Urich says, "playing a tough action detective in triple digit Vegas temps that convinced me it wasn't worth it. After three years of *Vega$*, I was an emotional and physical wreck. I was neverso close to falling into a deep, dark hole than after those years working in the desert heat in the daytime under a baking sun, and freezing at night. It finally took it's toll on me. I was mentally exhausted, too." Bob also says, "After the third year, our creative team began to 'fall apart.' The scripts got worse and I was rewriting more and more I screamed louder and louder, but I had no control over the show. I was locked in and contractually couldn't get out. I fought against the massacre episode which opened with seven people getting killed in the first 30 seconds. It received our lowest rating. I used to fight for comedy and fun," the actor laments, "but I finally got worn down and worn out. I was sick with the flu, thirty pounds over-weight and in terrible shape. When producer Aaron Spelling called to say the show was cancelled, I immediately got over the flu, and began exercising again. I felt human again."

"When we finished the third and final season of *Vega$*, in March of 1981," says Urich. "I locked the doors on our Vegas home and drove across country to our peaceful place on the lake in Ontario Canada."

Life After *Vega$*

The same day Bob Urich received word that *Vega$* had been cancelled, NBC called. "NBC offered me $75,000 an episode," Bob says, "to star in *McLaine's Law*[1] which was an enormous sum even by today's standards, but I turned it down." Reportedly, Bob took home around thirty-five thousand an episode as the star of *Vega$*, so this role would have paid him twice as much. Bob's reasoning for turning down the lucrative TV offer: "The only way to become a movie actor is to stay away from TV series for awhile, but even that is no guarantee. They offer you TV movies or roles in B movies, not A features which I was interested in."

"Bill Hayes,[2] who at that time had a hand in managing my career, advised me to parlay my strength from the series [*Vega$*] for a deal which would combine movie and TV in the same package."

The icing on the proverbial cake for Bob which got him to agree to terms was signing in Louis B. Mayer's[3] old office. Until signing with M-G-M, Bob's feature film career consisted of a five-line role as a rogue motorcycle cop in Clint Eastwood's *Magnum Force.*

---

1 *Gunsmoke* star James Arness was ultimately cast as Detective Jim McClain in the hour long police drama which had a relatively short life span on NBC, airing from November 1981 until August 1982.

2 Heather says she was not 'privy' to the arrangement Bob may have had with Bill Hayes and only recalls that Hayes handled some of their finances.

3 Louis B. Mayer (1882-1957) was the co-founder of Metro-Goldwyn-Mayer and was one of Hollywood's most powerful studio moguls.

Many motion picture studios lured a TV star with promises of movie roles, providing they star in a TV series. Reportedly, Urich's deal at M-G-M called for three feature films, a TV series with a two-hour pilot and a firm 13 week on-the-air commitment and part ownership. M-G-M also agreed to pay *Robert Urich Productions* for developing books and stories into movie properties. Bob completed his first feature film for the studio in 1982, starring as Ruben Castle in the 12-million dollar adventure-mystery, *Endangered Species*.

Bob's M-G-M Years

Bob had hoped to complete a second feature before beginning his new television series *Gavilan*, for M-G-M Television. The role had him playing an oceanographer with CIA operations. The hour long series aired from October 26, 1982 through March 18, 1983, but didn't catch on. To fulfill it's contractual obligation with Bob, the studio filmed 13 episodes, but NBC only aired ten, before taking it off the air.

Bob next starred in three additional feature films. The first was *Ice Pirates* as Jason at M-G-M, released in 1984. The space-sci-fi flick developed quite a fan following and today has become a cult-classic. Also in 1984, Urich starred as Matt Winslow in *Invitation to Hell* for Moonlight Productions, and in 1985, he co-starred with Tim Robbins in *Turk 182*[1] for 20th-Century Fox, playing Terry Lynch, a NYC fire-fighter. After Bob found himself turning down horrible film scripts and winding up in a medium series (*Gavilan*), he realized more than ever that you have to be careful what you wish for. After all, come hell or high water, Bob wanted to become a movie star. As an actor, he was also acutely aware of where his bread was buttered and how successful he was as a major player and star on television. It was right around that time that a character named Spenser came a callin.'

Getting to know Spenser!

Spenser, first name unknown, is a fictional detective character first brought to life in a series of novels created by mystery writer and Bostonian, Robert B. Parker.

---

1 In *Turk 182*, critics praise Bob's work. Some saying it was some of his best. Ironically, for his effort, he was awarded a raspberry award which is covered in 'The Films of Robert Urich' at the back of this book.

Spenser is a native of Laramie, Wyoming, who served as a combat infantryman in the lst Infantry Div. in the Korean War. He is intelligent, who quotes Shakespeare and is also a gourmet chef. Spenser maintains a committed relationship with one woman, Susan Silverman, a Harvard-trained Ph.D. psychologist who assists Spenser in his cases. Spenser received a football scholarship to Holy Cross where he played strong safety, but a knee injury forced him to drop out, because he didn't have funds to finish his schooling.

Spenser is a former State trooper who is assigned to the Suffolk County [MA] District Attorney's office.[1] For most of the television series he is basically described as a private eye."

The other primary character in the *Spenser* novels is his close friend, and sometimes, sidekick, Hawk, an African-American who is equally tough, but a little on the 'shady side' of Spenser. Having served in the French Foreign Legion, Hawk is a 'Gun for Hire' who lives by his own personal code. Spenser and Hawk met as boxing opponents in a preliminary bout in the Boston Arena and each man believes he was the victor. Both work out at Henry Cimoli's gym. They respect each other and are friends who understand the other's philosophy of how to conduct themselves in life.

Avery Brooks played Hawk in the *Spenser* TV series. Speaking about his role as Hawk, Brooks said, "I never thought of myself as a sidekick... I've never been the side of anything. I just assumed that I was equal." After *Spenser* was canceled, Avery received a spin-off of the series, *A Man Called Hawk*. Urich's older brother, Tom recalls, "Bob offered to make an appearance on Avery's new show as a kind gesture to his one-time co-star, but Avery turned down his offer." Brooks series only lasted seven months on ABC, January - August 31, 1989. As one TV critic aptly put it, "Hawk just didn't work without Spenser."

Spenser: For Hire

[**Bold typed words** are Bob's and taken directly from his personal journal.]

A glimpse into how Bob envisioned the City of Boston and *Spenser* being filmed for TV: **"I wanted *Spenser: For Hire* to have the feel, smell**

---

1 Some novels state that Spenser also worked out of the Middlesex County DA's office. The television pilot episode has him as a Boston Police detective who regularly seeks help from Martin Quirk [played by Richard Jaeckel] of the Boston Police Dept. Among Spenser's other police contacts are Sgt. Frank Belson and Det. Lee Farrell, both homicide investigators under Quirk's command.

and grit of Boston. Fog, fish markets, cobbled streets, tugboat horns and seedy Irish pubs. Rowdy, grand, saturated with history, and local shenanigans–and a little falling apart. Boston was a grand old dame in a drafty, ancient, decrepit house drinking gin from a bottle; a stevedore playing darts in a waterfront bar; a mischievous Revolutionary War ghost out for a good time. Boston would have to be one of the major characters in the series if it was going to work."

The Network [ABC] had started out by saying, "Bob, we'll shoot it in L.A. and get the second unit guys to cover the Boston locales."

"No, no, no," I said. "We're not going to do that this time. We're gonna use the real Boston beans and cod."

"Don't worry, Bob, it'll look just like Boston. You won't be able to tell the difference."

"It can't just sort of look like Boston. It's gotta *be* Boston. We're going to shoot it in Boston or I don't want to do it."

So, thanks to Bob's insistence and persistence, that's how and where *Spenser* was filmed, in and around the streets of Boston. **"It was almost like a shoot for a TV movie. In the series, I'm a streetwise PI, accompanied at most times by an enigmatic partner in crime, Hawk, played by Avery Brooks."**

The Birth of *Spenser*

[*Italicized words* are those of Spenser's Producer John Wilder.]

Another man who insisted *Spenser* be filmed on location in Boston is also the person responsible for bringing the show to television, John Wilder. The Tacoma, Washington native and one-time radio and television actor who performed using his real name, Johnny McGovern,[1] created *Spenser* for television and produced the series' first season in 1985.

A graduate of UCLA with a BA in English Literature, John lives with his wife and granddaughter in Santa Barbara, California, where he is a Writer in Residence and Adjunct Professor of English at Westmont College. Wilder is a recognized writer-producer of quality television programming, who has received numerous awards, including the Writers Guild of America Award for Best Long-Form Television Drama, the Western Writer's of America Award for Best Western script and film, two Western Heritage Awards for Best Western Drama, two Emmy

1 Johnny McGovern later had his name legally changed to John Wilder.

nominations for Best Television series and two Golden Globe nominations for Best Motion Picture Made for Television. Among the television shows he has written and/or produced and directed are *The Streets of San Francisco*, James Michener's *Centennial, Return to Lonesome Dove* and *Spenser: For Hire.*

Here, in producer John Wilder's own words, is how he developed *Spenser* for television:

"I was asked by the President of Warner Brothers TV, Alan Shayne, if I would develop a detective series based on the novels of a Boston writer, Robert B. Parker. My response was that I loved detective fiction and would read the novels. My wife and I were off to Europe and I packed the paperback books and began to read them on the flight. By the time we got back to the states, I had read them all, from The Godwulf Manuscript, *the first of the series, through* The Widening Gyre, *which had come out in 1983. I talked with Alan and said I'd be interested in developing a series from the books, if I could shoot them in Boston."*

According to Wilder, "*The request was problematic for the studio because Boston had a bad reputation in the film industry as being very difficult and expensive place to shoot. I told them, San Francisco had the same reputation when I went to work for Quinn Martin to do* The Streets of San Francisco, *but we were able to work with Mayor Alioto's office and negotiate arrangements that made it a very positive experience."*

"The Vice President in charge of production at Warner Brothers was a very savvy man named Gary Credle. Gary had cut his teeth in the business working with Fouad Said, the man who invented Cinemobile, a van-like vehicle that facilitated filming on location, and he knew that, if we could successfully negotiate with the labor unions, and I could pull in my production team from Streets of San Francisco, *we could deliver the same kind of production values that QM Productions delivered for ABC on* Streets."

John Wilder and Gary Credle flew to Boston to negotiate with the unions.

"We met with then Mayor Ray Flynn and Govenor Michael Dukakis, who both assured me we would get full cooperation from their offices. With the union concessions Gary got, and the guarantee of cooperation I obtained," says Wilder, *"Warner Brothers allowed me to line-up production for a pilot episode to be shot in Boston."*

Wilder selected the fourth book in Robert B. Parker's paperback series, *Promised Land* to adapt. *"I chose it because it introduced the character Hawk. I knew I wanted to feature Hawk alongside Spenser every week. It also had good material between Susan Silerman and Spenser that indicated he could be a one-woman guy."*

John wrote a two-hour pilot script based on Parker's *Promised Land*, but says, "he added material to make it more cinematic, while keeping the tone and moral depth of the novel, which he felt elevated the material to a level TV should always be striving for.

"The studio was happy with the script, the network [ABC-TV] was delighted, and we got a production order to shoot a pilot film," says Wilder.

The first thing John Wilder did was alert key crew members he had 'standing by' that they would be shooting in Boston in February.

"I wanted that bare-leafed, frosty-air feeling for the film," he recalls. "My production Manager from Streets, *Dick Gallegly signed on as the line producer [in Boston] and we got him off to Boston to find and secure a warehouse we could turn into a sound stage and offices. He found a great place on Soldier's Field Road* [next door to WBZ Radio & TV]. "Wilder flew back to give approval and to begin hiring key crew members.

John Wilder got one of his first Assistant Directors from *Streets of San Francisco* and *Centennial* to work on prepping a production schedule and contacted the director he wanted for the pilot, Lee Katzin.

"Lee was great with the camera and knew the city. He had done his undergraduate work at Harvard. ABC didn't approve Lee. They had several other people in mind. I fought for Lee and won. And, he shot a brilliant picture. Barry Meyer, the senior film exec at the studio [Warner Bros] said, when he saw it, that it was as good or better looking than any of the studio's theatrical releases that year."

While readying for actual production, Robert B. Parker and John Wilder began the casting process, beginning with Spencer.

"Bob [Parker] *and I talked about wanting a mature actor, as close to Robert Mitchum as we could find, Brian Dennehy had the quality but was too old* [he was 48 at the time]. *Ed O'Neill was someone the network was interested in. I like him a lot as an actor, but I wanted more of a leading man. There were lots of good ones around, but not many that could convey that they had been a heavyweight boxer.*

Alan Shayne at Warner Bros. asked John to consider Robert Urich.

"I knew him from his Vega$ *series, and my first reaction was that he was too handsome, too smooth. I remembered him as a young cop in* Magnum Force *as having some physicality, though, and it was on display even more in a TV movie he did about football player Rocky Bleier* [*Fighting Back–The Rocky Bleier Story*].

Wilder and Parker looked for several more weeks. "*We considered several more actors, before concluding that Bob was the best actor we could find for the role. Bob and I met at Alan's house. He was even more impressive physically in person, and had undeniable charm. He said, he loved the script and really wanted the role. I knew I had Alan's blessing, so I offered it to him on the spot.*"

After locking in Bob for the lead as Spenser, Wilder began searching for a 'Hawk' and a Susan Silverman.

"I had cast Barbara Stock on an episode of The Yellow Rose *the* previous year," Wilder says, and *after seeing a lot of actresses, felt she was our Susan. I had Marvin Hagler in mind as the physical presence Hawk required, and found out that he was actually interested in the part, but it didn't look like he was going to retire immediately* [from the boxing ring], *so, even if he proved he could act that wouldn't work. The image remained , though, and I read many actors and athletes for the role.*"

Casting Hawk on *Spenser*

John Wilder says the role of Hawk came down to a choice between an actor named Badja Djola and Avery Brooks.

"Both gave good readings in interviews. And, I took the two of them to read for the President of ABC-TV, Lou Ehrlich. When they had both read, Lou asked me who I wanted. I said, I liked them both, but wanted to go with Avery. He said, 'Do it.'"

When producer Wilder left the room, Alan Shayne, followed him out, urging him to go with Badja, who had a much fiercer presence than Avery.

"Alan had been a top-shelf casting director for years, and I respected his opinion immensely, but I explained that for me, while Hawk was an assassin, I wanted him to have an elegance about him, wanted him to be classier than the average hit man for hire. Alan felt Badja was the better choice. I asked him whose show it was. If it was the studio's, he could certainly override my decision and cast Badja. But, if it was my show, I wanted Avery. Alan said it was definitely my show. I went down the hall to speak with both actors. I thanked

Badja, who had done a terrific reading, and then went to Avery to tell him he had the part, if he would do one thing for me. He asked what that was, and I told him [still having that Marvin Hagler image in mind] that I wanted him to shave his head. Avery grinned, and said, "Well, John, I guess every man's head has a price on it."

John knew right then and there he had made the exact right choice for the role of Hawk.

"It was that literacy that Avery exudes, that wry humor," he says. "He was definitely the right man for the role. And, he proved it in each and every episode."

Wilder had cast well-known supporting actor Richard Jaeckel[1] in *Centennial*, and even though the character Marty Quirk in Parker's books is a different type, John liked Dick's 'crustiness' for the role of the recurring police lieutenant. Wilder says, his casting directors in New York, John Lyons and Donna Isaacson held readings for the other characters in the pilot.

"That's where I met Ron McLarty … and set [cast] him to play Sgt. Belson the day I met him. I set my friend Joe Torrenueva as Henry Cimoli [owner of the gym] and set my friend Chuck Connors as an Irish mob leader instead of the swarthy Joe Broz in Parker's novel.

Spenser's residence

[**Bold typed words** are Bob's - *italicized* words are John Wilder's.]

Spenser lived in Boston and after his first place of business goes up in flames, he moves into an abandoned firehouse given to him by grateful Boston firefighters for saving the life of one of their own. It is situated on the corner of River Street, near Mt. Vernon Square and Beacon Hill, and how it came to be used is explained by Wilder.

"My wife and I were walking down Charles Street [Boston] when I saw the abandoned firehouse. I asked the Boston Film Commissioner, Mary Lou Crane,

---

1 Richard Jaeckel was born October 10, 1926. He had a long successful career as a Hollywood actor, both in film and TV. Featured in war films like, *Guadalcanal Diary, Sands of Iowa Jima* and *The Dirty Dozen* to a variety of TV series, including his first starring TV role in 1951, on the *Bigelow-Sanford Theater* in the production 'TKO' on the DuMont television Network. He also was featured on *Banyon, Frontier Circus, Spenser: For Hire* and his last series, *Super Carrier*, in 1988 on ABC. He passed in 1997.

to find out if it could be leased. We filmed exteriors there, and built the interior on our sound stage on Soldier's Field Road."

In the novels, Spenser usually carried a Smith & Wesson Model 36, .38 caliber, and sometimes carried a .357 Magnum revolver which he usually kept in the top drawer of his office desk, simply for "just in case" situations. He also carried a small .32 caliber revolver that he used as a 'back up' weapon. Later, he carried a Browning hi-powered 9 mm semi-automatic pistol. On the TV series, Spenser carried a Beretta 92 9mm pistol.

"For the pilot," remembers John Wilder, "I had Bob Urich wear a scar on his cheek and put him in a stocking cap, sweaters, plaid shirts, jackets and jeans, looking to make him a little less Hollywood handsome and less Vegas snappy. The network loved the look, but Bob was uncomfortable with it, so we dropped the scar after the pilot. He didn't like driving the mildly-worn ivy green '66 Ford Mustang, my homage to Steve McQueen's car in Bullit, *which I put Bob in for the pilot, either, but I kept him in it for the first season.*

Bob writes in his journal about filming the Spenser pilot in Boston in frigid weather. **"It was February, freezing cold. Spinning cold. It's a sunny, brilliant day. We were just about finished with the pilot. There are just a few 'pick-up' shots left over. We're driving around the Boston Common. We needed to pick up a couple of close-up shots of me jumping over a turnstile at the entrances to the "T"[1] chasing bad guys. There was a lot of that stuff in *Spenser*. We do those and we're done."**

Spenser - on location, a fire!

"We used a big old work van to move around the city in. It carries sixteen people. It's usually a gun-shoot at that point. There's the director, the DP [director of photography] the sound guys, cameramen with their equipment in their hands, one lighting guy with a lighting gun–just getting down and dirty. Maybe somebody with a battery and a shiny board. They do their thing and they get out of there. So, that's what we're doing, spending the morning getting those last few shots."

They'll finish up around eleven or eleven-thirty and then Bob will go and meet his family at the Boston Ritz Hotel, where they are staying during filming.

---

1 The T is short for what Bostonians refer to as the MTA, the Massachusetts Transportation Authority.

"My children, Ry and Em were little then, between three and four years old. They were walking but still infants."

"I look over to my left and across the garden in the Common. The snow encrusted trees were bare...and beyond them, I see smoke!

"What is that I ask, to those around me?"

"Oh, there's a fire over there. The Ritz is on fire."

"What!" I exclaim. "My family is in that hotel."

"It started about thirty minutes ago and it's roaring."

"Get me over there," I insist.

"How you gonna do that, all the streets are blocked."

"I don't care how you do it, just get me over there *now*!"

John Wilder immediately took Bob over to a cop he knew.

"We climbed into a squad car and that officer took us on a siren-sounding, curb-jumping ride that delivered us to the Ritz with a sliding stop. We both hit the ground running, raced into the hotel and found our wives, and got them and Bob's children out while the BFD continued working to put out the fire."

Real life Suspense while filming Spenser

There were fire engines and fire trucks with sirens blaring and hoses all over the street. Bob had recently finished a movie called, *Turk 182,* in which he played a New York City firefighter, it was about to be released and there was a lot of press about it.

"We pull right up in front of the Ritz–it's all fenced off, with the sheriffs and cops yelling at me as I jump out wearing my black pea coat and watch cap. They look at me and say, 'Hey, is that the guy from the movie.' And while they're trying to sort out the movie from reality I rush into the burning hotel."

Bob's wife, Heather and their children were on the twelfth floor. When the alarm went off–so often in places like hotels they are false alarms–Heather opened the door and smelled smoke. She called down to the desk and the operator is screaming hysterically, "Oh my God! Oh my God! The hotel is on fire. I'm gonna die, it's on fire."

"Heather, as cool as they come, bundles the kids up and has one in each arm as she starts down the back staircase. She gets to about the fourth floor and the smoke is so thick she can't see. They are all coughing and just as it seems hopeless, she hears a voice below that says,

'Down here!' An arm reaches up out of the darkness. Some hotel person grabs her around the back and leads her down the last three flights and they burst into the lobby just as I run into the hotel.

Meanwhile, there's the *News Live at 5* and the cameras. Heather takes Ryan, our son, the heavier of the two, throws him into my arms. I said, 'Honey, just get out of here.' She heads out the side door of the Ritz. I turn and pop! A flash bulb goes off."

"The next day the front page of the Boston Herald reads, 'ACTOR ROBERT URICH SAVES UNIDENTIFIED CHILD FROM BURNING HOTEL.'

"Heather looks at the front page of the paper and says, 'It's always been the way with you. You've always been the guy with the luck. I do all the work. I save the kids and you're a hero with your picture about the fire on the front page of the newspaper.'"

Here is U.P.I.'s correspondent, Rich Nagle's account of the Boston Ritz Hotel fire[1]

Dateline: Boston, February 8, 1985

Byline: By Rich Nagle for United Press International

A smoky three-alarm fire in the laundry room at the swanky Ritz-Carlton Hotel Friday forced the evacuation of about 200 people into the bitter cold and 13 degree temperatures with fierce winds making it feel like 30 below zero, when smoke spread through the 58-year-old building, alongside Boston's Public Gardens. There were no injuries in the blaze at the 16-story hotel, which opened to much fanfare in 1927. The cause of fire was undetermined and damage was estimated at $25,000. A spokeswoman at the hotel, which is undergoing renovations, said the fire was "construction-related," but would not elaborate. The third floor contains offices. "A fire began in the laundry room on the third floor and there was some extension to the fourth floor," said fire commissioner Leo Stapleton. He said heavy smoke from the 10 a.m. blaze prompted evacuation of the 277-room hotel located in Boston's fashionable Back Bay area. The fire was controlled by 11 a.m. There was a fire drill yesterday which set off the system., but according to a guest, "the hotel said it wasn't a real

1 Thanks to writing friends, David Kruh and Stephanie Schorow for researching this fire story for the author. Dave and I worked together in Boston radio at RKO-General. He has written several books about Boston. Check him out at www.joeandnemo.com Stephanie's latest book is *Inside the Combat Zone*.

fire. Today, they didn't say that." Among the guests who fled the hotel was actor Robert Urich, who starred in the TV series, *Vegas* and has been filming a television movie in Boston.

Spenser: On Location in Boston

[*Italicized* words are those of John Wilder.]

When Spenser was about to go on the air, Producer John Wilder was told they couldn't use the title Spenser because NBC had a situation comedy using that title.

"I stewed over that for a while," recalls Wilder, "and then I thought of Graham Greene's novel, The Gun For Hire, *and came up with* Spenser: For Hire. *The first year was a good one. I wrote and directed the first episode, No 'Room At the Inn,' to get a handle on the crew. They were absolutely first rate. All had read Parker's books and were excited to be working on the series. It took awhile though, to convince Bob that Spenser was different from Dan Tanna on* Vega$. *He had such success in that role, that he wanted to bring facets of the character into our series. He would eventually see what the difference was and why I wanted it, and agree to what I had promised Bob Parker I would deliver and what the network was expecting. Primarily, it was keeping the toughness that impressed the network so much in the pilot on camera, and is at the core of Parker's books.*

Wilder gives mucho kudo's to Urich as television's Spenser.

"He worked very hard, was always prepared and seldom needed more than one take, which is a huge asset to a production company, and greatly appreciated by producers and directors because there is precious little time for rehearsing scenes in television. We shot our episodes in 7 days, while most series at that time were going 8-9 days, a few even took double digits to shoot. Bob had a great sense of humor and was always really good to the crew, which he soon came to realize was the best he'd ever worked with.

I had hand-picked my key people and they had all hand-picked the people they supervised. Ron LaTour was our director of photography, and one reason I picked him For Spenser was that he was comfortable working with available light, and with two cameras, which allowed us to get two angles at the same time, saving an extra set-up."

Bob Urich was one of those special individuals who lived his life according to his faith. He was true to his core values, including his strong Catholic faith. Not even a TV script could get him to compromise on his principles. Take, for example, an episode of *Spenser: For Hire*. Spenser learns that his girlfriend Susan Silverman [Barbara Stock] is pregnant and that he is the father. Spenser wants her to have the baby but she opts for an abortion. "When Bob read that," says his wife Heather, "his first response was 'no way, I can't go along with this! He wanted no part of any premise involving abortion." Producer Wilder also spoke out on the hot issue.

In an article by Morgan Gendel, dated October 24, 1985 (published a few days before the series moved to its new Tuesday night at 10 time slot with this bombshell of an episode), producer John Wilder noted, "One reason we went for this theme is that it's controversial. It also gets to the theme of the character, *Spenser*, in the Robert B. Parker novels in which he *originated*, is a strong proponent of 'the individual's right to choice.'" Wilder says that both the pro-abortion and right-to-life sides (no doubt influenced at Urich's insistency) are strongly expressed in the episode.

The Joe and Andy Family

Another admirable quality of Bob's make-up was his strong loyalty to his friends. The author speaks from first-hand knowledge. He used his influence to gain access for me [the author] to appear in two episodes of *Spenser*. Nothing big or Emmy-worthy material, mind you, in fact, I was one step below an extra, playing a dude visiting a brothel in both episodes. (Talk about type-casting.) It was a fun part and was far removed from the straight-laced morning-drive guy that our listeners knew. The appearances brought lots of attention to our morning-drive radio show, *The Joe and Andy Family,* and certainly helped our ratings, too.

Another episode of *Spenser* shows more of Bob's loyalty to his friends. Bob is in Boston Police headquarters talking with Sgt. Frank Belson [Ron McClarty]. Belson looks up from his desk and says to Spenser, "Don't you ever listen to so and so?" Bob as Spenser, standing directly in front of his desk, shakes his head no, and smiles while holding one of our Joe and Andy coffee mugs. Our faces depicted as catoonish looking chaps are emblazoned on either side of the mug. Spenser says, "No, I listen to *Joe*–while slowly turning the mug for the camera…and *Andy*.
[*Words in italics are those of John Wilder.*]

The Author spent over 40 years as a radio-TV personality and knows the value of free exposure on national TV. It's what every person in radio yearns to receive. It was another example of Bob going the extra mile for a friend. I will always be indebted to him for his kind gesture and friendship.

Spenser & Ron McLarty

"Bob was probably the nicest star I ever worked with," says Ron McLarty. "He was a genuine good guy. I first met him on *Spenser: For Hire*. He came to my trailer, knocked on my door and asked if I wanted to come over to his trailer and chat. I was bowled over by his generosity and kindness. I do remember something very special about the man. Bob would make special efforts toward the guest stars. He set the tone by speaking to all the regulars and reminding them that we were all lucky to have these fine actors working with us, and to make them feel comfortable and welcome. Believe me," McLarty says, "that is a rarity among stars on any series. Bob liked and respected other actors and knew how difficult it is to come onto a set and do only one episode in an ongoing series."

When *Spenser* was in the throes of being canceled after its first season, we in turn showed our loyalty and friendship to Bob by launching an extensive radio campaign involving Joe and Andy listeners to *Save Our Spenser*. It caused such an outcry of support for Bob and *Spenser* from our listeners and viewers which prompted ABC network execs to give a nod to a 2nd and 3rd season for the series.

The only real problem for John Wilder in filming Spenser in Boston were the streets and traffic problems.

"The primary issue with Boston was all the streets were built along old, winding cow paths, instead of being on a grid like most other cities. I wrapped a location on that first show at 9:30 one morning, and didn't get my first shot at the next location till 2:00 p.m."

"It took so long to move all the vehicles across town, we had to break for lunch before getting back to work. I immediately called my supervising producer, Bill Yates, in L.A. and told him to start cutting locations in the scripts that were in work. There could only ever be one location move in a day, whereas in other cities, you could make a second move without any real time problem."

If you lived in metro Boston while *Spenser* was on location filming, you no doubt found yourself caught in one or more traffic jams. It also probably made you a little hot under the collar, being stuck on Storrow Drive if you were trying to get to work on time or over to Fenway Park for the opening pitch of a Red Sox game. However, most locals didn't mind an occasional inconvenience. Bostonians wanted *Spenser* to do well. That's why then Gov. Michael Dukakis and other State House officials led *Spenser*'s popularity parade by hosting a reception for the cast and crew. *Spenser* meant revenue for Boston. In an article for the Boston Globe 'Living Section,' dated January 14, 1985, writer Mark Muro writes, "The reception took place a few days prior to filming the pilot, *Promised Land*, the Warner Bros. made for TV movie was filmed in and around Boston's Back Bay, and is based on author Robert B. Parker's 1976 detective novel.

"More than 150 film enthusiasts gathered not only to pay homage to the character, who will bring attention to their city, but because of the economic consideration it brings to the hub. The movie means work and business. *Spenser*'s translation to film during the 22 days spent on location in Boston and it's $3-million budget meant work for the actors, and 300-400 extras with money being spent at local restaurants and shops. 'Anything that brings more money into our coffers is just fine by me,' were the words of one-time Mass State Treasurer, Robert Crane. Still others saw a public relations boon to Boston. 'It's a chance to show off our city to the entire country,' said one Boston business leader.

"Americans will see a city in *Spenser* that's powerful, a city on-the-move that's filled with promise for tomorrow while in touch with its historical past. Still others were thinking bigger. 'They are looking to make a regular prime-time series out of this film,' said Roger Burke, former head of the Massachusetts Film Bureau. "'The series will be filmed entirely 'on location' here in Boston. They'll come and set up shop here and spend maybe $20 million a year.* That's big money!'

"Robert Parker said he'll be involved in the film, but added, 'Obviously they know more about making TV than I do. So, it's really their thing,' he insisted. 'The producers are very interested in Parker's opinion. How would Spenser do this? What would he say here? Would he wear this? But, in general," the author of a dozen *Spenser* books says, 'he'll let them do their work. They make movies. I write books. I've been given a rather handsome sum of money for this, which I haven't sent directly to the I.R.S.,' he says blandly. 'Beyond that, it'll be fun to watch the actors and watch the movie when it's on. But, I'm a novelist. People say, "Don't you mind if they screw up your book?" I say, "They *can't* screw it up. The movie and the book are entirely different artifacts. If it's a great success and all my books flourish, I'll be obscenely rich. I expect it to be good,the screenplay [written by John Wilder] is very nicely organized and has a good rhythm to it. I think Urich looks good. He's a big, athletic guy. He's been working out, boxing and lifting weights for this. And they're shooting on location shows a sign of commitment. It's not just an L.A. sound stage with a few gaslights on the corner. If it bombs," says Parker, "I'll still be doing what I've always done, writing novels.'"

"The Boston Battleaxe"

[**Bold typed words** are Bob's own, taken from his personal journal.]

"There was a wicked woman who once wrote for a Boston newspaper. She was so malevolent that if you'd just won the lottery, or won a shiny new Cadillac in a drawing, she would make it look like you had stolen it. She was the Boston Battleaxe. She looked for the negative spin on everything. I would not talk to her. People like, my radio pal, Joe Martelle would say, 'Did you see what she said about you today? Did you *really* do that?' This was not a person I had great affection for. I couldn't change my socks or paint my house without it being in the paper."

One day, Bob read in the paper where his kids went to school and what Mass they attended on Sunday. Bob was livid–and rightfully so.

"I thought, you know what? Now, you're jeopardizing the security of my kids. I decided to call her up. I said, 'I'll make you a deal. I'll give you all the Hollywood stories you want. I'll let you know what's happening before anybody else. I'll let you know when [*Spenser*] gets picked up. When a movie deal gets struck, you'll be the first to know, but, you've got to be mindful of my family. I don't want any details about their personal lives.' I guess I sold out in a way. I'd do it again."

She died a few months after *Spenser* ended its run. **"Some one came up to me, and asked, 'Did you hear about so and so?' I can't remember her name.[1] I don't *want* to remember it. She died, he told me. Cancer of the tongue."**

---

1 For the record, the reporter Bob refers to as the "Boston Battleaxe" was Norma Nathan, who for years was *The Eye*, a gossip columnist for the Boston Herald. It was her trademark to punctuate her observations with the exclamation 'Eye Say!' Sometimes, life makes for strange bedfellows and opposites attract. For 41 years, the woman known for her acidic writing style was married to one of Boston's best loved and respected radio personalities, Norm Nathan. Norma passed from cancer of the jaw,

Spenser's Cars

It's Friday night and it's already dark. The lights of Boston sparkle along the Charles River. Its mystique is beautiful. The crew from *Spenser: For Hire* is near the tunnel, going to Boston's Logan Airport. Right on the corner is a building that looks like the Flatiron building in New York, but this one was from a Colonial period.

"We'd dressed it up and use it as a police station. You come out of the tunnel [Sumner] and right on the corner--BOOM! There's the city and all the lights. One block away is the Italian section. It's a very colorful place. Overhead passes, boats going by on the river [Charles] and the lights of the city have just popped on. The director was Lee Katsin. He was a good director, but from the old school, which means he would not only yell and cuss and holler at people, but generally scream at them. But, we're in Boston, and they don't like this kind of overbearing behavior, especially teamsters. They are not used to people yelling at them."

The car Bob and the crew are using won't start. In fact, it was chronically malfunctioning and the further behind they got in the schedule, the more Lee Katsin screamed. Bob comes out to see what's going on and there is his driver Bobby McGuiness and his co-captain, Jim Murray.

"When you use a car in a movie [for example] that Pontiac gives you, here's the deal. Once you're done with it, it's got to be destroyed and pressed. You can't salvage anything. You can't even take the radio out. You can't take the steering wheel. It's all got to be there. But word had it that someone was accepting new cars from the manufacturer and using a double an old one in the stunt and then keeping the new cars and selling them." As far as is known, no one ever got to the bottom of it.

Spenser's Cars

"Murray is a beefy guy, probably three-hundred pounds, wearing a t-shirt, and it's freezing outside. When everybody is in Eddie Bauer down parkas, he would throw a flannel shirt over his t-shirt, or his long-sleeved underwear. When it got really cold, Murray had a little corduroy shirt he put on top of that. It's February in Boston and it's freezing cold, right on the water. And, these two guys are leaning

November 11, 1999 at a Beverly [MA] hospital. Her beloved husband Norm preceded her in death, three years earlier, on October 29, 1996.

against the hood of the car. This old mustang, tacky green, old beat-up Mustang that I drive in *Spenser*."

As Bob comes out of the building, heading for his dressing room, the two men nod towards the car. "Almost fixed, Rabbit."

Katsin, the director had been yelling at them all day. All week, actually, and they are looking kind of down about it.

"What's going on?" I asked.

"It's about that '65 Mustang, Rabbit."

"It's been a big problem, that caw," I said.

"Oh, it ain't the caw so much," they said, "it's Katsin. This friggin' Katsin guy and the car. If they spent a little dough we wouldn't have this trouble. Coulda told us earlier, we coulda put a new engine in it and we coulda made it brand new. It would run every time you start it. But they didn't want to spend any more money, Bob. We told them. We told them til we were blue in the face."

I said, "Look. We're almost done [with the pilot film] Just hang in there. We'll go to series [weekly] and we'll get a good car and we'll spend ABC's money."

"You only got to say the word, Rabbit and tomorrow morning, they'll find this friggin' car in the bottom of Boston Harbor–and for no extra charge, Lee Katsin will be in it." "Jimmy," I said, "This conversation did not take place."

"Rabbit, I never heard nothing,' I swear. You hear him say anything, Jim?

Fuggitaboutit, everything's gonna be okay."

Shooting Spenser on Location

Part of the charm of shooting *Spenser* in Boston was they got to do a lot of filming on location. That's how Bob met Larry Bird, on the floor at the Boston Garden during a pre-game warm-up. **"We were filming with the fans in the Garden at a real NBA game–the Celtics versus the Sixers. They were hiding cameras in popcorn vendor boxes. Back then, I wasn't a big NBA fan. To tell you the truth, I just didn't know the teams. Didn't know the players. I just didn't follow it. Now, I love it."**

Larry Bird was in his prime. He was the Celtics franchise and Bostonians loved him.

"He was a very friendly guy and I asked him if there was a sweat-shirt or something with the Celtics' logo on it that I can borrow for the scene. He takes off his warm-up jacket and hands it to me. 'Oh no,' I said. 'I couldn't do that.'

'Go ahead, I can get another one. I've worn this most of the season, but here, you take it and keep it.' I just couldn't accept it so I said, 'Thank you, but I can't.' So in the end, I didn't take it." Later, driving home, Bob told his driver Bob McGuiness how Larry Bird offered him his jacket but he didn't take it. McGuiness went crazy!

"Are you outta yer mind? Larry Bird offers you his personal jacket and you don't take it? Lemme tell ya somethin.' If Bobby Orr offers you a hockey stick, take it."

During the course of his stay in Boston, Bob did get to know Bobby Orr–and last I heard, that Bobby Orr autographed hockey stick was still kickin' around the Urich home.

[*Italicized words* are John Wilder's.]

Producing a series shot on the other side of the country can be a real problem, but John Wilder had produced *Streets of San Francisco* from Los Angeles and in the process had learned a lot about managing a shooting company that wasn't a short walk across the studio lot from his office.

"I went from SOSF for QM Productions to Universal Studios to produce the 26-hour miniseries I developed from James Michener's Centennial, *which I shot entirely on distant location. At one point, having units shooting concurrently in Colorado, Ohio, Kentucky and Texas. The key is to pick smart, hard-working people who are highly organized and not prone to panic to work your set, and having daily communication, instantaneous, if needed, with them.*

Dick Gallegly had been John's Unit Manager on *Streets* and fit that description to a T.

"Having Dick running the store in Boston made my life possible. I also had two good writers working with me developing material in L.A. and a good group of film editors working under an ace named Gary Griffin. Karen Pingatore, who ran post-production for Warner Brothers TV, was a seasoned vet who always had the machine well-oiled, so we never skipped a beat through the many steps between delivery of dailies through final Answer print and delivery to the network for airing. We worked a lot of long days, but never missed a delivery date.*

John Wilder made sure they had 8 finished final-draft scripts ready to shoot before he went off to shoot the first episode.

"That way," he explains, *"my Boston unit was never pressed to scramble into a show without adequate preparation. That saves time and money and guarantees quality.*

"Donna Isaacson and John Lyons in New York would read actors for the various roles each week and the episode's director would spend a day with them. I had Donna get photos and bio info on the top five picks for each part. Then I would talk to Donna, and pick the best actor I felt best about." Wilder says it was surprisingly easy, *"and he would argue that it was one of the best casts shows on the air."*

In checking the cast list from the first year of *Spenser: For Hire*, you will see a lot of then-unknowns who have gone on to big screen careers. [*Italicized words* are John Wilder's.]

"One of my mentors, Quinn Martin told me that Samuel Goldwyn told him, "To be a good producer, you must be a good story editor and a good film editor.

So John's primary responsibilities are always getting good, polished scripts ready for production and then sitting on the final editing of the film, the dubbing, scoring and timing of the answer [final] print before delivery.

John Wilder left as producer of *Spenser, for Hire* after the first season. In 2017, in a phone interview with the author, he reflected on his time spent with *Spenser*. "Spenser *was a good show and I probably should have stayed with it, but I had to see what was on the other side of the mountain.*" He soon found out the other side of the mountain included a ten-hour miniseries for ABC and three theatrical film scripts for Warner Bros, Columbia and Sony-Tri-Star.

"After I left," Wilder says, "I had to grin, at Bob getting rid of the Mustang I wouldn't let him out of, and losing Cimoli's gym as a set I loved to put Spenser in with Hawk. My supervising producer, Bill Yates, took over the series and it ran for two more years. Looking back, it was a good time and I always felt I was fortunate that Bob Urich was available. As much as I didn't see him as the ideal Spenser when I cast him, I really can't see anyone else in the part now. He was terrific."

Author Lee Goldberg, along with co-writer, William Rabkin, wrote four episodes for *Spenser: For Hire*. "Robert B. Parker had no day-today involvement in the series, at least as far as I know," says Goldberg. "Parker did not provide a character outline for the writers on the show." Lee Goldberg is a two-time Edgar & Shamus Award winner nominee who has written and/or produced scores of highly successful TV series. In addition to *Spenser*, his work includes, *Diagnosis Murder*, *Hunter*, and *Nero Wolfe*. "We actually wrote our first script *If You Knew Sammy* for the 2nd season of *Spenser* on spec, meaning no one hired us to write it or paid us to. We sent it to the *Spenser* producers. They liked it, bought it and shot it, which is almost unheard of," Goldberg exclaims. The episode aired April 4, 1987. "Then they hired us to write more episodes, launching our long television careers. For the next three scripts, we came up with stories, pitched them to the producers, then wrote the outlines, and the scripts." In 1987, The team of Goldberg & Rabkin wrote their 2nd and 3rd episodes for season three. *Sleepless Dream* aired November 8, 1987, and *Play It Again Sammy* aired January 30, 1988 which was also a pilot episode for an unsold spinoff series. The writing team also wrote a fourth unproduced script for the fourth season.* Lee Goldberg recalled meeting Urich in Boston in 1986 on the set of *Spenser*, while they were shooting *If You Knew Sammy*. "We basically hung out for a few days, watching the shoot and chatting with Urich between takes and over lunch. It was nothing formal, all work-related."

"Spenser is shuttled around the ABC schedule"

When *Spenser: For Hire* debuted September 20, 1985, the brass at ABC must have thought their new detective show was Superman and he would destroy all competition. Someone in their infinite wisdom slotted the series Friday night at ten opposite popular *Miami Vice* on NBC. Not a wise move. When the ratings came in, programming people who still had jobs, quickly moved the series beginning October 29, 1985 to Tuesday nights at ten, where it did well for eleven months. However, in September 1986 and the new fall TV season, *Spenser* was shuttled to Saturday nights at ten, opposite another hit series, *Twilight Zone* on CBS. Not a good situation for the new P.I. on the block. ABC realized the error of their ways and *Spenser* found himself back to his familiar Tuesday night at ten slot where it had done fairly well. However, it was only for the summer months of 1987.

Come fall, *Spenser* first aired Sunday nights at eight from September 1987 until January 1988, opposite the 4th most watched show in the country, *Murder She Wrote* on CBS. From January 1988 until June 1988, the P.I. found himself back on Saturday nights at ten. For the summer months, he was shuttled to Wednesday nights at ten. For his final network series appearance, our favorite sleuth was back on familiar turf, Saturday nights at ten but for just one month, August-September 1988, before finally being cut loose from ABC's weekly programming schedule. ABC-TV moved the series an astounding eight times during its three year run.

It's a shame that a quality program like *Spenser: For Hire* wasn't allowed one time slot to develop a loyal following and higher ratings. Instead, from season to season, *Spenser* was shuttled around ABC's schedule like an unwanted relative. Additionally, without high ratings, the Network's creative minds panicked and instituted whole sale changes. After the first season, Barbara Stock found herself without a job. She was replaced by Carolyn McCormick as ADA Rita Fiore. *Spenser,* still being shuttled about, didn't fare much better in the ratings and Rita was shown the door after the 2nd season. In all fairness to both capable actresses, McCormick and Stock, the series was still being moved to various nights with precious little time to build a loyal fan following.

For *Spenser's* third and final season, those in charge, decided to bring Barbara Stock back to the family fold. Stock had to know that Bob could have spoken up in her behalf.

After all, *Spenser* was *his* show.

However, it takes a big man to 'eat crow' and 'fess up' to one's mistakes, and to his credit, and being a stand-up guy, Bob admitted, "When she was let go. I didn't fight it. I'll take as much blame as anybody." Bob found himself dialing up his former co-star. "You might hang up on me," he recalled saying, "but this is what I propose. It's a new ball game here. We've got new people. If you can forgive me because I didn't have the foresight and courage to say, 'let's *ride it* out to the end,' will you come back?" Allegedly, Barbara asked him for time to think about it, and Bob said, he'd call her the next day. However, he couldn't wait and called her back an hour later. "I didn't do that very well, did I?" he asked. He must have done well enough, because Barbara returned, although, she never pretended to be overly sentimental about why. "I did it," she says, "because at the time, it was the right thing for me to do in my career."

During the 1980s, before the advent of the DVR, viewers made appointments with their favorite TV programs. They looked forward to watching a certain show at a certain time on a certain night. *Spenser* had done well in its original time slot, *Tuesday nights at ten.* Interestingly, the program that replaced *Spenser* on Tuesday nights at ten, which was supposed to garner high ratings, was *Jack and Mike.*[1] Jack and *Who?!?* It lasted seven months.

The End of Spenser

[**Words in bold type** are Bob's own and from his personal journal.]

In Bob's journal, he writes in detail how a series lives and quite often dies. **"When you do a successful hour show [like *Spenser*] you try to get four, five, six and seven seasons in the can. When you've been on-the-air for three seasons and the show is doing well in the ratings, it doesn't pay to stop. In financial terms, every additional season the show runs is an occasion to get all the money [invested in production, etc.] back.**

"The first season is all the nuts and bolts stuff. It's the press. It's all the talk shows. It's giving up your lunch to do a radio interview. On the weekends, it's flying somewhere to do promotional stuff. Then, there's the *Tonight Show* with David Letterman. All the interviews and newspapers. There's press junkets. They fly in press people [from] all around the country. The second year there's a whole new bath of shows. Your show is now in season two, and you have to figure out some way to create new excitement. You add a character. You add a story line that has people buzzing. You shoot on location in New Orleans, on a riverboat. They come up with stuff. Season three, if you are still maintaining your audience, you're there! You never cancel a show after three seasons. But that's happened to me twice (with Vega$ and *Spenser*). We were so confident that everything was going along fine that when we heard from the network [ABC] that we were going to take six weeks off and go back to work, and get a jump on the new season nobody thought twice about it."

According to Bob's entry in his journal, the beginning of the end with Spenser went down something like this: **"Out of the blue, the guy who was head of programming at ABC at the time starts asking alarming**

1 Jack and Mike was another attempt by ABC to produce a trendy, romantic drama along the lines of its popular *Moonlighting* series. Jack & Mike starred Shelley Hack and Tom Mason. It first aired for 7 months, Tuesday nights at ten, from September 1986-March 1987, and was moved to Thursday nights at nine for 2 months-April-May 1987 before being canceled.

questions. 'You know this *Spenser* show,' he says, 'do you like it? The reason I ask is that it's kind of hovered around the same number [ratings] all the time. We don't think it's a break-out show, a show that's going to give us a big, big, big return.'"

Note: Keep in mind, as previously metioned, Spenser was bounced around the network schedule like an out of control ping pong ball on steroids.

"Now, this is crazy talk because, meanwhile, we're beating our competition nine out of ten times. Fred Dryer had a show where he played a cop. We beat him, week in and week out. They moved Fred Dryer's time slot and he went on to star in that show [*Hunter*] for another four or five seasons[1] and became a multi-millionaire. I got cancelled.

"When the Warner Bros., execs went in to pitch *Spenser* for a fourth season, that's when the guys from ABC programming said, 'The show's been hovering around the same ratings number for a while now. We don't think it's a break-out show.' So, the guy from Warner's says, 'Well, what about Hawk [the second primary character on Spenser] as a show?'"

"The network went, "*Hawk* huh? Yeah, that's interesting."

So Warner Bros. said, "Yeah, okay. We'll do that. We'll give up *Spenser* if you buy *Hawk*. So, they sacrificed the *Spenser* franchise as a series to get another series on the air called *Hawk*. Avery Brooks is a wonderful actor, someone who could certainly carry his own show.[2] But, unfortunately for Avery it didn't work out either."

---

1 During it's first season, September 1984, *Hunter* was seen Tuesday nights at nine.

The police drama set in L.A. next aired Friday nights at nine. From March until August of 1986 it was slotted opposite *Spenser*, Saturday nights at ten. In March of 1986 it moved to Tuesday nights at nine, where it remained until August when it moved back to Saturday nights at ten. In December of 1987, NBC moved the show back to Tuesday nights at nine. From March 1988 until April 1990 it was back on Saturday nights at ten. For the next two seasons, *Hunter* primarily moved back and forth between Wednesday and Saturday nights at ten. It aired for a total of 7 seasons on NBC and like *Spenser* on ABC, *Hunter* also moved around its network's programming schedule like a volley ball. NBC moved the series 13 times during it's seven seasons on the network.

2 Avery Brooks went on to star and carry his own television show in 1993 in the syndicated series *Star Trek: Deep Space 9*. It was a spin-off series from *Star Trek: The Next Generation*. Brooks played Commander Benjamin Sisko in the highly popular science fiction series.

Spenser Meets the Kid

In May of 1988 it had just been announced that *Spenser* wasn't coming back. Bob, Heather and their children were still living on Boston's North Shore in Andover. **"I was asked by Ford to do a commercial,"** Bob writes in his journal. **"An industry promotion for Ford Mustang, because I had driven Fords in almost all of the shows I had done. So, without actually saying so, we were using the Ford Mustang from *Spenser*–Spenser's car. We're down on the docks with the Boston skyline in the back ground. In the commercial, I come screeching around the corner, sliding to a halt, get out of the car and then you see booms and cameras and dollies. I walk over and sit in a director's chair and talk about the tradition of Ford Mustang being a muscle car and so on. They're paying me a lot of money to plug their cars.**

"I'm finishing up. There were a couple of kids hanging around there. One of them was a little black kid. He couldn't [have been] more than seven or eight. It was cold and he [the little kid] was blowing on his hands. I said, 'Where are your gloves? Where's your hat?'

"Okay. Alright," he smiled. "You're Spenser, aren't you?"

"Well, I used to be," I said.

"What do you mean?" He's non-plussed.

"Well, there isn't going to be a Spenser anymore. They cancelled that show."

To make him feel better and to reassure him, I said, "But there is going to be a *Hawk* show."

"Hawk?" He said.

"Yeah, there were two of us. There was *Spenser* and then there was *Hawk*.

"Yeah. I know that man." This little black kid looks down at his feet and then looks back up at me and says, "I don't want no *Hawk* without *Spenser*."

For a minute, I couldn't swallow. This little kid, he just nails me. "I don't want no Hawk without Spenser." I thought, Geez…it's true. That's what made that show work was the two of us, the synergy of those characters."

Bob age 13, visited Boston, standing in front of Minute Man statue.

Spenser: for Hire *Producer, John Wilder with Robert Urich, courtesy John Wilder.*

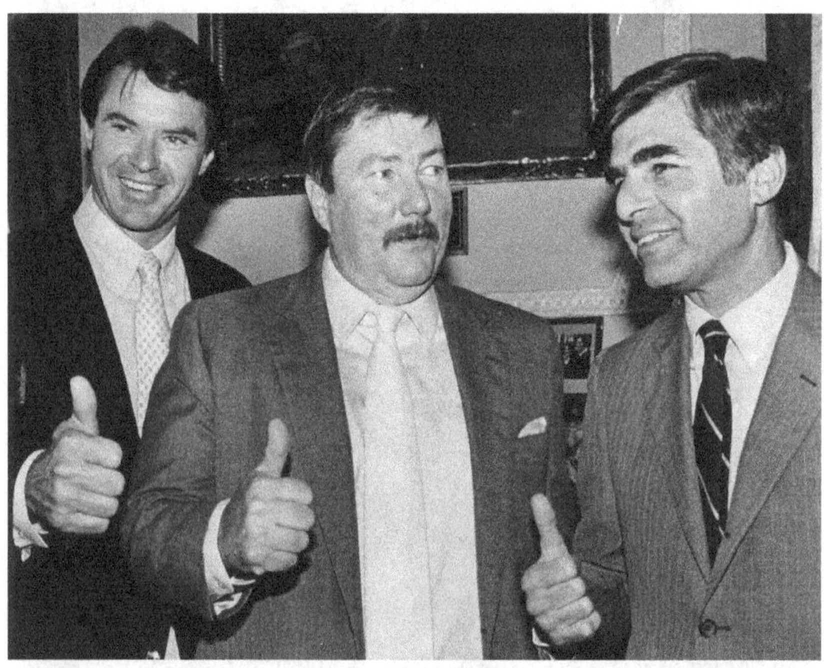

Bob with Spenser *author Robert B. Parker & former Gov. Mike Dukakis.*
Photo courtesy of author's private collection.

L-R, Avery Brooks as Hawk & Bob as Spenser, ABC-TV. Photo courtesy Heather Menzies Urich.

Barbara Stock as Spenser's love interest, Susan Silverman on Spenser.

, Bob as Spenser shooting action scene on roof of car.

Barbara Stock as Susan on Spenser with Author/Broadcaster Joe Martelle at promotional appearance for Spenser TV series, circa 1986.

Group shot of Spenser *cast members) L-R, Ron McLarty as Sgt. Frank Belson, Bob & Richard Jaeckel as Lt. Martin Quirk.*

Bob was actively engaged in supporting charities in the Boston area. In 1986, after filming his series Spenser *throughout the city, he made time that night to play in the annual WROR-98.5FM POLICE Vs. PRIESTS Annual charity softball game. Bob up at bat for the priests nearly hits one out as thousands cheer his plate appearance. Photo courtesy of Bob Joyce.*

L–R, Chuck Connors, guest star on Spenser, & former Celtics player, Celts super-star, Larry Bird & Bob. Photo courtesy Author's private collection.

John Wilder
Alan Shayne
and
Warner Brothers Television
cordially invite you to
the First Annual
Spenser: For Hire
Wrap Party
Saturday, March 22, 1986
7:00 - 11:00 pm
Michela's
245 First Street
Cambridge, Massachusetts

Rsvp. Janet - Mary 617-782-1526

courtesy of Author Joe Martelle

Invitation to Spenser *Wrap Party, after completing first year of filming in Boston – March 22, 1986.*

Chapter 21

Bob Loved Boston
This Olde House, Bob's Money Pit

"I don't miss the weather there but to this day, I miss the house."
- From the personal journal of Robert Urich

Bob and Boston

[**Words in bold type** are Bob's own and from his personal journal.]

When Bob worked in a long running series like *Vega$* or *Spenser: For Hire*, he and his family became residents of whatever city the series was filmed in.

"I move there [Boston] lock, stock and barrel and settle in. I become part of the local culture and willy nilly, get involved in some strange situations. Over the years, I've encountered a bunch of eccentric characters you've never likely to hear about who are as memorable as the guest stars on the shows. Boston is that place full of Characters."

The door swung open like it was jet-propelled and Jimmy Murray walked in.

"Good Morning, 'Rabbit,' he said." 'Rabbit': that's the way they pronounced Bob's name in Boston. Jimmy was a local guy who worked in special effects for the *Spenser: For Hire* crew. He had a rich Boston accent and he was good at blowing things up. He also was well-connected.

"What's up?" I said.

"They want you to be the Grand Marshal of the St. Patrick's Day Parade next weekend," he informed me enthusiastically.

In South Boston, there is no bigger event than the St. Pat's Parade and they wanted Bob for the figurehead. **"That's nice," I said, "but…"**

"Rabby, you realize what an honor this is? You are the first non-Irish Catholic to be asked to do this," he said, wanting me to understand the significance of the gesture. Sort of like being the first non-Catholic Pope."

"I'm honored Jimmy but I'm exhausted. I've done twenty shows in a row and I've got a few more to go. My mom's in town. Tell them thanks, Jimmy, but no."

Jimmy and Bob's driver, Bobby McGuiness, both teamsters, folded their arms across their chests and stared at Bob like he was out of his mind.

"In Boston, I was well aware, there is this blurred dividing line between the Irish Mob and the teamsters. They run things. They can do things for you. They can do things *to* you." Looking into the faces of Jimmy Murray and Bobby McGuiness, Bob quickly realized they were not making a request. It was an offer he couldn't refuse.

"I was going to be their parade marshal!"

On Sunday morning, they picked up Bob and his family at their home in Andover, MA. Bob's mom, wife and children rode together in a standard limo, but for 'Rabbit,' they had something really special.

"For me, they had a white Rolls Royce convertible–well guarded, of course. Riding on one fender was Tommy McNeely, who fought Floyd Patterson for the heavyweight championship in 1964 and lost. On another fender was the brother of the former Massachusetts Secretary of State, Whitey Bulger,[1] who had just gotten out of the Charles Street jail after doing time for second degree murder. Who else? Oh yeah, a guy named Six Button Louie from Philadelphia, and Joey the Frog from places unknown. Our driver was Jackie Hurley, who was certifiable. His father was President of the bartender's union. There were stories about Jackie tending bar on St. Paddy's Day wearing nothing but a white apron. I was in good hands."

The parade started and it was short and uneventful, which was unusual for this celebration. Nobody was hurt. At the end of the line, Mike Crawson, a Boston cop rushed up to Bob.

"Crawson was assigned to our show and had been assigned to me during the parade. "Ok, get outta the caw," he said.

"Why?""Get outta the f_ _ kin' caw," he reiterated. "Nobody threw a brick at you…no fights…so get outta the caw."

---

1 James Joseph 'Whitey' Bulger, born Sept. 3, 1929 in Dorchester MA, was an organized crime boss and F.B.I. informant who let the 'Winter Hill Gang' in Somerville MA. He was a fugitive and on the run for 16 years before being captured in California in June 2011. In 2013, he was convicted and sentenced to life in prison. Bulger who was in a wheelchair was fond dead on Oct. 30, 2018. He was killed by inmates within hours of his arrival at Hazelton Prison in W.V. He was 89.

"Alright, already, I'm getting out," I said.

The scene outside was getting a little inebriated and ugly. Reluctantly, with Mike yelling and pulling on Bob's arm, he got out of the *caw*. Bob looked at Jackie Hurley, hoping he would explain.

"I almost wish he hadn't," said Bob.

"Yeah, sorry," he said, "but we gotta have the caw back to the docks by *tree* o'clock.

It's gotta be on a boat to Saudi Arabia."

"What?" I exclaimed!

"Well, it's a very long story and I won't be bodderin' you with the details but to make it *shot* and sweet–it's not our caw. We just borrowed it."

"You *borrowed* it? How exactly do guys like you borrow a spanking new white Rolls Convertible?

"Yeah, we just went down there and told them which one we wanted and one of our friends, you know, gave it to us. But, it's gotta be back by...

"Yeah, I know, *tree* o'clock."

On the front page of *The Boston Herald* the next morning was a photo of *Spenser*–alias *Robert: For Rent*–riding in a stolen Rolls Royce with Joey the Frog on the fender. (See photo at the end of this chapter.)

Bob Versus the Redcoats

One winter Bob rented a new house in Weston, a suburb of Boston. They liked it so much, they thought maybe they should live there. **"We love it here," we said. "Let's put down roots. We loved the whole Boston pageantry. It's living history."**

Every weekend, Bob visited historic sites in Concord and Lexington to look around and explore. **"The battlefields, the shot heard round the world! I went through all the historical houses. I just loved all of that stuff."**

One weekend, Bob and his family went to see a Revolutionary War reenactment. **"They have these British soldiers who march through the town. They're actors telling the story. They start talking about how cowardly the colonials were. How they didn't have the proper protocol, they didn't know how to fight properly. Cowards hiding behind rocks shooting at them [the British]."**

A British officer was going off on the Revolutionaries. Finally, Bob had had enough. **"I get angry and my actor's imagination gets the better of**

me and I yell from the crowd at the British officers. "So what are you trying to say, buddy? You know what? You redcoats, you're the ones who behaved like sniveling cowards."

"My wife is pulling me away, pleading, 'Bob, please, it's a show. It's a performance. This guy works at Denny's. He's an actor.' And I hear one of the Denny's redcoats whispering, 'Hey, it's the *Spenser for Hire* guy!' But, I'm still telling them off. 'You damn redcoats. You imperialist bastards!' Now, the officer gets into it. 'Take this man to the brig,' he orders. And, suddenly, I find myself in a scuffle with a bunch of re-enacting actors, who are playing colonial soldiers. I was really upset. They didn't know what to make of me." Sometimes, Bob's quick-trigger temper got the best of him.

Bob's Quick-Trigger Temper

Bob Urich was a good and decent man[1] with numerous good qualities, and like most of us, he also possessed a few human faults. The kind we all try to live with and handle. Bob's one big shortcoming was his volatile quick-trigger temper which he did his best to keep under wraps. "Most of the time he was pretty calm," insists his wife, Heather. But, when he did become provoked and his fuse would hit the flash point, look out! When he would 'momentarily' lose it, it was usually the result of someone he witnessed acting really dumb or stupid," she says, "or someone being disrespectful to another.[2] His occasional outbursts prove one thing, Bob Urich was human, just like the rest of us.

When Bob filmed *Spenser* in Boston, he was a regular guest on the author's morning radio show, *The Joe and Andy Family*. One morning, following our show, my late partner Andy Moes and I were explaining to Bob our different roles on our show. "Joey is the good guy," says Andy. You know, All-American, clean-cut, apple pie type. The kinda guy you hope your daughter will marry. As for me, I'm a sleaze-ball, a first class rectal depression. Young children run and hide from me. Dads lock their daughters in a sealed room. Mothers scream in horror when I'm around and make sure their daughters are wearing their chastity belts. Bob laughed

1 Author's note: In the numerous interviews conducted for this book [over 100] most everyone said the same thing in describing Bob Urich. "He was a wonderful man, a loyal friend who dearly loved his wife and family. He also possessed a volatile temper.

2 Respect was Bob's by-word. *The Lonesome Dove* Ch.23 details Bob's feelings about being disrespectful.

and said something which knocked us over. "You know, it's funny. Most people believe I'm a good guy, but I'm not. I'm really not a nice guy." Both Andy and I were a little taken aback by his words. Let's face it, it's not exactly the kind of remark you'd expect to hear from good guy Robert Urich. We pressed him to explain his comment, but Bob just smiled and shook it off, apparently not willing to discuss it any further.

Bob's words have stayed with me [author] to this day. I've often wondered what he meant? Was it a momentary soul-searching revelation? A sort of a mea culpa on his part? While writing this biography, I ran the comment by Bob's wife. She lightly passed it off, "Oh, he was just messin' with you guys." Perhaps. . .or was his comment about "not being the nice guy the public perceives," made out of frustration and being tired of trying to live up in real life to the 'good guy' image he often portrayed on the screen? Library shelves are filled with books about celebrities who had difficulty trying to live up to their 'good guy' image. As one legendary screen star, said, "It's difficult living up to one's screen role as 'Mister nice guy' when you're feeling tired, your hemorrhoids are killing you and you're feeling a little jumpy and grumpy because you had a fight with your wife. Sometimes, people have a difficult time discerning between the person an actor plays on-screen with the real-life person."

The point being, everyone has their faults and both good and bad sides. Good or bad, it's what makes you *uniquely* "you." Most often than not, Bob Urich, did a good job of letting his 'good guy image and nice guy side' come shining through.

***

Bob and his family first lived in a little town in Weston [MA] and they fell in love with the area. The stone walls and the white-spired churches…

"And on the grounds of this little house I rented was a pond. I thought–Currier and Ives! We are going to ice skate and have a fire and the kids are going to roast chestnuts and it's going to be beautiful. They can have hot chocolate out there." Only one problem. The place was somewhat overgrown, there were branches sticking up.

Bob's Boston Life

Bob thought if he trimmed them, and then ran a garden hose out of the basement window, and let the water run all night, they'd get a nice, smooth skating pond.

"The first thing I've got to do, I thought is cut all these branches. So, I'm with my driver, Bobby McGuiness and we stop at Sears to buy a little cheap chain saw. But, by the time we get there, Sears is closed."

"Oh, Rabbit," he says, "It's just as well. Ya know, chain saws are dangerous things. We're all sort of depending on you, like, and what's to become of us if you cut your arm off. You're putting our kids through college now, ya know? We aren't driving beer trucks anymore. We got a nice cushy job here, Rabbit. We cahn't have you operating chain saws and heavy equipment.

"Look," I said. "I've got a little farm saw that I found in Canada. Use them all the time. I'll be careful. All right dear."

The stage for *Spenser: For Hire* was a warehouse on Soldiers Field Road in Boston. It was right down the street from Harvard University Stadium. Cramped parking. Bob had a trailer as a dressing room.

"Now the procedure is that when you do a scene in an hour show, you first go in and block it–which means you show all the departments where you'll be moving and stopping during the scene. And, while they are lighting it–which takes forty-five minutes to an hour sometimes–you go in and change clothes for that scene. The scene had been blocked. I went in to shoot the scene, which took an hour and a half. I come back in my trailer and when I open the door to my dressing room I trip over a brand new Black and Decker chain saw."

The chainsaw just fell off a truck

Bob asks Bobby McGuiness, "where'd the chain saw come from?

"Oh, Rabbit, remember you said you needed one."

"I know I did, but where did it come from?"

"Never you mind. You need a chain saw, you got a chain saw. Just be careful and don't cut your arm off. Remember what I told you. You got to keep taking care of us."

"Yeah, Bobby, but I just can't take the chain saw. What's the story? Did somebody get it for me? Did somebody buy it? I'll be happy to pay for it."

"It fell off a truck, ok? Don't worry about it. Just don't get hurt."

Bob said he would use the chain saw but he wasn't keeping it.

"The next Saturday, I went and trimmed all the branches and gave the chain saw back–because you don't keep stuff that fell off a truck."

Bob Builds his own Masterpiece

Bob writes in his personal journal about the historic dream home he eventually found in Andover, Mass. It was somewhat run down, but he had a vision for the grand ole dame. **"The ancientness seeped out of the house. It stood on ground that had been walked on by [native Americans], Revolutionary War soldiers, farmers and peddlers. It had a presence all its own, like a gnarled old apple tree. It had known all the winters, known the burning of leaves in autumn, wisps of smoke curling up around the corner of the house. When it rained, it was almost as if a collective shudder went up from the house as it pulled inside itself to get away from the rain."**

"Once you were inside, with the log fire burning in the grate, the rain lashing at the windows, there was no where you wanted to go. You only wanted to sit there and look out at the apple trees and the day lilies."

This is the way Bob first imagined this great brooding house and then like 'magic' it materialized. When they really decided to settle in the Boston area, Bob and Heather began looking for a great old New England house. The actual story of how he found his dream house is recorded forever in his journal.

"I was on location filming in a state park for an episode of *Spenser*, drinking coffee, musing aloud to a state trooper that I'd really like to find a great olde house in the area. 'My wife's a realtor,' he said. So, she came to the location site and on the way home showed me a few homes, but none of them anything near what I was looking for.

The next real-estate agent didn't even want to show me my soon-to-be ancestral house. 'Well, we do have a large older house in our listings, but you wouldn't be interested in it.' 'Why's that?' I asked. 'Oh, it's in terrible shape. It's dilapidated and falling down and overgrown.'" That immediately got Bob's attention. **"'Let's drive over and take a look,' I said. There it was, an old stick-and-shingle style house on nineteen acres, adjacent to the Philips Academy property. She was right about everything. It was dilapidated, falling down and overgrown."**

To Bob, it was beautiful. He didn't see a mere house. To him, it was a dynasty.

As soon as he saw it, he said, **"This is it!"**

The house came with wonderful stories.

It was said Doctor Spock had taught class in one of the upstairs rooms. World-famous architect Frank Lloyd Wright had once been a visitor, and upon viewing the massive corner fireplace, pronounced, "You might as well tear it down, it'll never draw." And, there were other intriguing rumors about the place that only increased it's appeal to Bob and Heather Urich. **"But, there was one big problem–it really was falling down! It had been occupied until recently by the curator of the local museum, who I think, had recently passed away. He and his daughter had lived there. The poor guy was an alcoholic and the plumbing had been organized in an alcoholic manner. All the pipes in the kitchen were exposed. Running through the ceiling and through the house. He had color coordinated them, the hot and cold and waste pipes. He had green, red and yellow pipes and holes in the plaster. You'd start pulling the plaster away and there would be empty whiskey bottles. In the attic, there were boxes of them under the eaves."** Strange as it may seem, none of this bothered ole Robert. He and Heather looked at the place as a homestead on nineteen beautiful acres.

"A stream ran through the property. You could dam it up way down in the woods to have your own pond. You could have a huge garden and an apple orchard with ancient specimen trees."

Later, Bob had a professor at Harvard University come out to their home and he told Bob, "Now this property, Mr. Urich, you don't know this, but it once used to be the Arboretum Society of Massachusetts. The very first one! So, there are specimen trees here that grow nowhere else in the country." Bob thought to himself, **"Gee, even the trees have pedigrees."**

Mr. Bob Finds his Dream House

It was an enormous house. Three stories with a slate roof. But, it was dilapidated. It was literally falling down before their eyes, but in typical Bob and Heather fashion, they could envision infinite possibilities. The entry was forty feet long and twenty-five feet wide with a marble fireplace at the end of it. Bob could imagine Christmas Eve and family showing up and the fire roaring in the entry. Later, reality hit Bob.

"I think given the ruinous state of the place, it would have been cheaper, had I just hired a draftsman to copy every detail of the house,

demolished it and re-built it. To take an old place like that and reinforce some of the stairwells with steel and do all the plasterwork–the lathe and plaster had to be torn off and redone. The slate roof had asbestos in it, so it had to be removed. It required special handling by guys in rubber suits. It was a nightmare!" But, Bob and Heather were determined to look at the positive side. Here they thought was an opportunity to create this great manse, like the *House of Seven Gables* in Hawthorne, a house that would stand forever. A house to be passed down for generations. **"Our kids would bring their kids and their kids' kids and they'd all cherish the ancestral home and its ancient apple orchard."**

Interestingly, before actually finding his dream house, I [the author] and a friend were invited to dinner at Bob and Heather's. At the time, they were renting a home in Andover, Ma. After a delicious meal of home-made soup, we all sat down to watch a movie. Believe it or not, it was *The Money Pit*![1] Little did we know at the time a 'fictional movie' would soon become reality, or nightmare if you will, for the Urich's.

Even though they made extensive renovations to the house–including a large room with a staircase and a turret at the top–they left the character of the house intact.

"We left the mantels from the original house, the old railings, the original spiral staircase that went up three stories and the old tea cupboard in the dining room. There was a little staircase in the garage that had been rubbed smooth with use, a hundred years of gloved hands from putting up horses polishing it. Our decorator wanted to strip it and repaint it. 'No,' I said, 'we'll keep it just as it is. All it needs is a good cleaning and oiling. We cut away some of the small growth on one side of an open field and found that the trees were not as old there as others in the area and as we cleared away the ground, we found the remains of a lawn tennis court.'"

All the walls of the house had to be demolished. The frame of the house stood, but if you stood at the foot of the stairs you could look straight through the house. All that was left were the studs and the two-by-fours and the stairwells. The fireplaces had to come down too. As Bob writes in his journal, **"They would have fallen down anyway."**

1 *The Money Pit* was released in 1986, starring Tom Hanks and Shelley Long. It's the story of a young couple struggling to repair a hopelessly dilapidated house.

Heather and Bob hired an architect, Nan Binkley, a young lady from Cambridge who was fresh out of architectural school. **"I described what I wanted and she drew all these spectacular turrets and towers. I said, 'Okay, build it.' She was stunned. 'What? You're actually going to build this stuff?' She couldn't believe that someone would actually say, yes, go ahead, let's build it. She was a student, and used to people having her design things and then making compromises."**

But once Bob saw her magnificent designs he thought, **"what she'd drawn was perfect. This was going to be where I would live forever!"**

Bob had seen a guy on *60 Minutes* build a stone wall by hand and asked his builder to track him down. **"It turned out, he lived just a few miles down the road."**

This Ole House Becomes a Money Pit

"This old Italian guy comes up to me and I explain to him what I want. Stone walls all around. I might even build a wooden gate at the entrance to the stone and put steps down to a lower area which had been the tennis court, which would become the perennial garden. He took the job and later that week, an enormous truck showed up and dumped a mountain of stones over the area. He would walk around mumbling in Italian, *Managgia la miseria*. Mumble, mumble. Then, he'd stop and he'd say, *Ecco*!!" *Ah, ere's a good one*!' He'd see a rock that would fit and he'd pick it up and he'd place it. Then, he would walk around again, and mumble, mumble, *Ecco*! And find another one and put that one in. He would do something like a foot of wall a day. He was there all summer building walls with one helper. A true craftsman, an artist. I got him to build stone walls around what had been the small tennis court to make it a perennial garden, with crushed gravel and walkways.

Bob's fancied his Andover dream house as an estate and seemingly at a fraction of the cost of anything he could afford to build in Bel Air or Hollywood.

One day, Bob was working in the fields, clearing the Arboretum with its wonderful specimen trees. His son, Ryan, who was just a little guy back then, shouts over to his dad.

"Look, I found these arrow heads." There was a stone wall behind the carriage house. **"I thought to myself, just a kid's imagination. They're just stones. But Ry insisted.**

'Dad, dad. You've got to come look.' Okay, I said. Ry was over in the corner of the property, where two stone walls had been erected, most likely during Revolutionary times. I was keeping an eye on him, of course, and could see him the whole time."

The Secret of the house is Revealed

Bob writes in his journal that he put down what he was doing and walked across the field to the foot of the stone wall where Ry had uncovered a little mound. **"It was full of arrowheads and flakes of broken stone where native Americans had made them. They had been there for how many hundreds of years? I don't know. 200, maybe?"**

Bob moved on to his next architectural project. The carriage house, which like the main house, was in total disrepair and falling down. But it was part of the master plan. **"It was a two-story building. I dreamed of making it into a workshop, or maybe even my office some day, the place where I would write the Great American Novel, and during slow periods of inspiration, get working on my mahogany boats. Just as they are shoring the thing up so it wouldn't fall down, the backhoe guy yells, 'Mr. Urich. You need to come see something.' What now, I'm wondering, as I walk over.**

'Take a look at this,' he says. 'It's a dress, an ancient dress.'"

"He's found some bones!"

"We took rakes and carefully cleared the earth away. We found a skeleton with clothes laid out. Strips of taffeta clinging to the bones. Both grisly and evocative of an ancient life. Somebody had been buried there. . .an old woman. "What are we gonna do? We should call some people," I said. "Oh no. That wouldn't be a good ideah, Mr. Urich. They'll shut us down. What earthly difference is it gonna make now," he insisted. "She's dead and buried anyway. You let this get out and you'll have guys from some university digging holes all over the property." "So now it's revealed," Bob states in his journal. **"There was a dead body and ghost. Some old Pilgrim but we left her there. We covered her up."**

Bob's Money Pit

Bob's Dream House was progressing into a Bostonian movie sequel to *The Money Pit*. **"It was one mistake after another. They have a phrase in Vegas to cover this notion. It's called chasing [after] bad money with**

good, and that's what we were doing. But, after you've made your first mistake, you keep on going. It would be a serious mistake to stop at that point, if you follow my logic. We had hard-wood floors flown in from South Carolina. American Chestnut floors.

Oh, it got worse and more expensive. Bob and company went to a quarry somewhere up in Maine where they fabricated a fifty foot front step out of a single piece of granite. Bob excitedly points out, **"They actually had to re-tool the mill to do it. It looked like some megalithic plinth from Stonehenge."**

"It was a big event for them. All their families came [to watch]. It was Robert Urich and Spenser and they came with cameras and the newspaper showed up. They brought this big crane over and loaded this thing." Bob makes a note in his journal which reads somewhat sarcastically, **"Ah, it was a beautiful sight to see. A front step made of a single granite slab."** The garage was a two-storied Dutch gambrel-roofed building.

"The upper floor I designed as one huge lodge. I wanted it to look like a carriage house. I used tongue-and-groove beam board. Ya know, the kind you see on turn-of-the-century porches. The interior of the garage was decorated with lanterns and gold filigree signs that said, 'Entrance.' It was just amazing. It was going to be my tribute to the family. The house itself was a huge lodge."

Bob's Dream House

"I once read somewhere Mark Twain had said the perfect winter scene for him was sitting in front of a fire and looking out the window at the same time." Bob mentions that he made the mistake of telling this to Nan Binkley, his architect. **"So, she designed a fireplace at the far end of this huge cathedral like room. The Grand Room. The Great Room. We called it The Lodge! The windows arched up and met almost at the roof peak, so you could in fact, look at the stone fireplace, look at the fire and watch the snow fall all at the same time. And, it was a good thing we had the [massive] fireplace, because the heating system never worked in that room! It wasn't just a plastered room. We studied old barns and decided to use the mortice-and-tenon timbers that couldn't be found anywhere else but in Washington State."**

These special one-of-a kind trees had to be hand cut down and shipped by rail all the way across the country to Bob's dream house in Massachusetts.

"Most ceilings you have rafters and then you plaster it and then you put a siding on it and you put wood up there if you want, and then, on top of the roof there's the plywood and tarpaper, and it's sealed, and then it's caulked and it's got your stainless or galvanized or copper flashing that you put on the roof. It's a slate roof, of course. There again, we're in New England. This beautiful green color." But, this wasn't good enough for our pal, Bob. **"You got it. Our roof had to be different. We found tongue and groove wood that must have been four inches thick and eight inches wide that locked together, and that was to be both the ceiling and the roof. The slate would be laid over that. So, it had to hold a certain amount of stress-weight. The slate per square foot is very heavy."**

A very 'expensive' roof

"All this special wood came from Washington [State] and to say the least, it was very expensive, of course.

It started to get winter and the project manager, Warren Sideri, kept saying, "All the materials will be coming in a couple of days. Meanwhile, we're going to put up the beams and wrap them with plastic in case we get any rain. We don't want them spotted before we get them stained. We're going to put a quick coat of sealer on it." Bob describes these huge beams going throughout an enormous room. **"It's fifty feet long, and they're all wrapped. Every day Bob would go to the house at five in the morning before anybody would show up and then late at night I would come by again, and Warren and I would walk through the site and finally, we would just sit in the big empty space."**

"You smell the plaster, the dirt and the dust and imagine what it's going to be like to live in this great place. Just one problem. The roof hasn't shown up and now, as Bob describes in agonizing detail, **"the plastic wrap is starting to be wind-tattered and it's starting to flap. I keep saying to the guy, "Warren, where's the roof? Where is the ceiling? "It's coming. It's coming."**

"Finally, on the Friday it's supposed to be there and it's not there, I said,

"Okay, Warren, what's the story with this friggin' roof?"

"Bob," he said, I've got to tell you. It's been here for a couple of days."

"It has? Where is it?"

"There's a wildcat strike down in Revere Beach at the rail yards. They can't unload it. We're really in trouble."

Bob's Dream House with NO roof

Dismayed and upset, Bob went to work and walks past the teamster captain, whose name is Billy Winn. According to Bob, if you looked down the list of teamsters working on location, it was all his brothers, all his kids. Whether they could even find the Mass Pike or not, it didn't matter–they were drivers. **"I was always friendly to those guys. As a matter of fact, a couple of weeks earlier I was on my way home, very tired after a long day of shooting and my driver, Bobby McGuiness says, 'We should stop by and see Billy.' 'Stop in where? I want to go home. I'm tired. It's dark. It's cold. I'm hungry.' 'Well, he's got a little trouble with da Feds, ya know? They confiscated his boat, something about he lent his sailboat to these guys and they found it full of guns headed for the Irish Republic. Imagine that?'"**

"Yeah, with these guys involved, I *could* imagine."

All through the summer Bob had heard a lot about this sailboat and its fate.

"They'd say, Let's go for a sail, Bob. Let's take the boat out. I always found a reason not to go. Then one evening when I felt like sailing across Boston Harbor, I heard the story. "I'm real sorry," Bobby told me, but da Feds handcuffed her and took her away to the holding tank, wouldja believe it?"

"Yeah, I'm sorry to hear about Arlene II getting confiscated, but what's that got to do with me?"

"Rabbit," he says very earnestly, "you gotta go. You should say hello, at the very least. You gotta pay your respects. You haven't been dere. You should really be dere. You shoulda been dere already." "Okay, okay. Just a couple of minutes. I'll shake hands, eat the eye of the lamb with him and we're outta there."

Bob and the cast of characters in Boston

"We drive down a dark street in Somerville, Mass, and pull up in front of this little brick affair, "Home of the Somerville gang." No win-

dows. Well, one little round window with a beer sign in it and a solid door. I said, "What kind of a place is this?" "This is his joint." Bobby starts laughing. So, we go up to the door and he gives a little rap. Someone peers through a little peek hole and lets us in. There are cards being played and stuff going on in the background. Serious guys playing cards. Billy spots us immediately. "What a wonderful surprise.," he says. "How wonderful that you would come and see me. Have a beer." "Well, okay, Billy, a quick one and then I've got to get home." "You are one stand-up guy, Robert, you know that? Everybody likes you. You're never any trouble and you're one of us."

"Oh great," I said. 'thanks for the beer. I've gotta go. God Bless you."

"He [Billy] takes out a business card, slides it across the bar and says, "If you have any trouble on the East Coast, on the Eastern Seaboard, you call that number. I don't care if you're sleeping drunk under somebody's dining room table. It doesn't matter how you got there. You don't have to remember any of it. But in fifteen minutes, somebody will be there to get you. No questions asked."

Bob carried that card around in his wallet forever. It was all tattered and worn. He kept it but never used it. The business with the roof was still bothering him. It occurred to him, Billy Winn is a teamster. He would surely know if a strike was taking place.**"Monday morning on my way to work, I knocked on his [Billy's] door and pushed it open. I go in and it's like going into a Secretary of State's office. Picture this old dilapidated warehouse with dust everywhere. But, inside, there is a real room."**

"There was a fish tank, five feet long, and badges from all the sheriff's departments around the country. The American flag, the Commonwealth [of MA] flag, and pictures of Billy with celebrities…and standing over in the corner is the head of the National Teamsters Union at the time.

"I don't mean to interrupt," I said.

"No, no, no Bob. Come in. Billy was just telling me what a stand-up guy you are and what's the deal? What's going on? Anything we can do for you?"

"Well, just answer a question for me. I'm building this house and I have this wood and it's on a rail car in the dust somewhere and they tell me that there is a wildcat strike and they can't off-load anything."

"Is that right?" The teamster boss turns around and says to a couple of his Lieutenants, "We got a wildcat strike goin' on over at Revere Beach?"

"Yeah, could be we got some trouble down there, they respond."

The guy picks up the phone and says, "This is a secure phone. Too bad the Feds can't listen in on this one." And, he calls down to the Union Hall. Here's the head of the Teamster's Union, on the phone to the Union Hall about my roof and asks, "Are we having a wildcat strike? We do? Is that right? Ok. Listen. I have some wood on one of these rail cars that belongs to Rabbit Urich."

"Rabbit, what's the name of the lumbah Company?" Anderson, I tell him. "Okay, listen," he says. "There's a guy with a truck. He'll be down there from Anderson Lumbah in about an hour. I want the wood off-loaded and delivered to Mr. Urich's house today."

Bob get his lumbah delivered

"He turns to me. "Okay. Anything else, Bob?"

"No. Thanks. I've got to go to work. It was nice to see you guys."

After work, Bob made his customary stop at his 'dream' house still without a roof. They had put up a big hurricane fence for insurance purposes–anything to keep people out of there. It was eight feet tall. It was already dark. Bob's headlights hit the fence and there's his guy, Warren, locking the place up.

"What's going on?" I ask.

"You are not going to believe this," he said. "Just before dark, about an hour ago, this truck comes roaring down the driveway and almost hits your dog [Jake]. I was about to lock it up."

"This guy says, "Open the gate, please. I gotta unload this wood for Mr. Urich.

Please, please you've got to help me. The load's got to me unloaded tonight. Look, [he continued in a pleading way] I've got a family. A wife and kids. You've got to let me unload this."

"So, Warren says, "the wood is in the garage and it's got a tarp over it. We're gonna put it up tomorrow."

***

"Robert Parker who wrote the original Spenser novels on which the TV series was based came to dinner with his wife, Joan, after the house

was finished. He'd lived in New England his whole life, and said, he's never been in a finer house than ours. "I want to preserve the patina of things rubbed smooth by use and time, I told him. "Isn't it a blast," he said to his wife, "to hear tough-guy Robert Urich say patina."

Bob had at long last created his own idyllic setting on twenty beautiful acres in Andover, Massachusetts, yet his life was not fulfilled, as he points out in his writings. The problem lied beyond his enclosed daydream of twenty acres.

"The house was my architectural poem–an epic, actually, in stone and ancient timbers–a tale to be told through countless generations of Urichs to come. The problem lied beyond my enclosed daydream of twenty acres. It wasn in the real world, a world in which we soon discovered we did not belong."

Bob riding in St. Patrick's Day parade in 'Southie' March 16, 1986. Photo courtesy Bill Belknap.

Bob & Heather in their 1895 reconstructed colonial home, 24 Phillips St., Andover, MA. known as 'The Dove-Hayes-Urich House'.

Chapter 22

So long, Spenser: Bye, Bye Boston
[The real reason Bob stopped living in the Boston area]

So Long Spenser: Bye, Bye Boston

[**Bold typed words** are Bob's–taken directly from his personal journal.]

Bob loved his time living in the Boston area, and thought, even if his show [*Spenser: For Hire*] was cancelled, he would stay there and raise his kids there. The schools are great. The question is: if he loved it so much, why did he leave?

"Eventually, I got tired of pulling up to a gas station and have some pimply faced kid say, "What are you doin' livin' heah?"

And I would say, "It's for the beautiful countryside and the history of the place…and great sports…a great city."

"Yeah," he'd say, "but you could live in Hollywood. What's a matta wich you?"

Pure and simply stated, Bob got tired of answering that question.

"The more I answered it, the less convincing I sounded to myself. I began to think, you know what? I really don't have a good reason to be here. For a grown man to be driving a road and not know where that highway goes, is a little weird. And I don't know where the Boston Post Road goes. "Where does that wind up?" I would ask. "What are you talking about? It goes out to Lincoln and you hang a right and you're at such-and-such avenue. You know where that is, right?" "Well, no, actually, I don't."

Bob actually believed there was some kind of synchronicity between TV series and property values. **"The minute we were cancelled, real estate went into a decline around Boston. We had only lived in the house a year or so, our dream home, with the porch, the carriage house, the arboretum. It took another two years to sell it, then [we] lost all the money I'd put in it. No problem. The show was cancelled in the spring and we spent an idyllic summer at our house on the lake in Canada."**

Bye, Bye Boston

The Urich family returned to Boston in the fall, and Bob thought, **"Well, I'll live here and have a nice Christmas. But, after Christmas, we all started to miss California. This coupled with my agent [Merritt Blake] saying, 'Bob, out of sight, out of mind.'"** But, the real clincher came when Bob and Heather took a skiing trip out West. **"As we stepped off the plane, we bore witness to the breath-taking expanse of the American West. At that moment, we looked at each other and realized we didn't belong in a New England clapboard house surrounded by woods in the wintertime, at heart, we were westerners."**

Timing is everything in life and, as it happened, the people Bob and Heather were skiing with were from Los Angeles, and told them about a house that was for sale. **"It belonged to Frank DeLeo, Michael Jackson's manager. We added a day to our trip and flew to L.A. We were immediately convinced that this was where we needed to be and made an offer on the house. It wasn't our dream house, but it was the place of our dreams. In our love-hate relationship with LA., love had won. We liked living in Boston, but we [felt] we were like freaks of nature. We would be invited to charity events and people would just look at us like–'Hollywood.' Maybe, that's why people like me end up living in Hollywood. There, you're just one of the freaks."**

Bob honestly felt that he and Heather were really never included. **"My kids went to this little [Catholic] school which had been in Andover, Mass. forever. Lovely priest. Great nuns, especially Sister Kathleen. Our kids were doing very well there, but it [the school] was really outdated. It was time to put some computers in there.**

It was time to replace the linoleum on the floors." When Bob mentioned it to Father Tom, he said, "Absolutely. You're dead right." So, Bob and Heather threw a big party at their house and invited all these lawyers and doctors who were Alumni [of the school]. **"Food, music and wine. The priest made a speech and we gave out donor cards to everyone. As they filed out at the end of the evening, all they said was, "Good luck with your project." Good luck on *our project?* I thought, what kind of place is this? We raised practically no money."**

In the final analysis, it was a case of not feeling like they were really accepted there, plus that pimply-faced kid, as Bob puts it, at the gas station, who kept asking him the same question. *Why ya livin' here when ya could be in L.A.?* **"One morning, he asked it once too often and I said, 'You know what? I have no idea why I'm living here.' So, the house went on the market."**

***

"I looked in the mirror one morning and I could see myself becoming old right before my eyes. My hair got gray and I was getting jowly–I had been looking forward to lobster pie at least once a week. I said, 'What's the matter with me?'The minute I left Boston and went out to California to do some interviewing and meet with people, the gray hair went away. It just kind of disappeared."

The house Michael Jackson's manager sold Bob was on just under an acre of land. **"You could barely walk around in it. I painted the walls because they were dirty. I had just come from an architectural gem. One of the most extraordinary houses on the East Coast, on 20 acres. Now, I'm in this little California ranch house and my kids are coming out in a week and I'm thinking, what have I done?"**

California livin' ain't always EZ

Following the kids' arrival from back East, Bob is up on the roof. His son Ryan, who was then around five or six, walks by, looks up and says, "Aw, Daddy. Aw Daddy. We're living way below your means."

"'Way below *your* means.' I thought we had gotten him out of Hollywood, and removed him from those values. I didn't want him thinking that private jet travel and a Mercedes were somehow an ordained right. That sense of entitlement so many children of the rich have, and here he was looking down his nose at a two-million dollar house because it wasn't a New England mansion."

Bob & J.W.

Bob met his future business partner J. W.[1] when they were still living in New England. **"His wife was my secretary. I was overwhelmed at the**

---

1 J.W. are the initials of a person Heather had a serious falling out with after Bob died. She asked me not to include him in the book, saying [quote] "If his name *never* appears in Bob's bio I'll be a happy lady." Here's my dilemna: Bob mentions J.W. in complimentary fashion in his journal, writing, "I owe my entire off-screen career to him," citing several examples. Therefore, I feel compelled to mention the fact. However because of my loyalty to Heather, and to honor her request, I will only refer to this person by his initials, JW.

time and really needed help. I hired a secretary and that was his wife, Liz. She was a pretty prim and proper New England raised girl. She came and sat in my living room with her hands folded. I was trying to interview her for the job as my secretary and every time I would say, 'One of the things you would do is take calls from my agent,' she would titter. She thought that was hysterical. I'd say, 'Then there will be the fan mail…' and she would just howl. She thought it was so amusing that someone would write somebody like me a letter."

Evidently, Bob wasn't at all turned off by her reactions to his questions, because Liz got the job and was Bob's secretary for a long time. It wasn't until the Urich's were about to move back to Los Angeles that Bob met her husband, J.W.

"One day, just before we moved I asked Liz what her husband did. 'Oh, you know,' she said, very matter-of-factly, 'He's that guy selling hot dogs over on Elm Street.' And, that's what he was, an old world hot dog vendor, selling hot dogs out of a van. These famous frankfurters were made using a closely-guraded recipe known to its employees as the SGT–the Secret Grease Formula. The trick was that instead of being boiled in water, they were cooked in some kind of oil seasoning mixture. Great, but you know, just a 911 heart attack as soon as you have a couple.

"So, there he was selling hot dogs out of a truck. He was nuts. A genius. He'd been an executive at Ralph Lauren's Polo at twenty-two. He's the guy who came up with the idea for their outlet stores. They opened them all over [the] country, but by twenty-four he was burned out from traveling around and leading a fast life. He then settled down selling hot dogs on a street corner. Had I known him when I lived in Massachusetts, we would probably have become fast friends and I might never have moved back to Hollywood. We could have made it happen from there. I didn't run into him until I was about to leave."

As Bob's business partner, J.W. managed certain aspects of Bob's career. He arranged all his speaking engagements, the commercial endorsements, like Purina Dog Chow, and he dealt with things like book deals. But, when Bob met him, he was selling hot dogs!

"Lawton's Famous Frankfurters had a hot-dog truck with a big hot dog painted on it. There's a gruesomely funny story connected to that truck. I had a little dog named Mimsy, that I'd had before I met Heather. A little

black Chihuahua. I got her from the pound when I was living in Chicago, back in the seventies. "

The hot-dog story & Mimsy

[**Words in bold type** are Bob's own and from his personal journal.]

"She was so tiny, she slept in my tennis shoe the first night. I took this dog everywhere. I named her for a character in a play I was in at the time, *Forty Carats*. It was a dog of a role, so...

Mimsy became very old and feeble. She was something like twenty years old and could barely walk, straighten her legs or even move. She used to sleep in the garage because it was warm under the car.

"One day, Heather jumps in her car, starts to back out of the driveway and...runs over Mimsy. The poor thing was on her last legs, anyway, but Heather, naturally, was hysterical. She was beside herself. She was shaking. She ran in the house–the kids had just got home from school and Heather was wondering how she was going to break the news to them. J.W.'s wife Liz was there, watching the kids while Heather was going to run an errand to the grocery store and back. **"Heather, calm down," says Liz. "I'll call my husband. He'll know what to do." Heather tells the kids that Mimsy, the dog is gone...'Sweethearts, our little Mimsy passed away. It's a very sad thing but she was very old and sick and now she's at peace.' And, as she is telling them how Mimsy has gone to doggy heaven, he** [J. W.] **drives up in the Lawton Famous Frankfurter truck, picks up Mimsy, slips her into a plastic bag, puts her in the back of the truck with a clunk and drives off. The kids are standing there with their faces at the window and are in shock.**

'Mommy! Mommy! He's going to make Mimsy into hot dogs!!'

They still haven't gotten over it."

***

California Here We Come!

Bob and Heather were at the point where they decided to move back to L.A. when he got a call from J.W. Actually, Bob writes in his journal, it was a couple of calls.

"You know, we're gonna come too," he tells me.

"Really? Why?" I ask.

"We've had it with New England and the weather and the people here and besides, I want to get away from my parents and the whole scene. I want to start fresh. So, we're coming to California."

Bob tried to tell him that they were going out there [CA] so he could start a new life and a new career. **"I cannot be responsible for you and your wife and Liz is pregnant. I don't honestly know that I can even keep Liz on. I'm going to need somebody eventually, but right now it's just not possible. I'm sorry."**

Bob says, **"He wouldn't take no for answer, which is actually one of his best assets." "We're coming," he insisted. "I'll do anything. I'll wash windows. I'll clean out dog dirt." All of which, to his credit, he did.**

The day the Urichs moved into their new home in sunny California, there he was, Mr. Moving-man, unpacking boxes, putting stuff away and taking garbage out.

"Look, Bob, don't you see how indispensible I am? I'll take care of everything around the house. I'll be Popeye and Mary Poppins combined–you won't have to do a thing. Pay me three-hundred a week and you've got yourself a full-service handyman. I'll be Aladdin and Mister Clean..."

"Alright, alright, I'm sold–you got your three-hundred a week."

"And, of course..."

"And, of course what?"

"Well, then there's Liz's four-hundred a week."

"Hey, that's seven-hundred a week!"

"All inclusive."

"They rented a little apartment. So, J.W. graduated from selling hot dogs to washing windows."

***

Time passes. A year later, Bob made a deal at MGM. They gave him a hundred-thousand dollars for developing projects, a secretary and a suite of offices. Bob hired some guy who had been in development to help him find properties, but he didn't work out. That's when he had a thought. **"Do you** [J.W.]**want the job? He went, 'Hell, yeah!' And, he never looked back."**

"He knew who the players are. He makes deals. He has the ability to take in everything. He's a quick study. He sees every movie, knows every TV star, every movie star. He has an I.Q. of something like 250.

He's one of the smartest guys I've ever met in my life. Has a mind like s steel trap."

The two were in New York once and after dinner, Bob said, "You know what I'd like right now is a good cigar." At the time it was getting late, around ten-thirty, a little late to go searching for the ultimate Havana hand-rolled cigar. But, Bob saw a light go on in J.W.'s head.

"Well, now, hang in there, Bob," he said, "Maybe Dunhills is still open."

"So, we head over there and the place is humming. People milling around, the press, TV cameras. We happened to be dressed in business suits, because we'd had a bunch of meetings that day, and this beautiful girl looks at us and says,

"Oh, hi. Come on in. Go right upstairs."

"Thank you," I said.

"You smoke cigars?" she asked.

"As a matter of fact we were just looking for a good cigar."

"Fantastic!"

"We go up and there is a huge champagne reception going on. A cocktail party for the opening of some movie, but without any movie stars there. The press are all there and being the only celebrity in the room, the news cameras are focused on me.

"What's going on?" I asked. "It's the new Merchant-Ivory movie," the PR lady tells me. I've no idea what she's talking about."

Just then, a suave gent introduces himself.

"I am Mr. Merchant, one of the producers. Very pleased to meet you, Mr. Urich. I'm so glad you could come. Would you care to say a few words about the film?"

"Whispering in my ear, he [J.W.] named all the movies they'd made and fed me my lines– "Their most recent is *Howard's End*, a masterpiece of period recreation and a flawless cinematic interpretation of the E. M. Foster novel."

Bob knew none of this but thanks to J.W.'s prompting, he came off sounding like an authority on the subject. He wound up on the five o'clock news speaking very articulately about the new Merchant-Ivory movie, and what a big fan he was of their period stuff.

"He saved many a day for me. I would be doing some interview, completely out to sea, and there he is, 'off-camera,' throwing out the

name, the word, the opinion I was grasping for. He has one of those kinds of brains. But, if you turned the camera on him, he would freeze. He always said, 'Coming up with the lines is easy–getting up in front of a camera–that I could never do.'"

"The truth be known, hc [J.W.] has been responsible for so much. I owe my entire off-screen career to him, and I made as much money off screen as I have on stuff that most people will never see. Industrial films, commercials, infomercials, speaking engagements. There were times when this was the only work I got."

***

When Bob went through *the cancer event*, as he referred to it, people began pulling things out, right and left. They cancelled his show, *The Lazarus Man.*[1] Ralston-Purina pulled his dog-food commercials. Bob writes about that stressful, bleak time in his journal. **"Oh God, it was horrible. I was unemployed. No jobs, no offers, the phone stopped ringing. He [J.W.] said, 'It's all going to be fine. This is what we are going to do.' He virtually invented a second career for me. Slowly, he started putting it all back together. I was still doing chemo. I'd done my last chemotherapy on the seventeenth, had five days of rest and he's on the phone saying,**

"Pack yout overrnight bag, we're going to Cleveland."

"We are?"

"Yes, indeed, beautiful downtown Cleveland, Ohio."

"Why would I want to go there?" I asked.

"Because you're gonna speak," he said, "and you're gonna make some money."

"You're gonna be able to pay your rent."

"Well, in that case, okay," I said,

"Let's go!"

***

Bob notes in his journal that **"He [J.W.] had been a loyal friend and a patriot, but he can also be very thin-skinned."**

1 *The Lazarus Man* is covered in detail in Chapter 24.

When Bob got his star on the Hollywood Walk of Fame,[1] he was asked to give a speech. **"I show up and there's crowds of people and news cameras, my agent [Merritt Blake] is there.** Bob's older brother Tom was also present.

"But my heart wasn't really in it. I wasn't really thinking. I gave a short speech. At the end I said thank you and what a great honor to be here--thanked my wife, my agent, and my brother Tom, but I forgot to thank him [J.W.] **His feelings were hurt and he went off in a huff."**

Bob recalls literally chasing him down the street.

"I caught up with him on Wilshire Boulevard. He admonished me for not thanking him in public, and I was shouting back what a jerk he was being. We were screaming at each other in the middle of the street. He's crying and I'm crying. We're hugging each other and crying and yelling right on Wilshire Boulevard.

Camera pulls back. End credits roll."

1 Robert Urich's star on the Hollywood Walk of Fame is located at 7083 Hollywood Blvd.

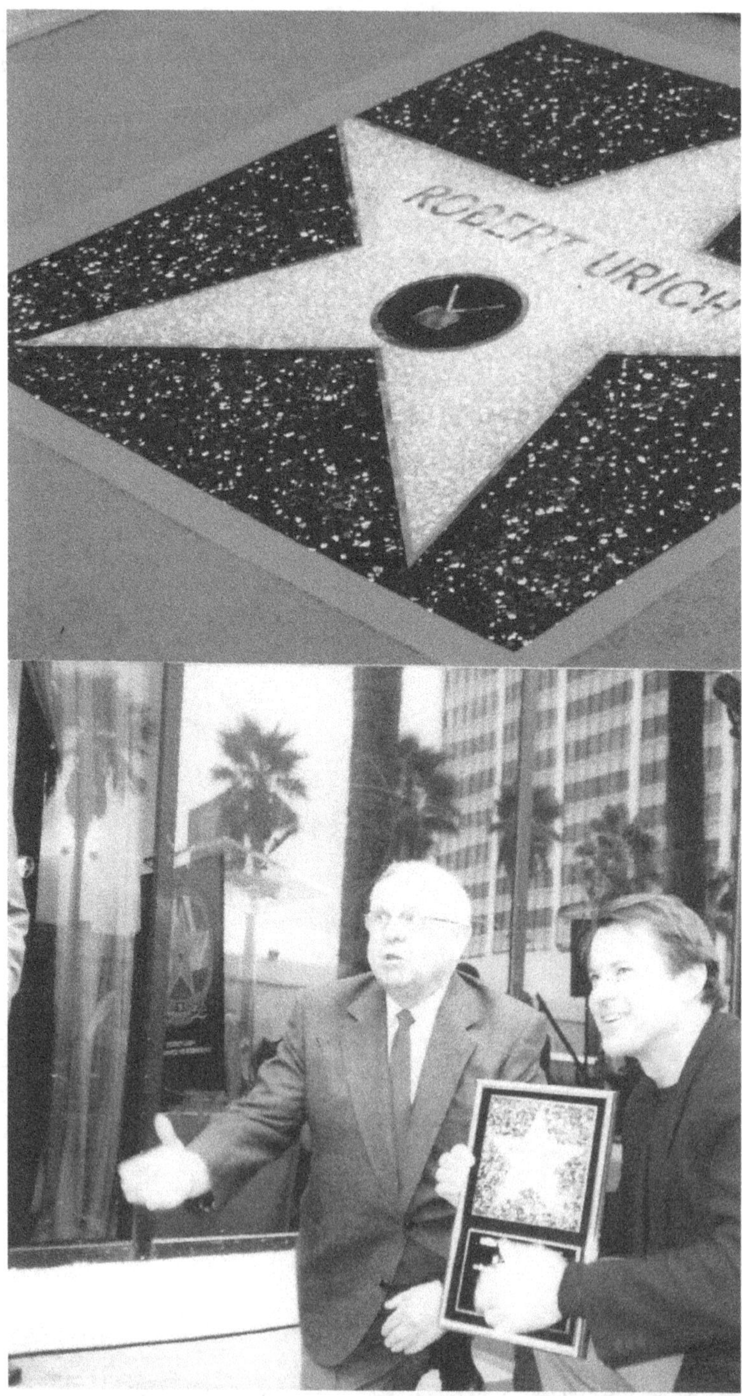

(Top) Bob's star on Hollywood Walk of Fame. (Bottom) Bob with Honorary Mayor of Hollywood, Johnny Grant.

PART IV
Chapter 23

Lonesome Dove - Bob's finest hour
On The Trail with Lonesome Dove
Battle of the Bob's

Lonesome Dove

[**Bold typed words** are Bob's–taken directly from his personal journal.]

Many critics and fans alike believe Robert Urich's finest role was his unforgettable portrayal of down-on-his-luck Texas Ranger Jake Spoon in the acclaimed 1989 CBS-TV miniseries, *Lonesome Dove.*[1] However, few know the popular screen star nearly passed on the project!

Bob's wife, Heather laughs at the thought. "Producers were wooing Bob to take the role, but he simply didn't want to do it. When he read the script and his character says, 'Hey Gus! Let's go jump some gullies!,' He kind of panicked." "Heather!" Bob cried out, "I DON'T jump gullies! I don't think so," and with the wave of his hand playfully tossed he script down beside him on the sofa. "'Besides," he adds, smiling, "I need a break after *Spenser*[2] I really don't want to be away from you and the kids for most of the summer. I want to go boating off Marblehead [Mass] in our new Boston Whaler." Bob loved boats. At one time, when he had six or seven, his business manager at the time said, "if you buy one more, you'll have a navy the size of a small country!"

Heather sensed her husband was tired and deserved a much needed rest. Three grueling years jumping off rooftops and driving cars at breakneck speeds while shooting *Spenser* on location in unpredictable Boston weather had worn him out. She understood, completely. "Okay, it's your

1 The TV miniseries was based on author, Larry McMurtry's best selling book.

2 Bob filmed *Spenser: For Hire* on location in the streets of Boston in all types of weather both winter & summer, during the 3 seasons it aired on ABC-TV from September 20, 1985 - September 3, 1988.

call," she told him. "But, I think you're missing the boat on this one." As his wife, she knew her husband always appreciated her input, but she also knew when it was a dead issue and no longer worth pursuing. This was one of those times. Once Bob's strong-willed mind was made up, that was that! She also knew she and the kids would miss him during his time away for the long filming shoot in Texas.

Lonesome Dove

That was the end of the story until one night when Bob's long-time agent, Merritt Blake called. "Heather, you've got to convince Bob to take this part. This has all the makings of a landmark miniseries," he insisted. "Have you seen the cast, Bobby Duvall, Tommy Lee Jones, Angelica Houston, one after another," Merritt excitedly reeled off the heavy-weight actors involved. "You need to talk some sense into this boy." She could almost see their agent and friend, on the other end of the phone, down on bended knee pleading his case trying to convince her to help sway Bob's decision. "Remember," she says, "Bob didn't want to go anywhere to do anything."

Heather admits Bob's love of Westerns, and told Merritt she would give it her best shot. After reading the script, Heather put her plan into action. She always believed Bob was a little afraid around horses, but would never admit it. "Let's be real," she says. "The word scared would be a little over-the-top for the image he portrayed as a strong, virile leading man. Let's just say that horses intimidated him a little and leave it at that," she laughs. She kept his feelings in mind, as she again broached the subject with her husband. Using one of Bob's own lines, she began, "Ok, this is what we are going to do," outlining her plan. "Look, I'll get my riding instructor, Pam Hunt[1] to give you a few riding lessons. She'll get you over some fences. The kids will come down on Spring break. I'll come down in between. We'll get someone to drive the whaler down to the Rio Grande and you and I can drive it back up to Massachusetts. What'd ya say?" With that, Bob gave in and accepted the role that he will perhaps be best remembered for.

---

1 Bob Urich was uneasy riding horses, so his wife Heather had her riding instructor, Pam Hunt from Cornerstone Farms in Haverhill Mass go over some basics about riding with Bob in Massachusetts [where they were living at the time] before he and his family left for Texas to join cast and crew for the shoot.

By the way, and just for the record, Heather did get an employee of theirs to drive the Boston Whaler down to Texas. "Then I went down," she says, "once with the kids and then when the series wrapped. We towed the Whaler back up to Boston through Hot Springs, Arkansas, which was amazing. It was part of my initial bargaining plan. We *loooved* Hot Springs Arkansas. The water is truly healing. What a fun road trip that was," and thinking back fondly says, "Bob did love his road trips."

***

There was one other incident involving Bob, through no fault of his own, and how he nearly didn't get the role on *Lonesome Dove*.

"It would have been during the 3rd season of *Spenser.*[1] I'd gone off on a hunting trip with some friends to Grand Rapids, Minnesota for the annual invitation only American Grouse Hunt. I'm not much of a hunter, to begin with–the reason I'd gone there in the first place was that I wanted a change of scenery." Trying to hit a grouse in the woods, Bob writes in his journal, **"is like trying to hit something with a pea shooter. I was exhausted. Checked in, laid down and slept for ten hours."**

The next morning, Bob's agent, Merritt Blake calls and says, **"Tim Masters at CBS just phoned me. He says he wants you to do this new big miniseries they are doing called *Lonesome Dove*. I'm tired, I told him. I don't want to work. I want some time off and the last thing I want to do is get involved with another series." "Bob, now wait a minute," he said. "You do want to do this. It's based on the Larry McMurtry novel and everybody in Hollywood wants this role they're offering you. I'm going to send you this script. You've got to read it as soon as you get it," says Merritt. "They want an answer right away."**

"Okay," I said. "I'll take a look at it as soon as it gets here."

A day goes by, two days go by. He calls me back.

"Bob, did you get the script? Did you get a chance to read it? I've not heard from you, so I was wondering." "I haven't gotten anything yet."

"But, I faxed it," he insisted.

---

1 It was the end of the 2nd season of *Spenser: For Hire*, 1987. The series had just wrapped. And Bob was tired and looking forward to some time away from acting to spend time with Heather and their family.

Come to find out, he had sent the script to Grand Rapids, Michigan. As opposed to its namesake. . .Grand Rapids, *Minnesota,* a small town. It went to the wrong state.

"Well, now that I know where you are, I'll fax it to you again," Blake said.

The Wagon Wheel Inn, where Bob was staying, was a little motel on the side of the highway–they didn't have a fax machine. That's how far out in the boonies Bob was. **"The only fax machine anybody could locate was at the Ford dealership out on the highway. The guy who was managing the event knew everybody in town and took me down to the dealership and got permission to send over four hundred pages through their fax machine."**

Bob used to joke that when the script finally got delivered to his hotel room, the car salesman showed up and said, "Mr. Urich, here's your script from Hollywood. I really don't have any problems with it, although Act One could use a little work."

Bob did get the script and began reading it. His initial reaction?

"Oh, my God. It's just wonderful. I loved the character I was playing, Jake Spoon."

A year or so earlier, Bob had done a film with Tommy Lee Jones about the American Revolution called *April Morning,* and the shot heard round the world. Bob was crazy about that era in American history. **"How could I resist a movie like that? During the filming, one day, I popped my head in Tommy Lee's trailer while we're shooting. 'Hey Bob,' he goes, 'Come on in. I'm reading our next one.' He was reading *Lonesome Dove* which I'd never gotten around to looking through. Later, is when I learned that Tommy Lee, Robert Duvall, Danny Glover and Angelica Houston were all going to be in it. The cast just went on and on. Diane Lane, D.B. Sweeney–just a wonderful cast. Maybe the greatest piece I was ever involved in. . .I think, hands down."**

***

Bob Urich's character, Jake Spoon, a former Texas Ranger, now a down on his luck cowpoke, takes up with Diane Lane's Lorena Wood, the only prostitute in the small one-horse town of Lonesome Dove, where the cattle drive begins. Desperate to leave the dusty town, she hitches a ride with the cattlemen on their trip to Montana. The ole West was often unforgiving and mighty cruel.

Our adventure begins as two former Texas Rangers and others embark on a treacherous 3,000-mile cattle drive from Texas to Montana. The main storyline of the eight-hour miniseries centers around the grueling cattle drive led by retired Texas Rangers Gus McCrae [Robert Duvall] and Capt. Woodrow F. Call [Tommy Lee Jones]. The year is 1876; now, in their senior years, their glory days far in their past, the 3,000-mile journey represents their last hurrah.

Along the Trail with Lonesome Dove

Along the trail, they encounter countless enemies and natural disasters as they make their way through the hazards of nature, surviving battles with white renegades and Indians, bar-room brawls and shoot-outs, stampedes and perilous river crossings filled with venomous water moccasins. Talk about high adventure with plenty of action: along the way, there's a run in with renegades, who rape Lorena "Lorie" Wood [Diane Lane] led by "Blue Duck" [Frederic Forrest], a notorious Mexican/Indian bandit from Gus and Call's Ranger days; a psycho band of bank robbers, led by a certified 'nut-job,' who hates sodbusters and winds-up shooting two in the back, hanging them and setting them on fire. Another cowboy is lynched by his friends [guess who?] and vultures pick at the deceased body of one of the series stars, after his body slips out of its coffin en route to a burial place. And for those who fancy a love scene or two, there's Angelica Houston as Clara Allen, the love of McCrae's life, whose ranch just happens to lie in Nebraska on the way to Montana. That's just a few of the scenes in this wonderful Western loaded with a superlative cast.

***

Lonesome Dove is more than a slice of the history of our American West. Much more.It is also a story of the human will to overcome whatever obstacles stand in their way. It is a story of determination, courage and the triumph of the human spirit.

The challenges of filming such a massive production were immense.

Shooting the epic production proved to be a monumental task for everyone involved. Filmed on location in just over sixteen weeks, the production carried with it a grueling shooting schedule which required meticulous preparations, involving dozens of sets and extensive location changes for both man and animal.

There was also an extremely large number of cast and crew with an astounding 89 speaking parts, 1000 extras, 90 crew members, 30 wranglers, 100 horses and up to 1400 head of stampeding cattle. It was difficult enough recreating stampedes, dust storms, and a blizzard, which Mother Nature lent a hand to with the changeable weather, but Indian battles and dangerous river crossings were also an ambitious undertaking.

Even more challenging were the various details involved in moving everyone from location to location. The schedule was rigorous, to say the least, but in the end, those who worked on the project deemed it rewarding.

Lonesome Dove was a TV production, but was shot like a feature film. Movie cameras were used, along with complex lighting techniques. Attention to detail was essential. Quite often, the staging was so complicated, it required scenes to be shot from a half-a-dozen different angles. "To the cast and crew's credit, no one approached the production like a television movie," scriptwriter William Wittliff remarked in an interview with *Newsweek*. "Everyone had such respect for the novel that they put their hearts and souls into it. I think that shows."

The huge success and popularity of *Lonesome Dove* lies with the actors, all of whom were equally committed to the quality of the production. In fact, Tommy Lee Jones, who raises horses and cattle on his own ranch in San Saba, Texas, insisted on doing all his own riding–including bucking scenes–instead of using a stunt double. Producer Dyson Lovell was not happy and feared Jones would injure himself. In the end, Jones won out. Many of the other actors really got into their roles.

Danny Glover prepared for his role by studying historical notes while 18 year old Rick Schroder, who plays Newt in the series, got some on-the-job training. "I didn't know how to ride a horse before this movie," he told *TV Guide*. "They took me out to Texas three weeks early and I learned how to ride, rope, bulldog, tie and run." he says. As the story goes, Rick later went on to shoot a rattlesnake with a bow and arrow. He ate it and took the skin to have boots made out of it.

In his journal, Bob writes of his first scene in *Lonesome Dove* as Jake Spoon, arriving at the ranch on horseback, where Tommy Lee Jones and Robert Duvall, as Woodrow F. Call and Gus McCrae, are holed up.

"They are all standing around the bunk house and way in the distance they see a rider coming and from quite a ways away and they recognize that it's Jake and they all give him a great greeting when he gets off

the horse. They invite him in to eat. I guess that travel in those days was such that it took such a long time to get from one place to another and you would say, 'I just got back from Montana.' To you and me that means transferring [by plane] **in Salt Lake and you're home by supper time. Those days it meant four months on the trail."**

In another poignant scene, Jake Spoon finally crosses over the line and the law and has to be hanged–by his friends. Robert Duvall did an interview with Bob Costas and he described that moment, the hanging of Jake as being one of the most piquant and moving scenes he had ever been involved with. 'It's one of the most perfect scenes on film," Duvall said. "The hair stood up on the back of my neck when I read the script," and I realized the only reason for me to take the part was that moment."

It's the scene where Jake's sitting on his horse with a noose around his neck.

"All the other outlaws have been hung and Duvall says, 'You crossed the line, Jake.' And Jake in some kind of stupor, in this reverie of his, says, 'I didn't see any line.' The following instance, Jake is digging his spurs into his horse so that it will gallop out from under himself, relieving his friends of the obligation of having to hang their friend."

"There I swung in the breeze with this harness and thing around my neck and Duvall stood there and it made the hair stand up on the back of all *our* necks."

Australian-born filmmaker Simon Wincer won an Emmy for his directing on *Lonesome Dove.* In an interview with *Cowboys and Indians* Magazine to commemorate the 25th anniversary of the making of the film, Wincer describes Bob's hanging scene as "one absolutely magic moment in the film. The scene where they hang Jake Spoon, played by Robert Urich when the horse runs forward and leaves Jake to hang, the reaction on Duvall's face is absolutely extraordinary. That's such a powerful moment in the movie. But, the thing is, when we showed him the first cut, we'd used a different take by sheer accident. I hadn't done the final cut yet, and I'm sure that we would have found that take eventually. But Duvall picked that up straight away. He asked us to please use that other shot of him. And, he was right." Critics and fans agree, it is one of the most powerful moments in the miniseries and without question, some of Bob Urich's best work.

At the time, Bob said he was "more concerned about what reaction my getting hung would have on my kids who were sitting over on one side while they were shooting."

"But, I didn't need to have worried–when I looked over they were giggling and laughing. They were so gleeful about my hanging I thought they might mess up this tense moment, so instead of being concerned about the effect my gruesome movie death might have on their little psyches, I now had to worry that their raucous laughter could blow the scene."

Heather was seated with their kids during the hanging scene.

"The kids and I sat in director's chairs on the set and watched them rig a pole up Bob's back which was attached to a rope around his neck. Because we saw all the safety measures in place we weren't concerned at all. The kids thought it was pretty cool."

Staying faithful to Larry's novel was a primary goal and nothing was taken lightly, said a member of the production staff. Painstaking efforts were made to match scenes and character descriptions from the Pulitzer Prize-winning novel. Historical accuracy was paramount and close attention was paid to the authenticity of props, from saddles to period clothing and guns. Historic Western photos proved helpful in offering a visual representation of the Old West. Vivid details from McMurtry's book served as a foundation of many locales used in filming the miniseries, including the dry creek bed which divided the town of Lonesome Dove which was constructed on a private site near Del Rio, Texas. Filming also took place at a ranch outside Santa Fe, and utilized a set from the movie *Silverado*.[1] With so much ground being covered as the characters migrated from Texas to Montana, many locales needed to be recreated. The only steadfast rule insisted by writer Bill Wittliff was that any scenes taking place in Texas had to be shot in Texas.

***

Today, because of its huge success, *Lonesome Dove* may seem like it was an easy sell getting it to the production stage. Not so. The miniseries that would go on to become a television Western classic nearly didn't make it to the tube at all.

---

1 *The Silverado* movie set was constructed on the site of The Hughes Ranch which later in Bob's career was used for filming scenes of his TV western series, *The Lazarus Man*.

At first, the vision and fortitude of Executive Producer, Suzanne de Passo, needed to jump a major hurdle: none of the three major TV Networks could see the potential of McMurtry's lengthy 1600-page publication manuscript. In fact, it was so lengthy, Suzanne recalls how it was rolled in to her office on a dolly. But, de Passo, President of Motown Productions at the time, read it just prior to publication and recognized an opportunity to make a Western classic. Therefore, she purchased the production rights for an unbelievable $50,000. "I had no idea it was going to be a best seller and win a Pulitzer," she recalls in an interview with *Newsweek*. "But, when it did," she adds, "The network doors suddenly opened." Motown made the miniseries for CBS with Robert Halmi Productions.

Lonesome Dove brought to life all of the magnificent drama and romance of the Old West. Hailed as a masterpiece by both critics and audiences alike, the television series was originally telecast on CBS from February 5-8, 1989, and drew a huge viewing audience with an estimated 26 million homes tuned in–an unusually high number for a Western. The miniseries received 18 Emmy nominations and 7 wins, including best director for Simon Wincer. *Lonesome Dove* also won two Golden Globes for best miniseries and best actor for Robert Duvall, the Western Heritage Award in 1990, the Director's Guild of America and Writer's Guild of America Award, and CBS was presented with a Peabody Award for Outstanding Achievement in Drama.

Lonesome Dove went on to capture the hearts and imaginations of millions of viewers and brought back to the screen a way of life seldom seen. The miniseries was faithful to author Larry McMurtry's best selling novel, and went on to become one of the greatest Western sagas of all time.

Bob writes in his journal that Tommy Lee Jones was a pleasure to work. **"I'd always heard that Tommy was tough. I guess in his early years he had been difficult. I don't know what caused all that, but if you go in with a set of preconditioned notions about people, you unbalance your relationship even before you start. I tried to put everything out of my mind I'd ever heard about him and I think he recognized that. That I had no bone to pick, no pre-conceived notions. He was just a blank slate to me in that regard. Whatever was going to happen between us on the film was what the relationship would be. I always found him to be–even from *April Morning*, the other film we did together–to be a gregarious guy, friendly, ready to talk to you."** Bob goes on to write that

Tommy Lee knew his stuff. **"He was always up for rehearsing and helpful and he was pretty much the same way when we did *Lonesome Dove*."**

The miniseries was a long shoot–three months–and Bob and Tommy often went out socially.

"We went to eat–and drink, in Mexico one night when I thought we all were not going to make it back. Tommy Lee said, 'You never had real Mexican food until you go over there'[across the border]. **So one night, we headed across the border** [to the town of Ciudad Acuna] **in search of fabled Mexican food, Tommy, D.B. Sweeney and me and a driver. I insisted on a driver. I had heard about their ability to consume Tequila." "We wound up at this dance hall size restaurant and had some good Mexican food, but D.B. Sweeney and Tommy Lee made an early start in the Tequila department. I'm just not a drinker. I might have one Margarita and only get through half of it–but I knew that one of us had to stay sober, because it looked to me like the driverwas matching them shot for shot, too."**

It's now getting late and time to head back over the border. The driver is taking them down dead-end roads that lead to the river, but no bridge and after a few wrong turns like that, Bob insists on driving.

"D.B. Sweeney is in the back yelling profanities out the window and I'm telling him to shut his mouth because we are all going to die in Mexico! 'D.B.,' I said, 'you keep that up and you can forget the film. We'll never make it out of here alive.' He quieted down some after that. I don't remember much about Tommy. He was just pretty sleepy by that point. I ended up driving the car back over the border and getting us back into Del Rio, Texas, which is not exactly your garden spot."

"Life is not so short that there is always time to be respectful." - Author

Trouble Along the Trail with Lonesome Dove

"During the course of that film I had an unfortunate confrontation-with Robert Duvall, who I think is one of the great American actors. Maybe the greatest." But, Bob, notes in his journal that Duvall's behavior changed. **"His behavior began to deteriorate during the shoot and he wasn't always as thoughtful to his fellow actors and to people as he could be."**

After three months of filming, they're doing Bob Urich's last scene to be shot. It's the scene where Duvall, Jones and Urich ride their horses across the border to Mexico to steal a bunch of wild mustangs.

"I remember Tommy Lee saying, 'Now Bobby, don't get perpendicular to these horses, cause if they turn on us, we're gonna go down and that wouldn't be good.' I'm not a big horse person. Duvall and Tommy both have their own ranches and probably ride their horses daily."

Bob Urich says he didn't have much to do in the scene, probably just a couple of lines. **"It was really a scene between the two of them. We'd do several versions of what they call the master which is a wide angle lens with everybody in the shot. Then we did four or five takes of Tommy Lee and then four or five takes of Robert Duval in close-up. It takes time for them to change the camera lens, especially for a close-up on a moving horse. They have to focus marks, so it's something you're acutely aware of. So, we'd done all of that for Tommy Lee and Duvall. Then it came time for my take. I had three lines and in the first take, the director said, 'Fine. Print.'"**

"Hold on," Duvall says. "I want more."

"Battle of the Bob's"

"The director, Simon Wincer, a wonderful Australian director tells Duvall, 'Well, Bob, the camera actually wasn't on you. It was on Robert here.' Meaning me. 'What?' says Duvall. 'Bob,' he tells Duvall, 'We already did your close-up. We did it second. We already got your close-up. This one was on Robert.' Duvall threw quite a tantrum at that, he behaved poorly. It was an embarrassing moment for the crew and for the director. When the filming was finished, I let Duvall know in no uncertain terms that I thought his behavior was disruptive. I said to Duvall, 'Bob, you know something? You're not the only one who cares about how good this is.'

'You talkin' to me?' He said. That kind of confrontational thing. Again, to him, I'm just this TV actor and he's a big movie star.

'You should know that we all want it to be good,' I told him. 'We all care about it. That's why we're all here–you're not the only one who wants to be great, and you blew my scene, you ruined the last moment of mine on the film. I've had a wonderful time on this movie and the whole moment was spoiled.'

He threw down his hat and was ready to fight.

'I don't think this is the way you want this to go,' I told him. 'You really don't.'"

Heather Urich was on the set of Lonesome dove when the incident occurred. She says her husband was quite upset and angry, and didn't mince any words directed at Bobby Duvall which, she recalls, went something like, "I'm going to pound your bald head into the ground. You do not speak to anybody like that. You earn respect. This man [the director] doesn't demand respect. He earned our respect."

Along the Trail with Lonesome Dove

According to Heather, "If someone was unprofessional, Bob would call them out. He had a very high confront level. He was not afraid of confrontation. He had no qualm about standing up to somebody who was disrespectful, like Bobby Duvall, and saying, "Look! What you just did is not o.k. I actually think Bobby [Duvall] respected Bob for what he did." Maybe, Duvall felt that way later, after he had time to cool down and think about it, but not when it happened.

"He [Duvall] reigned in his horse and galloped off into the night which no one was too happy about because they still had work to do. Simon Wincer said, 'Damn it, Bob. I've been kissing this guy's behind for eight weeks trying to get a movie made and you tell him off and off he rides.'"

"'I was only defending you,' I said. 'I'm just trying to keep some kind of integrity involved here.' The next morning, Tommy Lee filed a formal complaint with his agent that Duvall's behavior was starting to affect his performance. Duvall and I did not part on good terms."

Interestingly, later, in an interview, Robert Duvall describes the hanging scene with Robert Urich as Jake Spoon as one of the most poignant and moving scenes in the entire series.

On the 25th anniversary of the epic Western miniseries, *Cowboys & Indians* went behind the scenes with Simon Wincer. During the interview, the subject of his working relationship with Robert Duvall came up. "It's no secret that I had my share of conflicts with Robert Duvall," Wincer admitted. "But, I've since heard that he's had a rough ride with most of the directors he's worked with. I got along well with Tommy Lee and just about everybody else. But, look, that's just the way Duvall works.

You've got to accept that and get on with it. He's a wonderful actor–and really, that's all that counts."

Commenting in *Cowboys and Indians* with writer, Joe Leydon, Duvall says, "Hey look, I've worked with three Australian directors, and, I don't know, we didn't always see eye to eye. I don't know what the deal is. But, you know, sometimes, when you have a little turmoil, it can turn out better than if everything is in total harmony." Regarding the miniseries, Duvall says *Lonesome Dove* and his role as Gus McCrae is maybe his career high point. On the set one morning, he said, "Boys, we're making the *Godfather* of Westerns. *Lonesome Dove* has just gone on and on," the distinguished actor proudly boasts. "Wherever I go–from Alberta down to Texas, and even in big cities–people love *Lonesome Dove*. I hear there's a gaucho way out in Argentina who has worn out his videotape of the series. And, I know, cowboys love *Lonesome Dove*. I ran into a woman who was a Texas Ranger and she said, 'I wouldn't let my daughter marry her fiancé until he saw *Lonesome Dove*.'"

The Bob and Bobby Broohaha

By now the sun was coming up on the set of *Lonesome Dove*. They worked all night and Bob [Urich] was headed back to his trailer thinking about what had just happened. **"Outside my trailer is this young guy who was working for him** [Bobby Duvall], **shifting his weight from foot to foot. He hands me a piece of paper. 'This is a list of phone numbers Bobby wants you to have,' he said. 'This is his ranch in Virginia. And, this here is his place in L.A. and he has an apartment in NY and if you're driving back and want to stop on the way and you want to stay at the ranch, he would love for you to stay.' I figured I was the only guy who'd stood up to him, and maybe he [Duvall] respected that."**

A while later, Bob received an invitation to go to a promotional screening of the film. He hadn't yet seen it so he decided to attend.

"Duvall was there. We were asked to stand together in a group for the photographers, and all through it, Duvall's giving me these little funny looks but still not speaking to me. I couldn't figure out what was going on with him. A little later I saw him at an award show and he didn't speak to me again and I felt very bad about it. I harbored this bad feeling about Bob for years. Almost twenty years I had this feeling about Robert Duvall and what an SOB he was. A great actor, yes, but not very thoughtful."

Now, as they say in the movies, time marches on. It's eleven years later,[1] and Bob is doing the musical *Chicago*, and heading for Broadway. **"A lifelong dream of mine is to do a Broadway show. We're in Washington DC at The National Theatre. I had a day off so we went up to Middleburgh, Virginia, my wife and I and the baby and the nanny [Dee Dee]. We had lunch at the Red Fox Inn–it was a charming little town. We went into an antique shop and I knew that Duvall's place was somewhere near there. I didn't know exactly where, but it was on my mind."**

Out of the blue, one of the owners of the antique shop says to Bob.

"Didn't you do that Lonesome Dove thing with Robert Duvall?""Well, yes I Did," I said. It was as if he were reading my mind. "Doesn't he live around here?" Yes, not far. He comes in here all the time buying stuff. You should call him. I just saw him. I know he's in town. I bet he would want to see you."

Bob and Bobby "Friends again"

"I thought, "No, you're wrong about that. I'm pretty sure he *doesn't* want to see me." But, before I could say anything, the guy said, "Let me call him. He's got a little restaurant over in this town next door. The Whistle Stop or something, it's called. I was about to stop him but my wife looked at me in her very wise and quiet way, and said, "Let him call." We're still poking around in the store when the manager hangs up the phone and says, "Bobby would love to see you." "Heather and I drive over to this café, a ten-minute drive at most. We'd had lunch already, but we're sitting having coffee and in walks Duvall with a bunch of friends from Argentina."

Bob notes in his journal that Robert Duvall is known for being an avid Tango dancer and Argentina is the birthplace of the tango. He makes several visits a year to Argentina just to dance the tango. At the time, in 2000, Urich believes Duvall had finally raised the money to do the movie that he's always wanted to make about tango dancing.[2] Bob couldn't wait to see it.

---

1 In his journal Bob writes it was 20 years later, but in reality, *Lonesome Dove* aired in 1989, and his role in *Chicago* was in 2000. It may have felt like 20 years had passed, but in reality, it had only been eleven yrs.

2 Robert Duvall wrote, produced, directed and starred in his tango film, *Assassination Tango*. It featured Luciana Pedraza, who in 2004 would become Duvall's 4th wife. The film was released in 2002, the same year Bob Urich died.

"Duvall walks in, gives me a look and says, "Do you want to come to the farm?"

"Sure," I said. "C'mon then, follow us."

"He says goodbye to his friends, we get into our rental car and in another ten or 15 minutes we are driving through the rolling hills of Virginia, the most beautiful countryside you've ever seen. We enter his ranch through these big stone gates and beyond there are thoroughbred horses grazing. It was a very old house. George Washington spent a night there when he was a surveyor. This was Duvall's place."

"He had a big barn and a pavilion that he had renovated for tango dancing and the most classic, beautiful home on a hillside set in 250 acres. You walk in the entry with its amazing hard pine floors and antiques. Duvall introduces us to his significant other. She is from Argentina. I don't think they're married,[1] but they've been living together for several years."

Heather goes off to see the house and leaves Bob and Robert Duvall standing there, staring at each other. Duvall invites Bob into his kitchen.

"Now, Duvall is looking at his boots and shuffling his feet and I'm looking at the ground and shuffling *my* feet. There is a long dramatic moment of silence between us and finally, he says,

"Robert, I'm really glad you're here. I gotta tell you something. I thought all this time you were mad at me."

"That's funny," I said, 'cause I always thought *you* were mad at me."

"Aw, no," he says and gives me one of those old guy-hugs and we head into the kitchen and he makes tea. We sat at this big round wooden table and for the next three hours … all afternoon, we talked about *Lonesome Dove* and about acting and producing and careers and agents and candlesticks and kings. "Believe you me, everything I ever thought about Robert Duvall changed in that afternoon. Complicated man with lots to say and the power of an artist. It was one of those life lessons that you learn. You harbor things. You carry things around. Then you find out that other people are doing the same thing you are."

---

1 The woman is Argentina actress and tango dancer, Luciana Pedraza. She and Robert Duvall share the same birthday January 5, but she is 41 years younger than him. They lived together for 7 years before marrying on October 6, 2004.

Bob and Bobby

Bold typed words are Bob Urich's own.

An art director makes a proof sketch of every scene in a movie, such was the case on *Lonesome Dove*.

"There was one sketch of Robert Duvall and myself as Jake Spoon leaning against the well house, a shady spot on a hot afternoon. In the middle of the scene, Jake Spoon falls asleep. I saw this sketch–it looked like a blueprint–pinned on the back of the set. I asked the art director if I could have it and he said, 'Sure, but you know eventually it will fade away and it'll be gone. The ink just disappears. There is no way to preserve it. But, go ahead, take it.' I took it home and framed it and just last week I walked by that spot where it had been hanging on the wall and there was nothing there. It was gone. The picture just faded away ... like memory, like the old West itself."

Shortly before he passed on April 16, 2002, Bob walked past that spot and noticed the photo had faded way. This was one of his final entries in his journal.

L-R, Bob with Tommy Lee Jones on set of their film, April Morning. *During breaks Tommy was reading the script for proposed series* Lonesome Dove. *At that time, it was the first they heard of the series, neither knew later they would both be cast in the classic western series.*

Bob and his long-time agent Merritt Blake in Maine enjoying lobster. L-R, Merritt's son, Justin, Merritt wearing Yankee's cap, Ryan Urich, Heather and Bob standing in background.

Bob & Diane Lane, co-stars in Lonesome Dove. *During the 25th Anniversary and reunion of the series & cast, which took place 12 years following Bob's passing, Diane paid tribute to Bob, para-phrasing, I wish Bob were here to see how much his fans enjoyed his work.*

Bob as Jake Spoon in foreground in Lonesome Dove. *L–R, D.B. Sweeney, Tommy Lee Jones, unknown, Danny Glover and Ricky Schroder. Photo courtesy Heather Menzies Urich.*

Bob and Robert Duvall hangin' out on the set of Lonesome Dove. Photo courtesy Heather Menzies Urich.

Chapter 24

Bob, the American Dreamer
The Lazarus Man *wraps for season #1*
A lump is found, Bob has biopsy

Bob, *the American Dreamer*

One of the most approachable, down-to-earth guys in show business was Robert Urich. Sometimes, a role he played on television seemed like a thinly veiled extension of his own personality. This was particularly true of his role as Tom Nash on *American Dreamer*. Bob was perfectly cast and fit the mold to a T as a dreamer. In real life, he dared to dream great things. "He was always blue-skying it," says his wife, Heather. Meaning, he constantly day-dreamed about various projects and things he wanted to do.

The half-hour comedy, co-starring Carol Kane, Lillian Abernathy, Jeffrey Tambor and Margaret Welsh debuted September 20, 1990 on NBC. Susan Seeger created the series and Gary David Goldberg,[1] best known for creating the hit series *Family Ties* with Michael J. Fox, was executive producer. "Gary, or Gar, as we called him, was a great guy. Bob and I spent a week with him and his family in Vermont," recalls Heather. "Julia Louis-Dreyfus and her husband Brad Hall, who was a writer on *American Dreamer*, were also there.

Bob, as Tom Nash, was a foreign TV correspondent. Tom's wife was also a journalist who dies in Lebanon covering a story. After his wife's death, he quits his network news post and moves with his two children to a small Wisconsin town. His teenage daughter, Rachel, was played by Chay Lentin and son Danny by a young Johnny Galecki. Urich's real-life wife played his deceased TV wife in one episode. A creative feature of the show, from time to time, Nash spoke directly to the camera as characters from his past or present appeared behind him on a minimally lighted set.

---

1 Gary Goldberg passed away of brain cancer, June 22, 2013 at age 68, three days shy of his 69th birthday.

Bob loved the role and cast, especially Galecki, and said, "If I ever need a son in a series, I'm calling him!"

On September 20, 1990, Baltimore Sun TV critic, David Zurawik wrote a positive review of the show. "*American Dreamer* is one of the funnier and smarter sitcoms of the new fall season. It also introduces one of the most off-the-wall but engaging new characters on television, Lillian Abernathy, played by Carol Kane." Even though, the program was well-written and well acted, initially, it had a few problems. For example, because the show was loaded with bright talent, sometimes while watching it, you get the feeling it becomes a case of who will top whom with a funny line. The co-stars seem to overwhelm the central character, Nash, which at times became confusing, let alone irritating to the viewer. In time, things like 'timing' and chemistry between actors on a new show can usually be worked out. However, NBC did not appear to be in a giving mode–and did not grant the sitcom more time to work out some of the kinks. The network canceled *American Dreamer* after nine months.

Bob Urich was a versatile, affable leading man. A heart-throb to millions of women for more than a quarter of a century, while men looked at him as a guy they wanted to be pals with. According to the Guinness Book of World Records, during his 30-year acting career, Urich still holds the record for appearing as a regular in the most television series with 16 (a record previously held by actor Harry Morgan with 12). Bob attributes his longevity as a successful actor to his Ohio roots. "I come from a blue-collar town where I was raised to work hard and respect other folks. I know it sounds hokey, but I think ultimately, on television, you can't hide who you are. It's why people are always coming up to me, not to talk about my shows, but about their families, their pets, their lives. They obviously feel comfortable with me."

Bob, the Always approachable actor

Bob always treated his fans with respect and was most cordial. You could tell he felt grateful for their attention and support. Bob's easy-going style is what made him appealing to so many viewers. He made every character believable and accessible, someone you could identify with and, in most cases, liked. Of course, a few of the characters he played were polar opposites to his 'good guy' personas; for instance, playing convicted murderer Rob Marshall in the 1990 film, *Blind Faith.*[1]

A good deal of Bob's appeal is how he comes across as the kind of guy you want to hang out with. Someone you want as a friend. Someone you feel you can trust. Making people feel that way, who don't even know you–other than what they see on screen–is an awesome gift, and Bob had it. In a January 28, 1996 *Inquirer TV* article by critic Jonathan Storm, Urich says, "Quite frankly, I've been lucky." Instilled with a blue-collar work ethic [his father worked in a steel mill in West VA] and a potent dose of Catholic guilt, Bob figured it was the truth in his eyes that got him hired. "My parents raised me a certain way, and I've tried to bring that honesty and pursuit of the truth, and love for my fellow man, into the work." Urich's not exactly sure why some of his shows like *Gavilan*, *Crossroads* and *It Had to be You* were not successes, but believes that "sometimes it's political battles between studios and networks." As for *why* he kept getting opportunities, Urich told the *L.A Times* in September 1993, "I think people in the industry understand that many elements go into making a show succeed or fail. It can be a time slot, chemistry between actors, even the mood of the country."

The Lazarus Man

Bob Urich seemed to enjoy working in every series he was cast in, but he had a child-like enthusiasm for one particular television series he described as his all-time favorite: *The Lazarus Man*. Bob's wife, Heather says, "I think what people remember most about Bob's TV work is *Vega$* and *Spenser: For Hire*, but *The Lazarus Man* was his favorite."

The setting for the series is Texas, following the American Civil War. Lazarus, an Amnesiac, claws his way out of a shallow grave wearing a Confederate uniform and carrying a U.S. Army revolver. He is haunted by the memory of being attacked by a man wearing a derby. Calling himself Lazarus, after the man Jesus raised from the dead [John 11:41-44], he sets out on a long journey to discover his true identity and the reason he was buried alive.

The opening narration to the program goes like this…

"Something has happened to me which I do not understand.

---

1 Bob's film "Blind Faith" is covered in detail in Chapter 16, "Bob's Take on Acting.

All I know for certain is I am alive. How I got here? Who am I?
I do not know, but I must've seen or done something.
Something terrible to be buried alive…to be left for dead.

I can remember nothing of my life, my friends or my enemies,
But the key to my enemies lies somewhere out there.

I will search until I find the man I was. . .and hope to be again."

Bob often mentioned that starring in the hour-long Western drama was the fulfillment of his own boyhood dream. "I have a picture of myself taken in 1956, when I'm around ten," he says, "standing in my backyard in Ohio wearing my Hopalong Cassidy plastic pearl-handled cap guns with my little bandana and my black hat. My Uncle John used to call me Hoppy[1] because I would hop all around our neighborhood slapping my thighs, in lieu of a real horse."

In many ways, Bob believed *The Lazarus Man* was not much different from the array of Westerns he grew up watching as a kid like Gene Autry, Roy Rogers and his favorite, Hopalong Cassidy. However, Bob's Western series is considerably darker and more mysterious than one would find in a 1950s Autry, Hoppy or Roy vehicle that fed his fantasies. "There are good guys and bad guys, and like in the popular 60s TV series, *The Fugitive* starring David Janssen," Urich says, "a bad guy is after him and a mysterious woman from his past haunts his memories. Lazarus can't distinguish friends from enemies. It's not complicated with 20th-century sociological problems of child or spousal abuse." Lazarus also interacts with real characters from Western history. There are episodes where he meets Gen. Ulysses S. Grant and a young George Armstrong Custer.

During an interview in Santa Fe, where the series was filmed, Urich tells Hollis Walker of *The New Mexican*, "When I saw the script for *The Lazarus Man*, I was impressed and immediately said, yes." To prepare himself for the role, Urich read lots of Western history, including the *Oxford Encyclopedia of the American West*, to better portray his character and understand the nature of the times. Series producer Harvey Frand said, "Everyone involved in the series is reading. We're trying to depict historic events as accurately as possible. The pilot episode explores the

---

1 Hoppy is the nickname for popular 50's cowboy star Hopalong Cassidy made famous by film star, William Boyd. Growing up, Bob Urich was influenced greatly by Hoppy which is described in Ch. 4.

possibility that President Lincoln's assassination was the result of a conspiracy and not the act of one man. Many people believe John Wilkes Booth was a pawn," says the producer.

Near the end of the first season, Lazarus is revealed to be James Cathcart, a Captain in the U.S. Army and a member of President Abraham Lincoln's personal bodyguard detail. The memory that plagues him is from the night of April 14, 1865. Lincoln was shot and assassinated at Ford's Theater in Washington, DC. Cathcart, realizing the President was in danger, ran to stop the assassin, but was attacked by his superior officer, the treasonous Major Talley, who wanted to see Lincoln dead.

January 7, 1996
Pasadena, California

Bob Urich is up from Santa Fe doing a publicity appearance to promote *The Lazarus Man*. The sun is setting over the Pacific Ocean as Bob, his wife Heather and a small herd of TV critics ride their horses down from the Hollywood Hills. "Hey, someone, anybody," Bob cries out. "We've got a problem here." Urich's horse, Dutch is an ornery critter. He's been kicking some of the other horses and acting up, which makes Bob feel a little uncomfortable. In fact, he is downright nervous.He has lost his rein. Somehow, it just came off the bridle. A young wrangler rides up to him and saves the day, and Bob. "Actually," says Heather, "I think he's afraid of horses, but would never admit it."

The syndicated Western television series, featuring 22 hour-long episodes in the first Season, was created by Dick Beebe and produced by Castle Rock Entertainment. It first aired on T-N-T [Turner Network Television] on January 20, 1996.

The Lazarus Man received positive reviews. Here is one example. "This western is full of surprises, followed by a great plot which keeps you guessing and hanging onto every episode. Robert Urich puts depth into this character bringing this Lazarus to life. The series has morals and good family values. If you like Robert Urich, mysteries or westerns, it's a must see."

A little Lump

[Typed **Bold words** throughout this book are Robert Urich's, taken directly from his personal journal.]

Spring of 1996, Santa Fe, New Mexico, Heather Urich's notes.

Power walking together was something Bob and Heather always enjoyed doing together, wherever they found themselves. Heather was able to join Bob on location in Santa Fe for the filming of the TV series, *The Lazarus Man.* "Ever since his experience with Lonesome Dove," Heather says, "Bob was always looking for another good Western, and he finally found it! "We were still living in Park City, Utah at the time. The kids were away at school. We had rented a condo on a golf course in Santa Fe and Bob & I would power walk around the circumference of the course, almost daily, 'blue-skying' future plans and philosophical ideas."

Heather doesn't remember the beginning of one particular walk, nor does she recall the ending. However, she does remember the moment Bob told her he found a lump. "What lump? Where? I wasn't able to absorb the information. It's nothing, she told herself. It's a cyst and he's being a hypochondriac, or so I thought. He told me while he was showering, he discovered a small pea-sized lump on his scrotum and he was concerned. How could anything that small be a threat. Later, I poked and prodded and couldn't find anything. Maybe it's because I didn't want to find anything. But, I didn't doubt for a minute it was there. Bob and I agreed to have it checked out as soon as possible." Meanwhile, the end of the first season on *Lazarus* was near.

After *The Lazarus Man* wrapped for the season, Bob and Heather flew to Los Angeles to consult with a doctor who is a physician for the University of Southern California football team. The doc is accustomed to being around athletes, so with the background of his own gridiron glory days, Bob feels comfortable with him.

"I'm relieved when he doesn't seem overly concerned about the lump. "The needle he used was about the size of the Alaska Pipeline. He tried again and again to draw tissue and fluid from my abdomen, but just couldn't seem to get the right sample size he was looking for. Finally, he got a little something. "That's enough," the doctor says. "What do you think, I ask? I think that little tumor is going away because I've punched so many holes in it," he laughs. "It's going to just shrivel up. It's nothing to worry about." "Okay, I'm not in pain," I reply, and it's not a large lump. Maybe my white blood cells will devour what's left after the many needle punctures. "When will we know for sure?" "It takes three days for the biopsy," the doctor replies.

If there is an ordeal more trying than waiting for the results of medical tests, it isn't on this planet. And this wasn't Robert Urich's first experience with the excruciatingly long wait associated with test results. A year or so earlier, before starting *The Lazarus Man*, Bob was on location in Toronto [Canada] filming a *Spenser: For Hire* movie for the Lifetime Channel. Meanwhile back home in Utah, Heather was undergoing a routine gynecological exam. Her doctor was probing around down there and exclaimed, "What the hell is this?" Heather recalls that frightening moment. "She had found a tumor on my ovaries and I was rushed to the hospital for an ultra-sound that confirmed her suspicion. She scheduled emergency surgery the following morning."

Heather's health issue

Heather says, "the doctor told me to go home and not move around very much. . .to sit still, the tumor could burst. I got to my car and was unable to start it. I was unable to function, sobbing, I got word to Bob in Canada." Somehow, Bob managed to locate a charter plane service, booked a jet and flew all-night to Salt Lake City. Upon arriving at St. Mark's hospital, he was told the somber news.

Heather had undergone a complete hysterectomy.

Dr. Regla Burki pulled no punches.

"It looks like cervical cancer."

"When will be know the results?" a concerned Bob asks. "Well, it's a state holiday here in Utah, so I can't let you know until next Tuesday," she says. "You got to be kidding me! You're talking cancer and you expect us to tread water for three days?" Bob's patience obviously running out. "No way," raising his voice now and shaking his head in disbelief.

"There's no one around to do the lab work," insists the doctor.

Bob had just been paid his per diem for the week and had a little cash with him. He quickly pulled it from his wallet and began peeling off hundred dollar bills.

"There's one, two…how many is it going to take to get a technician down here?

There's three more…four…how many," he angrily asks?

Heather's friend, Ellen Kidwell, who was also by her bedside, dug through her wallet, too. "Over my drugged out body," she says, "They were counting bills on my stomach."

The doctor looks stunned. "Stop, stop, stop," she says."This is embarrassing."

"Yeah, it is," insists an upset Urich. "Is that enough?"

"I think so. I think that will be enough," the doctor responds, sheepishly. I don't know what this says about the medical system in this country, but as Bob tells it, she took the money and they had the test results in twelve hours.

"There was good news and bad news," recalls Heather. "The bad news was the tests were positive. The good news was the tumor was encapsulated which prevented it from metastasizing. It was the size of a grapefruit. Our son, Ryan," laughing as she retells the story years later, "wanted to put it in a mason jar and take it to his science class." One to two percent of women who are diagnosed with ovarian cancer are lucky enough to have the tumor encapsulated. But now the pieces of Bob's tissue were at issue. There was nothing they could do to accelerate the process. They tried to relax and enjoy themselves. Bob decides the Bel-Air Hotel in L.A. was as good a place as any to wait it out.

When Bob first hit LA, as a young, struggling actor in the 1970s, someone invited him to lunch at the Bel-Air. Later, an agent took him to dinner there. He thought it was paradise. "It measured up to my idyllic expectations of California," wistfully recalls Urich. "It was not the L.A. of Raymond Chandler,[1] which features dark alleys and soft ocean breezes of the Santa Ana winds and smog engulfing everything. This was different. White stucco and red tile roofs and bougainvillea hanging over the walls, along with black and white photos of stars on the walls in the lobby." Soon enough Robert Urich would run into the cold, hard reality of L.A., but the Bel Air Hotel remains one of those atmospheric pockets of old Hollywood which Bob and Heather loved. "I think we stayed in every room," she says. "One room is where Marilyn Monroe had stayed. That was special. We love the 'Old Hollywood' vibe of the place." "It holds a bitter-sweet memory for me," Heather adds, with a faraway somber tone. "It's where we were staying when we found out the severity of the Bob's cancer."

There were happy times when the Bel-Air was a favorite haunt of Bob and Heather's, particularly on special occasions–Mother's Day, anniver-

---

1 Raymond Thornton Chandler [July 23, 1888-March 26, 1959], An American novelist, writer of crime fiction featuring the private detective Philip Marlowe.

saries, Easter Sunday. "Sometimes, Bob would surprise me with a dinner there and then check us in for a romantic weekend away from the kids."

"They have an oval pool there with black and white pictures of Clark Gable, Myrna Loy, and other old movie stars sitting around that same pool. We had our favorite room with a veranda that overlooked the pool. Now, if it could only talk."

The glamorous hotel was a place the Urichs went to celebrate. Not so this time. They were a long way from their home in Utah. The Bel-Air is just another grim waiting room. Every minute is an hour and every hour is a day.

At last, the call comes. Bob's tests are negative. "Not life threatening," says the doctor. Nowhere near that. He tells Bob the lump will go away and not to worry about it. He repeats the stuff about how it's going away by itself because he cut so many holes in it. "Everything is fine," the doctor reassures Bob. "As we check out," Heather says, "I felt like I was doing the walk of shame, wearing the same clothes as when we checked in days earlier."

A short while later, Bob finds out he has more than one reason to celebrate. He has lunch with Russ Barry, the head of Turner Syndication, and Glen Padnick, the head of Castle Rock Television. They bring good news that things look good for a second season of *The Lazarus Man*. Still the show had lost seven million dollars its first year.

The Lazarus Man

[**Bold typed words** are Bob's own and taken from his personal journal.]

During lunch, the trio spent a lot of time talking about ways to cut costs–such as moving the location to Canada. They also emphasized how important it was for Bob to hit the road to promote the series.

No one wanted *The Lazarus Man* to succeed more than Bob did. To star in his own Western series was a dream come true.

As much as he needed a break at that point, he agreed to do whatever was necessary to promote the series, as he writes in his own words in his journal.

"Fourth and one? Put me in, coach. That's the nature of syndication. You are always trying to improve your position. Even if you're reaching eighty-five percent of the country, as they were, you constantly campaign to pick-up a station that has better coverage of a particular area,

or you try to persuade the ones you already have in house to give you a better time slot. Networks can pretty much dictate to their affiliates; syndicators have far less leverage. So, you schmooze and cajole and try to sell yourself."

Almost immediately following their luncheon meeting, Bob left for New York. He appeared on *Larry King'Live,' the Conan O'Brien Show, Regis and Kathy Lee*, *CNN Reports* and did several other interviews, all to promote *The Lazarus Man*. Bob remembers on the local Fox-TV station which carried the show he even did the Noon weather–all in pursuit of a better time slot.

"There's no question, it was an exhausting trip for me, but I was in a state of exhilaration. The lump is nothing and I have a good chance of a job for at least one more year."

After the whirlwind trip was over, a very tired Robert Urich felt the call of the wild. He needed to recharge at their summer place in Canada. Bob's father had recently passed away and Heather says, "Bob felt the need to go to a place where he had fond memories of him." Every summer the Urich family would pile in the car and make the 12-hour drive from Toronto, Ohio to Uncle Rudy's cottages on West Lake, in Ontario, Canada.

West Lake is an offshoot of Lake Ontario, separated from the big lake by a giant sand bar. It's adjacent to the Sandbanks Provincial Park, two and a half hours east of Toronto, the Canadian city where Heather was born. So, the Urichs were off to Canada!

Bob & cast of his TV series American Dreamer *on NBC-TV-1990. L-R, behind Bob, Johnny Galecki and Carol Kane, seated on Bob's right, Chay Lentin. Photo courtesy Heather Menzies Urich.*

Bob as star of his own western series on Turner Program Services, The Lazarus Man.

Chapter 25

Bob's Serene, Safe Sanctuary
'WEST LAKE'
CANADA

A safe blissful Sanctuary

After his bout with a lump, Bob & Heather retreat to the lake in Canada.

It's called West Lake: a part of a series of lakes and islands that step down to Lake Ontario. Bob's Uncle Rudy Halpate, his mother's brother, owned a cabin on the lake. It wasn't much to look at, but the Urich men loved hanging out there and fishing. When Bob and his younger brother David were youngsters, the Urich family vacations always centered around a trip to Rudy's cabin for swimming, fishing, boating and a good time in the fresh Canadian air. Picturesque West Lake Canada in Picton County, Ontario was Bob Urich's little piece of heaven on earth. It's where you usually could find he and his family, when a much-needed break was in order from the glitzy world of show business.

"We bought the cottage in Canada in 1979 during a major actor's strike. It's on a lake I had visited as a child. It's a place that touched my soul. A place of water, sky and sunsets that are so spectacular, you swear you hear music as the light fades and days succumbs to evening. In the summer time, the meteor showers offer a nightly astronomy lesson."
West Lake–Canada-1979

One lazy afternoon, Bob and Heather were jogging down the country road by Uncle Rudy's place when they noticed a foreclosure sign on a piece of property. "Bob and I stopped, and looked at each other, and we both had the same idea."It was the same piece of property that Bob and his Cousin Jo Jo had admired a few days earlier. "We were out fishing," says Jo Jo, "and we could see this house with a stone bank over across the lake. When we came back in, Bob said, 'Come on, let's get in the car. I wanna go take a look at that place.' And with that we drove on down the road."

Home at West Lake

"We went down and found a for sale sign out in front. It was owned by a newspaper Editor[1] in Picton, Ontario. Three days later, Bob owned it," says Jo-Jo with a chuckle.

As Bob and Heather wandered down the driveway to the house, they noticed it was being shown to someone by a real estate representative. "As it turned out, the 'someone' was a lawyer from Montreal. The property consisted of a four-bedroom log main house with a three-bedroom guesthouse and a large garage. It was right on the lake with a dock and boat-house overlooking the Sandbanks Provincial Park. It was a dream," Heather gushes, "and it was in foreclosure. Bob promptly asked the real estate person how much the bank was asking. Before she replied, she checked us out from head to toe. Here we were dressed in our ratty jogging outfits, covered with sweat and grime. 'It's VERY expensive,' she finally managed to say. Bob said, 'Well, how much is expensive?' She shot back with, 'Seventy thousand dollars.' Now, keep in mind back in those days you were talking about 35 Thousand American dollars. As my jaw nearly hit the ground," Heather says, "my dear husband said, 'Will you take a check?' Before she could answer, Mr. Lawyer Dude got his feathers all ruffled and began sputtering, 'Hey, you can't do that! This place was being shown to me and I was about to make an offer!' At that point, Bob turned to the man and very quietly informed him and the real estatewoman that 'whatever he offers, we'll top it. So, where would you like to start?'

***

"A short time later, we closed on our dream house on West Lake."

"Our business manager thought we were out of our minds," says Heather. "When are you going to get there? It's a five-hour flight from LA then a 2 ½ hour drive from the Toronto Airport. Good luck, but I don't think this is gonna work out!"

---

1 Al Capon in his *Reflections* column for *The County Weekly News* on Tuesday, July 31, 2012 writes about the history of the Urich home. "The house, a log and cedar 2 story home, on the shores of West Lake and overlooks the Sandbanks. There is also a spacious guest cottage on the property. Frederick Ward, a Picton lawyer had the original house built. His wife, Grace, designed it on the lines of a pioneer cabin. After Ward died, the house was sold to then county sheriff, Herbert Colliver, and later to Cornelius 'Chuck' Slik and then to newspaper publisher, Joseph Cembal."

Summer 2017

Happily, things did work out. For well over 38 years Bob and Heather's dream home on West Lake has been the Urich summer retreat. Of course, Bob went on to become a household name to millions of adoring fans, but in Picton County, he and Heather kept a low profile. People sometimes would do a double-take, she says, "but they got so used to seeing Bob around that it was no big deal. In fact, local folks were pretty protective of him. We attended church in Picton, went out to dinner at Angeline's in the nearby town of Bloomfield and were regulars at Canadian Tire." The only time their celebrity side came out is when they agreed to appear in a parade in August 1981, waving from a convertible as it drove through Cherry Valley. Speaking from a stage outside Athol Central School, Bob said, "Prince Edward County people were the friendliest people anywhere." He told the audience his wife was born in Toronto, Ontario to thunderous applause as he accepted the gift of a Canadian flag. "I was also born in Toronto," he said and after a long pause, added... Ohio. Donald King, former Mayor of Picton, mentioned he had presented Bob with a key to the town of Picton which made him an honorary citizen. Bob made two additional appearances in Picton. Once, he, flipped hamburgers at a Cancer Society fundraiser, and in 2000, while undergoing treatment of his own for the disease, Bob made an unannounced visit to Camp Trillium, a camp for children fighting cancer.

The Beauty of West Lake

The beauty and serenity of West Lake was also the location for the much acclaimed film, *Fly Away Home* from Columbia Pictures. It's the soaring adventure of a 13-year old girl (Anna Paquin) and her estranged father (Jeff Daniels), who learn the true meaning of family when they adopt an orphaned flock of geese who have forgotten their migratory route back down to the Carolinas. Father and daughter teach them how to fly using a light plane disguised as a goose. Bob Urich marveled at the glorious sight of a large flock of Canada geese winging their way north or south, depending on the season. "The flock in Flight," he'd say, "in a perfect V-formation is team-work personified! A vision of beauty." Another amazing, yet little known, fact about these beautiful winged warriors is when a goose becomes ill or wounded, it never falls from the formation alone. Two other geese also leave the group and fly with the ailing goose to the ground. Since geese, like doves, mate for life and are extremely loyal, one of them is usually the mate of the injured bird.

Once on the ground, the healthy birds protect and stand guard over the wounded bird as much as possible. Quite often, going to the extreme of placing themselves between the weakened bird and predators. The soldier-like birds stay with their fallen comrade, ever vigil, until he or she is able to fly again, or dies. Then and only then, do they 'fly away,' their loyal duty completed.[1] Bob Urich was always amazed at the awe-inspiring sight and protective nature of these great birds as he observed them 'close-up' at West Lake.

1979 Westlake, Prince Edward County, Ontario CANADA

Heather and Bob with baby Ryan arrived at the lake on a perfect spring day…

Home at West Lake

"The hillsides were awash with lilacs and here and there patches of daffodils competed for space. The purple martins were returning and they soared and glided above the water feasting on mosquitoes and other insects, singing in a deafening chorus which was joined by the barn finches and other birds native to the lake."

In the spring and summer, the roadsides leading up to their cottage are strewn with vegetable stands. Fresh morel mushrooms in May; a little later, asparagus and all the root veggies–potatoes, radishes and onions; then beans and strawberries in June; beets and squash and delicious sweet corn in late summer.

When they arrived at Bob's Uncle Rudy's cottage they were met by some of Bob's cousins from Ohio, including his cousin Jo Jo Urich. They enjoyed a wonderful week ofboating, hiking, fishing and as Heather proudly points out, "wolfing down the freshest corn on the planet."

Spring 2015

In the Spring of 2015, writer, Tom Cruickshank, interviewed Heather for *Watershed* magazine. "Heather was more than co-operative as I prepared the story," he wrote the author, "and I am more than happy to oblige you with any information on the area." Tom lived in Prince Edward County in the 1980s and is well acquainted with the area where Bob and

---

1 Usually, the geese will wait until another flock of geese flies overhead, and will join them. Giving credence to the expression: *safety in numbers.*

his family enjoyed their summers on West Lake. We took Tom up on his kind offer to act as our guide for a brief written history on the area Bob Urich loved so much.

"Prince Edward County, not to be confused with Prince Edward Island, was first settled in the 1780s and early 1800s," says Cruickshank, "but was always off the beaten path. Urban development eluded it, and it remained something of an agricultural backwater, and to some eyes, it still is. Tourism came to the County in the late 19th Century and it was felt mostly in and around West Lake and East Lake. Both lakes are separated from Lake Ontario by a narrow north-south sandbar and the beaches are exceptional. The West Lake sandbar, known as the Sandbanks is an amazing natural phenomenon with windswept dunes 25 or 30 feet high. They rise gradually from the Lake Ontario side and drop dramatically into the West Lake side. They say they are the largest complex of fresh-water dunes in the world."

The Sandbanks & Thieves in the night

Bob's cousin Jo Jo Urich remembers one adventurous night he and Bob shared involving those awe-inspiring sandbanks.

"I spent lots of time with Bob at his cottage on West Lake. We were fishing buddies and had lots of fun together. We pulled off some wild things," says Jo Jo. "One time, Bob decided he needed sand for his son Ryan's sand box. He was around two at the time; Ryan, not Bob," he laughs. "We took three large industrial size trash cans, loaded them in the boat and took off for the sandbar. There we were with flashlights and shovels in the dark of night loading sand in the trash cans from this pristine sand bar–which was illegal. Man, if we ever got caught, we'd still be serving time. But that was Bob's way of having a little fun. He was always looking for another adventure."

Writer Tom Cruickshank adds, "the sandbanks are the largest complex of fresh-water dunes in the world and are well protected by law. Back in the day," he says, "there were several resort hotels near the dunes, but in the automobile era, West Lake became prime real estate for cottage development, and today West Lake is rimmed with summer homes on narrow frontages."

"In all honesty," Tom adds, "it's probably overdeveloped, but it's easy to see its appeal. Traditionally, the lion's share of tourists and weekenders hail from Toronto, which is about 2½ hours west. Some come from Ottawa and Montreal and there has always been a small but significant number of Americans, especially from Ohio and Pennsylvania, although I'm sure the numbers are dwindling, partly because of traffic congestion and also thanks to border security. You need a passport to cross into Canada these days.

"When Bob and Heather first arrived in 1979, West Lake was probably much like Bob remembered it as a kid. Since then, the County has gentrified some…in fact, a lot. In the early 90s, some enterprising vintners started to experiment with wine grapes." "Since then," Cruickshank[1] continues, "Prince Edward has established itself as Ontario's newest wine country. With it has come better restaurants, boutique shopping, organic farms and more Mercedes than Pontiacs. Most of this is north of West Lake in Hillier. It isn't exactly Napa Valley yet, but there has been a noticeable upscale trend. This was already underway at the time of Bob's passing and I'm sure he must have noticed it.

"The most desirable cottage locations are in the southwest corner of West Lake, facing west with a brilliant sunset view towards the Sandbanks. And, that's exactly where the Urich property is located. Lest I forget," says Tom, "for anyone who likes fishing, as Bob did, it's a great destination, for most of West Lake is quite shallow and weedy."

[**Bold typed words** are Bob's own and taken directly from his personal journal.]

Bob's cousin Jo Jo Urich spent many a day out fishing with Bob in and around those weedy spots. "I had a fishing lure I really liked," he recalls. "Bob called it a retarded rudder. If you catch something on that thing, I'll buy you a new Cadillac," he said. "So, one day, I went out fishing with Bob's neighbor, Eric Caley and I used that lure. I caught about a 4½ pound bass on it. I left the lure in the bass' mouth and took it to show Bob. 'That's not fair. I gotta be with you! You probably caught that on something' else and stuck that lure in it's mouth,' he laughed. We had some good times together but come to think of it, I never did get that Cadillac."

West Lake - Ontario CANADA

---

1 The author is deeply appreciative to Tom Cruickshank for his invaluable input on West Lake and Prince Edward County, Ontario Canada.

Summer 1996

The Urich family cottage at West Lake has been a blissful sanctuary for Bob and his family, a place to recharge, rejuvenate and restore their perspective and equilibrium. There were canoes, a catamaran, jet skis and an old cedar strip boat that belonged to his uncle. **"It must be fifty years old, but I have buffed and sanded and varnished it back to life. We have bonfires at night and we read and spend hours discussing with each other things we have read."**

Bob hadn't gotten the call yet from anybody about the show [*Lazarus Man*] being picked up officially but there were more signs that it might be.

"They were telling me, 'we started late, Bob, so there's really no reason to get picked up yet.'

"Yeah," I said, "but it's hard to turn down offers from other shows when you don't know what is happening."

[A Blissful Safe Sanctuary–West Lake]

They hadn't been to the cottage in quite awhile, so their friend Roger Hobson stopped by to lend a hand cleaning up to make the place livable. **"The cottage had been sort of a symbol of stability and solidity in our lives, and Roger was a part of that. He had traveled a bit, but still lived in the farmhouse where he was born. I've always envied people who found their way home and stayed there."**

Roger Hobson was a handy-man, who looked after their place when they were away, but he was also their trusted friend.

"Bob never looked at Roger as an employee," says Heather. "He was a friend, and Bob's motor-cycle riding partner. The twosome covered many a mile over numerous back roads on the Harleys which Bob owned and loved to ride. Bob's motorcycle adventures ended," she laughs, "when our son, Ryan was old enough to ride. Always, the protective dad, Bob feared Ry, who was fearless, would wrap himself and the bike around one of the numerous pine trees which lined the country roads around the lake."

"The first couple of days back at the cottage were very, very busy. I was trying to get a new coat of varnish on the boat and with Roger's help, flip mattresses, shake dust out of the rugs and a dozen other chores. So, Roger is there and Heather's down in the kitchen, putting her new kitchen together and Roger's upstairs in one of the other bedrooms and he and I are turning over mattresses and beating the dust out of them. And the phone rings."

A few seconds later, my wife said, "Ted Turner is on the phone."

I looked at Roger and said, "Did you hear that? Ted Turner is calling me."

He said, "Who's Ted Turner?"

I laughed and said, "Oh, just the fellow I work for."

"I took the phone without any trepidation. The show [*Lazarus Man*] was being renewed.

"Hey, Bob, congratulations," Turner said. "How about that *Lazarus Man*, eh? I love that show."

"Me too," I said.

"We lost seven million dollars last year," he said. "Next year we can lose about five million. Maybe we will break even. I don't know. But I love that show and maybe we will start making millions...ten million, twenty million, thirty million, forty, fifty, a hundred million. I've really got to go. I like that show. Gotta go, Bob. Bye."

By the time Bob mumbled, **"Bye, Mr. Turner, sir,"** he had already hung up.

"Roger was standing nearby.

"Now, who was that?" he asked.

"Ted Turner...the cable television tycoon."

"Well, it wasn't a very long conversation, "Roger said.

'Ted's a very busy guy," I said. "He has to get back to buying whatever parts of Montana he doesn't already own and single-handedly saving the buffalo herd in America, or trying to re-introduce the sweet red fox or some other critter into his habitat in Montana. The local ranchers will love that. The man's got no time to spare for small talk. Roger shook his head and grinned, probably thinking that we were all just a little flaky."

Ted Turner's call was the official confirmation of what Barry and Padnick had already told Bob. With no worries, the Urich's could settle in now for a really lovely summer.

***

Bob's youthful adventures at West Lake usually were happy moments; however, one summer, he did have one extremely painful experience.

"For days my dad has tormented us–my mother, my younger brother David and myself. We're going to Canada to vacation–fishing and boating for two weeks and then we are not. My mother knows him too

well and secretly continues preparing for the trip, paying the utility and phone bills, scrubbing the kitchen floor on her hands and knees, crying, for the last thing my father has said before he leaves the house is that we are not going! We can't afford it and that's that! And, I cannot understand his anger that at times borders on rage. Years later, I know now that it was the alcohol, and exhaustion and constantly doing a job he did not want to do."

***

"The car is loaded, our father is dressed in a white short-sleeve shirt and tie, to look presentable, if we stop for lunch at a roadside restaurant."

For the first hour of their 12 hour drive the highway follows the river and Bobby sits in the back seat, wondering about all that anger.

***

Bob, then age nine, was excited to be at West Lake with the entire Urich clan. "Our dad and Uncle Rudy were coming in from fishing," recalls David, "Bob and I were running down to meet them. The docks at that time were anchored to the lake bottom with one-inch steel pipe slipped through a sleeve, attached to the dock and driven into the lake bottom with sledge hammers. Obviously," he says, "when this was done, the pipes were split at the ends, complete with a jagged edge. The top of the pipe was a couple of feet above the surface of the dock.

"Like any other red-blooded athletic youngster, Bobby thought he could easily jump over the pipe and into the cool lake water. He made a quick decision. Trying his best to convince himself, 'this is a piece of cake,' he murmured to himself, 'I can clear this easily, no sweat.' With that, Bobby hurled himself up and over the end of the ragged pipe! Now, sometimes, in life, even our best intentions can go awry. Bobby didn't make it. Nope. In fact, he landed squarely on the pipe! Not over it, but on it, and in doing so promptly snagged his 'private parts. Ouch!"

Not exactly a pleasant way to begin a summer vacation! Bobby's injury required him to make a quick trip to the local hospital, Picton General, where attentive nurses and doctors cared for a tearful Bobby Urich.

Ahh, the healing power of youth. A few hours later, after getting stitched-up, Bobby was begging to be allowed to go swimming. Thankfully, unlike Bob's encounter with an immoveable object, the pipe, most of his memories of youthful summers spent at West Lake are happy one's. One particular blissful time was the summer of 1960.

Young Lovers at West Lake

Bob was fourteen. His trusty Hopalong Cassidy cap-pistols, no longer in use, were carefully packed away in a chest with his other boyhood toys. Now, a robust, exuberant teenager, he was ready to explore new adventures. He was ready to take on the world, or at least Toronto High School in the fall as a freshman. But, at the moment, it was summertime and fun time at West Lake. Bobby's hormones were jumping and he had his eye on a new girl at the lake...Francie Weeks.

To Bob and his younger brother, David, who also had a crush on her, Francie, with her long dark hair and medium height was a living doll ... a vision of loveliness ... a Mona Lisa in a pony tail. The summer of 1960 was also when young Bob Urich's thoughts of becoming a Catholic priest went straight out the camp window.

Bob served as an altar boy at St. Joseph's Byzantine Church. Later, as an adult, he says, his early religious training had a profound effect on him, which offered him an appreciation of ritual, tradition and closeness to God. "There was a time Bob gave serious consideration to become a priest," says his younger brother, David. "The Franciscan seminary in the neighboring town of Steubenville had a Boy Scout camp on the grounds which Bob visited, and there were talks about Bob and the seminary around our home."

Oh, Bob didn't lose his virginity that summer of 1960. No way. He was a good Catholic boy and was saving himself for marriage. In fact, there wasn't any heavy petting or even a tender first kiss with Francie, not that he wouldn't have minded one, but his strict Catholic upbringing kept him on the straight and narrow. He played by the rules.

However, he had lusted in his heart for Francie, and that in itself was a sin in Bob's mind. How big a sin was another question.

"How do I confess this to Monsignor Beros at St. Joseph's Church?" he asked himself. After all, he was an altar boy and his parish priest easily recognized his voice including when he went to confession. Rolling back the screen in the darken confessional, Bob would begin, "Bless me Father, for I have sinned."

"'Hello, Robert," the priest would always cheerfully reply. How is your mother, Cecelia? 'Oh man,' Bob thought, 'I'm dead meat! This is different than receiving a few Hail Mary's for confessing to slugging my brother, David, or for taking the Lord's name in vain. No sir! This was the Holy Grail of all sins. . .lusting after a woman, or a girl who was going to become a woman someday."

Bob sweated over it, doing his best to convince himself that, perhaps, it's not quite a mortal sin for any healthy, young man of 14 trying to handle a dose of jumping hormones. Maybe, it's more like a venial sin. Finally, Bob reached an epiphany of sorts. He realized one important thing. Whichever way you want to label it, lusting after any woman other than your wife is wrong. At least that's what our parish priest preached. But, just as importantly, Bob Urich made another decision in his young life. He decided he could never become a priest.[1] He liked girls too much and therefore, could never be celibate. Rubbing his chin, and grinning from ear to ear, Bob asked himself, "Now, how do I break this bit of news to Monsignor Beros?"

Heather shares happier moments at West Lake
Spring 2015

Tom Cruickshank writing for *Watershed Magazine* shared Heather's happier days on West Lake. "Above everything else," she says, "our cottage was a gathering place, especially for the kids and their friends. The kids have friends at West Lake they've known their whole lives.

"We've done a lot of fixing up to the place since back then. We took the little galley kitchen and made it into a gourmet chef's dream. A lot of fabulous meals came out of that little galley kitchen," she says, laughing. "When the kids were teenagers, we built a new garage and put a giant recreation room on top, 'The Loft.' It had rows of bunk beds, TV, refrigerator, ping pong table, popcorn machine...the works. We built it so I could get all those teenagers from up and down the lake out of my

---

1 Heather Urich says, "Bob was around 16 or 17 when he realized he couldn't be a priest. He had a huge crush on Francie Weeks, but I'm not sure there was ever a first kiss between them. I think Bob was 21 before he lost his virginity. I'm not sure of the circumstance," she adds. . .it may have been Barbara [Bob's first wife] but I'm not 100% positive." Later in his life, in an interview, Bob admitted that he kissed a girl for the first time at West Lake. Could it have been Francie?

kitchen. I was finding it difficult to get to my own refrigerator. I would go up to the loft, sometimes in the morning, and find about 20 or so bodies sprawled out all over."

She laughs as she recalls doing the dishes one day when an Ontario Provincial police car came down their driveway. "I looked up and as he was parking, I thought to myself, 'Crap, we've been here so many years without a single problem . . . Now what? What have they got themselves into?'" She went out to meet the uniformed officer and he introduced himself. "'Hi, I'm Mick Chalmers. . .I live across the lake. I've just come to pick up my kids.' Out from the loft, stumble his kids, Ben and Melinda. They are still two of our kids, Ryan and Emily's best friends. Mick and Delores have since become good friends and neighbors," and speaking in a hushed almost faraway voice says, "Mick became a golfing buddy of Bob's."

Heather reminisces about happier times at West Lake

"There were always quite a few folks around the dinner table. Afterward, we would light a fire in the pit, and Bob would show us how to make really good smores while we solved all the world's problems as the sun went down to a spectacular Canadian sunset. I miss watching those glorious sunsets with Bob. Somehow, they are no longer the same."

"Summers are different these days," Heather says with a slight air of remorse. "Our two oldest children, Ry and Em are both married with families of their own. Their busy lives and careers don't permit them to spend as much time at the lake as they once did...usually, just a few weeks in the summer. Our youngest daughter, Allie is away at college. It was so traumatic for me, when she got an apartment of her own. It hit me harder than I ever expected. My sister, Sheila visits me and sometimes a few old friends, who remember fun times sitting by the fire pit with Bob and me, will spend a few days, but for the most part, I'm alone up here with just my memories, and being alone a lot is not a good thing. The ole cottage which once echoed with happy voices and laughter just isn't the same these days. This was Bob's sacred place, where he felt most like himself. It was the complete opposite of L.A. Bob's spirit is still here. I can feel it," she says.

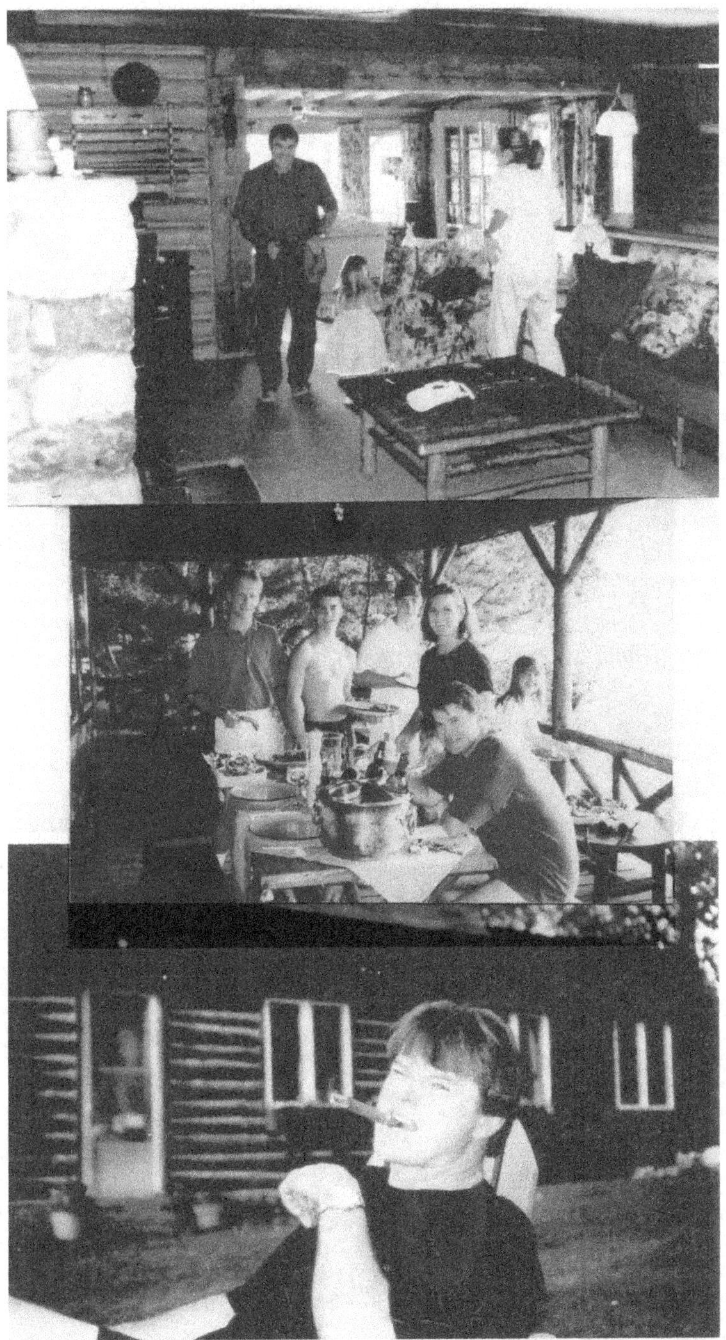

Top: Bob dancing with Allie–2001. Center: dinner on front porch. Bottom: Bob occasionally enjoyed a good cigar!

Bob & brother David (behind him), waving from boat in Canada; their dad, 'Papa' John is handling the motor and their uncle Mike is wearing a hat.

Heather & son Ry on picnic table at Uncle Rudy's. 1970's.

Bob holding baby Ry, Heather on far right in front with family members at Uncle Rudy Halpate's camp, West Lake Canada. 1970's.

Urich family home at twilight -West Lake Ontario Canada.

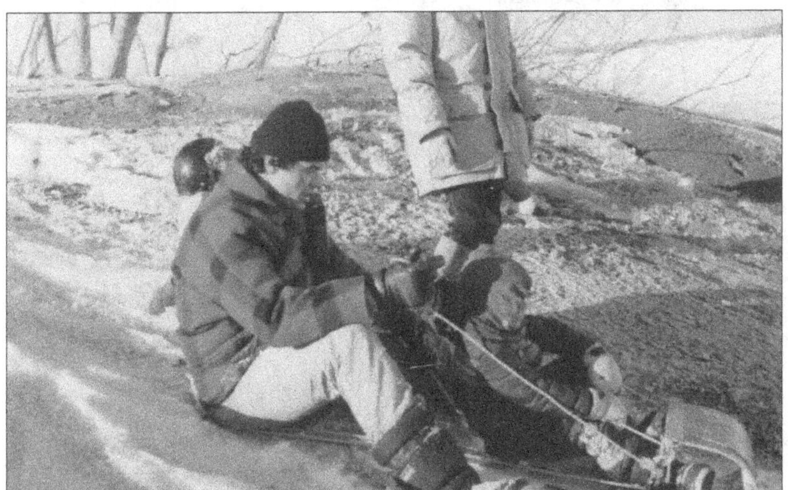

Bob sledding down the sand banks on West Lake.

... and where they landed after sliding down the banks.

Bob –doing what he loved to do---fishing!
Top left-Bob, age 12 bags the 'Big One' fishing with younger brother David in Canada. Top right, Bob fishing with his cousin Jo-Jo; Middle left: L-R, Bob, Alan Vint & Eric Caley; middle right: Bob deep sea fishing in Hawaii; Bottom left, Bob & his catch Virgin Gorge, Utah; bottom right: another one of Bob's favorite hobbies, fly fishing.

Chapter 26

Cause for Concern
Cancer Strikes !
Dream Sequence

"Courage is not the absence of fear, but the mastery of it."
- Mark Twain

The Lump !

[**Bold typed words** are Robert Urich's, taken directly from his journal.]

As the weeks passed at the lake, Bob and Heather kept watching the lump. "I could see and feel it now," she says. "Cancer is like that, sneaking in like an unwanted intruder, taking up residence like a poltergeist underneath the floorboards of your house." Their doctor in L.A. had said that it would probably disappear but it seemed to be growing.

"We weren't terribly concerned, because it had already been diagnosed as negative. However, Bob came to me and said, 'Heather, I'll have a window of time when we get back to L.A. before I have to go to work. I think I want this out of my body.' We called Dr. Bob Saffian, Bob's urologist. We had known him for years and reached him at his office in L.A. After a few questions regarding the presence of any discomfort, Dr. Saffian said, 'I can't diagnose it from across the country. But, I will tell you that twenty-five percent of all adult males will find a lump like that in that region of the body–all about your age. I take one out a week. It's probably just a little duct that fills up with tiny fatty deposits, and it sort of starts to grow and takes on a life of its own. Don't worry about it. When you get some time, come in and we'll check it out.'

"What can be done about it?" I asked.

"If you want to, we can take it out," he says. "If not, just leave it there. It's not going to hurt anything."

"But it's gotten a little bigger."

"If it bothers you, come on in and we'll take it out."

"It sounded so innocuous, like pulling a tooth or removing a mole," says Heather.

Cause for Concern

"We were scheduled to start filming the second season of *Lazarus* in Calgary in three weeks. Horses and dolly tracks and most of the crew were already there. We were going to do twelve shows and finish up around Thanksgiving, before the Winter snows disabled everything."

"Can I have this out and be in the saddle in three weeks?" I ask him.

"Oh, yeah, no problem," he says.

Bob and Heather flew back to Los Angeles and met with Dr. Saffian at Encino Tarzana Medical Center. His manner was reassuring. "We figured it would be an out-patient procedure and we could go home and resume our lives," says Heather.

Waking up in a hospital room after anesthesia, says Bob, can be very unnerving.

"At first, you don't know where you are or what you're doing there and then slowly you realize that you are practically naked, bandaged and surrounded by an eerie assortment of machines, wires and tubes. Then you start to remember and you're grateful to be alive to remember anything.

"As soon as Dr. Saffian walked in, my stomach knotted. He didn't have to say anything. The look on his face was enough.

"I think we've got a problem," he said. "My pathologist thinks this is something we need to check out further."

"The room, a dreary, austere whitewash of tile and disinfectant, seemed to turn black, like a burned-out tenement."

"We are sending it to Dr. Juan Roussi at Sloan Kettering in New York," he said.

As soon as Bob heard "Sloan Kettering" his worst fears were confirmed.

"We weren't talking about fibrous tissue here. We were talking about cancer.

"So great was the paradigm shifts within myself that the room seemed to roll with the motion. Everything that I have ever believed to be true about myself changed in that moment. A 180 degree turn, that's what a paradigm shift is."

In 1996, when first diagnosed with synovial cell sarcoma, a rare form of cancer, the words hit Bob right between the eyes. "It can't be," he thought. "After all, I have so much going for myself, and so much to live for; a loving wife and family, solid friends, the adulation of millions of loyal fans. . . and financial security. No! There must be some mistake." The world was his, or at least he thought so. Up until the time of his illness, Robert Urich appeared to be indestructible.

Dr. Roussi had written the book, literally, on synovial cell sarcoma. It's a soft-tissue cancer that often results in large tumors wrapped around muscle masses. It can spread throughout the body and when it is present in the limbs, can often result in amputation. It is a very rare, but very treatable form of cancer–at least that's what the doctor told Bob.

Heather walked into Bob's hospital room as he was waking from surgery. "There was a nurse in the corner of the room fiddling with some tubes and wires. She looked up at me with a look that said she would rather be anywhere else. She actually seemed to be willing herself to disappear. I hated her presence. She was an intruder. She knows something that will change my life. If she weren't in the room none of this would be happening."

Heather remembers Bob being under a drug-infused blur. "He was speaking in a garbled halting manner saying things like, radiation, chemotherapy, and we have a problem. I wanted the nurse to evaporate. I stood at the end of the bed trying to comprehend what he was trying to say. My soul resisted with every fiber. NO, NO, NO! He's wrong, confused, he's drugged... But the nurse's eyes said it all."

"I'm the leader. The guy on the white horse. The guy who wins the day. That same guy was being asked to head over to Cedars Sinai Comprehensive Cancer Center and start preparations for a series of treatments that were not going to be pleasant. Throughout my life, even when I had very little to show for it, I believed myself to possess personal power, the power of the love of my parents, the power of having had the right kind of teachers and coaches, the power of friends and faith. The power of believing that no matter what the situation, this guy Robert Urich could deal with it. Never in my mind was there a doubt that someday I would do something significant. . .not just in the way of

professional accomplishment , but in a way that meant something to other people."

As an actor Bob thrived on portraying heroic guys capable of going the distance, tough guys with compassion. **"At the top of every movie script you ever get–as soon as your character is introduced, there is a brief character description. My character in *Spenser: For Hire* said, 'He is capable of going the distance whatever the distance might be. He is handsome without knowing it.' What did that mean? How do you play that? But those were my roles–guys who had what it took, and I certainly thought of myself as a guy in control."**

Cause for Concern
August 1996

Lying in that hospital bed, Bob felt he was stripped of all that. A loss of control is terrifying, as he writes in his journal. . .

"The anchor line has been severed and you are at the mercy of the raging gales and the angry seas. You can't be talking about me. I've got cameras and dolly tracks and horses and wranglers and stunt men and assistant directors calling me. There are scripts arriving for my notes. You can't be talking about me. I'm Dan Tanna. I'm Spenser. I'm the Lazarus Man. No. I'm Robert Urich. I've got cancer."

Holding his wife Heather's hand, Bob began to cry. It's no shame for a man to shed tears particularly when hearing such devastating news: "You have cancer." Besides, crying can help you get through a difficult time. Tears can be shared and *sharing* helps one get through a life threatening illness. Bob let his tears flow, but only for a few minutes did he permit himself to be caught up in the emotional moment. Quickly gathering his composure, and with his infectious grin, he said to his adoring wife, "Okay, honey, now I'm ready to fight this disease!"

Heather remembers that defining moment and spoke freely about it in Daniel Howard Cerone's poignant article in the November 9, 1996 issue of *TV Guide*. "Personally, the most difficult part of it was just seeing this invincible, problem-solving, bigger-than-life loving human being be so vulnerable," she says. "That's been the most difficult day-to-day adjustment for this whole family."

The Bel Air Hotel[1] in all its splendor and celebratory atmosphere became a tomb, recalls Heather. "Our days were spent waiting for the pathologist report. We already knew the results but prayed they were wrong."

"Our friend, Dr. Dyrk Halstead flew in from Nashville to be with us while we waited. His lap top computer in hand, researching everything he could find about this rare type of sarcoma. People were lazily lounging by the pool. I was aware of bits and snippcts of laughter, and conversation…the clinking of silverware from the lunch service. We waited…and waited. The phone call finally came. Bob was sitting on the edge of our bed in the hotel room. I could see the air go out of his body as he received the diagnosis. When he hung up the phone there was resolve. After the onslaught of tears from the both of us, he became a man bent on fighting a war! The next thing I knew," she says, "he was making appointments at the hospital and planning protocol for his treatment. He was ready to slay this savage beast."

Sunday Evening, July 10, 2016 - The night Bob "spoke" to the author

Call it being too fixated on writing the bio of his life, or whatever, but Robert Urich actually reached out to me. Oh, to be sure, it was in a dream all right. The man passed away fourteen years ago, but nevertheless, he seemed to be real. Bob not only appeared to me, in a series of dream sequences, but conversed with me. The sequences seemed so real that it was almost as if he were trying to tell me something. I believe what happened earlier that Sunday had something to do with my dream. I had been cleaning the mess in my office, going through mountains of papers, trying to decide what to do with it all.

That's when I came across a stack of notes and research I had written earlier about Bob.

Now, we are not talking about a few pages, either. The stack was well over two feet high. How it got there in the first place is anyone's guess. The pile was haphazardly located under some magazines on a bookshelf. Somehow, I had overlooked it. The papers were filled with invaluable info

1 The Bel-Air Hotel with its 103 rooms and 45 suites is a secluded hillside retreat at 701 Stone Canyon Road in Bel-Air, Calif. The hotel's charm and seclusion reflects 'old Hollywood' complete with it's eleven acres of exquisite tropical gardens. Anyone who is anyone in Hollywood has stayed at the posh Hotel which closed for renovations in 2009, reopening in October 2011 with 12 new rooms built into the hillside offering sweeping canyon views. The Hotel also featured a new spa and fitness center.

about Bob's life. Notes which I desperately needed to accurately tell his story. While thumbing through page after page of the misplaced information, I asked myself, over and over, why hadn't I been able to finish this project?

At that time, it had been well over two years since I originally decided to write the book about my late friend's life and career. I had conversed by phone or e-mail with his wife, Heather and practically every member of the Urich family, along with friends and co-workers. Surely, you would think enough info had been gathered about Bob Urich to fill several volumes. To support this claim was the huge stack of papers I found myself staring at.

There is little doubt in my mind the events of the day led to my unexpected 'visit' that evening from Bob.

The first dream sequence took place in an upscale restaurant, city unknown. My wife Kimmie and I had joined Bob's wife, Heather, and some of her friends. I noticed Bob had walked over and sat down at a nearby table. He looked great, healthy and looked quite resplendant in uniform. It may have been a pilot's uniform or what the captain of a ship would wear. Now, in retrospect, his attire reminds me of two of Bob's final roles; the TV series, *Love Boat: The Next Wave*, as the ship's Captain, Jim Kennedy, and another Captain, Glen 'Lucky' Singer, an airline pilot in the TV movie, *Final Descent*.

In my dream, Bob looked over at me, nodded and smiled that infectious grin of his. I thought it peculiar that he didn't join us at our table, nor did he acknowledge Heather or any others. Dream sequence one fades to black as Bob laughs and jokes with those seated at his table.

My second dream sequence involving Bob had to do with his athletic ability. He was demonstrating his ability on ice skates and how to skate and pivot with ease. He was doing remarkably well, until he collapsed withering in pain, and holding his left side. His young son Ryan, perhaps four at the time, was with us, and immediately ran to get some sort of drink for his dad. Ry tripped and fell and spilled the brownish-yellow liquid, which looked to be apple juice or iced tea. Bob asked me to get him a Bud from the family refrigerator. Apparently, the scene changed from an ice arena to his family kitchen. I looked but couldn't find any. There isn't any Bud, how about an ale–I can't recall the brand. Quizzically, he looked at me and said, "look in the cupboard." I did but still no Bud. Dream sequence two fades to black.

The third dream sequence involving Robert Urich shows him driving up to me in a black Thunderbird convertible. [Remember that Bob drove a red T-Bird convertible on his series *Vega$*.]

"Get in," he smiles. He moves over to the passenger side. I get behind the wheel, but don't drive. Looking over at him, I ask, "why are you so rude to everyone?" Evidently, I was referring to the restaurant, where he didn't speak to us, and ice skating scenes where he didn't acknowledge or speak to anyone, but me. "You come back and you don't acknowledge your loving wife or son, or speak to anyone but me." A look of total surprise and shock is written all over Bob's face. Softly, he says, "you have more stories to tell about me, right Joe?" "Yes, I do, but do you have any idea how difficult it is to make sure I'm writing an accurate description of you? If I write that you throw a chair in anger on the set of one television episode, people may think you are a total hot head and completely out of control. I know that's not you. One misplaced, or inaccurate word can make all the difference in how readers perceive you and what you're all about. Bob smiles and says, "Tell the truth. I know you will," as dream sequence three fades to black.

In my final dream sequence, number four, Bob and I are in a house. There is lots of wood. Maybe knotty-pine. We are in a stairwell, watching Heather prepare a meal in the kitchen area–it is an open room. It may be stew or salad. She keeps going back and forth to the refrigerator getting veggies. A tall teenager comes in –his name may be Mark, or Mike–he has some sort of bug hanging from a fishing hook. Heather, barely looking up, asks him to take it outside and he leaves. Bob continues watching his beloved wife move around the kitchen. With tears in his eyes and once again, speaking ever so softly, he says, "She wants me to come back but I can't. I just can't."

Pleading with me, he continues, "please tell her [Heather] I'm o.k."

In my dream, it finally sinks in that no one else can see or talk with Bob in the dream except me.

My final dream sequence fades to black.

Waking up, I instinctively rub my eyes and feel I too have been crying.

Author's note:

After confiding in Heather about Bob appearing in my dream sequences the night before, she listened rather intently and then made a few comments. She said the kitchen scene with all the wood had to be their cottage at the lake in Canada. Bob loved to fish at West Lake where their cottage is located. Incidentally–I had neither seen nor visited the place.

As far as the skating portion of my dream, she said, "Bob wanted the role in the 1977 hockey film, *Slap Shot,* but he wasn't very good on ice skates. *So, he* rented time at an ice skating rink at 3 o'clock in the morning. It was the only time available. This is another example of how much effort Bob put into his acting career. After a few falls, he felt confident enough to hit the ice for the audition. But, later as he pointed out to me, "as soon as Paul Newman took to the ice, it was all over and the part went to him."

Heather's concluding comment to me is enough to make the hair stand up on the back of your neck:

"There's no way you you could have known about Bob's attempt at ice skating, because until this very moment, no one knew about it except me." Heather added, "he was channeling you, Joe. He was channeling you."

The Lazarus Man - Lawsuit

"The Lazarus Man" was cancelled just weeks before production was scheduled to begin on a second season, right after Bob revealed that a month earlier [July 1996] he had been diagnosed with synovial cell sarcoma [for the first time]. In the November 9, 1996 issue of *TV Guide,* speaking with Daniel Howard Cerone, Urich says Turner Broadcast Services sent him a press release to approve the announced cancellation. "They were pushing me in a direction I didn't want to go. 'Due to personal and medical reasons, I am withdrawing from . . .' I said, 'Bull_ _ _ _! That is NOT my attitude, and I'm not going to say that.' Because I believe we could have saved the show."

"They didn't even ask me if I planned to work while undergoing treatment! In fact, they didn't ask if I was even going to have treatment." His chemotherapy treatment involved nine days on, then three weeks off and doctors cleared him to work in between. Bob even volunteered to give up $50,000 of the $73,000 he was to receive per episode to make it happen. But one executive remarked that there was simply too much uncertainty surrounding Urich's illness and how he would respond to treatment. The

$20 million necessary to produce a second season was too steep to play the 'what if' game and they pulled the plug. "Bob loved that role more than most," says Heather. "It broke his heart when they canceled the show because of his diagnosis. Bob really didn't want to go after Castle Rock Productions after they canceled *The Lazarus Man*. This was done on the advice of his agent at the time, Sylvia Gold at ICM."[1]

"The statute of limitations* had passed, but the disrespectful way they treated Bob really bugged me," she says. "At the time, I was not aware of the Americans with Disabilities Act. This Act makes it illegal to fire a person upon a diagnosis of ANYTHING, which is basically what they did. I ran it by a friend, who just happened to be a lawyer, and he agreed with me that there could be something there. I really just wanted to make a point that what they did was not right," Heather stresses.

"We convinced Bob to jump in and give it a shot." Bob had always maintained that the producers jumped the gun before finding out his prognosis. As it turned out, his condition was treated successfully, and he returned to work in various film and TV series including a pilot for a daily TV talk show.

The actual lawsuit, filed by Urich stated the following: On April 11, 2000,[2] Robert Urich sued Castle Rock over cancellation of his TV series, "The Lazarus Man." In the suit, Urich sued Castle Rock Television charging that the production company terminated his TV series, and refused to pay him because he had cancer. Castle Rock exercised the option for the first season of "The Lazarus Man" in September 1995 and for the second season in June 1996.

In July of 1996, Bob informed Castle Rock that he had cancer and would have to undergo treatment, but according to the complaint at no time was he [Urich] unable to perform under the agreement, and Castle Rock had no information that would have created a reasonable apprehension about Urich's ability to perform.

Bob maintained that although he was undergoing cancer treatments, he never informed Castle Rock that he would be unable to perform in the series. Castle Rock went ahead and cancelled the series anyway and failed

---

1 Bob had taken a sabbatical for a while from his long-time agent, Merritt Blake.

2 No definitive reason was given for the 4 year gap between the cancellation date of the series and Urich's lawsuit. It may have been primarily, because Bob was not the type of person to sue anyone. He also may have been concerned about not obtaining future work, as an actor, for suing a major production company.

to pay Urich the $1.47 million he was to be paid, $73,000 per episode,[1] for a second season. The complaint also says that Castle Rock terminated the agreement a month later.

***

The lawsuit was later settled with both parties agreeing not to publicly disclose the terms of the settlement. Heather admits, "We were both happy with the outcome. If we hadn't waited until the statute of limitations had expired,* we would have received the full amount which was 1.4 million. As it was," she says, "I don't remember how much it was [the settlement] but it was enough to make us want to go out and celebrate. We were in the lawyer's office after the entire mediation was over and wanted to go out to our favorite restaurant *Peppones Ristorante*, a legendary Italian restaurant in Brentwood, Calif. to celebrate. We loved the place with its cozy red leather booths, soft music and candlelight. The walls were adorned with beautiful paintings, and of course their delicious home-cooking and great wine. We were salivating and could hardly wait to head out," she says. "Our lawyer, Frank Hobbs called to get us a reservation and was told they were booked solid. Not one to easily accept the word, 'no,' Bob called and got right in." Heather laughs, "Frank witnessed a good dose of celebrity privilege."

Bob, preaches the Gospel of Survival

Bob had to undergo his cancer treatments without the one thing he had for over 25 years–a steady job. His respite from working did give him needed time to reflect on his life and how he wanted to spend what he referred to as his "second adulthood."

"The biggest thing I need to do now is be quiet enough to listen to that inner voice, and the spirit of God," he says. "I don't know what's next. I don't want to do the same old stuff, you know?"

***

Never one to quit. Bob Urich fought his illness with everything he had. He refused to become a victim and was determined to beat the odds. After surgery and chemo, he did beat the odds and was free from his disease . . . at least for awhile longer.

---

1 Bob reportedly was paid $70,000 per episode for the first season on *The Lazarus Man.*

Bob Urich would soon learn that his next role in life would be, perhaps, his most important one.

1998, Bob after being diagnosed with a rare form of cancer [synovial cell sarcoma] preaching the Gospel of survival at Truman State University.

PART V
Chapter 27

Bob Through Heather's Eyes

"True love begins when nothing is looked for in return."
- Antoine de Saint-Exupery

Bob Through Heather's Eyes

If anyone knew Bob best, it was his soul-mate and devoted wife, Heather.

In the following pages, as you read her own words, you will see why Bob was so special in her eyes. Her personal comments will give you first-hand knowledge of what Bob was all about and what made him tick. Some of her words will make you smile, while others may bring a tear or two, but all will give you a better understanding of Bob Urich's unique personality. As told by the woman who loved him completely, and so passionately, not only during their 27 years as husband and wife, but following his death in 2002. You see, Heather always felt she was still married to 'her Bob,' and she carried her deep love for him in her heart until her own passing in 2017.

***

"Let me begin with one important thing about Bob," she says, laughing. "No, he did NOT leave the cap off the toothpaste. He also took great care in respect for his surroundings. The first thing that impressed me about Bob other than the fact he was impossibly handsome complete with his hazel eyes, is how he treated me with such enormous respect. However, I think the biggest thing that drew me to Bob is how he talked about his family in such a loving way. It was quite obvious how much he loved them. Bob also had tremendous respect for his parents and his family. Bob was a go-getter. When I first met him, I knew whatever he did, whatever he chose to do, he would make it work and be successful. I admired that about him.

"Bob was very affectionate and very much a 'hugger.' When he met my mom for the first time he wrapped her in a bear hug. Her Scottish self was really taken a back. Over time, she came to know and love him and actually looked forward to his big bear hugs!

"He loved his soup and his mother, Cecilia made the best chicken soup around. She was a fantastic cook, and I'm sure Bob picked up his cooking skills from her.

On one of our first dates he cooked me chicken soup prepared the way his mom made it. Later, he taught me how to make it. It's soooo good. Bob was not very good about fixing things around the house, but man, he could make a mean chicken soup. I'd say a homemade bowl of soup was his favorite meal. He preferred a hamburger to hot dogs. Actually he preferred hamburger to steak.

"As mentioned, his mother got him into cooking which he enjoyed, especially on the holidays. They were always big festive events with specialty dishes, cabbage rolls, shredded pork chops, the works. Delicious Slovak dishes. He loved my spaghetti which brings to mind a funny incident. One day, before he came home from work, I got a call from his agent at the time, Sylvia Gold.[1] She was kind of panicky. 'Heather,' she said,

'We need to help Bob watch his weight.' I thought, Oh great. How do I handle this one. He did get a little lazy about taking care of his weight and being in shape and that annoyed me. I would get irritated when he would go into McDonald's or something like that. Anyway, back to my spaghetti story. Bob had had a particularly bad day at work. That night, I served spaghetti and when he went for a second helping, I said, 'Do you

1 Heather says, "Bob got wooed away from his long-time agent, Merritt Blake by Sylvia Gold at ICM. She and Alan Berger banged on his door, promised him all kinds of sh_ t, excuse the vernacular. She was wonderful but Bob really didn't need an agent. People would come to him. The agent was really the conduit. There was no animosity when Bob left Merritt. "I was just a one-person office," Merritt said, "If Bob can get with a major company like ICM, go for it." I represented Bob Duvall and he left. I wished him well. It's part of being an agent." Out of the blue one day, Merritt got on a plane, flew to Toronto Canada, rented a car and drove 3 hours to our place," recalls Heather. We sat by the camp fire and talked. He told Bob, "You are a huge success and I want to kick you into the next realm. I want to be part of that." Being a compassionate man, Bob was moved by Merritt's sincere gesture. Merritt stayed 4 or 5 days and convinced Bob to come back. Bob said, "If he's willing to go to all this trouble then I want to work with him"

think you really need that?' Oh boy! There was a look of fire in his eyes! He took the plate of spaghetti and threw it against the wall."

"The kids just stared at him. I looked at him and said, 'I'm not cleaning it up. The mop and bucket are right over there. Go to it,' and went back to eating my spaghetti. Whenever Bob had one of his explosive moments,[1]like the spaghetti incident, which thankfully didn't happen very often, they were over about as quickly as they began. Immediately after, he was always contrite that it happened in the first place.

"Bob loved his coffee and loved grinding fresh beans to make it. To this day, hearing the sound of coffee beans being ground in the kitchen makes me tear up. Our kitchen was one of the first places he'd head for in the morning to make coffee. He liked it with a touch of milk. When we were at a hotel, for some reason, it was always cream in his coffee. I would always request that the cream was heated. When a few of our coffee mugs showed up missing, I always knew where to find them. In his garden. He loved gardening and always had one wherever we lived. He bought land close by our place in Canada, just so he could buy a John Deere tractor. He'd jump on board and drive around the fields.

"Bob liked breakfast. Sometimes it was just toast or eggs. Not so big on pancakes. He looooooved," she emphasizes, "the Canadian peameal bacon.[2] I had a button when he would make a sandwich for lunch and leave crumbs all over the counter. I would give anything to have those crumbs today.

"Dinner was always an event at our house. It was so important to him for us to have a family meal every night of the week when he was in town. He would call me every day at noon and say, 'O.K. Heather, what's the answer to the question of the day?' The answer would always be *what's for dinner*?

"When we lived in Boston, he would call me from the set of *Spenser* and we'd talk about what we were going to have for dinner that night. 'You get this and I'll get that...and we'll do this,' he'd say. On his way home, he would stop at our local grocery store and pick up whatever we needed for dinner. Sometimes, we'd shop together.

---

1 Bob's shortcoming was his explosive temper, which he tried hard to keep under wraps.

2 Canadian peameal bacon is also known as cornmeal bacon. It's made from lean boneless pork loins, trimmed fine, wet and rolled in cornmeal. It was developed by a Toronto Ontario ham curer, William Davies.

"He wasn't a big sweet eater, but with all modesty, I make the best apple pie on the planet. He enjoyed that and once in a while with ice cream. Chocolate ice cream was probably his favorite ice cream, but he wasn't the type who only liked one flavor. He liked to try different ice cream flavors.[1]

"Bob really wasn't a drinker, but every once in awhile, he'd have a glass of Scotch. He didn't really enjoy champagne and seldom drank beer, but when he did, it was always a good German beer. He liked a good glass of wine and liked to spend good money on it.

"Bob could have been the model for the perfect male. He was tall, 6'2" ruggedly handsome with an award-winning smile and boyish grin. He consumed life. Whenever he was having fun, you could see the child-like joy written all over his face.

"He was very passionate on so many different levels. . .he was passionate with me, and his family, his work, fishing and really good food. Once, we were in France having dinner at a restaurant. I think it was San Simeon, located between Paris and Deuville, I saw him actually shed tears of joy over a piece of fillet of sole. I'm not kidding. Bob actually cried. 'Oh, Heather, This is so good, as tears streamed down his cheeks.'

"His wallet was an on-going deal, because he was always losing it in the house. We would be heading out the door and he'd say, 'Heather, I can't find my wallet.' He didn't have anything surprising in there. A bit of money and credit cards, but he was always asking me to hold it for him when we went anywhere. Usually, it's the other way around for a couple.

"Bob was definitively a man's man, loved to fly-fish, and golf, but he also had the reputation of being the male Martha Stewart, which our friends teased him about. One time, he didn't come with me to a dance class at our friend, Joe Malone's. Yes, I actually got Bob to take a few dance lessons, even a couple of ballet classes. This particular night, Joe asked, 'Where's Bob?' Another friend chimed in and said, 'Oh, he's probably home wallpapering the driveway.' He loved decorating and he was good

---

1 Author's note: When we both lived on Boston's North Shore, the Urich's in Andover and we lived in W. Boxford, we would meet up at Benson's Ice Cream Stand in West Boxford. My friend, Alan Benson had the best homemade ice cream around. Bob would be hunched down behind the steering wheel of their blue SUV wearing sun glasses and a baseball cap, doing his best not to be recognized. Heather and the kids would be waiting in line to order. All Bob wanted to do was enjoy an ice cream cone with his family, but his visibility was high and people wouldn't leave him alone. According to Alan Benson, Bob's choice of ice cream on that summery Sunday afternoon was a double dip cone of strawberry and vanilla.

at it. Bob had very specific tastes. He knew what he liked and what he didn't and had a very expensive sense of style.

Bob couldn't sit still. He always had to be busy. He rearranged our furniture so often, guests would get confused as to where to sit. I would go with the flow with his fixation about rearranging the furniture which he was constantly doing. Friends would teasingly say, 'What's next, Bob? Will you rearrange our cars in your driveway.' He enjoyed buying something for the house. I usually made the bed but he always wanted to wash the sheets and put clean ones down sooner than I cared to.

He liked to hunt and fish. I'm sure it's hard to envision him killing anything, and you need to know he did not hunt animals. He was a member of Ducks Unlimited and believed it was a way to control the duck population. He was a bird and duck hunter, but eventually gave that up, too because he felt uncomfortable about it. He never caught anything he didn't eat," says Heather.

"I remember once, eating quail with pellets through it. It's not very appetizing and a good way to lose all your teeth.

"His favorite place to hang out was our cottage on West Lake in Canada. He had gone there as a kid and always felt it was his safe sanctuary. His passion was fishing and golf. Bob had his favorite fishing spots on West Lake and why he requested that some of his ashes be spread over them. He'd go out fishing by himself early in the morning and come back with a string of walleye. He taught our daughter Em how to fish and was in the process of teaching our youngest daughter, Allie. Our son Ry was more into fly-fishing.

Golf was Bob's favorite hobby. He loved the game. I couldn't begin to count how many different sets of golf clubs he owned. Funny, if he had a bad round, he would blame the clubs, and go out and buy a new set. I took it up so that I wouldn't be a golf widow. I enjoyed playing with him because he would let me get away with not keeping score and taking mulligans. I only played with him and I don't play anymore. Bob probably would have pursued a golfing career if he hadn't been a successful actor.

"He was always the athlete, and enjoyed playing one on one basketball with friends, like Robby Benson. He loved watching sports on TV. The Olympics were his favorite, also football, which he played in high school which earned him a football scholarship to Florida State. My God, whenever there was a game on TV. Holy Crap!, especially if it was

F.S.U., Oh, my God. If a play didn't go right, he would get up and leave the room. I'd say, 'Honey, it's only a game.' 'No, it's not,' he'd yell back. 'You don't understand.'

"In 1970, after Bob graduated from F.S.U. and grad school at Michigan State, the Viet Nam War was raging. Bob didn't serve because of a football injury he received at F.S.U. He woke up in the hospital, four days after being injured in a game with a contusion of the mid-brain. I think, that's a fancy description for a blood clot on the brain, which gave him headaches for the rest of his life, plus a 4F status in the military. He couldn't have served even if he wanted to."

"Oh, a cute side note," Heather says, "The first time Bob was on national TV was playing football for Florida State in the Tangerine Bowl. I think they retired his number #55, but I'm not sure. Bob followed basketball, too. When we were in Utah, we went to the Jazz games, because he knew one of the players, John Stockton. They were golfing buddies. We'd go to the games and hang out after. You tend to follow a team when you live in an area[1] and know the people in it.

"He loved to camp, especially going up to Big Sur. Camping is something he began doing as a teen growing up in Ohio. He would garb his knapsack and his uncle's WWII Army tent and hike up into the Allegheny mountains for a few days all by himself.

"Bob did not like profanity and seldom if ever used foul language. He used to say, 'when people use foul language its because of a lack of knowing how to express themselves.' He would not have the F word used around him. I think I said it once in front of him and that was the last time. He turned off *The Sopranos*. He wouldn't watch it because of the foul language. He had a real problem with vulgar language.

"Bob had a great work ethic which I'm sure stemmed from how he was raised, in a very middle class family. His father was a foreman in a steel mill."

Heather says, "Bob and his siblings were raised in a very modest house on a modest street in a very ethnic neighborhood made up of lots of folks

---

1 When living in the Boston area, Bob followed the Celtics. Back then, he was a Danny Ainge fan and wanted to meet him. During the NBA season, Danny did a feature on our morning radio show, *The Joe and Andy Family,* so thanks to Celtics PR guy, Jeff Twiss [in 2018 he was still with the Celtics as V.P. of Media Relations, marking over 30 years with the team] I arranged to have Bob & Danny meet after a home game. I'm not sure who was more excited to meet whom, Danny or Bob? As I recall, it was a mutual feeling.

from the 'old country,' very Catholic and Slovak...in the small Midwestern town of Toronto Ohio.

"We went to the movies a lot. He walked out of *Basic Instinct*, claiming, 'If I wanted to see a blue movie, I'll go see a blue movie.' He ended up revisiting the movie years later and thought it was pretty good. Speaking of blue, it was Bob's favorite color. He had old fashioned standards. I guess, you could say, growing up, he was an 'old soul'at a young age. Lots of his traditions and standards remained with him throughout his life. Having said that, this may shock some of you, but Bob was on the cover of *Playgirl* once and never regretted it. To him, it was just another magazine. I never regretted being in *Playboy* either, but my Presbyterian parents weren't too pleased. It didn't bother me, because it's the main reason Bob wanted to go out with me in the first place. His friend and neighbor, actor Tim Matheson, showed him the magazine before we met and did the Libby's commercial together. Later, I was told Bob's initial reaction was...

'Oh, so THAT'S Heather.'

***

"We went to Mammoth ski resort on our honeymoon. My sister Sheila, who tagged along, and I had never skied before so that was a comedy act. That has changed. I'm pretty good at it now. Our son Ryan became an expert skier.

"The first year we lived in Park City [Utah] I skied every single day. The ski resort stayed open longer that winter, because we had so much snow. Bob was in L.A. shooting his TV series *It Had to Be You*. My friends wanted me to go skiing, so I did. It was the last run on the last day the resort was open for the season.

"It was getting a little fluffy and I hit a snow slope. I went to do a turn and nothing. I broke my left leg from the knee down. It was eight weeks in a cast and it bothered me for a long time. It took about a year for the pain to completely go away and not swell up any longer. Bob preferred water-skiing to snow skiing. He probably would be doing wade-boarding by now because its kind of become the sport of the day. Even though, we lived on a ski slope in Park City, Bob kinda got bored with it. 'O.k., one run, and I'm done,' he'd say.

"One of Bob's strong suits was his humor. He was very quick witted and smart as a tack. He found joy and humor in just about everything. He wasn't the least bit reserved. He was always trying to pull me out of my shell. I was painfully shy as a kid. When Bob started to become successful a certain amount of attention was placed on him wherever we went, especially at network functions we would have to attend. People would clamor around him and my penalty would be to let him do his thing and I'll just step over here. He would literally grab my arm, pull me back and say, 'Stay right here.' He did that and in doing so made me feel I had more to give than I believed I had. Bob never lost awareness of my presence. He needed and wanted me by his side, which I appreciated. He would verbally say to me, 'I need you here. I want you right by my side, and you are just as important as I am.' Bob really made me feel important and really helped bring me out and in doing so, made me a better person. In the summer of 2017, I was emcee for a charity auction at a theater in Picton, Ontario. I was worried about being able to pull it off, because I had to get up on stage before an audience all by myself. . .and then I remembered his words, 'I've got this. I can do this.' I got up there and this calm came over me. I had the best time, and It was like Bob was standing right there beside me."

"Bob was big about staying 'in touch' while at work. Throughout the day, he would call me. There would be 4 or 5 phone calls, sometimes just to say 'hi' and to tell me he loved me. He couldn't tell me enough how much he loved me. . . every day. The word adoration was tossed about minute by minute. He would always say that EVERY day was Valentine's Day. We couldn't pass each other in the kitchen or hallway without touching,a hug…a kiss. It was always hands on with us.

"We didn't 'spat'. . .we had discussions. He would spat with our son, Ryan though. But, Bob and I had a rule that neither one of us could leave the room until the discussion was over and agreed upon. Raising voices and slamming doors was NOT an option. We agreed upon that before we got married. We had a whole set of by-laws that we stuck by. I only violated that once in all our years together and that was just before Bob passed.[1]

"Date nights for us were always pretty spontaneous. We were never able to conceive the traditional way, hence all three of our children are adopted. I made it to four months once! I feel as though if we had been able to do it the conventional way it would have been a crying shame, because

1 You can read more about it in Chapter 29, Bob's Final Days.

we wouldn't have the kids that we do have. However, Bob and I had a lot of fun trying. He would book a sitter and surprise me with a night out.

"Bob was a very unique type of person who had many different interests. He was clever beyond measure, and was always 'blue-skying' it as he referred to his countless dreams and ideas for future projects. Bob was a TV newsperson rather than reading a newspaper. I was always the one who grabbed the paper. He was an avid reader and collected Asprey leather bound lst edition copies of the classics. He was also very well-read, so you didn't really want to get 'into it' with him unless you knew what you were talking about.

"Bob was extremely intelligent, brilliant. He was always seeking wisdom. He was a huge Joseph Campbell fan and always read his books and discussing philosophy. Bob loved reading Steven Cutty type of books, too. Back in the day, we both loved Sidney Sheldon books. We actually got to meet him. He sent Bob a letter inviting us to dinner at his place, simply because he wanted to meet Bob. We accepted of course and headed over one evening for dinner. Sidney lived in a big mansion on Sunset Boulevard. It was just Bob and I, Kirk and Ann Douglas,[1] Don Rickles and his wife, Barbara and Sidney Sheldon and his wife. We had dinner and watched a movie. For the life of me, I can't remember the movie because the whole time I was thinking, *What am I doing here?*

"Bob was not into pop culture at all. When it came to music, he was always singing. He loved the standards, anything by Dean Martin and Frank Sinatra, especially *the Sinatra Songbook*[2] with songs like *Fly Me To The Moon*, *Witchcraft+* and one of his all-time favorites, *Someone to Watch over Me*. Bob also loved Christmas music. I've got so many Christmas CD's, I don't know what to do with them all," she says.

"What Bob and I liked to do the most was to be in the same room. I know that probably sounds silly, but it's the truth. He loved to just 'hang out' with me. He enjoyed shopping, something I can't stand. He would

---

1 Kirk Douglas had a pool house on Canon Drive. I knew his son, Michael. As kids, we would all hang out at Michaels. I had never met his famous father and one day, in walks Kirk. I was just paralyzed. He looked at me and said, "What's the matter, cat got your tongue." I was so embarrassed.," Heather says.

2 *Fly Me To The Moon* was written in 1954 by Bart Howard; *Witchcraft* was composed by Cy Coleman with lyrics by Carolyn Leigh and *Someone to watch over me* was composed by George Gershwin with lyrics by Ira Gershwin in 1926 for the musical, "Oh Kay. All three hits were recorded by Frank Sinatra.

usually pick out most of my clothes. If I went shopping, he would insist going with me, because he didn't trust my judgment when it came to my clothes. As for what he wore, he liked tailored clothing."

"Bob also loved window shopping and antiquing... just poking around. He appreciated the finer things in life, art work and well-crafted things. He had a good eye. I bought this print when I was in Vienna [Austria], a lithograph and had it framed. Bob hated the frame, saying, 'The frame is too much. It detracts from the lithograph.' I said I paid $700.00 for that frame. 'It's a crappy frame. It's horrible,' he insisted. I gave the frame to my friend, Angela [Cartwright], and he went out and bought another one. And, you know what? It looked great! He was always right," she says, laughing.

"We liked to walk together. In Canada, we have an 8k loop that we would power walk. No walkman allowed. No headsets with music. He would talk the entire time.

"Our dance classes at Joe Malone's at the Performing Arts Center in Northridge were until 8 p.m. Then we'd head over to the Beverly Hills Playhouse and Milton Katselas' acting class until midnight. Bob and I enjoyed working together. There was a tremendous amount of mutual respect in that arena [acting class].

"Bob never really played card games. You'd think after being in *Vega$* and playing Dan Tanna it would have rubbed off on him, but that just wasn't the case. He did play backgammon. At one time, we were all into playing Uno, but Bob wasn't really into card games, or playing chess or checkers.

We were always taking photos of the kids. In fact, while going over all our photos for the book makes me realize what an amazing life we had together and how much Bob loved his family and worshipped his kids.

"He enjoyed hangin' out with *Average Joes* rather than celebrities. In fact, he really didn't care much for the Hollywood lifestyle. He'd rather be fly-fishing with his friends, or spending time with us at our cottage in Canada where he could relax and be himself.

"Here's a little something I bet you didn't know about Bob..." she says. "He was extremely claustrophobic, especially on elevators. He avoided small places like the plague, which is probably why we lived in big houses. He took up a lot of spiritual space.

"Bob was a big dog person, but loved all animals. He had a huge heart when it came to our four-footed friends. When he did a series of Purina commercials, he came home with the Springer Spaniel he worked with that day. There was a time when we had three dogs, four cats, two horses, three iguanas and a hamster or two. We would take the dogs up to Canada with us every summer. Jake, our golden Retriever, who you remember Joe [again referring to the author], was a stray someone found wandering in our neighborhood. The owner couldn't be found, so he moved in with us. Coco was a chocolate lab. All our cats were strays that just found us.

"At one time, we owned six horses. Bob gave one away. It was a horse that starred with him in the movie *A Horse for Danny*. It was a horse headed for the glue factory, but Bob loved him too much to let him go. After filming wrapped, he purchased the horse, whose given name was Tom Thumb, as a gift for me. I had hoped to use the horse in hunter/jumper competition, but he just wouldn't cooperate. So, $10,000 dollars worth of vet bills later, Tom Thumb, when last I heard, was happy, healthy and living in Colorado.

"Bob was somewhat apolitical but didn't pretend to know about something if he didn't have the information. He was a man of his own convictions. When it came to voting, he always voted for the man, rather than the party. When living in Boston and he was filming the TV series *Spenser: For Hire*, Bob campaigned for Gov. Mike Dukakis. They attended a few barbecues together.

"However, on voting day, he told me he didn't vote for him. When I said, but you campaigned for him, Bob's reply, 'He's not the right man for the job.'[1]

"In *Vega$*, Bob's star really began to rise and people would actually come looking for him. It was like finding Mickey Mouse at Disneyland. Where is he? We ran out of something in Vegas, and had to go to the mall to buy socks or something. We had to leave because they swarmed all over him. I remember sending Bob out to buy some diapers. He came back and said, 'Don't ever do that to me again.' He just wanted to grab a box and come

1 Bob was probably initially pursued by the Dukakis campaign to make personal appearances in behalf of the Governor, because of his status as a major celebrity, who was highly visible at that time as *Spenser* on TV. However, from the time he campaigned for then Gov. Dukakis, they attended a few barbecues together until election day, a lot of things happened which came to light during the campaign which may have influenced Bob's voting decision.

back. He was exhausted. Women were all over him. He would forget and think he was still Bobby Urich from Toronto, Ohio.

"Boston was pretty much the same story. High visibility, little privacy. He knew that as as soon as he stepped out the door of our home, his privacy ended, but it still bothered him. It really troubled him, and he'd often say, 'In L.A., I'm just another working actor, here I'm the celebrity guy.' He didn't really like that.

'At our son Ryan's 5th or 6th birthday party, we put a specific time on the invitations of when to drop the kids off and when to pick them up. Hours after the party ended, and now in the early evening, Bob arrived home from work, dog-tired, and some of the women were still waiting–with their kids in tow–to see him. It drove him crazy. 'I can't even go in my own G.D. house,' he said.

"Bob was very sensitive, but a strong sensitive.

"He was also extremely perceptive, almost bordering on clairvoyance. He instinctively sensed what was about to happen, like a bear catching a whiff of a scent in the wind. Bob also had ESP. When we lived in Vegas he owned a Datsun for a short time and gave it to his brother, David. Then, Bob had a very vivid dream about the car being in an accident. He called David and told him to get rid of the car, which David did, no questions asked. Later, when they were filming an episode of *Vega$* in a junk yard, Bob spotted the car completely mangled. How's that for some ESP!

"Bob was also very spiritual and religious. We regularly attended Mass as a family, but he didn't go much for confession. He truly believed he didn't have any sins to confess.

"He wasn't easily depressed but could get down in the dumps occasionally. He was really depressed one December when we lived in Boston. I finally said, 'What the heck is wrong with you?' 'I can't believe I'm going to be forty,' he said. 'You're not going to be forty,' I answered. 'You're 38.' He spent his 50th birthday curled up in a dark room recovering from a chemo session.

"I guess Bob's biggest mistake was not being more judicious about money. I'm more conservative than he was when it comes to money. After all, I am a Scot," she says with a laugh. "I have to admit, one of his downfalls was being extravagant. He had the need to 'have' not one Rolex, but several. Of course, he would occasionally give one away to friends. Bobby McGuiness, his driver in Boston received one after filming was finished on *Spenser*, as a way of thanks for carting Bob all over Boston. Today, our son Ryan has the Rolex's. Bob was always raising the bar as far as 'havingness' was concerned. In addition to *having* to own several expensive wristwatches, he also was very car fickle.

I don't know how many cars he went through, but I know, at one point, he had three Harley's. He sold them because he didn't want Ryan riding them and wrapping himself around a tree.

"After Bob passed, I asked his brother David to come out and go through some of Bob's fishing equipment, since I really didn't know its value or what to do with it all. David found, 'among other things, 30 or 35 handmade bamboo rods that were probably worth around two-thousand bucks a piece.' Proving again Bob's need to have the best.

"We lived in a beach house for awhile in Oxnard [Calif] and had a 32 foot sail boat, but nobody ever wanted to go sailing with him. I got horribly seasick and the kids thought it was boring. As far as boats were concerned, Bob had his own small Navy; two Boston Whalers, a Pony, a row skiff, a Hobie cat, a canoe and an old wooden cedar strip boat that his Uncle Rudy had owned in the Fifties. I gave the cedar strip to our neighbor and one of Bob's fishing pal's, Eric Caley, because he helped Bob restore it.

At one point, I had to put the brakes on his spending and actually took over paying the bills. After I took over handling our money from EBM [Executive Business Management], he had to ask me before he purchased anything. It didn't bother him. He was very happy about me taking over. He told me, 'I should have done this years ago.' EBM always told me it was far too complicated, because we had both corporate and personal accounts, but with the adage of Quicken, it's actually quite easy.

"Bob was generous to a fault with his siblings, mostly his younger brother, Dave. He had a net under him that I feel prevented him from succeeding on his own merit. He finally stopped after I took over the money and wouldn't let him do it anymore.

Bob asked me what I wanted for our 10th Wedding Anniversary. I said, please take my wedding ring and have it cleaned. Bob bought it for me when we got married. He would tease and say, 'You need a magnifying glass to see her diamond,' but my ring was very sentimental to me and I love it. Besides, at the time, we were struggling actors with little money. We were surviving off veggies from our garden.

"The evening of our anniversary, we were out to dinner and he said, 'Oh, by the way, I have your diamond,' and handed me a box. I said, 'Great,' thinking he remembered to get it cleaned. When I opened the box I was so surprised. He had bought me a brand new diamond... a very expensive one which is lovely. However, I could never part with my old diamond. I had it made into a necklace and still have it.

"One Christmas, we were living in Andover Mass, he surprised me by buying a two-seater Mercedes...wrapped it in a big bow and had it secretly driven in our garage to surprise me on Christmas morning. I appreciated his thoughtfulness but with two small children a two seater just wasn't practical, so I sold it. Yes, Bob spent a lot, but I figured, he worked hard and earned it. His mantra was always 'First class portal to portal.' Hey, you can't take it with you, and he left me and the family plenty to live on for the rest of our lives.

"Bob was never self-centered and not all about himself. He cared about other folks. He cared about his fans and would engage complete strangers in conversation who approached him on the street or at an airport. Bob always made time for them. Towards the end of his life, while undergoing his own treatment for cancer, and speaking in behalf of the American Cancer Society, he always made time for those who came up following his speech to chat or have their photo taken with him.

"Bob treated everyone with respect but he believed that respect was something that was earned. I remember an assistant director yelled at me because he thought I was an extra on the show and was parking in the wrong spot. Bob's elderly mom was with me who couldn't walk very far, so Bob told me to park by his trailer. The guy was gone the next day. The lesson here–everyone is treated with respect on the set until they give a reason not to be.

"Bob didn't typically let things slide. If someone said something to him that he felt was disrespectful, he would rise up. I had a guest role on Bob's TV series, *American Dreamer*, I was in the next dressing room to Bob's rehearsing my lines. The walls were paper thin. He was talking to the director. They were going back and forth over something on the show. All of a sudden, I heard the director say, 'What difference does it make. It's only television.' I remember thinking, Oh boy, look out, you asked for it, pal." Heather says her ears are still ringing all these years later from Bob's explosive reaction.

"Bob had the ability to make people feel like they were life-long friends, but he could also intimidate the hell of them, too. He had a thing about teenagers wearing ball caps in our house. If they walked in wearing one, Oh God. He'd actually rip them off. He went out of his way to do that. Bob felt that wearing a hat in someone's else's home showed a lack of respect. I told him one day, 'Bob, these kids are scared to death of you,' and he said, 'Well, that's a good thing.' He could be a very imposing figure.

"Sometimes, it was difficult to know if he was teasing you or was serious with his comments. I knew the difference, but I saw him do it with other people and saw the look they gave him. I'd say, 'Honey, come on. Stop.'

"Bob was strong-willed, stubborn and head-strong. If I had an idea about something, there were times when I would go through the back door and make him think that it was his idea. He really didn't like to accompany me on some of my personal appearances for *The Sound of Music*. Of course, I wanted him with me. We were scheduled to appear in the U.K. Bob declined to go. Now, keep in mind Bob was an avid golfer and there are some gorgeous golf courses in Scotland and Ireland.

"I called my brother Neil, and asked, 'What is the most expensive golf course to play in Scotland?' He said, 'Gleneagles.' 'Not St. Andrew's?' I asked. 'No, that's old line,' he said. 'If you want a really expensive course, it's definitely Gleneagles.'[1] I thanked him, hung up and booked two rooms at Gleneagles. One for me, and one for my brother. Smiling, I thought to myself, when Bob finds out where we're headed it will be the last time he'd refuses to go with me. Actually, Bob and I usually went everywhere together. We didn't want to be apart for very long. He just didn't seem to enjoy going with me when it involved my *Sound of Music* appearances.

"Bob didn't really like the idea of any type of party for himself. I think he felt it was a bit embarrassing for him. Although, he had no qualms about throwing them for me. On my birthday or our anniversary, he would surprise me by getting a sitter for our kids and take me someplace really nice, like Chasen's.[2] A funny story about Chasen's. The first time Bob and I dined there, we had no idea they didn't accept credit cards. This

---

1 Gleneagles Golf Club in Perthshire Scotland is a golfers paradise, set among ridges and hollows with copious quantities of heather. When pro golfer Lee Trevino first played Gleneagles, he remarked, "If Heaven is as good as this, I sure hope they have some tee times left."

2 Chasen's, a popular celebrity restaurant on Beverly Boulevard, was a popular hang-out for scores of Hollywood luminaries from 1936 until it closed in 1995.

was before the kids came along and early in our careers. We had both been booked into jobs and wanted to celebrate at a really nice restaurant and Chasen's was it.

"Back in the day, the studio gave actors perdiem money for gas, food, etc. I just shoved mine in my purse and forgot about it. When we realized Chasen's didn't accept credit cards, we frantically were opening our little brown envelopes out of sight underneath the table so nobody would see us. This was the days before ATM machines. We had enough money between us, but were really sweating it out for awhile and, of course, laughed about it after.

"Bob loved being married and having kids. That is the essence of what he was all about, and what was most important to him. Acting was just something he did for a living. He never brought his work home.

"I called him my Eagle Scout because he was always thinking of fun things to do with the kids, whether it was water skiing, snow skiing, hiking. He grew up knowing how to do all those things. He taught Em how to fly-fish and Allie how to water ski. Our son Ryan became an expert skier and loved to surf, which Bob tried to do, so he could spend more time with Ry, but he nearly killed himself and that was the end of that adventure for him.

"Bob often said the worst part of his job as an actor were the creative fights. There are hurt feelings involved and I hate it, but I always feel better when it's over.'

"Another time, once again after he had a particularly bad day, He came home grumpy and broke a window in our kitchen with his fist. I glared at him and in no uncertain terms said, 'We don't act that way around here. Don't ever do that again,' and he never did.

"He was never conceited; in fact, Bob was the total opposite. He was a very humble guy, which I'm sure stemmed from his upbringing. Any accomplishment he was involved with he always gave credit to the other guy.

"I wouldn't describe him as being argumentative, but he wasn't one to hide his feelings. If someone crossed him or me, they were gone in the blink of an eye with not a moment of questioning, so he wasn't real forgiving. But he was very generous to his family and those in need.

"Bob was always watching out for me and our children.

"I remember when we were living in Andover [Mass], we had gone out for a bike ride. We were standing with our bikes on a crosswalk. A driver, who was going really fast, nearly hit Ry and Em. Bob was furious! He picked up his bicycle and threw it at the car and driver. I completely understood his anger. The A-hole driver could have killed our children, but I said to Bob, 'What if you had hit someone else with your bike and caused an accident.' He was very protective of us. Sometimes, even when I didn't need him to be.

"Another time, I was in extreme pain from an ulcerated hemorrhoid and Bob was driving me to the hospital. I could barely sit in the car and he is driving really slow, trying not to hit any bumps and doing his best not to jar me around too much. We were on our way to the UCLA Medical Center. Some guy behind us is honking his horn. Bob stops the car, gets out and goes back to the guy. He wanted to reach in the car and kill this person. This was during *Spenser: For Hire* time, and the guy recognizes Bob right away.

"'Jesus C,' he says to Bob. 'What have I done.' Later, I said, you don't ever want to do that–approach someone like that when you're angry–what if he had a gun? It's times like that when Bob would have a short fuse, but actually he had more patience than I did. Most of the time Bob was a pretty calm guy. His faith kept him together.

"If someone was disrespectful or if somebody did something that was unprofessional, Bob would call them out. He was not afraid of confrontation, at all. He wasn't afraid about going for it. He had no qualms about standing up to somebody and saying, 'Look, what you just did is not o.k.,' and he wouldn't avoid that. If something or someone bugged Bob, he was very vocal about it. I remember him standing in this little bathroom in the house we were remodeling in Andover. He was talking with our contractor, who hadn't done what he wanted. I heard, Bob say, 'I want a window right here!' And with that he took a hammer and smashed a hole in the wall.

"There was another incident involving our home in Deer Valley Utah. Bob wanted a fireplace built in the main room. He sent word to the construction guys, through his brother David, not to start the fireplace until he was home the next weekend. Bob wanted to make sure the rocks were exactly the ones he wanted and each one placed exactly where he wanted them to go. While he was away, the contractor insisted on starting the fireplace to give him [Bob] some idea of how it would look. This was a very bad idea. When Bob arrived home that weekend, he took one look at the fireplace and in his booming voice, yelling for all to hear, especially David, 'I told you I wanted to be here when this was built.' Bob took a pick-axe and tore it all out, every rock and threw it all over the banister. 'Now, tell them to come back, and we're gonna do it the way I said, we're gonna do it!' Bob wasn't one to hide his feelings," Heather says.

"When faced with a huge problem, whether it be financial, health related or whatever, and this also applies to problems our friends were dealing with, Bob was the type of person who wanted to 'own the problem. He wanted to take control and not leave it to somebody else to fix."

Heather says, "Bob realized early on when he was diagnosed with cancer that he needed to grab that bull by the horns and handle it himself, which he did. He was a kind soul, who felt compelled to hand advice out to others, whether they wanted it or not," she says, laughing. "I can't tell you how many people, since he's passed, have come up to me and said how much Bob helped them by saying the right thing, at the right time, and just when they needed to hear it. One lady, Lisa, a writer, had written a book and Bob witnessed that she was being disrespected by her significant other. Bob pulled her aside and said, 'You're better than that. You don't have to put up with that sh_ t.' She never forgot it and reminded me of it recently when we had lunch. I hear stories like that sort of thing every once in a while and it makes me feel so good.

"Back then, Bob did not have many male friends and I remember wishing he had had a few more, so I could have lunch with my girlfriends once in a while. Now, I'd be happy to spend ALL my time with *just* him," says Heather. "He always wanted to be with me. He loved to walk and talk. He never wore a headset when we were out walking or talking. He talked the entire way. I was headed out one day to a dance class and Bob said, 'Please, stay home and talk with me.' He loved just hanging out, or to go antiquing–just poking around. Bob was always thinking of ways to reach out and make his 'blue ski' thoughts, inventions and creations become reality. Some landed and some didn't," she readily admits. "One of his closest guy friends was Nashville physician, Dr. Dyrk Halstead. Bob and Dyrk used to go duck hunting and fly-fishing excursions together. They shared the love of the outdoors.

"They were really good buddies and were well-read intellectuals, and one reason why they went into the publishing business together. Bob's favorite book of all time was *The Wind in the Willows* by Nash Buckingham. Bob and Dyrk founded Beaver Dam press with their mutual admiration for the author with hopes of publishing old Buckingham novels. I think," Heather recalls, " they published two of his works."

Dyrk and Bob also had another business together. They developed Cyber Angel, which Heather describes as kind of the Lojack for lap tops. "It went under because," she says, "Dyrk got too big, too fast and got bought out by another company." Strangely enough, Bob was not a computer person. "You'd think because of his partnership in Cyber Angel he would be, but that was Dyrk's doing. Bob never would have come up with that one on his own.

"Dyrk remained a loyal friend. He flew out the second he found out about Bob's diagnosis and was there at the end. He was very helpful when Bob was first diagnosed with synovial cell sarcoma with info on the disease. He helped us do research on what was going on. He gave advice to our son when Ry was going into a residency program.

"Bob was a good listener in Milton Katselas's acting class. He was very engaging and very vocal, always adding different perspectives. He got to the point where he could actually teach the class. Bob was great at working with young talent and helped them whenever he could. I would go to him if I were auditioning for something and have him work with me. He was such a brilliant actor, and worked hard at his profession. He liked it and it afforded us a nice, comfortable lifestyle, but he *loved* his family more and couldn't wait to spend time with us.

"Bob's favorite movie role was probably playing Pittsburgh Steeler great, Rocky Bleier in *Fighting Back*. Having played high-school football and also at F.S.U., he was excited to star in a movie about a sport he loved. Growing up just 40 miles west of Pittsburgh, Bob was also a huge Steeler fan, so the role was very meaningful and important to him. He said the Rocky Bleier story[1] is one of the most inspiring in the history of sports. Little did Bob know at the time, that in just a few years, he would be living his own true-life *Fighting Back* story in his battle with cancer.

"I think Bob regretted not doing more major films," says Heather. "He felt like he was sort of stuck in TV land and even though he was suc-

1 Read more about the film Fighting Back and comments from Rocky Bleier in Ch. 9.

cessful doing television, he was upset that he was never able to make that jump. He once said to me in a bit of frustration, 'I'm more than just a 'good lookin' guy.' It wasn't said in a boastful way, he meant, he went deeper in his profession as an actor, and was not just another pretty boy. I believe Bob deserved more credit for his acting ability. He did have a few shots at major movies. To name two, *Endangered Species* and *Turk 182,* the latter presented him with the dubious distinction of a Razzie. Funny, critics called it some of Urich's best work. Go figure. However, his film attempts on the big screen were not big enough winners at the box office.

Was Bob jealous of the success of his friends who made it in film?

"Jealousy is born out of insecurity," says Heather. "Sometimes, I think he had a hard time comparing his success to other people's, like his friends Burt Reynolds and Tom Selleck. He wasn't jealous of those who made it on the big screen, and he never looked at himself as being better than them. However, I believe, he felt he was as good as them, and that's what he had a difficult time accepting. He struggled with it."

What was Bob's favorite TV role?

"That's a tough one," she replies. "He had fun doing *Vega$* and *Spenser* in Boston, and was pleased with his performance as Jake Spoon in *Lonesome Dove,* the TV western miniseries which drew praise from fans and critics alike, but I'd have to say his favorite series was *The Lazarus Man.*

"Bob always wanted to do a Western series of his own and jumped at the opportunity to be *The Lazarus Man.* In July of 1996, Bob had just completed his first season on the series when he learned he had cancer. That was the first time he was hit with the disease. During the next six years, the disease would come back three additional times. The first time, upon learning of his illness, the producers of *Lazarus Man* canceled the show. It broke Bob's heart. He loved doing *the Lazarus Man.*

"Most people remember Bob from television and his numerous roles–sixteen different series is a record which still stands to this day, but he was also a great stage actor as well. He loved doing theater. In the summer of 1977, Bob co-starred with Sally Field in *Bus Stop* at our friend Burt Reynolds' dinner-theater in Jupiter, Florida. Bob loved doing that play. Sally was wonderful and we had a great time hanging with she and her kids in Florida. It was pretty funky, because a train would go by during a specific spot in the play, EVERY night, and the cast would have to improvise until the train went by and the noise stopped.

"In the early 1980s, Bob and I worked together on stage in *Barefoot in the Park* on the Kenley Players Circuit in Ohio," says Heather. "It was lots of fun. [See photo] We also appeared together at Burt Reynolds' dinner theater in Jupiter Florida in *The Hasty Heart*, which we also performed in Washington [D.C.] at the Kennedy Center.

"Burt is a wonderful director and even though he didn't direct the play *Hasty Heart,* he produced it. Whenever we had problems, Burt would help us through the confusion. One evening following our performance at the Kennedy Center, President Ronald Reagan and Nancy came backstage to meet us. During his acting years, the President had played a Yank in the film version. It was exciting and an honor for Bob and me to meet them. [see photo]

"Before Bob passed, he got to live one of his dreams by appearing on Broadway. He starred as Billy Flynn in *Chicago*, the musical. As fate would have it, Bob began his acting career on stage in Chicago in *the Rainmaker* and ended on stage in the musical, *Chicago."*

Heather always felt that Bob would have been a wonderful director, but he never did direct anything. "I was always prodding him, but he would tell me, 'Heather, I don't want to be the first one on the set and the last one to leave.' Bob did produce the film, *Miracle on the 17th Green* with Chris O'Donnell. He bought the rights to the book and pitched it to the network and they bought the idea. Bob was really good at pitching," she says.

"He enjoyed guest hosting daytime TV talk shows, and turned down being the regular host on *Good Morning America* when David Hartman left. He was a regular fixture on late night television as a guest on Johnny Carson, Jay Leno, David Letterman, all the talk shows. Bob filled in for Regis Philbin on *Regis & Cathy Live.* He got along great with Cathy. He figured out her MO rather quickly. 'She is pretty strong-willed,' he said, 'so, itwas really important to give her *her* space, don't try to compete with her or control her, just let her go.' Early in his career, Bob co-hosted with Mike Douglas for an entire week."

What do you think Bob would be doing today?

"If Bob had lived he would have gone on to do all kinds of things. He was always reinventing himself, and coming up with all sorts of things, not just acting. One time he was being courted as the host on *Good Morning America*. I don't know what type of offer was put on the table, but I do know he was being courted. It would have been a perfect fit for him. He was well read and so good with people.

"*National Geographic* wanted Bob exclusively to be their on-air commentator. He didn't want to do that because he still wanted to act. He couldn't continue acting, if he exclusively signed to do either program. He turned them both down, because acting is something he loved to do more than anything else as a profession. Bob also did a pilot for a TV talk show. I think for Disney. It was taped over three days at a small theater in North Hollywood. They took segments and made one show. Bob's brother Tom was the announcer. The opening showed a person knocking on the doors of many stars including Tom Selleck, Jo Anne Worley, William Shatner and others. They would slam the door with comments like, 'Why would I want to be on a show with *him*!' or 'NO!' or, 'Who the hell is Robert Urich?' It was very funny. There was a segment called, 'Bob Does Your Job.' They shot it at Bob's Big Boy, a hamburger stand. There were plans to have him pilot a Riverboat on the Ohio River and other things. There was a band and Bob even got to sing. He had quite the voice. Another funny segment, on his projected TV Talk Show, showed clips of him kissing girls 5 or 6 times and clips of him getting punched by different guys. His comment to the audience, 'Everyone is asking me why I'm doing this show. Well, because I was getting tired of this [clip of him being punched].' And my wife, Heather was getting tired of this [clip of him kissing a girl].' The audience loved it. Bob came across as warm, charming and sincere. One of his strong suits was his wit and self-deprecating humor. The producer of the pilot show had been in news and cut out all the entertaining and funny stuff. It didn't sell and Bob was sorry it didn't. He was a natural talk show personality."

Thinking back when she and Bob first met, Heather says, "I initially met Bob through our mutual friend, David Hayward, who was in our acting class. During a break, I was walking to the bathroom and David was in the hallway talking to Bob. He said, 'Hey, Heather, this is Bob...Bob this is Heather.' I said, 'Hi' and that was it and went on my way. Little did I know the guy I said hi to, and continued on my way, was to be the love of my life. Funny thing, later, Bob and I both remembered that fleeting moment."

If Bob were with us today, she says, "he would have been wonderful in character roles. Maybe doing more Broadway shows, like *Man of La*

Mancha or *Music Man*. He'd love it. Then again, maybe he wouldn't be acting at all. He was so gifted and talented, it's really hard to say what Bob would be doing today. A couple of things I do know. For one, he'd be spending as much time as possible at his favorite place to be with his family, our lake-side cottage in Canada. That's where he could kick back, relax, be himself away from the spotlight, enjoying an occasional cigar by our fire pit. And, best of all, no one would bother him. You may spot him having dinner at Angeline's, our favorite restaurant in Bloomfield, the next town over, or at Sunday Mass at St. Gregory's Church in Picton. And, if you're an early riser, you may even spot Bob casting out in the cat tails on West Lake, coffee cup in one hand, fishing rod in the other. Yes, it's difficult to say what Bob would be doing today, but as Heather enthusiastically points out, "one thing I do know, whatever he did…he would be great at it."

Just before Bob passed, Heather says, "He told me that everything I've ever said to him he had taken to heart and learned from my wisdom. Funny, I always thought he was so much more wiser than myself, and come to find out he felt the same way."

November 2017

Bob has been gone for 15 years and Heather is still missing him. . .so much. Some family members say, Bob was the glue which kept everything together and that things seemed to fall apart after he died, including Heather's closet drinking, which she kept hidden from nearly everyone, until the very end. Having worked with her on the story of Bob's life exclusively via e-mail and with phone calls, for nearly four years, I was completely in the dark that she had a drinking problem. Perhaps, it's because we always set a day and time in advance of when I would call. I only recall once, in the evening, when we spoke that she was slurring her words slightly. Not being judgmental, I thought she probably enjoys a glass of wine at night. I did make a promise to myself, not to call her again in the evening with any questions about Bob for the book. Only when she was hospitalized, at the end of her life, did I first I learn of Heather's drinking problem. Evidently, her day would begin with vodka and end with wine. Sadly, it had been going on for quite some time. Some say as long as four or five years. When family or friends would speak to her about her excessive drinking, like so many alcoholics, and speaking from first-hand knowledge, she simply wouldn't listen. Her daughter

Emily tried to intervene which resulted in her mom getting angry and not speaking to her for weeks.

I may not have been aware of Heather's drinking problem, but one thing I do know is how much she missed Bob. She told me so nearly every time we talked, and we chatted frequently about Bob for the book.

Therefore, and in no way making excuses for her alcohol abuse, I can empathize with her need to escape the harsh realities of life without him. Bob and Heather's love for each other was truly special. She missed him so much and suffered from a broken heart for fifteen agonizing years. Try as she may to move on with her life, supported by loving family and friends, her broken heart just wouldn't cooperate.

***

In November 2017, just a few weeks before she was diagnosed with inoperable brain cancer and one month before her own passing, Heather sent me the following e-mail...

"It's so difficult for me to accept the fact that Bob's gone. He was so strong in every way. I never thought anything would ever be able to bring him down. I miss him."

Bob & Heather were always hugging 1970's.

Bob & Heather kissing – daughter Em on left–Christmas 1995

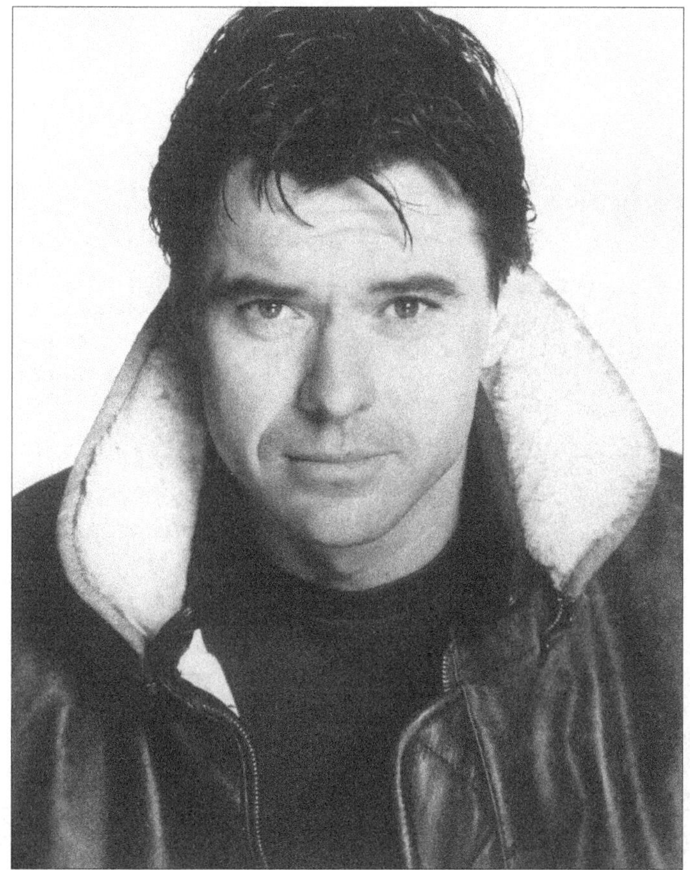

Heather's fave head shot of her Bob.

Bob golfing (one of his passions) in So. Africa.

Bob with friend & long-time agent Merritt Blake- late 70's.

Ryan & Emily as teens outside family home in Utah

Bob & Heather skiing outside their Park City Utah home.

Bob hosting pilot for his proposed TV talk show.

Bob loved the water. Here he is on right scuba diving for Nat'l Geo *episode in Cayman Islands.*

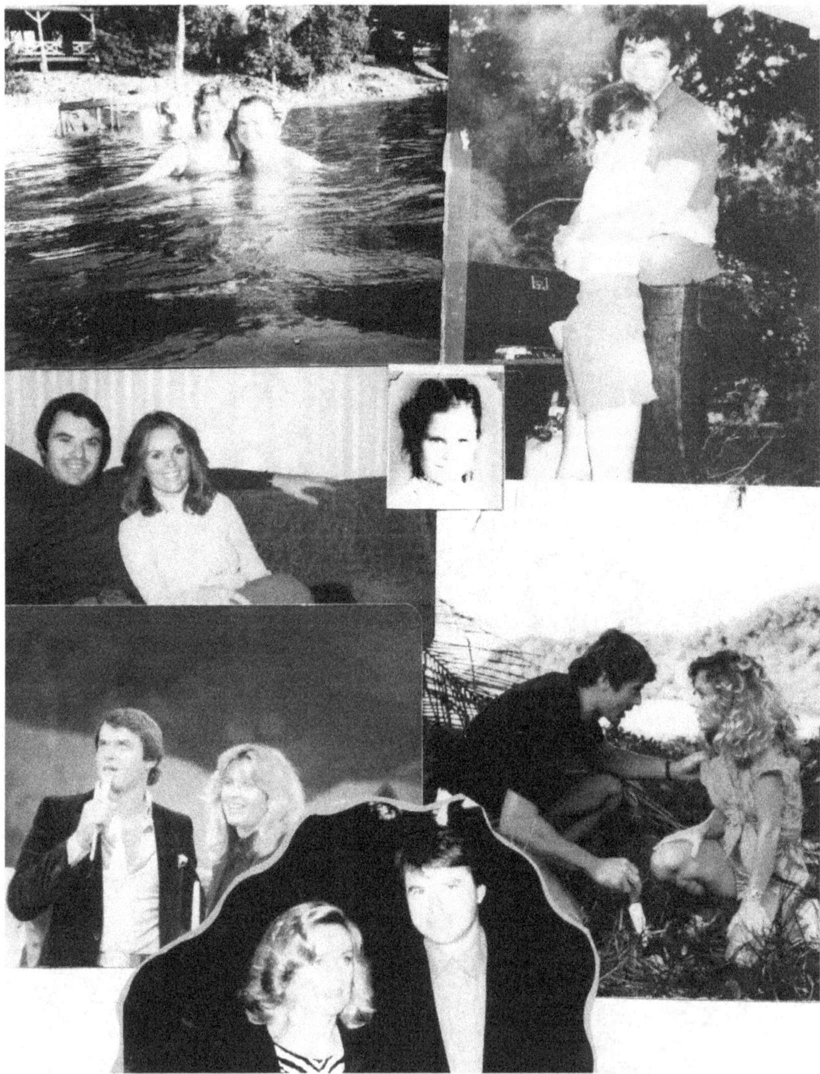

Bob & Heather 'always and forever' love birds. Top left, swimming in front of their cottage West Lake summer 2001–the year before he passed; Top right, they were always in hug mode; Left center, together at Christmas 1975; small insert Heather age 3 yrs; Lower left: Bob holding mic hosting Grand Ole Opry. He brought Heather on stage because it was their first wedding anniversary; Lower right: scene from Bob's TV series Gavilan. Heather was a guest star on this 1982 episode filmed in the Virgin Islands; Bottom center: Bob & Heather at his 26th class reunion from Toronto Ohio, graduating Class of 1964.

Heather relaxin' on hammock at her home on West Lake, summer of 2017. No one including me (author) ever thought she would be gone in just 4 months. Photo courtesy Christa Bindokat Williamson.

Chapter 28

Bob's Diagnosis
His Life living with Cancer
THE WILL to WIN & SURVIVE

"Charge forward with hope in your heart."

Bob always played to win, regardless of whatever he attempted, Sports, acting, and particularly his six-year-long battle with cancer...

In July of 1996, Bob had just completed his first season on the TV series he loved, *The Lazarus Man,* when he first learned he had cancer.

Bob had been diagnosed with synovial cell sarcoma, a rare form of cancer that attacks the soft tissue of the body. Less than 800 cases are diagnosed yearly worldwide.[1] Being a stand-up guy and straight-shooter, he told the producers of his cancer. Upon hearing the news, they fired him. Bob was devastated and hurt. Heather admits being angry. "Canceling the show broke his heart. I was furious. They didn't even ask how he planned to undergo treatment, and if he was going to continue working. He never

---

1 Considering how rare synovial cell sarcoma is, with less than 800 cases diagnosed yearly from all over the world, three other people, in addition to Bob, were diagnosed with this rare cancer in the Tri-State area, all within a 50 mile radius of Toronto, Ohio [Ohio, W.VA and PA] where Bob grew up. The author asked Dr. Charles Forscher of Cedars Sinai, one of the doctors who treated Bob for his illness to comment on the subject. His reply, in February 2016...

"It is interesting that 3 synovial sarcomas are seen in a small town [area]. There are no specific environmental risk factors for synovial sarcoma, but there is an increased risk for development of soft tissue sarcomas in general with exposure to herbicides and pesticides. If this area of Ohio is a farming community, there might be some connection." Bob's older brother, Tom says, "Toronto, Ohio was not a farming community but within 20 miles there were farms. Everyone had a victory garden, as they were known after WWII. I can remember my dad spraying powder on his tomato and green bean plants to keep the bugs away. Don't know if it was pesticides."

said he couldn't perform, and never expected them to act the way they did. But Bob didn't want to go after them, saying, "It's in the past."[1]

He continued working while undergoing treatment for his illness and became an advocate for finding a cure for cancer. Along the way, he won an award from the John Wayne Cancer Institute and also received the Gilda Radner Courage Award. "It was around that time," says Heather, "that Bob and I founded the Urich Fund to raise money for cancer research."

"Bob was both a gladiator and courageous," says Heather, "especially with the cancer monster bearing down on him. He was gallant and valiant, always the knight in shining armor on a white horse. I'm sure he had fears, but tried his best to rise above them. He never allowed himself to be a victim and was always in control. He was pretty scared of that cancer but was so courageous in his battle with it. I only saw him lose it once and that was when he first received the devastating news. Bob describes that moment in his journal as, 'the lowest point of my life.' Once he was over the initial shock of it, he took a deep breath and said… 'OK, now it's time to go to war.'"

Of course, *The National Enquirer* received the information first. "They had Bob with six weeks to live on the front cover. We were fielding calls from everyone we've ever known."

Heather remembers, "Our son, Ryan was away on a National Outdoor Leadership school trip on the Wind River Range in Wyoming. He had been gone for a month and was scheduled to come down from the mountain in a couple of days. There is no communication between students and parents while they are up there.

Emily, our daughter, was in summer school at Phillips Academy in Andover, Mass. We had lived in the town of Andover when Bob was filming the TV series *Spenser: For Hire* and still had friends there. I was able to get hold of Em's first grade teacher and now longtime friend, Sister Kathleen Leary. She kindly went over to be with Em when I phoned her with the news. Sister Kathleen's arms around Em would be my arms.

"I envisioned Ryan coming down from the mountain and being greeted with the front page of the *Enquirer*, or even being greeted by someone who had seen the front cover. I flew to our home in Park City [Utah] and

1 Eventually, the Urich's filed a lawsuit and were happy with the results. You can read more about the Urich-Castle Rock lawsuit in Chapter 26.

the next day got in my car and drove to Lander, Wyoming. I sat on the trail head waiting all day with a book to keep me company, actually to keep me sane. I wasn't exactly sure when he would emerge.

"Hours later, he came trudging down with his backpack, not having showered or shaved for a month. I was the last person he expected to see. He stopped in his tracks and started to back up, instinctively knowing something was very wrong. There was a look of horror in my child's eyes. I managed to put my arms around him all the while saying, 'It's OK, it's OK. . .' I don't remember the words I used to tell him, but made a beeline to the nearest pay phone to call Bob. Our son needed to hear his dad's strong voice. . .to be reassured. Whatever was said on the other end of the phone line made Ryan believe that our knight in shining armor will never be taken from us.

"Back in California, we had rented a small bungalow close to the hospital, so Bob could receive treatment at Cedars Cancer Center. It was a former home of Dudley Moore's in Toluca Lake. It was a quaint little place covered with climbing roses with a pool out back. Swimming was a form of therapy for Bob, especially during this time. He was a water baby. Can I say that I was actually sick of the room service menu at the Bel Air Hotel where we had been staying, awaiting Bob's biopsy report. How is it possible to dislike anything about that grand hotel?

"Emily flew in from Andover," recalls Heather. "I picked her up at the airport and we headed to the little cottage we were renting on Navajo Ave. Bob would be finished with his treatment for the day and join us there. Emily adamantly declared she needed to go straight to where her dad was.

"She wanted to see him and wrap her arms around him. So, reluctantly, I drove her to the basement at Cedars. We arrived towards the end of the cycle. When one is undergoing chemotherapy, at least the kind of chemo that Bob was being administered, one is brought to the brink of death. . .only to be revived again so the cycle can begin a new.

"Emmy walked in at the end of the first cycle and it was not a pretty sight. She entered her daddy's cubical to see him hooked up to all sorts of machines, wires everywhere. His skin tone was of a waken alien color. He still had hair but the texture had changed. Emmy fell into her daddy and sobbed and sobbed. She was fifteen.

***

"One day, we were driving home, after he had gone through the first chemotherapy," says Heather. "We were stopped at a crosswalk in Thousand Oaks. There was this old guy–he looked to be about 90–walking across the cross walk. He had a walker. He would walk 2 steps, pause and walk another 2 steps and so on. We sat there and watched him go across the cross walk so slowly. Eventually he made it to the other side. Bob never took his eyes off him and said with a sigh, 'I envy him.'

"In 1998, Bob was declared 'cancer free' and became the national spokesperson for the American Cancer Society. He enjoyed traveling all over the country with his numerous speaking engagements, speaking to those who were also trying to cope with catastrophic illness. They had to provide him with a private jet, because sometimes, there was no way he could make it from one venue to another in time. Bob enjoyed telling audiences, 'it was part of my deal I made with God to spread the word that cancer is survivable, that this notion of being cancer free is one that you can achieve.'"

Bob became known for 'Preaching the Gospel of Survival.' He always made time for those who came up to him following his talk to chat or have their photo taken with him.

"I was at one of his speeches," says a cancer survivor. "I was too shy to talk to him, so I just stood off to the side and watched how he interacted with his fans. He treated everyone with kindness and asked how they were feeling. I was impressed with the man."

Bob was a giving person. He donated the $125,000 he won by appearing on the TV show *Who Wants to be a Millionaire* to cancer research.

Heather recalls, ""When Bob was going through chemo, he acquired some medicinal pot. I laughed and blurted out, 'well, you're not doing that by yourself.'"

***

During the filming of *The Love Boat* [98-99], the insidious lump paid a return visit. It was localized and was in the same spot as the first one. "This time I could feel it," Heather says. The doctors decided to surgically remove it and forgo any other treatment. "If we hadn't been in a haze of denial, we might have interpreted that as a portent of doom. The chosen physician was Dr. Frederick Eilber at UCLA Medical Center. He was a highly regarded surgical oncologist. We met with him at UCLA several times before the surgery.

"I had Allison with me during one of our last meetings. She was five months old and in a little carrier basinet. When Dr. Eilber saw the baby, there was a look of astonishment, mixed with guarded horror. I knew," says Heather. "No words were exchanged. What are these people thinking was written all over his face. I look back on that fleeting moment when I knew. I dismissed the truth with a flash of anger. This doctor had penetrated my world of denial for an instant. How dare he?"

"After the surgery, life and *The Love Boat* continued. Bob took a couple of days off and then went right back to the set with blood dripping down his leg. We started plans to look for a place to buy," says Heather. "And decided instead to build out in Lake Sherwood, a golf community in Thousand Oaks. Designing a house on a golf course was a dream come true for Bob and he was certainly determined to live out his dreams after being given a second chance at life.

"*The Love Boat* survived for a season and then was docked for good. No worries. . .there will always be something around the corner. Bob had always dreamed of doing a musical on Broadway. Just before he entered into *Lazarus Man* there had been talk of a revival of *Man of La Mancha*. Bob obtained the score and was working with a coach when word came that *the Lazarus Man* TV series had been picked up. Now was the perfect opportunity. Ryan and Emily were now away at college and protected from the concern hanging over our heads, and little Allison wasn't in school yet. Bob never wanted to take off and be away from them for the kind of time commitment a Broadway show would demand. He was offered the role of Billy Flynn in the revival of *Chicago*. We would travel all over the country and end up on Broadway for 8 weeks. Meanwhile, our house at Sherwood would be built and finished by the time the tour ended.

"The thing I loved about Bob being in *Chicago* was not just his performance of course, but knowing him as well as I did, there was this twinkle in his eyes the entire time, almost as if to say, 'Hey, look at me. Look at what I'm doing.' You could see how much he enjoyed doing it.

Sandy Duncan co-starred with Bob in *Chicago* at the Schubert.

"Sandy knew Bob could sing and dance, but also realized how nervous he was before their opening night performance. She took him aside and said, 'Look Bob, if the jokes don't go over as you think they should, or if you flub a line, don't worry. The theater is filled tonight with Japanese tourists and they won't understand a word.'

"As it happened, Bob didn't flub a line or miss a beat and for good reason: he'd been singing since he was a kid and had been taking dancing lessons; more proof that Bob was constantly re-inventing himself and to do what it takes to improve his performance.

"Sometime during the tour, around Detroit, he discovered another lump. Won't this insidious thing ever go away! It was in the same spot as before, in his scrotum. Still isolated. A small marble-sized lump. So small. After researching around, we discovered the amazing resource of the University of Michigan Comprehensive Cancer Center in Ann Arbor. They claimed to be at the forefront of research when it came to synovial cell sarcoma. The professionals determined it would be all right for Bob to finish his tour before starting treatment. They recommended the repeat of chemotherapy followed by radiation treatments. We had been in New York City for a number of weeks when halfway through the Broadway run, we realized his tumor was growing at an unacceptable rate. After conferring with the doctors in Michigan and the producers of the show, it was decided the treatment couldn't wait and Bob had to bow out of the run.

"The University of Michigan Comprehensive Cancer Center had a state of the art radiation machine, a new technology. Off Bob went to Ann Arbor, where he stayed with our friend, Janet Roth and her family.[1]

He went through three weeks[2] of constant radiation after a grueling repeat of chemotherapy. Bob described the experience this way, "A doctor takes a hammer to your toes and says, 'I know that really hurt, but I'm going to have to do it again.'"

When someone is undergoing treatment for cancer that person doesn't necessarily curl up in a fetal position in some dark room somewhere. People who undergo treatment can still be productive members of society. They can work, raise their kids and live pretty normal lives. "The first time Bob's hair started to fall out," says Heather, "he decided to shave it off right away. Our son, Ryan got the clippers and after a shared beer he shaved his dad's head.

"Bob never stopped working the entire time he was going through treatment. This is what I what I mean, about him being a gladiator and

---

1 Read more about Bob's stay with the Roth family in Chapter 29- Bob's final days.

2 In Chapter 29, Bob recalls the treatment lasted for 6 weeks.

so courageous. 'Give me the ball,'" he'd tell Heather. "'I can do this.' Bob would just slap on a wig and off he'd go! Sometimes, he wouldn't wear the wig. He'd just be bald in whatever program it was. Granted there were times when, during a chemo treatment, he felt as though he had swallowed pool chemicals, or eaten a rotten egg sandwich. But, remember, we had 'you will beat this' card in our hip pocket. I think Bob thought it was a small price to pay in order to live.

"Our house in Lake Sherwood was finished. We decided to have the chemotherapy treatments at Cedars-Sinai in LA., so we could move into the house," says Heather. "We moved in with little Alli, who was almost two at the time. The reoccurrence of Bob's cancer was not broadcast all over CNN, like before. This time the ordeal was on a need to know basis. Hollywood wants their leading men to be strong and tough." A diagnosis is a sign of weakness. At least it appears to be that way in show biz circles. It's almost acceptable to have a drug problem and be out of rehab. Don't worry, we will shut down production until you are out of jail. Not so with cancer.

"Bob would have treatments in the middle of the night so Alli wouldn't know he was gone. She had no concept of cancer. Daddy is just off to work. He has a dragon to slay."

[**Bold typed words** are Robert Urich's, taken directly from his journal.]

There is no better example of Bob's wit and story-telling ability then his encounter with a snake...and in his own backyard in Sherwood, no less...

This morning I woke up and found a rattlesnake on my back porch. Well, not actually on the back porch. It was curled up in a cozy corner of the brick patio, down by the barbecue, close enough to being on the porch–you get the picture. Now perhaps seeing a snake should not phase a boy who was raised on the flood plain of the Ohio River. As boys we tramped around all day in grass well over our heads with nothing but blue jeans and tennis shoes between us and the venomous water moccasins and copperheads, but this was the first time I'd seen a great western diamondback rattlesnake close up!

It was my turn to get up with baby Allison, then twenty-six months old. She was my itsy bitsy, blue-eyed blonde Marilyn Monroe. A baby of infinite splendor, conceived in another galaxy where people smile all day long and sport perfect dispositions."

Bob and Alli were out on their early morning rounds, outside at 6:00am, up the driveway to get the newspaper, pick a weed or two, and water the geraniums. She ran ahead of her daddy, around the side of the house, scampering through the wet grass.

"I called her to stop, to wait for daddy, as I stepped up and over the short wall that separates the rest of the patio area from the grassy slope that drops down sharply to the lower yard. Something distracted her for a moment. I moved ahead to begin putting the cover over the barbecue, having let it cool down from the night before. When I looked down, eighteen inches away from the right cuff of my pants was a snake. I swooped up the baby in one movement and raced in the house and up the front staircase, my feet barely landing as I came crashing into our bedroom, depositing her on the bed and announcing to my half-asleep wife that there was a rattlesnake on the porch. Well, you know, not on the porch, but on the patio down by the barbecue." Bob headed back down the stairs, a chorus of "Oh, my Gods" echoing down the hall as he considers the ramifications of being bitten by a rattlesnake.

"Just two nights earlier I had completed the second major chemotherapy course during the most recent and hopefully, final phase of my cancer treatment. It consists of poison being pumped non-stop into your heart for distribution throughout the rest of your body, all the while being monitored to make sure your kidneys continue to function properly. It's really a pharmaceutical race to the death. The chemo kills all the cells in your body, good and bad. The cancer cells, which inherently receive the chemo at an accelerated rate, quite simply die faster than the good ones. This involves eighteen hours of constant infusion by a pump about the size of a walkman that you wear around your waist, followed by a visit to the hospital for four to six more hours of fluids and anti-nausea medicine. All things considered, it seemed to be prudent to avoid the venom of a poisonous snake."

The guy who installed Bob's TV cable told him a friend of his, a big guy, six-feet-two, 240 pounds was reaching down to open a sprinkler valve the other day and got bit by a snake that uncannily matches the color description of the one on his patio. The bite put the guy in the hospital for four days. Bob listens to the story and shudders to think of what a poisonous snake bite could do to a two year old.

"Cautiously, I move out the back door, checking in all directions lest the beast had moved. There he lay where I had left him, in a comfortable ball, oblivious to the histrionics he had created. Now my reaction, or over-reaction, to the presence of this snake can only be fully understood in the vernacular context of the Bible. I was raised in a strict Catholic family and I had heard many times the story of the snake in the garden, and how the snake in the garden was evil. The snake was, in fact, Satan and therefore was worthy of our loathing and fear."

An interesting facet of Bob's career was his involvement with the National Geographic Society as host of their Emmy award-winning programs, *Explorer* and *On Assignment* for several years. **"I traveled from the paw of the Sphinx on the Giza plateau in Egypt to the rain forests of Central America which incidentally has more than its share of venomous snakes. I've learned that it's not scientifically proper to anthropomorphous animals to give them human traits and characteristics. After all, it's just a rattlesnake sleeping on my back porch, the warmth of the sun collecting in those bricks helps this new-born reptile to regulate its body heat. They're really quite docile, I've since discovered and strike only when disturbed, like perhaps when you happen to step on one in your pajamas."**

As if out of nowhere, Jorge materializes. He has been working on the irrigation system in the new yard and offers, in the most nonplussed manner, to dispose of the snake. A brief exchange in Spanish and one of his men disappears and returns promptly with a bamboo pole. Bob offers a shovel with a nice, narrow sharp end.

"He says he has only seen and used such a shovel as mine in central Mexico where he is from. It is indeed a very fine shovel. I ask him if he has ever used one to take the head off a monster. He grins and moves towards the task at hand as I hurry back indoors and the relative safety of the kitchen."

Bob looks up from pouring his first cup of coffee, and through the screen door, hears Jorge say something in Spanish. They share a laugh and Jorge's man heads down under the oaks and the stone path that leads away from the house.

"I can see the soft white underbelly of the snake as it dangles lifelessly at the end of my 'very fine' shovel. I feel no remorse. The serpent is dead."

Later that morning, Bob calls to Don Rowe across the backyard fence. Don's the construction foreman on the house they're building next door, and he did a fine job of building the Urich home, too. He's a lanky cowboy from East Texas with a slow drawl.

"Hey Don, what do you tell new residents, you know folks like us who've just moved in, I mean what do you tell them about rattle snakes?" Don looks at his boots and kicks softly into the dirt. A grin begins to form on his face. He's heard this question before. 'I tell' em, they live in the country now. Surrounded by the Santa Monica Conservatory in the Conejo Valley and you now live adjacent to thousands of acres of wilderness.'"

Bob had seen deer in the early twilight, eating grass under the large oak across the street, and heard the shrill howling of coyote packs in the hills as they closed in on their prey late at night. There's also plenty of skunk, raccoons and lots of rabbits. **"I've also seen bobcats and have heard locals talk about an occasional mountain lion sighting, but right now, I wanted the lowdown on rattlesnakes.**

"Where was he?" Don asked.

"Right here in the corner by the barbecue," I said. "I almost stepped on him!"

"Good thing you didn't," Don answered, "That could ruin your day. The little ones don't know how to regulate their venom yet, so they just give you all they got. Caught a six-footer over on lot fifty-four the other day. The word 'caught' stopped me. It suggests an intention to catch a rattlesnake–an idea that has always escaped me, I had done the story of the rattlesnake round-up in Sweet Water, Texas for National Geographic on countless occasions. They were constantly recycling their stories and the one about cowhands in pick-up trucks.

"How did you catch them Don," I asked.

"Just got a stick behind his head and picked em' up and threw him up on the hillside in the brush."

Bob says he asked the next question as honestly as he could.

"Don, when you throw a rattlesnake, which end do you let go first? Anything other than split scone timing seems like it could be an invitation to disaster. Could it be as difficult as hitting a golf ball 300 plus yards down the center of the fairway? It takes a tremendous amount of eye-hand coordination to accomplish such a feat. Some say hitting

a baseball traveling 97 miles per hour as it travels some sixty feet from the pitcher's mound to home-plate is the most difficult task in all of sports. But, for my money, it's throwing a rattlesnake and letting go of the head and tail at exactly the same time."

"Don looked at his boots again and started to laugh.

"Gotta go, Bob, be careful of those rattlers.

He headed back up the hill to his pick-up truck, and I could hear him laughing as he repeated the question to himself, "Which end do you let go first?" He got to his truck before he turned and yelled back to me.

"You know, Bob, some people think it's good luck to see a snake like that."

"Who Don," I yelled back.

"Who?" He laughed some more, got in his truck and drove away."

For, if truth be told, I am afraid of snakes–even the non poisonous varieties, the same way I am now afraid of cancer. I wasn't always afraid. When the doctors first told me of this virulent sarcoma they said that I had a better chance of winning the lotto than getting this rare cancer. Maybe eight cases a year in the United States. That's out of one-point-four million diagnoses of all kinds of cancer in this country a year. I've always been such a lucky guy.

Dr. Gerald Rosen of Oncology at Cedars-Sinai Medical Center described it like this:

"Bob, on a scale of one to four, one being a smoldering little fire and four being a raging forest fire, this is a four. This fire is raging throughout your body and we have to stop it now." I wasn't afraid at first, because his prognosis was good. If we executed the course of treatment, radiation, surgery and chemotherapy, there was a good chance we'd never see it again.

Then came appearances with Larry King Live on CNN and Diane Sawyer's Dateline NBC. I felt like an imposter when they talked of the integrity and courage with which I was handling this event and how I must be an inspiration to millions of Americans who are now currently fighting this dreaded disease. I knew we would treat this disease and that it would go away never to return.

That was before it came back again... and again...and again, and now for the fourth time. That was before the additional radiation therapy at

the University of Michigan and four more surgeries, and still more chemotherapy after which my hair fell out again.

I no longer feel like an imposter."

"That night in bed I promise my wife that everything is going to be alright, that this is the end of it.

Later, she falls asleep in my arms and I brush a curl of hair from her forehead and pray to God that I'll be able to keep my promise.

Finally, I fall asleep. . .and dream of snakes.

Well, you know, some say, it's good luck.

***

When Bob was first diagnosed, Heather says she wasn't afraid, "Not then anyway, because his prognosis was good. We were told Cedars was at the forefront when it came to synovial cell sarcoma research. Dr. Gerald Rosen, MD was one of the first guys we saw. Dr. Rosen is one of the most respected physicians in his field.

"I credit him and his wisdom, along with other cancer specialists, for adding a few years to my husband's life. He said some things that put our rattled nerves at ease a bit. One of the first things he asked us was, 'Were we scared?' 'Uh. . .YAH!'

"He told us the prescriptive protocol he recommended was very aggressive because Bob's cancer was *very* aggressive. On a scale of one to five, Bob was a stage four, a raging forest fire. However, if he followed the plan. . .he would beat this. Those were Gerald Rosen's very words. In hindsight was he giving us hope that would instill strength?

"There are opposing opinions regarding how much a patient should be told regarding their chances of survival when facing a serious illness which sometimes is terminal. Some physicians believe the less the patient understands the odds, the more they will fight to live. Others believe the patient has the right to know everything. . .including how much time is left. I've searched my soul and asked again and again the same question, almost pleadingly says Heather, 'Why didn't they let us know what the chances were? How would that information change the outcome?' He might have died at home surrounded by loved ones instead of clinging to life on a ventilator in a strange hospital. The information may have given us time to say goodbye. Ultimately, I don't think Bob wanted to say goodbye. He always believed he could beat his illness.

"Were we given false hope? I don't know. What I do know," says Heather, "we left that doctor's office that day with *Robert* feeling like an imposter. Everyone was in a state of alarm. . .friends, family, media. But, we were armed with, 'If you do what I ask you to do, you will beat this.'"

Author's note: in our many hours of conversations and numerous e-mails, to the best of my recollection, this was the only time Heather ever referred to Bob as "Robert," at least in conversing or writing me.

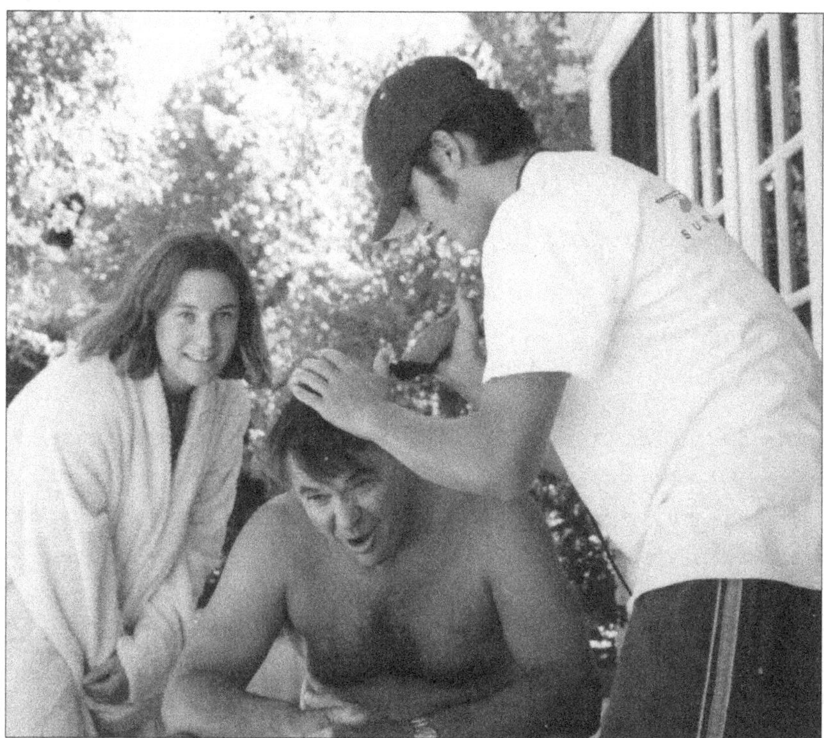

Bob's son Ryan shaving his dad's head after chemo. Em lending moral support. This was Bob's first round of chemo in 1996.

Bob backstage during his starring role in Chicago-The Musical. *Pictured here with fellow actor Ray Bokhour*

Chapter 29

Bob's Final Days
Thinking back over his 6 year long battle with cancer
His Will to Live

Robert Urich didn't want to die. He always thought he could beat his cancer. "I'm not going anywhere," he would tell his adoring wife, Heather. "Do everything you can to keep me alive," he urged her. "Try everything possible, every new treatment!" He did NOT want to leave her and their children.

"Bob kept telling me he wasn't going any where," said Heather, "that he was going to be fine. I'm not stupid. He was NOT fine. I could see it. He was in bed and looking horrible. It was like this fast-forward photography where he was aging before my very eyes. He slowly got up. His shoulders were slumped and he was kind of shuffling around. The doctors weren't saying anything to me, and I said to Bob, 'Please be honest with me. What's going on here?' He looked at me and put his finger in my face, and said, 'I am NOT going anywhere!' I kinda snapped a little and said, 'O.K., if you're fine and NOT going anywhere, then put your shoulders back and step up the pace! What protocol is gonna reverse what I'm seeing and what's happening before my very eyes?' That's when I left the room and slammed the door. That was a no-no. Before, we got married, we promised each other never to get up and leave in the middle of an argument and no slamming doors. I wasn't mad at him, but at the situation. I felt bad about the incident and so did he. It was a stressful time. It didn't help that I didn't know what was going on and he wouldn't tell me."

A life-threatening health issue can be part of coping with life. However, there is a danger in not sharing the illness with those who love you. If you don't share your troubles and concern, you really aren't being fair with those who love you. After all, shouldn't they be given a chance to shower you with all the love and care you deserve? How can they possibly do that if they don't know what's going on? For reasons known only to himself, Bob kept his own feelings about the seriousness of his disease to himself. Perhaps, he didn't want his wife and family to worry about him. One thing is for sure, he never wanted to be labeled a victim. "Bob never complained or talked about his illness," insists Heather. "He never painted himself as a victim. He never complained and would always find humor in every aspect of it [his illness]. Bob was a gladiator."

In researching his life story, a few facts have surfaced that leave little doubt that Bob may have known he was terminal. To begin with, his rare type of cancer kept coming back and in the same spot. Another point was his deteriorating physical appearance, which did little to convince others that he was healthy; his once handsome face was now pale, thin and drawn; some observers refer to it as a 'death mask.' Bob also continued losing weight and dropped nearly forty pounds. He was down from his usual weight of around 218 on his 6 foot-2 frame to 170. Not since his college football playing days at Florida State had he weighed 170. In February, two months before he passed, Bob told Heather that he wanted to go to Hawaii *one last time* before he died. He also informed her and their son Ryan of his wish to be cremated. If Bob truly believed he could 'beat' his cancer, why would he mention his desire to be cremated? Of course, this is all conjecture, but it does make one wonder if Bob was more concerned about his illness and dying than he let on.

Bob's friend, Dr. Dyrk Halstead feels Bob always thought he could beat the cancer. "He was the kind of guy you just couldn't keep down. And after surgery and chemo and going five years being cancer-free, he felt he had overcome the odds."

In an odd way, Bob believed that something deep inside himself made him superior to circumstances. After all, his parents never told him that he couldn't achieve anything that he put his mind to. Bob was a master at turning a stumbling block into a stepping stone. On to life's next adventure could easily have been his manfra.

Bob approached his cancer the same way he approached everything in life. "I will love the light for it shows me the way. Yet, I will endure the darkness for it shows me the stars."

Heather says, "Bob would never admit to us [the kids and me] that he wasn't gonna make it. Although, he must have had some sort of deep down feeling, because a few months earlier, he told me that he wanted to visit Hawaii one more time...which we did. Strange as it was, considering that he really didn't want to talk about him dying, but we did discuss that he wanted to be cremated. The only time I got any hint of admission from him that things might go south was that Saturday in April when blood started coming out of his mouth.

"A few days earlier I was at my friend Angela Cartwright's house. We were working on a project for *The Sound of Music*. I had a premonition something was wrong and called home. Bob answered but his voice was weak and it sounded like he was gasping for air.

'Are you okay," I asked.

"No, I'm not. I'm having difficulty breathing."

I said, "I'll be right home."

"I took him to the hospital. That's when we learned that the tumor he was scheduled to have removed the following Monday at Cedars-Sinai in Los Angeles was pressing on his diaphragm. They didn't admit him, and sent us home with oxygen. That afternoon, a company brought more [tanks] over to our house." Shaking her head in a disbelieving way, Heather says, "Bob Urich on oxygen. I know that's really hard to picture."

Bob's surgery on that coming Monday, April 15, was to be a very innovative procedure to eliminate the tumor. They weren't going to eliminate the cancer, but try to buy him more time by removing the tumor. This was Friday. and their daughter Emily remembers, "I should have known things weren't looking good for dad, because there were oxygen tanks there. He couldn't go up the stairs because he had difficulty breathing." That night, he said to Heather, "Just let me sleep in the guest room tonight." Yes, he was surrounded by oxygen tanks, but up until then," she says, "he appeared to be fine. I said, "Okay."

Saturday - April 13, 2002, mid-morning
Sherman Oaks, California

Robert Urich sat on a swing on the portico at the rear entrance of their Sherman Oaks home. Bob loved swing sets and the homes they owned had to have at least one. Half a cup of coffee was clutched in his right hand. His body slightly stooped over. His head and shoulders slumped forward as he stared off into space. No doubt pondering what life had in store for him on this Saturday in April. Fatigue is written all over his once handsome face, now thin, pale and drawn. His weight once well over 200 pounds is now down to 170. He had to know he was losing his battle with cancer which was slowly eating away at his body.

A few months earlier in February, Heather's sister, Sheila Menzies, had paid them a visit. "When I saw Bob, he looked very ill. I knew he was dying. I cried all the way home. Funny," she recalls, "when he was on chemo, he never looked sick. I saw him again at Easter, and he looked worse. The strange thing about his illness," says Sheila, "nobody was talking about it."

Leaning back in his chair, Bob closes his eyes, his thoughts drifting back to five years earlier, when this rare form of cancer first attacked him.

"Lying in the hospital bed, holding my wife Heather's hand, I began to cry. It's no shame for a man to shed tears particularly when receiving such devastating news. Besides, crying is good. It can help you get through difficult times. Tears can be shared and *sharing* helps you get through a life threatening illness. I remember letting my tears flow, but only for a few minutes did I permit myself to be caught up in the emotional moment. Trying to gather my composure, I said to Heather, "okay, honey, now I'm ready to fight this disease! I was a man ready to go to War!"

It's Saturday Morning, April 13, 2002, and Bob Urich is alone on his back porch. Deep inside, he feels time is against him, but is unaware he only has a few more days to live, to share this elegant home of his dreams with his wife and family. He is thinking how hard he fought his disease. He wants to live. He does not want to die. When faced with adversity and the biggest challenge of his life, cancer, Bob put one foot in front of the other every single day, and did his best to live life to the fullest in spite of personal pain and discomfort.

His insidious disease, synovial cell sarcoma, attacks the soft tissue of the joints and can spread to the lungs. Bob's surgery and treatment, the first time, included a grueling eight months of chemotherapy and radiation at UCLA's Medical Center.

"A full recovery was expected." Bob's stoic attitude should serve as an inspiration to others dealing with terminal illness. He always believed he would be cured of his cancer and approached his treatment with positive vibes. Courage is more than sheer bravado, shouting, I know I can do this ... True courage is manifest when a person like Bob makes a conscious decision to take a difficult course of action, simply because it is the right thing to do.

Courage can manifest itself in many ways. There is physical courage and there is moral courage. Then, there is still a higher form of courage. The courage to brave pain, to live with it, to never let others know of it–including our closest family members and loved ones. This is what Bob did. No one knew how much pain and discomfort he struggled with every day. He lived with it and yet he still found happiness in life; he woke up early in the morning to show up first at the hospital for treatment with enthusiasm for the day ahead. Smiling, and announcing to the staff, "I'm here to be the first one cured today!" That takes courage. Miraculously, three weeks after his surgery, doctors told Bob they found no evidence of cancer or a tumor. Bob remembered how good it felt when his doctors gave him the good news. "Bob, your cancer is in remission." He had battled back and won! It had been a glorious time to celebrate, even though he knew the insidious serpent could rear it's ugly head at any moment. Sadly, he was right.

The cancer came back a second time. . .and a third, and when it reappeared for a fourth time, it hit him with a vengeance. Almost like a pissed-off monster from another galaxy. Bob shuttered, as if he could almost hear this vicious creature speak to him. "How dare you try and beat me! You mere mortal. I'll show you!"

Bob, always the heroic warrior, was worn down from his six year long battle. He was exhausted. Never a quitter, he always believed he could beat anything handed him. Heather remembers him saying, "Nobody or anything is going to intrude upon my sense of well being." All he had to do was set his mind to it.

But this time, on this Saturday Morning in April, he felt a little differently. He was beginning to believe that the odds were not in his favor; that the deck was stacked against him. Earlier, Emily, on her way to her girlfriend's house, said goodbye. "Love you" were the last words her dad would ever hear from her. She did not know the seriousness of his condition, or she would have stayed by his side. "Love you, too," he said.

It's now mid-morning, Bob is sitting outside admiring his lilacs which have just bloomed. His deep thoughts are interrupted as his son Ryan, home from college for the weekend, joins him on the porch, just as his dad begins coughing up blood.

"I really thought it was congestion, or blood from his nose," Ryan recalled. "Looking back, I should have know better.[1] "Dad, are you o.k.?" "Ya, fine," he answered, and as Bob often did, quickly changed the subject away from himself and any health issues. The man always tried to protect, or 'insulate' his family and most of his close friends from what was going on with his illness.

Never a whiner or complainer, Bob's health issues were something he simply kept to himself. It was not something he easily liked to discuss. "Hey, Ry," grinning at his son, "did you notice my flowers are finally in bloom." It puzzled Bob as to why his beloved daffodils and calla lilies were not happening. After all, it was spring in California and his flowers, including his prized lilacs, should be showing off their best side.

"Kind hearts are the gardens. Kind thoughts are the roots. Kind words are the blossoms. Kind deeds are the fruits." Kirpal Singh(1894-1974)[2]

Little did Bob know, this would be the last time he would see his beautiful flowers, let alone work in his beloved garden. Some of his happiest times were spent right in his own backyard, gardening. It was a long-time hobby which brought him peace of mind. When working the soil, he could almost forget his cancer. Almost, that is.

"Bob loved puttering around his garden," says Heather. "Talk about a green thumb. He grew beautiful flowers and delicious veggies. Is there anything more tasty than a tomato directly from the garden, Bob would proudly boast. If he were here with us right now and the subject of gardening came up," she laughs, "I feel confident, he'd smile, and say, in the springtime at the end of the day, you should smell like dirt!"

Bob Urich wasn't alone with his love of gardening. The great actress Helen Hayes once described working in Mother Earth this way: "All through the long winter, I dream of my garden. On the first day of Spring, I dig my fingers deep down into the soft earth. I can feel its energy and my spirits soar."

---

1 Ryan Urich is a graduate of Ross University School of Medicine (June '04) and is working as an infectious disease hospitalist at Lovelace Medical Center in Albuquerque, N.M. He and his wife, Michaela (Micki) have three children, two girls and a boy.

2 Kirpal Singh was a spiritual master, born in Indiaon February 6, 1894. His mission in life was to fill the human heart with compassion and universal love, which should radiate all countries, nations and people of the world. He passed away on August 21, 1974.

"I'm hungry," Ryan says. "Think I'll make some stir fry. Are you interested, dad?"

"No thanks, your mother is making me some home made chicken soup. They say it's good for what ails you. Hey, I'll try anything these days," Bob says with a smile.

"Thanks, dad, but I prefer stir fry," as he opens the backdoor and disappears inside. His father is left alone again with his thoughts about his long struggle with cancer.

Sitting for a long time in the chair, Bob's long legs feel stiff and are cramping up on him. He stretches them out trying to get a little more comfortable.

Fast rewind to 1999, when the cancer returned again. Bob thinks back to how difficult it was leaving Heather and their infant daughter Alli, behind at their home in Canada, while he underwent treatment in Michigan. It was a 6-week program, yet seemed longer, because they missed each other so much. It helped flying home on weekends to see them, even though sometimes he felt nauseous from the treatment. The flight was only about 45 minutes, so that wasn't too bad, he reasoned.

Bob remembers undergoing radiation treatment at the University of Michigan in Ann Arbor. The strange feeling he had as a man loyal to Michigan State, where he received his Masters, to be roaming around the grounds of his alma mater's bitter rival. Grinning, he recalls putting the passionate school rivalries aside, and was grateful to have been there. The University of Michigan has one of the finest cancer research centers in the world. Bob's thoughts drift to Janet Roth. She was on the development team at the hospital and was assigned to him to make sure all went well with his doctor appointments. He recalled how she generously allowed him to stay in their guest room. It was a more comfortable arrangement than staying at a hotel. He was grateful to be staying with Janet and her husband. He enjoyed being with them and the feeling was mutual.

"Bob was so much fun," says Janet. "Sometimes, when people would visit us, he wouldn't let on who he was and introduced himself as *Bob Brown*, or, just a friend. One day a friend stopped by to see if I was home. Later, she called me at work and excitedly said, "Do you know Robert Urich is washing your floor?'" Bob was a great cook and made some wonderful meals. He even helped our son with his homework. He wasn't a guest, he was more like family.

"I always knew when Bob was feeling good after undergoing treatment," Janet says. "When I walked in our home and saw that he had rearranged my entire kitchen. I knew he had a good day. When he wasn't feeling so good, he would read. Bob could be very decisive on what he wanted," she says.

"One afternoon, he asked me to join him for a trip to the local paint store in Ann Arbor. He spent hours looking at paint chips. He couldn't decide which color *blue* he wanted. He'd hold one up and say, 'Janet, look at this shade of blue. Now what do you think compared to this one,' and he'd hold up another. To me they both looked the same, but not to Bob. It had to be the perfect shade for what he had in mind. I was ready to scream and wanted to leave," Roth says, laughing.

***

It's Saturday morning, April 13, 2002. Bob Urich is sitting outside on the veranda of their Sherwood home. . .his long struggle with cancer fills his every thought. He smiles thinking about the deal he made with God, way back when he was first diagnosed and heard those three ugly words, *synovial cell sarcoma.* Heal me, Oh Lord and I shall go forth over the land from sea to shining sea, spreading the Gospel of Survival, in your name. So, following his own diagnosis and treatment with cancer, he kept true to his promise to God that, if cured, he would do his best to reach others suffering from disease to serve as an inspiration to them. His message–never lose hope and fight on. Bob Urich preached *the gospel of survivability* throughout the country in a thought-provoking way, sprinkled with humor.

As a guest on CNN's *Larry King Live*, Bob spoke candidly and openly about his condition.

"I've been flying around the country for the last year talking to groups. It's part of the deal I made with God to spread the word that it is survivable, that this notion of 'cancer-free' is one that you can achieve."

Bob sighs, thinking to himself, well, it worked fine [his speeches] for awhile. And, what about all those visits to so many cities. I did my best to keep our end of the bargain.

June 1998

In 1998, two years following his original diagnosis, Bob recalls being the keynote speaker at the University of Chicago Hospital's ninth annual

Celebration of Life, a recognition of National Cancer Survivors' Day. The hospital's event was held at the Westin Hotel on Michigan Avenue from noon to 3:00 p.m. on Sunday, June 7. The theme was *It's A Wonderful Life (*the title borrowed from the Frank Capra Christmas classic).[1] "During that speech, I revealed that I decided early on that I wasn't going to be a victim. I chose to go public with my cancer diagnosis [an unusual decision for an actor in the prime of one's career]. I took an active role in my care, becoming a partner with my doctors in affecting my cure. I drew from my strong Catholic upbringing and concluded with the words, 'There is a reason for all this to be happening. You will become a better human being and you will see the spiritual brilliance of it all.'"

In Wisconsin in 2001, Bob remembers telling a large gathering, many of whom had been diagnosed with serious health issues, to charge forward with hope, urging them to "never give up and get the best medical advice you can. Talk to your family, friends, and neighbors. Together, you can attack it," he said.

In May 2001, the *Bangor Daily News* mentioned that Bob Urich was a guest speaker at the Aroostook Medical Center in Presque Isle, Maine. Speaking at the podium before a packed auditorium, he laughs, remembering how he began his speech with a light-hearted jab at the venue's remoteness which prompted a huge laugh from the audience. "I spent a weekend in Camden [ME], but I've never been to a place where I needed to go to the end of an interstate." For those unfamiliar with Maine's topography, Presque Isle is about as far North in the state as you can go before hitting the Quebec border and Canada.

Speaking without any notes,[2] Bob recalled telling the audience, that after being told of his cancer, he skipped the denial and disbelief stages and went straight to the "deal-making" stage with God. "When I tell you that was a dark hour for me–that was an understatement of a lifetime. At first the doctors thought the lump in my groin was nothing to worry about, but, the tests came back saying the disease was ravaging my body and we have to stop it now. It was a shift in my life of monumental proportions."

1 Coincidentally, the film debuted in theaters across America in December 1946, the same week Robert Urich was born.

2 Bob was a master at ad-libbing. Quite often when they were headed to one of Bob's speaking engagements, Heather would notice he didn't have any prepared notes. "What are you going to talk about," she'd ask." Oh, I don't know. I'll think of something," he'd say.

On the evening of his speech in Maine in May 2001, Bob also made mention that a recent check-up showed he continued to be cancer-free, but the thought of the disease recurring continued to be in the back of his mind. "That is a challenge," he added with a smile, "but we can't always control what happens to us, but we can control how we react to what happens to us." He also quoted Don Quixote from the musical *Man of La Mancha*, and even sang a portion of "Dulcinea"[1] from the show's musical score to illustrate his philosophy of pursuing his personal quest with dedication.

"I come to preach the gospel of love, to support each other." Thinking back to that night and how perfectly still the audience in the auditorium was, Bob remembers how he quickly changed gears, laughed and said, "I also believe in the scientific methods of treatment: 'Show me the drugs!'"

It is mid-morning, **Saturday, April 13, 2002.**

Bob is reflecting on key moments in his six-year long battle with cancer.

"In 2001, I preached the Gospel of Survival,[2] because it appeared I had won the biggest challenge of my life and my battle with cancer. The serious health issue was a life altering change for me. You see, I've always felt that my priorities were in proper alignment [which the actor revealed in an America Online interview in 1996]. Flirting with cancer only reinforced my desire to live every day to the fullest. It also forced me to look at using my talents in other areas. My illness also makes me realize that I needed to rededicate myself not only to do quality work, but enjoy my family, and my friends, moment to moment...each day of my life. It's a sobering experience, as anyone can tell you who has experienced a life-threatening illness. I can truly tell you that it has changed my life for the better.

"Yes, every time the disease came back, I fought it with a vengeance and won. Like the time in 1998, I returned to the work I love, acting.

---

1 *Man of LaMancha* is a 1964 musical based on the book by Dale Wasserman. Dulcinea del Toboso is an unseen fictional character in Miguel de Cervantes novel *Don Quixote*, a 17th Century masterpiece.

2 Bob Urich's optimism about his battle with cancer made him a popular lecturer. His nation-wide speaking tour covered the U.S.A. In a three-year period, he spoke more than 60 times to over 200,000 people. Bob did his best to instill hope in others going through similar situations. His audiences ranged fromc support groups to Fortune 500 Companies. His fee of $30,000 per speaking engagement helped defray his medical expenses, while providing his family with a quality of life far above the average American family.

I was reunited with my old boss from my *Vega$* days, Aaron Spelling. I owe so much to the man. He not only launched my TV acting career with *S.W.A.T.* and *Vega$*, but in spite of my illness, he signed off on me [forinsurance purposes] and cast me as Captain Jim Kennedy III on *Love Boat: The Next Wave*. I love the man." Bob's tenacity for life was evident for both cast and crew to witness. He always showed up on time on the set of his latest production, even though hours earlier, he had received a round of chemo which left him nauseous and feeling lousy.

"He never allowed himself to use his illness as a way of seeking pity or to cast a dark cloud over the set," says actor/director Anson Williams, who played 'Potsie' on ABC's long-running TV series, *Happy Days*, and directed Bob in two episodes of *Love Boat: The Next Wave*. "He never allowed himself to become a victim. He brought an air of professionalism to the set," says Williams. "He was always smiling and friendly, and served as an example to others on how it was done."

Thinking back to his days on *Love Boat*, Bob felt that the cast and crew would be watching him. "I knew every time I walked on that set, I had to believe in myself that in spite of my illness, I could compete well with the other actors in the cast. A few times, I discovered my biggest rival was myself, because I always strived to do my best and be great."

Bob's Final Days

Left on the back porch, alone with his thoughts, Bob thinks back to spreading the good word of staying positive[1] when hit by illness by appearing on countless television programs including *Oprah*, *The Today Show*, *Good Morning America*, *Larry King Live* and a prime-time live interview with *Diane Sawyer*.

"Diane Sawyer came to our cottage in Canada and did an hour long, very emotional interview with me. She asked what was it like to be facing this frightening diagnosis. I answered, 'It was like being in the bull ring. I am staring down into the eyes of the raging bull and all I have for him is steel. It was horrifying contemplating the physical effects of what was to come, hence the emotion in the interview.'"

1 No doubt drawing on his Catholic faith, Bob also never ruled out alternative methods of treatment including praying for patients suffering from life-threatening disease.

In the summer of 2001, five years after seemingly beating his disease Bob Urich's cancer returned with a vengeance. They found some lumps, but a wonder drug had cleared them up, or at least he thought so.

Glancing down at his Rolex, Bob suddenly realizes how long he's been sitting outside. His mind is weary from recalling so many memories of days gone by. Some good, others painful and not so good. Oh well, that was then, he thinks shrugging his broad shoulders, and this is now. Homemade chicken soup is calling him. Besides, he wants to watch the Masters to see how Tiger Woods is hitting the ball. Easing himself up and out of his chair, Bob takes one last look at his beautiful now-blooming lilac bushes, smiles, opens the patio door and steps inside.

Saturday April 13, 2002
late morning

"I was in the kitchen making him chicken soup," says Heather. "By the way, it doesn't cure anything," she says in a feeble attempt at humor while retelling a difficult time in their lives. "Bob was down the hall from me in our guest bedroom. He had been on oxygen watching the Masters and Tiger Woods vying for the green jacket.

"Suddenly, I heard him coughing." Instinctively, Heather had a bad feeling and rushed down the hall to check on him. Their son Ryan was home from college for the weekend–he did that occasionally because it was close by. He recalls that anxious moment and hearing his mom's footsteps. "I heard mom's clogs echoing in the hallway as she ran to check on dad. It told me something was radically wrong."

Heather raced in the bedroom. One look at Bob told her, all too well, that her beloved husband, who had endured so much during the past six years, was in tough shape.

"I know this sounds awful, and this is really graphic," as she recalls that frightening moment, "but blood was spewing from his mouth. I was totally panic stricken." Doing her best to remain calm, and hoping Bob could not read the fear in her eyes, she simply asked,

"Do you need me to call 9-11?"

"Yes," was his one word reply.

That single word, 'yes,' said so much. It told her that Bob knew the severity of his situation. "That was the only time, I got any admission from him that things were gonna go south." she says with a deep sigh.

***

Heather told her son Ryan to take Alli, who was almost four, upstairs.

"You don't need to see this. He was like freakin' out, so he grabbed his little sister and headed upstairs. Up until that horrifying moment," she says, "doctors were saying surgery on Monday. We have a plan here in place, until then, that's what they were saying. But, then, it was just like a house of cards. . .it all went south.

"The emergency people arrived, ambulance, fire trucks and everything else. One of the fire-fighters who was there was an angel."

"Allie had come back downstairs and I shouted to Ryan, 'Get her back up there.'

"The firefighter said, 'no, no, bring her over here.' Ryan went and got her. This guy was an angel. He put little Allie up on top of the gurney with her daddy. He said, 'Let her say bye bye to her daddy.' They all seemed to know what was going on–I didn't but they sure did. So, she said goodbye and Bob whispered in her ear, 'I will be back.' Allie never forgot that," says Heather, "and she really believed for a very long time that her daddy was coming back.

The firefighter took Allie and let her climb all over his fire truck. He was so kind and thoughtful and gave her a teddy bear which she has to this day. Allie says, 'Yes, I still have it, minus a few parts that I think our dog enjoyed."

"I am so grateful to that man," says Heather. "I followed the fire-truck to Los Robles hospital.

"We got Bob checked in and as comfortable as possible. We planned to go back to see him the next day, still thinking, 'o.k., I'll just deal with this and we'll get him to Cedars on Monday morning for his surgery.' I thought maybe he had burst a blood vessel, because he had been coughing so much. So, I dropped him off, got him settled in, comfy, we were huggy and lovey and then headed for home."

"As we walked across the hospital parking lot, Ryan said, 'Mom, we didn't say good-night to dad.' I didn't turn around and go back, because I knew in my heart that he was going to be o.k. When I left him in the hospital room, I never imagined in a million years that would be the last time I would see him awake. It had been a long day. I kissed him good night. It was always 'love you, love you, too,' and I told him I'd be there first thing in the morning. That's why I didn't stay in the hospital with Bob that

Saturday night. I really thought that he was going to be fine. Over the ensuing years, it's something I've wrestled with so many times: Should I have stayed? What if I stayed? We could have said our goodbyes."

***

"The hospital called me in the middle of the night. 'Mrs. Urich, Bob is having difficulty breathing,' which I already knew. 'We are giving him oxygen,' which I also knew. That's what they told me. If I knew then that they were going to put him on life-support, I would have made a mad dash to the hospital, but they didn't tell me that. They didn't tell me they were putting him on life-support, but that they were giving him a breathing apparatus to make it easier for him. Ryan heard the phone ring and told his mom, 'I'm going to go be with daddy.' I couldn't go with him because I had Allie, who was almost four at the time, and obviously I couldn't leave her alone. Ryan packed some things in his knapsack that he thought his dad would want, including three of his watches. Your mind travels in strange ways when under stress. Ryan flew to the hospital and got a speeding ticket on the way. He didn't try to explain to the officer why he was driving so fast, just admitted to the offense, took the ticket so he could be on his way to the hospital.

He spent the whole night sleeping on the floor of his dad's room.'

"In the morning, I called Allie's sitter, Dee Dee, and when she arrived, I headed straight for the hospital. I got there at six in the morning and that's when I learned Bob was on life-support. I was so upset.

The weekend passed ever so slowly. It seemed like an eternity for Heather. "I was in a state of total disbelief and shock. My emotions were all over the place," she recalls. Totally confused by the sudden turn of events, a few days ago, the were planning surgery to give Bob more time ad now he was on life support. It was surreal. It hurt so much to see the man she loved lying motionless in a hospital bed. Word got out that Bob was in the hospital. Difficult calls were made to family members and friends. The sad news was passed on. He was not expected to live. Now was the time to come and say goodbye.

***

Heather remembers that painful moment.

"Oh God, it was so hard to deal with the decision to take Bob off life support. You have no idea. To this day, I'm still living with the nightmare of that moment. It's like having this poltergeist underneath the floor boards of your home, every day.

"Bob fought like a son of a bitch to beat his illness," she says. "So many painful memories of his six-year long battle against his insidious disease flooded my confused mind. His words came pouring back to me. At one point, he said, 'Heather, I want you to do every thing for me. I DO NOT want to die. Pull out all the stops. I want you to do whatever you can.' He told me that! It was so difficult. Bob's brother, Tom recalls, 'The doctor showed us the x-rays of the two big masses in Bob's chest. The planned surgery to remove the tumor – which had now burst was no longer an option. He told her it was hopeless. She had to make the decision.'"

After some time, the doctors said to Heather, "How long do you want to do this? We'll sit here with you as long as you want, but our recommendation is to let him go."

***

When Heather finally made the difficult decision to remove her beloved Bob from life-support, life was taken from the man, who at one time seemed so indestructible, who had fought so valiantly to prove in real life that he had the strength he portrayed in countless screen roles. Tom Urich was standing right there when his younger brother took his final breath. "I stood ten feet away; couldn't get any closer because their children and their friends circled my brother with their hands touching him."

"They turned off the machine and it scared the children, because Bob sat up with a gasp...then died."

Each of us have our own finish line in life. Robert Urich passed his at 1:15a.m., the morning of Tuesday, April 16, 2002. His final television performance aired the night before, *Night of the Wolf,* in which he starred with Anne Archer. As fate would have it, it's a story of triumph and survival. Robert Urich will always survive as an American icon.

Robert Urich had the will to win. The will to survive. He never quit. He never gave up. Bob fought his disease with every ounce of strength he had right up until the very end. The man simply couldn't accept not fighting. He didn't ask for a bag of 'never-say-die' spirit. It wasn't for sale. It was a quality he honestly felt he was born with. He fought hard to live, never losing his faith in God and believing strongly in the power of prayer. Throughout his six-year-long battle with cancer, he only asked for one thing...the courage to endure the struggle. He did just that, and in doing so not only brought honor to himself, but he also brought hope to everyone of us who may be dealing with illness and fighting our own battles each and every day.

At Bob's bedside at Los Robles Regional Medical Center in Thousand Oaks, California were his loving wife, Heather, son Ryan, and daughter Emily. Their youngster daughter Allison was just four at the time. The decision was made that she was too young to grasp the meaning of what was happening with her daddy. Also present were Bob's brother Tom, his wife, Judy, and many of their children's friends.

***

Bob had the right attitude about living life. He believed the purpose of life is to contribute in a positive way, to be useful, to be responsible, to be honorable, to be compassionate. He always believed this way but even more so, after being diagnosed with cancer.

"Leading a productive, useful life is what truly matters," he said, "if a life is to matter, to count, to stand for something, to have made a difference that you lived at all." As a devout Christian and Catholic, Bob frequently read the words of great men who have gone before us, like Cardinal John Henry Newman, who wrote about life and dying. "Fear not that your life shall come to an end, but rather that it shall never have a beginning." Bob Urich's life not only had a beginning but his life was filled with joy and happiness which he willingly shared with his family and friends and those he never knew, the millions of television viewers who enjoyed his numerous roles and performances.

The year 2015 marked the 20th anniversary of the television miniseries, *Lonesome Dove.* Actress Diane Lane who played opposite Bob in the award winning miniseries paid her co-star a touching tribute in an article for *American Cowboy* magazine.

"I wish Robert Urich, who played Jake Spoon was still with us, so he could experience the gratitude from all the fans for his work. But, the wonderful gift of film is that the grave has no sway. You are forever in that encapsulated bubble and that's a brilliant gift that film gives back to people who work in that medium. Your work [like Bob's] can live forever." Thanks to Robert Urich's extensive body of film and television preserved on film, Bob will be with us forever.

Today, Robert Urich's bravery and courageous strength in battling his illness lives on to give hope to millions who witnessed his struggle, and who also suffer from serious illness of their own. And, because of the fund for cancer research,[1] which Bob and Heather established before his death, future generations will not have to face their serious illness without the benefit of the latest medical research.

In the 1700's, over 200 years before Bob Urich as *Spenser* roamed the cobblestone streets of Boston, Benjamin Franklin wisely wrote in *Poor Richard's Almanac,* "Wish not so much to live long as to have lived *well.*"

Robert Urich lived well and touched many lives and in doing so led an extraordinary life.

Joe Martelle
Mon. March 19, 2017
4:05 p.m. M.T.

---

1 Robert Urich cancer fund information is available on-line at www.roberturich.com.

Bob kneeling at one of his speaking engagements as spokesperson for American Cancer Society, 1997. He inspired thousands to never give up hope.

Bob with youngest daughter Allison, taken in 2001.

One of the last publicity photo's taken of Bob in 2001. His hair is growing back following a 2nd round of treatment.

Chapter 30

Bob's Family and Friends Remember Him

Bob's Memorial Service- Funeral Mass

St. Charles Borromeo Catholic Church on Moorpark St. in North Hollywood, ten a.m. on Friday April 19, 2002

Services at West Lake, Picton County, Ontario Canada

Final resting place, ashes spread over his favorite fishing spots on, the lake, and also some ashes interred at church cemetery near the Urich cottage

Bob remembered by family and friends, and how some heard the news of his passing.

Bob's friends remember him

Bob Urich accomplished many great things in his relatively short life, including starring in a record sixteen television series* and over fifty films which earned him several awards, including a star on the Hollywood Walk of Fame. However, in the 'book of life' it's *not what you accomplish in life that counts, it's what you overcome which ultimately defines who you are and what you are all about as a person.* Bob gets high marks in this all important category. This was particularly true when he was diagnosed with a rare form of cancer which he heroically battled for six long years.

Bob was a good son and brother; a loving and caring husband and father, who was exceptionally loyal to his family and friends, who always did his best to treat everyone in a respectful manner.

Bob was always ready and willing to lend a hand to his friends. Tony Hillary[1] is one who felt the warmth of Bob's hand in friendship.

---

1 Tony Hillary started a non-profit program for school children in NYC, called, "Harlem Grown." He says, "I went from a 2 million dollar a year limo company to running a non-profit organization. Tony teaches school children how to grow their own veggies. The profits pay for the children's school supplies and helps them go through school." Bob would be proud of his accomplishments.

"Bob got me started in the limo business. He opened my eyes to so many things about life. From the first time I received a call from him to pick him up at JFK Airport." Tony had been driving for another company in New York City.

One day, Bob called from L.A. and said, "Tony, I'm coming to New York and I need you to pick me up at the airport." At that time, Tony didn't have a car of his own.

"Bob, I don't have a car," he said. "Get a bicycle," Bob replied, laughing.

Tony managed to come up with something. "I think it was a used town car. I picked Bob up at the airport. How well, I remember our first meeting. Bob could be gruff and intimidating. I thought, "Oh boy, this is gonna be a long ride from JFK to the hotel with this guy. But, I was so wrong.

"Bob was a big ole teddy bear. He was the complete opposite of my initial reaction. Bob began talking about family and life in general. He could talk to you about anything and that's what I really admired about him. We would talk about politics, sports, religion, our families. You name it. We became 'fast friends.' Meeting the man for the first time is like reconnecting with an ole friend. He made my heart warm, because he called me friend. Here I am, a little black guy in New York giving this guy a ride and he wants to be *my* friend. Bob wasn't the big fancy Madison Avenue type. He was a regular guy. You won't find any dirt on him. That's not his DNA," says Hillery. "He loved life and living it. Let's face it, if you had a billion dollars, you wouldn't be driving a VW. Bob liked the finer things. What a watch collection he had and so many leather jackets. He wore fine-tailored clothing. He was first class all the way. That was one part of him, but once you got past that surface stuff, Bob was the most genuine down to earth guy you would ever meet. He and I would laugh and just have a great time. 'I'm hungry,' he'd say.' Let's go get something to eat.' Man, could that man eat! Oh. My goodness, gracious. We went to San Marino and he knew I couldn't eat that much and he was eating off my plate! After eating, we'd get in the car and he'd say, 'I know a great place for dessert.' Dessert? I'm thinking, if I try and eat any more, I'm gonna pass out.

"Bob would go into a meeting and I'd go in with him. 'No way are you sitting alone outside in the car,' he'd tell me. 'Come inside with me.' I never forgot his kindness and generosity. He was my 'Broadway Bob,'"

Tony says. "That's what I called him. He was so fancy, so hi-class. He took me into places I never heard of and I grew up in New York.

"During the horrific day that was 9-11, Bob was in New York on business endorsing a cholesterol lowering butter. He was right off Madison Square Garden, right on 33rd Street and 7th Avenue. That morning, I was sitting outside listening to Howard Stern and somebody said, 'Hey, a plane just hit the Trade Center!' I'm thinking it's a small sight-seeing plane. I got out of the car and walked over to 7th Avenue. Just as I look up, the second plane hit the building. I ran inside and said, 'Bob, we gotta get outta here right now!' He said, 'No. What'd ya mean, we gotta go. No!' I grabbed him, pulled him outside and shoved him in the car, explaining, as best I could, what was going on. We shot uptown. Bob was staying at the St. Regis Hotel. We were driving uptown when the building [the World Trade Center] came down. It was a nightmare."

Tony Hillery was always looking out for his friend, *Broadway Bob* Urich. Whenever Bob had business in New York, he'd say, "I don't want anybody to drive me, but Tony." After Bob, Tony began picking up other celebrity clients like Brad Pitt, Keanu Reeves, Nicole Kidman, Edward Norton and many others.

"Bob invited me out to his home in California. The one on the golf course [Sherwood Country Club]. Who the f_ _ k does that," Tony laughs with a tone of sincere appreciation. "And, when you do visit him, it's not some superficial B.S. We had lunch and Bob says, 'Stay for dinner. Stay with us, don't go back to the hotel in L.A. Stay here with us,' he insisted. Who does that?" Tony asks. "Bob was one of a kind. A very special man. I loved him. He gave me a couple of his over-night luggage bags. He was always such a generous guy.

"When he died, Heather gave me one of his leather coats. He was twice my size, but I'd just roll up the sleeves and wear it. I know he's smiling' down, sayin' 'that's my boy.'"

Tony Hillery says, "Bob Urich is one of my favorite subjects in the world, next to my Harlem kids. He understood the game. Let's face it, with a lot of aging TV stars the work is just not there like it was, and that's why a lot of guys get so bitter. Agents, who once loved you, now don't even have the decency to return your calls. But with Bob, it didn't sour him one bit. ,'Well, you gotta keep goin,' is what he'd say. To this day, I run with that and what he showed me by example. If we all had Bob's attitude, the world would be a better place. He was such a great influence on me and my life.

I miss him."

Actress Joni Darling was Bob's acting coach. She remembers her friend Bob.

"When he first got sick, I had a long talk with him on the phone. . . offering whatever comfort I could, admiring his determination. We even sent him some books to the Bel Air Hotel where they were staying when he was initially treated. Don't know if he ever got them.[1] Later, we visited Bob and Heather at their house at Sherwood. He showed us around. I still have the picture of him, in my head, sitting in the living room, and he and Heather realizing that he had to go to the hospital. It brings tears to my eyes to this day. Shortly thereafter, I heard that he had gone into the hospital and died. Heather gave us some details of his [Bob's] failing and they were so sad and awful to me," she says.

"I was pretty much up to date the entire time Bob was ill," says actress and director Joanna Kerns. "I directed Bob on *The Love Boat* and he shared what many didn't know at the time about his treatment. Aaron Spelling was the one that stood up to insure him and for that Bob was very grateful. Bob and I worked together for the first time on the miniseries *Blind Faith.* He played Robert Marshall, who to this day is on death row for murdering his wife, Maria Marshall. I played Maria," says Kerns. "Bob was wonderful in the part but was troubled by it and the man he was asked to play. Robert Marshall murdered his wife, the mother of his children, on her birthday. Bob had a difficult time getting his head around that.

"We became good friends. He was the most handsome leading man, funny with self-deprecating humor. He was also really smart and kind. He loved his family and over time, I got to know his wife, Heather as well." "He was also a guy's guy, if you know what I mean. He was a sportsman, fished, skied, played golf, he loved houses. . .just an all around good guy.

---

1 When asked about the books, Heather says they never received them, but thanks Joni was the kind gesture.

"I visited him at the hospital [Cedars-Sinai] the week before he passed. Heather was very generous about my time spent with Bob and I was able to sit with him for about an hour. I can still hear his voice. Loved his voice. I had a big crush on Bob, but who didn't. He just looked at me and said, 'I just didn't believe this cancer could get me. I thought I could beat it.' I remember him saying how he had always been able to overcome any challenge he set his mind to. And, then Bob laughed in that way that he did. I totally understood, because he was so strong and honorable and he played by the rules.

"Bob did everything the doctors told him to do but the cancer was tougher than he was. At that point, he knew he was going. . .and we were able to say good bye. I played opposite Bob but never got to kiss him. In the hospital as we said 'goodbye,' I kissed him on the forehead. Then Heather and I went out in the hallway and cried, so we wouldn't break down in front of him. What a guy, such a beautiful man inside and out. I miss him and I am so happy I got to know him, work with him and laugh with him. We laughed a lot. He was a funny guy with a great sense of humor. He was also a family man and loved Heather and his children dearly. There was nothing Hollywood about him. I think that's what I liked about him the best," says Joanna Kerns.

Bob Urich's long-time pal, and one-time business partner,[1] Dr. Dyrk Halstead says, "Bob was a great friend, who loved and respected his wife, Heather, and therefore, always conducted himself in a positive way," The Nashville operating physician continues, "Bob always thought before he acted. He never wanted to say or do anything that may impact in a negative way, or possibly embarrass his wife. Before doing anything, he would ask himself, 'How will this affect Heather? How will she feel if I do this?' He loved and respected her so much and therefore, always conducted himself in a positive way. He had this wonderful, unselfish way of behaving. It was one of his best qualities."

Dr. Halstead was also Bob's fishing and hunting companion and unequivocally declares, "There's no doubt in my mind, Bob was completely faithful to his wife. Virtually all our trips, whether it was fishin' or

1 They jointly owned Beaver Dam Press to primarily publish some of the works of their favorite author, Nash Buckingham. They also owned 'Cyber Angel,' a short-lived computer software company.

huntin' was usually just he and I, so I got to observe the man close-up and personal. I got to see how he interacted with folks." In a phone conversation with the author in February 2016, Halstead said, "You know there was one thing that was unique about Bob. I met a lot of other celebrities through him, Tom Selleck and others. But, having traveled extensively with Bob and going through airports and stuff like that, I can tell you, the women were all over him. I remember once we were in a small town in South Dakota, and we went to a locally famous steakhouse. This was during his hey-day and, of course, it didn't take long for a lot of people to recognize him. They were so polite and didn't want to interrupt our dinner.

"One of the waitresses, came over to our table and said to Bob, 'Can I have your autograph?' He smiled and said, 'Absolutely, sure, sure.' He was so friendly. Well, by then, two or three other waitresses came over and wanted the same thing and within five minutes, there was a friggin line at our table. They wanted Bob to hold their baby so they could get a picture of both of them. Of course, this was before digital cameras and it took a while to pose and set things up. He was always so gracious about it. Bob certainly had this air of being a ladies' man, but I'll tell you this, no man present was ever offended by that. Why? Because, Bob was always so polite and courteous. I say this figuratively, if you're lookin' for dirt on Bob Urich, you're talkin' to the wrong guy. If he ever wanted to screw around, get drunk or do drugs, believe me, I would have known about it and that was never, ever an issue with Bob." Bob may have been tempted on numerous occasions, by his many female admirers, but his fidelity and devotion to his wife never wavered. Heather was his one and only true love.

"He was not afraid to die, but he wasn't resolved to his fate either," says Halstead. "He always believed he could beat it, especially after being 'cancer/tumor' free for five years. No, Bob was not afraid to die, but he wasn't going to pick up the phone and call Oral Roberts or the Pope for a divine intervention on his behalf either."

Your author can vouch for Bob's ability to keep his life and career in check. One day, we were coming out of a popular Boston restaurant. There were a bunch of college-age co-eds standing there. They immediately descended on Bob. They were hangin' all over him. The young ladies wanted their picture taken with him, but he politely declined. "No, no, he smiled, but I'll be more than happy to sign something for you," which he did. Laughingly, and teasing me, he said, "you want to line-up here next to

Joe. He's a radio pro."They all laughed over that. Truth be told, they could have cared less about having their photo taken with me.

As we walked away, I asked Bob, "why didn't you want your photo taken with them?"This was in the mid-1980s during the height of his popularity on ABC-TV's *Spenser: For Hire*, which was filmed entirely on location in and around Boston.

"Because, Joe," he replied, "Six months or even a year from now that photo will end up on the front page of the *Enquirer* with some bizarre headline and then I'm in trouble."

That's when I knew Bob Urich was wise beyond his years.

Bob's first wife, actress Barbara Rucker, remembers when she heard Bob had come down with cancer. "I started getting phone calls from everybody, people in Chicago and LA. I had been through breast cancer the year before, and wanted to speak with him." The couple hadn't seen or spoken to each other since their divorce in 1974. "I managed to locate him through a friend in Chicago. So, I called Bob and we talked for 3 hours.

"We talked about the enormity of cancer, how do you handle it and what it's going to do to you. It was so healing for me [the call] I don't know if he appreciated it. I was trying not to cry but I did. He was going to be a guest on *Oprah.* He said, "I want you to meet my wife, Heather. You guys are gonna get along great." So, we made an appointment for lunch in downtown Chicago. I was a Mary Kay [cosmetics] director at the time, so I brought my girlfriend with me, because I was a little nervous about seeing him again after all these years. Everyone got along beautifully and it was no big deal. I thought Heather was adorable. It was very healing for me and I hope it was for him."

Merritt Blake, Bob's long-time agent, says, "I knew he was seriously sick and visited him at Cedars-Sinai Hospital a few days earlier. I was in Northern California when I heard the news of his passing on the radio. I was shocked and saddened by the news."

In 1992, Dylan Daniels was a young boy when he appeared with Robert in the film *Survive the Savage Sea.* "I knew he was battling cancer but didn't know it was that bad. I had brought my car to the dealership that morning to get it tuned-up. I was sitting in the waiting room watching

TV when it came on the news that he had passed away. I was in total shock and started to cry. People were looking at me weird, so I stepped outside and called my mom and told her while crying and waiting for my car. It was a total shock and gut punch to see that news report."

When Bob passed in April of 2002, Burt Reynolds made the following statement. "Robert Urich was an athlete, artist, a wonderful friend and he was one of those rare people who never said anything unkind about anybody."

Actor Chick Vennera was Bob and Heather's friend. He was also best man at their wedding. "I was at home. The phone rang and Heather told me what was happening with Bob. At that time, their son Ryan was in my acting class. There were a few students that were close to Ryan and they went to the hospital with him. I taught that night and waited for Heather to get back to me. When the phone rang again, I knew what to expect. I heard the news from her that Bob had slipped away."

Duke Vincent was the producer on Bob's TV series, *Vega$*. "Unfortunately, I was out of the country at the time in Greece. I knew nothing until I got back and heard the sad news from the studio."

Bob's Toronto [Ohio] High School classmates share their stories of how they received the tragic news of his passing:

Bill Hutchison was a tri-captain, along with Tim Seese and Bob on the Toronto High Red Knights football team. "I heard about Bob's passing from the news. I was very surprised that his condition had become so grave. When I had talked with him, after his cancer was in remission, it looked like he had beaten it and was really getting back to his active lifestyle. Bob's passing has stayed with me from that time on."

Terry Hunter was working in a TV newsroom in Hawaii at the time of Bob's passing. "I believe someone in the newsroom told me about his death before I read about it on one of the wire services. I was surprised and saddened but not very shocked because what little I did know about his health hadn't been good."

Gregg McElvey and Bob had been friends going back to grammar school and all through high school. "We were living in Mingo Junction, Ohio at the time. It's about five miles south of Steubenville, which is about 15 miles south of Toronto. I knew Bob wasn't doing well and I heard about his death on the local news since he was so well-known in our local area. I really didn't know that he wasn't expected to live so his death really shocked my wife Chris and me."

Eric Caley was Bob's fishing pal and neighbor at West Lake in Canada. "Fishing was our big connection and we totally became best friends. The best fishing took place in Eastern Lake Ontario for small mouth bass, and the Bay of Quinte for walleye where I knew the 'spots.' It was a lot of fun and the best memories I have to this day were those excursions where Bob and I trailered and launched in different waters. He was quite the fisherman. Bob's favorite lure was a top water Heddon injured minnow which took finesse and skill to cast working in weed infested shoal water, but Bob made it look easy. He always enjoyed watching the strike and the hook up...and the fight that ensued. His reward was the frying pan afterwards. Bob was the best cook I have ever met when it came to fish frying. We generally did well fishing, just seemed we couldn't get out enough as there was always something going on. Bob was also a conservationist[1] and really cared about the environment.

"We remember well that evening when Rodger Hobson, Bob's full-time local Carpenter, phoned and told us Bob wasn't expected to survive the night. He had reached Heather and got the bad news. We hadn't talked with Bob in about three weeks and didn't have a clue of his health issues. We were in total shock and disbelief. Despair and helplessness sunk in. Cathy and I walked in darkness to Bob's boathouse overlooking the lake. West Lake was flat calm, silence. You could sense that he was there! We prayed for him and cried. We were shedding tears in the sadness that we were losing the nicest guy in the world," continues Caley. "It's still not the

---

1 Bob volunteered to help spotlight the conservation accomplishments of sportsmen and woman and was honorary chair person one September for the annual National Hunting and Fishing Day event which is celebrated the fourth Saturday of every September. It remains the most effective grassroots efforts ever undertaken to promote outdoor sports and conservation. Other past chairpersons include George Bush, Arnold Palmer, Tom Seaver, Terry Bradshaw, Tracy Byrd, Louise Mandrell, Jeff Foxworthy and others.

same here even nowadays. This was his getaway home. He loved the area and the lake. So many good memories. I'm still hurting thinking about Bob, it just doesn't go away."

Bob's 16th and last TV series was the sitcom *Emeril.* He played Jerry McKinney, a co-worker to popular chef Emeril Lagasse. The show centered around the chef [guess who] of a popular cooking show and his dealings with his producer and stage manager. Emeril debuted in the fall of 2001 on NBC. "Bob and I became instant friends," says Lagasse. "He was so approachable, friendly and although he looked like a tough guy, his energy and compassion were undeniable. After being with him for a few hours, then days, then weeks, we were attached to each other. Bob had more of a glass overflowing with personality. He was funny and made the work days energetic and easy going. His warmth and personality made you just love him. He was a true gem." How the man managed to maintain such a high energy level after fighting cancer for five long years was an inspiration to all. "Bob's on-screen character was much like his off-screen character," Lagasse continues. "His display of courage in his roles was the same display of courage in his daily life. He was so strong; he never thought of giving up and was always ready to fight his illness. He was positive that he would beat the cancer again."

Emeril's viewers were encouraged to create their own spice blends. Bob wanted in on the fun. "He created his own spice and called it Kapow. We used to joke that he had Kapow and I had Bam. Robert was a great cook and we loved to cook together. We spent many nights having a drink, laughing and cooking together at he and Heather's home. I felt I knew the man all my life."

Heather Urich's sister, Sheila Menzies, says she received a call from David Urich's former wife, Ann. "She told me that Bob was in the hospital in Thousand Oaks and was on life support. This was a couple of days before he died. I said my goodbyes the night before he died. His room was packed with people, at least 20. I didn't know most of them. I know Bob wouldn't have wanted all those people in his room watching him die. My brother Neil called me around 1:30 in the morning [Tuesday, April 16] and told me Bob had died. I've never felt that kind of sadness. This bigger than life personality was gone. He was the glue that held the family together.

"Maybe a month or so after he died, I had a dream about Bob. He was wearing his flannel and corduroys. He looked to be in his 30s, and looked healthy and happy. I felt like he was in the room. I didn't feel as sad as I had been feeling. I knew he was o.k."

Bob with his sister-in-law, Sheila Menzies.

Bob embracing his Heather.

Robert Urich's Memorial Service

Friday, April 19, 2002

Robert Urich's funeral was held at 10:00am at St. Charles Borromeo Catholic Church on Moorpark Street in North Hollywood. Blue was Bob's favorite color and almost like a heavenly tribute to the man, the skies over California that April morning were bluer than blue, with big fluffy white clouds.

Bob and Heather's long-time friend Tom Selleck spoke to reporters gathered outside the church, but did not speak at the services.

The Church is ornate in the traditional sense, with intricate molding adorning the high ceilings. A wooden crucifix is surrounded by dark wood carvings.

All of Bob's nephews were pall bearers. His casket[1] was covered in Bob's favorite flowers, lilacs. Heather was in a dazed, stunned state. She sat white-faced and expressionless with her children. She had to be handled like a child and left most of the funeral arrangements to her brother-in-law Tom Urich.

The priest who spoke at the service had also baptized Bob and Heather's four year old daughter, Allison. He spoke of that special day four years earlier as a day filled with much happiness. After the baptismal, he had gone to a gathering at the Urich home where he observed a private moment between Bob and baby Allison. "It was just the two of them. He was playing with her, and was beaming with a father's special joy."

The priest did his best to console the gathering of Bob's family and friends, saying, "We shouldn't feel cheated because Bob was taken from us too soon. If we live to be 20, 50 or 80 years, it still is an instant when compared to eternity with the Lord."

A number of guest speakers shared stories of Bob's life, including Bob and Heather's son Ryan. He mentioned how much his father spoiled him and how he resented it when his friends teased him about it, but knew it was because his father loved him so much. Ryan showed the congregation

---

1 Because Bob was to be cremated, a casket was rented for the funeral from Pierce Brothers Valley Oaks Mortuary in Thousand Oaks, CA.

a ukulele his dad had bought him a short time ago in Hawaii. "My dad loved Hawaii and wanted to visit there one more time. He brought this home for me. I searched and searched the internet for info on how to play it." And, with that, he played it a little.

Bob's brother Tom also spoke. He shared the story of a game they played as kids called mumblypeg:

"You had to flip a pocket knife off your arm, chin, or any other part of your body. It had to land blade first in the dirt. Whoever won planted a matchstick. Whoever lost had to dig it up with their teeth! Since Bob was so much younger, he was usually the 'dirt-eater.' Later," Tom continued, "when Robert was cast as Dan Tanna in *Vega$*, I was a guest villain. Dan was supposed to chase the bad guy and tackle him.

"When the scene was shot, Dan [Bob] chased me, caught me, turned me around and punched me in the stomach–knocking the wind out of me. That's when he whispered in my ear, 'this is for making me eat dirt.'" A tearful Tom then added, "if we could have you back, I'd eat dirt every day for the rest of my life."

Jim Lowery was another Toronto High classmate of Bob's. They also played football together. "Bob's cancer was a shock to all who knew him," he says, "but in typical Bob Urich fashion, he fought it courageously. We all thought if anybody could beat it, Bob could. It was a sad day for all who knew him when he passed and at such a young age."

"My wife Carol and I attended his funeral," says Lowery. "I spoke with his brothers Tom and David before the service and to his mom afterward. She remembered me right off and we talked of things she remembered we did during our high school days, and how much fun we all had hangin out in their basement rec room. Bob is greatly missed and so is his mom, Cecelia."

Bob's high school girl-friend and classmate, Candy Mindigo, and her husband Richard were also in attendance. "After the services," she says, "I saw Mrs. Urich [Bob's mom] and we hugged. I vividly remember the moment we approached Heather. Her greeting to us was choked with emotion, 'Oh, you're here. I can't believe it.'

"We hugged and I said, 'How could I not be here.' Heather looked at me through tears and said, 'You can't imagine how hard this was.' She didn't say anything else, but her eyes told me so much. It was so hard for her to see Bob go before her very eyes. To have the painful experience of watching someone you love so deeply, slowly deteriorate, day after day and then leave you is more than one can handle. That's what Heather was saying to me with her eyes," says Candy. "I could feel it."

***

Tragedy compounded by overwhelming grief can cause even the strongest person to act in unusual ways. Bob was cremated. His brother Tom had picked up the urn at the mortuary. "I was somewhat surprised by their seemingly insensitive attitude, when they handed me the urn and said, 'here's your brother.'"

Heather, understandably, was an emotional wreck. She couldn't quite comprehend that her once strapping, physically fit husband was now reduced to ashes and placed in an urn. She didn't know what to do, let alone what to do with the urn containing Bob's remains. Once again, it was brother Tom who rose to the occasion and provided his assistance. Tom kept his brother's ashes safely stored away in the front hall closet of their home for three months. In August, Heather's brother Neil picked up the urn and placed it in the trunk of his car for the arduous cross-country drive from Los Angeles to Ontario Canada for Bob's memorial services at West Lake.

Bob & his older brother Tom is a scene from Vega$ *episode Judgement Pronounced which aired on ABC-TV, May 27, 1981.*

Bob's Final resting place: his sacred sanctuary,
West Lake, Ontario CANADA
"Ashes to ashes, dust to dust"

Heather says, "Amazingly, Bob and I did talk about having his body cremated, and that Catholics don't like that, but I'm sorry, that's what he wanted. It was his decision. What Bob wanted was to be in his sacred place. . .the lake." "'I want to be in the lake,'[1] he insisted. I said ok, if that's what you want, but part of you has to be across the street from us in the church cemetery with a monument."

Even though Bob was Catholic, he did not have a problem with being cremated. However, his mom did. She did not approve of the cremation idea one bit.

"Bob's mom, Cecelia, was a strong Catholic.

There's a lane where you pull off into where our house is and there's a church and cemetery right on the other side. I went and bought a plot," says Heather, "and we saved some of Bob's ashes and buried them in the urn. His mom was happy with that."

Rev. Danny Smith was pastor at the West Lake Church of Christ, from August 1989 until June 2005. He was a neighbor of Bob's and officiated at his Lake memorial service.

"My family and I moved to the parsonage in August 1989. I met Bob the next summer. We were neighbors. Bob was always friendly. Never stand-off-ish as, perhaps, some might think a celebrity was. He pretty much kept to himself enjoying the quiet that the cottage gave him. He once remarked to me how different it was being in the County [Picton Ontario] and not having to worry about his children, compared to where they lived in LA, and having to have security guards for the children. At West Lake, his kids played with and hung out with local neighbourhood kids.

Bob was very generous. Every July 1 or July 4, and sometimes both days, he would have an outstanding fireworks display off his floating dock. He'd let all the neighbors know and we'd gather down on the shore and watch a great display as big as any in the area." Local legend has it that the fireworks were imported from the states in 'somebody's trunk.' How they got through customs is a mystery. Some say, Bob had his ways.

August 2002

Pastor Danny Smith at Christ Church in West Lake Canada is remembering his neighbor, Bob Urich:

"I remember one conversation we had when he was going through treatment for cancer and things were pretty bleak. I asked him if I could pray for him and he said yes, and added that he had friends of all differ-

1 What is somewhat confusing is Bob also mentioned to Heather that he wanted to be buried in the West Lake Church of Christ cemetery which is directly across the street from the Urich property.

ent faiths praying for him and his mother who was a strong Catholic was offering enough prayers that he should be well covered.

"I was pleased to conduct a simple committal service in their back yard," says Pastor Smith, "for a small gathering of family and a few friends. Then a few of the family were taken by boat out on West Lake to where they cast Bob's ashes upon the waters."

***

Heather recalls that sorrowful August day. "It was gray and over-cast. We had waited for summer for Bob's memorial service, so everyone could be with us. Pastor Danny Smith gave a blessing before we left the dock. Sixteen of us went out on the lake in three Boston Whalers, Bob's favorite boat. I said to Bob's cousin, Jo Jo Urich, 'why don't you take Bob's brother's Tom and David in your boat and you and Eric Caley, another of Bob's fishing pals and neighbor, pick a spot for his ashes on one of his favorite fishing spots. You both know the lake better than anybody else.'"

Eric Caley remembers the place they picked. "It was about two miles out, on the northern side of West Lake, in a remote less-traveled area where cattails made up the shoreline. It's not more than six feet deep and prime bass habitat. Bob loved fishing at that spot. It was a place where you can actually walk out to the cat tails where we would go fishing," says Jo Jo Urich. "It took us about 15 minutes to get there. We were in no rush. It was a sad fleet.

"Roger Hobson was piloting Heather's boat. Ryan and Emily were with her. All three boats were joined together," recalls Eric Caley, "and the poly bag with Bob's ashes was passed to each boat and everyone shared in putting him to rest. It tore my heart out, the hurt of saying farewell and everyone participating in the solemn event was weeping. The sadness was overwhelming. We slowly trolled apart to some distance away to let Heather and the kids share a private moment in their farewell and prayers."

It was at that point, an unexplained and extraordinary event occurred.

"A large dark cloud approached the lake from the west, and was nearing us," Caley recalls. "It looked like rain was coming. We drifted several hundred yards from Heather's boat, still in tears, when suddenly, a hole in that cloud opened directly in the center and sunshine beamed through. The narrow beam of light, which was like a spotlight, only illuminated Heather's boat. The rest of the lake was in darkness. When my wife Cathy and I saw it, we knew it was a sign from God and the heaven above that Bob was o.k. He was in God's loving arms. We were all crying. The hurt of saying good-bye was overwhelming."

Bob's younger brother David was in one of the other boats. "What was amazing is that beam of light stayed only on Heather and her boat. Everybody in the other boats were saying, 'Oh my God, do you see that? This is crazy. What on earth is going on here?' It was if Bob was reaching out[1] to Heather to tell her he was o.k."

Everyone in the three boats felt Bob's presence. His cousin, Jo Jo Urich, says, "it was like Bob was up there orchestrating the whole thing. Almost as if to say, 'this is what I want.' It was a few moments of pure joy and wonder and was truly a miracle. Bob was at rest. You could almost feel the warmth of his smile. It was God blessing them and Bob saying, 'It's o.k., I'm home.'"

Later, upon reaching the dock, Eric told Heather what had occurred, but she was unaware of the event. "No," she says, "I wasn't aware of any beam of light; I guess I was so focused on the moment and emotionally over-whelmed with everything."

Afterwards, they placed the urn containing Bob's remaining ashes under his Monument[2] in the West Lake Church's cemetery."

On April 9, 2016, Heather sent the author the following text message . . .

"*Most of us live out our lives as if change were an interloper, something that goes against the way things are supposed to be. We expect life to remain static, stable and predictable. Many of us live as if we will never have to let go of anything. We will never become ill, face the loss of an important relationship, lose ones to death, start over again in our career or suffer the loss of material possessions or financial security. Just look to nature and the seasons to understand change is the natural order of things.*

"*It is only our arrogance and insistence that things stay the same that keeps us from this full realization.*" Robert Urich - 2002

---

1 It was not the only time Bob reached out to Heather following his passing. When she moved to the cottage from Utah, she was unpacking some boxes. Inside the first box she opened, on the very top of the contents was a letter in Bob's handwriting. She had packed that particular box and had no recollection of any letter, particularly from Bob, being included. She never revealed the contents of the letter and I never asked.

2 Ryan Urich designed his father's head stone. [see attached photo].

Monument to Robert Urich in church cemetery which is a short walk from the Urich home at West Lake – Canada. The headstone was designed by Ryan Urich.

Epilogue

Update on Synovial cell sarcoma: Cigall Kadoch, September 4, 2016

Cigall Kadoch has accomplished a tremendous amount in her young career—at just 28 years old, she is an Assistant Professor of Pediatric Oncology and Principal Investigator at the Dana-Farber Cancer Institute in Boston, MA, along with an Institute Member of the Broad Institute of MIT and Harvard.

In 2013, Cigall earned her Ph.D. in less than three years at Stanford. According to an article by Richard Saltus, writer for the Dana-Farber Cancer Institute, "Kadoch vaulted into a position in Dana-Farber/Boston Children's department of Pediatric Oncology, and as assistant professor at Harvard Medical School where at age 27, she was one of the youngest scientists ever appointed to the Harvard Medical Faculty.

"In 2014, she opened her own lab at Dana-Farber. As the lab director, she is younger than several of the trainees she brought on-board. Cigall, utilizing her creative mind has funded her lab through various awards, and grants, along with philanthropic gifts from donors who become interested after hearing her positive explanation about her research involving new ways to fight cancer.

"Also in 2014, she received a $1 million-dollar Research Scholar Award from the American Cancer Society, and a $2.5 million innovator award from the National Institute of Health. Around the same time, she was honored to be named to *Forbes* Magazine's list of '*30 under 30*'–the top people under age thirty who are making an impact on the world. In heading her own research laboratory, Cigall is deeply dedicated to find a cure for synovial sarcoma, the insidious disease, which took actor Robert Urich's life at age 55, in April 2002."

Cigall Kadoch's research has uncovered several surprising classes of genes not previously known to play roles in cancer. "This has resulted in providing us," she says, "with a powerful foundation toward understanding the oncogenic mechanisms directed by altered chromatin remodeling complexes."

In layman's terms, she is not so interested in how good genes go bad, but in how mistakes in regulation of DNA structure can cause 'normal' genes to be activated at the wrong time, in the wrong place, or NOT activated when they are needed. "This process," Kadoch says, "begins in the structure that stores our genes, called *chromatin*. Our entire human genome–a thin, 6-foot-long thread of DNA carrying about 20,000 genes–is squeezed into each cell's nucleus, a structure about 1,000 times smaller than the head of a pin." Once again, putting things in layman's terms, Cigall's team hopes to determine what turns these genes on and off, which causes cancer. "If we can understand how the flawed architecture of the '*chromatin complex*' can cause cancer, we can hopefully design specific therapeutic strategies against it."

The author asked Cigall on September 4, 2016 if Bob Urich and others were diagnosed with synovial sarcoma today, would the end results be the same? "The sad news is yes, about the same," she says, "because we are still treating sarcoma the conventional way with surgery, chemo, radiation, and so on. There are few biologics which have proven to work well in this context. The good news is 'down the road,' if we continue to stay on track as a field, translating genetics into biochemical mechanisms with clear, disease-specific targets, we will have a strong chance to find a cure for synovial sarcoma and other cancers."

NOTE: Bob Urich told his wife Heather over and over that he didn›t want to die. He wanted her to try every possible cure known to keep him alive. Based on what Cigall Kadoch has said, along with the comments from other physicians who attended Bob, including, Doctors Larry Baker & Charles Forscher, I hope Heather had peace of mind knowing she did everything possible, medicine-wise, to adhere to Bob's wishes. Faced with his failing health and fragile condition, and as difficult and heartbreaking as it was, she did the only humane thing possible for Bob to be out of pain. She let him go.

Twenty years ago, when Bob was first diagnosed with synovial cell sarcoma, surgery, chemotherapy and radiation were the most common forms of treating this insidious disease. Today, thanks to Cigall Kadoch's lab and her continued research, progress continues to be made to hopefully one day find a cure.

Update: Synovial cell sarcom

On **Thursday, March 22, 2018,** I received an update from Cigall Kadoch regarding "more" research funding made available for synovial cell sarcoma.

Now, at age 32, Cigall Kadoch is one of biology's rising stars. She continues to be an Assistant Professor of pediatric oncology at Dana Farber Cancer Institute in Boston, where she operates a 24-person lab that delves into how altering the chemical packaging surrounding DNA can alter the way genes work. She founded a new biotechnology company, Foghorn Therapeutics. In March 2018, the company received a grant of $50 million from Flagship Pioneering. This means Cigall and her team can continue their important research on what causes disease in a cell and open new ways to think about how to treat serious diseases like cancer and, in particular to readers of this book, synovial cell sarcoma. What she has learned from her on-going research is that the chromatin packaging is controlled by genes and that a form of pediatric cancer, synovial cell sarcoma, was caused by changes in a complex of proteins that regulated *chromatin*.

Changes in that regulatory system of cells appear to be involved in at least 20% of cancers, including common ones like non-small cell lung cancer, and in other ailments, including degenerative disease of the brain.

The first drugs won't begin human tests for a year or more, but the company has been building a team of employees. Its experimental medicines are in the process of lead optimization, meaning that molecules have been developed but need to be improved. Diseases being targeted: synovial sarcoma, along with prostate cancer and non-small cell lung cancer. Cigall says her company, Foghorn, likens its work in chromatin to developing an air-traffic control system–it refers to it as "gene-traffic control" and has trademarked the phrase.[1] No amount of money can buy a cure, but it does give Cigall Kadoch and her team of researchers more options, which gives hope to millions suffering from cancer and other serious health issues.

Cigall Kadoch would like to keep you informed of her labs latest findings. Her website is www. Kadochlab.org

1 Matthew Herper of the Forbes staff reported on some of the information included.

Afterword:

Tribute to Heather Menzies Urich

"Heather's loss and God"

"whoever believes in Him shall not perish, but have eternal life" John 3:15

Few events in life are as painful as the death of a spouse. The pain is so over-whelming, you are uncertain you will ever survive such a hurtful loss. At times, you may be unsure you even have the energy or desire to survive, much less try to heal.

Bob Urich was more than a husband to Heather. He was all the things one could ever hope to have in a marital partner; a best-friend, lover, protector and provider. Bob was also a loving, caring father to their three children, Ryan, Emily and Allison. Robert Urich displayed all these wonderful qualities and a lot more. As Heather often pointed out in describing their twenty-seven years as husband and wife, "I felt like a princess, surrounded by a moat."

Bob's deep love for Heather was in evidence for all to see. He worshiped her and told her how much he loved her every single day. They never parted even for a few hours without telling each other, "love you … love you, too."

***

Immediately following Bob's passing, Heather found herself in the midst of intense personal grief. She felt like she was drowning in a sea of turbulent emotions. "It was frightening," Well-intentioned family and friends urged her to hang on to her faith and to pray. Sage advice, but sometimes easier said than done.

Heather hardly knew her own name, let alone what to ask or say to God. Besides, she was angry with God and disappointed that her prayers for Bob's healing went unanswered. She admitted to family and close friends that she was having difficulty believing God would do anything for her ever again. She shed so many tears her eyes were swollen and stinging with pain.

"I really wasn't sure I could possibly carry on."

Repeatedly, she asked herself the same questions, over and over:

Where was God when she and her children needed Him most?

Why did He turn a deaf ear to my prayers? Question after question repeatedly rolled around in her tired mind, but no answers were forth-coming.

Heather truly believed that her life would never be the same again. "Nobody gets a dress rehearsal for this," tears flowing as she spoke. "You don't get to practice this emotional scene." How could she carry on, without Bob by her side? At times, the pain was so incredibly real, she felt as if she were losing her mind and going crazy. Heather admits she felt suicidal. "I thought I may need to be institutionalized. I needed help and reached out to a therapist. Meds helped somewhat. At least they helped me fall asleep," she says, "but when I awoke the same dreadful loss was there hitting me squarely in the face. I was desperate. Friends tried to help. My next door neighbor at Sherwood, Sarah Carlson, came over almost every morning and dragged my sorry ass out of bed and around the golf course on a walk. If not for her help, I probably would have stayed in bed forever."

One morning, shortly after Bob's passing, Heather, overcome with grief, broke down at the breakfast table. "It was an ocean of tears," she painfully recalls. "I was sobbing uncontrollably." Their youngest daughter Allie (Allison) was four at the time. Sensing her mommy's sadness, she put her arms around her mom, and pointing to her own tiny heart, said, "Don't worry mommy, daddy's in here and you can hug him."

"I completely melted at her words, and hugged my daughter ever so tightly," she says.

Sometimes, the words an actions of an innocent child can work wonders to help heal. Suddenly, it became quite clear to Heather that she had to get control of her life. She had this precious child to care for and look after.

***

In 2017, Heather admitted she doesn't attend church services regularly. "I go with my friend, Judy [Rice] occasionally and it all depends on the priest as to what kind of an experience it is.

"I still have faith, but it continues to be shaken. I read a book called *The Shack*[1] and saw the movie. Perhaps," she says, "I need that kind of experience to bring me back." Heather's dear friend, the very Reverend Gary Hall, head of the National Cathedral in Washington, D.C. had a discussion with her about this one day and he said, "We can get you back."

Death ends a life, not a relationship, a feeling, nor a great love

When it comes to losing someone you deeply love, nothing on earth can make up for the loss of someone who has loved you. Heather could have given up on life. She could have easily given up. It's the easy way out, but holding it together when everyone around you would understand if you fell apart, that's true strength. "There are times," she says, "you have to put your boots on and cowboy up. It's by no means easy, I mean, how can you possibly get over 'it' when 'it' is the one you loved?"

People we love who pass on, do not immediately die for us. "It has been said that time heals all wounds. I don't agree," says Heather. "As Rose Kennedy reminds us, "'Time–for the mind, and protecting its sanity–covers the wounds with some scar tissue and the pain lessens, but it is never gone."

July 13, 2017

"He's with me every moment of every day in everything I do, "Heather says. "He's right in here," pointing to her heart. He continues to live in her heart, and occupies her thoughts in the very same way as when he was alive. It is almost as if Bob is away from her…traveling somewhere.

Author's note:

In her numerous conversations with me, as the author of Bob's story, she shared some moments which were particularly painful for her; like being alone at their lakeside cottage in Canada, which she admitted was not good for her. Too many memories. It was too difficult for her to handle being alone. She no longer wanted to view the spectacular Canadian sunsets that she and Bob enjoyed watching together. They brought back too many memories of happier times. She began drinking more to ease her pain and to escape the harsh reality of life. Heather also talked about how Bob always made her feel safe and secure regardless of what was happening in the world. Following the Presidential election of November

---

1 *The Shack* is a best selling novel about hope in the middle of despair written by William Paul Young.

2016, Heather was feeling uncertain about the state of our nation and wrote about how she was feeling in an e-mail to the author.

Mon. November 14, 2017

2:23 p.m. New York City

"I was missing Bob today, probably because I have been so depressed over the election and worried about the direction this country is headed with some of Trump's choices in his cabinet appointees. He [Bob] *always gave me such comfort. I miss him."*

"I miss the sensation of his touch and having him with me physically," she says, "but if I close my eyes I can see him…and almost feel his warm, gentle embrace."

In November 2017, Heather Menzies Urich was diagnosed with terminal brain cancer. She died on December 24, 2017. She was 68 years old.

They are together again … this time, for keeps.

Bob & Heather together again, and always in love! Photo courtesy Richard Reinsdorf.

Bob with his award winning grin–the way we will always remember him!

A Complete listing of Robert Urich's Television series, guest appearances and films

Robert Urich had an extraordinary television and film career that has never been given proper attention until now, probably because he never enjoyed talking about it. Unlike many stars, Bob never craved attention or being in the limelight. He was often described as being non-egocentric and non-neurotic–words seldom used to describe a star of his magnitude. Bob preferred to be known as just a good ole boy from Ohio.

For three decades, Robert Urich's name was synonymous with weekly network television entertainment in America, but Bob was more than an actor. He was a personality who was one of TV's most popular performers. His TVQ[1] index rating of recognition and likeability was one of the highest ever in the history of the medium.

Robert Urich's earliest TV roles

Year	Title of Program	Net	Guest role he played	Title of episode
1972	*The F.B.I.*	ABC	Davie Stroud	"The Runner"
1973	*Kung Fu*	ABC	Greg Dundee	"Blood Brother"
	Owen Marshall-Counselor at Law	ABC		"A girl named Tham"
	Marcus Welby	ABC	Mike Lowery	"Death is only a side Effect"
1974	*Nakia*	ABC		"Beginning in the Wilderness"
1975	*The Specialists* [TV pilot]		Dr. William Nugent[2]	Billed as Robert York

1 The Q Score, more popularly known as the Q rating is a measurement of the familiarity and appeal of a Celebrity, brand, company or entertainment product. The higher the "Q" score, the more highly regarded the person or item is among the group familiar with them, The Q Score, developed in 1963 by John Landis is used today by Marketing Evaluations Inc.

2 Jack Webb, star & producer of *Dragnet* on radio and TV, produced this pilot starring Bob and Maureen Reagan as epidemiologists working to track down health risks to the public. The pilot aired in January 1975, titled, *The Specialists* part of an NBC Double-feature with another unsold pilot called *Target Risk*. *The Specialist* was never sold as a series and the program was never picked up. Webb thought 'Urich' sounded

	Gunsmoke	CBS	Manolo Etchahoun	"Manolo"

Robert Urich's earliest TV roles as a guest performer

Year	Title of Program	Net	Character he played	Title of episode
1977	*Bunco*	[TV pilot]	Walker [Bob co-starred with his pal, Tom Selleck]	
	The Love Boat	ABC		episode # 14 January 1977
1978	*Charlie's Angels*	ABC	Dan Tanna	"Angels in Vegas"
1980	*The Love Boat*	ABC		episodes # 23 & #5
1981	*The Love Boat*	ABC		episode #14
1982	*The Love Boat*	ABC		episode # 9
1983	*The Love Boat*	ABC		episode # 17

There was a time when no fall television launch seemed complete if it didn't include at least one series starring Robert Urich. The popular actor was once referred to as "Television's Teflon Man," for his uncanny ability to rise from the ashes from the demise of many of the ambitious series he starred in. Over and over again, he would come back to star in another series. Kinda like the regenerative nature of the character he played in one of his final television series, *The Lazarus Man*. The good looking, good-natured Urich was always more popular than many of his TV series.

"He was always a draw," says ABC-TV executive, James W. Duffy.

"Bob was money in the bank for our network and our sponsors." says network executive Robert Murphy.

Many of Bob's TV series had short runs[1]but the failure always seemed to be more a rejection of the program and not the star. A testimony to the likeable actor from his legions of loyal fans, they may not have always liked the story-line of a series, but they always loved the man and enjoyed his performances.

Name of Program	Net	Years on-air	Character played	No. of episodes
1. *Bob & Carol*	ABC	Sept. 73- Nov73	Bob Sanders	12

too ethic and convinced Bob to change it to 'York.' Bob only used the name change for this planned series.

1 When a TV series is canceled, it could be for a variety of reasons: poor writing, terrible time slot [against well-established competition] chemistry problems between cast members, etc.

&Ted & Alice Sit-com			Urich's sitcom debut	
2. *S.W.A.T.* police action	ABC	Feb 75- Jun 76	Off. Jim Sweet	37
3. *SOAP* sit-com	ABC	Sep 77- Apr 81	Peter Campbell the tennis pro in season 1	8
4. *Tabitha* sit-com	ABC	Nov 77- Aug 78	Paul Thurston	12
5. *Vega$* Detective/drama	ABC	Sep 78- Sep 81	Dan Tanna	69
6. *Gavilan* Adventure	NBC	Oct 82- Mar 83	Robert Gavilan	8
7. *Spenser: For Hire* Detective/drama	ABC	Sep 85- Sep 88	Spenser	65
8. *National Geographic Explorer* Documentary	Nick- TBS	Apr 85 -Feb 86 Feb 86 to present	Bob hosted 91-94	
9. *American Dreamer* Sit com	NBC	Sep 90- Jun 91	Tom Nash	17
10. *Crossroads* Adventure	ABC	Sep 92- Jul 93	Johnny Hawkins	9
11. *It Had to be You* Sit com	CBS	Sep 93-Oct 93	Mitch Quinn	6
12. *The Lazarus Man* western	TNT	Jan 96-Nov 96	James Cathcart	20
13. *Boat Works*	PBS	Oct. 96	host, 13 part series	
14. *Vital Signs*	ABC	Feb 97	host, 6 part series	
15. *Love Boat- The Next Wave* Sit com	UPN	'98-99	Capt. Jim Kennedy III	25
16. *Emeril* Sit com	NBC	2001	Jerry McKenney Bob's final series	10

Robert Urich's Additional Television Work

"Talent only gives you the opportunity to succeed. You need to work hard to achieve success"

Bob was featured in leading roles in five miniseries for television. Many say his best work was as Jake Spoon, a down-on-his-luck former Texas Ranger, in *Lonesome Dove,* based on the Larry McMurtry novel about a grueling cattle drive. The epic western miniseries first aired on CBS in 1989.[1] However, *Lonesome Dove* was not the only TV miniseries which utilized Urich's talents.

Amerika aired on ABC-TV as a 12-hour miniseries, on February 15, 1987. The series dealt with America being taken over in a bloodless way by the Soviet Union, which leads to slave labor camps for some, collaborative efforts for others and rebellion by still others. Robert Urich played Peter Bradford with Kris Kristofferson as Devon Milford. *Mistral's Daughter* aired on September 24, 1984 with Bob playing Jason Darcy and appearing in 3 of the 4 episodes.

Princess Daisy is set in the 1940's and based on the Judy Krantz novel about the lovely Frencesca Valenski [Lindsay Wagner] an American actress who meets, falls in love with and marries a Russian prince Stash Valenski [Stacy Keach]. The two have twin girls, Daisy and Danielle. Danielle is mentally challenged from birth and Stash has her secretly institutionalized. He believes it's insanity which runs in his family, which he is greatly afraid of. When Francesca hears what her husband plans, she takes both her daughters and flees for America. Robert Urich plays Patrick Shannon, a business tycoon who falls in love with Daisy, but that doesn't happen until later. In the meantime, there are many subplots, and twists and turns in this 3-hour romantic miniseries. *Princess Daisy* was telecast November 6 and 7, 1984 on NBC. *Blind Faith*[2] aired as a two-part TV miniseries.

Additional guest roles and television appearances by Robert Urich

Year	Date	Title of Program and Network
1973		*Match Game* as panelist CBS
1975	9-8-75	*Match Game 1973* as panelist CBS

1 *Lonesome Dove* is covered extensively in Ch. 23.

2 *Blind Faith* is covered in Ch. 16, Bob's take on acting.

	11-3-75	*Tattletales* as panelist with wife Heather Menzies CBS
		The Showoffs Bobby Van as host of this panto mime game show ABC
1976		*The Cross Wits*, a crossword puzzle game show, Ralph Edwards Ex. Prod.Bob appeared on 3 episodes between 1976-77 on this syndicated show
		The Riddlers as panelist, David Letterman was host of this pilot Quiz show which never found a spot on the network schedule
	8-13-76	*Dinah*, daytime talk show starring Dinah Shore with Bob as guest, SYN
1977	5- 5-77	*Richard Pryor Special* - NBC
	7-20-77	*Tattletales*, panelist, CBS
	9-19-77	*$20,000 Pyramid* with Anne Meara ABC
	10-19-77	*Merv Griffin Show* as guest SYN
	11- 7-77	*$20,000 Pyramid* panelist along with Lee Meriwether ABC
	12-12-77	*Tattletales*, panelist CBS
		Alan Hamel Show as guest
1978	2-13-78	*$20,000 Pyramid* as panelist with Lori Nettleton ABC
	5- 8- 78	*$20,000 Pyramid* as panelist along with McK-
enzie		Phillips ABC
	7-21-78	*Dinah* ! As guest SYN
	7-27-78	*The Mike Douglas Show* as co-host, SYN by Group W [Westinghouse]
	11-18-78	*Battle of the Network Stars* - ABC, Bob was member of ABC team
	11-20-78	*Tonight Show starring Johnny Carson*, guest NBC
	11-21-78	*The Mike Douglas Show* co-host SYN-Westing house Broadcasting
	11-23-78	*Good Morning America* as guest - ABC
1979	1- 1-79	*The Merv Griffin Show*, SYN [syndicated] guest
	1-15-79	*The Mike Douglas Show*, Bob was host for the entire week of 1-15
	2-10-79	*Mike Douglas Show*, again Bob was guest host for the wk of February10,

	2-26-79	*Good Morning America*, guest star ABC
	2-28-79	*The Merv Griffin Show*, guest star SYN
	3-24-79	*Paul Lynde at the Movies* ABC, guest
	4-23-79	*Password Plus*, NBC, guest star
	5- 7- 79	*Battle of the Network Stars*, Bob was on the ABC team
	5- 7- 79	*$20,000 Pyramid*, guest panelist with his wife Heather ABC
	5-14-79	*TV Annual*- ABC
	6- 4-79	*The Mike Douglas Show*, guest host for the week of 6-4, SYN
	10-10-79	*The Mike Douglas Show*, guest host for the week of 10-10, SYN
	11- 8- 79	*Dinah* ! Guest SYN
	11-16-79	*Celebrity Football Classic* NBC
	12-14-79	*Merry Christmas from the Grand Ole Opry*, host ABC
	12-24-79	*Christmas Special* - Mac Davis with Love, guest, NBC

<u>**Note:**</u> the 1979 television season was a busy one for Robert Urich. He also appeared on the *31st Annual Emmy Awards*, and the *5th Annual People's Choice Awards*. In addition to starring in his weekly TV series, *Vega$* and starring in one made for TV film, *When She Was Bad* for ABC-TV.

Year	**Date**	**Title of Program; and Network**
1980	3-17-80	*Bob Hope Special - Star Makers,* guest NBC
	4-30-80	*The Merv Griffin Show,* guest SYN
	5- 9- 80	*Dinah!* guest SYN
	9-10-80	*The Merv Griffin Show*, guest SYN
	9-21-80	*The John Davidson Show*, guest SYN
	10- 1- 80	*Hour Magazine,* guest SYN

Note: there is a possibility Bob Urich also appeared on another Bob Hope Special in 1980, *Bob Hope for President*. This could not be verified. Urich also appeared On *the 37th Annual Golden Globe Awards* Show

1981	11-18-81	*Bob Hope's 30th Anniversary Special*, guest NBC
	3-27-81	*The Midnight Special*-hosts: Skip Stevenson and Byron Allen, guestNBC
	5-4-81	*60 Years of Seduction, Hollywood*, host ABC

	5-8-81	*Battle of the Network Stars*. team capt. ABC
	5-25-81	*All Star Comedy Birthday Party from –West Point*, guest
1982	1-2- 82	*Billy Crystal Comedy Hour*, guest on 2 eps. NBC
	3-9- 82	*Entertainment Tonight* SYN
	3-16-82	*The John Davidson Show*, guest SYN
	3-20-82	*Saturday Night 'Live'* host NBC
	5-11-82	*Richard Pryor Special*, guest NBC
	10-18-82	*Tonight Show starring Johnny Carson*, guest NBC
1983	11-29-83	*Rodney Dangerfield: I can't Take it No More* ABC guest
1984	5-21-84	*Funniest Joke Ever Heard*, host ABC
	8- 2-84	*Entertainment Tonight* SYN
1985	2-20-85	*Late Night with David Letterman*, guest NBC
	3-11-85	*Night of 100 Stars II* ABC
	4-15-85	*Bob Hope's Comedy Salute to the Soaps* NBC
	9- 6-85	*Entertainment Tonight* SYN
	9-15-85	*ABC-All Star Spectacular Fall Season Preview*, host ABC
	11-24-85	*Start of Something Big*, guest SYN
1986	1-19-86	*Funny* ABC
	2- 1-86	*Lifestyles of the Rich and Famous*, guest SYN
	11- 86	*Philadelphia Thanksgiving Day Parade*
1987	2-13-87	*Good Morning America*, guest ABC
	4-14-87	*Late Show starring Joan Rivers*, guest NBC
	7- 4- 87	*A Star Spangled Celebration*, co-host ABC
1988	1- 7- 88	*Cheers*, as *Spenser* , Season 6, eps. 3 Woody for hire meets Spenser NBC
1989	?	*Audio Robert Ludlum's The Hallcroft Covenant*- narrator
	?	*All Star Tribute to Kareem Abdul Jabbar*
	7-14-89	*Arsenio Hall Show*, guest SYN
1990	1-26-90	*Pat Sajak Show*, guest CBS
	2- 8- 90	*Arsenio Hall Show*, guest SYN
	?	*2nd Annual Valvoline Nat'l Driver's Test*
	5-26-90	*Carol & Company*, eps: Fabulous Bicker Girls, guest NBC
	9- 17-90	*Tonight Show starring Johnny Carson*, guest NBC

	10- 9- 90	*Arsenio Hall Show* SYN
	11- 6- 90	*Tonight Show starring Johnny Carson*, guest NBC
	11-21-90	*Circus of the Stars*, ringmaster CBS
	11-22-90	*Macy's Thanksgiving Day Parade*, host
	11-22-90	*Late Night with David Letterman*, guest NBC
	12- 1- 90	*Carol & Company*, eps: Mr. Carmen, guest NBC
1991	1-1- 91	*People's Choice Awards-17th Annual*
	1-23-91	*Tonight Show starring Johnny Carson*, guest NBC
	?	*48th Annual Golden Globe Awards*
	11-29-91	*One on One with John Tesh*, guest
	12- 3- 91	*Arsenio Hall Show*, guest SYN
	?	*Fantasies*
1992	8-30-92	*National Geographic: Egypt, Beyond the Pyramids*, host TBS
	?	*The Canine Connection*, host
	?	*The Bat, the Cat and the Penguin*
	11-10-92	*Where in the World is Carmen San Diego*, eps. The lipstick UP/WQED
	?	*Volga, the Soul of Russia, host* TBS
1993	1- 4- 93	*Evening Shade*, eps. Frieda and the preacher, guest role CBS
		15th Annual Cable Ace Awards
		Antarctica: Life in the Freezer, host TBS
	9-21-93	*Late Show with David Letterman*, guest [repeat] NBC
	12-18-93	*A Musical Christmas at Walt Disney World*, host
1994	?	*Made in the U.S.A.*
1995	?	*Alien Encounters: From New Tomorrow land*, narrator Disney
1996	5- 6- 96	*When Animals Attack* , host FOX
	5-16-96	*Live! With Regis and Kathy Lee*, guest [*Kelly & Michael*] SYN
	5-18-96	*Hidden Secrets* , host NBC
	8-22-96	*Family Film Awards*, presenter/nominee
	9- 4- 96	*Prime Time- Live* ABC
	9- 18-96	*When Animals Attack II*, host FOX
	10-11-96	*Larry King Live*, guest CNN

	10-15-96	*3rd Annual Screen Actor Guild Awards*
	10-27-96	*World's Greatest Magic*, host FAM
	11- 2- 96	*Houdini: Unlocking his secrets*, host FAM
	12- 6- 96	*The WEB-the site*, guest C/NET

Also: *The Ultimate Stuntman*: Dar Robinson, *Plugged In: A Parents Guide to TV* and *Close Calls-Cheating Death* are three additional programs Robert Urich is credited in some listings as being a guest on.

1997	2-17-97	*When Animals Attack III,* host FOX
	2-19-97	*The Nanny*, eps: Samson he denied her, Bob as Judge Jerry Moran CBS
	2-25-97	*The Tonight Show*, guest NBC
	3-27-97	*Oprah*, guest SYN
	3- 97	*Geraldo Rivera*, guest SYN
	4- 7 - 97	*Larry King Live*! Guest CNN
	4-25-97	*Live! With Regis and Kathy Lee*, guest SYN
	5-14- 97	*When Stunts go bad , host*
1998	?	*Invasion America*, animated series, Bob was the voice of Briggs in 13 eps.
	4-13-98	*Rosie O'Donnell Show*, guest SYN
	?	*Late Show with Conan O'Brien*, guest NBC
	5-13-98	*Live! With Regis & Kathy Lee* [Regis & Kelly], guest SYN
	9-28-98	*Live! With Regis & Kathy Lee* SYN
1999	?	*Building Pyramids*
	4-25-99	*Intimate Portrait of Lindsay Wagner*, Bob as narrator
	11-16-99	*Live! With Regis & Kathy Lee*, guest SYN
	12 - 99	*67, Annual Hollywood Christmas Parade*, Grand Marshall KTLA/SYN
2000	1- 7 - 00	*Live! With Regis & Kathy Lee*, guest SYN
	?	*Ultimate Explorer*
	2-13- 00	*E! True Hollywood Story*: eps 9 - The Mod Squad
2001	9-11-01	*The View*, guest,
	10-1 -01	*The late, late show with Craig Kilborn,* this was Bob's last guest appearance on a nationally viewed television talk program. He passed away, 6 months later, on April 16, 2002.

Note: To insure this listing of Bob Urich's television series work, films and guest appearances is comprehensive, every resource has been checked for accuracy. However, we may have missed a few. If you know of any additional appearances not listed here, please contact the author at his publisher's website, **http://www.bearmanormedia.com/**. One additional point regarding Bob's local radio and TV appearances: He did so many interviews around the country with numerous air personalities, it is virtually impossible to track them all down. If you had the good fortune to have Bob as a guest on your local radio or TV show, we'd love to hear from you as well.

The Films of Robert Urich

Throughout his 30-year acting career, Robert Urich moved effortlessly between dramas and comedy, action thrillers and period Westerns, on both TV and in film. He appeared in a total of 55 films – 51 made for TV, and 4 on the big screen.

It all began for Bob in 1973, playing a motorcycle cop in one of Clint Eastwood's blockbuster films.

Year Film Title, date released, length Urich's role Story synopsis-notes

1973 *Magnum Force*, WB, released, 12/25, [124 mins], Mike Grimes
Bob's screen debut
#1

This action film is the 2nd to feature Clint Eastwood as maverick cop, Dirty Harry Callahan. Ted Post who also directed Eastwood in his TV series, *Rawhide* and the feature film *Hang 'Em High*, directed the film. The movie features early appearances by Tim Matheson , Kip Niven, David Soul and Robert Urich. The four play motorcycle cops and members of a sub-organization called *Magnum Force.* Their mission: to wipe out crime in San Francisco at all cost. The group strike Callahan as a young, idealistic group of officers with promising futures. In return, they look up to Harry, but he refuses to support their tactics. Lt. Briggs [Hal Holbrook] is a by-the-book police administrator who is disgusted with Callahan's 'dirty' tactics. One death squad motor cycle officers, Red Astrachan [actor Kip Niven] is named after a popular apple grown in central California. Suzanne Somers is in the film, too, but don't blink, or you'll miss her. Directed by Ted Post and written by Harry Julian Fink and Rita M. Fink. Music by Lalo Schifrin *Magnum Force* was filmed at various sites in San Francisco, and in Oakland and Richmond, Ca.

1974 *Killdozer*, released, 2/2, [74 mins], Universal, Mack McCarthy
Film for TV, ABC
#2

This horror/sci-fi film centers on a small construction crew on an island which is pursued and terrorized by a strange spirit-like being that takes over a large bulldozer and goes on a killing rampage. Clint Walker plays

Lloyd Kelly. Neville Brand also co-stars. Directed by Jerry London, known for his work on the TV series *Diagnosis Murder* and *Hogan's Heroes*. The teleplay was by Theodore Sturgeon and Ed Mackillop. Science fiction writer, Edward Hamilton Waldo contributed to the project. He is known for his TV work on *The Invaders*, *Twilight Zone* [1985] and the original *Star Trek*. In an interview with Leonard Nimoy, who played Spock on the series, credits Waldo for coining the phrase "*live long and prosper* "which was used for the first time on the premier episode of the 2nd season of Star Trek. *Killdozer* was filmed at Indian Dunes, California.

1975 *The Specialist*, a proposed but unsold TV pilot, [73mins], produced January 6, 1975.
#3

Dragnet creator and star Jack Webb produced this film via his Mark VII Ltd productions. He also convinced Bob to change his name to Robert York, believing Urich was too ethnic sounding. Bob obliged, but only for this film. Bob plays Dr. William Nugent, assisted by Maureen Reagan as Dr. Christine Scofield. Both work for the U.S. Public Health Service trying to track down the cause of a rash of mysterious ailments suddenly popping up amongst the general populace. The film co-stars Jack Hogan as Dr. Edward Grey. Filmed in Atlanta, this pilot film never sold or got picked up.

1977 *Bunco*, produced by Lorimar, [48 mins], Bob plays Walker on proposed TV pilot
#4

This pilot for a proposed TV series is about two L.A. police officers, 'Walker' [Bob Urich] and 'Gordean' [Tom Selleck] who as members of the Bunco squad are in charge of nabbing con men, cheats and swindlers and bust scams. Donna Mills plays 'Frankie' an undercover Police officer. Bob and Tom play well off each other. Directed by Alexander Singer and written by Jerrold L. Ludwig. Rumor has it, this pilot was not picked up by the network because it was believed the co-stars lacked the necessary charisma required to maintain audience interest. It was a terrible error in judgment by programming execs, because both Selleck and Urich went on to become huge stars., and although friends, remained competitive with each other. In 1981, they were opposing team captains, Bob for ABC, Tom for CBS on *Battle of the Network Stars.* Four years after Bunco, Donna Mills would also become a star for her role on *Knots Landing*.

1978 *Leave Yesterday Behind*, 5/14, [100 mins], one of Bob's first film roles for ABC, Bob plays David Lyle
#5

This story concerns a young man in his prime of health and lust for life, Paul Stallings [John Ritter] a horse riding polo trophy winner who receives a back injury and becomes paralyzed from the waist down. Dealing with despair from his life in a wheelchair, he meets by accident Marnie Clarkson [Carrie Fisher] who befriends him after an initial confrontation when Stallings nearly causes her to have a similar accident. They become friends which develops into romance and overcome obstacles in pursuit of 'real love.' It is a warm story which deals with life's love, loss tragedy and triumph of the human sprit. Bob Urich, in one of his first screen roles makes a guest appearance as Marnie's fiancée. The supporting cast includes Buddy Ebsen as Doc and Ed Nelson as Mr. Clarkson. The film is directed by Richard Michaels and written by Paul Harrison. Filmed in Carmel Valley, Davis, Elk Grove and San Juan Bautista, Calif.

1979 *When She Was Bad*, 11/25, [100 mins], Bob plays Bob Morgan, ABC
#6

David Ladd produced this made for TV drama which was directed by Peter H. Hunt and written by Carmen Culver. David Ladd's former wife, Cheryl Ladd, fulfills a life-long crusade to prevent child abuse in this film. Robert Urich and Ms. Ladd give great performances in bringing attention to child abuse which is going on behind closed doors every day in American homes. Most of the action is verbal, with the exception of one physical scene that sends Robbie [Nicole Eggert] to the hospital. Urich, as Bob Morgan, and his poignant reaction is some of his best work. Only help from her friends, family and counselors can stop her from harming Robbie and herself. One reviewer says "The superb acting supported by the film's important message is well worth seeing."

1980 *The Shadow Box*, 12/28, [96 mins], Bob is unaccredited in this TV film, ABC
#7

Three terminally ill cancer patients live in separate cottages on a hospital's grounds, where they are attended and visited by both family and close friends. Written by Michael Cristofer, directed by Oscar winner Paul Newman and stars his wife, actress Joanne Woodward, Christopher Plummer and Valerie Harper. Music by Henry Mancini. Filmed at the Salvation Army Camp in Calabasas, California.

1980 *Fighting Back-The Rocky Bleier Story*, *12/7 , [95 mins], Bob plays Rocky TV film
#8

MTM Enterprises on ABC Bob Urich, who plays Rocky, was well-suited in the role, having played high school football which won him a scholarship to Florida State. Urich calls the film one of the best inspirational stories in the history of sports. Little did Bob or anyone else know at the time they were shooting this film, that later in life, Rocky's positive attitude of never giving up would be helpful to Bob as he waged his own courageous battle against cancer. Written by Jerry McNeely and Rocky Bleier and Directed by Robert Lieberman. 21 Steeler players play themselves in the film. **Note:** *Read more about Rocky Bleier in Ch. 9.*

1981 *Killing at Hell's Gate*, 10-31, [96 mins], Bob plays Charles Duke
#9

In this action-thriller, filmed on the Rogue River in Oregon, a rafting party is terrorized during a trip down the river. The 'bad guys' are local wood-cutters, upset by the fact their factory is to be closed down. Directed by Jerry Jameson, written by Lee Hutson. The film co-stars, Deborah Raffin, Lee Purcell and one of Hollywood's outstanding supporting actors, Harry Carey, Jr. Heather Urich says, "Deborah was a great girl. She and her husband flew all the way to Columbus Ohio to see Bob and me in *Barefoot in the Park.* The last time I saw her I did a reading for a film that a mutual friend wrote. She was set to direct it and I was going to co-star. It never got off the ground. I never knew she was battling leukemia." The disease took her life in 2012 at age 59.

1982 *Endangered Species*, 9/10, [97 mins], Bob plays Ruben Castle feature film, M-G-M
#10

This Sci-Fi film based on a true story is one of the truly great conspiracy/mystery thrillers. The story is set in Colorado and revolves around the true story of mysterious cattle mutilations in the American West. Questions are whispered about…are they acts performed by devil worshipers, aliens from outer space, perhaps, even Soviet spies? Whatever the theory, the film is a depiction of a skillful, powerful, high tech entity that threatens to destroy the townsfolk, along with the ranching industry. Written by Judsin Klinger and Richard Clayton Woods and directed by Alan Rudolph who does a great job and his skills are ranked with John Carpenter and Michael Mann. One reviewer says, "Robert Urich proves his acting ability goes far beyond the TV screen and is well suited for more big screen roles." Another writes, "Urich is great as Reuben Castle, the retired alcoholic police lieutenant out visiting the town with his tomboy daughter. At first, he stays out of the case but finds himself involved after the mysterious death of his friend, Joe Hiatt [Paul Dooley]. Doing his best to stay sober, Castle finds himself in danger and in love, as he works with the attractive female sheriff, Harriet Purdue [JoBeth Williams] to get to the bottom of the mystery." Also in the cast, Hoyt Axton, Peter Coyote, John Considine and Harry Carey, Jr. Filmed in Colorado, Bob had the misfortune of having one of his few major motion pictures released the same night as the blockbuster *E.T.*

1982 *Take Your Best Shot*, 10/12, [1 hr 36 mins], Bob plays Jess Marriner TV film, CBS
#11

This comedy/drama is about an actor, Jess Marriner, whose career has gone 'down the tubes.' He resolves to pursue a more stable occupation while also trying to save his troubled marriage, Jess' wife Carol is played by Meredith Baxter [Birney]. Produced by Robert Dapefizian, directed by David Green and written by Richard Levinson and William Link.

1984 n*The Ice Pirates*, 3/16, [91 mins], Bob plays Jason, feature film, M-G-M
12

M-G-M's The Ice Pirates is a tale of smuggling and slavery in an intergalactic setting with profiteer Jason [a role reportedly turned down by Kevin Costner] and his band of brigands, including Angelica Huston and Ron Perlman. They are searching for a lost planet whose vast reserves of water could help refresh a dry cosmos and come in contact with Princess Karina [Mary Crosby]. Produced by John Foreman, Stewart Raffill directed and also was the writer, along with Stanford Sherman. Urich's comedic side comes bursting through in this campy and fun film which spoofs *Star Trek* and *Star Wars*. Some critics and fans refer to the film as Monty Python in Space. The picture earned $14 million on a budget of $9 million. Location sites include, L.A., Santa Clarita, Van Nuys, and Verona, Calif. Some scenes were shot at the Anheuser Busch Brewery and Bethlehem Steel Plant.

1984 *Invitation to Hell*, 5/24/84, [96 mins], Bob as Matt Winslow, film for TV, ABC
#13

This film was made shortly after Director Wes Craven completed *Nightmare on Elm Street*. It is another creepy tale written by Richard Rothstein. Scientist Matt Winslow and his wife Patricia [Joanna Cassidy] and their family move to a town where Jessica Jones [Susan Lucci] director of the Steaming Springs Country Club invites them to join. Matt is suspicious, but his wife and children are befriended by Jessica and convinced to join the club. Matt feels the change in behavior of his family and decides to investigate the club. In doing so, he uncovers an evil secret about Jessica and the members. Excellent cast members include Joe Regalbuto, Kevin McCarthy and Patty McCormick. This horror film is filled with excellent acting, directing and special effects. The health club set was erected with three thicknesses of plaster wall board covering the wooden stage flooring set, required for the controlled fire effects when Lucci as Jennifer introduces her 'hellish' character's charms. The translucent vacuum-formed panels used in the walls actually started to melt from the intense heat radiated from the gas-line-pipes which were positioned to create the aisle of fire Susan Lucci walked through. The fire sequence took several re-takes, causing the plastic material to melt. When watching the sequence you can actually see the vacuum formed 4" deep pyramid pattern-plastic design sag on camera. Susan Lucci's hair and costume were singed and scorched from the intense heat.

1984 *His Mistress*, 10/21/84, [100 mins], Bob plays Allen Beck
#14

An older man is unhappy in his marriage and meets a lovely, young sweetheart in whom he discovers his own youth. He dumps his wife and family and begins living with his new girl-friend. That's when problems begin. Bob Urich is Allen Beck, Julianne Phillips as Anne Davis, along with Cynthia Sikes, Paula Schuster, Linda Kelsey and Katherine Beck. A Robert Papazian Production, Directed by David Lowell Rich and written by Beth Sullivan. Bob's sister-in-law, Sheila Menzies is a stand in.

1985 *Scandal Sheet*, 1/21/85, [101 mins], Bob plays Ben Rowan, film for TV, ABC
#15

The publisher of a celebrity scandal tabloid newspaper sets out to destroy an aging actor, who is battling alcoholism while his career is going down the tubes. Directed by David Lowell Rich [he also directed Bob the previous year in '*His Mistress*'] and written by Howard Rodman. Bob Urich gives a strong performance as Ben Rowan. His co-stars include movie icon, Burt Lancaster, who Bob enjoyed working with; also Lauren Hutton and Pamela Reed. Filming location was Aqua Dulce Air Park, California. **Note**: Henry Winkler [Fonzie on TV's *Happy Days*] was the producer. According to Heather Urich, "Henry called the house trying to get Bob involved in the project. It was something he did quite often [calling Bob]. This time, he was successful."

1985 *Turk 182*, 2/15/85, [102 mins], Bob plays Terry Lynch, 20th-Century Fox
#16

Director Bob Clark [The Christmas Story] filmed one of the best with *Turk 182*. An off-duty fire-fighter, Terry Lynch [Urich], injures his back while off-duty when he performs a rescue of young children, only to go through all sorts of trouble trying to get a disability pension. Turk referred to the character's nickname and 182 was his ID number with the fire department. Timothy Hutton plays Bob's younger brother, Jimmy, who does his best to get some justice for his brother, but is rebuffed by everyone including the arrogant mayor [Robert Culp] of NYC. Darren McGavin and Peter Boyle play police officers, with contrasting personalities. Kim Cattrall also co-stars. There is a good moral to this 'feel good' story written by James Gregory Kingston, who also wrote the screenplay. Urich turned in some of his best work, but was still nominated for a Golden Raspberry. Five filming locations were used: Kaufman Astoria Studios 3412 36th St. Astoria, Queens, Giants Stadium in the Meadowlands, East Rutherford, N.J., Hoyt-Schermerhorn St. Subway Stn. Brooklyn, Spadaro Airport, Eastport, Long Island, N.Y., and Woodside, Queens New York.

1986 *The Defiant Ones*, 1/5/86, [100 mins], Bob is Johnny 'Joker' Johnson, film for ABC
#17

A great human interest story of relationships, racism, conflict and ultimately two individuals who must depend on each other to survive. Two convicts, one white Johnny 'Joker' Johnson [Urich] and one black, Cullen Monroe [Carl Weathers] escape from a chain gang. Each loathes the other but chained together, they must stick together. Once again, Bob is directed by David Lowell Rich [marking their 3rd film together]. Writers are James Lee Barrett and Harold Jacob Smith. Weathers and Urich are both listed as co-producers. The original film was released in 1958 starring Tony Curtis and Sidney Poitier. 20 years later, Curtis would play Urich's Casino boss on *Vega$*. See Chapter 17.

1986 *Young Again* , 5/11/86, [85 mins], Walt Disney's Wonderful World of Color, ABC
#18

Robert Urich plays Michael Riley, age 40. Keanu Reeves appears in this film in one of his earliest roles. He plays the younger Riley in this feel good movie written by Barbara Hall and David Steven Simon, and directed by David Hilliard Stern. A 40 year old bachelor doesn't want to celebrate his 40th birthday on his own and yearns for his childhood sweetheart. An angel grants him his wish to be 17 again. However his childhood sweetie, Laura Gordon [Lindsay Wagner] hasn't gone back in time and also has a 16 year old daughter, Laura [Jessica Steen], her spitting image. The young Riley [Reeves] begins dating the daughter but longs for her mom. He wishes for another miracle and all works out well. One of the most heartwarming scenes is when the mom realizes it's her old boyfriend in a young man's body. Even though Reeves was 22 at the time, his boyish features allow him to pass for 17. *Young Again* was filmed in Georgetown Ontario Canada.

1988 *April Morning*, 4/24/88, [100 mins], Bob plays Joseph Simmons, *Hallmark* on CBS
#19

This April morning in the film version of Howard Fast's 1961 novel revolves around the start of America's Revolutionary War on April 19, 1775 in which the infamous 'Shot heard Round the world' was fired, signaling the start of the American Revolution. The story is not your typical 'shoot-em-up' battle tale but is an insightful look at people and their involvement, who were caught up in a series of events, particularly a 15 year-old farm by from Lexington, Mass. played by Chad Lowe as young Adam Cooper, who wants nothing more than to earn his father's respect. Urich plays Joseph Simmons, Tommy Lee Jones is Moses Cooper. The film also stars Susan Blakely, Rip Torn and Meredith Salenger. Filmed in Quebec, Canada, directed by Delbert Mann, James Lee Barrett penned the teleplay. The film aired on CBS in April 1988 and was the 157th Hallmark Hall of Fame presentation. It also marked the first time Bob and Tommy Lee Jones worked together. One year later [1989] they would appear together again in the critically acclaimed Western miniseries, *Lonesome Dove*. One day, on the set of *April Morning* Bob visited Tommy's trailer to find him reading the script for *Dove*. Little did they know then that they would be working together on the Western, which is covered extensively in Chapter 23.

1989 *The Comeback*, 1/8/89, [94 mins], Bob plays Scotty Malloy, made for TV film, CBS
#20

Once again Bob's athletic ability comes into play as Scotty Malloy, a former NFL player who travels around the world without a care. He decides to come back to Minneapolis to settle down to start a life for himself and falls in love with Jessica [Chynna Phillips], his son Bo's girlfriend. Jessica takes a liking to Scotty and they begin a relationship behind Bo's back. Needless to say, problems arise which prevents 'Scotty' from making the 'comeback' of his life. Directed by Jerrold Freeman and teleplay by Percy Granger. Comeback was filmed in Minneapolis at the Lumber Exchange Building on Hennepin Avenue.

1989 *She Knows Too Much*, 1/29/89, [96 mins], Bob as Harry, made for TV film, NBC
#21

Meredith Baxter [Birney] plays Samantha White, a woman who because of a rough childhood grows up to be as tough as nails and becomes a career criminal. She is a cat burglar with a long rap sheet. As the film opens, she is serving a long prison sentence and has a reputation as someone not to mess with. A fictitious Federal Agency [S.O.B.] gets her released in the custody of one of their agents, Robert Urich as 'Harry,' a bumbling stumbling guy. Why? For her assistance on a project which her special 'talents' as a 2nd -story person are needed. Directed by Paul Lynch and written by Michael Norell

1989 *Murder By Midnight*, 7/19/89, Bob plays Allan Strong, MCA/ Universal-Showtime
#22

A man inadvertently gets caught near a car explosion and after he recovers from his injuries realizes he has amnesia. Soon evidence begins to show that he could be the 'Claw Hammer Killer,' a serial murderer who targets for death the former patrons of a particular restaurant called 'Puzzles.' Also in the cast is Kay Lenz and Michael Ironside as Det. Carl Madsen. Directed by Paul Lynch , who also directed Bob 6 months earlier in *She Knows Too Much.* Written by Allan B. McElroy. Filmed in Toronto Canada. This is the first time Bob deals with memory loss on film. The second time was in 1996 in his Western series *The Lazarus Man.*

1989 *Dragon Fight* , 9/1/89, [96 mins], Bob has a minor role as an airport police officer
#23

This action Hong Kong film stars Jet Li as Jimmy Lee and Dick Wei as Tiger Wong. Two martial arts performers from China appear in a show in the U.S.A. Trouble begins when one of them decides to defect and stay in America. Directed by Hin Sing 'Billy' Tang, the screen play is by James Yuen and Sally Nichols. Filmed in Glen Canyon Utah and San Francisco, Calif.

1989 *Night Walk*, 10/1/89, [100 mins], Bob plays Simon, TV film, CBS #24

Bob's real-life son Ryan, who was ten at the time, makes his acting debut in this film as Matt. Widowed police detective Lt. Bob Simon [Urich] protects an unhappily married woman Geneva Miller [Lesley Anne Down] who insists she has seen a murderer. Directed by Jerrold Freeman, writers: Renee and Harry Longstreet. Ryan Urich says, "I really didn't enjoy acting all that much, but it gave me an opportunity to spend more time with my dad."

1989 *Spooner*, 12/2/89, [98 mins], Bob as Harry Spooner, Walt Disney TV film NBC
#25

Escaped forger Harry Spooner poses as a high school teacher and wrestling coach. It's a story of redemption and goodness combined with some great wrestling scenes. Once again, Bob's athletic ability shines in this film and his wrestling ability is convincing. (Note: in real-life, Bob's son Ryan competed in wrestling in high school.) Co-stars include Barry Corbin, Katie Barberi, Conrad Bachmann and Gary Bairos. *Spooner* is directed by George Miller and written by Peter I. Baloff.

1990 *Blind Faith*[1], 2/1/90, [190 mins], Bob plays Rob Marshall, TV Movie, NBC
#26

This story is based on the 'real-life' book by Joe McGinniss. The teleplay is by John Gay. Directed by Paul Wendkos, who directed many TV series, including, *Hawaii Five-0, The Invaders The Untouchables, I Spy, the F.B.I., Dr. Kildare* and others. A wealthy businessman, Rob Marshall, is accused of murdering his wife Maria [Joanna Kerns*] to collect insurance money [$1.5 million] to pay his gambling debts[$335,000]. Although his three

1 Read more about Joanna Kerns in chapter 30.

sons believe in their father's innocence, his actions and court evidence soon begin to prove otherwise. Bob is excellent as the weak and self-centered husband and father. This film hits an emotional home run in telling the victim's side of the story. The loving relationship between Maria Marshall and her 3 sons is the cornerstone of the film which makes the viewer realize the depth of suffering one endures with such a senseless crime. The mother is contrasted with her husband's self-absorbed obsession with his own needs. Caught in the middle are their three innocent sons, who are devoted and loving to both parents. Joanna Kerns says Bob had a difficult time getting his head around this role, because he could find no redeeming qualities about the man's character to draw from. Robby, one of the three Marshall sons, to insure the films accuracy, agreed to coach Bob and Joanna on his parents' mannerisms. "He [Urich] wanted to know what my father drank, how much ice he'd have in his glass," he says. "All the stuff that makes the story real." One critic wrote, "If *Blind Faith* isn't Urich's best work it has to rank near the top." The setting for the true crime story is Ocean County in Toms River, New Jersey. Felice, the other Woman, is played by Robin Strasser. A poignant scene is when a bubbly Maria [Kerns] is driving her 3 sons home and Supertramp's 1979 hit song, "Take the Long Way Home" is playing on the radio. The Marshall sons are played by Johnny Galecki as John, Jay Underwood as Chris and David Barry Gray as Robby. Note: The imprisoned Robert Marshall began writing Bob Urich pleading his innocence and asking for his help.

1990 *A Quiet Little Neighborhood*, 10/14/90, [100 mins], Bob as Ross Pegler, TV NBC, *A Perfect Little Murder*
#27

Anson Williams, 'Potsie' from *Happy Days,* directed Bob in this made for TV film. Later, he directed Urich n two episodes of *The Love Boat-The Next Wave.* Mark Stein wrote this amusing film that spoofs soap operas. Marsha Pegler [Teri Garr] moves to the suburbs with her hubby, Ross Pegler [Urich]. Marcia's new baby monitor system begins picking up conversations between a mysterious Don and Judy, leading to a murder plot. As Marcia becomes the town's newest detective, the plot thickens but becomes more like a soap opera than reality.

1990 *83 Hours Til Dawn*, 11/4/90, [90 mins], Bob plays Bradley Burdock, TV film, CBS
#28

A wealthy man's teenage daughter is kidnapped and placed in a box with just enough air for 83 hours. Peter Strauss plays Wayne Stracton, an unscrupulous psychopathic criminal responsible for the dastardly deed. Also in the cast, Paul Winfield as Dr. Dantley and Shannon Wilcox. Locations shot included Long Beach, Calif. The story is based on the 1971 biography of Barbara Jane Mackle, who was kidnapped in 1968 and buried alive for 83 hrs. in a wood and fiberglass capsule. Gene Miller adapted the story for television, directed by Donald Wrye.

1991 *Stranger At My Door*, 9/27/91, [100 mins], Bob as Joe Fortier, TV Movie, NBC, also listed as *Dead Run*
#29

Joe Fortier [Urich] a cop on the run from his mob boss "in-laws," tries his best to begin a new life on a deserted farm with his two kids. Things become complicated when Sharon Dancey [Markie Post] shows up. She is injured and her husband Jimmy Lee Dancey [Michael Beck] is a bad guy and wife abuser. Fortier and his kids take her in until she is located by a bounty hunter. Markie and Bob work well together. Nick Stahl plays Robert Fortier and Lauren Stanley is Cindy Fortier. Written by Peter S. Fische, and directed by Vincent McEveety, who has a multitude of TV directing honors on numerous detective/crime series, including, *Diagnosis Murder, Murder She Wrote, Columbo, Simon and Simon, Magnum PI, Kolchak, The Fugitive, The Untouchables* and others. *Stranger At My Door* was filmed on location in Austin, Texas.

1991 *And Then She Was Gone*, 9/29/91, [100 mins], Bob as Jack Bauer, TV Film, NBC, also known as *In A Stranger's Hand*
#30

Jack Bauer is a sort of nerdy computer exec and a workaholic, who accidentally gets involved in a case of child kidnapping when he returns a doll found in the subway. Our friend, Bob gets quite the work over in this suspenseful and exciting film, complete with a doozy of a shiner early in the film. At least in three different scenes, he is chased, and in return chases the real kidnapper. Also in the cast, Megan Gallegher as Laura

Mckillin and Erica Dill as Carla. One reviewer says, "Robert Urich who is quite at ease playing tough guys like Dan Tanna and Spenser gives a skillful performance as a nerdy guy." Another critic says, "this is some of Bob's best work." Directed by David Greene; writers, Matt Benjamin and Matthew Bombeck.

1992 *Survive the Savage Seas**, 1/6/92, [120 mins], Bob as Jack Carpenter, TV film, ABC
#31

Jack [Bob] and Claire [Ali MacGraw] Carpenter realize a life-long dream of his by selling their family farm and uprooting their four children; Susan, decides to take a job in a port. Her place on board is taken by Wally Hudson, [David Franklin] who wanted a lift to Tahiti. The Carpenters three sons are Gary [Mark Ballou], Brian [played by Urich's real-life son, Ryan] and Timmy, played by Dylan and David Daniels]. Read more about Dylan Daniel's take on working with Bob and the film in Chapter 15. This adventure is directed by Kevin James Dobson, written by Dougal Robertson and based on his book, *Survive the Savage Seas* with teleplay by Fred Haines. The film is based on Robertson and his family's true-life experience of spending 37 days a drift in the Pacific Ocean after their boat was attacked by a pod of killer whales. One critic calls the story, "one of the best disaster films to come out in the early 1990's. It depicts survival and courage at its best and whether it's because Robert Urich is right at home on the water, or what, but this movie is Urich at his best. It shows the human spirit at its best, too." It was filmed in Queensland, Australia.

1992 *Blind Man's Bluff*, 2/19/92, [86 mins], Bob as Prof. Thomas Booker, Paramount
#32

Written by Joel Gross and directed by James Quinn, Bob is co-producer on this film. He also plays professor Thomas Booker, who was blinded by an accident and plunged into a world of total darkness which robbed him of his sight, his girlfriend Carol [Lisa Eilbacher] and his dreams. After extensive rehabilitation and psychoanalysis, Booker puts his life back together and comes to terms with both his vision loss and the loss of his girlfriend to his best friend, Frank Carrillo [Ron Perlman]. But, Booker's stable existence is rocked to pieces when he learns his next door neighbor Mary–who is also Carolyn's aunt–has been murdered and he is the prime suspect. One reviewer says, Ron Perlman and Robert Urich play well off each other and project nice screen chemistry. The viewer has no problem believing these characters are brothers by friendship. This is the 2nd film both actors have appeared together in. Their first was *Ice Pirates* for M-G-M.

1992 *Double Edge*, 3/22/92, [100 mins], Bob plays Harry Carter, TV Movie, CBS, also known as *Hit Woman*
#33

This film features two look-alikes, one an FBI Agent , Maggie Dutton, the other Carmen Moore, a hit woman, both played by actress Susan Lucci. A romance develops between Maggie and fellow agent Harry Carter played by Bob. Directed by Steven Stafford, written by Joe Reb Moffly. It also stars Michael Woods and Kevin Dunn. One reviewer calls it, "a terrific suspenseful movie."

1992 *Revolver*, 4/19/92, [96 mins], Bob plays Nick Sastre, Columbia Pictures
#34

Depending on which press release you read, Bob plays Nick *Sastre* or Nick *Suster*. The film is directed by Gary Nelson and was shot entirely in Barcelona and Catalonia Spain, beautiful locations by the Mediterranean. A secret intelligence agent paralyzed by an assassin's bullet sets out to track down the assailant, and in the process uncovers a major arms smuggling operation that threatens international security.

1992 *Jock: A True Tale of Friendship*, 12/22/92, [91 mins], A Major film, Alternative title: *Jock of the Bushveld*
#35

In 1886, 20 year old Percy Fitzpatrick [Sean Gallagher] heads out from Kaapstad [Cape Town] for the Transvaal to dig for gold. On his way, he helps save a sickly puppy from drowning. *Urich* makes a brief cameo appearance as Rocky Mountain Jack. The film features beautiful scenery, shot in South Africa. Directed by Danie Joubert and Duncan MacNellie, written by Johann Potgieter and Duncan MacNellie. Featured in the cast,

Fay Masterson as Lilian Cubit, Wilson Dunster as Ted, Sello Sebotsane as Jim Makokela, and Sean Gallagher as Percy Fitzpatrick.

1993 *Deadly Relations*, 5/22/93, [91 mins], Bob plays Leonard Fagot, TV movie, ABC
#36

This film is based on a true story of a domineering, sociopathic father who both terrorized and coddled his four daughters. Bob plays Leonard Fagot, a successful attorney, who is both strict and loving towards his four daughters. As teenagers, the former Marine, inspects their rooms daily, while showering them with expensive gifts. As they grow-up, he struggles with keeping them near him, even building houses for his daughters and their families after they marry. His wife Shirley [Shelley Fabares] suffers in silence for most of their marriage, secretly enduring his many extra-marital affairs. Leonard loves his daughters so much, he usurps his control over them, and lets them know in no uncertain terms how he feels about the men they date. If he disapproves of them, he probably will have them killed to get them out of their lives. Writers are Carol Donahue, who wrote the book, and Shirley Hall. Directed by Bill Condon, who has directed five different actors in Oscar-nominated performances (Lynn Redgrave, Ian Mckellen, Laura Linney, Eddie Murphy and Jennifer Hudson, who in 2006, won for best performance in *Dream Girls). Deadly Relations* also features a young Gwyneth Paltrow, and Mathew Perry, along with Georgia Emelin, Jillian Boyd and Joy Farmer. Filmed in Atlanta, GA.

1993 *Spenser: For Hire 'Ceremony'*, 7/22/93, [1 hr 35 mins], Bob as Spenser, Lifetime Ch
#37

Spenser is hired to locate April Kyle [Tanya Allen], the missing daughter pf Harry Kyle [Dave Nichols], millionaire and candidate for Governor. Spenser and his 'sometimes' partner Hawk [Avery Brooks] travel from Boston's combat zone to Providence in search of the missing teen, who now has taken to a life in the streets, a seemingly unimportant runaway whom nobody wants found. Her discovery leads to the truth about a prominent politician who has a taste for teenage prostitutes. Directed by Paul Lynch and Andrew Wild, Mike Maschio is the producer. The story is based on characters by Robert B. Parker. Barbara Williams plays Spenser's love interest Susan Silverman. Note: the radio station the author worked at [WROR-Boston] held a contest and the winner got to make a 'walk on' appearance in the film, along with the author. Toronto subs as Boston, even though the Canadian combat zone is twice the size of the original.

1994 *Spenser: For Hire*, January 2, 1994, [90 mins], Bob as Spenser, TV Film, Lifetime
#38 *Pale Kings & Princes* Urich was co-executive producer

When one of Susan Silverman's [Barbara Williams] former patients, a news reporter, turns up dead on the outskirts of Wheaton, the cocaine capitol of Massachusetts, she and Spenser head out to Wheaton to find out what happened and why he was killed. Hawk tags along to provide a little muscle, if needed, and they wind-up getting involved with Felipe Esteva, the head of the cocaine smuggling ring, who just happens to have the whole town in his pocket. The Director is Vic Sarin, from Kashmir India, one of Canada's most celebrated directors of photography. Written by Robert B. Parker. The book upon which this film is based marks the first appearance by Rita Fiore, who had been portrayed by Carolyn McCormick in the 2nd season of the *Spenser* television series. Interestingly, McCormick has played the same character, Dr. Elizabeth Olivet, in five different TV series, *Law & Order* [1990], *Undercover*[1994], *Law & Order: Special Victims Unit* [1999], *Law & Order: Criminal Intent* [2001] and *Law & Order: Trial by Jury* [2005]. *Pale Kings and Princes* was filmed in Paris, Ontario Canada.

1994 *To Save The Children*, 4/5/94, [92 mins], Bob plays Jake Downey, TV Film, CBS
#39

Teacher Jake Downey [Urich] has relocated to a small town in Wyoming hoping to escape the urban problems of his last assignment. His myth of rural bliss is shattered when a former police officer comes unglued and takes Jack's class hostage. Directed by Steven Hilliard Stern. Written by James Henderson [teleplay] and Hartt Wixon and Judene Wixom.

1994 *A Perfect Stranger*, 9/12/94, [105 mins], Bob as Alex Hale, TV Film, NBC
#40

Based on the Danielle Steel novel, teleplay by Jan Worthington and Directed by Michael Miller. Robert Urich's handsome features makes him a natural to be cast in Steel's romantic novels. In this one he plays Alex Hale, a lawyer in love with a woman who is married to a dying millionaire. Co-starring, seasoned actor Darren McGavin as wealthy John Henry Phillips and Stacy Haiduk as his wife, Raphaella. Stacy is known for her role on CBS-TV's *The Young and the Restless*, and as Hannah Nichols on *All My Children*. Filmed in San Francisco. A reviewer said, "Robert Urich's performance is fantastic; as usual he pulls the audience in and allows it to feel what he is feeling, whether it's laughing or crying. His eyes look so deep and easily enter your heart. This role allows Urich to express the sensitivity and caring that he had in real life. He is superb."

1994 *Spenser: For Hire - Judas Goat*, [12/1/94, [1 hr 31mins], Bob as Spenser, TV Film
#41

Spenser and Hawk [Avery Brooks] are hired by Hugh Dixon [Leon Pownall] to find out who murdered his wife and children. Their investigation eventually leads the two crime-busters to a white supremacist-terrorist who is plotting the assassination of a prominent African leader. Wendy Crewson as Susan Silverman gives a strong performance. One reviewer said, "No other actor captured the true essence of Robert B. Parker's Spenser better than Robert Urich." Joseph L. Scanlan directed and the teleplay is by Nahum Tate based on a novel by Robert B. Parker. Patrick Doyle is the producer and Michael J. Maschio was executive in charge.

1995 *Spenser: For Hire*, 1995, [90 mins] Bob as Spenser, ABC Cable-Hallmark Ch., *A Savage Place* also Lifetime
#42

This film marks Bob's final appearance as Spenser. It is loaded with lots of second appearances for a few members of the cast and crew. For openers, Joseph L. Scanlan directs his 2nd *Spenser* and Nahum Tate pens his 2nd Spenser story based on Robert B. Parker's novel. And, Wendy Crewson makes her 2nd appearance as Susan Silverman. Candy Sloane [Cynthia

Dale], a news reporter that Spenser used to date, hires him as back-up while she investigates a credit card fraud ring that could be operating out of a previously bankrupt movie company.

1995 *A Horse For Danny*, 4/8/95, [92 mins], Bob plays Eddie Fortuna, TV Movie
#43

Danny is a bright little eleven year old girl [Leelee Sobieski]. She lives at the race track with her uncle Eddie Fortuna, played by Bob, who is a horse trainer. Danny knows her uncle needs only one great horse to make a name for himself. Directed by Dick Lowery, and written by Remi Aubuchon. It was filmed in Kentucky. After filming was completed, Bob purchased the horse, Tom Thumb, as a gift for his wife Heather. She hoped to use the horse in hunter/jumper competition, but it didn't work out. "Yeah," she says, "every once in a while a bell would go off in his head and he thought he was racing. I just couldn't trust him. 90% of the time he was fine, and then he would just try to run away with me. He did it once," she says, "out in the flats of Santa Fe where there are so many gopher holes. Tommy came to L.A. with me and I tried to rein him to show jump but he just had too much race instinct in him. He threw me once when I was trail riding alone, which I know is not a smart thing to do. I turned him over to my trainer but eventually he went to a ranch in New Mexico," she believes. "Today, Tom Thumb is living in Colorado. They simply took his shoes off and retired him. "I think they must have had him drugged during the filming," says Heather, "even though the wranglers said they didn't."

1995 *She Stood Alone:*, 5/22/95, [90 mins], Bob plays Admiral Williams, TV Movie, ABC, *Tailhook Scandal*
#44

This film is a dramatized account of a female U.S. Naval officer's ordeal of being sexually harassed at a naval convention and her legal retaliation. It stars Gail O'Grady as Lt. Paula Coughlin, Bess Armstrong, Cameron Bancroft, Matt Clark, Hal Holbrook, Rip Torn, Michael Knight and James Marshall. Bob plays against his usual persona as Rear Admiral Williams who reluctantly is in charge of the investigation, a man who is a chauvinistic defender of an all-male fighting force. Urich's diverse acting talent shines through in this film. *She Stood Alone* is directed by Larry Shaw and written by Suzette Couture.

1996 *Captains Courageous*, 4/21/96, [93 mins], Bob as Dan Troop, TV Film, Family Ch.
#45

Harvey Cheyne, Jr. [Kenny Vadas] second richest person in the world, orphaned and spoiled Rotten, is at sea on an ocean liner bound for a prestigious boarding school in England. Seasick from smoking a cigar, he falls over-board and is rescued by Dan Troop [Urich] of a Gloucester fishing boat. Three months at sea, under a firm but fair Capt. Troop, fair wages for the lad are $10.50 a month. It proves to be a hard life and a dangerous one for the boy who grows up fast. "If you don't work, you don't eat!" Filmed on board *The Rotterdam* sailing vessel, it's a great story with a convincing cast. Directed by Michael Anderson, John McGreevey wrote the teleplay. Kaj-Erik Eriksen is also in the cast which enjoyed a picturesque shoot in Vancouver B.C. Canada. One critic wrote," This is the type of movie that you never want to end. Michael Anderson's directing and John McGreevey's script along with Robert Urich's fine acting tear at your heart. The film is faithful to the original Kipling classic novel." **Note:** The original film [1937] starred Academy Award winner Spencer Tracy and Freddie Bartholomew. In 1977, another version was filmed for television starring Karl Malden, Jonathan Kahn and Ricardo Montalban. Norman Rosemont was the Producer and Harvey Hart directed. John Gay wrote the teleplay. The author of this book wrote an article about the production and was on-board the *Roseway* during some actual filming scenes off the coast of Camden/Rockport Maine.

1996 Angel of Pennsylvania Avenue, 12/15/96, [92 mins], Bob as Angus Feagan, Hallmark
#46

Directed by Robert Ellis Miller, the writers were Rider McDowell and Michael De Guzman. This is a heartwarming story about three determined depression-era kids. Robert Urich plays their father, Angus Feagan, an unemployed Detroit worker who is arrested for a crime he didn't commit. His three children are determined to get him out of jail in time for Christmas even if it means hitch-hiking, or sneaking on board trains, and traveling all the way to Pennsylvania Avenue and the White House to see President Hoover. En route, the youngsters meet some colorful characters. The movie is based on the true-life story of Bernice Feagan. Diana Scarwid plays Angus Feagan's wife, Annie. The three children are Tegan Moss as Bernice, Britt Irvin plays Lilly Feagan, and Alexander Pollock as Jack Feagan. Thomas Peacock plays a convincing Pres. Herbert Hoover.

Note: This film is based on a true-life incident which occurred during Hoover's Presidency. He was going into what was an unsuccessful re-election campaign being portrayed as an uncaring incumbent. The story was published in the memoirs of Hoover's Press Secretary, Theodore Joslin [*Hoover Off the Record*] who served in the last two years of his presidency [1931-33]. The memoir depicts a more human side to Hoover. In 1934, when the book was first published, Herbert Hoover was in need of all the good publicity he could get, but instead of thanking Joslin, he never spoke to him again. Hoover, a very private man, felt he had been betrayed instead of helped. *Angel of Pennsylvania Avenue* is the perfect story at Christmas time or anytime. It shows real people, three youngsters, barely existing during the tough economic times following the stock market crash of the late 1920s, who refuse to give up in pursuit of helping their father.

1997 *Final Descent*, 10/12/97, [100mins], Bob as Capt. Glen 'Lucky' Singer, TV Film
#47

This film is based on the book *The Glass Cockpit* by Robert P. Davis, Roger Young wrote the teleplay. Directed by Mike Robe. An airliner collides with a light plane following take-off causing the air-craft's elevators to jam in full climb position. The plane will crash as soon as the fuel runs out unless some drastic measures are taken. Urich plays Capt. Glen 'Lucky' Singer. The cast also includes Annette O'Toole and John de Lancie. Interestingly, later in his career, de Lancie plays an air-traffic controller who causes two planes to crash in an episode of *Breaking Bad* in 2008. *Final Descent* was filmed in Vancouver B.C. Canada

1999 *Final Run*, 10/10/99, [89 mins], once again Bob plays Capt. 'Lucky' Singer, TV film
#48

A new computer-controlled train loses control due to an error in the system and speeds out of control. Our hero, Bob Urich, cast once again as Capt. Glen 'Lucky' Singer, attempts to stop it. Also starring Cathy Lee Crosby, Patricia Kalember and John de Lancie. Directed by Armand Mastroianni and written by Michael Braverman, this Silver Screen Pictures Production was also filmed in Vancouver British Columbia, Canada.

1999 *Miracle on the 17th Green*, 12/19/99, [100 mins], Bob as Mitch McKinley, TV Film
#49

Bob Urich bought the rights to the book and pitched it to CBS. His wife Heather says, "Bob was really good at pitching." Urich and fellow actor Chris O'Donnell were co-producers on this film made for CBS-TV. A 50-year-old man adman [Urich] loses his job. Rather than trying to find new employment, he decides to try and make it on the Senior Golf Tour. An avid golfer off-screen, Bob often blue-skied the thought of being a semi-pro golfer. In this film, his dream causes him to neglect his wife [Meredith Baxter] and his family. James Patterson and Peter DeJong wrote the novel and Wesley Bishop the teleplay. Michael Switzer directed. Pro-golfer Lee Trevino plays himself. Heather Urich says, "If Bob wasn't a successful actor, he would have been a pro golfer." *Miracle on the 17th Green* was also filmed in Vancouver B.C. Canada.

2000 *Clover Bend*, 6/14/02, [89 mins], Bob plays Bill Clayton
#50

Heading out on a camping trip, a newly married cop's family is caught up in a gas station robbery where his wife is seriously injured, and the drama unfolds from there. This film shows the depth of Bob's acting ability which plays on your emotions and tugs at your heartstrings. Critics believe it is one of his best performances in his 30-year career. The story shows the pain a family goes through when they lose someone they love and there is little someone can say or do to help ease the pain. Directed by Michael Vickerman, Bob plays Bill Clayton, Marnette Patterson is Claire and David Keith plays a man who exudes hatred and pure evil.

Heather Urich and their daughter Emily were on-set for this one. "Bob was kind of going downhill healthwise," Heather says, "and I wanted to keep a close watch on him. I recall he loved working with David Keith." One reviewer writes, "To see the pain on Robert Urich's face when he realizes that there was so much to be said but so little time to do it. This film is a must see for every Robert Urich fan. Director Michael Vickerman makes sure Bob and the other cast members play on your emotions, and it works."

2001 *Late Boomers*, TV Pilot 2001, [30 mins], A never-aired series produced for CBS
#51

This unaired TV film [pilot] for CBS was produced by ATG [Artists Television Group] with Patricia Fass Palmer as Producer, and written by Executive Producers Nat Bernstein and Mitchel Katlin. Burt Reynolds was originally cast as Teddy Barnett, but was replaced by Scott Bakula of *Quantum Leap* fame, after creative differences with producers. Urich played Dennis; the cast also included Adam Arkin, Markie Post and Joe Regalbuto [the intense reporter Frank Fontana on *Murphy Brown*]. Regarding the project, Bob said that the sitcom was perfect for his long-time friend, Burt and he was the primary reason he agreed to do the series. "It just didn't work without him." The premise of the show was great. Robert Urich was a former NFL football player and his interaction with his friends, played by Alan Arkin and Joe Regalbuto, as well as his 20-something daughter and his wife, played by Markie Post, is hilarious. One reviewe viewed the pilot program this way, "the constant one-liners and back and forth barbs and bantering of the three friends was fantastic." But, as Urich said, "it just didn't play well without Burt. The program was really designed with him in mind."

2001 *For Love of Olivia* , 3/18/01, [120 mins], Bob plays Horton Roundtree, TV Film
#52

To protect his wife's 'secret' a small-town Southern lawyer in the 1960's decides to defend a young man accused of murder, while running for Congress and dealing with personal threats against his family. Directed by Douglas Barr, and written by H. Haden Yelin. Bob plays Horton

Roundtree, Louis Gossett Jr. plays Daniel Stewart, Lonette Mckee as Olivia Stewart and Kathryne Dora Brown as Camille Stewart

2002 *The President's Man*, 1/20/02, [90 mins], Bob as Pres. Adam Mayfield, TV Film, CBS, *A Line in the Sand*
#53

This action thriller, filmed in the Dallas Texas area, was released three months before Bob Urich's passing. A counter terrorism specialist is assigned by the President of the United States, Adam Mayfield, played by Urich, to track down a terrorist who is suspected of planning to set off a nuclear device somewhere in the United States. Directed by Eric Norris, son of Chuck Norris, who stars as Joshua McCord. Writers are Bob Gookin, John Lansing and Bruce Cervi. Other cast members, include, Texas Senator Kay Bailey Hutchinson as herself, Judson Mills as Deke Slater, Jennifer Tung as C. McCord, Roxanne Hart, Lydia Mayfield and Joel Swetow as Rashid. This is a very good action flick for fans of that genre. Bob is not the headliner in this film–that credit goes to action star Chuck Norris of '*Walker-Texas Ranger*' fame–but Urich does look very presidential in his role and is quite convincing. Bob is a little heavier than usual, most likely due to the meds he was on at the time as he was in the final days of his battle with cancer.

2002 *Night of the Wolf*, 4/15/02, [89 mins], Bob plays Purley Owens, Animal Planet
#54

This film aired early in the evening of the night that Bob passed. Directed by David S. Cass, Sr. and written by Paul W. Cooper, it stars Anne Archer, as Claire McNichol, Michael Shamus Wiles as Crawford, Peter Dobson as Rucker and Sally Kirkland as Rose Handy. Kirkland speaks fondly of Bob, "He was always so kind and treated me with respect," she recalls. The story is about a widowed rancher Claire McNichol and her teenage son, Jesse [Zachary Bostrom] and the dramatic events that cause them to reevaluate their relationships with one another and the world around them. Set against a rugged, rural setting, Claire and Jesse along with their longtime friend and ranch foreman Purly Owens [Bob] work the cattle ranch that Claire once shared with her husband who was killed in a ranching accident. A life-threatening accident strands her deep in the wilderness with only a wild wolf, whom she fears the most, as company. It's only fitting that Bob's final film which aired the night he passed is a western.

2003 *Aftermath*
#55

Was filmed in 2001, obviously before Bob passed, but its content, sexual abuse, at the time was deemed questionable for viewing audiences. Therefore, it wasn't released until January 2003, nearly a year following Bob's passing. The film starred Bob as 'Jack,' along with Meredith Baxter Birney and Diane Ladd. Family members struggle to heal their emotional wounds after an incident of sexual abuse. It also aired on the Lifetime Channel. Filmed in Phoenix, AZ.

In addition to his success in series television, and his extensive film work, Robert Urich also performed on stage in numerous productions, including *The Rainmaker* in Chicago, thanks to movie icon Burt Reynolds who cast Bob to play the part of his younger brother and in doing so helped launch his career.

Bob and his wife Heather Menzies starred together in *the Hasty Heart*, both in Florida and in Washington, DC. In the 1980's, the couple also appeared together in Ohio in the Kenley Players' summer theater production of *Barefoot in the Park*. In 1977, Bob also appeared on stage with Sally Field in *Bus Stop* and later with Teri Garr in *Love Letters*. Urich's final stage role was as Billy Flynn in the touring company of *Chicago*–the musical, which had a successful run on Broadway.

Amazingly, during a six-year period –1996 to 2001– between the time when Bob's cancer was first diagnosed in 1996, treated and was in remission, only to have it return in 2001, the stalwart actor turned out a tremendous volume of work in both series and films made for television. Critics say his body of work during that period was some of his best.

Bob Urich also made countless speaking engagements spreading the word of survival. From coast to coast, speaking in front of audiences, he served as an inspiration and gave hope to those dealing with their own serious illnesses.

No one is certain exactly where Bob gathered the energy, and stamina to accomplish so much while not feeling in top shape. One can only assume his strength came from within. One thing is certain: Robert Urich was a courageous man who never quit on anything he endeavored to do.

Robert Urich Awards:

Nominated Golden Globe-1980 for Best Performance by an actor in a TV series-drama, for *Vega$* [78]. In 1981, he was nominated a second time for a Golden Globe for Best TV Actor again for *Vega$*. The same year, Bob received a Bravo Award in Germany for Best Actor for *Vega$*

In 1992, he won a Cable Ace Award as Informational host for National Geographic Explorer and a News and Documentary Emmy as narrator for National Geo Explorer: *U-Boats Terror on Our Shores.*

In 1997, Urich won a Golden Boot Award for his appearances in Westerns, *Lonesome Dove* and *The Lazarus Man* among others.

In December 1995, Urich was awarded the 2,059th Star on the Hollywood Walk of Fame for television. His star is located at 7083 Hollywood Blvd.

Bob won the Gilda Radner Courage Award from the Roswell Park Cancer Institute along with the John Wayne Cancer Institute Award.

In 1998, he was named national spokesperson for the American Cancer Society.

A star athlete at Toronto [Ohio] High School, he won a football scholarship to Florida State Univ.

For his outstanding achievement, Robert Urich was inducted to the Lou Holtz Upper Ohio Valley Hall of Fame in 2002.

Robert Urich Bibliography

The primary source of material used in this book was from the personal journal of Robert Urich. Numerous sources are cited in the footnotes at the bottom of each page. I did my best to include every newspaper article, periodical, fan magazine, and book which I poured over during my four years of research and writing.

Primary sources are listed below.

American Cowboy Magazine, "Lonesome Dove," Diane Lane comment on Bob, pg.

American Film Magazine,

American Weekly Magazine, 1950's

Arizona Republican Newspaper

Atlantic Monthly

Archerd, Army, *Variety*, April 22, 2002

Atlanta Journal Constitution

Baltimore Sun – TV Critic, David Zurawik, Sept. 20, 1990

Bangor Me. Daily News, May 2001

Beaver County Times, Ed Bark, April 17, 2002

Bleier, "Rocky" – *Don't Fumble Your Retirement*

Boston Globe – Living Section – Mark Muro, "Spenser Reception," Boston Herald – "Spenser in St. Patrick's Day Parade,"; Norma Nathan,

Boston Magazine

Bronson, Fred – *Billboard's Book of #1 Hits – 1989*,

Brooks, Tim F. and Marsh, Earle F. *The Complete Directory of Prime Time Net & Cable Shows, 33,642 TV shows – 1946-present,* Ballantine Books

Buckingham, Nash, *Wind in the Willows*

Cable Ace Awards

Campbell, Joseph. *Power of the Myth*

The County Weekly News, Capon, Al , history of the Urich home on West Lake

Carpatho-Rusyn American Newspaper

Cerone, Daniel Howard – *TV Guide*, "Robert Urich," Nov. 9, 1996

Chandler, Raymond – *Philip Marlowe*

Chicago Daily News

Chicago Herald American

Chicago Sun Times

Chicago Tribune, "Bob Urich," 1986

Cleveland Plains Dealer

CNN – Apr. 16, 2002, *Robert Urich Dead at 55*

CNN Transcripts – Larry King 'Live'

Cosmopolitan – The Sound of Music, cast reunion

Columbia Pictures – *Fly Away Home*

Costas, Bob, TV interview with Robert Duvall

Cowboys & Indians Magazine, 25th Anniversary of *Lonesome Dove*

Watershed Magazine, Cruickshank, Tom – Heather Urich interview, Spring 2015

Daily Oklahoman Newspaper

Dallas Morning News

Denver Post, Dillard, Sandra C., "All Jazzed Up – Robert Urich," Oct. 17, 1999

Durant Daily Democrat – "Urich Only Wants Movie Roles," Feb. 19, 1982

Encyclopedia of Homosexuality – Wayne R. Dynes & William A. Percy, 1989
Entertainment Tonight
Entertainment Weekly Magazine, Apr. 26, 2002
Film Daily
Film Quarterly
Florida State Univ. Voles Fans website, Perrone, Bob
Forbes Staf-Herper, Matthew, "Medical Funding, Cigall Kadoch"
Ft. Worth Ledger
Gaschnig, Mary Ann – *Carpatho-Rusyn American*, 1989 interview w/ Robert Urich
Gendel, Morgan, *Spenser: For Hire* episode on abortion,
Gilda Radner Courage Award – presented to Robert Urich
Golden Boot Award, presented to Robert Urich, 1997
Golden Globe Award
Goodwin, Joseph P., *More Than You'll Ever Be*
Guinness Book of Records, Urich appears in the most TV series
Hanrahan, Michael, *National Enquirer*- Urich article , Apr. 30, 2002
Hollywood Citizen
Hollywood Reporter
Holtz, Lou, Upper Ohio Valley Hall of Fame – 2002
Houston Chronicle
New York Daily News, Huff, Richard –*Versatile, Engaging Robert Urich*, Apr. 17, 2002
Jones, Kenneth, Playbill.com, *New Tour Chicago Begins with Robert Urich*
Jordan, Larry, *Midwest Today*, June 1998
Kadoch, Cigall, researcher – Dana Farber Cancer Inst. Boston,
Kansas City Star Newspaper
Los Angeles Times, King, Susan, Robert Urich Obituary, Aug. 17, 2002
Las Vegas Review Journal, Bob & *Vega$* crew
Las Vegas Sun News, A.P. report on *Vega$* filming at Rancho Circle
Cowboys & Indians Magazine – Leydon, Joe, *Duvall interview*
Lipton, Michael, *People* – "Bright Knight-Robert Urich"
Lodi News – Sentinel, *Robert Urich dies of cancer*, Apr. 17, 2002
London Times
Los Angeles Daily News
Los Angeles Examiner
Los Angeles Times
Lowell Sun Times
Major League Baseball Hall of Fame
Marincolo, Sebastian, *Dr. High: Insights on Marijuana*
Martelle, Joe, *Radio Pro-How to be a Real Radio personality*, Bear Manor Media 2013
McMurtry, Larry, *Lonesome Dove*
Miami Herald
Middleboro Daily News, *Urich Dies at Age 55*, Apr. 18, 2002
Midwest Today
Nagle, Rich, Urich Talks About Grueling schedule on *Vega$*
National Enquirer, Bob's cancer
Nelson, Jim, *National Enquirer* - Urich article, Apr. 30, 2002
NBC Film Productions – "Hopalong Cassidy Outdraws Them All- 1953"
New Mexican
Newsweek, interview w/ William Wittcliff of *Lonesome Dove*
New York Evening Herald
New York Post
New Yorker
New York Times
New York Tribune
Nielsen Ratings, Sept. 1948

Nowinski, Chris, *Dr. Head Games*
New York Post
O'Haire, Patricia, New York Daily News, "Chicago is Urich's Kind of Show," Jan. 11, 2000
Ohio High School St. Ath. Assoc. Tim Stried & Dale Gabor, Reverse Hurdles Dale
Orlando Sentinel
Oxford Encyclopedia of the American West
Palm Beach Post
Parade Sunday Magazine
People Weekly Mag. Apr. 29, 2002
Phoenix Sun
Pittsburgh Post Gazette, *2nd Chances*, Nov. 3, 1999
Playboy '74 issue, "Whatever Happened to the Stars of the Sound of Music"
Playgirl, April '80 issue with Bob Urich on cover
Poor Richard's Almanac, Benjamin Franklin quote
Providence Journal
Reilly, Sue, *People* Mag. Robert Urich article, Oct. 23, 1978
Rinker, Harry L., *Hopalong Cassidy –King of the Cowboy Merchandisers*, Schiffer Pub. Ltd. Copyright 1995 U.S. Television Office, Inc. pg. 57
Sanello, Frank, interview w/Bob Urich, "In The Hot Seat," Apr. 1990
San Francisco Call & Post
San Francisco Chronicle
Scott, Vernon- The Durant Daily, "Snubbing TV Offers," Feb. 19, 1982
Spokesman Review, Urich Suing over Lazarus Man, Apr. 14, 2000
Star Magazine, "$100. Letter," May 28, 1998, also article on Urich, Oct. 8, 1991
Steubenville Herald, interview w/Bob Urich, 1990
Storm, Jonathan, *National Enquirer*, Robert Urich article, Jan. 28, 1996
Sunday Herald Star Steubenville Ohio
TCM, Osborne, Robert, interview with actor Peter O'Toole
Texas Monthly
Thomas, George M. – Pittsburg Post-Gazette, "2nd Chance," Nov. 3, 1999
Toronto High Alumni Assoc.
Toronto High School Commemorative booklet
Toronto High School Mirror, interview w/Robert Urich, Dec. 18, 1981
Toronto Ohio Historical Society, Carolyn Walker
Toronto Ohio Tribune, 1990 interview w/Robert Urich
Towle, Patricia, *National Enquirer*, Urich, Apr. 30, 2002
Tribune News Service
TV Daily
TV Guide, "Lonesome Dove," 1988
TV Week
Urich, Robert, personal journal
USA Today
U.S. News & World Report
Vanity Fair- cast *Sound of Music* Reunion
Variety
Wall Street Journal
Washington Post
Welkos, Robert W. – Los Angeles Times, interview w/Duke Vincent
Whitburn, Joel, *Billboard Book of Top-40 Hits 7th Edition*
Worcester-Telegram & Gazette
Young, William Paul, *The Shack*

Index

Numbers in **bold** indicate photographs

Aftermath 190-191, 532
Ainge, Danny 413
Ali, Muhammad 231, 246-247
American Dreamer 205, 209, 370-371, **380**, 421
Amerika 501
Ames, Ed 11
And Then She Was Gone 520-521
Anderson, Michael 210, 527
Anderson, Ron 76-77
Angel of Pennsylvania Avenue 7, 527-528
Ansell, Betty 74, **112**
April Morning 354, 359, **367**, 516
Archer, Anne 148, **153**, 165, 186, 209, 466, 531
Astrin, Marv 138-139
Axelrod, Jonathan 176

Baquet, James 267-269, 270
Barefoot in the Park 209, **224**, 428, 511, 532
Basic Instinct 414
Bedelia, Bonnie 103, 104
Benson, Alan 411
Benson, Robby 412
Berger, Alan 409
Binkley, Nan 332, 334
Bird, Larry 309-310, **332**
Birney, Meredith Baxter 190, 512, 517, 529, 532
Blake, Merritt 188, 228, 342, 349, 352, 353, 354, **367**, 405, 409, **433**, 477
Bleier, Rocky 102-104, **111**, 298, 426, 511
Blind Faith 215-216, **225**, 372, 474, 501, 518-519
Blind Man's Bluff 521-522
Bob & Carol & Ted & Alice 148-150, 151, **153**, 166, 176, 500
Bokhour, Ray **451**
Bowden, Bobby 119, 120
Boyd, Grace Bradley 29, 30
Boyd, William 19, 24-30, **31**, 373
Boys from Syracuse, The 39
Bradway, Lois "Burchfield" 66-67
Brando, Marlon 191
Braverman, Bart 228, 229, 244, **261**
Brooks, Avery 294, 295, 298-299, 315, **319**, 523, 525
Buckingham, Nash 426, 475
Bunco 195, 499, 509-510
Burke, Roger 306
Burki, Dr. Regla 376
Bus Stop 427, 532

Caesar, Sid 141, 231
Caley, Eric 386, **396**, 420, 479-480, 487
Campbell, Alan 255
Cannonball Run 52-53
Captains Courageous 185, 210-211, 527
Cardhart, Billy xviii, xix, xxi
Carlson, Sarah 494
Cartwright, Angela xiv-xv, 417, 454
Cerone, Daniel Howard 189, 400, 404
Chaffey, Don 247, 248
Chalmers, Mick 392
Chalpty, Michael 12
Charlie's Angels 221, 235, 248, 253, 499
Chicago 4, 280, 364, 428, 442-443, **451**, 532
Clark, Bob 187, 514
Clayton, Dick 146, 148, 183-184
Clover Bend 529-530
Cluett, Tom 158
Cohen, Burt 232, 233

Cohen, Deidre "Dee Dee" Miller 280-282, 364, 465
Comeback, The 516-517
Connors, Chuck 299, **322**
Cope, Ralph 74-75
Coppa, Larry 57
Costas, Bob 357
Coulter, Tom "Chip" 70-72, 76-77, 92
Crane, Robert 306
Crawford, Dohrman 61, 69-70
Crawson, Mike 324-325
Credle, Gary 296
Crucible, The 147
Cruickshank, Tom 384-386, 391-392
Crystal, Billy 178, 179-180, **182**, 504
Curtis, Tony 230, 243, **261**, 515

D'Amico, John 184-185
Dailey, John 72, **82**
Daniel Boone 11
Daniels, Tom 2,
Daniels, Dylan 44, 211-214, **224**, 477-478, 521
Darling, Joni 156, 158, 184-185, 474
Davies, William 410
Davis, Phyllis 244, **261**
De Passo, Suzanne 359
Deadly Relations 523
Defiant Ones, The 515
DeLeo, Frank 342
DeLopez, Tom 121-124, 127
Dennehy, Brian 297
Dern, Bruce 216-217
DeVito, Joanne 174
Djola, Badja 298
Don't Take My Penny 61, **64**, 87
Double Edge 522
Douglas, Kirk 416
Douglas, Michael 158, 255, 416
Douglas, Mike 428, 502, 503
Dryer, Fred 315
Duffy, James W. 499
Duffy, Patrick 176
Dugan, Dennis 218
Dukakis, Mike 296, 306, **318**, 418
Dunaway, Faye 207
Duncan, Sandy 442-443
Duvall, Robert 282, 352, 354, 355, 356, 357, 359, 360-366, **369**, 409

Eastwood, Clint 154, 184, 188, 292, 508
Ehrlich, Lou 298
Eilber, Dr. Frederick 441-442
Emeril 196, 480, 500
Endangered Species 189, 293, 427, 512
Eriksen, Kaj-Erik 210-211, 527

Fantasticks, The 63
Father of the Bride 142-143, 148
FBI, The 148, 184, 498, 518
Fenwick, Jack 119, 120, 121-124, 126-129, **131**, **133**
Field, Sally 188, 427, 532
Fighting Back: The Rocky Bleier Story 102-104, **111**, 298, 426, 511
Final Descent 402, 528
Finch, Peter 219
Fly Away Home 383
Forrest, Steve 167, **169**
Forscher, Dr. Charles 438, 491
Foy III, Eddie 125, 126

Gabor, Dale 106-107
Galecki, Johnny 209-210, 370-371, **380**, 519
Gallegly, Dick 297, 310
Garr, Teri 519, 532
Garwood, Bret 229-230
Gaschnig, Mary Ann 13
Gavilan 241, 248, 293, 372, **436**, 500
Gendel, Morgan 304
Glass, Roy 69, **97**
Glover, Danny 354, 356, **369**
Gold, Sylvia 405, 409
Goldberg, Gary David 205, 370
Goldberg, Lee 311-312
Goldwyn, Samuel 311

Good Morning, America 428-429, 462, 502, 503, 504
Green, H.F. 141
Grill, S. A. 90, **96**
Gunsmoke 166-167, 292, 499

Hagler, Marvin 298, 299
Hall, Reverend Gary 495
Halpate, Rudy 34, 379, 381, 384, 389, **394**, 420
Halstead, Dr. Dyrk 89, 401, 425-426, 453, 475-476
Hamilton, Bob 185
Hamilton, Shirley 140, 144, 183
Hammond, Kathyrn 66
Hampton, Mark 141-142
Harris, Tyrone 99
Harrison, Gregory 177, **181**
Hartman, Lisa 178, 179, 239
Harvilak, Dave 72, 93, 94, 95, **97**
Hasselhoff, David 142, 148
Hasty Heart, The 118, **145**, 193-194, **198**, 428, 532
Hayes, Bill 292
Hayes, Helen 457
Haynes, Jackie 74, **112**
Hayward, David 158, 429
Hillery, Tony 471, 472, 473-474
Hinkle, Clarke 65, 98
His Mistress 514
Hitchcock, Alfred 216-217
Hobbs, Frank 406
Hobson, Roger 387, 479, 487
Hoover, D.W. Don 74-75, 93
Hoover, Herbert 528
Hopalong Cassidy 16, 19, 24, 25, 26, 27-28, 30, **31**, 373, 390
Horse for Danny, A 418, 526
Hughes, Bob 66, 67, 106
Hughes, Howard 176, 230, 232, 233
Hunt, Pam 352
Hunter 312, 315
Hunter, Terry 62, 76, **97**, 478
Hurley, Jackie 324, 325
Huston, Angelica 352, 354, 355, 513
Hutchison, Bill 62, 67, 70, 72, 77, 100, 101, 106, 108, **109**, 478
Hutton, Timothy 192, 266, 514

Ice Pirates, The 188, **197**, 293, 512-513, 522
Invitation to Hell 293, 513-514
Isaacson, Donna 299, 311
It Had to Be You 207, 372, 414, 500
Jaeckel, Richard 294, 299, **320**

James Dean Story, The 174
Joe & Andy Family, The ix, x, **xiii**, 304-305, 326-327, 413
Johnson, Don 128
Jones, Tommy Lee 176, 352, 354, 355, 356, 359-361, 362, **367**, **369**, 516
Jordan, Larry 3, 61

Kadoch, Cigall 490-492
Kane, Carol 370, 371, **380**
Katselas, Milton 165, 174, 176, 178-179, 184, 185-187, 209, 220, 221, 263, 417, 426
Katsin, Lee 297, 308, 309
Kenley, John 209
Kerns, Joanna 216, **225**, 474-475, 518, 519
Kidwell, Ellen 376
Killdozer 166, 508-509
Killing at Hell's Gate 511
King, Donald 383
Kirkland, Sally 531
Kung Fu 148, 498
Kupcinet, Irv 137, 138

Ladd, Cheryl 165, 186, 220, 221, **225**, 510
Ladd, David 165, 221, 510
Ladd, Diane 190, 532
LaGasse, Emeril 196, **200**, 480, 500
Lamantia, Joel 67, 106, 108
Landers, Judy 244, **261**
Lane, Diane 354, 355, **368**, 467

Lane, Johnny 237-242, 257, **260**
Last Tango in Paris 191-192
Late Boomers 203, 530
LaTour, Ron 303
Lazarus Man, The xviii-xix, xxi, xxv, xxvi, **xxvi**, 25, 30, **31**, 214, 268, 348, 358, 372-376, 378-379, **380**, 387-388, 400, 404-406, 427, 438, 442, 499, 517, 534
Leak, Jennifer 164
Leary, Sister Kathleen 342, 439
Leave Yesterday Behind 510
Lehrer, Tom 62
Lentin, Chay 370, **380**
Liss, Ted 140, 183
Live! With Regis and Kathie Lee 379, 428, 505, 506
Locke Brothers xix, xxiii, 56-59, 69
Lockwood, Gary 244
Logan's Run 176, 177, 178, **181**, 263
Lonesome Dove 105, 195, 282, 326, 351-366, **367**, **368**, **369**, 375, 427, 467, 501, 516, 534
Lonn, David 143-144
Love Boat, The 228, 499
Love Boat: The Next Wave 68, 223, 266, **286**, 402, 441, 442, 462, 474, 500, 519
Love Letters 532
Lovell, Dyson 356
Lovers and Other Strangers 143, 183
Lowery, Jim 14, 72, 75, 99, 100, 105, 484
Lucci, Susan 189, 513-514, 522
Lupton, Katie Brunk 277-279
Lynde, Paul 149, 503
Lyons, John 299, 311

MacGraw, Ali 211-212, 521
Magnum Force 154, 184, 292, 298, 508
Magnum, P.I. 195, 230, 257, 520
Man Called Hawk, A 294, 315, 316
Man from Atlantis 176
Man of La Mancha 442, 461
Mann, Michael 233, 234, 512
Mansha, Vaughn 120
Marcus Welby M.D. 148, 166, 498
Margulies, Julianna 245
Marincolo, Dr. Sebastian 166
Marshall, Robert 215, 216, 372, 474, 518, 519
Martin, Dean xix, 4, 231, 253, 416
Martin, Quinn 296, 311
Martin, Strother 166, 174
Masters, Tim 353
Matches, Pete 57, 58, 59
Matheson, Tim 154-155, 156, 159, 163, 164, 166-168, 170, 217, 414, 508
Mazeroski, Bill 17-18
McClain's Law 292
McCormick, Carolyn 313, 524
McDonald, Joe 71
McGinniss, Joe 215, 518
McGreevey, John 210, 527
McGuiness, Bobby ix-x, 308, 310, 324, 328, 336, 419-420
McHattie, Steven 174
McKelvey, Chris 91-92, **97**
McKelvey, Gregg 17-18, 68, 69, 78-79, 90, 91-92, 95, **97**
McLarty, Ron 299, 304, 305, **320**
McMurtry, Larry 351, 353, 358, 359, 501
Melhorn, George 4, 92-93, 94
Menzies, George 171, **180**
Menzies, Heather xi, xii, xiv, xv, xvi, xvii, xx, 1, 4, 5, 6, 7, **10**, 36, 43, 44, 52, 70, 76, 78-80, 88-89, **97**, 104, 123, 126, 127, 128, 134, 151, 156-163, 164, 165, 166, 167, 170-180, **180**, **181**, 184, 185, 186-187, 188, 189, 190, 193, 194, 196, **198**, 205, 209, 210, 211, 215, 217, 220, 222, **224**, 232, 237, 239, 242, 252, **260**, 263-267, 268, 269, 271-272, 273, **274**, 276, 279-280, 281, 282-285, **290**, 292, 301-302, 304, 316, 326, 329, 330, 331, 332, 342, 343,

344, 345, 351-353, 358, 362, 264, 365, **367**, 370, 372, 374, 375, 376-378, 379, 381, 382-383, 384, 386, 387, 391-392, **394**, 397, 398, 399, 400, 401, 402, 403-405, 406, 408-431, **432**, **434**, **436**, **437**, 438-441, 442, 443-444, 449-450, 452-454, 455, 456, 457, 458, 460, 463-464, 465-466, 467, 468, 473, 474, 475, 477, 478, 479, 480, **482**, 483, 484-486, 487, 488, 491, 493-496, **497**, 502, 503, 511, 514, 526, 529, 530, 532
Menzies, Mary 171-172, 173, 174, **180**
Menzies, Neil 171, 173, **180**, 422, 480, 485
Menzies, Sheila 52, 173, **180**, 240, 265, 266, 283-284, 392, 414, 455, 480-481, **481**, 514
Merry Christmas from the Grand Ole Opry 7, 503
Miami Vice 128-129, 312
Mindigo, Candy Patrick 63, **64**, 74, 85-88, 89, 90, 91, **96**, 123, 484-485
Mindigo, Richard 85, 88, 484
Mira, George 114
Mira, Joe 114
Miracle on the 17th Green 428, 529
Mistral's Daughter 501
Mod Squad 228, 506
Moes, Andy ix, x, **xiii**, 304, 305, 326, 327, 413
Muro, Mark 306
Murphy, Megan 164
Murphy, Robert 499
Murray, Jim 308, 323, 324
Murray, Kay Gilchrist 69
Musical Christmas at Walt Disney World, A 7, 505

Nagle, Rich 302-303
Nathan, Norma 307
National Geographic 5, 429, 446, 447, 505, 534
Nelson, Janey 125
Newman, Cardinal John Henry 467
Newman, Paul 166, 404, 511
Newton, Wayne 246, 255
Night of the Wolf 466, 531-532
Night Walk 518
Nimoy, Leonard 509
Notaro, Steve 276

O'Donnell, Chris 428, 529
O'Leary, George 147
O'Neill, Ed 297
O'Toole, Peter 217
Orr, Bobby 310
Osborne, Robert 217
Owen Marshall: Counsel of Law 148, 184, 498

Padnick, Glen 378, 388
Paige, Janis 143
Parker, Robert B. ix, 190, 291, 293, 296, 297, 298, 299, 303, 304, 306, 307, 311-312, **318**, 338-339, 524, 525
Pedraza, Luciana 364, 365
Penn, Leo 149
Perfect Stranger, A 525
Perrone, Bob 122
Personal Appearance 143
Peterson, Bill 117-118, 119, 120, **129**
Pfeiffer, Michelle 186, 187
Plaza Suite 141
Pletz, Rudy 24-25, 34, 56, 57, 68
Popovich, Lynn Vannich 69
President's Man, The 531
Princess Daisy 501
Promised Land 291, 297, 306

Rabkin, William 311, 312
Raffin, Deborah 511
Rainmaker, The 125, 144, 146, 183, 428, 532
Ralston, Dave 93, 94, 95
Rauch, Conrad 46, **54**
Ray, Jim 72-73, 79, 80, 92

Reagan, Maureen 498, 509
Reagan, Ronald and Nancy 194, **198**, 428
Reynolds, Burt 52-53, 72, 120-121, 144-145, **145**, 146-147, 150, 167, 183-184, 188, **198**, 203, 427-428, 478, 530, 532
Rich, David Lowell 513, 514, 515
Robards, Jason 166
Rooney, Art 102
Rosen, Dr. Gerald 448, 449
Rosenfelt, Dr. Robert 250
Roth, Janet 443, 458, 459
Roussi, Dr. Juan 398, 399
Rowe, Don 447
Rucker, Barbara 88, 140-141, 142, 144, **145**, 146, 147, 150-152, 155, 160, 164, 185, 391, 477
Ryan's Hope 217

S.W.A.T. 127, 167, **169**, 170-171, 174, 188, 190, 462, 500
Saffian, Dr. Bob 397, 398
Sampson, Will 243-244, **262**
Samstag, Teri Volsky 16-17, **21**, **22**, 61, 90
Sawyer, Diane 448, 462
Scandal Sheet 514
Schinholster, Jack 121
Schroder, Rick 356, **369**
Scott, Vernon 291
Seeger, Susan 370
Seese, Tim 14, 45, 49, 62, 68, 72, 73-74, 77-78, 91, 100-101, 106, **109**, **112**, 478
Selleck, Tom 7, 148, 165, 186, 195, **198**, 230, 237, **260**, 427, 429, 476, 483, 499, 509-510
Shayne, Alan 296, 298
She Knows Too Much 517
Sheen, Bishop Fulton J. 18
Sheldon, Sidney 416
Shore, Dinah 147, 502
Sideri, Warren 335
Silverado xxiv, 358
Silverman, Fred 230
Simon, Neil 140, 205, 209
Sinatra, Frank 4, 252-253, 416
Six Feet Under 53
Slap Shot 404
Smith, Pastor Danny 486-487
Smith, Tom 73, 116
Snedleton, Rhoda 144
SOAP 178, 179, **182**, 228, 500
Sothern, Ann 142, 143
Soul, David 148, 154, 255, 508
Sound of Music, The 88-89, 123, 156, 172, 173, **181**, 422, 454
Specialists, The 166, 498
Spelling, Aaron 167, **169**, 190, 221-222, 228, 231, 234, 235, 246, 250, 256-257, 265, 266, 292, 462, 474
Spenser: For Hire ix-x, **xiii**, 128-129, 157, 188, 190, 195, 232, 241, 244, 248, 254, 269, 271, 273, 283, 291, 293-316, **318**, **319**, **320**, **321**, **322**, 323, 325, 326, 328, 329, 334, 338-339, 341, 351, 353, 372, 376, 400, 410, 418, 420, 424, 427, 439, 468, 477, 500, 504, 521, 523-524, 525-526
Stallworth, Stephanie 246
Stephenson, Jonathan 117, 118, 194
Stern, Bill 15
Stern, Howard 473
Stern, Robert AM 282-283
Stock, Barbara 298, 304, 313, **319**, **320**
Stockton, John 413
Storm, Jonathan 372
Stried, Tim 106
Survive the Savage Seas 44, 521
Sweeney, D.B. 354, 360, **369**
Syatt, Dick ix

Tabitha 178, 179, 228, 500
Tambor, Jeffrey 205, 370
Tarr, Linda 74
Taste of Toronto, A 41
Taylor, Jackie Haynes **112**

Thomopoulous, Tony 256, 257
Torrenueva, Joe 299
Trevino, Lee 422, 529
Turk 182 187, 189, 192, 266, 293, 301, 427, 514-515
Turner, Ted 388
Twiss, Jeff 413

Urich, Allison **10**, 266, 267, **274**, 279-285, **289**, **290**, 392, **393**, 412, 423, 442, 444, 464, 465, 467, **469**, 483, 493, 494
Urich, Cecelia Halpate xx, 7, 13, 14, **20**, 25, 28, 32, 33, 36, 37, 39, 41, 42-43, 44, **45**, 46, 75, 86, 87, 105, 108, **111**, 115, 135, 170, **260**, 265, **288**, 324, 391, 409, 421, 484, 486
Urich, David xii, 8, 14, 15, 16, **20**, 24, 34, 35, 36, 39, 41-42, 43, 44, 48, 49-52, 53, **55**, 381, 389, 390, 391, **394**, **396**, 419, 420, 424-425, 480, 484, 487, 488
Urich, Emily 7, **10**, 211, 266, 269, 271, 273, **274**, 275-279, 282, 284-285, **288**, **289**, **290**, 301, 392, 412, 423, 424, 431, **432**, **434**, 439, 440, 442, **451**, 454, 456, 467, 487, 493, 530
Urich, Janet 53
Urich, Jo Jo 79, 381-382, 384, 385, 386, **396**, 487, 488
Urich, John Paul 13, 14, 17, 32, 33, 34-35, 36, 37, 38-40, 41, 42, 44, **45**, 46, 50, 74, 77, 86, 105, 170, 171, 265, 271, 389, **394**, 438
Urich, Judy 48, 49, **54**, 63, 275, 467
Urich, Mikey 8
Urich, Monica 14, 15, **20**, 35, 38, 40, 46-47, **54**, 134
Urich, Ryan 7, **10**, 187, **197**, 211, 212, 213, 237, 253-254, **260**, 265, 266, 267, 268-272, 273, **274**, 275, 276, 279, 282, 283, 284-285, **287**, **289**, **290**, 301, 302, 332-333, 343, **367**, 377, 384, 385, 387, 392, **394**, 402, 412, 414, 415, 419, 420, 423, 424, 426, **434**, 439, 439-440, 442, 443, **451**, 453, 456-458, 463, 464, 465, 467, 478, 483-484, 487, 488, **489**, 493, 518, 521
Urich, Tom xvii-xviii, 6, 11, 14, 15, 16, 18, **20**, 32-33, 34-35, 36, 39, 41-42, 44, 45, 47-49, **54**, **55**, 62, 63, 68, 79, 90, **96**, 134, 179, 207, 294, 349, 429, 438, 466, 467, 483, 484, 485, **485**, 487

Vega$ xi, 7, 40, 44, 52, 78, 100, 103, 127, 128, 148, 187, 188, 190, 195, 220, 221, 222, 227, 228, 229-335, **336**, 237-259, **260**, **261**, **262**, 263, 265, 291, 292, 298, 303, 314, 323, 372, 403, 417, 418, 419, 427, 462, 478, 484, **485**, 500, 503, 515, 534
Vennera, Chick 174, 186, 189, 190, 220, 244, 245, **260**, 478
Vincent, Duke 100, 148, 188, 190, 230-233, **236**, 242-244, 247-248, 251, 256, 478

Waldo, Edward Hamilton 509
Walker, Carolyn 2-3, 33-34, 65, 68-69, 77, 90, **113**
Walker, Hollis 373
Webb, Jack 166, **169**, 498, 509
West Side Story 62, 173
When She Was Bad 220-221, **225**, 503, 510
Wilder, John 195, 295-300, 301, 303-304, 305, 307, 310-311, **318**
Williams, Anson 68, 93, 223, 462, 519
Wincer, Simon 357, 359, 361, 362-363
Wind in the Willows, The 210, 426
Winkler, Henry 68, 514
Wiseman, Sam 205
Wisley, Admiral Denny **236**
Wittliff, William 356, 358
Wright, Abby 276-277

Yates, Bill 305, 311
Young Again 515-516

Zurawik, David 371

CPSIA information can be obtained
at www.ICGtesting.com
Printed in the USA
BVHW042254051021
618221BV00002B/33

9 781629 334578